CAMBRIDGE
UNIVERSITY PRESS

Accounting

for Cambridge International AS & A Level

COURSEBOOK

David Hopkins, Deborah Malpas, Harold Randall & Michael Seagrove

CAMBRIDGE
UNIVERSITY PRESS & ASSESSMENT

Shaftesbury Road, Cambridge CB2 8EA, United Kingdom

One Liberty Plaza, 20th Floor, New York, NY 10006, USA

477 Williamstown Road, Port Melbourne, VIC 3207, Australia

314–321, 3rd Floor, Plot 3, Splendor Forum, Jasola District Centre, New Delhi – 110025, India

103 Penang Road, #05–06/07, Visioncrest Commercial, Singapore 238467

Cambridge University Press & Assessment is a department of the University of Cambridge.

We share the University's mission to contribute to society through the pursuit of
education, learning and research at the highest international levels of excellence.

www.cambridge.org
Information on this title: www.cambridge.org/9781108902922

© Cambridge University Press & Assessment 2022

This publication is in copyright. Subject to statutory exception
and to the provisions of relevant collective licensing agreements,
no reproduction of any part may take place without the written
permission of Cambridge University Press & Assessment.

First published 2012
Second edition 2017
Third edition 2022

20 19 18 17 16 15 14 13 12 11 10 9 8 7 6 5 4

Printed in Italy by L.E.G.O. S.p.A.

A catalogue record for this publication is available from the British Library

ISBN 978-1-108-90292-2 Coursebook with Digital Access (2 years)
ISBN 978-1-108-82870-3 Digital Coursebook (2 years)
ISBN 978-1-108-82126-1 eBook

Additional resources for this publication at www.cambridge.org/9781108902922

Cambridge University Press & Assessment has no responsibility for the persistence
or accuracy of URLs for external or third-party internet websites referred to in this
publication and does not guarantee that any content on such websites is, or will
remain, accurate or appropriate. Information regarding prices, travel timetables,
and other factual information given in this work is correct at the time of first
printing but Cambridge University Press & Assessment does not guarantee
the accuracy of such information thereafter.

....

NOTICE TO TEACHERS IN THE UK
It is illegal to reproduce any part of this work in material form (including
photocopying and electronic storage) except under the following circumstances:
(i)   where you are abiding by a licence granted to your school or institution by the
      Copyright Licensing Agency;
(ii) where no such licence exists, or where you wish to exceed the terms of a licence,
      and you have gained the written permission of Cambridge University Press;
(iii) where you are allowed to reproduce without permission under the provisions
      of Chapter 3 of the Copyright, Designs and Patents Act 1988, which covers, for
      example, the reproduction of short passages within certain types of educational
      anthology and reproduction for the purposes of setting examination questions.

....

Cambridge International copyright material in this publication is reproduced under licence
and remains the intellectual property of Cambridge Assessment International Education.

Exam-style questions and sample answers have been written by the authors. References to
assessment and/or assessment preparation are the publisher's interpretation of the syllabus
requirements and may not fully reflect the approach of Cambridge Assessment International
Education.

Cambridge International recommends that teachers consider using a range of teaching and
learning resources in preparing learners for assessment, based on their own professional
judgement of their learner's needs.

DEDICATED TEACHER AWARDS

Teachers play an important part in shaping futures. Our Dedicated Teacher Awards recognise the hard work that teachers put in every day.

Thank you to everyone who nominated this year; we have been inspired and moved by all of your stories. Well done to all of our nominees for your dedication to learning and for inspiring the next generation of thinkers, leaders and innovators.

Congratulations to our incredible winner and finalists!

WINNER

Patricia Abril
New Cambridge School, Colombia

Stanley Manaay
Salvacion National High School, Philippines

Tiffany Cavanagh
Trident College Solwezi, Zambia

Helen Comerford
Lumen Christi Catholic College, Australia

John Nicko Coyoca
University of San Jose-Recoletos, Philippines

Meera Rangarajan
RBK International Academy, India

For more information about our dedicated teachers and their stories, go to
dedicatedteacher.cambridge.org

CAMBRIDGE
UNIVERSITY PRESS

Brighter Thinking
Better Learning
Building Brighter Futures Together

> Contents

> How to use this series

This suite of resources supports learners and teachers following the Cambridge International AS & A Level Accounting syllabus (9706). All of the components in the series are designed to work together and help learners develop the necessary knowledge and skills for this subject.

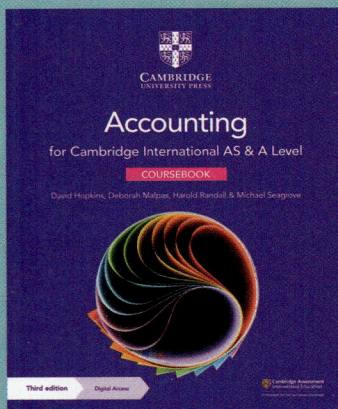

The coursebook is designed for learners to use in class with guidance from the teacher. It offers complete coverage of the Cambridge International AS & A Level Accounting syllabus.
Each chapter contains in-depth explanation of Accounting concepts with a variety of worked examples and activities to engage learners, help them make real-world connections and develop their analysis and evaluation skills.

The teacher's resource is the foundation of this series because it offers inspiring ideas about how to teach this course. It contains everything teachers need to deliver this course, including teaching guidance, lesson plans, suggestions for differentiation, assessment and language support, answers and extra materials including downloadable worksheets and PowerPoint presentations.

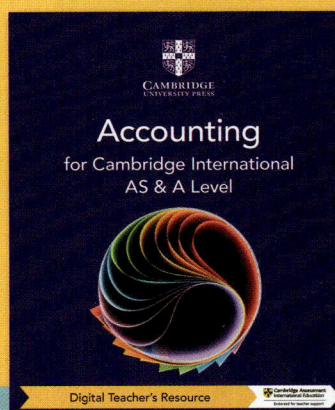

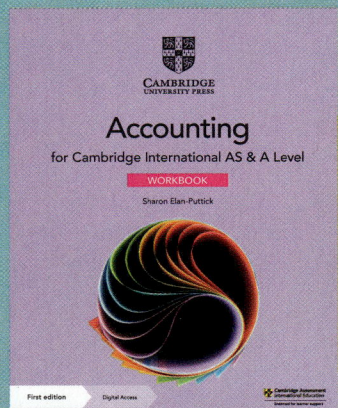

The workbook provides further practice of all the skills presented in the coursebook and is ideal for use in class or as homework. It provides engaging exercises, worked examples and opportunities for learners to evaluate sample answers so they can put into practice what they have learnt.

> How to use this book

Throughout this coursebook, you will notice recurring features that are designed to help your learning. Here is a brief overview of what you will find.

LEARNING INTENTIONS

Learning intentions open each chapter. These help you with navigation through the coursebook and indicate the important concepts in each topic.

ACCOUNTING IN CONTEXT

Accounting in context introduces you to the content in a chapter. These place some of the key ideas contained in the chapter into real-world accounting scenarios. They raise important issues for discussion, with questions that allow you to look in more detail at the topic.

TIPS

Tips are provided throughout this coursebook to help with your learning. The tips might cover how to avoid common errors or misconceptions, advice on difficult accountancy problems, evaluation and analysis skills, or guidance on how answers are arrived at.

ACTIVITIES

There are various activities throughout this coursebook. These include short case studies with evaluative or analytic questions, as well as opportunities to practice a variety of accounting processes and solve problems either individually, in pairs or in groups.

REFLECTION

Reflection questions direct you to look back on an activity and encourage you to think about your learning. You will reflect on and assess the process that you used to arrive at your answers.

WORKED EXAMPLE

Worked examples offer a clear step-by-step breakdown of complex accounting processes to show you how an outcome is achieved.

KEY TERMS

Key vocabulary and formulas are highlighted in the text when they are first introduced. An accompanying definition explains the meanings of these words and phrases. You will also find definitions of these words in the Glossary at the back of this book. There is also a separate appendix for all key formulas.

KEY CONCEPT LINKS

These explain how the coursebook's topics are integrated with the key concepts in the Cambridge International AS & A Level Accounting syllabus.

THINK LIKE AN ACCOUNTANT

Think like an accountant provides you with an opportunity to apply your accounting skills to current events across a variety of international settings. You will be encouraged to look at the world through an accounting lens. Designed to be thought-provoking and encourage discussion, the short case studies and questions raised will help you to make connections between your studies and the world of work.

PRACTICE AND EXAM-STYLE QUESTIONS

At the end of each chapter, you will find either informal practice questions to practice the skills and processes you have learned, or exam-style questions to check your understanding and help you prepare for your examinations. You can find the answers to the activities and exam-style questions in the digital coursebook.

SELF-EVALUATION CHECKLIST

At the end of each chapter, you will find a series of statements outlining the content that you should now understand. You might find it helpful to rate how confident you are for each of these statements when you are revising. You should revisit any topics that you rated 'Needs more work' or 'Almost there'.

> Introduction

Who is this book for?

The third edition of this coursebook accurately and comprehensively supports the updated Cambridge International AS & A Level Accounting syllabus (9706) for examination from 2023. If you are a learner following this syllabus, or a teacher guiding learners through it, you can be confident that the book fully covers the syllabus content to the appropriate level. Others following different A Level or equivalent courses should also be able to benefit from the subject content, activities and exam-style questions that this book contains.

What makes this book different?

The key distinctive features of this book are its:

- international perspective
- focus on decision making.

The book contains a large number of case studies relating to the different aspects of financial or management accounting contained within the syllabus, many of which are based on genuine examples from around the world. While laws in different countries may be quite different, accountants across the world are governed by one international regulatory framework. This means that, theoretically, accountants should be treating particular issues in a standard way.

While needing to a master a range of numerical techniques is essential in order to achieve success on this A Level programme, you will also need to:

- understand the nature of the problems or issues that have made those techniques necessary.
- be able to interpret the result of applying those techniques.
- understand the benefits and limitations arising from accounting information.
- be able to draw conclusions from accounting information and make appropriate recommendations.

This book provides a large number of activities, practice questions and some exam-style questions which will help you develop your ability to explain, analyse and evaluate – skills that are highly valued by employers!

Using the book

Even the keenest learner is unlikely to read this coursebook from cover to cover. Instead, use it to support and guide you in each section of the syllabus as you progress through this Accounting course. While it is expected that you will work through the many activities, practice questions and exam-style questions contained within each chapter, it is hoped that you will devote effort to attempting the new features like 'Accounting in Context' and 'Think like an Accountant'. These are designed to encourage you to think about why accountants do what they do and hopefully will increase your background knowledge and understanding of the subject matter. The 'Reflection' feature is designed to encourage you to evaluate how effectively you have grasped a topic and identify whether there are areas that require further work – and if so, ways of addressing those weaknesses.

To support your progress even further, test your understanding and gain more experience at demonstrating the key subject skills, by using our Cambridge International AS & A Level Accounting Workbook. This has revision questions, exam-style case studies with questions, and sample answers for you to improve on and assess.

Enjoy your studies in Accounting and use this book as an invaluable resource, guide and support towards achieving success on your course. While it is expected that you will work through the activities, practice questions and exam-style questions contained within each chapter, it is hoped that you will devote effort to attempting the new features like 'Accounting in Context' and 'Think like an Accountant'.

Syllabus reference guide

Chapter	Syllabus reference
Chapter 1 Double-entry bookkeeping: Cash transactions	Part of AS Level 1.2
Chapter 2 Double-entry bookkeeping: Credit transactions	Part of AS Level 1.2
Chapter 3 Books of prime entry	Part of AS Level 1.2
Chapter 4 Balancing accounts	Part of AS Level 1.2
Chapter 5 The classification of accounts and division of the ledger	Part of AS Level 1.3
Chapter 6 The trial balance	Part of AS Level 1.2 and 1.4
Chapter 7 Statement of profit or loss	Part of AS Level 1.5
Chapter 8 Statements of financial position for sole traders	Part of AS Level 1.5
Chapter 9 Accounting concepts	Part of AS Level 1.2
Chapter 10 Accruals and prepayments (the matching concept)	Part of AS Level 1.5
Chapter 11 Accounting for the depreciation of non-current assets	Part of AS Level 1.3 and 1.5
Chapter 12 Irrecoverable debts	Part of AS Level 1.5
Chapter 13 Bank reconciliation statements	Part of AS Level 1.4
Chapter 14 Control accounts	Part of AS Level 1.4
Chapter 15 The correction of errors	Part of AS Level 1.4 and 1.5
Chapter 16 Incomplete records	Part of AS Level 1.5 and A Level 3.1
Chapter 17 Incomplete records: Further considerations	Part of AS Level 1.2, 1.5 and A Level 3.1, 3.2
Chapter 18 Partnership accounts	Part of AS Level 1.1 and 1.5
Chapter 19 Partnership changes	Part of A Level 3.1

Chapter	Syllabus reference
Chapter 20 Manufacturing accounts	Part of A Level 3.1
Chapter 21 An introduction to limited company accounts	Part of AS Level 1.1, 1.5 and A Level 3.1, 3.2
Chapter 22 Limited companies: Further considerations	Part of AS Level 1.5 and A Level 3.1, 3.2
Chapter 23 Non-profit making organisations (clubs and societies)	Part of A Level 3.1
Chapter 24 Statements of cash flows	Part of A Level 3.1 and 3.2
Chapter 25 Auditing and stewardship	Part of A Level 3.2
Chapter 26 International accounting standards	Part of A Level 3.2
Chapter 27 Computerised accounting systems	Part of AS Level 1.2 and all of A Level 3.4
Chapter 28 Business acquisition and merger	A Level 3.3
Chapter 29 Ethics and the accountant	Part of A Level 3.2
Chapter 30 Accounting information for stakeholders	AS Level 1.6
Chapter 31 Analysis and communication of accounting information	A Level 3.5
Chapter 32 Costing of materials and labour	AS Level 2.1
Chapter 33 Absorption costing	Part of AS Level 2.2
Chapter 34 Unit, job and batch costing	Part of AS Level 2.2
Chapter 35 Marginal costing	Part of AS Level 2.2
Chapter 36 Activity-based costing (ABC)	A Level 4.1
Chapter 37 Budgeting and budgetary control	A Level 4.3
Chapter 38 Standard costing	A Level 4.2
Chapter 39 Investment appraisal	A Level 4.4

David Hopkins, Deborah Malpas, Harold Randall & Michael Seagrove

> Introducing command words

The command words and definitions in the following table are taken from the Cambridge International syllabus (9706) for examination from 2023. You should always refer to the appropriate syllabus document for the year of your examination to confirm the details and for more information. The syllabus document is available on the Cambridge International website at www.cambridgeinternational.org. The guidance that appears in this table has been written by the authors.

Questions in exam papers typically start with a command word. For Cambridge International AS & A Level Accounting, the command words are shown in the table below. In time and with experience, it will become easy to understand which skills need to be demonstrated in response to different types of questions.

Command word	Definition
Advise	write down a suggested course of action in a given situation
Analyse	examine in detail to show meaning, identify elements and the relationship between them
Assess	make an informed judgement using evidence
Comment	give an informed opinion
Compare	identify/comment on similarities and/or differences
Define	give precise meaning
Describe	state the points of a topic/give characteristics and main features
Discuss	write about issue(s) or topic(s) in depth in a structured way that develops each point
Evaluate	judge or calculate the quality, importance, amount, or value of something
Explain	set out purposes or reasons/make the relationships between things evident/provide why or how and support with evidence
Identify	name/select/recognise
Justify	support a case with evidence/argument
State	express in clear terms
Suggest	apply knowledge and understanding to situations where there are a range of valid responses in order to make proposals/put forward considerations

There are a number of command words that relate more to numerical elements of examinations – and in some cases, to particular topics. These are provided in this table:

Allocate	charge overheads that can be directly attributed to a specific cost centre to that centre
Apportion	charge overheads that cannot be directly attributable to a cost centre, to other centres using that overhead, on an appropriate basis
Calculate	work out from given facts, figures or information
Prepare	present information in a suitable format
Re-apportion	recharge overheads from non-production cost centres on an appropriate basis
Reconcile	process two sets of figures to confirm their agreement

Additional guidance, e.g. phrases such as 'To what extent …?', may also be seen.

> Part 1

The accounting system

> Chapter 1

Double-entry bookkeeping: Cash transactions

This chapter covers part of syllabus section AS Level 1.2

LEARNING INTENTIONS

In this chapter you will learn how to:

- describe how every financial transaction a business makes has two sides to it
- describe how double-entry bookkeeping records both sides of a transaction
- describe how each side of a transaction is recorded in its own ledger account, which has two sides
- describe how cash transactions involve immediate payment
- use ledger accounts to record cash transactions.

ACCOUNTING IN CONTEXT

Keep a record

Millions of new businesses start up every year across the globe. There are around 100 000 registered start-ups in India and 400 000 in South Africa alone. Whatever the industry or country, every new business should keep a record of its financial transactions.

Running out of cash is one of the biggest worries of new business owners as it can be the reason for business failure. Understanding how to record and manage money is a priority for many new business owners.

There is plenty of financial advice available. An internet search will provide information on common financial issues including opening a bank account, borrowing money and taking care of day-to-day spending. Banks, such as Barclays and HSBC, offer business accounts to start-ups. Many banks also offer information and advice to help with planning future income and expenditure and calculating profits.

Figure 1.1: Every new business should keep a record of its financial transactions.

Discuss in a pair or a group:

- What does a new business owner need to know about accounting when they start up?
- Why do banks provide free financial information and advice?
- What other organisations might offer free advice about money?

1.1 What is double-entry bookkeeping?

Every business uses an **accounting system** to record its financial transactions. This system can be used to make decisions or report on the financial performance of the business. The accounting system is based on **double-entry bookkeeping**.

For example, you give your friend $5 in exchange for his book. From your point of view, the two sides of this financial transaction are:

1   you are *giving* him $5 (one aspect)

2   you are *receiving* a book worth $5 (the other aspect)

Every transaction involves giving and receiving. It is important that you *recognise* and *record* both sides of each transaction in your bookkeeping. The term double-entry bookkeeping comes from the fact that both sides are recorded. The two entries to record the two sides are made in *ledger accounts*.

1.2 Ledger accounts

Financial transactions are recorded in **ledgers** in **ledger accounts**. These accounts are sometimes called T accounts because each one looks like the capital letter T.

KEY TERMS

accounting system: a system of collecting, storing and processing financial information and accounting data used by managers.

double-entry bookkeeping: a system of recording financial transactions that recognises there are two sides to every transaction.

KEY TERMS

ledger: a book or computer file containing accounts.

ledger account: a history of all financial transactions of a similar nature.

TIP

It is important to remember that every transaction is recorded twice in the double-entry system.

Layout of a ledger account

Account name, e.g. Sales					
Debit (dr)			Credit (cr)		
Date	Details	Amount $	Date	Details	Amount $

The two sides of an account separate what is received from what is given. The **debit side** records what is received into the account. The **credit side** records what is given.

When there is a financial transaction, one ledger account will have an entry on the debit side and one account will have an entry on the credit side. This is how we record financial transactions in the double-entry system.

In a ledger account, the date of a financial transaction is abbreviated with only three letters for the month. For example, 1 April is written Apr 1. The details (or narrative) state where the other entry is recorded.

1.3 Recording cash transactions

When a financial transaction involves money being paid or received straightaway, it is known as a cash transaction. Payments and receipts either through the bank account or as notes and coins are all considered cash transactions.

Bookkeeping treats the business as separate from the business owner(s). For example, if Haziq is a trader, all his financial transactions are recorded as those of the business and not as Haziq's personal financial transactions.

> ### WORKED EXAMPLE 1

Financial transaction 1

1 April. Haziq starts a business by paying $10 000 into a new business bank account.

The two sides of this transaction are:

1   the business bank account receives $10 000

2   Haziq gives the business $10 000 **capital**

The double-entry for this transaction is:

1   debit the bank account

2   credit the **capital account**

To record the transaction the business must first open ledger accounts for capital and bank. Then the following two double-entry bookkeeping entries are made on 1 April:

Bank account					
Debit (Dr)			Credit (Cr)		
		$			$
Apr 1	Haziq – capital	10 000 [1]			

Note: this is the business's bank account, not Haziq's personal bank account.

KEY TERMS

debit side: left-hand side of an account where what is received is recorded.

credit side: right-hand side of an account where what is given is recorded.

TIP

All financial transactions are recorded from the point of view of the business, not from those of its customers and suppliers or the business's owner.

KEY TERMS

capital: the money invested in a business by its owner(s).

capital account: the account that records the money invested in a business by its owner(s).

CONTINUED

Haziq – capital account			
Debit (Dr)		Credit (Cr)	
	$		$
		Apr 1 Bank	10 000 [2]

Notes:

[1]   The business has received $10 000, which has been paid into the business bank account, hence that account has been *debited*.

[2]   Haziq has given the business $10 000, hence his capital account has been credited. Entries in ledger accounts are known as **postings**, and bookkeepers are said to 'post' financial transactions to the accounts.

Financial transaction 2

2 April. Haziq buys a motor vehicle for the business and pays $2 000 from the business's bank account.

The two sides of this transaction are:

1   the business receives a $2 000 motor vehicle

2   the business bank account gives (pays out) $2 000

The double-entry for this transaction is:

1   debit the motor vehicle account

2   credit the bank account

The bank account already exists and a motor vehicles account must be opened. Then the following two bookkeeping entries are made on 2 April.

Bank account			
Debit		Credit	
	$		$
Apr 1 Haziq – capital	10 000	Apr 2 Motor vehicles	2 000

Motor vehicles account			
Debit		Credit	
	$		$
Apr 2 Bank	2 000		

Financial transaction 3

3 April. Haziq buys goods that he will resell in the normal course of trade for $3 000 and pays out of the business bank account by debit card.

The two sides of this transaction are:

1   the **purchases** account receives $3 000 of goods

2   the bank account gives $3 000

The double-entry for this transaction is:

1   debit the purchases account

2   credit the bank account

A purchases account must be opened to record the goods being bought. Then the following two bookkeeping entries are made on 3 April.

KEY TERM

posting: the process of recording financial transactions in ledger accounts.

TIP

In Worked example 1, financial transactions are all recorded in ledger accounts.

KEY TERM

purchases: goods bought from suppliers that will be resold to customers.

CONTINUED

Bank account					
Debit			Credit		
		$			$
Apr 1	Haziq – capital	10 000	Apr 2	Motor vehicles	2 000
			Apr 3	Purchases	3 000

Purchases account				
Debit			Credit	
		$		$
Apr 3	Bank	3 000		

Financial transaction 4

4 April. Haziq sells a quantity of the goods for $800 and pays the money into the bank.

The two sides of this transaction are:

1   the bank account receives $800

2   the sales account gives $800 of goods to customers

The double-entry for this transaction is:

1   debit the bank account

2   credit the sales account

A sales account must be opened to record the goods being sold. Then the following two bookkeeping entries are made on 4 April.

Bank account					
Debit			Credit		
		$			$
Apr 1	Haziq – capital	10 000	Apr 2	Motor vehicles	2 000
Apr 4	Sales	800	Apr 3	Purchases	3 000

Sales account				
Debit			Credit	
		$		$
			Apr 4	Bank	800

Financial transaction 5

7 April. A customer returns some goods and receives a refund of $40.

The two sides of this transaction are:

1   the **sales returns (returns inwards)** account receives $40

2   the bank account gives $40 to the customer

Hence the double-entry for this transaction is:

1   debit the sales returns (returns inwards) account

2   credit the bank account

> **KEY TERM**
>
> **sales returns (returns inwards):** a customer who has already bought goods sends them back to the seller. A refund is given of any money already paid because goods are faulty or incorrect goods were delivered.

CONTINUED

A sales returns account must be opened to record the goods being returned to the business from a customer. This account is also known as the returns in account. Then, the following two bookkeeping entries are made on 7 April.

Bank account					
Debit			**Credit**		
		$			$
Apr 1	Haziq – capital	10 000	Apr 2	Motor vehicles	2 000
Apr 4	Sales	800	Apr 3	Purchases	3 000
			Apr 7	Sales returns	40

Sales returns account				
Debit			**Credit**	
		$		$
Apr 7	Bank	40		

Note: goods returned from a customer are debited to the sales returns account, not the sales account.

Financial transaction 6

8 April. Haziq returns some goods costing $100 to a supplier and receives a refund.

The two sides of this transaction are:

1   the bank account receives $100

2   the **purchase returns (returns outwards)** account gives $100 of goods back to the supplier

The double-entry for this transaction is:

1   debit the bank account

2   credit the purchase returns (returns outwards) account

A purchase returns account must be opened to record the goods being returned to the supplier. This account is also known as the returns out account. Then, the following two bookkeeping entries are made on 8 April.

Bank account					
Debit			**Credit**		
		$			$
Apr 1	Haziq – capital	10 000	Apr 2	Motor vehicles	2 000
Apr 4	Sales	800	Apr 3	Purchases	3 000
Apr 8	Purchase returns	100	Apr 7	Sales returns	40

Purchase returns account				
Debit			**Credit**	
		$		$
			Apr 8	Bank	100

Note: goods returned to a supplier are debited to the purchase returns account, not the purchases account.

TIP

Remember that sales returns are sometimes referred to as returns inwards and purchase returns are sometimes referred to as returns outwards.

KEY TERM

purchase returns (returns outwards): purchased goods that are sent back to the supplier who agrees to accept them back and return any money paid.

CONTINUED

Financial transaction 7

10 April. Haziq buys another motor vehicle for the business and pays $4 000 by cheque.

This financial transaction is similar in nature to transaction 2 on 2 April.

The double-entry for this transaction is:

1   debit the motor vehicle account
2   credit the bank account

No new ledger accounts need to be opened for this financial transaction as the business already has both a motor vehicle account and a bank account. The following two bookkeeping entries are made on 10 April.

Bank account					
Debit			Credit		
		$			$
Apr 1	Haziq – capital	10 000	Apr 2	Motor vehicles	2 000
Apr 4	Sales	800	Apr 3	Purchases	3 000
Apr 8	Purchase returns	100	Apr 7	Sales returns	40
			Apr 10	Motor vehicles	4 000

Motor vehicles account				
Debit			Credit	
		$		$
Apr 2	Bank	2 000		
Apr 10	Bank	4 000		

An account is a history of all financial transactions of a similar nature. Therefore, it is not necessary to open another account for the second motor vehicle. Similarly, all purchases of office equipment are posted to the office equipment account, and all purchases of office furniture are posted to the office furniture account.

Financial transaction 8

11 April. Tania lends the business $5 000. Haziq pays the money into the business bank account.

The two sides of this transaction are:

1   the bank account receives $5 000
2   the loan from Tania account gives $5 000 to the business

The double-entry for this transaction is:

1   debit the bank account
2   credit the Tania – loan account

CONTINUED

A loan account specific to Tania must be opened. Then, the following two bookkeeping entries are made on 11 April.

Bank account					
Debit			**Credit**		
		$			$
Apr 1	Haziq – capital	10 000	Apr 2	Motor vehicles	2 000
Apr 4	Sales	800	Apr 3	Purchases	3 000
Apr 8	Purchase returns	100	Apr 7	Sales returns	40
Apr 11	Tania – loan	5 000	Apr 10	Motor vehicles	4 000

Tania – loan account					
Debit			**Credit**		
		$			$
			Apr 11	Bank	5 000

Separate loan accounts are needed for each lender. If Tania lends the business more money in the future, another entry can be made into the 'Tania – loan account'. However, if Kim also lends money to Haziq's business, a new 'Kim – loan account' must be opened.

Financial transaction 9

12 April. Haziq pays rent for a warehouse by debit card, $1 000.

The two sides of this transaction are:

1   the rent payable account receives $1 000

2   the bank account gives $1 000 for use of the warehouse

Hence the double-entry for this transaction is:

1   debit the rent payable account

2   credit the bank account

A rent account must be opened. This account is also known as the rent payable account. Then, the following two bookkeeping entries are made on 12 April.

Bank account					
Debit			**Credit**		
		$			$
Apr 1	Haziq – capital	10 000	Apr 2	Motor vehicles	2 000
Apr 4	Sales	800	Apr 3	Purchases	3 000
Apr 8	Purchase returns	100	Apr 7	Sales returns	40
Apr 11	Tania – loan	5 000	Apr 10	Motor vehicles	4 000
			Apr 12	Rent payable	1 000

Rent payable account					
Debit			**Credit**		
		$			$
Apr 12	Bank	1 000			

CONTINUED

Financial transaction 10

14 April. Haziq rents part of the warehouse to his friend Lee and receives a cheque for $300 for the rent. This is paid into the business bank account.

The two sides of this transaction are:

1   the bank account receives $300

2   the rent receivable account gives $300 of warehouse space to Lee

Hence the double-entry for this transaction is:

1   debit the bank account

2   credit the rent receivable

A rent received account must be opened. Then, the following two bookkeeping entries are made on 14 April.

Bank account					
Debit			Credit		
		$			$
Apr 1	Haziq – capital	10 000	Apr 2	Motor vehicles	2 000
Apr 4	Sales	800	Apr 3	Purchases	3 000
Apr 8	Purchase returns	100	Apr 7	Sales returns	40
Apr 11	Tania – loan	5 000	Apr 10	Motor vehicles	4 000
Apr 14	Rent receivable	300	Apr 12	Rent payable	1 000

Rent receivable account					
Debit			Credit		
		$			$
			Apr	Bank	300

> **TIP**
>
> Take care not to mix up rent (payable) with rent receivable. Rent is an expenditure of the business while rent receivable is income.

Financial transaction 11

15 April. Haziq pays wages by bank transfer, $1 200.

The two sides of this transaction are:

1   the wages account receives $1 200

2   the bank account gives $1 200 to the staff for wages

The double-entry for this transaction is:

1   debit the wages account

2   credit the bank account

CONTINUED

A wages account must be opened. Then, the following two bookkeeping entries are made on 15 April.

Bank account					
Debit			**Credit**		
		$			$
Apr 1	Haziq – capital	10 000	Apr 2	Motor vehicles	2 000
Apr 4	Sales	800	Apr 3	Purchases	3 000
Apr 8	Purchase returns	100	Apr 7	Sales returns	40
Apr 11	Tania – loan	5 000	Apr 10	Motor vehicles	4 000
Apr 14	Rent receivable	300	Apr 12	Rent payable	1 000
			Apr 15	Wages	1 200

Wages account			
Debit		**Credit**	
	$		$
Apr 15 Bank	1 200		

Financial transaction 12

16 April. Haziq withdraws $600 from the business bank account for personal use.

The two sides of this transaction are:

1   the **drawings** account receives $600

2   the bank account gives $600 to Haziq

Hence the double-entry for this transaction is:

1   debit the drawings account

2   credit the bank account

A drawings account must be opened. Then, the following two bookkeeping entries are made on 16 April.

Bank account					
Debit			**Credit**		
		$			$
Apr 1	Haziq – capital	10 000	Apr 2	Motor vehicles	2 000
Apr 4	Sales	800	Apr 3	Purchases	3 000
Apr 8	Purchase returns	100	Apr 7	Sales returns	40
Apr 11	Tania – loan	5 000	Apr 10	Motor vehicles	4 000
Apr 14	Rent receivable	300	Apr 12	Rent payable	1 000
			Apr 15	Wages	1 200
			Apr 16	Drawings	600

> **KEY TERM**
>
> **drawings:** money, goods or services the business owner takes out of the business for personal use.

CONTINUED

Drawings account			
Debit		**Credit**	
	$		$
Apr 16 Bank	600		

Note: money drawn out of a business by the owner for personal use is debited to a drawings account, not to the owner's capital account (see Chapter 8 for explanation of drawings).

KEY CONCEPT LINK

Business entity: The accounting records for a business consider the financial transactions from the business's point of view. As a result, money put into the business by the owner is treated as capital for the business and money taken out of the business for personal spending by the owner is treated as drawings.

ACTIVITY 1.1

Here are the financial transactions for Faris's new business. Open the necessary ledger accounts and post the following financial transactions to them. All financial transactions use the bank account.

June

1   Faris started a business by paying $14 000 into his business bank account.

Prisha lent the business $5 000.

Faris then had the following financial transactions:

2   Purchased equipment for business use, $10 000.

3   Paid rent, $700.

4   Paid wages, $600.

5   Purchased good to resell, $2 000.

6   Sold some goods for $1 500.

7   Refunds money to customer for goods returned, $300.

8   Returns goods to supplier and receives refund, $500.

9   Faris takes $400 out of the bank account for personal use.

REFLECTION

When answering Activity 1.1, how did you decide the account to debit and the account to credit? Did you get the account names correct? Were any of your debit and credit entries the wrong way round? If so, can you think of how to learn the correct debits and credits for the future?

ACTIVITY 1.2

Complete the entries for the following table with information taken from the accounts of a trader:

		Name of account to debit	Name of account to credit
1	Paid rent by cheque.		
2	Postage and stationery paid by cheque.		
3	Telephone bill paid from the bank account by standing order [1].		
4	Heating and lighting bill paid from the bank account by standing order.		
5	Paid wages by cheque.		
6	Rent received directly into the bank account.		
7	Bank interest received into the bank account.		
8	Business owner takes money out of the bank account for personal expenses.		
9	Loan received from a friend, Lee.		
10	Loan repayment made on the loan from Lee.		
11	Purchases paid by debit card.		
12	Sold goods and banked the takings.		
13	Returned goods to supplier and banked the refund.		
14	Refunded money to customer by cheque for goods returned.		
15	Carriage inwards [2] paid by cheque.		
16	Carriage outwards [3] paid by cheque.		

Notes:

[1] A standing order is a regular direct payment from a bank account.

[2] Carriage inwards is the delivery cost of bringing the goods from the supplier to the business.

[3] Carriage outwards is the cost of delivering goods to a customer (see Chapter 7 for explanation of carriage inwards and carriage outwards).

THINK LIKE AN ACCOUNTANT

Do you track your own finances?

Studying accounting sometimes makes people think more carefully about their own personal finances. Just as a business has lots of receipts and payments going in and out of its bank account, so too do many of us. Keeping track of our own personal income and spending habits can help us make more informed decisions about our finances. We may be less likely to run out of money.

You could set up your own double-entry accounts on paper or a spreadsheet. Alternatively, there are apps available to track personal spending. Is this something you do already? If not, you could try it for a month to see how useful it is.

Figure 1.2: Keeping track of our own spending habits can help us make more informed decisions about our personal finances.

PRACTICE QUESTIONS

1   Which of the following financial transactions is most likely to require a debit entry in the bank account?

   A   purchases

   B   rent receivable

   C   sales returns

   D   wages   [1]

2   Amir bought goods for resale and paid for the goods to be delivered. Which entries in Amir's books record the delivery cost?

	Debit account	Credit account
A	bank	carriage inwards
B	bank	carriage outwards
C	carriage inwards	bank
D	carriage outwards	bank

[1]

3   A trader takes money from the business bank account for personal use. Which entries record this in his books?

	Debit account	Credit account
A	bank	capital
B	bank	drawings
C	capital	bank
D	drawings	bank

[1]

CONTINUED

4   Below are the financial transactions for Mira's new business. Open the necessary ledger accounts and post the following financial transactions to them. All transactions use the bank account.

June

1   Mira commenced business by paying $20 000 into her business bank account.

Mira then had the following financial transactions:

2   Purchased machinery, $12 000.

3   Paid rent for office space, $1 200.

4   Bought goods for resale, $4 000.

Paid carriage inwards for delivery of goods supplied, $30.

5   Sold some goods for $3 500.

6   Paid for heating and lighting, $200.

7   Received rent for subletting part of the office, $300.

8   Bought more machinery, $800.

9   Bought more goods for resale, $2 000.

10   Sold goods, $2 050.

Paid carriage outwards for delivery to customer, $50.

11   Repaid by cheque to customers for goods returned, $100.

12   Bank interest received, $10.

[16]

SELF-EVALUATION CHECKLIST

After studying this chapter, complete a table like this:

You should be able to:	Needs more work	Almost there	Ready to move on
Explain that every financial transaction a business makes has two sides to it.			
Explain that double-entry bookkeeping records both sides of a financial transaction.			
Explain that each side of a financial transaction is recorded in its own ledger account, which has two sides.			
Explain that cash transactions involve immediate payment.			
Use ledger accounts to record cash transactions.			

> Chapter 2

Double-entry bookkeeping: Credit transactions

This chapter covers part of syllabus section AS Level 1.2

LEARNING INTENTIONS

In this chapter you will learn how to:

- use ledger accounts to record credit transactions and their payment
- distinguish between trade and cash discounts and record them in the ledger accounts
- distinguish between discounts allowed and discounts received and how to record each in the appropriate account.

ACCOUNTING IN CONTEXT

Buy now, pay later

7-Eleven is the largest chain of grocery and convenience stores in the world. It has thousands of outlets throughout North America, Asia, Europe and Australia and serves millions of customers. It sells a huge range of products from basics such as bread and milk to mobile phone accessories and newspapers.

Many manufacturers of convenience products are keen to have 7-Eleven as their customer. 7-Eleven selects its suppliers carefully so that it can ensure its stores are stocked with products that consumers would like to buy.

7-Eleven's customers must pay for the goods they buy immediately; sales are cash transactions. Suppliers to convenience stores such as 7-Eleven do not usually get paid immediately. Typically, there is a 30- to 60-day delay between the supplier supplying the goods and the supplier receiving payment for those goods. These purchases are credit transactions.

Figure 2.1: 7-Eleven is the largest global grocery and convenience store chain.

Credit transactions for both sales and purchases happen across industries especially when selling regularly to other businesses. Suppliers to 7-Eleven stores in Malaysia alone can be collectively owed more than $80 million at any one time. This delay in paying suppliers is common business practice in retailing.

Discuss in a pair or a group:

- Why does 7-Eleven require immediate payment from its customers?
- Why does 7-Eleven expect to delay payment to its suppliers?
- Why are credit transactions more common when selling to other businesses rather than to individuals?

2.1 What are credit transactions?

Businesses do not always require their customers to pay immediately for the goods they buy. Sometimes customers are allowed to pay a few days, weeks or even months later. When a purchase occurs but the payment happens later, it is known as a **credit transaction**.

For example, Lai sells goods to Chin for $500 on 31 May and gives Chin until 30 June to pay. The transaction is *on credit*, i.e. a credit transaction. The sale has taken place on 31 May and must be recorded in Lai's books of account *at that date*. No entries to record payment are made in Lai's books until the day that Chin pays Lai.

2.2 Recording credit transactions

A sale on credit is credited to the sales account and debited to an account in the customer's name. The customer who owes the business money is a **trade receivable**. When the customer (trade receivable) pays, their account is credited and the bank account debited.

A credit purchase is debited to a purchases account and credited to an account in the supplier's name. The supplier that the business owes money to is a **trade payable**. When the supplier (trade payable) is paid, their account is debited and the bank account credited.

KEY TERMS

credit transaction: a financial transaction where no money changes hands at the time of the transaction.

trade receivable: a customer that owes the business money.

trade payable: a supplier to whom the business owes money.

WORKED EXAMPLE 1

Lai owns a business that buys and sells on credit. This example shows Lai's ledger accounts.

Transaction 1: sales

31 May. Lai's business sells goods to Chin for $500 and gives Chin until 30 June to pay.

This sale is a credit transaction because the customer does not pay immediately on May 31. Instead, Lai's business is owed money by the customer, Chin, who becomes a *trade receivable*.

In Chapter 1 we saw that where sales are paid for immediately (a cash transaction) we debit the bank account and credit the sales account. However, for a credit sale the debit will not be to the bank account. Instead, it is entered in an account for the customer.

The double-entry for this transaction is:

1   debit Chin's account

2   credit the sales account

The following two double-entry bookkeeping entries are made on 31 May.

Chin account			
Debit		**Credit**	
	$		$
May 31 Sales	500		

Sales account			
Debit		**Credit**	
	$		$
		May 31 Chin	500

The debit entry in Chin's account shows that he is a *trade receivable* in Lai's books; Chin owes Lai $500 until he pays for the goods.

Transaction 2: purchases

31 May. Lai's business buys goods from Yan for $400 and is given until 30 June to pay. This purchase is a credit transaction because the supplier is not paid immediately on May 31. Instead Lai's business owes money to the supplier, Yan, a *trade payable*.

For a credit purchase, the credit is entered in the supplier's account.

The double-entry for this transaction is:

1   debit the purchases account

2   credit Yan's account

The following two bookkeeping entries are made on 31 May.

Yan account			
Debit		**Credit**	
	$		$
		May 31 Purchases	400

> **TIP**
>
> If a business buys on credit, check whether it is buying goods for resale. If the goods are for resale then they are entered into the purchases account. If the business buys something such as machinery, then it is entered into the machinery account.

CONTINUED

Purchases account			
Debit		**Credit**	
	$		$
May 31 Yan	400		

The credit entry in Yan's account shows that he is a trade payable in Lai's books; Lai owes Yan $400 until he pays for the goods.

Transaction 3: sales returns

4 June. Lai's customer, Chin, returns goods costing $100 to Lai because they are damaged.

This sales return (returns inwards) is on the credit sale made on 31 May. Hence, on 4 June Lai's business does not give the customer any cash. Instead the customer, Chin, will now owe Lai's business less money.

We saw in Chapter 1 that where sales returns come from cash sales, we debit the sales returns account and credit the bank account. For a sales return from a credit sale, the credit is entered in the supplier's account instead of the bank account.

The double-entry for this transaction is therefore:

1   debit sales returns account

2   credit Chin's account

The following two bookkeeping entries are made on 4 June.

Sales returns account			
Debit		**Credit**	
	$		$
Jun 4 Chin	100		

Chin account			
Debit		**Credit**	
	$		$
May 31 Sales	500	Jun 4 Sales returns	100

Transaction 4: purchase returns

5 June. Lai's business returns goods costing $200 to the supplier, Yan, because they are the wrong size.

This purchase return (returns outwards) is on the credit purchase made on 31 May. Hence, on 5 June Lai's business does not receive cash from the supplier. Instead, Lai's business will owe the supplier, Yan, less money.

CONTINUED

For a purchase return from a credit purchase, the debit is entered in the supplier's account.

The double-entry for this transaction is:

1 debit Yan's account

2 credit purchases returns account

The following two bookkeeping entries are made on 5 June.

Yan account					
Debit			Credit		
		$			$
Jun 5	Purchases returns	200	May 31	Purchases	400

Purchases returns account					
Debit			Credit		
		$			$
			Jun 5	Yan	200

2.3 Recording payments for credit transactions

Goods bought or sold on credit must eventually be paid for. Customers that buy on credit may be given a month or even longer to pay. The sale is recorded on the day of the sale. The payment is recorded later when the money is received.

Purchases on credit are treated in a similar way with the purchase being recorded on the day of the purchase. The payment is recorded later when the payment is made.

WORKED EXAMPLE 2

(continuing from Worked example 1)

Transaction 5: receipts from credit customers

6 June. Chin pays all money owed on 6 June.

Chin pays Lai's business $400 ($500 − $100).

Therefore, Chin's account gives $400 and the bank account receives $400.

The double-entry for this transaction is:

1 debit the bank account

2 credit Chin's account

The following two bookkeeping entries are made on 6 June.

Extract of the bank account:

Bank account				
Debit			Credit	
		$		$
Jun 6	Chin	400		

CONTINUED

Chin account					
Debit			**Credit**		
		$			$
May 31 Sales		500	Jun 4	Sales returns	100
			Jun 6	Bank	400

Transaction 6: payments to suppliers for goods bought on credit

7 June. Lai's business pays Yan all money owed on 7 June.

Lai pays Yan $200 ($400 − $200).

Therefore, the bank account gives $200 and Yan's account receives $200.

The double-entry for the payment to Yan of $200 is:

1 debit Yan's account

2 credit the bank account

The following two bookkeeping entries are made on 7 June.

Extract of the bank account:

Bank account					
Debit			**Credit**		
		$			$
			Jun 7	Yan	200

Yan account					
Debit			**Credit**		
		$			$
Jun 5	Purchases returns	200	May 31	Purchases	400
Jun 7	Bank	200			

2.4 Discounts

A customer may be allowed to pay less than the selling price for the goods they have bought. This is called a discount. There are two types of discount:

1 trade discount

2 cash (or settlement) discount

Trade discount

A **trade discount** is typically given where the buyer and seller are in the same line of business. It is given as a percentage reduction from the normal price of a product.

Businesses may choose to offer trade discounts when a customer buys a large volume of goods. Businesses may also offer trade discounts to a customer that buys goods regularly or frequently. As a result, customers may be encouraged to buy more goods or to buy more often, and so increase sales for the business.

For example, goods that Lai's business sold to Chin for $500 may have been sold normally for $625. Chin has been given a trade discount of $125 (20% of $625). Although the normal price of the goods was $625, the transaction was for $500 and only $500 is entered into the ledger accounts.

TIP

Trade discounts are used to calculate the value of a sale and are not recorded separately in ledger accounts.

KEY TERM

trade discount: a reduction in the selling price of goods made by one trader to another.

A trade discount is used to calculate the value of a sale, but it is not recorded separately in ledger accounts.

Cash (or settlement or prompt payment) discount

A **cash (or settlement) discount** is given to encourage a customer to pay quickly.

For example, Lai has given Chin one month to pay for the goods sold to him. Lai offers Chin a 5% cash discount on the amount due if Chin pays within seven days of the sale.

> ### WORKED EXAMPLE 3
>
> Transactions 5 and 6 would look very different if cash discounts had been allowed as shown next.
>
> **Alternative transaction 5: receipts with discounts allowed**
>
> 6 June. Suppose Lai has allowed Chin a cash discount of 5% provided Chin pays by 7 June. Chin pays on 6 June.
>
> When a customer pays for the goods they previously bought, we need to record the payment in the ledger accounts. If a cash discount is given then we must record this too. This is recorded in a **discounts allowed** account.
>
> Before the cash discount Chin owes Lai $400 ($500 – $100).
>
> Chin meets the condition of the cash discount by paying on 6 June.
>
> The cash discount is 5% of $400 = $20.
>
> He will therefore pay only $380 ($400 – $20).
>
> The double-entry for the receipt from Chin of $380 is:
>
> 1 debit the bank account
> 2 credit Chin's account
>
> The double-entry for the $20 discount allowed is:
>
> 1 debit the discounts allowed account
> 2 credit Chin's account
>
> The following *four* bookkeeping entries are made on 6 June.
>
> *Extract of the bank account:*

Bank account				
Debit			**Credit**	
		$		$
Jun 6	Chin	380		

Discounts allowed account				
Debit			**Credit**	
		$		$
Jun 6	Chin	20		

Chin account					
Debit			**Credit**		
		$			$
May 31	Sales	500	Jun 4	Sales returns	100
			Jun 6	Bank	380
			Jun 6	Discounts allowed	20

KEY TERMS

cash (or settlement) discount: an allowance given by a seller to a customer to encourage the customer to pay an invoice before its due date for payment.

discounts allowed: cash discounts allowed to the customer of goods for prompt payment.

TIP

Cash discounts taken are always recorded in ledger accounts at the payment date.

CONTINUED

Alternative transaction 6: payments with discounts received

7 June. Suppose Lai's supplier, Yan, has allowed Lai a cash discount of 5% provided Lai pays by 7 June, and Lai pays Yan on 7 June.

When a supplier is paid for goods they previously purchased, we need to record the payment in the ledger accounts. If a cash discount is given then we must record this too, in a **discounts received** account.

Before taking the cash discount, Lai owes Yan $200 ($400 − $200).

Lai meets the condition of the cash discount by paying on 7 June.

The cash discount is 5% of $200 − $10.

She will therefore pay only $190 ($200 − $10).

The double-entry for the payment to Yan of $190 is:

1   debit Yan's account

2   credit the bank account

The double-entry for the $20 discount received is:

1   debit Yan's account

2   credit the discount received account

The following *four* bookkeeping entries are made in Lai's business accounts on 7 June.

Bank account				
Debit			**Credit**	
	$			$
		Jun 7	Yan	190

Yan account				
Debit			**Credit**	
	$			$
Jun 5	Purchase returns	200	May 31 Purchases	400
Jun 7	Bank	190		
Jun 7	Discount received	10		

Discounts received account				
Debit			**Credit**	
	$			$
		Jun 7	Yan	10

> **KEY TERM**
>
> **discounts received:** cash discounts received from the supplier of goods for prompt payment.

> **TIP**
>
> Note carefully whether a cash discount is to be deducted from settlements; that checks whether one is being offered and whether the time condition has been met.

KEY CONCEPT LINK

Duality (double-entry): Where there is a payment with a cash discount applied, we need to recognise that two transactions are actually taking place: the payment itself and the cash discount. As a result, there are four entries in the ledger accounts.

ACTIVITY 2.1

Below are the financial transactions for Max's business. Post the transactions to the ledger accounts. All goods are bought and sold on credit.

October 1	Purchased goods from Tina that cost $2 000.
2	Sold goods to Ali for $300.
4	Returned goods to Tina that had cost $200.
8	Purchased goods from Lim that cost $2 400.
9	Sold goods to Omar for $1 100.
10	Returned goods to Tina that had cost $100.
11	All goods sold to Ali have been returned.

ACTIVITY 2.2

Below are the financial transactions for Peng's business. Post the transactions to the ledger accounts. All goods are bought and sold on credit.

November 1	Bought goods from Ting that cost $5 000 less trade discount of 15%.
5	Sold goods to Li for $1 000.
10	Returned goods costing $500 less discount to Ting.
15	Purchased goods from Wei that cost $4 800 before trade discount of 20%.
20	Paid Ting all money owed.
	Paid Wei for goods bought on 15 November.
25	Received full payment from Li.

ACTIVITY 2.3

Complete the entries for the following table.

		Name of account(s) to debit	Name of account(s) to credit
1	Sell goods to Diya on credit.		
2	Buy machinery for use by the business on credit from Joints Ltd.		
3	Purchase goods on credit from Alan. Trade discount received.		
4	Return goods bought on credit to Alan.		
5	Goods bought on credit returned by Diya.		
6	Return goods to a supplier and bank refund.		
7	Refund money to a customer by cheque for goods returned.		
8	Pay Joints Ltd for goods bought.		
9	Receive full payment from Diya less cash discount.		
10	Pay Alan for goods bought less cash discount.		

REFLECTION

When completing Activity 2.3 how did you decide which account to debit and which account to credit? Did you think about which account 'gives' value and which 'receives' value?

Discuss your approach in pairs or small groups.

ACTIVITY 2.4

Zoe's business usually sells to the general public. A new business customer is interested in buying from her but wants to buy on credit.

Discuss in a small group the factors Zoe should consider when deciding whether to agree to sell on credit.

THINK LIKE AN ACCOUNTANT

Who do we trust with money?

Trust is important where money is involved. Buying and selling on credit between businesses is common business practice. It can be very useful, but it can be risky for a business to sell goods one day but then wait a month before receiving payment from the customer. How can the business be certain that the customer will pay? Can the customer afford to pay? Is the customer trustworthy or might they try to avoid paying?

If you were selling one of your personal possessions, would you insist on immediate payment? If so why? If not, are there any circumstances where you might be willing to allow payment to be delayed, e.g. the value of the possession, how well you know the buyer or if you have made a written agreement? Why might this make a difference?

Figure 2.2: If you were selling one of your personal possessions, would you insist on immediate payment?

PRACTICE QUESTIONS

1   Which of the following transactions is most likely to require a credit entry in the bank account?

   A   cash discount

   B   cash sales

   C   payment by a customer

   D   payment to a supplier   [1]

2   Jose bought goods on credit from Maria for $200 less trade discount of $30. Which entries record this transaction in Jose's books?

	Account(s) to be debited	Account(s) to be credited
A	Purchases $170	Maria $170
B	Purchases $170	Discounts allowed $30 Maria $200
C	Purchases $200	Maria $200
D	Purchases $200	Maria $170

Discounts received $30   [1]

CONTINUED

3 Myra sold goods on credit to Zara on 1 July. The goods are priced at $1 000 but Myra allowed Zara a trade discount of 10% and offered a cash discount of 2% if she pays within seven days.

Which entries record this transaction in Myra's books on 1 July?

	Account(s) to be debited	Account(s) to be credited
A	Zara $880	Sales $880
B	Zara $882	
	Discounts allowed $18	Sales $900
C	Zara $882	Sales $882
D	Zara $900	Sales $900

[1]

4 Below are financial transactions for Rachael's business. Post all the transactions to the ledger accounts. All goods were purchased on credit.

January 1 Purchases from Yun: $800 less trade discount of 15%.

5 Purchases from Liyna: $1 000 less trade discount of 10%.

6 Returns to Liyna of $200 less trade discount.

9 Rachael settled her account with Liyna and was allowed 2% cash discount.

23 Rachael settled her account with Yun but was too late to receive a cash discount.

[10]

SELF-EVALUATION CHECKLIST

After studying this chapter, complete a table like this:

You should be able to:	Needs more work	Almost there	Ready to move on
Explain that credit transactions involve buying now and paying later.			
Explain that trade discounts are given by one trader to another.			
Explain that cash discounts taken are recorded in the accounts on the date of payment.			
Use ledger accounts to record credit transactions and their payment.			
Explain the difference between discounts allowed and discounts received and how to record each in the appropriate account.			

Chapter 3

Books of prime entry

This chapter covers part of syllabus section AS Level 1.2

LEARNING INTENTIONS

In this chapter you will learn how to:

- demonstrate that financial transactions are recorded in the books of prime entry before being posted to the ledger accounts
- demonstrate when to use the books of prime entry: the sales and sales returns journals, purchases and purchases returns journals, cash book and the journal
- demonstrate the purpose of a cash book
- demonstrate that cash discounts are recorded in the cash book then posted to the discounts allowed and discounts received ledger accounts
- demonstrate that contra entries are made in the cash book when money is transferred between the bank account and the cash account
- enter the transactions in the books of prime entry and post to the ledger from the books of prime entry
- record discounts allowed and discounts received in the cash book and ledger accounts.

ACCOUNTING IN CONTEXT

Cash or card?

Many small businesses use cash but also have a bank account. In Pakistan, cash is widely used by individuals and by many of its 3 million small- and medium-sized businesses. However, there has been a trend towards bank accounts and less reliance on cash.

A number of banks offer current accounts and other financial services to meet the banking needs of business customers. Habib Bank (HBL) is one such bank operating in Pakistan. It offers business customers a bank account designed for their needs, called the business freedom account. This account includes free cash withdrawals and deposits as well as a debit card so payments can be made directly from the bank account. This means that businesses that buy and sell using cash can put their money into a bank account regularly.

Figure 3.1: Many small businesses use cash but also have a bank account.

Discuss in a pair or a group:

- Which types of financial transaction do you think are mostly likely to involve cash?

- Why might small businesses regularly transfer money in and out of bank accounts?

3.1 What is a book of prime entry?

In Chapters 1 and 2, financial transactions were posted straight to the ledger accounts using double-entry bookkeeping. In practice, businesses have an additional step between the transaction and the ledger accounts. This additional step involves entering transactions into one of the **books of prime entry**.

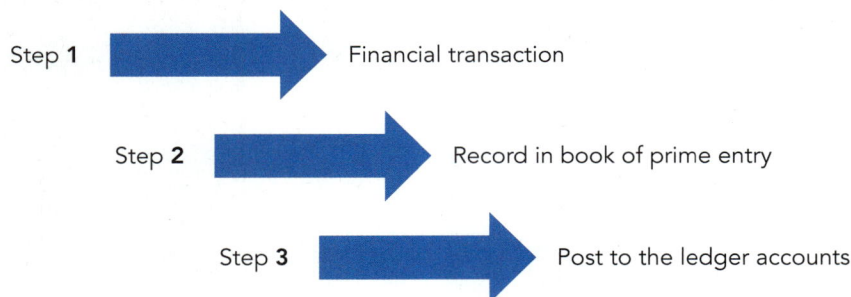

KEY TERM

book of prime entry: a book used to list all transactions of a similar nature before they are posted to the ledger.

Step **1** ➡ Financial transaction

Step **2** ➡ Record in book of prime entry

Step **3** ➡ Post to the ledger accounts

The books of prime entry are:

1 Sales journal

2 Sales returns journal

3 Purchases journal

4 Purchases returns journal

5 Cash book

6 Journal.

3.2 Using books of prime entry

Sales

When there is a credit sale, an **invoice** is *issued* to the customer. The invoice confirms that the customer must pay for the goods or services that the business has supplied and it states the amount owed and the payment deadline.

Once the invoice has been sent, an entry is made in the **sales journal** to record the sale.

> **WORKED EXAMPLE 1**

Khor has sent the following invoices:

Invoices sent to customers		Amount of invoice
		$
6 Sep	Anna	400
8 Sep	Baron	350
9 Sep	Anna	250

The invoices are entered into the sales journal. The sales journal is totalled periodically (weekly or monthly). The more entries a business has, the more frequently the sales journal is likely to be totalled. For example:

Sales journal		
		$
6 Sep	Anna	400
8 Sep	Baron	350
9 Sep	Anna	250
12 Sep		1 000

Posting from the sales journal to the ledger accounts

Each item in the sales journal is posted to the corresponding customer's ledger account following the procedure shown in Chapter 2.

Individual items are not posted to the sales account. Instead, the **total** of the sales journal is posted to the sales account.

Anna account					
Debit				**Credit**	
		$			$
Sep 6	Sales	400			
Sep 9	Sales	250			

Baron account					
Debit				**Credit**	
		$			$
Sep 8	Sales	350			

KEY TERMS

invoice: a document that a business issues to its customer asking the customer to pay for the goods or services supplied to them on credit.

sales journal: the book of prime entry used to record all sales made on credit.

CONTINUED

Sales account			
Debit		**Credit**	
	$		$
		Sep 12 Sales journal	1 000

Note: the detail given in the sales account is the 'sales journal'. This signals that the figure of $1 000 is the sum of numerous individual sales, as listed in the sales journal.

By using a sales journal, the number of entries that must be made in the sales account is reduced. In the example, there are three debit entries (in customer accounts) but only one credit entry (in the sales account). This meets the double-entry requirement because the total values of the debits and credits are the same.

KEY CONCEPT LINK

Duality: Once a journal entry has been made the next step is to use the double-entry system by entering the debit(s) and credit(s) into the ledger accounts.

Look closely at the dates recorded in the ledger accounts. Why are the dates entered in the customers' accounts those of when each sale took place? Why is the date in the sales account when the sales journal is totalled?

Sales returns

If a credit sale is returned, a **credit note** is issued to the customer that shows the amount credited to the customer's account for the return.

Once the credit note is sent, an entry is made in the **sales returns journal** to record the sales return.

WORKED EXAMPLE 2

Khor has sent the following credit notes:

	Credit notes sent to customers	Amount of credit note
		$
7 Sep	Anna	350
9 Sep	Baron	100
9 Sep	Anna	50

The credit notes are entered into the sales returns journal and totalled on 12 September.

	Sales returns journal	
		$
7 Sep	Anna	350
9 Sep	Baron	100
9 Sep	Anna	50
12 Sep		500

KEY TERMS

credit note: a document given to a customer when goods sold on credit are returned to the seller; the amount is deducted from the amount owed by the customer.

sales returns journal: the book of prime entry used to record all goods returned from credit customers.

CONTINUED

Posting from the sales returns journal to the ledger accounts

Each item in the sales returns journal is posted to the corresponding customer's ledger account. The *total* of the sales returns journal is posted to the sales returns account.

Anna account					
Debit			**Credit**		
		$			$
Sep 6	Sales	400	Sep 7	Sales returns	350
Sep 9	Sales	250	Sep 9	Sales returns	50

Baron account					
Debit			**Credit**		
		$			$
Sep 8	Sales	350	Sep 9	Sales returns	100

Sales returns account				
Debit			**Credit**	
		$		$
Sep 12	Sales returns journal	500		

Purchases

When a purchase is made on credit, an invoice is *received* from the supplier, which confirms that the business must pay for the goods or services supplies and states the amount owed and the payment deadline.

All invoices received from suppliers are entered into the **purchases journal** to record the purchase.

> **KEY TERM**
>
> **purchases journal:** the book of prime entry used to record all purchases bought on credit.

WORKED EXAMPLE 3

Khor has received the following invoices:

Invoices received from suppliers		Amount of invoice
		$
2 Sep	Marc	500
5 Sep	Sam	200
7 Sep	Marc	400

The invoices are entered into the purchases journal and totalled on 12 September:

Purchases journal		
		$
2 Sep	Marc	500
5 Sep	Sam	200
7 Sep	Marc	400
12 Sep		1 100

> **TIP**
>
> Never record cash discounts in sales or purchases journals.

CONTINUED

Posting from the purchases journal to the ledger accounts

Each item in the purchases journal is posted to the corresponding supplier's ledger account. The *total* of the purchases journal is posted to the purchases account.

Marc account				
Debit		Credit		
	$			$
		Sep 2	Purchases	500
		Sep 7	Purchases	400

Sam account				
Debit		Credit		
	$			$
		Sep 5	Purchases	200

Purchases account			
Debit		Credit	
	$		$
Sep 12 Purchases journal	1 100		

Purchases returns

If a business returns purchases made on credit to a supplier a credit note is *received* from the supplier that shows the amount entered to the supplier's account for the return.

Once the credit note is received, an entry is made in the **purchases returns journal** to record the return.

> **KEY TERM**
>
> **purchases returns journal:** the book of prime entry used to record all goods returned to suppliers that have been bought on credit.

WORKED EXAMPLE 4

Khor has received the following credit notes:

Credit notes received from suppliers		Amount of credit note
		$
6 Sep	Marc	100
7 Sep	Sam	200

The credit notes are entered into the purchases returns journal and totalled on 12 September:

Purchases returns journal		
		$
6 Sep	Marc	100
7 Sep	Sam	200
12 Sep		300

CONTINUED

Posting from the purchases returns journal to the ledger accounts

Each item in the purchases returns journal is posted to the corresponding supplier's ledger account. The *total* of the purchases returns journal is posted to the purchases returns account.

Marc account					
Debit			**Credit**		
		$			$
Sep 6	Purchases returns	100	Sep 2	Purchases	500
			Sep 7	Purchases	400

Sam account					
Debit			**Credit**		
		$			$
Sep 6	Purchases returns	200	Sep 5	Purchases	200

Purchases returns account					
Debit			**Credit**		
		$			$
			Sep 12	Purchases returns journal	300

TIP

Note whether an invoice or credit note is sent or received. This will help you to recognise the correct book of prime entry for each purchase, sale or returns transaction.

One of the advantages of using books of prime entry is to cut down on the number of individual entries in some ledger accounts. By posting only the *totals* of the sales, sales returns, purchases and purchases returns journals to the ledger, the numbers of entries in the sales, sales returns, purchases and purchases returns accounts are reduced.

As all transactions of a similar type are grouped together, it makes it easier to track them into their accounts in the ledger. This also works the other way; if there is an error in posting to the ledger account, it is easier to track it back to the appropriate book of prime entry.

3.3 The cash book

Some businesses put all their payments and receipts through the bank account. Other businesses make some payments and receipts through a bank account and some using cash.

In Chapters 1 and 2, when money was received or paid we only used the bank account. Now we will look closely at businesses that use both cash and bank accounts.

For example, an ice cream seller makes the following transactions:

1 Jul   Purchases $100 of goods for resale by debit card (a payment card that allows money to be taken directly from the bank account).

Sales of $150 in cash.

Pays wages of $60 in cash.

2 Jul   Puts all cash into bank account.

The entries in the bank account and cash account are:

Bank account					
Debit			**Credit**		
		$			$
Jul 2	Bank	90	Jul 1	Purchases	100

Cash account					
Debit			**Credit**		
		$			$
Jul 1	Sales	150	Jul 1	Wages	60
			Jul 2	Bank	90

Note: On 2 July the cash account gives $90 ($150 – $60) and the bank account receives $90.

The **cash book** is a book of prime entry *and* the cash and bank ledger accounts all in one.

When we use a cash book, separate cash and bank accounts no longer appear in the ledger.

The cash book is the only book of prime entry that is also part of the double-entry system. It contains debit entries for cash and bank and credit entries for cash and bank. It keeps the information about cash and bank account entries side by side. The cash columns are entered in exactly the same way as the bank columns. Cash received is debited, and cash payments credited, in the cash columns. Bank receipts are debited, and bank payments credited, in the bank columns.

For example, the two separate cash and bank accounts can be replaced with the cash book:

Cash book								
Debit					**Credit**			
Date	Details	Cash $	Bank $		Date	Details	Cash $	Bank $
Jul 1	Sales	150			Jul 1	Purchases		100
Jul 2	Cash		90		Jul 1	Wages	60	
					Jul 2	Bank	90	

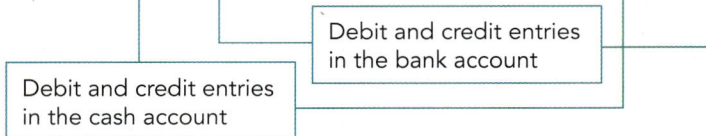

Debit and credit entries in the bank account

Debit and credit entries in the cash account

Removing the cash and bank account from the ledger helps to divide the work between a number of employees. One person could write up the cash book and another person could post the transactions to the appropriate ledger account. This form of internal control will help to prevent fraud, as one person does not have complete control over all the books of account. It should also help to locate errors in posting more easily.

3.4 Recording discounts in the cash book

The cash book is also used as the book of prime entry for cash discounts. An additional column on the left side of the bank account records *discounts allowed*, and an additional column on the right side records *discounts received*. This form of cash book is sometimes known as a three-column cash book as there are three columns of figures on both sides of the book.

> **KEY TERM**
>
> **cash book:** the book of prime entry used to record all bank, cash and cash discounts. It is also part of the ledger system replacing separate cash and bank ledger accounts.

When a payment is received from a customer who has deducted a cash discount, enter the amount of the discount in the discounts allowed column, next to the amount received in the cash or bank column.

Enter discounts received from suppliers in the discounts received column, next to the amount paid in the cash or bank column.

```
┌─────────────────────────┐        ┌─────────────────────────┐
│ List of discounts allowed│        │List of discounts received│
└─────────────────────────┘        └─────────────────────────┘
```

		(3-column) Cash book				
Debit			**Credit**			
Disc	Cash $	Bank $		Disc	Cash $	Bank $

Money in — Money out

TIP

Discounts are listed in the cash book because it is a book of prime entry. Discounts allowed and discounts received must still have their own separate ledger accounts.

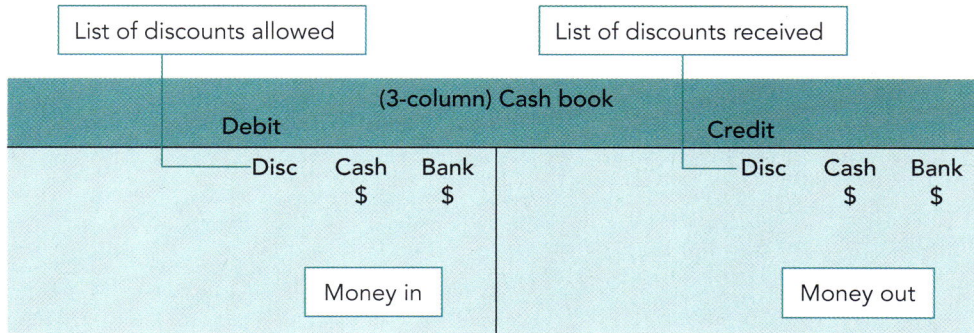

WORKED EXAMPLE 5

Continuing with the Worked example of Khor's business, all receipts from customers and all payments to suppliers were settled on 12 September through the bank account. In each case, a cash discount of 10% was allowed to customers and 5% was received from suppliers.

The ledger accounts to record the receipts from the customers and payments to suppliers are shown next.

Receipts and discounts allowed

Anna owes a net total of $250 ($400 + $250 − $350 − $50) before the cash discount is deducted.

Cash discount of 10% is $25 ($250 × 0.1)

Anna's payment is $225 ($250 − $25)

Both the payment made and the discount allowed to Anna are recorded on the *credit* side of Anna's account.

	Anna account				
Debit			**Credit**		
		$			$
Sep 6	Sales	400	Sep 7	Sales returns	350
Sep 9	Sales	250	Sep 9	Sales returns	50
			Sep 12	Bank	225
			Sep 12	Discounts allowed	25

Baron also owes a net total of $250 ($350 − $100) before the cash discount is deducted.

Cash discount of 10% is $25 ($250 × 0.1)

Baron's payment is $225 ($250 − $25)

CONTINUED

Baron account

Debit		$	Credit		$
Sep 8	Sales	350	Sep 9	Sales returns	100
			Sep 12	Bank	225
			Sep 12	Discounts allowed	25

Payments and discounts received

Bank payments and discounts received are both recorded on the *debit* side of suppliers' accounts. Marc and Sam are suppliers to the business.

Khor owes Marc $800 ($500 + $400 − $100) before the cash discount is deducted.

The cash discount is 5% of $800 = $40

He will therefore pay $760 ($800 − $40)

Marc account

Debit		$	Credit		$
Sep 6	Purchases returns	100	Sep 2	Purchases	500
Sep 12	Bank	760	Sep 7	Purchases	400
Sep 12	Discounts received	40			

Khor returned all goods bought to Sam, therefore he does not need to make any payment and will not receive any cash discount.

Sam account

Debit		$	Credit		$
Sep 6	Purchases returns	200	Sep 5	Purchases	200

The bank payments and receipts plus the discounts allowed and received are recorded in Khor's cash book.

Cash book

		Discounts (allowed) $	Cash $	Bank $			Discounts (received) $	Cash $	Bank $
Sep 12	Anna	25		225	Sep 12	Marc	40		760
Sep 12	Baron	25		225					
		50					40		

Note: the receipts from customers are entered on the debit side, together with the discounts allowed relating to them. Similarly, all the payments to suppliers are recorded on the credit side, together with the discounts received alongside.

3.5 Posting from the cash book to the discounts allowed and discounts received accounts

Entries in the discounts allowed and discounts received columns of the cash book are *not* part of the double-entry system in the cash book. They simply list the discounts allowed and received.

The discount columns in the cash book are totalled periodically. The *total* of the discounts allowed column in the cash book is posted to the *debit* of the discounts allowed account. The *total* of the discounts received column is posted to the *credit* of the discounts received account.

WORKED EXAMPLE 6

Continuing with the Khor business example, the postings for the discounts are:

Discounts allowed account			
Debit		Credit	
	$		$
Sep 12 Cash book total	50		

Discounts received account			
Debit		Credit	
	$		$
		Sep 12 Cash book total	40

The double entries for the discounts are summarised as follows.

For discounts allowed:

1   debit the discounts allowed with the total of the discounts allowed column in the cash book

2   credit the individual customer's accounts with the discount allowed to them when they made their payment

For discounts received:

1   debit the individual supplier's accounts with the discount they permitted you to take when you paid their account

2   credit the discounts received account with the total of the discounts received column in the cash book

ACTIVITY 3.1

Junior had the following credit purchases and purchase returns during the first 10 days of November:

1 Nov   Purchased goods from Cora for $10 000 less trade discount of 20%. Cora allowed a 5% cash discount for payment within 10 days.

2 Nov   Purchased goods from Prem for $14 000. Prem allowed a 2% cash discount for payment within 5 days.

4 Nov   Returned goods to Cora, cost $400 less trade discount.

5 Nov   Purchased goods from Cora for $16 000 less trade discount of 20%. Cora allowed a 5% cash discount for payment within 10 days.

9 Nov   Sent cheques in full settlement of their accounts to Cora and Prem.

Enter the transactions for November in Junior's books of prime entry and post them to the ledger accounts at 10 November.

3.6 Transfers between bank and cash accounts

A business may move money between cash and its bank account. This is a transaction and must be recorded in the cash book.

When cash is banked the double-entry for this transaction is:

- debit the bank account
- credit the cash account

When cash is withdrawn from the bank the double-entry for this transaction is:

- debit the cash account
- credit the bank account

This type of posting in the cash book is a **contra entry**. As an account has been debited (bank or cash) and another credited (cash or bank) the double-entry has been completed. There is no need to make any other postings in the ledger to record this.

> **KEY TERM**
>
> **contra entry:** the completing of both sides of the double-entry within one account or cash book.

WORKED EXAMPLE 7

The following transactions took place in Clara's business for the first week of March:

March

3   Cash sales of $2 000.

4   Paid postages of $40 in cash.

5   Banked $1 500 cash.

7   Paid $500 wages from the bank account.

CONTINUED

The cash book entries are recorded as follows:

Cash book									
Debit					Credit				
		Discounts (allowed) $	Cash $	Bank $			Discounts (received) $	Cash $	Bank $
Mar 3	Sales		2000		Mar 4	Postage		40	
Mar 5	Cash (C)			1500	Mar 5	Bank (C)		1500	
					Mar 7	Wages			500

Note: C (or ¢) is an abbreviation for 'contra', indicating that the double-entry is completed on the opposite sides of the bank and cash accounts.

ACTIVITY 3.2

Enter the following transactions in Lee's cash book:

April 1 Cash sales, $1 000.
2 Electricity paid in cash, $100.
3 Cash sales, $800.
4 Banked cash, $1 400.
5 Stationery paid in cash, $20.
6 Withdrew $900 from bank for the cash float.
7 Cash purchases, $600.

3.7 The journal

All transactions should be recorded in one of the books of prime entry before being posted to the ledger accounts. These non-regular items require entries in the **journal (or general journal)**:

- opening entries in a new business or new accounting year
- purchases and sales on credit of items for use in the business, e.g. machinery, delivery vans
- corrections of posting errors
- adjustments to accounts (which are dealt with in Chapter 7)
- transfers between accounts.

Each journal entry shows the account to be debited and the account to be credited. The value of the debits and credits should always be equal.

KEY TERM

journal (or general journal): a book of prime entry for recording transactions and events for which there is no other book of prime entry.

Layout of the journal

Date	Details	Debit	Credit
		$	$
	Name of account to be debited		
	Name of account to be credited		
	The narrative		

Although it contains the words 'debit' and 'credit' (or dr and cr), the journal is not part of the double-entry system. It is simply a book of instructions, telling the bookkeeper which account in the ledger to debit and which to credit.

3.8 How to make journal entries

The account to be debited is stated above the one to be credited. Every entry should have a narrative.

The journal is an important book and before the entries are posted the owner of the business or a manager should authorise them.

> **KEY TERM**
>
> **narrative:** something recorded under a journal entry to explain why the journal entry is being made.

> **TIP**
>
> Record the debit entry before the credit entry in the journal. This is normal accounting practice.

> **WORKED EXAMPLE 8**
>
> **Opening entries in a new business**
>
> 1 March. Akhona started a new business and put $20 000 into the business bank account.
>
> The journal entry will be:
>
> | Date | Details | Debit | Credit |
> |---|---|---|---|
> | | | $ | $ |
> | Mar 1 | Bank | 20 000 | |
> | | Capital | | 20 000 |
> | | Narrative: opening capital for the new business | | |
>
> After the entry has been made in the journal the debit and credit are posted to the cash book and the capital account.
>
> **Cash book**
>
> | | Debit | | | | Credit | | |
> |---|---|---|---|---|---|---|---|
> | Date | Details | Cash $ | Bank $ | Date | Details | Cash $ | Bank $ |
> | Mar 1 | Capital | | 20 000 | | | | |
>
> **Capital account**
>
> | | Debit | | | Credit | |
> |---|---|---|---|---|---|
> | | | $ | | | $ |
> | | | | Mar 1 | Bank | 20 000 |

CONTINUED

Purchase on credit of item for use in the business

4 June. Akhona bought a motor vehicle from A. Smith on credit for $7 000.

The journal entry for this purchase of a motor vehicle for use in the business will be:

Date	Details	Dr	Cr
		$	$
Jun 4	Motor vehicles	7 000	
	A. Smith		7 000
	Narrative: Purchase of vehicle registration no. WE123DSD from A. Smith. See A. Smith invoice no. A156 dated 4 June.		

Note: The narrative gives information to enable Akhona to check on the details later if necessary.

The postings to the ledger accounts are:

Motor vehicles account			
Debit		**Credit**	
	$		$
Jun 4 A. Smith	7 000		

A. Smith account			
Debit		**Credit**	
	$		$
		Jun 4 Motor vehicles	7 000

Correction of posting error

Akhona discovered that he had credited $100 that he had received from A. Williams on 1 May to an account for L. Williams in error.

The journal entry to correct the error will be:

Date	Details	Dr	Cr
		$	$
May 1	L. Williams	100	
	A. Williams		100
	Narrative: Correction of an error. A remittance from A. Williams on this date was posted incorrectly to L. Williams's account.		

Note: L. Williams account is debited because it was previously credited in error. The debit effectively cancels out the credit.

After the entry has been made in the journal the debits and credits are posted in the ledger accounts.

> **TIP**
>
> Post journal entries to ledger accounts only, never to other books of prime entry.

CONTINUED

The postings to the ledger accounts are:

L. Williams account			
Debit		**Credit**	
	$		$
May 1 A. Williams	100		

A. Williams account			
Debit		**Credit**	
	$		$
		May 1 L. Williams	100

ACTIVITY 3.3

Prepare journal entries for each of the following items.

1   Purchased motor vehicle for use in the business from Paul, which cost $14 000.

2   Purchase of office furniture for the business costing $6 000 has been debited to the purchases account instead of the furniture account in error.

3   A new business opens with $6 000 of equipment, $3 000 of furniture, $1 000 of stationery. It is paid for with $10 000 capital.

4   Credit note no. 34, for $170, received from B. Jones, a supplier, has been posted to C. Jones's account in error.

REFLECTION

When correcting errors such as in journal entries 2 and 4 in Activity 3.3, how did you work out which account to debit and which account to credit? What accounting skills did you have to use? Discuss in pairs/small groups other strategies you could use.

THINK LIKE AN ACCOUNTANT

Businesses need bookkeepers

Worldwide there is high demand by businesses for staff with relevant bookkeeping qualifications, training and experience. Posts such as sales ledger clerk, finance assistant and cash book supervisor are regularly advertised along with offers to support employees while they work towards bookkeeping or accounting qualifications.

Consider whether it is better for a business to train their own staff in the bookkeeping skills they require or to recruit people who already have the skills needed. What are the advantages and disadvantages of each option?

Figure 3.2: Businesses have a high demand for staff with relevant bookkeeping qualifications, training and experience.

PRACTICE QUESTIONS

1 Gina sold goods on credit for $950 less 20% trade discount. She allowed a cash discount of 2%. Which amount should be entered in her sales journal?

A $744.80

B $760.00

C $931.00

D $950.00 [1]

2 Sai received an invoice from Jaya for $2000 less 10% trade discount. Sai has forgotten to enter the invoice in her purchases journal. What effect will this have on Sai's accounts?

	Jaya's account		Purchases account	
	Debit	Credit	Debit	Credit
A		underadded $1800	underadded $1800	
B	underadded $1800			underadded $1800
C		underadded $2000	underadded $2000	
D	underadded $2000			underadded $2000

[1]

3 Deepak's transactions for May were as follows:

May 1	Bought goods from Bhanu for $1000 less 10% trade discount. Bhanu allowed 5% cash discount.
4	Sold goods to Krish for $2000 less 10% trade discount. He allowed 5% cash discount.
7	Bought goods from Adya for $900 less 20% trade discount. Adya allowed 5% cash discount.
8	Purchased equipment on credit from Sanjay for $4000, invoice no. 156.
14	Returned goods that had cost $100 to Bhanu.
19	Krish returned goods that had cost him $120.
20	Purchased goods from Adya for $1000 less 20% trade discount. Adya allowed 5% cash discount.
22	Sold goods to Nour for $2000 less 20% trade discount. He allowed 5% cash discount.
24	Krish returned goods that had cost him $100.
31	Deepak settled all accounts he owed by cheque and received cheques for all amounts owing by his customers. All discounts were taken.

Required

a Enter all the transactions for May into the books of prime entry. [10]

b Total the books as at 31 May and post the books of prime entry to the ledger accounts. [14]

4 Explain the difference between the sales journal and the general journal. [4]

SELF-EVALUATION CHECKLIST

After studying this chapter, complete a table like this:

You should be able to:	Needs more work	Almost there	Ready to move on
Explain that financial transactions are recorded in the books of prime entry before being posted to the ledger accounts.			
List and know when to use the books of prime entry: the sales and sales returns journals, purchases and purchases returns journals, cash book and the journal.			
Explain the purpose of a cash book			
Explain that cash discounts are recorded in the cash book then posted to the discounts allowed and discounts received ledger accounts.			
Explain contra entries are made in the cash book when money is transferred between the bank account and the cash account.			
Enter the transactions in the books of prime entry and post to the ledger from the books of prime entry.			
Record discounts allowed and discounts received in the cash book and ledger accounts.			

> Chapter 4

Balancing accounts

This chapter covers part of syllabus section AS Level 1.2

LEARNING INTENTIONS

In this chapter you will learn how to:

- demonstrate that all ledger accounts are balanced at least once during a trading period
- demonstrate that cash books have two balances, one for cash and one for bank
- balance ledger accounts that have debit or credit balances
- balance both the cash and bank accounts held in the cash book.

ACCOUNTING IN CONTEXT

Know your customers and what they owe

Paul has his own small, specialist engineering business advising companies on designs for new buildings; he offers a service rather than selling goods. He makes few purchases but does have some regular business customers that come for advice.

Like many small business owners, Paul knows a lot about the services he offers but less about keeping accounts. He also finds it difficult to keep his accounts up to date. Paul uses a local bookkeeper to check his ledger accounts a couple of times a year. The bookkeeper calculates the difference between the debits and credits to balance all the accounts and reports back to Paul.

Figure 4.1: Many small business owners know a lot about the services they offer, but less about keeping accounts.

Although Paul is happy for most of his accounts to be checked and balanced occasionally, he checks his bank account more frequently. It is important that he knows how much money is in the business bank account each month so that he knows whether he can afford drawings for his own personal use.

Every month, Paul checks the accounts of his trade receivables and works out how much his customers owe him. Paul sends invoices each time he makes a sale, but he also sends statements out to each regular customer monthly. These statements remind his customers what they have bought, what they have paid for and the outstanding balance on the account. This reminder often encourages his customers to pay.

Discuss in a pair or a group:

- Apart from bank and trade receivables, what other accounts is Paul likely to have?

- Why are some of Paul's accounts only checked a couple of times a year?

- Do you think bank and trade receivables are the most important accounts for all small businesses? Give reasons for your answer.

4.1 Why accounts need to be balanced

Ledger accounts are usually balanced once a month.

The ledger accounts are balanced to determine how much the business owes other people, how much it is owed and how much has been received from, or spent on, the various activities.

The cash book is balanced to determine how much money is in the bank account and how much cash the business has.

4.2 How to balance an account

The steps to **balancing an account** are:

Step 1   Add each side of the account to find the value of:

      i   the total debit entries and

      ii   the total credit entries.

Step 2   Calculate the balance, i.e. the difference between the two totals.

Step 3   Insert the balance on the side with the smaller amount to make both sides equal or, in other words, balance.

> **KEY TERM**
>
> **balancing an account:** the process of finding which side of a ledger account is the greater and by how much.

Step 4   Insert the total on each side of the account and carry the balance down to the other side of the account on the next day.

WORKED EXAMPLE 1

Balancing an account with a *debit balance*

Jai is a customer whose account is as follows.

Jai account					
Debit			**Credit**		
		$			$
Jun 6	Sales	900	Jun 7	Sales returns	300
Jun 10	Sales	3 000	Jun 12	Bank	570
Jun 21	Sales	2 000	Jun 12	Discount allowed	30

To balance Jai's account at the end of June:

Step 1

Add each side of the account to find the value of the debit and credit entries.

The debit side total is $5 900 ($900 + $3 000 + $2 000)

The credit side total is $900 ($300 + $570 + $30)

Step 2

Calculate the balance. This is the difference between the two totals.

Balance is $5 000 ($5 900 − $900)

Note: the debit side has the higher figure. This means that the account is going to have a debit balance.

Step 3

Insert the balance on the side with the smaller amount to make both sides equal, or, in other words, balance.

Jai account					
Debit			**Credit**		
		$			$
Jun 6	Sales	900	Jun 7	Sales returns	300
Jun 10	Sales	3 000	Jun 12	Bank	570
Jun 21	Sales	2 000	Jun 12	Discount	30
			Jun 30	Balance c/d	5 000

This is the balance carried down (c/d).

CONTINUED

Step 4

Insert the total on each side of the account and carry the balance down to the other side of the account on the next day.

Jai account					
Debit			**Credit**		
		$			$
Jun 6	Sales	900	Jun 7	Sales returns	300
July 10	Sales	3 000	Jun 12	Bank	570
Jun 21	Sales	2 000	Jun 12	Discount	30
			Jun 30	Balance c/d	5 000
		5 900			5 900
Jul 1	Balance b/d	5 000			

Carry the balance down to the other side of the account on the next day. This is the balance brought down (b/d).

Insert the total on each side of the account.

Note: the totals of each column ($5 900) are placed level with each other. In bookkeeping nothing is written against these figures. They are simply the totals of each column.

Jai's account has a **debit balance** at the end of June/start of July. This means that he owes the business $5 000 at this time; he is a trade receivable of the business.

WORKED EXAMPLE 2

Balancing an account with a *credit balance*

Deeba is a supplier whose account has been balanced at the end of May.

Deeba account					
Debit			**Credit**		
		$			$
May 8	Purchases returns	1 000	May 1	Balance b/d	500
May 29	Bank	1 470	May 5	Purchases	2 000
May 29	Discount	30	May 26	Purchases	3 000
May 31	Balance c/d	3 000			
		5 500			5 500
			Jun 1	Balance b/d	3 000

Note: the balance b/d at 1 May means that there were entries in the account before May that are not shown. The account was balanced at the end of April resulting in an opening balance on 1 May of $500 cr.

Calculations to balance Deeba's account at 31 May:

TIP

The balances carried down on accounts should always be shown as brought down on the accounts on the next day.

KEY TERM

debit balance: the amount by which the debit side of an account is greater than the credit side.

CONTINUED

Step 1

The debit side total is $2 500 ($1 000 + $1 470 + $30)

The credit side total is $5 500 ($500 + $2 000 + $3 000)

Step 2

Balance is $3 000 ($5 500 − $2 500)

Note: the credit side has the higher figure.

Deeba's account has a **credit balance**. This shows that Deeba is owed $3 000 at the end of June; she is a trade payable of the business.

> ### KEY TERM
>
> **credit balance:** the amount by which the credit side of an account is greater than the debit side.

WORKED EXAMPLE 3

Balancing an account with only one entry on each side

Hannah is a customer whose account is as follows.

Hannah account					
Debit			**Credit**		
		$			$
Jun 7	Sales	800	Jun 14	Bank	800

Note the underlining of the entries on both sides. There is only one entry on each side and they are equal, so there is no balance to carry down and it is acceptable to rule off the account in this way.

WORKED EXAMPLE 4

Balancing an account with equal entries each side

Aidan is a customer whose account for June is as follows.

Aidan account					
Debit			**Credit**		
		$			$
Jun 1	Balance b/d	300	Jun 24	Bank	1 500
Jun 9	Sales	400			
Jun 17	Sales	800			
		1 500			1 500

Note: the totals are underlined on both sides. When there is more than one entry on at least one side, and they are equal, there is no balance to carry down, so it is acceptable to total and rule off the account in this way.

WORKED EXAMPLE 5

Balancing an account with an entry on one side only

a   Maya is a supplier to a business. Her account is balanced at the end of August as shown.

Maya account					
Debit			**Credit**		
		$			$
Jul 31	Balance c/d	3 500	Jul 10	Purchases	3 500
			Aug 1	Balance b/d	3 500

The account was balanced by entering the balance carried down (c/d) on the debit side. The balance was brought down the next day to the credit side.

The only entry made in the account before it was balanced was the purchase of goods for $3 500.

Maya's account has a credit balance. This shows that Maya is owed $3 500 at the end of July; she is a trade payable of the business.

b   Office furniture account is balanced as shown.

Office furniture account					
Debit			**Credit**		
		$			$
Jul 4	Bank	6 000	Jul 31	Balance c/d	6 000
Aug 1	Balance b/d	6 000			

The account was balanced by entering the balance carried down (c/d) on the credit side.

The balance was brought down the next day to the debit side.

The only entry made in the account before it was balanced was the purchase of furniture for $6 000.

The office furniture account has a debit balance, which shows that the business owns furniture costing $6 000.

WORKED EXAMPLE 6

Balancing the three-column cash book

Balancing the three-column cash book is done as shown.

Cash book										
Debit					**Credit**					
		Disc	Cash	Bank				Disc	Cash	Bank
		$	$	$				$	$	$
May 1	Balances b/d		100	740	May 3	Postage			200	
May 3	Sales		440		May 5	Bank C			200	
May 4	J Stores	15		300	May 6	G Lee		20		520
May 5	Cash C			200	May 6	Purchases			160	
May 7	A Ltd	10		230	May 7	Cash C				400
May 7	Bank C		400		May 7	Wages			300	
					May 7	Balances			80	550
		25	940	1 470				20	940	1 470
May 8	Balances		80	550						

Both the cash and the bank accounts have debit balances. This means that the business has $80 in cash and $550 in the bank account at the start of 8 May.

Balances in the cash account are always debit balances. There can never be a credit balance in the cash account because receipts must be equal to, or greater than, payments, i.e. it is not possible to have a negative amount of cash.

It is possible to have a credit balance in the bank account. It happens when payments are greater than receipts. In this case it means that the business has a negative amount of money in the bank. This is called an **overdraft**.

TIP

If a business does not keep a cash book, then the bank account and the cash account will be balanced in the same way as any other ledger account.

TIP

Remember from Section 3.4 (Recording discounts in the cash book) that the discount columns are not balanced. The totals are posted to the discounts allowed and discounts received accounts.

KEY TERM

overdraft: a bank account that has a negative balance. Payments out of the account are greater than receipts into the account.

ACTIVITY 4.1

Jana's business has opening balances at 1 October of $1 000 cash and $2 500 in the bank account. There are no balances on any other accounts. She has the following transactions for the first week of October:

October		$
1	Jana put her own money into the business bank account	8 000
2	Bought goods for resale on credit from Dev	5 000
2	Paid rent by debit card	1 000
4	Sales on credit to Yash	3 000
4	Cash sales	700
5	Put cash into bank account	500
6	Paid Dev money owed by cheque, after deducting a 5% cash discount	
6	Paid for stationery by cash	30

a   Prepare the ledger accounts and cash book to record the transactions.

b   Balance the accounts at 7 October and bring down the balances.

REFLECTION

When answering Activity 4.1, why did you find some accounts more straightforward to balance than others? Did you use a different approach when balancing the cash and the bank accounts in the cash book?

4.3 When are accounts balanced?

Each business will make its own decision about how often their cash book should be balanced. Typically, the cash book may be balanced at weekly intervals in small businesses and daily in large ones because it is always important to know how much money is in the bank account. A business that relies heavily on cash may choose to balance even more frequently.

Accounts for customers and suppliers are balanced monthly because of the practice of sending and receiving statements of account. The statements are copies of the accounts of customers in the sellers' books and are sent to customers so that they can check their ledger accounts with those of their suppliers. Any differences can be queried and an agreement reached between supplier and customer. The statements also remind customers that payment of outstanding balances is due.

The other accounts are balanced as and when required; this will always be when a trial balance is being prepared. Trial balances are explained in Chapter 6.

ACTIVITY 4.2

Some ledger accounts have debit balances; other ledger accounts have credit balances.

a   List the accounts that have debit balances. Do the same for accounts that have credit balances.

b   In small groups, compare your lists to see whether you agree.

THINK LIKE AN ACCOUNTANT

What's it worth?

Balancing accounts allows a business to know the value of what it owns or owes. As individuals we could do this too, but would it be useful for us?

Consider how you feel if you own, or might own, a valuable asset such as a house? Would you want to know what it's worth? If you have a loan to help you buy the house, would you want to know how much you owe at any point in time?

How do you feel about owning items that are less valuable such as a pen or a book? Would you still be interested to know its worth? If not, why not?

Figure 4.2: If you owned a valuable asset such as a house, would you want to know what it's worth?

PRACTICE QUESTIONS

1   Which of the following accounts is most likely to have a credit balance?

   A   capital

   B   discounts allowed

   C   office equipment

   D   rent   [1]

2   When must the balance of each account be known?

   A   each day

   B   each week

   C   when a bookkeeper is available

   D   when a trial balance is being prepared   [1]

3   Balance the following accounts at the end of September:

Discounts allowed account			
Debit		**Credit**	
	$		$
Sep 1 Balance b/d	60		
Sep 30 Cash book	174		

Discounts received account			
Debit		**Credit**	
	$		$
		Sep 1 Balance b/d	110
		Sep 30 Cash book	20

J and P Ltd account			
Debit		**Credit**	
	$		$
Sep 8 Purchases returns	240	Sep 1 Balance b/d	700
Sep 29 Bank	500	Sep 15 Purchases	640

A and B Ltd account			
Debit		**Credit**	
	$		$
Sep 7 Sales	450		
Sep 18 Sales	300		
Sep 21 Sales	400		

CONTINUED

George account

Debit		$		Credit	$
Sep 12	Sales	2 300	Sep 28	Bank	2 208
			Sep 28	Discounts allowed	92

Motor vehicles account

Debit		$		Credit	$
Sep 4	Bank	12 000			

Cash account

Debit		$		Credit	$
Sep 4	Capital	800	Sep 7	Stationery	45
Sep 23	Sales	100	Sep 24	Sales returns	20
			Sep 26	Wages	200

Bank account

Debit		$		Credit	$
Sep 1	Balance b/d	3 000	Sep 8	Motor vehicle	5 000
Sep 5	Sales	450	Sep 25	Purchases	200
Sep 9	Purchases returns	50	Sep 25	Sales returns	100

[8]

4 Explain why trade receivables accounts have debit balances while trade payables accounts have credit balances. [2]

SELF-EVALUATION CHECKLIST

After studying this chapter, complete a table like this:

You should be able to:	Needs more work	Almost there	Ready to move on
Explain that all ledger accounts are balanced at least once during a trading period.			
Explain that cash books have two balances, one for cash and one for bank.			
Balance ledger accounts that have debit or credit balances.			
Balance both the cash and bank accounts held in the cash book.			

Chapter 5

The classification of accounts and division of the ledger

This chapter covers part of syllabus section AS Level 1.3

LEARNING INTENTIONS

In this chapter you will learn how to:

- classify ledger accounts into assets, liabilities, income, expenses, capital and drawings
- sub-divide assets into non-current assets and current assets; sub-divide liabilities into non-current liabilities and current liabilities
- group accounts in terms of personal accounts and impersonal accounts
- divide the accounts into several ledgers, each containing transactions of a similar nature
- classify accounts and divide the ledger to improve the organisation of accounting information and reduce the likelihood of errors.

ACCOUNTING IN CONTEXT

Anyone for coffee?

Nisha owns and runs a mobile coffee business. She set up five years ago with a van that she fitted with storage, fridge and coffee making equipment. She sells many types of coffee and other hot and cold drinks and snacks.

She started with one van in a market in town that she operated herself. It is successful with lots of regular customers who enjoy her coffee and excellent service. Nisha has steadily grown the business. She now owns several similar vans operated by employees in neighbouring towns. The vans can also sell its products at shows and events.

Nisha is well organised. When the business first started, she only needed a few accounts, which were kept in one ledger. As the business grew, she found that the number of transactions and accounts needed also grew. Eventually Nisha bought an accounting software package that kept all the supplier accounts together in a purchases ledger.

Figure 5.1: Nisha has steadily grown her mobile coffee business and now owns several similar vans in neighbouring towns.

Discuss in a pair or a group:

- List items that Nisha's business is likely to own. Split your list into those items the business will keep for more than one year and those items the business will keep for one year or less.

- What ledger accounts might Nisha's business use?

- Why might it be useful for a business to keep all its supplier accounts together?

5.1 Classification of accounts

Businesses have many ledger accounts. Accounts that have transactions of a similar nature will be treated in a similar way in the ledgers.

It can be helpful to group accounts together into categories that have similar features.

The main groups are:

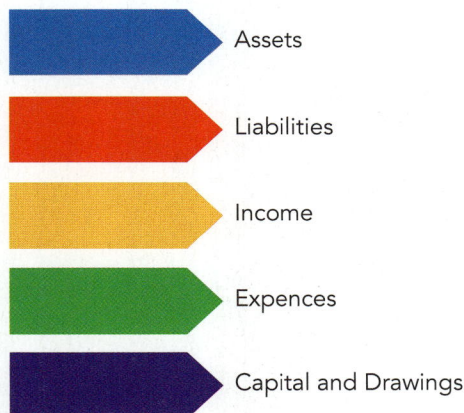

- Assets

- Liabilities

- Income

- Expences

- Capital and Drawings

> **TIP**
>
> It is useful to learn which types of account typically have debit balances and which have credit balances. This will help with your double-entry skills.

Assets

Assets including vehicles can be owned by a business; trade receivables owe money to a business.

Assets are further subdivided into:

- **Non-current assets**, for example property, machinery, vehicles, office furniture and equipment. These assets are intended to be used in the business for more than one year.
- **Current assets**, for example inventory and trade receivables. These assets will be turned into cash within one year.

Asset accounts have debit balances.

Liabilities

Liabilities, for example loans, trade payables and overdrafts, are split into:

- **Non-current liabilities**, i.e. amounts owing that do not have to be paid within one year, such as a long-term loan.
- **Current liabilities**, i.e. amounts owing that must be paid within one year, such as trade payables and bank overdrafts.

Liability accounts have credit balances.

Income

This group includes revenue from sales and other income. Other income can be from rent receivable, discounts received and interest receivable.

Income accounts have credit balances.

Expenses

Expenses accounts are items such as rent, wages, salaries, heating and lighting, postage and stationery. These are costs that are incurred in running the business on a day-to-day basis.

Expense accounts have debit balances.

Capital and drawings

The owner's capital and drawings accounts do not fit neatly into these categories but are equally important.

KEY TERMS

assets: items that are owned by or owed to a business.

non-current assets: items bought by a business that are intended to be used in the business for more than one year.

current assets: cash and other assets, typically inventory and trade receivables, which are expected to be give rise to cash within 12 months.

liabilities: amounts owed by a business.

non-current liabilities: amounts owed by a business that are repayable in more than one year.

current liabilities: items that the business is due to pay within 12 months.

expenses: expenditure incurred in running a business on a day-to-day basis.

The capital account will have a credit balance and the drawings account will have a debit balance.

The balances for the types of account are summarised as follows:

Types of account with debit balances	Types of account with credit balances
Expenses	Liabilities
Assets	Income
Drawings	Capital

ACTIVITY 5.1

Complete the table, ticking the boxes that describe the given accounts in the books of a business.

The first one is completed for you.

Account	Asset	Liability	Revenue or other income	Expense
Delivery vehicles	✓			
Rent				
Loan				
Interest received				
Interest paid				
Trade receivables				
Inventory				
Discounts allowed				
Postage				
Bank				
Rent receivable				
Trade payables				
Computers				
Wages				
Discounts received				

KEY CONCEPT LINK

A true and fair view: Organising the information in the accounts makes it easier to work out the value of a business's assets, liabilities and other types of account. This helps owners, lenders, accountants or anyone else who sees the information to get a *true and fair view* of the business.

An alternative way that accounts can be classified is to put them into one of two classes: a **personal account** or an **impersonal account**.

a   *Personal accounts* include:

- accounts for trade receivables

KEY TERMS

personal account: an account relating to a person.

impersonal account: any account other than a personal account.

- accounts for trade payables
- the owner's capital and drawings accounts.

b   *Impersonal accounts* include:

- asset accounts including both non-current and current assets
- **nominal accounts**, which include expenses accounts, revenue accounts or accounts with credit balances.

5.2 Division of the ledger

It was explained in Chapter 1 that a ledger is a book (or computer file) containing accounts. Except in very small businesses, there are too many accounts to be kept in a single ledger. It is usual to divide the accounts among several ledgers.

Ledger	Use
Sales ledger	For the accounts of customers that buy on credit.
Purchases ledger	For the accounts of suppliers from whom the business buys on credit.
General (or nominal) ledger	For assets, liabilities, revenue and other income, expenses and capital.
Private ledger	For accounts of a confidential nature, such as the owner's capital and drawings accounts and loan accounts; also the statements of profit or loss and statements of financial position (see Chapters 7 and 8).
Cash book	For the bank and cash accounts.

Businesses do not need to use all the ledgers listed. Businesses will choose to use the ones that are useful to them. For example, the business owners might want to keep a private ledger as they would not want their employees to know how much the business had borrowed, or how much profit the business makes and how much the owner has taken from the business as their private drawings. Other business owners choose not to have a separate private ledger but will keep these accounts within the general ledger.

The division of the ledger is essential in a business that employs several bookkeepers, as the work may be divided between them so that they do not all need to be working on the same ledger at the same time. It makes sense to group items of a similar nature, for example all sales are together in one ledger, the sales ledger. This allows staff to be trained in different aspects of the business. Most importantly, it helps to detect and prevent errors occurring in the books of account. It may also help to detect and prevent fraud by the accounts staff. This is a form of internal control.

KEY TERMS

nominal account: an account used to record the revenue and expenses of a business. It also relates to an account or accounts that record the revenue of the business from sales.

sales ledger: the book that contains the individual accounts of all the business's credit customers.

purchases ledger: the book that contains the individual accounts of all the business's credit suppliers.

TIP

Although individual customer accounts are in the sales ledger, the sales account itself is in the general ledger.

Equally, supplier accounts are in the purchases ledger, but the purchases account is in the general ledger.

ACTIVITY 5.2

In which ledger would you expect to see the following accounts?
The first one is completed for you.

	Ledger
Motor vehicles	General
Capital	
A customer who buys goods on credit	
Supplier of office equipment	
Bank	
Wages	
Sales	

REFLECTION

When answering Activity 5.2, how did you decide on the correct ledger? Explain to another learner how you made your choices. Was your knowledge of classifying accounts into assets or liabilities etc. useful when choosing the appropriate ledger?

ACTIVITY 5.3

Complete the following sentences by inserting the correct word from the following list:

non-current	expense	purchases	general	sales

a   The _____ ledger contains the accounts of suppliers from whom the business buys on credit.

b   The heating and lighting account is stored in the _____ ledger and is an example of a _____ account.

c   Goods bought on credit are recorded in the _____ ledger.

d   A _____ asset is bought for use in the business for a long period of time.

THINK LIKE AN ACCOUNTANT

It's good to be organised

Classifying accounts into types with similar features helps with their organisation. This makes it easier to track the value of a business's assets and liabilities and to assess whether its revenue is greater than its expenses.

Grouping information into types is not just done in accounting; it's done in many ways that people come across in both their personal and working lives. Examples of organising information include books in a library, clothes of different size and style in a shop and organising your study notes into topics.

Imagine being in a book shop or library where the books were not organised. What might be the consequences? Think of three more examples of information that you have seen grouped into types. What possible advantages come from organising information? Can you think of any disadvantages?

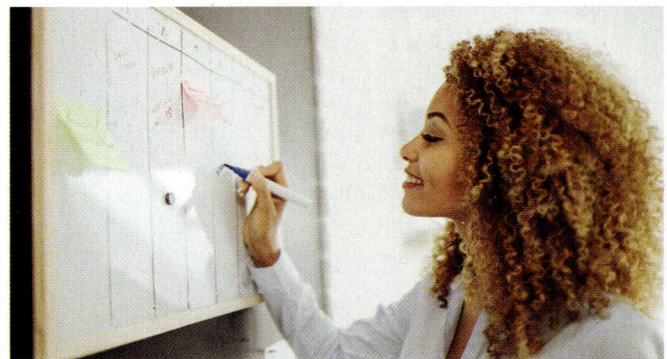

Figure 5.2: Classifying accounts can make it easier to track the value of a business's assets.

PRACTICE QUESTIONS

1   Which account is most likely to be kept in a private ledger?

  A   drawings

  B   interest received

  C   rent

  D   sales   [1]

2   How should cash discounts be classified?

	Discounts allowed	**Discounts received**
A	asset	liability
B	expense	income
C	income	expense
D	liability	asset

                                                                                  [1]

3   Explain why it can be useful to group accounts into different categories.   [4]

4   Discuss why a business may use more than one ledger.   [6]

SELF-EVALUATION CHECKLIST

After studying this chapter, complete a table like this:

You should be able to:	Needs more work	Almost there	Ready to move on
Classify ledger accounts into assets, liabilities, income, expenses, capital and drawings.			
Sub-divide assets into non-current assets and current assets; sub-divide liabilities into non-current liabilities and current liabilities.			
Group accounts in terms of personal accounts and impersonal accounts.			
Divide the accounts into several ledgers, each containing transactions of a similar nature.			
Classify accounts and divide the ledger to improve the organisation of accounting information and reduce the likelihood of errors.			

Chapter 6

The trial balance

This chapter covers part of syllabus sections AS Level 1.2 and 1.4

LEARNING INTENTIONS

In this chapter you will learn how to:

- apply a range of techniques to find missing figures in order to produce financial statements
- ensure that in any trial balance, the total of the debit balances equals the total of the credit balances
- work out that if the debit and credit totals are not equal then there must be at least one error
- demonstrate that if the debit and credit totals are equal then the trial balance may be correct
- make checks to help find trial balance errors.

ACCOUNTING IN CONTEXT

Big business needs accurate accounting

Unilever is one of the world's largest producers of consumer goods. It manufactures a wide range of products from food and refreshments to personal and home care. Unilever owns many well-known brands including Magnum, Dove, Lipton and Lux. These goods are sold in over 190 countries.

Like other large companies, Unilever produces an annual report that summarises its finances. Unilever's report for 2018 showed that its profit before taxation rose to over $13 billion and its total assets were worth about $66 billion. Many transactions and bookkeeping entries underlie these figures. Unilever requires a carefully thought-through accounting system. This reduces the likelihood of errors and fraud, giving confidence that the figures in the annual report provide a true and fair view of the finances for the business.

Producing a trial balance is an important part of any robust accounting system and can help to find some of the most common mistakes that can occur when recording transactions.

Figure 6.1: Unilever owns many well-known brands including Magnum, Dove, Lipton and Lux.

Discuss in a pair or a group:

- What is fraud? Have a look in a dictionary or do an internet search to find out.
- What kind of errors do you think bookkeepers might make when entering transactions into books of prime entry and ledger accounts?
- Why is it important that businesses of all sizes are concerned with avoiding errors in their accounts?

6.1   What is a trial balance?

In Chapter 3, we saw that the documents used in transactions, such as invoices and credit notes, are recorded in the books of prime entry and then posted to the accounts. This chapter introduces the next step: preparing a **trial balance**.

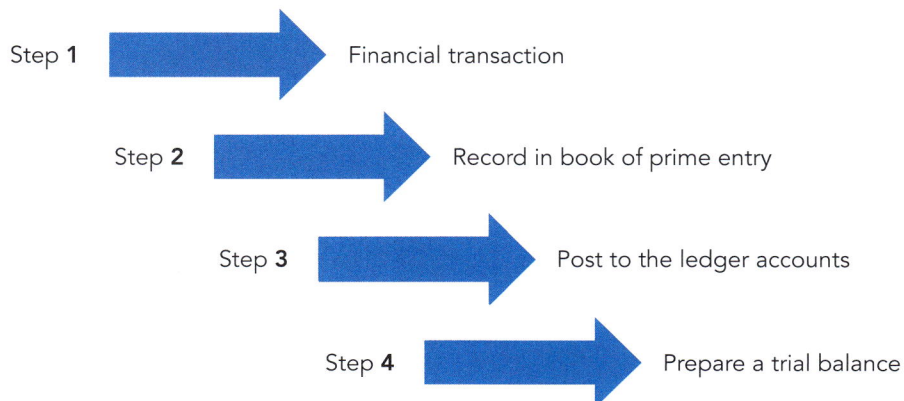

Step **1** → Financial transaction

Step **2** → Record in book of prime entry

Step **3** → Post to the ledger accounts

Step **4** → Prepare a trial balance

KEY TERM

trial balance: a list of the balances on each account extracted from the ledgers at a particular date. Its purpose is to check the arithmetical accuracy of the double entry in the ledger.

The principle of double-entry determines that the debit balances and credit balances should agree. If the totals do not agree there must be an error somewhere in the bookkeeping.

The size of the business affects how often a trial balance is prepared. All businesses must prepare a trial balance at least once a year so that it can be used to produce the financial statements (see Chapters 7 and 8). For a **sole trader**, once a year is probably enough. For a large company it would be more usual to prepare a trial balance at least every month in order to prepare monthly reports for managers that help in making decisions about the business.

If the accounts are kept using a computerised accounting system, a trial balance can be prepared easily at any time simply by using the function in the accounting package.

KEY TERM

sole trader: a business that is owned by one person.

6.2 How to prepare a trial balance

The steps to prepare a trial balance are:

Step 1 Balance all the ledger accounts including the cash book (see Chapter 4).

Step 2 List all the accounts putting the debit balances in one column and the credit balances in another column.

Step 3 Add up the debit column and add up the credit column. The total of the debit balances should equal the total of the credit balances. If the totals are equal, the trial balance agrees.

TIP

Any account that does not have a balance, where the value of the debit and credit entries are the same, is not included in the trial balance.

WORKED EXAMPLE 1

Darsha has balanced the accounts in her ledgers at 31 March 2021.

The following accounts have debit balances:

motor vehicles $25 000; machinery $15 000; office furniture $8 000; purchases $22 000; sales returns $1 000; rent payable $16 000; wages and salaries $12 000; heating and lighting $900; insurance $1 800; cash $1 200; bank $4 700; drawings $6 000.

She also has total trade receivables of $6 400. This is the total of all the balances on the customer accounts in the sales ledger.

The following accounts have credit balances:

sales $68 000; purchase returns $2 000; bank loan $12 000; capital $33 000.

She also has total trade payables of $5 000. This is the total of all the balances on the supplier accounts in the purchase ledger.

Prepare a trial balance for Darsha at 31 March 2021.

Step 1

Balance the accounts. The balances have been provided in the question.

CONTINUED

Trial balance extracted from the books of Darsha at 31 March 2021		
Account	Debit balances	Credit balances
	$	$
Motor vehicles	25 000	
Machinery	15 000	
Office furniture	8 000	
Sales		68 000
Sales returns	1 000	
Purchases	22 000	
Purchases returns		2 000
Trade receivables	6 400	
Trade payables		5 000
Rent and rates	16 000	
Wages and salaries	12 000	
Heating and lighting	900	
Insurance	1 800	
Cash	1 200	
Bank	4 700	
Bank loan		12 000
Capital – Darsha		33 000
Drawings	6 000	
	120 000	120 000

Step 2 Accounts with debit and credit balances are listed in separate columns.

TIP

It is vital that the correct date be given in the title of the trial balance. This confirms the date at which all the accounts have been balanced and will be relied on when producing the financial statements (see Chapters 7 and 8).

Step 3 The debit and credit columns are both totalled.

The total of the debit balances and credit balances agree at $120 000. The trial balance balances. This means that for every debit entry made in the ledgers, an equal and opposite credit entry has been made in the ledgers. This helps to confirm the accuracy of the bookkeeping.

Note: the total trade receivables figure goes in the trial balance instead of all the individual customer account balances, and the total trade payables figure goes in the trial balance instead of all the individual suppliers account balances. This helps to reduce the number of accounts in the trial balance. This is explained further in Chapter 14.

KEY CONCEPT LINK

Duality: Double-entry means that for every debit entry made in the ledgers, an equal and opposite credit entry has been made in the ledgers. As a result, a correctly drawn up trial balance will always show that the totals of the debit balances and credit balances agree.

ACTIVITY 6.1

Prepare a trial balance from the following balances that have been extracted from the books of a small online retailer at 31 December.

	$
Property	100 000
Motor vehicles	18 000
Office furniture	14 000
Computer	2 000
Sales	40 000
Sales returns	600
Purchases	6 000
Purchases returns	500
Motor vehicle expenses	4 000
Advertising	1 600
Office expenses	1 000
Stationery	400
Cash	200
Bank	300 (credit)
Capital	110 000
Drawings	3 000

REFLECTION

When answering Activity 6.1, you were not told which accounts had debit balances and which accounts had credit balances. Explain to another learner how you decided whether each account was debit or credit. You were told that the bank account had a credit balance; why was this necessary?

6.3 Benefits of a trial balance

The trial balance is an essential link between the ledger accounts and the financial statements of a business. The main benefits of a trial balance are as follows:

1 To check that the total of the debit balances equals the total of the credit balances.

2 It will help to uncover many types of error in the ledger accounts and can make it easier to find and correct the errors (see Chapter 15).

3 To provide a summary of all the ledger accounts and their balances in one document.

4 It is used for preparing the financial statements (see Chapters 7 and 8).

6.4 Limitations of a trial balance

If the debit and credit totals in a trial balance do not agree (they are different), there must be at least one mistake somewhere in the bookkeeping.

If the debit and credit totals in a trial balance do agree (they are the same), it proves that for every debit entry an equal credit entry has been made. Unfortunately, there can still be errors!

There are six types of error that can occur even when the debit and credit totals in the trial balance agree. They are as follows:

Type of error	Explanation	Example
Errors of omission	A financial transaction omitted completely from the books results in there being neither a debit nor a credit entry for the transaction. This could happen if a transaction is not entered in a book of prime entry.	$100 of equipment is bought for cash. The transaction is forgotten and not entered in the equipment or the cash account.
Errors of commission	A financial transaction is posted with the correct amount to the correct side of the wrong account, but the account is in the same class.	The payment for stationery is posted in error to the advertising account. Stationery and advertising are both classed as expenses.
Errors of principle	A financial transaction is posted with the correct amount, to the correct side of a wrong class of account.	Payment for fuel for a vehicle has been debited to the motor vehicles account instead of the motor vehicles running expenses account. Motor vehicles expenses are classed as expenses while the motor vehicles are non-current assets.
Errors of original entry	A wrong amount is entered in a book of prime entry for a financial transaction.	A purchase invoice for $100 is entered in the purchases journal as $10.
Complete reversal of entries	An account that should have been debited has been credited, and the account that should have been credited has been debited.	A payment made to Sam is debited to the bank account and credited to Sam's account.
Compensating errors	Two or more errors that cancel each other out.	An invoice for $1 200 in the sales journal is posted to the customer's account as $1 000. At the same time, the sales journal total is **underadded** (too low) by $200. The debit balance on the customer's account and the credit balance on sales account will both be underadded by $200.

Note: a number that is underadded is incorrect and is smaller than the correct figure. A number that is **overadded** is also incorrect but is larger than the correct figure.

It is important to consider these six types of error. When errors are found they must be corrected using the journal (see Section 3.7). If errors are not corrected, then they will result in inaccurate figures in the accounts.

> ## KEY TERMS
>
> **underadded:** a figure that is found by adding up two or more figures but which is lower than the correct figure.
>
> **overadded:** a figure that is found by adding up two or more figures but which is higher than the correct figure.

ACTIVITY 6.2

State which type of error each of the following represents:

		Type of error
1	A customer's invoice has been omitted from the sales journal.	
2	A purchase of goods for $100 has been entered in the purchases journal as $1 000.	
3	Discount received from Marie has been debited to Maya's account.	
4	Payment of advertising has been debited to the bank account and credited to the advertising account.	
5	Entries were $100 too high (overadded) on both the heating and lighting account and the sales account.	
6	Entries were $50 too high (overadded) on the heating and lighting account and $50 too low (underadded) on the rent payable account.	
7	The purchase of office furniture has been debited to the office expenses account.	

TIP

Learn the six types of error that do not affect the trial balance. You must be able to give examples of them.

6.4 What to do if the trial balance fails to agree

If the debit and credit totals on a trial balance are not the same, then there must be an error. If errors are not corrected, they will result in inaccurate figures in the financial statements.

There are many different possible reasons for errors. It is worthwhile carrying out some simple checks first before spending a lot of time checking all your postings.

Simple checks to find trial balance errors:

1 Check the additions of the trial balance.

2 Check that all accounts have been entered in the trial balance and are correctly entered in the debit or credit column.

3 If the difference between the debit and credit totals is divisible by nine, two figures may have been transposed in a balance (e.g. $269 may have been copied as $296).

4 If you still haven't found the cause of the imbalance, go back to the start and check the balances on each of the accounts and that you have transferred them correctly to the trial balance.

ACTIVITY 6.3

An inexperienced bookkeeper has extracted the trial balance at 31 December 2021. It does not balance.

Rewrite the trial balance and correct the errors.

Trial balance at 31 December 2020		
Account	Debit balances	Credit balances
	$	$
Plant and machinery	50 000	
Loan from David	10 000	
Office equipment	10 000	
Wages	9 400	
Rent and rates		3 000
Cash		1 200
General expenses	2 200	
Sales		97 000
Purchases	60 000	
Discounts allowed		460
Discounts received	360	
Bank	3 000	
Trade receivables	11 000	
Trade payables		6 000
Purchases returns	600	
Sales returns		800
Rent receivable	1 400	
Capital		70 000
Drawings		34 300
	157 960	212 760

THINK LIKE AN ACCOUNTANT

Attention to detail

When employers want to recruit new workers, they often provide a person specification to potential applicants as well as other information about the job. A person specification states the personal qualities and skills that the employer is seeking in the successful applicant.

The qualities sought when selecting a new bookkeeper or accountant will vary from business to business. However, the nature of the work means that there are some qualities that are very commonly found in person specifications for accounting staff. These include attention to detail, being well organised and having good communication skills. Why do you think that attention to detail is an important skill for a bookkeeper? What other skills do you think would be useful for a bookkeeper to have and why?

Figure 6.2: Attention to detail, organisation and communication are all highly valued skills in the field of accounting.

PRACTICE QUESTIONS

1 An invoice has been recorded in J. Smith's account instead of A. Smith's account. What type of error has occurred?

   A   commission

   B   compensating

   C   original entry

   D   pinciple   **[1]**

2 Discounts received of $100 for January have been posted to the debit of the discounts allowed account instead. What effect has this had on the trial balance?

   A $100 too little debit and $100 too much credit

   B $100 too much debit

   C $100 too much debit and $100 too little credit

   D   no effect on the trial balance   **[1]**

3 Which of the following is *not* a reason to prepare a trial balance?

   A   to check that the total of the debit balances equals the total of the credit balances

   B   to help find errors in the accounts

   C   to increase the sales of a business

   D   to prepare monthly reports for managers   **[1]**

4 The following balances at 31 December 2021 have been extracted from Lee's books.

	$	
Sales	120 000	
Sales returns	1 800	
Purchases	76 000	
Purchases returns	3 000	
Wages and salaries	30 000	
Heating and lighting	4 400	
Rent payable	8 000	
Rent receivable	2 000	
Travelling expenses	3 400	
Telephone expenses	2 400	
Discounts allowed	1 000	
Discounts received	700	
Plant and machinery	60 000	
Cash	400	
Bank	3 200	(debit)
Trade receivables	18 000	
Trade payables	15 500	
Loan from Ting	10 000	
Drawings	6 000	
Capital	?	

Prepare a trial balance at 31 December 2021 for Lee's business and calculate the balance on his capital account. **[8]**

SELF-EVALUATION CHECKLIST

After studying this chapter, complete a table like this:

You should be able to:	Needs more work	Almost there	Ready to move on
Explain that a trial balance is a list of the balances on each account extracted from the ledgers at a particular date.			
Ensure that in any trial balance, the total of the debit balances equals the total of the credit balances.			
Work out that if the debit and credit totals are not equal then there must be at least one error.			
Work out that if the debit and credit totals are equal then the trial balance may be correct.			
Make checks to help find trial balance errors.			

> Part 2

Financial accounting

> Chapter 7

Statement of profit or loss

This chapter covers part of syllabus sections AS Level 1.5

LEARNING INTENTIONS

In this chapter you will learn how to:

- describe what a sole trader is
- prepare a basic statement of profit or loss from a trial balance
- account for returns, discounts and other income
- describe unlimited liability
- identify that a statement of profit or loss shows the revenue and expenses of the business, the gross profit and the profit for the year.

ACCOUNTING IN CONTEXT

Cycle sales

Sunil has run his own business since he gave up a full-time job nearly a year ago. He operates as a sole trader, buying and selling a variety of goods related to bicycles.

Sunil thought that he would enjoy running his own business but he has found it hard work and spends much of his time worrying about things that he had never considered. Not only does Sunil have to make all of the decisions, but he is also responsible for keeping detailed records of his financial transactions, making sure he obeys the law and produces financial statements to show whether he has made a profit or not.

His accountant also warned him that, as a sole trader, he has 'unlimited liability' – it is this that worries Sunil the most.

Figure 7.1: Sunil operates as a sole trader, buying and selling a variety of goods related to bicycles.

Discuss in a pair or a group:

- What does it mean to be operating as a sole trader?
- Why would a sole trader want to run his or her own business?
- What is profit and why is it important to a sole trader?
- What is 'unlimited liability' and how might it affect the sole trader?

7.1 Sole traders and profit

A sole trader might employ people to work for the business, but they will have total responsibility for making any decisions.

Many people run their own business, and some of the advantages of being a sole trader include:

- being in full control of their own business – only the sole trader will be making the decisions and so can run the business in a way that suits their values and objectives
- running a business that is linked to one of their hobbies or interests – for example, a keen cricketer might like the idea of owning a shop that sells cricket equipment
- hoping that it will provide them with a large income and – this is probably the biggest and most common objective when a sole trader starts in business.

Whether the sole trader earns an income will largely depend on whether the business makes a **profit** or a **loss**. While making a profit is important for any business, it is vital for a sole trader for two reasons:

- the profit belongs to the sole trader
- sole traders have **unlimited liability**.

If the business does not have the resources to pay off debts and losses, then the people owed money can take legal action to claim the sole trader's assets, e.g. houses, cars and personal possessions, in settlement of any debts. The sole trader may face personal bankruptcy. This is different from limited companies (see Chapter 21) where the debts of the business remain with the business and its owners could only lose the value of their investment.

> **KEY TERMS**
>
> **profit:** the amount by which the income (or revenue) exceeds the expenses of the business.
>
> **loss:** the amount by which expenses exceed the income (or revenue) of the business.
>
> **unlimited liability:** the owner of a business is personally responsible for all the debts and losses of that business.

There are a number of other disadvantages to being a sole trader, including:

- a limit on how much finance can be introduced to the new business – the sole trader may be reliant on savings and it may be difficult for them to convince banks or other investors to help them

- having to work very long hours – if the sole trader takes time off (holidays or sickness) there may be no-one to take the day-to-day decisions

- being expected to have a wide range of skills and knowledge to run every aspect of the business. It may be difficult and expensive to find people to help cover any areas where they do not have the expertise

- not having another owner to discuss ideas with when they are considering several possible alternatives.

7.2 Statements of profit or loss

The profit or loss of a sole trader is found by preparing a **statement of profit or loss** (also referred to as a statement of profit *and* loss in many countries). This is prepared at the end of a one complete year but may be produced more frequently.

The trial balance is used as a starting point from which the statement of profit or loss can be produced.

The statement of profit or loss will show several things:

- **Gross profit** – the amount of profit made on the goods themselves. It is the difference between the **revenue** earned from selling those goods and the cost of selling those goods (**cost of sales**). Revenue is calculated as the total sales less any refunds and is known as **net sales**

- **Profit (or loss) for the year** – the 'bottom-line profit or loss' made by the business when all of the day-to-day running costs (expenses) have been deducted

- Expenses – the costs that the owner must incur for the business to function. Many expenses will involve regular outflows of cash, e.g. wages, or the payment of bills, e.g. electricity.

We shall now see how a statement of profit or loss is produced from a trial balance.

> ### KEY TERMS
>
> **statement of profit or loss:** an account prepared periodically to find the profit or loss made by a business.
>
> **gross profit:** the profit calculated by deducting the cost of sales from the net sales in the statement of profit or loss.
>
> **revenue:** the sales of goods or services made by a business.
>
> **cost of sales:** the net cost of the goods sold to customers.
>
> **net sales:** the difference between the original sales made and the amount of refunds that were given.
>
> **profit (or loss) for the year:** the profit (or loss) calculated by adding other income to the gross profit and deducting the business expenses.

WORKED EXAMPLE 1

Pavol is a sole trader who buys and sells clothing. His trial balance at 31 December 2019 contained the following:

	$	$
Heat and light	3 640	
Purchases	32 700	
Purchase returns		1 230
Rent and rates	9 870	
Sales		70 200
Sales returns	2 980	
Wages and salaries	24 190	

Step 1

Transfer the balances from the nominal ledger accounts to the statement of profit or loss. In most cases, this will 'close off' the accounts so that they can start the new period with a zero balance:

CONTINUED

Heat and light account

X			
X	Statement of profit or loss		3 840
3 840			3 840

Sales account

		X	
Statement of profit or loss	80 200	X	
	80 200	80 200	

Note: items that have a credit balance, e.g. sales will need to be debited to the statement of profit or loss while those with a debit balance will need to be credited.

Step 2

Make the entries in the statement of profit or loss and balance off to identify the gross profit and the profit for the year:

	$		$
Sales returns	2 980	Sales	80 200
Purchases	32 700	Purchase returns	1 230
Gross profit c/d	45 750		
	81 430		81 430
Heat and light	3 640	Gross profit b/d	45 750
Rent and rates	9 870		
Wages and salaries[2]	24 190		
Profit for the year[1]	8 050		
	45 750		45 750

Notes:

[1]   The business has made a profit, which belongs to the sole trader and would increase the owner's capital balance by making the following entries:

   Debit: Statement of profit or loss   8 050

   Credit: Capital   8 050

[2]   If the wages and salaries had been $34 190, then the statement of profit or loss would have looked like this:

	$		$
Sales returns	2 980	Sales	80 200
Purchases	32 700	Purchase returns	1 230
Gross profit c/d	45 750		
	81 430		81 430
Heat and light	3 640	Gross profit b/d	45 750
Rent and rates	9 870	Loss for the year	1 950
Wages and salaries	34 190		
	47 700		47 700

CONTINUED

While the entries made in the nominal ledger accounts have not changed, the layout of the income statement and some of the terms used have changed considerably. A vertical layout is now more common, which would look like this:

	$	$
Revenue		80 200
Less: Sales returns[1]		(2 980)
		77 220
Less: Cost of sales		
Purchases	32 700	
Less: Purchase returns[1]	(1 230)	
Cost of sales		31 470
Gross profit[2]		45 750
Less: Expenses		
Heat and light	3 640	
Rent and rates	9 870	
Wages and salaries	34 190	
Total expenses		(47 700)
Loss for the year		(1 950)

Note:

[1] Sales returns are deducted from the sales (revenue) because they represent a correction to the overstatement of some original sales caused by:

- customers being charged on the original invoice for goods that were not supplied or missing
- customers being charged the wrong price or not being given the correct trade or bulk discount

  Purchase returns are deducted from the purchases figure for exactly the same reasons except that in this situation, the business is the customer not the seller.

[2] If the business is offering a service rather than selling goods, then there would be no need to include cost of sales and a calculation of gross profit. The expenses would be deducted from the revenue to arrive at the profit for the year.

ACTIVITY 7.1

Shola is a sole trader who buys and sells shoes. The trial balance at 31 March 2020 contained the following:

	$	$
Delivery costs	8 645	
Office expenses	23 180	
Purchases	57 210	
Purchase returns		1 605
Rent and rates	12 870	
Sales		134 520
Sales returns	3 040	
Wages and salaries	53 985	

Required

Produce a statement of profit or loss for Shola that shows the gross profit and profit (or loss) for the year.

7.3 Returns, discounts and other incomes

There are a number of items that might require adjustments to be made to the statement of profit or loss. These include:

- inventory
- carriage inwards and outwards
- discounts allowed and received
- other income.
- sole traders removing goods for their own use
- wages paid to rework goods

Inventory

Many customers will not place orders. They will visit the business expecting goods to be instantly available, and if those goods are not in stock, sales will be lost and the customer may never return.

The sole trader will try to hold enough **inventory** to ensure that demand can be met but not too much that large amounts of cash are tied up. This means that inventory levels at the beginning and end of the accounting year could be different and this will mean that the cost of sales figure will not be the purchases figure. As will be seen in Worked example 2, the cost of sales will involve the following calculation:

Opening inventory + purchases – closing inventory = cost of sales

This is because most businesses will attempt to sell the oldest inventory first before moving onto the replacement inventory (purchases). The closing inventory is deducted because, if it is still in the warehouse, it hasn't been sold.

Carriage inwards and outwards

When goods are transported, costs are incurred that might be passed onto the buyer. These **carriage inwards** costs represent an addition to purchases.

KEY TERMS

inventory: the unsold goods of a business involved in buying and selling at a particular point in time.

carriage inwards: the additional delivery cost paid by a business in excess of the purchase price of the goods purchased for resale. It is added to the cost of goods by the supplier.

carriage outwards: the additional cost charged by the seller to deliver goods sold.

Some businesses do not pass transportation costs onto the customer. These **carriage outwards** costs are shown as an expense in the statement of profit or loss.

Note: both carriage inwards and carriage outwards are debit balances in the trial balance because they both represent costs to the business.

Discounts allowed and received

Many businesses sell goods on credit. Credit is often only given to customers who have proved to be reliable and the business may have carried out checks before deciding to offer credit terms. The business will decide when the customer will pay for those goods and will often set a credit limit.

Unfortunately, getting paid on time – or at all – is not guaranteed and this can make it difficult for the business to pay for its purchases and day-to-day expenses. One approach to encouraging customers to pay on time is the use of *cash (or settlement) discounts*.

A cash (or settlement) discount involves the customer having the option of paying a smaller amount if payment is made before a specified date.

If the customer pays quickly, then the amount of money deducted is a *discount allowed*. This is recorded as an expense in the statement of profit or loss and is kept separate from any sales figures for two reasons:

- the discount is dependent on payment and not on the sales – these are seen as different transactions and so the value of the sale itself is not considered to have changed

- theoretically, when a discount is offered, there is no guarantee that the customer will take advantage of it. The value of the sale itself should not be based on when the customer decides to pay for the goods.

The business may buy goods and find that the supplier offers a discount to encourage prompt payment. This works in the same way as discounts allowed. If the business chooses to pay quickly then the amount deducted is a *discount received* and is kept separate from any purchases figures. As will be seen in Worked example 2, discounts received are added to the gross profit figure.

WORKED EXAMPLE 2

Kolla is a sole trader who buys and sells hats. The trial balance at 31 March 2020 contained the following:

	$	$
Carriage inwards	880	
Carriage outwards	540	
Discounts allowed	2 020	
Discounts received		1 635
Heat and light	2 380	
Inventory at 1 April 2019	23 190	
Purchases	135 420	
Purchase returns		2 390
Rent and rates	22 200	
Sales		246 750
Sales returns	1 760	
Wages and salaries	37 625	

Note: inventory at 31 March 2020 was valued at $19 875.

CONTINUED

The statement of profit or loss would appear as follows:

Statement of profit or loss for Kolla for the year ended 31 March 2020			
	$	$	$
Revenue			246 750
Less: Sales returns			(1 760)
			244 990
Less: Cost of sales [4]			
Opening inventory		23 190	
Purchases	135 420		
Carriage inwards [1]	880		
Less: Purchase returns	(2 390)	133 910	
		157 100	
Less: Closing inventory		(19 875)	(137 225)
Gross profit			107 765
Discount received [2]			1 635
			109 400
Less: Expenses			
Carriage outwards		540	
Discounts allowed		2 020	
Heat and light		2 380	
Rent and rates		22 200	
Wages and salaries		37 625	
Total expenses			(64 765)
Profit for the year [3]			44 635

Notes:

[1] Carriage inwards is taken as part of the *cost of sales*, not an expense.

[2] Discounts and any **other income** received should be added to the gross profit.

[3] The *profit for the year* figure is important and will be needed when the statement of financial position is produced (see Chapter 8).

[4] If the business doesn't buy and sell goods but provides a service (e.g. an accountant), then there will be no cost of sales or gross profit. The income (revenue) will be shown and the expenses will be deducted from this to give the profit for the year.

KEY TERM

other income: income earned by the business from sources other than its main activities.

ACTIVITY 7.2

Bikram is a sole trader who buys and sells books. The trial balance at 31 March 2020 contained the following:

	$	$
Carriage inwards	2 305	
Carriage outwards	1 234	
Discounts allowed	1 888	
Discounts received		2 067
Heat and light	3 765	
Insurance	4 760	
Inventory at 1 April 2019	34 096	
Motor expenses	5 269	
Purchases	245 110	
Purchase returns		5 620
Rent and rates	14 400	
Sales		354 987
Sales returns	3 985	
Wages and salaries	67 109	

Note: inventory at 31 March 2020 was valued at $29 143.

Required

Produce a statement of profit or loss for Bikram that shows the gross profit and profit (or loss) for the year.

7.4 Other operating income, drawings and direct wages

Other operating income

Many businesses aim to earn their income from selling goods or providing a service. However, it is quite possible that income may be earned in other (sometimes unexpected) ways including:

- interest on bank accounts
- commission earned
- rental income.

As these incomes were not what the business was set up for – and may be quite minor when compared to the main sources of income – these are kept separate from the main revenue. These are added to gross profit, alongside items such as the discounts received.

> **KEY CONCEPT LINK**
>
> **Business entity:** A business is a separate legal entity from the owner of a business. The accounting records must relate only to the business and not to the personal assets and spending of the owner.

Drawings

Some sole traders might take goods rather than cash for their own use, e.g. food from the shelves of a food shop. The double-entry to record this would be:

- Debit: drawings
- Credit: purchases

Wages and cost of sales

It is possible that the business might buy in goods that are not yet in a condition to be sold. Employees' time might be used to get these goods into a condition where they can be sold. In that situation, it would be appropriate to add the wages relating to this work to the cost of sales, together with any materials that might have been used, e.g. paint or new packaging.

WORKED EXAMPLE 3

Izzi is a sole trader who buys and sells household cleaning products. Her trial balance at 30 June 2020 contained the following:

	$	$
Administrative expenses	47 520	
Carriage inwards	2 134	
Carriage outwards	1 908	
Discounts allowed	3 319	
Discounts received		4 107
Drawings	27 145	
Heat and light	6 603	
Interest received		2 890
Inventory at 1 July 2019	32 985	
Motoring expenses	9 703	
Purchases	204 320	
Purchase returns		1 247
Rent and rates	21 600	
Sales		302 389
Sales returns	5 731	
Wages and salaries	52 680	

Notes:

1. Inventory at 30 June 2020 was valued at $27 659.
2. Izzi took goods valued at $1 800 for her own use.
3. 20% of the wages and salaries had been paid to staff for getting the goods in a saleable condition.

CONTINUED

The statement of profit or loss would appear as follows:

Statement of profit or loss for Izzi for the year ended 30 June 2020			
	$	$	$
Revenue			302 389
Less: Sales returns			(5 731)
			296 658
Less: Cost of sales			
Opening inventory		32 985	
Purchases	204 320		
Carriage inwards	2 134		
Less: Purchase returns	(1 247)	205 207	
		238 192	
Wages paid to prepare goods (20% × 52 680)[1]		10 536	
Drawings[2]		(1 800)	
Less: Closing inventory		(27 659)	(219 269)
Gross profit			77 389
Interest received			2 890
Discount received			4 107
			84 386
Less: Expenses			
Administrative expenses		47 520	
Carriage outwards		1 908	
Discounts allowed		3 319	
Heat and light		6 603	
Motoring expenses		9 703	
Rent and rates		21 600	
Wages and salaries (80% × 52 680)		42 144	
Total expenses			(132 797)
Loss for the year			48 111

TIP

Tick off items from the trial balance when you have used them. Most items appear only once in the financial statements and it will help to ensure that you haven't missed anything.

Notes:

[1] You will be told if any of the amounts paid for wages should be entered in the cost of sales section of the statement of profit or loss. If no instructions are given, you should show all of the wages as an expense in the statement of profit or loss.

[2] Be careful! Although drawings should never be included in the 'Less: Expenses' section of the statement of profit or loss, they can appear in the 'Cost of sales' section because it is quite common for business owners to remove goods for their own use (for example, food if the business is a food shop) and these cannot remain as part of cost of sales.

7.5 Service Businesses

Other operating income

When the income statement is prepared for a business that provides a service, there is one major difference that stands out. Unlike a business that buys and sells products, there is no need for a cost of sales section that can be subtracted from the sales (revenue) figure to find the gross profit.

Example: The Income statement for Mike Graham Consultancy Services for the year ended 31 December 2020 might look like this:

Year	$	$
Revenue		275 200
Less: Expenses		
Wages and salaries	112 760	
Heat and light	8 735	
Rent, rates and insurance	21 340	
Administrative expenses	57 230	
Depreciation	14 405	
Motoring expenses	9 870	(224 340)
Profit for the year		50 860

7.6 The full trial balance

So far, only the parts of the trial balance that are relevant to the statement of profit or loss have been provided. In practice, an accountant will have the full trial balance and so will need to be able to identify those items that should be included in the statement of profit or loss and those that will need to be included in the *statement of financial position* (see Chapter 8), which is a statement showing the assets, liabilities and capital of the business.

WORKED EXAMPLE 4

A trial balance had been prepared for Samarah, a seller of women's clothing, at 30 April 2020.

A first step in preparing the statement of profit or loss is to sort the items in the trial balance into two categories – those that will appear in the statement of profit or loss and those that will appear in the statement of financial position (these are shaded in the table).

	$	$	Category	Does it go in the statement of profit or loss?
Rent and rates	480		expense	yes
Motor vehicles	7 400		asset	no
Fixtures and fittings	2 530		asset	no
Trade payables		1 900	liability	no
Discounts received[1]		50	revenue	yes
Carriage outwards	310		expense	yes
Sales		40 800	revenue	yes
Inventory at 1 May 2019	2 100		expense	yes
Bank loan (repayable 2022)		2 000	liability	no
Electricity	1 180		expense	yes
Capital at 1 May 2019		7 980	capital	no
Sales returns	320		revenue	yes
Commission received		2 340[3]	revenue	yes
Purchase returns		510	expense	yes
Discounts allowed	60		expense	yes
Purchases	22 600		expense	yes
Trade receivables	3 400		asset	no
Wages	9 700		expense	yes
Drawings	4 000		capital	no
Carriage inwards[1]	220		expense	yes
Motor expenses	660		expense	yes
Bank	620		asset	no
	55 580	55 580		

Inventory at 30 April 2020 was valued at $3 760[2].

Notes:

[1] There is more than one way to categorise items, e.g. it could be argued that items like carriage inwards could be labelled as 'cost of sales' rather than expenses. Discounts received has been categorised as a revenue when in practice, it might be better described as a reduction to an expense or cost. This is not as important as ensuring that you have correctly identified which items should be included in the statement of profit or loss.

[2] Closing inventory is the one item that will appear in the statement of profit or loss, even though it is an asset. As will be seen in Chapter 8, it will also be included in the statement of financial position.

[3] The commission was money that Samarah earned by selling goods on behalf of another company, for which she received a fixed percentage of the selling price.

ACTIVITY 7.3

Produce a statement of profit or loss for Samarah that shows the gross profit and profit (or loss) for the year.

REFLECTION

Consider any items that are shown in the statement of profit or loss that you struggled to account for correctly. Why do you think that was? Discuss with another learner what strategies you could use to deal with those items correctly.

TIP

Give all statements of profit or loss proper headings. Remember that with any financial statement, you need to show 'who, what and when'.

THINK LIKE AN ACCOUNTANT

All that hard work!

Sunil's statement of profit or loss was showing that he had made a profit for the year, although it wasn't as large as he had hoped.

'All that hard work and so little reward!' said Sunil to his wife, Anuja.

'Don't worry, most businesses don't make much money when they start up. You've done the hard part and things will get better!' said Anuja.

Why do many businesses struggle to make a good profit in their first year? What factors might Sunil consider when deciding what level of profit he would regard as acceptable?

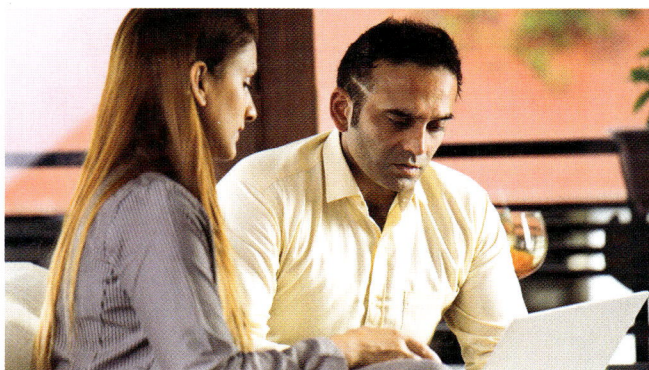

Figure 7.2: Many new businesses struggle to make a profit in their first year.

EXAM-STYLE QUESTIONS

1   Which of the following should *not* be recorded as an expense in the statement of profit or loss?

   A   delivery costs   C   drawings

   B   discounts allowed   D   insurance   [1]

2   Which of the following is included in the calculation of the cost of sales?

   A   carriage inwards   C   discounts allowed

   B   carriage outwards   D   discounts received   [1]

3   The initial profit for the year in the statement of profit or loss was $17 500. However, a number of items had been omitted:

   Carriage inwards $1 800

   Discounts received $6 200

   Sales returns $4 100

   What was the revised profit for the year once these omissions had been corrected?

   A $5 400   B $17 800   C $26 000   D $29 600   [1]

CONTINUED

4   The trial balance extracted from Umi's books at 31 March 2020 is as follows:

	$	$
Bank		31 044
Bank loan (repayable 2025)		116 997
Capital at 1 April 2019		142 450
Carriage inwards	4 128	
Carriage outwards	5 077	
Discounts allowed	1 009	
Discounts received		2 348
Drawings	31 380	
Fixtures and fittings	21 263	
Heating and lighting	7 256	
Inventory at 1 April 2019	24 671	
Land and buildings	174 500	
Office expenses	22 034	
Office furniture	17 815	
Trade payables		39 670
Purchases	253 142	
Purchases returns		3 987
Trade receivables	54 072	
Sales		394 201
Sales returns	5 230	
Wages	109 120	
	730 697	730 697

During the year, Umi had taken goods costing $2 775 for his own use. This has not been recorded in the books. Inventory at 31 March 2020 cost $19 813.

Required

Prepare Umi's statement of profit or loss for the year ended 31 March 2020.   [15]

SELF-EVALUATION CHECKLIST

After studying this chapter, complete a table like this:

You should be able to:	Needs more work	Almost there	Ready to move on
Explain that a sole trader is a person that owns and runs a business on his or her own.			
Prepare a basic statement of profit or loss from a trial balance and know how to account for returns, discounts and other income.			
Understand that unlimited liability means that a sole trader is personally responsible for paying off any debts incurred by the business.			
Understand that a statement of profit or loss shows the revenue and expenses of the business and enables the sole trader to identify the gross profit and the profit for the year.			

> Chapter 8

Statements of financial position for sole traders

This chapter covers part of syllabus sections AS Level 1.5

LEARNING INTENTIONS

In this chapter you will learn how to:

- explain that businesses produce a statement of financial position at the end of an accounting year that shows the value of the business in terms of its assets, liabilities and owner's capital
- prepare a statement of financial position for a sole trader
- explain that profit (or loss) for the year produced by the statement of profit or loss belongs to the sole trader and is added to (subtracted from) the owner's opening capital
- describe how the statement of financial position and the statement of profit or loss are linked
- explain that drawings are always a subtraction from the owner's capital, whether a profit or a loss for the year is reported.

ACCOUNTING IN CONTEXT

Sunil revisited

Sunil was worried. Even though his business appeared to have made more profit than he had expected, there had been several times when he wondered whether there was going to be enough cash to pay the day-to-day expenses. His accountant had mentioned something called a 'statement of financial position' that would tell him whether his business was in a healthy state or not.

Discuss in a pair or a group:

- What is a statement of financial position?
- What items from a trial balance are shown in a statement of financial position?
- What will a statement of financial position tell sole traders like Sunil?

Figure 8.1: A statement of financial position can show how well, or how badly a business is performing.

8.1 What is a statement of financial position?

A **statement of financial position** can provide the sole trader – or anyone else – with useful information including an indication of the size and value of a business. It can be analysed using ratio analysis to determine whether the business is financially stable or not.

One major difference between the statement of profit or loss and the statement of financial position is what happens to the ledger balances. In the statement of profit or loss, most of the balances are transferred to the statement of profit or loss and so those accounts will start the new accounting year with a zero balance. However, the items that are included in the statement of financial position are assets, liabilities and items related to capital, and so the closing balance at the end of one period will represent the opening balance at the start of the next period.

Another difference is that, while the statement of profit or loss could be presented as an account with debit and credit entries, the statement of financial position is never thought of as an account – it just lists the balances from a large number of other accounts.

The statement of profit or loss and statement of financial position are known collectively as the **financial statements** of a business. For a sole trader, these two statements are generally sufficient. They also complement each other; the statement of profit or loss shows whether the business has performed well or badly, while the statement of financial position shows whether the business is in a healthy position.

8.2 What does a statement of financial position contain?

The statement of financial position uses the following items:

- *Non-current assets* – examples include land and buildings, plant and machinery, motor vehicles, fixtures and fittings, and office equipment.
- *Current assets* – examples include inventory and trade receivables as well as cash and (positive) bank balances, which are sometimes combined and called 'cash and cash equivalents'.

KEY TERMS

statement of financial position: a list of the assets, liabilities, capital and reserves of a business at a particular point in time.

financial statements: the statements that a business is required to produce, normally at the end of an accounting year.

- *Current liabilities* – examples are trade payables and, if the bank is overdrawn, the bank overdraft. Note that the bank account is one of the few items in an accounting system that can be either an asset or a liability – you should pay attention to whether it has a debit or credit balance in the trial balance.

- *Non-current liabilities* – examples include long-term loans and mortgages. Most non-current liabilities are paid off in monthly instalments and become current liabilities when they will be paid off within 12 months. Non-current liabilities can be secured or unsecured. Secured means that the loan is secured to an asset that the borrower owns, often the asset that the loan is being used to buy, such as a property. Secured borrowing gives the lender the right to repossess assets should the borrower fail to make the repayments on time. Unsecured means that the borrowing is not linked to specific assets – smaller bank loans are often unsecured. If the borrower fails to keep up with repayments, the lender will take action to recover money owed, rather than assets..

- *Capital* – as will be seen, this will change as a result of the profit or loss made by the business, and drawings or additional investment made by the sole trader.

8.3 Updating the owner's capital

Preparing the statement of financial position involves listing items, as well as the calculation of the owner's capital. This can be calculated in two ways:

Method 1: preparing a capital account and making the necessary entries.

Method 2: using an arithmetical listing approach.

If you are preparing the statement of financial position from the trial balance, then it is more likely that you will need to present the changes to the owner's capital using the 'listing approach'.

WORKED EXAMPLE 1

Kenzo, a sole trader, had a capital account balance of $176 400 on 1 January 2019. The business made a profit for the year ending 31 December 2019 of $37 200 and during the year made drawings of $41 500.

The capital account would look like this:

Capital account					
Debit			**Credit**		
		$			$
			1 Jan 2019	Balance b/d	176 400
31 Dec 2019	Drawings	41 500	31 Dec 2019	Statement of profit or loss	37 200
31 Dec 2019	Balance c/d	172 100			
		213 600			213 600
			1 Jan 2020	Balance b/d	172 100

Note: the statement of profit or loss when presented as a ledger account will have had a credit balance, so the full double-entry would be:

- Debit: Statement of profit or loss $37 200

- Credit: Capital account $37 200

CONTINUED

If the business had made a loss of $37 200, then the capital account would look like this:

Capital account					
Debit			**Credit**		
		$			$
			1 Jan 2019	Balance b/d	176 400
31 Dec 2019	Drawings	41 500			
31 Dec 2019	Statement of profit or loss	37 200			
31 Dec 2019	Balance c/d	97 700			
		176 400			176 400
			1 Jan 2020	Balance b/d	97 700

WORKED EXAMPLE 2

Still using the example of Kenzo, a sole trader, the presentation of how the profit (or loss) and drawings will have affected the amount of his capital will look like this:

Capital at 1 January 2019	176 400
Plus: Profit for the year	37 200
	213 600
Less: Drawings	(41 500)
	172 100

Or if a loss had been made:

Capital at 1 January 2019	176 400
Less: Loss for the year	(37 200)
	139 200
Less: Drawings	(41 500)
	97 700

ACTIVITY 8.1

Jana, a sole trader, had a capital account balance of $89 350 on 1 April 2019. During the year, Jana made drawings of $22 720.

a   Prepare the capital account, if a profit for the year of $26 390 had been made.

b   Calculate the closing capital using the listing approach, if a profit for the year of $26 390 had been made.

8.4 Preparing the statement of financial position

Having prepared a statement of profit or loss – and closed off many of the ledger balances – the process of preparing the statement of financial position largely involves placing the remaining items into the main categories. You will need to memorise headings, know which items appear under which headings and be aware that there is an accepted order in which items should be listed.

Note: sole traders are not required to set out their financial statements in a particular format, so you may encounter a variety of acceptable layouts.

WORKED EXAMPLE 3

James is a sole trader. The items taken from the trial balance at 30 April 2020 that relate to the statement of financial position are:

	$	$
Bank	9 550	
Bank loan (repayable 2024)		57 120
Cash	260	
Capital at 1 May 2019		210 890
Drawings	19 865	
Motor vehicles	25 345	
Office equipment	47 150	
Premises	162 000	
Trade receivables	21 560	

The profit for the year was $24 190. Inventory at 30 April 2020 was valued at $34 075.

> **TIP**
>
> Profit increases capital and losses reduce capital. The owner's drawings are then deducted. This gives the closing balance on the capital account, which will be carried forward as the opening capital for next year.

CONTINUED

Suppose the following information has been extracted from the statement of financial position of a sole trader. The statement of financial position would look as follows:

Statement of financial position for James at 30 April 2020		
	$	$
Non-current assets		
Premises	162 000	
Office equipment	47 150	
Motor vehicles	25 345	234 495
Current assets		
Inventory	34 075	
Trade receivables	21 560	
Cash and cash equivalents	9 810	65 445
Total assets		299 940
Capital and liabilities		
Capital at 1 May 2019	210 890	
Add: Profit for the year	24 190	
	235 080	
Less: Drawings	(19 865)	215 215
Non-current liabilities		
Bank loan (repayable 2024)		57 120
Current liabilities		
Trade payables		27 605
Total capital and liabilities		299 940

TIP

Give every statement of financial position a proper heading, which should include the name of the business and the date.

There are certain conventions that must be observed and issues that must be considered.

- Non-current assets are always listed first, and within that category it is customary to list either the largest items first or those with the longest remaining useful life first.

- Current assets are listed in the order that reflects how long it might take to turn them into cash:

  - inventory is listed first as it must be sold and then the money needs to be collected

  - trade receivables just need to be collected

  - cash and cash equivalents just need to be withdrawn from the bank or taken out of the safe.

- The calculation of the owner's capital is shown in full, not just the closing balance.

- Current liabilities list payables followed by the bank overdraft if there is one (a credit balance in the trial balance).

- Non-current liabilities contain the bank loan because it is repayable after more than 12 months. If repayment had been due in October 2020, then this would have appeared as a current liability.

KEY CONCEPT LINK

True and fair view: Financial statements are designed to give a true and fair view of the financial position, performance and changes in financial position of the business to internal and external stakeholders. Who are some of these internal and external stakeholders? Why is it essential that the financial statements give a true and fair view of the business?

The accounting equation

This states that:

Assets = liabilities + capital   or

Assets – liabilities = capital

Provided the rules of bookkeeping are followed, no matter how complicated the affairs of a business might be, this equation always holds true. It also means that if two of the three items are known, the other one can be deduced.

Suppose a sole trader has assets of $32 000 and liabilities of $13 000, then:

Assets – liabilities = capital

32 000 – 13 000 = capital of $19 000

ACTIVITY 8.2

Raza is a sole trader. The items taken from his trial balance at 31 May 2020 that relate to the statement of financial position are as follows:

	$	$
Bank	3 245	
Bank loan (repayable 2024)		144 150
Bank loan (repayable 2020)		28 330
Cash	510	
Capital at 1 June 2019		169 945
Drawings	33 450	
Fixtures and fittings	44 125	
Trade payables		33 075
Premises	197 600	
Trade receivables	36 085	

The loss for the year was $9 145. Inventory at 31 May 2020 was valued at $51 340.

Required

Produce a statement of financial position for Raza at 31 May 2020.

TIP

If the current assets are lower than the current liabilities, the business is more likely to struggle to pay its day-to-day expenses and suppliers on time. This might mean that the sole trader could be forced to sell non-current assets to pay his or her trade payables. This is not a good position to be in as the non-current assets will soon run out and are likely to be needed for the business to be able to operate.

KEY TERMS

accounting equation: an equation that represents the relationship between assets, liabilities and capital.

8.5 Preparing the statement of financial position from the full trial balance

So far in this chapter, only the parts of the trial balance that are relevant to the statement of financial position have been provided. In practice, an accountant will have the full trial balance and so will need to be able to identify those items that should be included in the statement of financial position as well as those that will need to be included in the statement of profit or loss (see Chapter 7).

In simple terms, if an item can be identified as an asset, a liability or something linked to the owner's capital, it will appear in the statement of financial position.

WORKED EXAMPLE 4

We are now going to revisit the trial balance prepared for Samarah at 30 April 2020, as shown in Worked example 4 in Chapter 7.

This time we are going to prepare the statement of financial position. Again, a logical first step is to place the items in the trial balance into logical categories:

	$	$	Category	Does it go in the statement of financial position?
Rent and rates	480		expense	no
Motor vehicle	7 400		asset	yes
Fixtures and fittings	2 530		asset	yes
Trade payables		1 900	liability	yes
Discounts received		50	revenue	no
Carriage outwards	310		expense	no
Revenue		40 800	revenue	no
Inventory at 1 May 2019	2 100		expense	no
Bank loan (repayable 2022)		2 000	liability	yes
Electricity	1 180		expense	no
Capital at 1 May 2019		7 980	capital	yes
Sales returns	320		revenue	no
Commission received		2 340	revenue	no
Purchase returns		510	expense	no
Discounts allowed	60		expense	no
Purchases	22 600		expense	no
Trade receivables	3 400		asset	yes
Wages	9 700		expense	no
Drawings	4 000		capital	yes
Carriage inwards	220		expense	no
Motor expenses	660		expense	no
Bank	620		asset	yes
	55 580	55 580		

Inventory at 30 April 2020 was valued at $3 760.

From Activity 7.3 in Chapter 7, we know that the statement of profit or loss produced a profit for the year of $9 830.

ACTIVITY 8.3

Produce a statement of financial position for Samarah using the information in Worked example 4.

REFLECTION

Do you think the layout of the statement of financial position is logical? Why do you think that all of the assets are listed in the top half and all of the capital and liabilities in the bottom half?

THINK LIKE AN ACCOUNTANT

How much is my business worth?

Sunil was looking at his first statement of financial position, which showed that the assets of his business were worth nearly $150000. However, he noticed nearly two-thirds of this figure was accounted for by liabilities – one large bank loan and several current liabilities. Should Sunil be worried that two-thirds of the assets of his business seems to be accounted for by liabilities? Why/why not? Which would be preferable, a long-term bank loan or current liabilities? Why?

Figure 8.2: Should Sunil be worried that liabilities accounts for two-thirds of his business assets?

EXAM-STYLE QUESTIONS

1   The owner of a business has taken goods for her own use but no entry has been made in the books to record this. Which row will show the effect of this on the statement of financial position?

	Inventory	Capital
A	no effect	no effect
B	no effect	it will be too large
C	it will be too large	no effect
D	it will be too large	it will be too large

[1]

2   The following information has been extracted from a statement of financial position at 31 March 2020.

Non-current assets	275000
Current assets	54000
Current liabilities	28000
Long-term loan	67000
Profit for the year	31000
Drawings	42000

What was the balance on the capital account at 31 March 2020?

| A | $234000 | B | $245000 | C | $256000 | D | $318000 | [1] |

CONTINUED

3   Which of the following statements is *not* correct?

   A   assets = liabilities + capital

   B   capital = assets – liabilities

   C   capital – liabilities = assets

   D   liabilities = assets – capital   [1]

4   The following trial balance has been extracted from Xand's books at 31 December 2019:

	$	$
Advertising	9 145	
Bank	8 802	
Capital		71 400
Discounts received		1 670
Drawings	51 500	
Equipment	42 190	
Fixtures and fittings	29 234	
Heat and light	7 226	
Inventory at 1 January 2019	31 675	
Loan from bank (repayable 2023)		46 006
Motor vehicles	17 459	
Office expenses	54 025	
Trade payables		42 397
Purchases	127 081	
Purchase returns		2 246
Trade receivables	26 043	
Revenue		276 320
Sales returns	1 842	
Wages and salaries	33 817	
	440 039	440 039

Inventory at 31 December 2019 cost $35 331. Profit for the year was $50 756.

Required

Prepare Xand's statement of financial position for the year ended 31 December 2019.

[15]

SELF-EVALUATION CHECKLIST

After studying this chapter, complete a table like this:

You should be able to:	Needs more work	Almost there	Ready to move on
Understand that businesses produce a statement of financial position at the end of an accounting year that shows the value of the business in terms of its assets, liabilities and owner's capital.			
Prepare a statement of financial position for a sole trader, applying the layout and knowing it is a representation of the accounting equation.			
Explain that profit for the year produced by the statement of profit or loss belongs to the sole trader and is added to the owner's opening capital. A loss for the year is subtracted from the owner's capital.			
Understand how the statement of financial position and the statement of profit or loss are linked and that they complement each other; the statement of profit or loss shows how the business has performed while the statement of financial position shows if the business is in a healthy position.			
Know that drawings are always a subtraction from the owner's capital, whether a profit or a loss for the year is reported.			

> **Chapter 9**

Accounting concepts

This chapter covers part of syllabus section AS Level 1.2

LEARNING INTENTIONS

In this chapter you will learn how to:

- explain that, without accounting concepts, accountants might apply different methods to accounting for items in the financial statements and the consequences of this

- use the most important accounting principles and concepts

- describe how, when individual concepts appear to contradict each other, a decision is made about which takes priority.

ACCOUNTING IN CONTEXT

Sunil's confusion

Sunil had started to think that every item in the financial statements could be dealt with in a number of ways. Given the same information, would different accountants use different methods and arrive at completely different profit figures? Could an accountant use different methods to suit their clients' needs – a larger profit figure to improve the chances of getting a bank loan or a smaller profit figure to reduce the amount of tax paid?

Sunil believed that his accountant was trustworthy and honest, but it did seem that as individual accountants were using their professional judgement, the process of preparing financial statements was less precise than he had originally thought.

Figure 9.1: Given the same information, would different accountants use different methods and arrive at different profit figures?

Discuss in a pair or a group:

*   What problems could arise if accountants are allowed to use their judgement when preparing financial statements?

*   What are the ethical or legal implications for an accountant producing a profit figure to enable his client to obtain a bank loan or pay less tax?

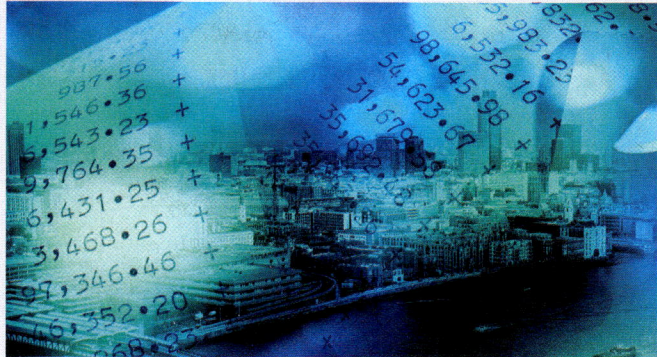

9.1 The need for rules

Accountants worldwide follow international accounting standards (IASs). The main objective is to help accountants apply the same concepts and methods and ensure that the financial statements produced are accurate and can be meaningfully compared. We will look at some of these later in the book.

9.2 Accounting concepts

Accounting concepts are necessary to ensure that accounting records provide information that is reliable. Anyone using the financial statements to make decisions will want to know that comparisons between different businesses or between different accounting year are meaningful because, as far as is possible, the same approaches or methods have been used by all of the accountants involved.

All businesses should apply the concepts in their financial statements. The following are the most important of these concepts and should be learned, understood and applied when preparing financial statements.

Duality

The concept of **duality** (double-entry) is the basis of the accounting equation covered in Chapter 8.

Business entity

Every business is regarded as having an existence separate from that of its owner. Information can only be entered into the accounts if it has a direct impact on the business and must be done so from the business's point of view.

KEY TERMS

accounting concepts: basic rules for recording financial transactions and preparing financial statements. They are sometimes known as principles.

duality: this recognises that there are two aspects to each financial transaction, represented by debit and credit entries in accounts.

This is particularly important when considering transactions between the owner and the business and might explain why many transactions seem to treat the owner as a 'friendly liability'. For example:

1 The owner puts $10 000 into the business bank account.

 Debit: Bank $10 000

 Credit: Capital $10 000

 The owner has effectively lent the business some money.

2 The owner removes $2 000 for his own use.

 Debit: Drawings $2 000

 Credit: Bank $2 000

 The owner has effectively been repaid $2 000 that he is owed by the business and drawings reduces the capital figure.

3 The business makes a profit of $5 000.

 Debit: Statement of profit or loss $5 000

 Credit: Capital $5 000

 The profit belongs to the owner and increases what the business owes to him.

4 The owner inherits $100 000 from his uncle.

 No entries would be made as this does not affect the business unless the owner decides to put it in the business bank account.

5 Owners might be tempted to use the business bank account to pay for their personal expenses. These would have to be removed or treated as drawings because they do not relate to the business. Failure to do this might seriously distort profit figures as well as figures in the statement of financial position. If the owner has knowingly put these items through the business and does not intend to treat them as drawings, he or she is committing fraud.

Money measurement

Only transactions that can be expressed in monetary terms are recorded in ledger accounts. Goods, non-current assets, trade receivables and expenses may be recorded in ledger accounts because they have resulted from transactions that can be expressed in monetary terms.

There are some things that cannot be expressed in monetary terms, such as the skills of workers or the business having a good reputation. This means that a business might be worth a lot more than the value of the items shown in the statement of financial position.

However, these items are *subjective* and so getting a valuation is difficult. Accountants take the view that something is worth what someone pays for it – as soon as money changes hands, there is a valuation that can be recorded in the accounts.

WORKED EXAMPLE 1

A sole trader wants to sell her business. The assets in the statement of financial position are valued at $500 000 but the sole trader feels that the skills of workers and the good reputation that her business has, are worth $200 000. She has offered the business for sale at $700 000 and a potential buyer has made an initial bid of $550 000.

What is the business worth? According to money measurement, it is worth $500 000 and that is all that can be shown in the statement of financial position. The $550 000 offer is just an initial bid and cannot be accounted for.

Suppose, after negotiations, the business is sold for $600 000. Then the money measurement concept will allow the business to be valued at $600 000 – the skills and reputation have definitely been valued at $100 000 because something is worth what someone has paid for it.

ACTIVITY 9.1

Discuss in a pair or a group:

Your favourite football team has just paid $50 million for a player that you do not think is very good. Under money measurement, how much is the player worth?

Historic cost

Financial transactions are recorded at their cost to the business. Cost cannot be disputed as invoices or other documentary evidence may be produced to support it. Recording financial transactions in this way is said to be *objective* because it is based on fact and not on opinion. Like the money measurement concept, **historic cost** tries to ensure that opinion is minimised when valuing items. This can be applied to purchases of non-current assets and inventory or expenses and, as we saw under money measurement, could be applied to the valuation of a whole business.

Recording transactions at their historic cost has two disadvantages:

- it does not allow things that cannot be expressed in monetary terms to be recorded in accounting

- **inflation** means that prices rise and the value of money falls. Using historic cost might cause a distortion.

> ### KEY TERMS
>
> **historic cost:** financial transactions are recorded at their original cost to the business.
>
> **inflation:** this is a general rise in the level of prices.

WORKED EXAMPLE 2

A sole trader bought an item for $200 five years ago and sold it for $350 yesterday. He knows that replacing that item would cost $250 now. How much profit did he make on the sale of that item?

Answer: $350 – $200 = $150.

However, he might argue that he has to replace that item at a cost of $250 and so has really only made a profit of $100. He may even base future selling prices on the replacement cost which, in a cost and management accounting situation, would be entirely fair.

Realisation

Realisation is where something has actually happened and is a fact. If a customer offers to buy something, that does not represent a sale – it can only be accounted for and said to have been *realised* when payment has been made (cash transaction) or when an invoice or bill has been issued (credit transaction). Transactions are realised when cash or a trade receivable replaces goods or services.

This concept prevents revenue from being credited in the accounts before it has been earned and before it has become a certainty.

Goods on sale or return (and sold on commission)

When a trader sends **goods on sale or return** to a customer, no sale takes place until the customer informs the seller that she or he has decided to buy them. The customer has the right to return the goods to the trader.

WORKED EXAMPLE 3

Jemima runs a shop that sells shoes supplied by Heels Unlimited who originally delivered 500 pairs. Each month, Heels Unlimited sends someone to Jemima's shop to check how many pairs have been sold, replace them and to produce an invoice for the sold items. This raises several questions:

* Should Jemima include the 500 pairs of shoes in her inventory valuation – do they belong to her?

* How many pairs of shoes has Heels Unlimited sold?

* Suppose Heels Unlimited asked Jemima to stock their shoes and would pay a commission on anything sold. How would this be accounted for?

Jemima cannot include any goods still held on sale or return as part of her inventory, as they still belong to Heels Unlimited. If she sells 20 pairs of shoes, then she can account for the revenue in her statement of profit or loss and, when invoiced for those 20 pairs, can include the cost in her cost of sales.

If items are being sold on commission, then the amount earned by Jemima would represent 'other income', which is added to the gross profit figure in the statement of profit or loss. The shoes would not represent part of Jemima's inventory and the money received from customers visiting the shop would not represent Jemima's revenue. She should keep that money separate from her main cash as most of it would not belong to her business.

KEY TERMS

realisation: revenue is recognised or accounted for by the seller when it is earned whether cash has been received from the transaction or not.

goods on sale or return: this is not a concept but a very important point in relation to ownership of goods relating to a transaction. When a trader sends goods on sale or return to a customer, no sale takes place until the customer informs the seller that she or he has decided to buy them.

WORKED EXAMPLE 4

Heels Unlimited has sent goods on sale or return to Jemima for $7 500 and treated the transaction as a sale. Jemima has not yet accepted the goods. The goods cost Heels Unlimited $4 800. The following balances have been extracted from the Heels Unlimited trial balance: sales $200 000; trade receivables $56 000. Inventory on hand has been valued at $31 500.

The following adjustments must be made to the financial statements.

Revenue		Trade receivables		Inventory	
	$		$		$
Per trial balance	200 000	Per trial balance	56 000	As given	31 500
Less:	(7 500)	Less:	(7 500)	Add:	4 800
Corrected revenue figure	192 500	Corrected receivables figure	48 500	Corrected closing inventory figure	36 300

Heels Unlimited would have to make adjustments that would remove the $2 700 unrealised profit that an uncorrected statement of profit or loss might have shown.

Consistency

Financial transactions of a similar nature should be recorded in the same way (consistently) in the same accounting year and in all future accounting years. For example, the cost of redecorating premises should always be debited to an expense account for the redecoration of premises and charged to the statement of profit or loss. It would not be correct the next time that the offices are redecorated to debit the cost to the premises (non-current assets) account.

As will be seen in later chapters, where there are several acceptable methods for dealing with an accounting item, **consistency** would demand that once a method has been adopted, the business will continue to use that method.

Accountants are always trying to ensure that the accounts of a business represent a **true and fair view**. If an alternative method does give a better representation of what is going on, then a change can be made. What is not acceptable is changing methods to get a desired result, e.g. changing an inventory valuation just to increase or decrease profit, which might be fraudulent too.

Consistency in the treatment of transactions ensures that the profits or losses of different periods, and statements of financial position, may be compared meaningfully.

Materiality

An amount may be considered *material* in the accounts if the way in which it is treated or even its omission or inclusion in the statement of profit or loss or statement of financial position would change the way in which people would read and interpret those financial statements. Whether something is material is a matter of opinion and its application might depend on factors like the size of the business. For example, a self-employed builder might spend $200 on some tools intending to keep them for a number of years. He would treat them as a non-current asset in the statement of financial position. A large building company might spend $200 on the same tools for use on a particular project and might choose to write them off as an expense at the end of that job.

Many businesses will set out guidelines or monetary limits to help staff apply a consistent approach. A limit of $200 might mean that the purchase of some boxes of computer CDs for $120 would be written off as a computer expense, but a computer printer costing $250 would be treated as a non-current asset.

> ## KEY TERMS
>
> **consistency:** financial transactions of a similar nature should be recorded in the same way (that is, consistently) in the same accounting year and in all future accounting years.
>
> **true and fair view:** the financial statements are accurate and faithfully represent the financial performance and position of the business.

Matching

The matching concept is often referred to as the accruals concept and many accountants consider this to be one of the most important concepts. It is responsible for many of the adjustments made to the basic financial statements that you saw in Chapters 7 and 8.

Under this concept the financial statements should show the revenue earned and the expenses incurred during an accounting year. This is significantly different from just recording the amount of cash flowing in and out of the business and can be seen in Worked example 5.

WORKED EXAMPLE 5

A business occupies premises at an annual rental of $4 800. In one year it paid $5 600 because it paid two months' rent in advance. It also used $2 700 worth of electricity but it paid only $2 250 because it has not paid the latest bill for $450. Its gross profit for the year is $12 000.

Statements of profit or loss prepared on (a) a 'cash basis', that is, on the actual payments made, and (b) on a matching basis, would look as follows:

	Cash basis		Matching basis	
	$	$	$	$
Gross profit		12 000		12 000
Less: Rent and rates	(5 600)		(4 800)	
Electricity	(2 250)	(7 850)	(2 700)	(7 500)
Profit of the year		4 150		4 500

The matching basis is the correct one as it records the actual costs incurred in the period for both expenses.

Statements of profit or loss should be prepared on the *matching* basis so that expenses are matched to the revenue earned; that is, expenses should be shown in the statement of profit or loss as they have been *incurred* rather than as they have been paid.

Prudence

The **prudence** concept is intended to prevent profit from being overadded. If profit is overadded, a trader may believe that her income is more than it really is and may withdraw too much money from the business. That would lead to the capital invested in the business being depleted. If it happens too often, the business will collapse because there will not be enough money to pay trade payables or to renew assets when they are worn out.

Showing an overadded profit may also cause the owner to be over-ambitious and result in her making poor decisions, which might also harm the business.

The concept can be applied in two ways:

- If there is an event that will potentially improve profit, it cannot be accounted for until it happens – this is the realisation concept being applied.
- If there is an event that will potentially reduce profit or result in losses, it should be provided for as soon it is *recognised*.

KEY TERM

prudence: profits should not be overadded and losses should be provided for as soon as they are recognised.

TIP

Learners often make the mistake of saying that the prudence concept means that profits must be underadded. That is not so; the concept is meant to ensure that profits are realistic without being overadded.

Going concern

A business is a **going concern** if it has the resources to continue operations for the foreseeable future and there is no intention to discontinue it. However, if a business is short of cash or access to credit and the owner is unable to put more money into it himself (or find someone who will), it may be unable to pay its day-to-day costs or its trade payables and be forced to close.

The going concern concept can sometimes appear to contradict the prudence concept. For example, suppose a business is struggling and it is quite possible that it will close down. The owner might know that the proceeds of selling the non-current assets for scrap might be significantly lower than their current value. If the sale is forced, the proceeds arising from the sale of inventory and other assets might also be very low.

The prudence concept would require that the value of the assets in the statement of financial position be reduced. However, this reduction in the value of the business assets might panic the owners, investors and trade payables into trying to get their money back and anyone who might have wanted to buy the assets might realise that the business is in trouble and could offer less for them than they might have done. The result of applying the prudence concept might be that the possible closure actually happens when it might have been avoided. In this case, going concern takes priority over prudence – the assets in the statement of financial position should be valued as if the business were expected to continue operating.

Substance over form

This is the accounting treatment of something that does not reflect the legal position; there are times when applying a strict legal approach will not provide a 'true and fair view' of what is really going on.

For example, a machine bought on hire purchase remains the property of the seller until the final instalment has been paid. If the purchaser fails to pay the instalments as they become due, the seller may reclaim the machine. That is the legal position, or the 'form'. Strictly speaking, as the machine may not belong to the business for several years, the machine should not be included in the statement of financial position as a non-current asset.

However, had the machine been bought and paid for immediately, then the business would have owned it from the start and would show it as a non-current asset.

In practical terms, the only difference is the payment method. The machine will be used in the same way, it will **depreciate** (lose value – see Chapter 11) in the same way and the business will need to carry out the same maintenance on it.

Substance over form will allow the business to show the item as a non-current asset immediately because, in practical terms, the machine bought on hire purchase is effectively being owned straightaway – this is the 'substance' of the matter. In other words, the practical view (the substance) is preferred to the legal view (the form) in the accounting treatment.

Objectivity

The objectivity concept is a principle which states that financial statements should not be influenced by personal opinions and bias. Instead, they should be prepared using solid evidence. This is why only information that has been entered into the books of prime entry and then the ledgers can be used in the preparation of the financial statements.

> ### KEY TERMS
>
> **going concern:** when there is no intention to discontinue a business in the foreseeable future.
>
> **depreciate:** measuring the loss in value of a non-current asset as a result of factors including age, and wear and tear.
>
> **substance over form:** the economic substance of the transaction must be recorded in the financial statements rather than its legal form.

THINK LIKE AN ACCOUNTANT

Why do we need a consistent approach?

When accountants prepare the financial statements, they will be aware that there are many people or organisations who will be relying on those statements representing a 'true and fair view' of the performance and state of that business. They will want to be assured that the accountant has followed recognised concepts and applied the appropriate methods when carrying out their work. How would you feel if you thought that your accountant had applied 'his own ways of doing things' that were different to the methods demanded by the accounting authorities? Which people or organisations

Figure 9.2: Organisations rely on statements to represent a 'true and fair view' of their business.

rely on the financial statements of a business to be accurate and produced in accordance with accounting standards and the law? Why do these people or organisations need those financial statements to be accurate and produced in accordance with accounting standards and the law? What could be the consequences if the financial statements have not been produced accurately and in accordance with accounting standards and the law?

REFLECTION

Which two accounting concepts covered in this chapter do you think are the most important?

Discuss your choices with another learner. Do you agree with each other's choices? Why/why not?

EXAM-STYLE QUESTIONS

1   The owner of a business paid for some repairs made on his wife's car out of the business bank account. The amount was debited to his drawings account. Which concept was applied?

    A   business entity

    B   matching

    C   prudence

    D   realisation   [1]

2   A trader paid $700 for business insurance but $100 of this related to the first two months of next year. Which accounting concept has been applied?

    A   historic cost

    B   matching

    C   money measurement

    D   prudence   [1]

CONTINUED

3   The balances in a sales ledger total $24 000. A customer who owes $1 500 is known to be in severe financial difficulties and may go out of business. The figure of trade receivables shown in the statement of financial position is $22 500. Which concept has been applied?

A   matching

B   prudence

C   realisation

D   substance over form   [1]

4   A trader sends goods on sale or return to a customer. When the trader prepares her statement of financial position at 31 March 2020, the customer has still not indicated that she has accepted the goods. Which concept should the trader apply when she prepares her accounts at 31 March 2020?

A   consistency

B   matching

C   prudence

D   realisation   [1]

SELF-EVALUATION CHECKLIST

After studying this chapter, complete a table like this:

You should be able to:	Needs more work	Almost there	Ready to move on
Know that without accounting concepts, accountants might apply different methods to accounting for items in the financial statements that make those statements less reliable and make it more difficult for people to meaningfully compare the accounts of different businesses.			
Apply the most important accounting principles and concepts: duality, business entity, money measurement, historic cost, realisation, consistency, materiality, matching, prudence, going concern and substance over form.			
When individual concepts appear to contradict each other, explain how a decision needs to be made about which takes priority.			

> Chapter 10

Accruals and prepayments (the matching concept)

This chapter covers part of syllabus section AS Level 1.5

LEARNING INTENTIONS

In this chapter you will learn how to:

- apply the matching concept
- record accruals and prepayments in ledger accounts
- explain that recording money received as income and amounts paid as expenses in the statement of profit or loss means that both figures can be distorted by the time the money is received or paid
- show accrued expenses and prepaid income in the current liabilities section of the statement of financial position
- show prepaid expenses and accrued income in the current assets section of the statement of financial position
- calculate inventories of consumables in the ledger and statement of financial position
- demonstrate various methods to adjust for accruals and prepayments in a trial balance.

ACCOUNTING IN CONTEXT

A matter of timing?

Some business owners do not have a good understanding of accounting and believe that only those bills that they have actually paid will count as expenses in their accounts. They might see their revenue increasing but their expenses increasing at a faster rate. So they might wonder whether delaying the payment of some of their bills until after the year end will make their accounts look better. When they present their records to their accountant for the year-end accounts to be produced, they could be in for a shock!

Discuss in a pair or a group:

- Will not paying the bills until next year improve this year's profit figure?

- If a business owner has paid for a full year's insurance, three months before the end of the year, would the fact that they have nine months left increase their expenses for the year and reduce their profit?

- Which accounting concept is an accountant likely to refer to when judging whether the business owner's plan to delay paying some of the bills is actually good or not?

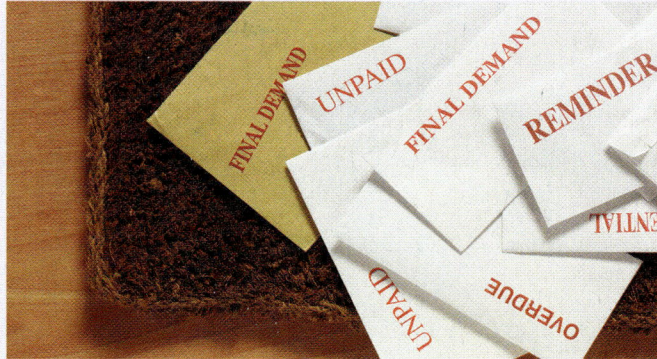

Figure 10.1: Some businesses might wonder whether delaying bill payments until after the year end will make their accounts look better.

10.1 What are accruals and prepayments?

Accruals (accrued expenses) – for example, an unpaid electricity bill is an accrued expense; the electricity has been consumed (the cost has been incurred), but not paid for. Sometimes when a payment is late, it is said to be *in arrears*.

Prepayments (prepaid expenses) – for example rent, because it usually has to be paid in advance. Insurance is another example as the insurance premium for the year may have to be paid *in advance*.

10.2 How to treat accrued expenses in an account (end of year)

An accrued expense is one where we have had the benefit of that expense but have not yet paid for it. We owe somebody money and, as we are almost certainly going to have to pay them within 12 months, that means we have a current liability. Liabilities have credit balances.

KEY TERMS

accrual: an expense that is due within the accounting year but has not yet been paid.

prepayment: a payment made by a business in advance of the benefits to be derived from it.

WORKED EXAMPLE 1

The accounting year of a business ended on 31 December 2019. During the year, payments from the bank totalling \$960 for heat and light had been made. At 31 December 2019 there was an unpaid bill for \$320.

How much expense should be shown in the statement of profit or loss?

Step 1

Enter the bank payments into the heating and lighting account.

CONTINUED

Step 2

Enter the closing balance b/d figure below your sub-total figures – this is a liability so will be a credit entry.

Step 3

Enter the closing balance c/d figure above your sub-total figures but on the other (debit) side.

Step 4

Add up the total of the entries on each side of the account and use the larger figure as your sub-total.

Step 5

Find the missing figure on the smaller (credit) side – this is your expense figure that will appear in the statement of profit or loss.

Heat and light account					
Debit			**Credit**		
		$			$
Various	Bank (1)	960	31 Dec	Statement of profit or loss (5)	1 280
31 Dec	Balance c/d (3)	320			
	(4)	1 280		(4)	1 280
			1 Jan	Balance b/d (2)	320

Note: even though only $960 has actually been paid, the amount of expense incurred is $1 280. The $320 owing at the end of the period will appear in the current liabilities section of the statement of financial position.

10.3 Opening and closing accrued expenses in an account

The situation becomes complicated when there are unpaid bills at both ends of the accounting year. Suppose someone receives a bill for an expense covering the period 1 January to 31 December 2018 and pays for it on 15 January 2019. Therefore, there is a liability. When they get the bill for 2019, they will likely pay for it in January 2020, so there is another liability. This might make it difficult to calculate how much expense has been incurred.

Fortunately, the use of ledgers can help us to calculate the correct figure and we will now look at an adapted version of the previous example to show how.

WORKED EXAMPLE 2

The accounting year of a business ended on 31 December 2019. At 1 January 2019, there had been an unpaid bill for $250. During the year, payments from the bank totalling $960 for heat and light had been made. At 31 December 2019 there was an unpaid bill for $320.

The approach is identical to Worked example 1, except that the opening accrual needs to be entered on the credit side (referred to as step 0).

Heat and light account					
Debit			**Credit**		
		$			$
Various	Bank (1)	960	1 Jan	Balance b/d (0)	250
31 Dec	Balance c/d (3)	320	31 Dec	Statement of profit or loss (5)	1 030
		(4) 1 280			(4) 1 280
			1 Jan	Balance b/d (2)	320

Note: even though only $960 has actually been paid, the amount of expense incurred has dropped to $1 030 because $250 of that has been used to pay for 2018 expenses.

The $320 owed at the end of the period will still appear in the current liabilities section of the statement of financial position because that is still the amount of money that we owe.

TIP

Remember that accrued expenses are liabilities and therefore any balance b/d figure will be on the credit side.

ACTIVITY 10.1

Kumar has a business whose accounting year ended on 31 March 2020. During the year, payments from the bank totalling $14 200 for rent had been made. At 1 April 2019 there was an unpaid bill for $3 430 and at 31 March 2020, there was an unpaid bill of $2 180.

Required

Using a rent account, show the amount of rent for the year that will appear in the statement of profit or loss.

10.4 How to treat a prepaid expense in an account

The person to whom a payment has been made in advance owes the business money because they owe it the services that have been paid for. An example is insurance where a year's cover has been paid for and the insurance company owes us a year's protection. As time passes, the amount that is owed will reduce as the amount of protection that the business (in months) is entitled to, falls. The business has an asset that is represented on the expense account by a debit balance carried down.

As with the accrued expenses, the amount of expense incurred is calculated using a ledger account. We shall also consider a situation where there are closing prepaid expenses and one where there is a prepayment at the beginning and end of the accounting year.

WORKED EXAMPLE 3

During 2019, Yousif made bank payments relating to advertising costs totalling $5 200.

a   At 31 December 2019, he calculated that he had paid $740 relating to advertisements that would not appear until 2020.

b   In addition to the $740 mentioned in **a**, Yousif realised that on 1 January 2019, there had been prepaid advertising expenses of $410.

How much expense should be shown in the statement of profit or loss?

The steps involved are very similar to those for accrued expenses, except that we are dealing with an asset.

Step 1

Enter the bank payments into the advertising account.

Step 2

Enter the closing balance b/d figure below your sub-total figures – this is an asset so will be a debit entry.

Step 3

Enter the closing balance c/d figure above your sub-total figures but on the other (credit) side.

Step 4

Add up the total of the entries on each side of the account and use the larger figure as your sub-total.

Step 5

Find the missing figure on the smaller (credit) side – this is your expense figure that will appear in the statement of profit or loss.

a

Advertising account					
Debit			**Credit**		
		$			$
Various	Bank (1)	5 200	31 Dec	Statement of profit or loss (5)	4 460
			31 Dec	Balance c/d (3)	740
		(4) 5 200			(4) 5 200
1 Jan	Balance b/d (2)	740			

Note: even though $5 200 has actually been paid, the amount of expense incurred is only $4 460 because the $740 paid at the end of the year relates to next year's expenses.

The $740 owing at the end of the period will appear in the current assets section of the statement of financial position.

The approach when faced with an opening prepaid expense is exactly the same as for the accrued expenses except that you first have to put the opening balance on the debit side to reflect the fact that we are dealing with an asset at the start of the year.

CONTINUED

b

Advertising account					
Debit			**Credit**		
		$			$
1 Jan	Balance b/d (0)	410	31 Dec	Statement of profit or loss (5)	4870
Various	Bank (1)	5 200	31 Dec	Balance c/d (3)	740
		(4) 5 610			(4) 5 610
1 Jan	Balance b/d (2)	740			

TIP

Remember that prepaid expenses are assets and therefore any balance b/d figure will be on the debit side.

Note: the expense figure has increased because the business has also incurred $410 of advertising expenses, which were actually paid for in 2018.

The $740 owing at the end of the period will still appear in the current assets section of the statement of financial position.

10.5 Mixed balances

Sometimes, the business will have an expense where there is a prepayment at the start of the period and an accrual at the end of the period. It could also be the other way around.

This is not a problem as long as you remember that prepayments are assets and have debit balance b/d figures, while accruals are liabilities and have credit balance b/d figures.

WORKED EXAMPLE 4

During 2019, Keira made bank payments for office expenses that totalled $15 280. On 1 January 2019 there had been an unpaid bill of $895 and at 31 December 2019 $2 035 had been paid in advance.

What office expenses would appear in the statement of profit or loss?

The order in which the entries were made is shown in brackets.

Office expenses account					
Debit			**Credit**		
		$			$
			1 Jan	Balance b/d (0)	895
Various	Bank (1)	15 280	31 Dec	Statement of profit or loss (5)	12 350
			31 Dec	Balance c/d (3)	2 035
		(4) 15 280			(4)] 15 280
1 Jan	Balance b/d (2)	2 035			

Note: do not be alarmed that there are three entries on the credit side of the account and only one on the debit side. Had there been an opening prepayment and a closing accrual, then there would have been three entries on the debit side and only one on the credit side.

ACTIVITY 10.2

During 2019, Benji made bank payments for motor expenses that totalled $7 605. On 1 January 2019, $1 180 had been paid in advance and at 31 December 2019, there had been an unpaid bill of $755.

What was the motor expenses that would appear in the statement of profit or loss?

10.6 Groupings of expenses

It is possible that a business might put several expenses under one category, e.g. rent, rates and insurance, which makes it possible that there might be more than two adjustments. As long as you apply the previous concepts, applying your double-entry concepts in a ledger account will enable you to identify the amount of expense that will appear in the statement of profit or loss.

WORKED EXAMPLE 5

Pip is a sole trader who repairs computers. During the year ended 31 December 2019, he made bank payments for rent, rates and insurance of $19 680.
The amount of accrued and prepaid expenses at 1 January 2019 and 31 December 2019 were:

	1 January	31 December
Insurance	$750 prepaid	$820 prepaid
Rent	$1 100 accrued	$2 340 accrued

What was the rent, rates and insurance expense that would appear in the statement of profit or loss?

	Rent, rates and insurance account				
	Debit			Credit	
		$			$
1 Jan	Balance b/d – insurance (0)	750	1 Jan	Balance b/d – rent (0)	1 100
Various	Bank (1)	19 680	31 Dec	Statement of profit or loss	20 850
31 Dec	Balance c/d – rent (3)	2 340	31 Dec	Balance c/d – insurance (3)	820
		(4) 22 770			(4) 22 770
1 Jan	Balance b/d – insurance (2)	820	1 Jan	Balance b/d – rent (2)	2 340

10.7 Calculation of accruals and prepayments

So far, the value of the accrued or prepaid expense has been given to you. However, it is possible that a payment may cover a period of time rather than a definite expense and in some cases, that period of time might span parts of two accounting years.

Let us consider a variety of situations and use them to establish the steps needed to identify:

- whether we need to adjust for an accrual or prepayment and
- the size of that adjustment.

In every case, the business has a year end of 31 December 2019.

Situation 1:

Payment of $2 760 is made on 13 January 2020 covering the three months, October to December 2019.

This is straightforward. The payment has been made after the year end, so this is an *accrued expense*. All three months relate to 2019 so the value of the accrual is the whole $2 760.

Situation 2:

Payment of $1 440 is made on 21 November 2019 covering the three months, January to March 2020.

This is straightforward. The payment has been made before the year end, so this is a *prepaid expense*. All three months relate to 2020 so the value of the prepayment is the whole $1 440.

Situation 3:[1]

Payment of $1 890 is made on 22 February 2020 covering the three months, November 2019 to January 2020.

This is not so straightforward. The payment has been made after the year end, so this is an *accrued expense*. However, only two out of the three months covered by the payment relate to 2019 (November and December), so we must calculate the accrual on a proportional basis:

$$\frac{2}{3} \times \$1\,890 = \$1\,260$$

Situation 4:[2]

Payment of $3 210 is made on 11 December 2019 covering the three months, November 2019 to January 2020.

This is not so straightforward. The payment has been made before the year end, so this is a *prepaid expense*. However, only one out of the three months covered by the payment relate to 2020 (January), so we must calculate the prepayment on a proportional basis:

$$\frac{1}{3} \times \$3\,210 = \$1\,070$$

Notes:

[1] **Situation 3:** had the payment been made before 31 December 2019, then one month would have been paid early and this would have been a prepayment of $630.

[2] **Situation 4:** had the payment been made after 31 December 2019, then two months would have been paid late and this would have been an accrual of $2 140.

The adjustment is carried out in exactly the same way as in the earlier examples.

ACTIVITY 10.3

Calculate the value of the accrual or prepayment in the following situations. In every case, the accounting year ended on 31 December 2019:

Situation 1: Payment of $720 is made on 14 November 2019 covering the three months, December 2019 to February 2020.

Situation 2: Payment of $1 140 is made on 3 January 2020 covering the three months, December 2019 to February 2020.

Situation 3: Payment of $2 730 is made on 27 October 2019 covering the six months, August 2019 to January 2020.

10.8 How to record inventory of consumables on expense accounts

Some expense accounts represent inventories of consumables, for example stationery and fuel for motor vehicles. Inventories of consumable stores may be unused at the year end. According to the matching concept, these inventories should not be charged against the profit for the year – they are an asset and not an expense at the year end. Carry them down as a debit balance on the account. This may result in an expense account having debit and credit balances at the year end.

In the statement of financial position, the inventories of unused consumable stores will appear under current assets. They should be shown under their own headings and not be included with the closing trading inventory in the statement of profit or loss, or inventory of goods for resale in the statement of financial position.

WORKED EXAMPLE 6

In the year ended 31 December 2019, a trader had paid $1 525 for stationery. At 31 December 2019, he owed $420 for stationery and had an inventory of unused stationery, which had cost $280.

Stationery account					
Debit			**Credit**		
		$			$
Various	Bank (1)	1 525	31 Dec	Statement of profit or loss	1 665
31 Dec	Balance c/d (3)	420	31 Dec	Balance c/d (3)	280
	(4)	1 945		(4)	1 945
1 Jan	Balance b/d (2)	280	1 Jan	Balance b/d (2)	420

Note: in the statement of financial position at 31 December 2019, the inventory of unused stationery, $280, will be shown under current assets as inventory of stationery. The amount owing of $420 will be shown as 'other payables' under current liabilities.

The closing balances in 2019 will be the opening balances in 2020.

10.9 How to adjust income for accruals and prepayments

Some income accounts, such as **rental income** or **interest earned**, may need to be adjusted for income received in advance or in arrears. Just as a trader might pay for an expense early or late, it is possible that people will pay us in the same way. The way to deal with accruals and prepayments for different sources of income is to recognise whether we are dealing with assets or liabilities.

Prepaid incomes are *liabilities* – because we have been paid for something that we have not yet provided. We owe somebody that something.

Accrued incomes are *assets* – because we are owed money for something we have provided.

> ### KEY TERMS
>
> **rental income:** the income earned from allowing someone to use your premises.
>
> **interest earned:** the income earned from monies that have been invested or lent.

WORKED EXAMPLE 7

In the year ended 31 March 2020, Martin had received $6 800 in rental income and $720 for interest on a loan. The amounts prepaid and accrued at the beginning and end of the year were as follows:

	1 April 2019	31 March 2020
Rent received	$1 100 prepaid	$570 prepaid
Interest on loan	$60 accrued	$75 accrued

Rent received account

Debit			Credit		
		$			$
31 Mar	Statement of profit or loss (6)	7 330	1 Apr	Balance b/d (1)	1 100
31 Mar	Balance c/d (4)	570	31 Mar	Bank (2)	6 800
	(5)	7 900		(5)	7 900
			1 Apr	Balance b/d (3)	570

Interest received account

Debit			Credit		
		$			$
1 Apr	Balance b/d (1)	60	31 Mar	Bank (2)	720
31 Mar	Statement of profit or loss (6)	735	31 Mar	Balance c/d (4)	75
	(5)	795		(5)	795
1 Apr	Balance b/d (3)	75			

Note: all of the entries are on the opposite side to those made for expenses. The double-entry relating to the money coming into the business is:

Debit   Bank

Credit   Income account (rental income, interest received and so on)

The entry in the statement of profit or loss will be a credit because it is an income that is increasing profit.

ACTIVITY 10.4

In the year ended 30 June 2020, Rajesh had received $8 260 in rental income and $5 120 for **commission received**. The amounts prepaid and accrued at the beginning and end of the year were as follows:

	1 July 2019	30 June 2020
Rent received	$840 prepaid	$1725 prepaid
Commission received	$315 accrued	$360 accrued

Required

Prepare the rent received and commission received, showing the amount of each income that would appear in the statement of profit or loss.

KEY TERM

commission received: a form of income that is often earned as a result of selling goods on behalf of somebody else.

10.10 How to adjust a trial balance for accruals and prepayments

You will come across trial balances where you need to adjust expenses and incomes to reflect both accruals and prepayments. The ways in which the various items should be treated are as follows:

Item	Treatment in statement of profit or loss	Treatment in statement of financial position
Accrued expense (you are paying someone late)	*Add* to figure shown in the trial balance – this will increase the expense to show the total amount of expense incurred.	Show as other payables under current liabilities.
Prepaid expense (you are paying someone early)	*Deduct* from amount in the trial balance – this will reduce the expense to show the total amount of expense incurred.	Show as other receivables under current assets.
Accrued income (someone is paying you late)	*Add* to figure shown in the trial balance – this will increase the income to show the total amount of income earned.	Show as *other receivables* under current assets.
Prepaid income (someone is paying you early)	*Deduct* from amount in the trial balance – this will increase the income to show the total amount of income earned.	Show as *other payables* under current liabilities.

The terms 'other receivables' and 'other payables' are used to describe money owed to the business or money owed by the business that is not the result of the buying and selling of the main product – they relate to day-to-day expenses and other income such as rental income or interest received.

All items appearing as other receivables should be combined and presented as one figure and the same should be done for the other payables.

KEY TERMS

other payables: the current liability (money owed by the business) arising from late payment of expenses or early receipt of an income.

other receivables: the current asset (money owed to the business) arising from early payment of expenses or late receipt of an income.

KEY CONCEPT LINK

Money measurement: Why is it important to only include items in the financial statements that can (definitely) be expressed in terms of money?

WORKED EXAMPLE 8

A sole trader extracted the following trial balance from his books after he had prepared the trading account section of his statement of profit or loss for the year ended 31 March 2020:

	$	$
Bank	6724	
Capital at 1 April 2019		236694
Commission received		1230
Drawings	34560	
Gross profit		93777
Insurance	3760	
Inventory at 31 Mar 2020	24921	
Motor expenses	11044	
Non-current assets	181600	
Office expenses	16277	
Rent received		3820
Stationery costs	1329	
Trade payables		19762
Trade receivables	32150	
Wages and salaries	42918	
	355283	355283

Additional information

1 The inventory figure shown is *closing* inventory.
2 The following amounts were owing at 31 March 2020: commission earned $354 and motor expenses $863.
3 The following amounts had been paid in advance at 31 March 2020: rental income $550 and insurance $1255.
4 The inventory of unused stationery on hand at 31 March was valued at its cost of $510, but suppliers of that stationery were still owed $325.

Required

a Prepare the statement of profit or loss for the year ended 31 March 2020.
b Prepare the statement of financial position at 31 March 2020.

The treatments of the accruals and prepayments is as follows:

	$	$	Expense/income		Asset	Liability
Commission received		1230	+354	= 1584	354	
Insurance	3760		−1255	= 2505	1255	
Motor expenses	11044		+863	= 11907		863
Rental income		3820	−550	= 3270		550
Stationery costs	1329		−510 +325	= 1144	510	325
					2119	1738

CONTINUED

Statement of profit or loss for year ended 31 March 2020		
	$	$
Gross profit		93 777
Commission received		1 584
Rent received		3 270
		98 631
Less: Expenses		
Insurance	2 505	
Motor expenses	11 907	
Office expenses	16 277	
Stationery	1 144	
Wages and salaries	42 918	
Total expenses		(74 751)
Profit for the year		23 880

Statement of financial position at 31 March 2020		
	$	$
Non-current assets		181 600
Current assets		
Inventory	24 921	
Trade receivables	32 150	
Other receivables (354 + 1 255 + 510)	2 119	
Bank	6 724	65 914
Total assets		247 514
Capital and liabilities		
Capital at 1 April 2019	236 694	
Add: Profit for the year	23 880	
	260 574	
Less: Drawings	(34 560)	226 014
Current liabilities		
Trade payables	19 762	
Other payables (863 + 550 + 325)	1 738	21 500
Total capital and liabilities		247 514

THINK LIKE AN ACCOUNTANT

Accruals and prepayments

Accountants make adjustments for accruals and prepayments in order to ensure that the statement of profit or loss reflects the amount of income earned and expenses incurred. It also ensures that, as far as possible, the matching concept is being observed. Apart from not following the matching principle, what problems might arise if a business puts some of this year's expenses into next year's accounts?

Figure 10.2: Adjustments for accruals and prepayments help to make sure the statement of profit or loss reflects the income and expenses of a business.

REFLECTION

Do you think that making adjustments for accruals and prepayments makes the financial statements more or less useful? Why/why not? Discuss your views with another learner.

EXAM-STYLE QUESTIONS

1   A trader prepares her accounts annually to 31 March 2020. On 13 April 2020 she made a payment of $1 500 relating to rent and rates, which covered the three months ending 30 April 2020.

Which of the following should be included in the statement of financial position for the year ended 31 March 2020?

   A $500 accrual in the current liabilities

   B $500 prepayment

   C $1 000 accrual

   D $1 000 prepayment   [1]

2   A trader commenced business on 1 June 2019. During the year ended 31 May 2020, he made bank payments of $1 510 for heat and light. These payments included one for $420 that covered the three months, April to June 2020.

Which amount for heat and light should be shown in the statement of profit or loss for the year ended 31 May 2020?

   A $1 090

   B $1 370

   C $1 650

   D $1 930   [1]

CONTINUED

3   The accounts of a business have been prepared, but no adjustments have been made for accrued expenses at the end of the year. What effect will these omissions have on the accounts?

	Profit for the year	Current assets	Current liabilities
A	overadded	no effect	underadded
B	underadded	no effect	overadded
C	overadded	underadded	no effect
D	underadded	overadded	no effect

[1]

4   Xand extracted the following trial balance at 30 June 2020:

	$	$
Bank		4 188
Capital at 1 July 2019		117 640
Discounts allowed	1 754	
Discounts received		2 301
Drawings	20 000	
Inventory at 1 July 2019	18 365	
Mortgage (repayable 2027)		118 467
Motor expenses	17 437	
Motor vehicles	25 600	
Office equipment	19 240	
Office expenses	26 759	
Premises	160 000	
Purchases	217 044	
Purchase returns		2 243
Rent received		8 712
Revenue		320 857
Sales returns	1 709	
Trade payables		11 066
Trade receivables	13 444	
Wages and salaries	64 122	
	585 474	585 474

The following information at 30 June 2020 was also provided:

1   inventory was valued at $20 170.
2   office expenses of $1 100 had been paid in advance.
3   wages and salaries of $3 280 was owing.
4   rental income of $1 450 had been paid in advance.

Required

a   Prepare the statement of profit or loss for the year ended 30 June 2020.   [15]
b   Prepare the statement of financial position at 30 June 2020.   [15]

[Total: 30]

SELF-EVALUATION CHECKLIST

After studying this chapter, complete a table like this:

You should be able to:	Needs more work	Almost there	Ready to move on
Apply the matching concept, which requires a business to make adjustments for accruals and prepayments so that income and expenses reflect the income earned and expense incurred during a particular period.			
Record accruals and prepayments in ledger accounts to help identify the correct amount of income or expense in the statement of profit or loss.			
Know that recording money received as income and amounts paid as expenses in the statement of profit or loss means that both figures might be distorted by the time the money is received or paid.			
Show accrued expenses and prepaid income in the current liabilities section of the statement of financial position.			
Show prepaid expenses and accrued income in the current assets section of the statement of financial position.			
Account for inventories of consumables in the ledger and statement of financial position – they are an asset and not an expense at the year end.			
Use various methods to adjust for accruals and prepayments when dealing with a trial balance.			

> Chapter 11

Accounting for the depreciation of non-current assets

This chapter covers part of syllabus sections AS Level 1.3 and 1.5

LEARNING INTENTIONS

In this chapter you will learn how to:

- describe 'capital' expenditure and 'revenue' expenditure
- explain that depreciation is an expense in the statement of profit or loss and reduces the value of the non-current assets in the statement of financial position
- explain the matching concept
- calculate depreciation using the straight-line, reducing balance and revaluation methods
- calculate the profit or loss on disposal of non-current assets and show this in the statement of profit or loss
- prepare financial accounts that include depreciation.

ACCOUNTING IN CONTEXT

Sunil's new van

Many new businesses start up by just buying an old van, hoping to replace it one day with a new one or even more than one if business is going really well. Once a business has been growing for a while and the latest statement of profit or loss is showing a good profit figure, it might be time for them to look at increasing the size of the business. This could be achieved by buying a new van to make delivering the goods to their customers easier.

Sunil is making a good level of profit now and is trying to decide whether to buy a brand new van or a second-hand one to help his business to grow. But after discussing it with a friend, he is worried that a new van could lose a lot of value in a short period of time and not really be worth spending the money on.

Discuss in a pair or a group:

- Would a new van lose large amounts of value and, if so, why?

- Would this also apply to other non-current assets like equipment or machinery?

- If a non-current asset is being used to help the business make a profit, should any loss in value be considered in the financial statements?

Figure 11.1: Many new businesses buy an old van, hoping to replace it with a new one, or several if the business goes well.

11.1 What is depreciation?

Depreciation applies to most non-current assets and needs to be accounted for in the financial statements of any business.

Assets may depreciate for many reasons:

- *Wear and tear*: assets become worn out through use. The value of a car is not just determined by its age – the mileage is considered too because the further a car is driven, the less life it is likely to have left. It will probably need to be repaired more often than a new car and may be less efficient in terms of fuel consumption.

- *Obsolescence*: sometimes, more efficient technology has been developed or the goods that they helped to produce have been replaced, which means that they are no longer needed even though they are physically capable of being used for a number of years.

- *Passage of time*: a non-current asset acquired for a limited period of time, such as a lease of premises for a given number of years, loses value as time passes.

- *Depletion (exhaustion)*: non-current assets like mines, quarries and oil wells depreciate as the minerals/resources are extracted from them. For example, a coal mine that has no coal left will be worthless.

KEY TERM

depreciation: the loss in value of a non-current asset as a result of usage, wear and tear, obsolescence or the passing of time.

KEY CONCEPT LINK

True and fair view: Why do you think that accounting for depreciation improves the way in which the financial statements give a true and fair view of the business?

11.2 Capital and revenue expenditure

To calculate the amount of value lost by a non-current asset, we need to know how much it was worth when first acquired: the (historic) cost or the cash price. However, when buying non-current assets, there are often other costs associated with those assets where a decision needs to be made about whether they should be treated as capital or revenue expenditure.

An item that is treated as **capital expenditure** is often said to be **capitalised** and will probably be subject to depreciation.

Expenditure needed to get a non-current asset into a state where it can be used for the first time will also be regarded as part of the original cost of the asset and will be capitalised.

Revenue expenditure items will appear as expenses in the statement of profit or loss.

KEY TERMS

capital expenditure: expenditure incurred in the purchase or improvement of a non-current asset.

capitalised: recording an item as a non-current asset and showing it in the statement of financial position.

revenue expenditure: expenditure on the day-to-day running costs of the business.

WORKED EXAMPLE 1

During the last two years that Jahendra has been a manufacturer of children's clothing, she has made purchases relating to non-current assets.

Premises: When purchased on 15 April 2018, this building was not in a state where Jahendra could have used it to conduct her business. Jahendra occupied the premises and started trading on 24 June 2018.

		$
April 2018	Cash price	320 000
April 2018	Legal costs	14 000
April to June 2018	Repair and decorating costs	27 500
May 2018	Installation of double-glazing windows and doors	41 000
October 2020	Replacement of curtains and carpets	18 700

Machinery: Purchased on 11 July 2018.

		$
July 2018	Factory floor re-concreted and installation of fixings for machines	14 600
July 2018	Cash price	175 000
July 2018	Installation costs	9 250
July/August 2018	Costs of training staff to use new machinery	11 400
July 2018	Two years' insurance and warranty on new machine	22 100
February 2020	Training of six new employees to use machinery	4 800

Which items should be treated as capital expenditure and which as revenue expenditure?

Premises: Capital expenditure is $402 500 – the first four items.

Capital expenditure: The cash price and the legal costs are essential in buying the premises. The poor state of the buildings justifies including the $27 500 repairs and decorating costs. The double-glazing could be capital expenditure if it is either:

- essential to make the building usable or
- represents significant 'improvement' to the asset – an extension to an existing building is an improvement and therefore capital expenditure.

Revenue expenditure is $18 700 – the amount spent on replacing the curtains and carpets. It is assumed that Jahendra has replaced what was fitted in April–June 2018. Whether those have worn out or Jahendra wanted to change the colours, these costs would be recorded as a 'repairs and renewals' expense in the statement of profit or loss.

TIP

Consider what the money is being spent on. If it is the cash price, legal or physical costs of acquiring it or expenditure on making it usable, it should be treated as capital expenditure. If the expenditure is significantly improving the non-current asset, it should be treated as capital expenditure.

The timing of the replacement of the curtains also counts against it being capital expenditure as it happened two years later rather than close to the date of acquisition.

Machinery: Capital expenditure is $210 250 – the first four items.

Capital expenditure covers the work on the factory floor, the purchase price and the installation. Any testing would also be regarded as capital expenditure.

The training would also be included if it were essential to the staff being able to use the machinery and was carried out at that time.

Revenue expenditure would probably be $26 900. The insurance and **warranty** would be regarded as an ongoing expense – spread over two years with a prepayment running into the second year while the $4 800 spent on training again happened a long time after the machinery was acquired and with staff that were not employed at the time of the acquisition.

Notes:

1   Materiality is often used when deciding whether to capitalise an item. Businesses may decide that if the amount of expenditure is relatively low, then writing it off as an expense might be more appropriate. For example, buying a cheap printer for $100 might be considered by a large business as being an item small enough to be written off as 'computer expenses' while a small business might decide to capitalise it.

2   If the items had been bought on finance, any interest or other charges would have been regarded as a revenue expenditure and treated as an expense. Only the actual cash price of the item can be regarded as capital expenditure and included in the value of the non-current asset.

> **KEY TERM**
>
> **warranty:** a type of arrangement where the owner of a non-current asset obtains a form of insurance that will pay out for the cost of parts or repairs if there is a problem with the asset.

11.3 How does depreciation of non-current assets affect the accounts?

When accounting for depreciation, we will be trying to achieve two things:

1   *Apply the matching principle*: if we own a non-current asset for five years and it is used to generate revenue throughout that time, the matching principle requires that we spread the total cost across the whole life of the non-current asset rather than treat the whole amount as an expense in the first year.

    If we did treat the whole amount as an expense in the first year, then the profit for that year would be underadded and those in the next four years would be overadded as there would be no expense.

2   *Valuation of the non-current asset*: if the non-current asset is losing value across the five years and no depreciation is applied, then the valuation shown in the statement of financial position would be overadded. If the whole loss in value was applied in the first year, then the value of the non-current asset might be grossly underadded.

    As both the statement of profit or loss and the statement of financial position are influenced by our treatment of depreciation, it is very important that we account for it properly.

11.4 How to account for depreciation

The most common methods to calculate depreciation are:

- straight-line method
- reducing balance method
- revaluation.

11.5 Straight-line depreciation

With **straight-line depreciation**, the total amount of depreciation that an asset will incur is estimated as the difference between what it cost and the estimated amount that will be received when it is sold or scrapped at the end of its **useful life** – its **residual value**. The total depreciation is then spread evenly over the number of years of its expected life.

Calculation: Depreciation per year $= \dfrac{(\text{cost} - \text{residual value})}{\text{estimated useful life in years}}$

WORKED EXAMPLE 2

Fred owns a taxi company (a service business) and on 1 January 2018 bought a motor vehicle for $30 000, paying by cheque. It is expected to have a useful life of five years, at the end of which it will have no residual value. His year end is 31 December.

There are several steps involved in accounting for this non-current asset:

2018

Step 1

Prepare the journal for the purchase of the motor vehicle:

Date	Details	Dr $	Cr $
	Motor vehicles at cost	30 000	
	Bank		30 000
Narrative: Purchase of motor vehicle.			

Step 2

Calculate the depreciation charge for the year:

$30 000 \times 20\% = \$6 000$ (it will be this every year)

Step 3

Produce the journal to record the depreciation charge for the year:

Date	Details	Dr $	Cr $
	Statement of profit or loss (this is shown as an expense)	6 000	
	Accumulated depreciation on motor vehicles		6 000
Narrative: Depreciation charge for the year.			

For straight-line depreciation, this will be the same every year.

KEY TERMS

straight-line depreciation: a method of applying depreciation that assumes that the loss in value will occur at a constant rate.

useful life: the amount of time that the business expects to keep the asset – this may be significantly less than its physical life.

residual value: the amount that a business will receive for the asset at the end of its useful life – used to be known as scrap value.

accumulated depreciation: the cumulative total of all the depreciation that has been charged on the non-current assets.

CONTINUED

Step 4

Make the postings in the nominal ledger:

Motor vehicles at cost account				
Debit			**Credit**	
	$			$
1 Jan 18 Bank	30 000	31 Dec 18 Balance c/d		30 000
	30 000			30 000
1 Jan 19 Balance b/d	30 000			

Accumulated depreciation of motor vehicles account				
Debit			**Credit**	
	$			$
31 Dec 18 Balance c/d	6 000	31 Dec 18 Statement of profit or loss		6 000
	6 000			6 000
		1 Jan 19 Balance b/d		6 000

Step 5

Prepare the statement of profit or loss (the other items have been made up to show the context):

Statement of profit or loss for the year ended 31 December 2018		
	$	$
Less: Expenses		
Rent and rates		
Heat and light	1 800	
Depreciation of motor vehicles	4 300	
Wages and salaries	6 000	21 600
Profit for the year	9 500	?? ???

Step 6

Prepare the statement of financial position:

Statement of financial position at 31 December 2018	Cost	Accumulated depreciation	Net book value
	$	$	$
Non-current assets			
Motor vehicles	30 000	6 000	24 000
Current assets			
Inventory		x	
Bank		x	

CONTINUED

2019 and 2020

Suppose that on 31 March 2019, Fred bought another taxi for $36 000. This one was expected to last for five years, at the end of which it was expected to have a residual value of $4 000.

Step 1

Prepare the journal for the purchase of the vehicle:

Date	Details	Dr $	Cr $
	Motor vehicles at cost	36 000	
	Bank		36 000
Narrative: Purchase of vehicle.			

Step 2

Calculate the depreciation charge for the year.

One feature of straight-line depreciation is that many businesses will apply it on a fractional basis – so if they own an item for a fraction of a year, it only receives that fraction of the depreciation charge. In this case, Fred owned the second taxi for nine months of 2019.

Taxi 1: $30 000 × 20% = $6 000 (it will be this every year)

Taxi 2: $\dfrac{(\$36\,000 - \$4\,000)}{5 \text{ years}}$ = $6 400 for a full year (which will apply in later years)

$$= \frac{9}{12} \times \$6\,400 = \$4\,800$$

TIP

Look for when the year end is – it doesn't have to be 31 December and this will make a difference if you are having to count the months in order to apply straight-line depreciation on a fractional basis.

Step 3

Produce the journal to record the depreciation charge for 2019:

Date	Details	Dr $	Cr $
	Statement of profit or loss (this is shown as an expense)	10 800	
	Accumulated depreciation on motor vehicles		10 800
Narrative: Depreciation charge for 2019.			

Note: in 2020 and later years, the expense will be $12 400 unless other taxis are purchased.

CONTINUED

Step 4

Make the postings in the nominal ledger (2019 and 2020 only):

Motor vehicles at cost account					
		$			$
1 Jan 18	Bank	30 000	31 Dec 18	Balance c/d	30 000
		30 000			30 000
1 Jan 19	Balance b/d	30 000		Balance c/d	30 000
31 Mar 19	Bank	36 000	31 Dec 19	Balance c/d	66 000
		66 000			66 000
1 Jan 20	Balance b/d	66 000	31 Dec 20	Balance c/d	66 000
		66 000			66 000
1 Jan 21	Balance b/d	66 000			

Accumulated depreciation on motor vehicles account					
31 Dec 18	Balance c/d	6 000	31 Dec 18	Statement of profit or loss	6 000
		6 000			6 000
			1 Jan 19	Balance b/d	6 000
31 Dec 19	Balance c/d	16 800	31 Dec 19	Statement of profit or loss	10 800
		16 800			16 800
			1 Jan 20	Balance b/d	16 800
31 Dec 19	Balance c/d	29 200	31 Dec 20	Statement of profit or loss	12 400
		29 200			29 200
			1 Jan 21	Balance b/d	29 200

CONTINUED

Step 5

Prepare the statement of profit or loss:

Statement of profit or loss for the year ended 31 December 2019		
	$	$
Gross profit		?????
Less: Expenses		
Rent and rates	1 800	
Heat and light	4 300	
Depreciation of motor vehicles	10 800	
Wages and salaries	9 500	26 400
Profit for the year		?? ???

Step 6

Prepare the statement of financial position:

The asset will be expressed in terms of three figures:

- *Cost* – which is the original amount paid for the non-current asset.
- *Accumulated depreciation* – which is a total of all the depreciation ever charged on that type of non-current asset.
- **Net book value** – which is the remaining value of the non-current asset and cost minus accumulated depreciation.

> **KEY TERM**
>
> **Net Book Value (NBV):** the remaining value of the asset (cost – accumulated depreciation).

Statement of financial position at 31 December 2019			
	Cost	Accumulated depreciation	Net book value
	$	$	$
Non-current assets			
Motor vehicles	66 000	16 800	49 200

Statement of financial position at 31 December 2020			
	Cost	Accumulated depreciation	Net book value
	$	$	$
Non-current assets			
Motor vehicles	66 000	29 200	36 800

11.6 Reducing balance depreciation

Using the **reducing balance method**, depreciation is calculated as a fixed percentage of the net book value of the non-current asset at the start of the year.

It makes the assumption that either:

- the non-current asset will provide more benefit in the early part of its useful life because it is more efficient or cheaper to operate, or

- the loss in value is high in the early part of its useful life and becomes more gradual as time passes.

KEY TERM

reducing balance method: depreciation is calculated as a fixed percentage of the written-down (or net book) value of the asset each year.

WORKED EXAMPLE 3

On 1 January 2018, Fred bought a taxi for \$30 000, paying by cheque. His year end is 31 December. On 31 March 2019, Fred bought another taxi for \$36 000.

Depreciation is applied at a rate of 30% per year using the reducing balance method. A full year's depreciation is applied to all taxis owned at the end of each year.

Most of the steps that we used when depreciation was straight-line are the same when dealing with the reducing balance method. The one major difference is that we need to keep a record of each asset's net book value so that we can arrive at the correct depreciation expense.

Year	Taxi 1 (\$30 000)	Taxi 2 (\$36 000)
2018	30% × \$30 000 = \$9 000 (leaves \$21 000)	No depreciation
2019	30% × \$21 000 = \$6 300 (leaves \$14 700)	30% × \$36 000 = \$10 800 (leaves \$25 200)
2020	30% × \$14 700 = \$4 410 (leaves \$10 290)	30% × \$25 200 = \$7 560 (leaves \$17 640)
2021	30% × \$10 290 = \$3 087 etc.	30% × \$17 640 = \$5 292 etc.

Note: during the first year of an asset's life, the percentage is applied to cost as that is the same as the net book value.

The change in depreciation method is not going to change the cost of the taxis bought by Fred, so the motor vehicles at cost account will be the same as before:

Motor vehicles at cost account					
		$			$
1 Jan 18	Bank	30 000	31 Dec 18	Balance c/d	30 000
		30 000			30 000
1 Jan 19	Balance b/d	30 000		Balance c/d	30 000
31 Mar 19	Bank	36 000	31 Dec 19	Balance c/d	66 000
		66 000			66 000
1 Jan 20	Balance b/d	66 000	31 Dec 20	Balance c/d	66 000
		66 000			66 000
1 Jan 21	Balance b/d	66 000			

CONTINUED

The change in depreciation method will give different figures in the accumulated depreciation account, for the expense in the statement of profit or loss and the net book value in the statement of financial position:

Accumulated depreciation on motor vehicles account					
31 Dec 18	Balance c/d	9 000	31 Dec 18	Statement of profit or loss	9 000
		9 000			9 000
			1 Jan 19	Balance b/d	9 000
31 Dec 19	Balance c/d	26 100	31 Dec 19	Statement of profit or loss	17 100
		26 100			26 100
			1 Jan 20	Balance b/d	26 100
31 Dec 19	Balance c/d	38 070	31 Dec 20	Statement of profit or loss	11 970
		38 070			38 070
			1 Jan 21	Balance b/d	38 070

Statement of financial position at 31 December …			
	Cost	Accumulated depreciation	Net book value
	$	$	$
Non-current assets			
2018: Motor vehicles	30 000	9 000	21 000
2018: Motor vehicles	66 000	26 100	39 900
2018: Motor vehicles	66 000	38 070	27 930

ACTIVITY 11.1

Wesley started his business cleaning and valeting cars on 1 January 2018 and purchased the following machines:

Machine A: Cost $12 000 on 15 January 2018

Machine B: Cost $16 000 on 13 April 2019

Depreciation is to be applied at 40% per year using the reducing balance method.

Required

a   Prepare the machines at cost account and the accumulated depreciation on machines account for 2018, 2019 and 2020.

b   Show how the machines will appear in the statements of financial position at 31 December 2018, 2019 and 2020.

11.7 Comparing straight-line and reducing balance methods of depreciation

Both methods are designed to achieve the same thing: to distribute the cost of the non-current asset over its useful working life and to match the depreciation charge with the revenue earned in the accounting year.

If applied properly, both methods account for all of the loss in value of the non-current asset, but they do this in very different ways.

WORKED EXAMPLE 4

A business bought equipment for $60 000 on 1 January 2017 and expects it to have a useful life of four years. The residual value is expected to be $7 780.

Suppose depreciation is applied at:

a   25% per year using the straight-line method

b   40% per year using the reducing balance method.

How does the depreciation expense compare for each year?

Year	Straight-line	Reducing balance
2017	25% [1] × (60 000 − 7 780) = $13 055	40% [1] × 60 000 = $24 000 (leaves $36 000) [2]
2018	$13 055	40% × 36 000 = $14 400 (leaves $21 600)
2019	$13 055	40% × 21 600 = $8 640 (leaves $12 960)
2020	$13 055	40% × 12 960 = $5 180 [3] (leaves $7 780)

Notes:

[1]   The straight-line percentage is lower because the 25% is being applied to the same (high) total loss in value whereas reducing balance is applying the 40% to a net book value that will become quite small.

[2]   The depreciation expense will always be higher during the early part of the asset's useful life and so any business that has a high proportion of new items will always suffer more depreciation than a business with lots of old non-current assets.

[3]   There is $4 of rounding.

11.8 Choice of depreciation method

Providing for depreciation is an application of the matching principle, and the method chosen for any particular type of asset should depend on the contribution the asset makes towards earning revenue.

• The *straight-line method* should be used for non-current assets that are expected to earn revenue *evenly* over their useful working lives, or whose value will decline gradually over their useful lives. It is also used where the pattern of a non-current asset's earning power is uncertain. It should always be used to amortise (write off the cost of) assets with fixed lives, such as leases.

- The *reducing balance method* should be used when it is considered that a non-current asset's earning power will reduce as the asset gets older. This method is also used when the non-current asset loses more of its value in the early years of its life (e.g. a vehicle).

11.9 Which assets should be depreciated?

All non-current assets that have a limit to their useful lives should be depreciated. Therefore, depreciation should be provided on all non-current assets except freehold *land*, which does not have such a limit.

Freehold *buildings* will eventually need to be replaced and should be depreciated. In this sense 'freehold' means that the business has complete ownership of the land or buildings and, subject to any government regulations, can decide freely how these non-current assets are used. This differs from leasehold land or buildings where a landlord owns the land or buildings and may restrict what it is used for.

11.10 The revaluation method of depreciation

With some items treated as non-current assets it is sometimes difficult to keep track of them. An example would be loose tools in a manufacturing business. The individual tools may not cost enough to treat them as separate non-current assets. Each tool may have a different useful life. However, their total value may be quite large. In this case, the **revaluation method of depreciation** is used to find out how much to charge as an expense to the statement of profit or loss. It is calculated as:

Opening valuation + purchases made during the period – closing valuation
= depreciation charge for the period.

KEY TERM

revaluation method of depreciation: used to calculate the cost of consumption in the accounting year of small non-current assets such as power tools.

WORKED EXAMPLE 5

Lily runs a small manufacturing business. At 1 January 2019, she valued her loose tools at $4 000. During the year ended 31 December 2019, Lily bought more tools at a total cost of $900. At 31 December she valued the total loose tools at $3 700.

Calculate how much Lily should charge for depreciation of loose tools in her statement of profit or loss for the year ended 31 December 2019.

	$
Cost at 1 Jan 2019	4 000
Add: Additions during the year	900
	4 900
Less: Valuation at 31 Dec 2019	(3 700)
Charge to statement of profit or loss	1 200

In this case, the sum of $1 200 is charged as an expense in the statement of profit or loss. The total valuation of $3 700 will appear in Lily's statement of financial position at 31 December 2019. Where this is shown will vary from business to business. However, the most usual place to record the value is as a current asset – often labelled as 'inventory of loose tools'.

11.11 Other important issues

A non-cash expense: depreciation is not a cash expense – the only movements of cash are when the item is bought and any proceeds if it is sold at the end of its useful life. Money is not set aside to pay for a replacement when the non-current asset reaches the end of its useful life.

End of useful life: while many businesses might base their assessment of useful life on industrial averages, there are no guarantees that this will be accurate. It is possible that depreciation will be fully applied over say five years and the non-current asset continues to provide benefits for years 6, 7 and 8. As the business has already recorded the depreciation in its accounts, it cannot go back and change any figures. The non-current asset will be retained and will appear at its (zero) net book value until it is disposed of.

Part-year depreciation: earlier examples included non-current assets being purchased part-way through a year and there is nothing to stop a business disposing of those non-current assets during the year either. The issue is, how should depreciation be treated in the year of acquisition and in the year of disposal?

There are two main possibilities:

- A full year's depreciation is taken in the year of acquisition, but none in the year of disposal.

- Depreciation is calculated from the date of acquisition; in the year of disposal, depreciation is calculated from the commencement of the year to the date of disposal, that is, only a proportion of the annual depreciation will be provided. This is sometimes referred to as a 'month-by-month basis'.

Consistency

The chosen method of depreciating a non-current asset should be used consistently to ensure that the profits or losses of different periods of account can be compared on a like-for-like basis.

A change in the method of calculating depreciation should only be made if the financial results and position of the business would be stated more fairly. A change should never be made in order to manipulate profit.

TIP
If you are given the dates of acquisition and disposal, calculate depreciation on a monthly basis for the years of acquisition and disposal. Otherwise, calculate depreciation for a full year in the year of acquisition, but not for the year of disposal.

11.12 The disposal of non-current assets

Many non-current assets will eventually be sold, traded in or scrapped – we call this a *disposal*. Often this will be at the end of their useful lives although sometimes a non-current asset may be sold or traded in because the business wants to upgrade or change the way it operates.

It is essential that any record of the non-current asset being disposed of be removed. It is likely that the amount of money received from that disposal will be different from the net book value at that time despite having applied depreciation to that asset. That difference between the proceeds from the sale and the net book value is the profit or loss on disposal.

Before we carry out any double-entry, we must firstly create a disposals account. As we shall see, this is a temporary account that will ultimately 'disappear' with a zero balance.

The steps involved in a disposal of a non-current asset are as follows:

Step 1 Remove the cost of the non-current asset from the assets at cost account.

Debit: Disposals account

Credit: Assets at cost account

Step 2 Remove all of the depreciation that has ever been charged on the non-current asset being disposed of.

Debit: Accumulated depreciation account

Credit: Disposals account

It may be that the amount of depreciation has been given to you, although sometimes you may have to work it out for yourself.

Step 3 Record the proceeds from the disposal.

Debit: Bank or Trade receivables

Credit: Disposals account

Step 4 Tidy up the disposals account by transferring the balance to the statement of profit or loss. There are two likely outcomes:

a Debit: Disposals account

Credit: Statement of profit or loss (this will be a profit on disposal)

b Debit: Statement of profit or loss

Credit: Disposals account (this will be a loss on disposal)

In Worked example 6, we have assumed that the business has several of each non-current asset and that we are disposing of one of them.

WORKED EXAMPLE 6

At 1 June 2020, a motor vehicle which had cost $32 000 was sold for $7 500. A total of $26 200 had been provided for depreciation on that motor vehicle.

Motor vehicles at cost

Debit		$	Credit		$
1 Jan	Balance b/d (given)	74 100	30 Jun	Disposals (1)	32 000
			30 Jun	Balance c/d	42 100
		74 100			74 100
1 Jul	Balance b/d	42 100			

Accumulated depreciation on motor vehicles

Debit		$	Credit		$
30 Jun	Disposals (2)	26 200	1 Jan	Balance b/d (given)	57 500
30 Jun	Balance c/d	31 300			
		57 500			57 500
			1 Jul	Balance b/d	31 300

Disposals of motor vehicles

Debit		$	Credit		$
30 Jun	Motor vehicles at cost (1)	32 000	30 Jun	Accumulated depreciation (2)	26 200
30 Jun	Statement of profit or loss (4)	1 700	30 Jun	Bank (3)	7 500
		33 700			33 700

CONTINUED

Note: this is a *profit on disposal* because the proceeds ($7 500) were more than the net book value at that time (32 000 – 26 200 = $5 800). This would appear in the statement of profit or loss as an addition to gross profit – alongside items like discounts received and rental income.

Suppose the proceeds had been $4 500, then the disposals account would have looked like this:

Disposals of motor vehicles					
Debit			**Credit**		
		$			$
30 Jun	Motor vehicles at cost (1)	32 000	30 Jun	Accumulated depreciation (2)	26 200
			30 Jun	Bank (3)	4 500
			30 Jun	Statement of profit or loss (4)	1 300
		32 000			32 000

Note: this is a loss on disposal because the proceeds ($4 500) were less than the $5 800 net book value at that time. This would appear in the expenses section of the statement of profit or loss.

Proceeds do not have to be the result of a sale. If the non-current asset is destroyed, then the amount paid out by an insurance company is the proceeds.

ACTIVITY 11.2

On 30 April 2020, a motor vehicle belonging to Donata's business was completely written off in an accident. Details of this vehicle were as follows:

Cost: $18 000 on 31 May 2017

Expected useful life: 5 years

Proceeds of sale: a cheque for $4 400 had been received from the insurance company

Depreciation method: reducing balance at a rate of 40% per year (three years had been applied).

Balances at 1 January 2020: Motor vehicles at cost $42 900

Accumulated depreciation on motor vehicles $27 200

Required

a   Calculate the total depreciation charged on the non-current asset.

b   Make the necessary entries in the motor vehicles at cost, accumulated depreciation on motor vehicles and disposals accounts relating to the disposal.

Part exchanges

A new non-current asset may be acquired in part exchange for one that is being disposed of. The steps required to deal with this are very similar to those we have already encountered.

Step 1   Remove the cost of the non-current asset from the assets at cost account.

Step 2   Remove all of the depreciation that has ever been charged on the departing non-current asset.

Step 3   Record the proceeds from the disposal – *this is slightly different*.

Debit: Asset at cost

Credit: Disposals account

Step 4   Tidy up the disposals account by transferring the balance to the statement of profit or loss.

Step 5   Record the remaining cost of the new non-current asset.

Debit: Asset at cost

Credit: Bank or payable

WORKED EXAMPLE 7

A business bought new equipment costing $40 000 on 30 September 2019. The business part-exchanged old equipment that had originally cost $27 000 and that had been depreciated by $23 600. The supplier gave the business $6 000 for the part-exchange and the rest was paid by cheque.

The ledger balances on 1 January 2019 were as follows: equipment at cost $54 300 and accumulated depreciation on equipment $40 800.

Equipment at cost					
Debit			**Credit**		
		$			$
1 Jan	Balance b/d (given)	54 300	30 Sep	Disposals (1)	27 000
30 Sep	Disposals (3) trade-in	6 000	30 Sep	Balance c/d	67 300
30 Sep	Bank (5)	34 000			
		94 300			94 300
1 Oct	Balance b/d	67 300			

Accumulated depreciation on equipment					
Debit			**Credit**		
		$			$
30 Sep	Disposals (2)	23 600	1 Jan	Balance b/d (given)	40 800
30 Sep	Balance c/d	17 200			
		40 800			40 800
			1 Oct	Balance b/d	17 200

Disposals of equipment					
Debit			**Credit**		
		$			$
30 Sep	Equipment at cost (1)	27 000	30 Sep	Accumulated depreciation (2)	23 600
30 Jun	Statement of profit or loss (4)	2 600	30 Sep	Equipment at cost (3)	6 000
		29 600			29 600

ACTIVITY 11.3

On 31 March 2020, Wilhelm bought new machinery costing $48 000. The business part-exchanged an old machine that had originally cost $31 700 and had been depreciated by $29 500. The supplier gave the business $5 000 for the part-exchange and the rest was paid by cheque.

The ledger balances on 1 January 2020 were as follows: machinery at cost $101 300 and accumulated depreciation on machinery $65 800.

Required

Show the machinery at cost, accumulated depreciation on machinery and disposals of machinery accounts after recording the part-exchange.

11.13 Depreciation, trial balances and the financial statements

You may need to account for depreciation when faced with the trial balance.

WORKED EXAMPLE 8

The following extract was taken from a trial balance:

	$	$
Premises	140 000	
Plant and machinery at cost	71 600	
Accumulated depreciation on plant and machinery		35 200
Motor vehicles at cost	53 200	
Accumulated depreciation on motor vehicles		29 900

Additional information

1   Plant and machinery is to be depreciated using the straight-line method at a rate of 20% per year.

2   Motor vehicles are to be depreciated using the reducing balance method at a rate of 35% per year.

Required

a   Show the depreciation expense for the year as it would appear in the statement of profit or loss.

b   Show the non-current assets section of the statement of financial position.

a   As no residual value has been provided, the depreciation on the plant and machinery can be calculated by multiplying the percentage by the cost:

Depreciation = 20% × 71 600 = $14 320

The depreciation on the motor vehicles can be calculated by multiplying the percentage by the net book value at the start of the period, which in this case is:

Depreciation = 35% × (53 200 − 29 900) = $8 155

The total expense appearing in the statement of profit or loss = 14 320 + 8 155 = $22 475

b   The accumulated depreciation figures in the statement of financial position need to be updated by adding this period's depreciation to the total from the previous year that is shown in the trial balance.

TIP

Take great care in identifying which depreciation method should be applied to each type of asset.

Accumulated depreciation on plant and machinery = 35 200 + 14 320 = $49 520

Accumulated depreciation on motor vehicles = 29 900 + 8 155 = $38 055

The non-current assets section of the statement of financial position will look like this:

Statement of financial position at …			
	Cost	Accumulated depreciation	Net book value
	$	$	$
Non-current assets			
Premises	140 000	–	140 000
Plant and machinery	71 600	49 520	22 080
Motor vehicles	53 200	38 055	15 145
	264 800	87 575	177 225

Note: Premises has not had any depreciation applied on it so the net book value and the cost are the same. However, there is nothing to prevent a business charging depreciation on a building.

11.14 Provisions for depreciation and the accounting concepts

Provisions for depreciation are made to comply with the following concepts:

- *Matching*: the cost of using non-current assets to earn revenue should be matched in the statement of profit or loss to the revenue earned.

- *Prudence*: if the cost of using non-current assets was not included in the statement of profit or loss, profit and the value of assets in the statement of financial position would be overadded.

Whichever method of depreciation is chosen for a non-current asset, it should be used consistently and not changed unless there is a very good reason to do so. As we have seen, applying the various depreciation methods can result in very different expense figures, which will affect the amount of profit or loss for the year. The accumulated depreciation and net book value of the non-current assets could also vary considerably depending on the depreciation method used. All of this could affect how the performance and value of the business is viewed by its owner and others who relying on the financial statements to make decisions.

Example: Suppose a business buys a machine for $60 000 and decides to depreciate it using the straight-line method at a rate of 20% per year. At the end of Year 2, the owner decides to change the depreciation method to the reducing balance method at a rate of 20% per year.

The depreciation expense will be as follows:

Year		Expense (not changing method) $		Expense (changing method) $
1	20% x 60 000 =	12 000	20% x 60 000 =	12 000
2	20% x 60 000 =	12 000	20% x 60 000 =	12 000
3	20% x 60 000 =	12 000	20% x (60 000 – 24 000*) =	7 200
4	20% x 60 000 =	12 000	20% x (60 000 – 31 200*) =	5 760
5	20% x 60 000 =	12 000	20% x (60 000 – 36 960*) =	4 608

*this is the accumulated depreciation from all previous years.

If we now work on the principle that in each of the years 1 – 5, the profit for the year excluding the depreciation on this machine was $100 000, then the difference that the change in method is obvious:

Year		Profit (not changing method) $		Profit (changing method) $
1	100 000 – 12 000 =	88 000	100 000 – 12 000 =	88 000
2	100 000 – 12 000 =	88 000	100 000 – 12 000 =	88 000
3	100 000 – 12 000 =	88 000	100 000 – 7 200 =	92 800
4	100 000 – 12 000 =	88 000	100 000 – 5 760 =	94 240
5	100 000 – 12 000 =	88 000	100 000 – 4 608 =	95 392

Clearly, using the reducing-balance method for years 3, 4 and 5 would make a significant (and increasing difference) to the profit for the year. It would also have an impact on the value of the machine in the statement of financial position.

This change of method would almost certainly represent a breach of the consistency principle, particularly if that change was being used to provide a profit figure that might please the business owner or impress possible investors. The only circumstances under which it might be considered acceptable is, if the accountant could demonstrate that the new method represented a more 'true and fair view' of the way in which the machine was losing value.

THINK LIKE AN ACCOUNTANT

What if we don't apply depreciation?

Most non-current assets lose value and accounts apply depreciation both to reflect this as well as ensuring that the matching concept is being followed. In order to try to ensure that the level of depreciation provides a 'true and fair view', accountants will consider the cost, useful life and residual value of the asset as well as which method should be used. What effect would it have on the financial statements if accountants did not apply depreciation?

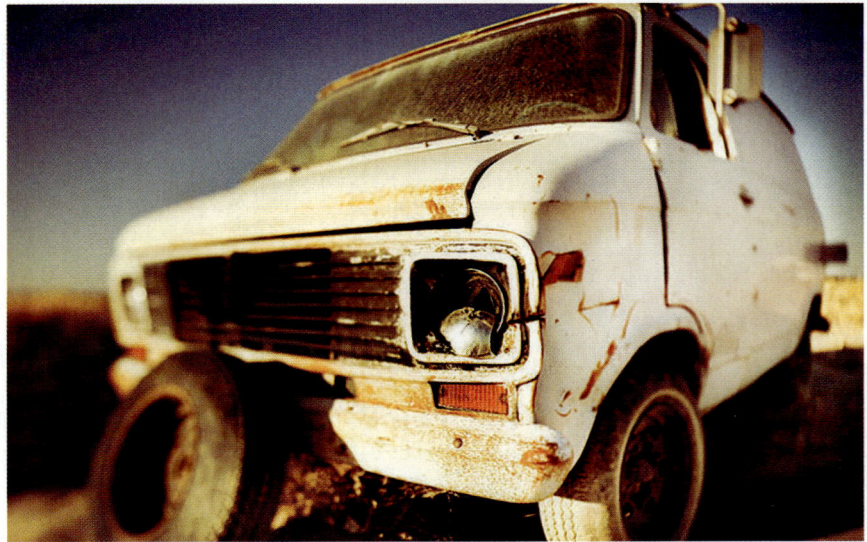

Figure 11.2: As we have seen, applying the various depreciation methods can result in very different expense figures, which will affect the amount of profit or loss for the year. The accumulated depreciation and net book value of the non-current assets could also vary considerably depending on the depreciation method used. All of this could affect how the performance and value of the business is viewed by its owner and others who relying on the financial statements to make decisions.

REFLECTION

Applying depreciation is an application of the accruals or matching concept. Why shouldn't businesses just record the purchase price of a non-current asset as an expense in the statement of financial position in the year in which the asset was bought? Discuss your views with another learner.

EXAM-STYLE QUESTIONS

1   Why should a business account for depreciation on its non-current assets?

   A   so that if the non-current asset is sold, the business owner will know how much money to ask for

   B   it will enable the business to match the non-current asset's loss in value to the periods in which that asset helped to generate revenue

   C   it will help the business to identify when the non-current asset is reaching the end of its useful life

   D   the business needs to ensure that it has enough cash to pay for the depreciation expense.   [1]

2   A business bought a van for $24 000 on 1 January 2017. The business applies depreciation at a rate of 30% per year using the reducing balance method.

   What is the depreciation expense for the year ended 31 December 2019?   [1]

CONTINUED

3   A business part-exchanged a motor vehicle on 2 April 2019. The motor vehicle had originally been bought for $21 500 and had been depreciated by $15 400 at the time of disposal. A loss on disposal of $1 750 was recorded.

What was the part-exchange value on the motor vehicle?   [1]

4   On 30 June 2019 a business sold a motor vehicle that had originally cost $16 300 and had been depreciated by $14 800. A cheque for $2 500 was received.

Balances on 1 January 2019 were as follows:

Ledger balances		
	$	$
Motor vehicles at cost	54 000	
Provision for depreciation on motor vehicles		37 200

Required

a   Explain why businesses might apply different methods of depreciation to different types of non-current asset.   [5]

b   Prepare the following accounts to record the disposal of the motor vehicle:

i   Motor vehicles at cost   [3]

ii   Provision for depreciation on motor vehicles   [3]

iii   Disposals of motor vehicles.   [4]

SELF-EVALUATION CHECKLIST

After studying this chapter, complete a table like this:

You should be able to:	Needs more work	Almost there	Ready to move on
Know that 'capital' expenditure is incurred in the purchase or improvement of a non-current asset whereas 'revenue' expenditure relates to the running costs of the business.			
Understand that depreciation is an expense in the statement of profit or loss and reduces the value of the asset in the statement of financial position.			
Understand that the matching concept requires all costs to be matched to the periods in which they were used by the business to make a profit or generate income – so depreciation must be accounted for.			
Calculate depreciation using the straight-line, reducing balance and revaluation methods, applying the one that provides a true and fair view.			
Account for the disposal of non-current assets, showing the profit or loss on disposal in the statement of profit or loss.			
Prepare financial accounts that include depreciation due to factors including usage and age.			

> Chapter 12

Irrecoverable debts

This chapter covers part of syllabus section AS Level 1.5

LEARNING INTENTIONS

In this chapter you will learn how to:

- distinguish between an irrecoverable debt and a irrecoverable debt
- account for irrecoverable debts and irrecoverable debts recovered
- calculate the provision for irrecoverable debts
- explain that the trade receivables in the statement of financial position are valued at the balance on the sales ledger control account minus the allowance for irrecoverable debts.

ACCOUNTING IN CONTEXT

Can't pay or won't pay?

The number of customers of Ricardo's clothing company stopped growing a year ago. Ricardo realised that, in order to attract new customers, he needed to offer credit terms. His bank manager advised him of ways to establish whether new customers were trustworthy by running credit checks. He was also advised to offer new customers small amounts of credit at first and then increase the amounts.

Ashton, who had been placing large orders for several months, suddenly went out of business owing Ricardo $10 000. Ricardo had not heard from another customer, Niteen, who owed $8 000 (when his credit limit was $5 000) for several months despite attempts to contact them.

What worried Ricardo most was that he had just received invoices from his suppliers for many of the goods he should have been paid for.

Figure 12.1: Credit checks can be an effective way to establish whether new customers are trustworthy.

Discuss in a pair or a group:

- What are irrecoverable debts and why do they happen?
- Why do businesses suffer irrecoverable debts despite carrying out credit checks?
- Why are irrecoverable debts a problem to a business owner like Ricardo's?

12.1 Irrecoverable debts

An **irrecoverable debt** may happen for many reasons. The customer's business may be in financial difficulties and be unable to pay. Some customers may be dishonest and may buy large amounts of goods with little intention of paying. If someone is trading with customers from another part of the world, there may be political or other events that mean that debts will not be paid.

If a business regularly sells goods on credit to a large number of customers, it is almost certain that some irrecoverable debts will happen even if the business has carried out checks – like using credit-rating systems or seeking references – to determine whether the customers are likely to be trustworthy. However, these checks only show whether someone has a history of payment problems. Even if someone has a perfect record of paying on time, there is no guarantee that they will not experience financial difficulties in the future.

When an irrecoverable debt happens, it needs to be recorded in the accounts. There are two impacts:

- an asset (the trade receivable) is now worthless
- a loss has been incurred.

KEY TERM

irrecoverable debt: a debt due from a customer that it is expected will never be paid by them.

WORKED EXAMPLE 1

Ricardo is owed $10 000 by Ashton and $8 000 by Niteen. Ashton has gone out of business and Niteen cannot be found. Ricardo has decided to write off both debts as irrecoverable on 30 April 2020.

	Dr	Cr
2020	$	$
30 Apr Irrecoverable debts account	18 000	
Ashton		10 000
Niteen		8 000

Narrative: Writing off outstanding balances for Ashton and Niteen who are not expected to pay

Given that the sales ledger control account should match the combined total of the individual receivable subsidiary ledgers, it is important these be credited with the amounts being written off.

Ashton Debit	$	Credit	$
Balance c/d	10 000	30 Apr Irrecoverable debts	10 000
	10 000		10 000

Niteen Debit	$	Credit	$
Balance c/d	8 000	30 Apr Irrecoverable debts	8 000
	8 000		8 000

When Ricard prepares his annual accounts at the end of that accounting year, he will transfer the balance on the irrecoverable debts account to the statement of profit or loss as an *expense*. This too is done using a journal entry:

	Dr	Cr
2020	$	$
30 Apr Statement of profit or loss	18 000	
Irrecoverable debts		18 000

Narrative: Irrecoverable debts for the year written off.

This will close off the irrecoverable debts account, which means that the next accounting year will start with a zero balance.

12.2 Irrecoverable debts recovered

It is possible that money written off may actually be paid at a later date. If a business has failed it is possible that its assets will be sold off and there may be money to enable the trade payables to be paid off, either in full or in part.

WORKED EXAMPLE 2

Suppose the assets relating to Ashton's business had been sold and on 17 November 2020, a cheque was received for $2 400.

The journal used to record the recovery of an irrecoverable debt would be:

Date	Details	Dr	Cr
		$	$
17 Nov	Bank	2 400	
	Irrecoverable debts recovered		2 400

Narrative: The recovery of $2 400 of the Ashton balance written off in April.

At the end of the year, this would be transferred to the statement of profit or loss using a journal:

Date	Details	Dr	Cr
		$	$
17 Nov	Irrecoverable debts recovered	2 400	
	Statement of profit or loss		2 400

Narrative: The transfer of recovered debt to the statement of profit or loss.

TIP

Never show the amount recovered as a negative expense.

This item would appear in the statement of profit or loss alongside other incomes and discounts received that for Ricardo in 2020 might look like this:

	$	$
Revenue		287 300
Less: Cost of sales		
Opening inventory	19 765	
Purchases	214 860	
	234 625	
Closing inventory	(23 285)	
Cost of sales		(211 340)
Gross profit		75 960
Irrecoverable debts recovered		2 400
		73 560
Less: Expenses		
Irrecoverable debts	18 000	
Office expenses	21 740	
Wages and salaries	32 185	
Total expenses		(71 925)
Profit for the year		1 635

12.3 Allowance for irrecoverable debts

Irrecoverable debts may only be written off many months after the sale. Many firms attempt to get the customer to pay first, sending reminders, threatening legal action and then taking legal action to recover the money.

It is likely that there will be debts relating to sales made during this accounting year that will not become irrecoverable debts until the next accounting year. This causes two possible problems:

- the business may not be applying the matching principle

- the trade receivables figure shown in the current assets part of the statement of financial position will be overstating the amount that we actually expect to get, which may not be applying the prudence concept.

In order to account for these **irrecoverable debts**, a business will create and maintain an **allowance for irrecoverable debts**.

KEY TERMS

irrecoverable debt: a debt due from a customer where it is uncertain whether or not it will be repaid by them.

allowance for irrecoverable debts: the amount of irrecoverable debts relating to this period's sales and trade receivables figure that a business has estimated it will suffer during the next accounting year.

WORKED EXAMPLE 3

Janine started a business in 2015 and as a result of some irrecoverable debts, decided in 2017 to create an allowance for irrecoverable debts that was based on a percentage of trade receivables at the year end.

The following information was available for the years ended 31 December 2017, 2018 and 2019.

	2017	2018	2019
	$	$	$
Irrecoverable debts written off	$2 400	$3 500	$3 150
Year-end trade receivables figure (after write-offs)	$32 000	$36 000	$29 000
Allowance for irrecoverable debts (% of receivables)	2%	4%	3%

The entries in the irrecoverable debts account will be:

Irrecoverable debts account					
Debit			**Credit**		
		$			$
31 Dec 17	Debtors Chang and Wallace written off	2 400	31 Dec 17	Statement of profit or loss	2 400
31 Dec 18	Debtor Hooley written off	3 500	31 Dec 18	Statement of profit or loss	3 500
31 Dec 19	Debtors Rishi and Sachin written off	3 150	31 Dec 19	Statement of profit or loss	3 150

Note: the debit entries in the statement of profit or loss represent expenses.

The entries in the **allowance for irrecoverable debts account** will be:

1 Calculate the size of the new allowance and enter it on the credit side of the allowance for irrecoverable debts account below the 2017 sub-totals – the allowance for irrecoverable debts account has a credit balance because it represents a reduction in the value of an asset (trade receivables).

2 As there is a credit balance b/d, there must be a debit balance c/d on the credit side above the sub-total lines.

3 Insert the statement of profit or loss entry on the credit side – it is making up for the lack of value on that side and making sure that both sides add up to $640.

KEY TERM

allowance for irrecoverable debts account: the account used to account for possible irrecoverable debts that may not be seen until the next accounting year.

CONTINUED

These steps are repeated for 2018 and 2019.

Allowance for irrecoverable debts account					
Debit				**Credit**	
		$			$
31 Dec 17	Balance c/d (2)	640	31 Dec 17	Statement of profit or loss (3)	640
		640			640
			1 Jan 18	Balance b/d (1)	640
31 Dec 18	Balance c/d	1 440	31 Dec 18	Statement of profit or loss	800
		1 440			1 440
31 Dec 19	Statement of profit or loss	570	1 Jan 19	Balance b/d	1 440
31 Dec 19	Balance c/d	870			
		1 440			1 440
			1 Jan 20	Balance b/d	870

2017: The allowance is 2% × 32 000 = $640. This represents the amount of the 2017 trade receivables figure that Janine thinks will be written off during 2018. The credit balance in the allowance for irrecoverable debts account represents a reduction in the asset of trade receivables while the debit entry in the statement of profit or loss represents *extra expense* for 2017.

2018: The allowance is 4% × 36 000 = $1 440. This represents the amount of the 2018 trade receivables figure that Janine thinks will be written off during 2019. The credit balance in the allowance for irrecoverable debts account represents a reduction in the asset of trade receivables while the debit entry in the statement of profit or loss represents *extra expense* for 2018.

2019: The allowance is 3% × 29 000 = $870. This represents the amount of the 2019 trade receivables figure that Janine thinks will be written off during 2020. As for previous years, the credit balance in the allowance for irrecoverable debts account represents a reduction in the asset of trade receivables.

However, the statement of profit or loss entry is different because the allowance has got smaller:

Debit: Allowance for irrecoverable debts

Credit: Statement of profit or loss

This means that we are dealing with a reduction in our overall expense for irrecoverable debts.

To avoid confusion about why increasing the allowance means more expense and reducing the allowance means less expense, it may be helpful to think of the situation in terms of 'new irrecoverable debts'.

In 2017, the irrecoverable debts written off were $2 400 and these were all 'new' in that they had not been accounted for. The allowance had only just been created (and increased from 0 to 640) so all $640 were also 'new'.

CONTINUED

In 2018, the irrecoverable debts written off were $3 500, but $640 had already been accounted for in 2017, so the amount of 'new' irrecoverable debts from those write-offs was $3 500 – $640 = $2860 and we need to add the revised allowance of $1 440 to arrive at the total expense of $4 300.

In 2019, the irrecoverable debts written off were $3 150, but $1 440 had already been accounted for in 2018, so the amount of 'new' irrecoverable debts from those write-offs was $3 150 – $1 440 = $1 710 and we need to add the revised allowance of $870 to arrive at the total expense of $2 580.

When preparing the statement of financial position, remember that the business has decided that some of the trade receivable balance will never be received. The allowance for irrecoverable debts at the end of the year needs to be deducted to arrive at the expected value of the trade receivables, as shown next. This is also an application of the prudence concept as the possibility of not receiving all of the money has been accounted for by the business as soon as Janine recognised that there might be a problem.

2017	$	$
Trade receivables	32 000	
Less: Provision for irrecoverable debts	(640)	31 360
2018		
Trade receivables	36 000	
Less: Provision for irrecoverable debts	(1 440)	34 560
2019		
Trade receivables	29 000	
Less: Provision for irrecoverable debts	(870)	28 130

ACTIVITY 12.1

Rudolph decided at the end of 2017 to create an allowance for irrecoverable debts that was based on a given percentage of trade receivables at the year end.

The following information was available for the years ended 31 December 2017, 2018 and 2019.

	2017	2018	2019
	$	$	$
Irrecoverable debts written off	$1 630	$1 575	$2 350
Trade receivables at 31 December	$11 800	$14 000	$15 000
Allowance for irrecoverable debts (as % of trade receivables)	5%	3.5%	4%

Required

a   Make the relevant entries in the irrecoverable debts and allowance for irrecoverable debts accounts for 2017, 2018 and 2019.

b   Show the irrecoverable debts expense figure that will be put in the statement of profit or loss for 2017, 2018 and 2019.

c   Show the trade receivables figure that would appear in the statement of financial position at the end of 2017, 2018 and 2019.

12.4 Calculating the provision for irrecoverable debts

The calculation of a provision for irrecoverable debts depends on the type of provision required:

- *General*: calculated as a percentage of the total trade receivables. The average percentage of debts by amount that prove to be irrecoverable is used. Many businesses might adjust the percentage to reflect factors like the state of the economy, adjusting the percentage upwards if the economy is entering into a recession or reducing it during times of prosperity.

- *Specific*: certain debts are selected from the sales ledger as doubtful. The provision will be equal to the total of those debts. The amount of the provision is based on specific knowledge the business owner has of each particular customer's financial position.

- *Specific and general*: made up of the debts that are thought to be doubtful plus a percentage of the remainder.

WORKED EXAMPLE 4

Rachel maintains a specific and general provision for irrecoverable debts. The general provision is based on 3% of trade receivables after deducting irrecoverable debts.

At 31 December	Total receivables	Irrecoverable debts	Provision Specific	Provision General	Total
	a	b		c	
	$	$	$	$	$
2017	28 500	2 000	2 000	795	2 795
2018	37 300	2 800	2 800	1 035	3 835
2019	32 400	2 600	2 600	894	3 494

The calculation of the general provision is [column (a) – column (b)] × 3% = column (c).

TIP

Specific provisions must always be deducted from trade receivables, first, before the general provision is calculated.

ACTIVITY 12.2

Ronal maintains a provision for irrecoverable debts in his books. It is made up of a specific provision for irrecoverable debts and a general provision equal to 2.5% of the remainder. The following information is extracted from Ronal's books:

At 31 March	Total trade receivables	Irrecoverable debts (included in total trade receivables)
	$	$
2018	21 000	2 200
2019	26 400	4 400
2020	28 300	3 500

Required

a   Calculate the total provision for irrecoverable debts for each of these years.

b   Prepare the allowance for irrecoverable debts account for each of the years. (Assume that Ronal had not made an allowance for irrecoverable debts before 31 March 2017.)

12.5 Trial balances and the financial statements

Sometimes a trial balance will include notes on irrecoverable debt adjustments that need to be made.

> ### WORKED EXAMPLE 5
>
> **A trial balance had been produced at 31 May 2020. Some of the balances were as follows:**
>
> | | Debit | Credit |
> |---|---|---|
> | | $ | $ |
> | Trade receivables | 41 260 | |
> | Irrecoverable debts | 2 380 | |
> | Allowance for irrecoverable debts | | 1 092 |
>
> **Notes:**
>
> 1 A customer had gone out of business owing $1 610 – nothing had been recorded in the books.
>
> 2 The allowance for irrecoverable debts is to be adjusted to 4% of trade receivables.
>
> **Step 1**
>
> Account for the irrecoverable debt first:
>
> > Debit: Irrecoverable debts $1 610
> >
> > Credit: Trade receivables $1 610
>
> This will increase the irrecoverable debts to $2 380 + $1 610 = $3 990 (which will be debited to the statement of profit or loss as an expense).
>
> This will reduce the trade receivables to $41 260 – $1 610 = $39 650
>
> **Step 2**
>
> Calculate the new allowance for irrecoverable debts and identify the amount of change that has taken place:
>
> > 4% × $39 650 = $1 586 . This is an increase of $1 586 – $1 092 = $494.
>
> The double entry to adjust for this is:
>
> > Debit: Statement of profit or loss $494
> >
> > Credit: Allowance for irrecoverable debts $494
>
> **Step 3**
>
> Identify the total expense in the statement of profit or loss:
>
> > $3 990 + $494 = $4 484
>
> **Note:** had the new allowance for irrecoverable debts been smaller than the trial balance figure, then the entry in the allowance for irrecoverable debts account would have been a debit and the amount of reduction would have been deducted from the $3 990 to give the amount of expense in the statement of profit or loss.
>
> **Step 4**
>
> List the remaining trade receivables and the revised allowance in the statement of financial position.
>
> | | $ | $ |
> |---|---|---|
> | Trade receivables | 39 650 | |
> | Allowance for irrecoverable debts | (1 586) | 38 064 |

ACTIVITY 12.3

A trial balance was produced at 31 May 2020. Some of the balances were as follows:

	Debit	Credit
	$	$
Trade receivables	29 640	
Irrecoverable debts	1 186	
Allowance for irrecoverable debts		1 400

Required

In each of the following cases, show the:

- revised trade receivables figure
- revised irrecoverable debts figure
- revised allowance for irrecoverable debts figure
- total irrecoverable debts expense
- trade receivables figures appearing in the statement of financial position.

a   A customer had gone out of business owing $840 – nothing was recorded in the books. The allowance for irrecoverable debts is to be adjusted to 3% of trade receivables.

b   A customer had gone out of business owing $880 – nothing was recorded in the books. The allowance for irrecoverable debts is to be adjusted to include a specific allowance for irrecoverable debts of $1 200 and 2% of remaining trade receivables.

12.6 Provisions for irrecoverable debts and the accounting concepts

A provision for irrecoverable debts complies with the following accounting concepts:

- *Prudence*: amounts expected to be received from trade receivables should not be overadded in the statement of financial position. The statement of profit or loss should provide for the loss of revenue and not overstate profit.
- *Matching*: the possible loss of revenue should be provided for in the period in which the revenue was earned, not in a later period when the debt becomes irrecoverable.

KEY CONCEPT LINK

Consistency: Consistency in the treatment of financial transactions enables the performance of a business to be compared meaningfully over different time periods. Can a business ever justify changing the way it calculates the allowance for irrecoverable debts at the end of an accounting year? Why/why not?

REFLECTION

What measures could a business that sells goods on credit use to reduce the level of irrecoverable debts that it suffers? Discuss your suggestions with another learner.

THINK LIKE AN ACCOUNTANT

Calculating the provision for irrecoverable debts

Writing off an irrecoverable debt when it happens should be a straightforward process of making the bookkeeping entries to record the expense and remove assets that no longer have any value. However, trying to create an allowance for irrecoverable debts that accurately reflects the likely amount of irrecoverable debts that will only be seen in the next accounting year is difficult. It may involve the accountant and the business owner making an educated guess, which could turn out to be very inaccurate. What approaches can be used to try to ensure that the allowance for irrecoverable debts is as accurate as possible? What will be the effects on the financial statements if the balance on the allowance for irrecoverable debts account turns out to be significantly larger (or smaller) than it should have been?

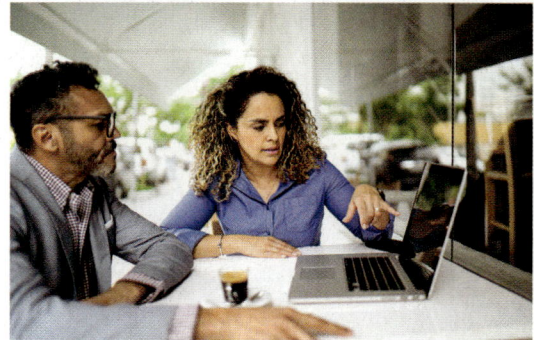

Figure 12.2: Creating an allowance for irrecoverable debts accurately can be very difficult.

EXAM-STYLE QUESTIONS

1   A trader has decided to maintain a provision for irrecoverable debts. Which of the following concepts are being applied when he does this?

   i   going concern   **ii**   matching   **iii**   prudence   **iv**   realisation

   A   i and iii

   B   i and iv

   C   ii and iii

   D   ii and iv   **[1]**

2   At 1 May 2019, a business had an allowance for irrecoverable debts of $1 200. At 30 April 2020, the allowance was adjusted to $900. How did this adjustment affect the financial statements?

	Profit for the year	Net trade receivables
A	decrease by $300	decrease by $300
B	decrease by $300	increase by $300
C	increase by $300	decrease by $300
D	increase by $300	increase by $300

   [1]

CONTINUED

3   Before any end-of-year adjustments were made, the trial balance of a business at 31 May 2020 included the following:

	Debit	Credit
	$	$
Trade receivables	25 400	
Allowance for irrecoverable debts		920

At 31 May 2020, the allowance for irrecoverable debts was adjusted to 4% of trade receivables.

A debt of $635, which had been written off as irrecoverable in January 2019, was recovered in January 2020. What was the effect of these events on the profit for the year ended 31 May 2020?

A   Decrease profit by $731

B   Decrease profit by $539

C   Increase profit by $539

D   Increase profit by $731   [1]

4   A trial balance was extracted for Tait at 30 June 2020:

	Debit	Credit
	$	$
Administration costs	71 685	
Allowance for irrecoverable debts		700
Bank		9 280
Business rates	45 630	
Capital at 1 July 2017		164 865
Drawings	75 000	
Equipment at cost	64 000	
Accumulated depreciation on equipment		19 200
Heat and light	13 890	
Inventory at 1 July 2017	65 105	
Irrecoverable debts	11 420	
Land and buildings	270 000	
Mortgage on land and buildings (repayable 2029)		217 500
Office furniture at cost	45 000	
Accumulated depreciation on office furniture		11 250
Purchases	428 990	
Purchase returns		6 545
Revenue		765 430
Sales returns	5 980	
Trade payables		26 795
Trade receivables	37 800	
Wages and salaries	87 065	
	1 221 565	1 221 565

CONTINUED

Additional information at 30 June 2020:

- Inventory was valued at $78 615.
- An irrecoverable debt of $3 600 had not been recorded at all.
- An unpaid heat and light bill for $4 275 was still outstanding while business rates of $3 510 had been paid in advance.
- Depreciation was to be charged on the following basis:
  - equipment 30% using the reducing balance method
  - office furniture 25% using the straight-line method.
- The allowance for irrecoverable debts was to be set at 2.5% of trade receivables.

Required

a   Prepare a statement of profit or loss for the year ended 30 June 2020.   [14]

b   Prepare a statement of financial position at 30 June 2020.   [16]

SELF-EVALUATION CHECKLIST

After studying this chapter, complete a table like this:

You should be able to:	Needs more work	Almost there	Ready to move on
Distinguish between an irrecoverable debt and a irrecoverable debt, remembering that irrecoverable debts may relate to sales made in the previous accounting year.			
Account for irrecoverable debts and irrecoverable debts recovered – irrecoverable debts and adjustments to the allowance for irrecoverable debts are an expense in the statement of profit or loss. If money is recovered from a customer who was previously written off as an irrecoverable debt, this is shown as an addition to gross profit in the statement of profit or loss.			
Provide for irrecoverable debts, remembering that the matching and prudence concepts require an attempt to be made to anticipate irrecoverable debts – the use of the allowance for irrecoverable debts helps to do this.			
Know that the trade receivables in the statement of financial position are valued at the balance on the sales ledger control account minus the allowance for irrecoverable debts.			

> Chapter 13

Bank reconciliation statements

This chapter covers part of syllabus section AS Level 1.4

LEARNING INTENTIONS

In this chapter you will learn how to:

- prepare a bank reconciliation
- explain what a bank reconciliation statement is and how it is used
- describe how the bank balance in the cash book equals the correct balance of cash at bank
- identify the correct bank account balance that should go into the statement of financial position
- discuss the benefits and limitations of preparing a bank reconciliation statement.

ACCOUNTING IN CONTEXT

Where's my money gone?

At the end of last month, Jules, who sells sporting goods, decided to confirm that the balances in his cash book were correct. He counted the physical amount of cash in the cash box and found that it matched exactly with the balance in the cash book and was delighted.

However, when Jules looked at the bank statement for the previous month, he got a shock. Not only were the closing balances different but the bank statement showed a large overdraft while his cash book indicated that he had large amounts of cash in the account. What was worse was that the bank had charged him interest for being overdrawn.

Figure 13.1: Jules's bank statement provided a very different picture of his business to his cash book.

Discuss in a pair or a group:

- Why do Jules and his bank have such a different view of the balance of his bank account?

- Had there been a terrible mistake made by Jules or the bank? Was there a reasonable explanation for the difference?

13.1 What is a bank reconciliation statement?

The **bank reconciliation statement** is used to reassure the business that the differences are not the result of errors committed by its accountants or the bank.

If any business records a large number of transactions in its bank account during the course of a month, then it is very likely that the cash book and the bank statement will show very different balances. There are two main reasons for this:

- **omitted items**: examples include **standing orders** and **direct debits**, bank charges, interest and electronic transfers.

- **timing differences**: for example, a cheque has to find its way back to our bank before the money actually changes hands, and this can take days.

It is therefore very likely that we will have recorded payments near to the end of the month that will only appear on next month's bank statement because, at the end of the month, our bank did not yet know about that payment. Our supplier will also find that his or her bank may not have recorded the receipt either and therefore his or her cash book will record money going into the bank account while the bank statement will not show it.

The situation is further confused by the fact that the business and the bank look at a bank account from the opposite point of view.

KEY TERMS

bank reconciliation statement: a statement prepared periodically to ensure that the bank account in the business cash book matches the business bank account shown on the bank statement.

omitted items: payments and receipts made by the bank that have not been recorded in the cash book.

standing order: an electronic payment where the payer gives instruction for his or her bank to pay a regular amount. The amount paid is always the same and takes place on a specific date.

KEY TERMS

direct debit: a regular electronic payment where the payer gives written permission (a direct debit mandate) for the person receiving the money to claim the money by presenting the 'bill'. Usually used where the timing of the payment or the amount is likely to vary.

timing differences: the delay between items recorded in the cash book and their appearance on the bank statement.

WORKED EXAMPLE 1

What happens if a trader opens a bank account and:

1 deposits $500 into the account then

2 takes $350 of it out and later

3 takes another $400 away?

Answer

1 The business has an asset because it has lent the money to the bank and shows the deposit and the resulting balance as a debit. The bank will regard the account as a liability and will record the transaction and the balance as a credit.

2 The business will record the transaction as a credit as it is reducing the size of the asset (to $150) while the bank will show the transaction as a debit because it is reducing its liability.

3 The account is now $250 overdrawn. The $400 is a credit entry and the resulting balance is credit, reflecting the fact that the business now has a liability. The bank regards the transaction as a debit because it is reducing the liability and then increasing the asset while the resulting overdraft represents an asset as the business owes it $250.

Banks use the terms **deposit** and **withdrawal** instead of 'debit and credit'. They also use 'O/D' for overdraft (a debit balance) and nothing for a credit balance. However, the deposit column is often on the credit side and the withdrawal column on the debit side – so you need to take care when reading your bank statement.

When the balances in the cash book and bank statement do not agree, the correct balance must be found by preparing a bank reconciliation statement.

13.2 Preparing a bank reconciliation statement

Follow these three steps:

Step 1 Compare the entries in the cash book with the bank statements. Tick items that appear in both the cash book *and* the bank statement. Be sure to tick them in both places.

Step 2 Enter in the cash book any items that remain unticked in the bank statement. Then tick those in both places. Then calculate the new cash book balance.

Step 3 Prepare the reconciliation statement. Begin with the final balance shown on the bank statement and adjust it for any items that remain unticked in the cash book. The result should equal the balance in the cash book.

KEY TERMS

deposit: money being paid into the bank account.

withdrawal: money being taken out of the bank account.

TIP

Show bank overdrafts as current liabilities in statements of financial position, never as current assets.

The cash book balance will now be the correct balance of cash at bank. This figure can then be used to record the bank figure in the statement of financial position. If the final balance in the cash book is a debit then it will appear under current assets, together with the cash in hand. This is headed 'cash and cash equivalents'. If the final balance in the cash book is a credit, it will appear under current liabilities as 'bank overdraft'.

WORKED EXAMPLE 2

Step 1

The cash book (bank columns only) for Felix for May 2018 and the bank statement were as follows. Tick all of the items that appear on both.

Cash book for Felix for May 2018					
Debit			**Credit**		
		$			$
1 May	Balance b/d	2396 ✓	2 May	Laker (446)	2673 ✓
4 May	May	772 ✓	9 May	Bedser (447)	518
10 May	Cowdrey	1916 ✓	13 May	Trueman (448)	99 ✓
15 May	Dexter	3525 ✓	21 May	Lock (449)	1094 ✓
22 May	Bailey	337 ✓	29 May	Watson (450)	2186
30 May	Evans	1006			

Bank statement for Felix for May 2018				
Date	Details	Withdrawals	Deposits	Balance
		$	$	$
01.05	Balance b/d			2396 ✓
03.05	Cheque 446	2673 ✓		277 O/D
05.05	Deposit		772 ✓	495
07.05	S/O – Business rates	800		305 O/D
12.05	Deposit		1916 ✓	1611
15.05	Cheque 448	99 ✓		1512
16.05	Deposit		3525 ✓	5037
24.05	Deposit		337 ✓	5374
25.05	Cheque 449	1094 ✓		4280
28.05	Bank charges and interest	45		4235
30.05	Credit transfer – Tyson		1200	5435

Step 2

All of the items that do not have a tick against them in the statement must then be added to the cash book to ensure that it is complete. Now that the items appear in both the cash book and the bank statement, they can be ticked off. The cash book can now be balanced off.

CONTINUED

Updated cash book for Felix for May 2018						
Debit			**Credit**			
		$				$
1 May	Balance b/d	2 396 ✓	2 May	Laker (446)		2 673 ✓
4 May	May	772 ✓	9 May	Bedser (447)		518
10 May	Cowdrey	1 916 ✓	13 May	Trueman (448)		99 ✓
15 May	Dexter	3 525 ✓	21 May	Lock (449)		1 094 ✓
22 May	Bailey	337 ✓	29 May	Watson (450)		2 186
30 May	Evans	1 006	7 May	Standing order – Business rates		800 ✓
30 May	Credit transfer – Tyson	1 200 ✓	28 May	Bank charges and interest		45 ✓
			31 May	Balance c/d		3 737
		11 152				11 152
1 Jun	Balance b/d	3 737				

Notes: the other half of the transaction needs to be recorded so there should be:

1   A debit entry of $800 should be made in the business rates account

2   A debit entry of $45 should be made in the bank charges and interest account

3   A credit entry should be made in the trade payables control account, assuming that Tyson was a supplier.

Step 3

Prepare the reconciliation statement. This will include all of the unticked items in the cash book and will be a combination of:

• **payments unpresented**

• **receipts unpresented**.

Bank reconciliation statement as at 30 May 2020		
	$	$
Balance per bank statement		5 435
Add: Receipts not presented:		
Name: Evans	1 006	
Total to add		1 006
Less: Payments not presented:		
Name: Bedser	518	
Name: Watson	2 186	
Total to subtract		(2 704)
Balance as per cash book		3 737

Note: overdrawn balances should be shown as negative numbers.

These outstanding items should appear on the June bank statement and will need to be ticked off next month.

KEY TERMS

payments unpresented: payments of money from the bank account that have been recorded in the cash book but have not yet appeared on the bank statement.

receipts unpresented: deposits of money paid into the bank account that have been recorded in the cash book but have not yet appeared on the bank statement.

13.3 Different opening balances

If the closing balances in one month are different in the cash book and on the bank statement, it follows that the opening balances at the start of the next month will be different.

Step 1   Identify and tick off the items that are causing the opening difference. In practice, we should have last month's bank reconciliation statement, but in the absence of this, we can use common sense to make some deductions.

For example, if the first cheque written out this month is number 771, then it follows that any cheques with a lower number must have been completed earlier (last month) and so can be ticked off as it helps to explain the difference in the opening balances.

Items from last month are likely to appear early in this month's bank statement.

Then we can proceed as normal.

WORKED EXAMPLE 3

The cash book (bank columns only) for Moores for May 2020 was as follows.

	Cash book for Moores for May 2020					
	Debit			**Credit**		
		$				$
1 May	Balance b/d	845 ✓	7 May	Motor expenses (771)		233 ✓
3 May	McGarry	3 131 ✓	10 May	Office expenses (772)		1 478 ✓
6 May	Cook	1 786 ✓	18 May	Napier (773)		577
11 May	Pettini	1 305 ✓	19 May	Middlebrook (774)		882 ✓
17 May	Flower	1 167 ✓	24 May	Foster (775)		1 950 ✓
29 May	Irani	611	27 May	Westfield (776)		1 500
			30 May	Wages and salaries (777)		3 201

The bank statement relating to that month was as follows:

	Bank statement for Moores for May 2020			
Date	Details	Withdrawals	Deposits	Balance
		$	$	$
01.05	Balance b/d			1 620
02.05	Cheque 769	1 489 ✓		131
03.05	Deposit		714 ✓	845 ✓
04.05	Deposit		3 131 ✓	3 976
08.05	Deposit		1 786 ✓	5 762
10.05	Cheque 771	233 ✓		5 529
13.05	Deposit		1 305 ✓	6 834
14.05	Cheque 772	1 478 ✓		5 356
17.05	S/O – Office expenses	600 ✓		4 756
19.05	Deposit		1 167 ✓	5 923
21.05	Cheque 774	882 ✓		5 041
27.05	Cheque 775	1 950 ✓		3 091
28.05	Bank charges and interest	33 ✓		3 058

> **CONTINUED**

Notes:

1   The **blue** ticks represent the items from April that have only appeared in the bank statement – you need to identify these early. If you don't and you don't use them to update the cash book, then you will never be able to reconcile the cash book with the bank statement.

2   The **red** ticks represent the normal elimination of the items that initially appeared on both the cash book and the bank statement.

Updated cash book for Moores for May 2020						
Debit			**Credit**			
		$			$	
1 May	Balance b/d	845 ✓	7 May	Motor expenses (771)	233	✓
3 May	McGarry	3 131 ✓	10 May	Office expenses (772)	1 478	✓
6 May	Cook	1 786 ✓	18 May	Napier (773)	577	
11 May	Pettini	1 305 ✓	19 May	Middlebrook (774)	882	✓
17 May	Flower	1 167 ✓	24 May	Foster (775)	1 950	✓
29 May	Irani	611	27 May	Westfield (776)	1 500	
			30 May	Wages and salaries (777)	3 201	
			17 Apr	S/O – Office expenses	600	✓
			28 May	Bank charges and interest	33	✓
		10 454			10 454	
			1 Jun	Balance b/d	1 609	

> **ACTIVITY 13.1**

The cash book for June 2018 was as follows:

Cash book for Arial for June 2018					
Debit			**Credit**		
		$			$
1 Jun	Balance b/d	9 720	2 Jun	Rawson (158)	1 746
3 Jun	Catley	2 531	6 Jun	Motor expenses (159)	423
8 Jun	Gill	1 475	11 Jun	Dinnes (160)	2 872
17 Jun	Williams	1 684	13 Jun	Office expenses (161)	564
30 Jun	Curtis	871	17 Jun	Gray (162)	3 523
			21 Jun	Drawings (163)	2 750
			24 Jun	Smith (164)	1 245
			30 Jun	Wages and salaries (165)	4 511

CONTINUED

The bank statement relating to that month was as follows:

Date	Details	Bank statement for Arial for June 2018 Withdrawals	Deposits	Balance
		$	$	$
01.06	Balance b/d			6 027
02.06	Cheque 155	883		5 144
03.06	Deposit		4 576	9 720
04.06	Cheque 158	1 746		7 974
04.06	Deposit		2 531	10 505
07.06	S/O – Rent and rates	350		10 155
09.06	Cheque 159	423		9 732
10.06	Deposit		1 475	11 207
13.06	Cheque 160	2 872		8 335
15.06	Cheque 161	564		7 771
18.06	Deposit		1 684	9 455
23.06	Cheque 163	2 750		6 705
27.06	Cheque 164	1 245		5 460
29.06	Bank charges and interest	27		5 433

Required

a   Tick off the cash book against the bank statement.

b   Update the cash book and balance it off.

c   Produce a bank reconciliation statement for Arial as at 30 April 2020.

KEY CONCEPT LINK

Planning and control: Management accounting provides a framework for a business to plan and control its finances and enables informed decision making. How does the process of producing a bank reconciliation statement improve the business's ability to plan and control its affairs?

13.4 Benefits and limitations of bank reconciliation statements

The process of preparing a bank reconciliation statement has a number of benefits:

- *Ensures the cash book is up-to-date*: the unticked items on the bank statement are entered into the cash book, which ensures that the cash book is kept up-to-date and the correct balance is shown in the statement of financial position.

- *Ensures that all transactions involving the bank are recorded*: if the other half of the entries are made, then other account balances will also be up-to-date and the trial balance will be accurate.

- *Helps to detect errors*: if the bank reconciliation agrees, it can reassure the business that errors have not been committed – by the bank or the business. If the bank reconciliation does not balance, then it can identify where errors have been made or where items need to be investigated.

All three of these benefits also provide **verification** of whether values shown for the bank account (and other ledger balances) are accurate and up-to-date by using external evidence – the bank statements.

- *Assists management of cashflow*: the business can avoid unintended overdrafts on the bank account – the cash book may highlight an overdraft before the bank becomes aware of it and the business may be able to pay money into the bank to avoid the overdraft. It can also highlight a surplus of cash at the bank that could be used to earn interest.

- *Strengthens* **internal controls**/*helps to prevent fraud*: the bank reconciliation might not be prepared by the same person who maintains the cash book, which would increase the possibility of any unusual activity being detected and reported.

Auditors refer to the dividing up of tasks between several people as **segregation of duties** and regard this as a strong form of internal control. One person might be able to commit fraud and conceal it quite easily, but if several people are involved then it is more likely that problems will be noticed and reported. The increased chance of being discovered might discourage someone from committing fraud in the first place.

There is also one major limitation that can arise from preparing a bank reconciliation:

- *Erroneously cancelling cheques*: one might expect that a vast majority of cheques that have not cleared will be those that were issued late in the month and have not cleared. However, there may be earlier cheques that have still not cleared. While it is likely that the cheque has arrived safely and it is just the supplier taking time to pay it into the bank account, it could possibly have been lost or stolen. The accountant could ask the bank to cancel the cheque only to find that the supplier pays it in later and it doesn't clear.

While the bank reconciliation is useful for identifying items that are taking a long time to clear, it does mean that the accountant needs to use their judgement. In this case, the most sensible decision would be to contact the supplier to ensure that the cheque has arrived safely. If the cheque has not been received at all, then asking the bank to cancel it is appropriate.

13.5 Identifying and adjusting balances

You will need to be able to identify the correct bank account balance that should go into the statement of financial position. This may involve you having to work backwards from the bank statement balance. You also need to make adjustments to ledger balances or the trial balance.

A bank account with money in it will be regarded as a current asset by the business (a debit balance) while the bank will regard it as a current liability (a credit balance) because the business has effectively lent the bank money. The following are saying the same thing:

- Cash book has a debit balance of $600 while the bank statement has a credit balance of $600 – both are claiming that there is money in the account.

- Cash book has a credit balance of $800 while the bank statement has a debit balance of $800 – both are claiming that there is an overdraft.

KEY TERMS

verification: the process of establishing the truth, accuracy or validity of something.

internal controls: the presence of systems or procedures that make it more difficult for people to make serious errors or commit fraud without it being detected.

segregation of duties: the dividing up of tasks or an accounting function between two or more people in order to strengthen internal controls and reduce the risk of fraud or error.

TIP

Always check if the balances given for the cash book or bank statement are overdrafts.

WORKED EXAMPLE 4

Situation 1: The balance on a bank statement at 31 March 2020 was $680 credit. The following items were entered in the cash book in January but did not appear on the bank statements:

1 amount paid into the bank $800

2 cheques sent to customers $1 235.

Required

Calculate the cash book balance at 31 March.

Answer

The bank statement is stating that there is a positive balance of $680 (a debit balance in the cash book).

The $800 will increase the balance, but the cheques sent to customers will have reduced it by $1 235, so the cash book balance is:

$680 + $800 − $1 235 = $245 (a debit balance as there is money in the account).

WORKED EXAMPLE 5

Situation 2: The bank balance in a cash book at 30 April 2020 was $570 (debit). The following items did not appear in the bank statement at that date:

1 cheques totalling $1 610, which had been paid into the bank on 30 April 2020

2 cheques sent to customers in April 2020 totalling $680.

Required

Calculate the bank statement balance at 30 July 2020.

Answer

The bank does not yet know about these two items so the statement will not be giving the benefit of having received the $1 610 and the effect of having paid out the $680. We therefore have to behave as if neither has taken place. The bank statement balance is:

$570 − $1 610 + $680 = overdraft of $360 (a debit balance on the bank statement).

WORKED EXAMPLE 6

Situation 3: At 31 March 2020, a cash book showed an overdraft of $240. On the same date the bank statement balance was $1 155 (credit). When the cash book was compared with the bank statement, the following were found:

1 A cheque sent to a supplier for $1 720 had not been presented for payment.

2 A cheque for $250 paid into the bank had not been credited on the bank statement.

3 Bank charges of $75 were omitted from the cash book.

Required

a Calculate the corrected cash book balance at 31 March 2020.

b Prepare a bank reconciliation statement at 31 March 2020.

CONTINUED

Answer

a   The cash book needs to be updated with the omitted payment and the revised balance is:

−$240 − $75 = −$315 (an overdraft)

This can be inserted in the bank reconciliation statement.

b

Bank reconciliation statement at 31 March 2020	
	$
Balance per bank statement	1 155
Add: Unpresented receipts	250
Less: Unpresented cheques	(1 720)
Balance per cash book	(315)

Note: notice that the final figure is in brackets. This identifies that the balance in the cash book is overdrawn.

WORKED EXAMPLE 7

Situation 4: The following balances were extracted from the trial balance of a business at 31 May 2020:

	$	$
Bank	765	
Rent and rates	3 600	
Trade payables		8 760
Trade receivables	11 245	

The bank statement for May 2020 showed that the following items had not been entered in the cash book:

1   An electronic payment to a supplier for $1 340.

2   An electronic receipt from a customer for $880.

3   A cheque from a credit customer for $655 that had been **dishonoured**.

4   A standing order paying $500 for rent and rates.

Required

Prepare the adjusted trial balance to include the items omitted from the cash book.

Answer

All of these items affect the bank balance and another account. If a payment is dishonoured, (the cheque has 'bounced') then the money is owed again.

The adjustments will result in the trial balance looking like this:

	$	$
Bank (765 − 1 340(1) + 880(2) − 655(3) − 500(4) = −850)		850
Rent and rates (3 600 + 500(4))	4 100	
Trade payables (8 760 − 1 340(1))		7 420
Trade receivables (11 245 − 880(2) + 655(3))	11 020	

TIP

Complete the double entry for all items entered in the cash book. Amend the other balances in the trial balance.

KEY TERMS

dishonoured cheque: a cheque that is not paid, usually because there is not enough money in the payer's account to cover it.

ACTIVITY 13.2

The bank balance in a cash book at 29 February 2020 was $2 345 (debit). The following items did not appear in the bank statement at that date:

1   cheques totalling $1 305 that had been paid into the bank on 29 February 2020.

2   cheques sent to customers in February 2020 totalling $3 010.

Required

Calculate the bank statement balance at 29 February 2020.

ACTIVITY 13.3

The following balances were extracted from the trial balance of a business at 31 March 2020:

	$	$
Bank		5 760
Trade payables		11 285
Trade receivables	8 435	
Wages and salaries	27 120	

The bank statement for March 2020 showed that the following items had not been entered in the cash book:

1   An electronic payment for wages and salaries of $4 115.

2   An electronic receipt from a customer for $2 390.

3   A payment to a supplier of $940.

Required

Prepare the adjusted trial balance to include the items omitted from the cash book.

TIP

When preparing the financial statements for a business, you may discover some deposits or cheque payments have not been recorded in the books of account. You will therefore need to adjust the bank balance (cash and cash equivalents figure) in the trial balance.

THINK LIKE AN ACCOUNTANT

Elusive cheques

Jules had just produced his first bank reconciliation statement and it agreed – there were five unpresented receipts and three unpresented payments that explained the difference between the bank balance in his cash book and that on the bank statement! There was only one thing that seemed odd. Two of the cheques that had not appeared on the bank statement had been written early in the month – what could have possibly gone wrong? Why have those cheques not appeared on the bank statement? What should Jules do to see whether something has gone wrong?

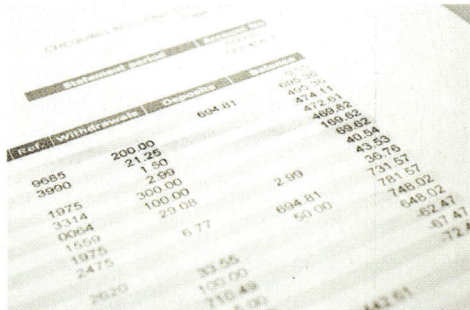

Figure 13.2: Jules produces a bank reconciliation statement to identify the discrepancy between his bank statement and cash book.

REFLECTION

How often do you think that a business should produce a bank reconciliation statement? Why? Discuss your suggestion with a friend.

EXAM-STYLE QUESTIONS

A business had a debit balance in the cash book on 31 October of $3 060 while the bank statement had a credit balance. Investigation revealed the following differences:

a   cheques totalling $2 540 paid into the bank on 30 October had not appeared on the statement

b   a direct debit payment made by the bank for $550 had not been entered in the cash book

c   a cheque payment of $1 150 had been made on 29 October but this had not appeared on the bank statement either

d   a cheque payment to a supplier for $680 had been incorrectly entered into the cash book as $860

e   bank charges and interest of $210 had not been entered into the cash book.

1   Which of the following statements are true?

A   The cash book balance indicates money in the account and the bank statement balance also indicates that there is money in the account.

B   The cash book balance indicates money in the account but the bank statement balance indicates that the account is overdrawn.

C   The cash book balance indicates that the account is overdrawn but the bank statement balance indicates that there is money in the account.

D   The cash book balance indicates that the account is overdrawn and the bank statement balance also indicates that the account is overdrawn.   [1]

2   Which items might be described as omitted items?

A   a and c

B   b and e

C   d

D   b, d and e   [1]

3   What will be the cash book balance when it has been updated and any corrections have been made?

A   debit balance of $2 480

B   debit balance of $3 060

C   debit balance of $3 220

D   debit balance of $3 640   [1]

CONTINUED

4   The following balances were extracted from the trial balance of a business at 30 June 2020:

	$	$
Bank	12 163	
Bank charges and interest	231	
Rent and rates	7 200	
Rental income		2 150
Trade payables		13 027
Trade receivables	16 728	
Wages and salaries	31 076	

The bank statement for March 2020 showed that the following items had not been entered in the cash book:

1   An electronic payment for wages and salaries of $2 189.
2   An electronic receipt from a credit customer for $4 010.
3   An electronic receipt of $375 relating to rental income.
4   A payment to a supplier of $1 274.
5   Bank charges and interest of $87.
6   A cheque from a credit customer for $329 had been dishonoured.

Required

Prepare the adjusted trial balance to include the items omitted from the cash book.   [8]

SELF-EVALUATION CHECKLIST

After studying this chapter, complete a table like this:

You should be able to:	Needs more work	Almost there	Ready to move on
Explain that it is necessary to produce a bank reconciliation using external sources, to verify whether values for the bank account are accurate and up-to-date.			
Explain what a bank reconciliation statement is and how it is used to ensure that the cash book is up-to-date and the items yet to clear are identified.			
Ensure that the bank balance in the cash book equals the correct balance of cash at bank – there will often be items that have not been recorded in the cash book and unpresented items that have not appeared on the statement because the bank does not yet know about them.			
Identify the correct bank account balance that should go into the statement of financial position – this may involve making adjustments to ledger balances or the trial balance.			
Explain the benefits and limitations of preparing a bank reconciliation statement, including that it will help deter fraud or detect it.			

> Chapter 14

Control accounts

This chapter covers part of syllabus section AS Level 1.4

LEARNING INTENTIONS

In this chapter you will learn how to:

- identify and explain entries in control accounts, including how control accounts can help detect errors
- prepare sales ledger control accounts and purchases ledger control accounts
- explain methods using internal procedures and external documentation to identify errors
- identify the effect on the financial statements of the correction of errors
- explain the benefits and limitations of control accounts
- reconcile the control account balance with the total of the individual ledger balances.

ACCOUNTING IN CONTEXT

Guiseppe's garage

Guiseppe has a garage that carries out car repairs. During the last few months, Giuseppe has started to allow his customers to buy goods on credit and he now has more than 50 such customers. While one or two of his customers are late payers, Guiseppe has not yet suffered any irrecoverable debts.

Giuseppe has set up a sales ledger for each credit customer to record every financial transaction. These ledgers help Giuseppe to establish who owes him what and enables him to chase up late payers.

Unfortunately, sometimes he forgets to enter transactions into the ledgers and this has led to him chasing people who have already paid. He wonders whether there is a quick way to find out how much he is owed in total to check that his sales ledgers are accurate.

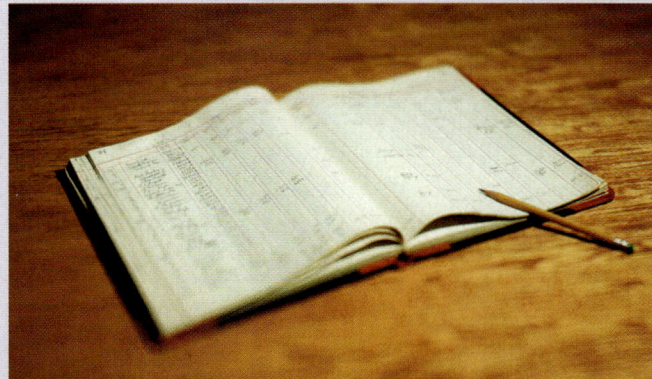

Figure 14.1: Giuseppe has set up a sales ledger for each credit customer to record every transaction.

Discuss in a pair or a group:

- Why is Giuseppe unable to find out easily the amount owed by all his customers in total?
- Why is Giuseppe only finding out about errors when he has an embarrassing encounter with a credit customer?
- What could happen if this situation continues?

14.1 What is a control account?

A **control account** can be used in many parts of an accounting system, but two of the most common are for the sales and purchases ledgers.

Control accounts are prepared at the end of an accounting year and use the totals from the books of prime entry.

The balance on a control account should equal the total of the balances in the ledger it controls. For the purposes of this syllabus, we regard the individual sales (and purchase) ledgers as part of the main double-entry system and regard the Control accounts as **memorandum accounts** that are prepared using double-entry bookkeeping principles.

They fulfil two main functions:

1 as an arithmetical check on the accuracy of the bookkeeping
2 as a summary of the part of the accounting system, enabling one total balance to be entered into the trial balance rather than lots of balances.

14.2 The sales ledger and its control account

When businesses sell goods on credit, one of the biggest concerns is ensuring that payment is made and on time. Keeping an accurate and up-to-date record of how much is owed is an essential part of this and so a **sales ledger** will be maintained for each customer.

These accounts show the value of the asset represented by the amount that each customer owes.

KEY TERMS

control account: a ledger account containing only total amounts – one entry for each type

of transaction rather than the details of each individual financial transaction. The two most commonly used are the purchase ledger control account and the sales ledger control account.

memorandum accounts: ledger accounts that are not regarded as part of the main double-entry system even though they are produced using double-entry principles. They are produced to check the accuracy of parts of the accounting system.

sales ledger: an account relating to one item – for example, each credit customer will have its own sales ledger.

A list of the most common items that you will encounter are:

Debits		Credits	
Balance brought down (b/d)	The amount that the customer owes	Sales returns	Initially recorded in the sales journal
Sales	Initially recorded in the sales journal	Receipts	Initially recorded in the cash book
		Discounts allowed	Initially recorded in the cash book
		Irrecoverable debts	Initially recorded as a journal

If the individual sales ledgers represent assets (money owed by each credit customer), then the **sales ledger control account** can be regarded as a summary of all of these assets. It is therefore logical to apply the same double-entry principles to this account as we apply to the individual sales ledgers. The balance b/d figures will be on the debit side. Anything that increases the amount that customers owe will be a debit entry, while anything that reduces how much customers owe will be a credit entry.

This account is about customers owing the business money and so only credit sales should be entered into the individual ledgers and the control account.

KEY TERM

sales ledger control account: summarises the transactions involving sales on credit.

WORKED EXAMPLE 1

A business has four credit customers whose balances at the start of the month were:

	$
Bray	275
Murtagh	1330
O'Brien	885
Rankin	410
	2900

The entries in the journals for that month were:

Sales journal	$
Bray	1440
Murtagh	2045
O'Brien	1060
	4545

Sales returns journal	$
Bray	90
O'Brien	110
	200

Details taken from the bank were as follows:

	Received $	Discount allowed $
Bray	880	
Murtagh	1310	20
O'Brien	1240	25
	3430	45

CONTINUED

In addition, Rankin was written off as an irrecoverable debt. The sales ledgers for each customer are:

Sales ledger – Bray account			
Debit		**Credit**	
	$		$
Balance b/d	275	Sales returns	90
Sales	1 440	Bank	880
		Balance c/d	745
	1 715		1 715
Balance b/d	745		

Sales ledger – Murtagh account			
Debit		**Credit**	
	$		$
Balance b/d	1 330	Bank	1 310
Sales	2 045	Discount allowed	20
		Balance c/d	2 045
	3 375		3 375
Balance b/d	2 045		

Sales ledger – O'Brien account			
Debit		**Credit**	
	$		$
Balance b/d	885	Sales returns	110
Sales	1 060	Bank	1 240
		Discount allowed	25
		Balance c/d	570
	1 945		1 945
Balance b/d	570		

Sales ledger – Rankin account			
Debit		**Credit**	
	$		$
Balance b/d	410	Irrecoverable debt	410
	410		410

Note: the total of the balances in the individual sales ledgers is 745 + 2 045 + 570 = $3 360.

TIP

The sales ledger control account provides some assurance of accuracy, but there are errors that might have been made even if the subsidiary ledger totals agree with the control account.

CONTINUED

The sales ledger control account is produced by posting the total for each transaction into it:

Sales ledger control account				
Debit		Credit		
	$			$
Balance b/d	2 900	Sales returns		200
Sales	4 545	Bank		3 430
		Discounts allowed		45
		Irrecoverable debt		410
		Balance c/d [1][2]		3 360
	7 445			7 445
Balance b/d	3 360			

Notes:

[1] This equals the total of the balances on the individual customers' accounts and so the sales ledger reconciles with the sales ledger control account.

[2] This reconciliation means that we can be fairly confident that the trade receivables figures is accurate, although it is possible that a transaction may have been posted to the wrong individual sales ledger, so there could be two individual balances that are incorrect. This would be an error of commission (see page 67). For example, if the sales return of $110 had been credited to the Murtagh sales ledger account instead of O'Brien's, then the balances for all of the customers would have been:

	Correct balances	Incorrect balances
	$	$
Bray	745	745
Murtagh	2 045	1 935
O'Brien	570	680
Rankin	0	0
Subsidiary ledger total	3 360	3 360
Sales ledger control account	3 360	

Reconciling the total of the individual sales ledgers with the balance on the sales ledger control account will not show up the problem. However, if the two totals disagree, then we know that there is definitely a problem that needs to be corrected.

14.3 Some unusual items

Dishonoured cheques

It is possible that a customer will have paid by cheque but does not have enough money in the account to cover that amount. In this case, the cheque will be dishonoured and the business will not be paid.

If the original payment has been recorded, the entries would have been:

Debit: Bank

Credit: Individual customer's account

And the appropriate credit entry would be made in the relevant individual sales ledger.

These entries need to be reversed because the money is owed again.

Debit: Individual customer's account

Credit: Bank

Credit balances

Most credit customers will have debit balances because they owe us money or zero balances because they have paid everything that they owe. However, it is possible that a customer may have a credit balance because they have:

- overpaid their sales invoice
- paid in advance or have paid a deposit before the delivery of the goods and the creation of the invoice
- paid the invoice in full but a problem discovered later has resulted in a credit note being issued.

Some businesses will offset those credit balances against the debit balances to arrive at one figure while others keep them separate.

Contras

It is also possible that two businesses might supply goods or services to each other on credit and so owe each other money.

For example, Business A might have sold stationery to Business B for $1 000 and Business B might have sent a bill for $800 to Business A for carrying out some repairs. If neither amount has been paid, then each business will have a trade payable who is also a trade receivable.

In this situation, the two businesses might agree to set off the lower of the two balances ($800) so that the only payment that needs to be made would be by Business B for the remaining $200. The $800 would be entered as a **contra (set-off)** and the entries needed to record this in the books of Business A would be:

Debit: Business B purchase ledger $800   Credit: Business B sales ledger $800

When producing the control accounts, Business A's bookkeeper would make the following entries:

Debit: Purchase ledger control account $800   Credit: Sales ledger control account $800

In all cases, the entries made should always reduce the balance on that account.

> **TIP**
>
> Contras reduce what the customer owes and are therefore credit entries in both the control account and the relevant individual sales ledger.

> **KEY TERM**
>
> **contra (set-off):** these arise when two people or businesses owe each other money because they have bought goods or services from each other and they agree to reduce both balances by the lower amount outstanding. Contra entries involve making a debit entry in the relevant purchase ledger and a credit entry in the relevant sales ledger as well as adjusting the purchase ledger and sales ledger control accounts.

WORKED EXAMPLE 2

A business had the following information relating to April 2020:

	$
Total of individual sales ledger balances at 1 April 2020	5 980
Receipts from credit customers	4 137
Irrecoverable debts	515
Sales journal total	6 109
Sales returns journal total	662
Dishonoured cheques	387
Discounts allowed	273
Contra (set-off against purchases ledger control account)	706

The total credit balances on the individual sales ledgers was $1 025.

The steps involved in creating the sales ledger control account are as follows:

CONTINUED

Step 1

Enter the opening balance and the summary of each transaction into the control account – debiting or crediting on the basis of whether the item increases the amount owed (asset) or reduces it.

Step 2

Enter the total credit balance b/d below the sub-total and the debit balance carried down (c/d) above the sub-total.

Step 3

Balance off the control account and check that it agrees with the total of the individual sales ledger balances.

Sales ledger control account			
Debit		**Credit**	
	$		$
Balance b/d (1)	5 980	Sales returns (1)	662
Sales (1)	6 109	Cash book (1)	4 137
Bank (dishonoured cheque) (1)	387	Discounts allowed (1)	273
		Irrecoverable debts (1)	515
		Contra (set-off) (1)	706
	1 025	Balance c/d (3)	7 208
Balance c/d (2)	13 501		13 501
Balance b/d (3)	7 208	Balance b/d (3)	1 025

The business will be hoping that the total of the debit balances on the individual sales ledgers is also $7 208.

> **TIP**
>
> The credit balances should be entered into the control account before the control account is balanced off.

ACTIVITY 14.1

A business had the following information relating to April 2020:

	$
Total of individual sales ledger balances at 1 April 2020	8 133
Receipts from credit customers	11 009
Irrecoverable debts	724
Sales journal total	10 817
Sales returns journal total	992
Dishonoured cheques	1 314
Discounts allowed	805
Contra (set-off against purchases ledger control account)	650

The total of the debit balances on the individual sales ledger balances was $7 029.

The total of the credit balances on the individual sales ledger balances was $945.

Required

Produce a sales ledger control account for April 2020 to see if the closing balance agrees with the total of the individual sales ledger balances.

14.4 The purchases ledger and its control account

When a business buys goods on credit, it needs to know when the purchases were made and how much is owed to each supplier so that the right amounts can be paid at the right time. It is therefore important that a ledger is kept for each supplier and many businesses will set up a series of individual ledgers in the same way that they did for credit customers.

However, the business does not wish to have lots of these ledgers appearing in the trial balance and so these individual balances will need to be totalled up so that one figure can be included. The business would also like to be assured that the bookkeeping has been accurate and that this total figure for its trade payables is reliable.

A **purchases ledger control account** will be used to provide a summary of all transactions relating to the buying of goods and services on credit. The balance on this account can then be compared (and reconciled) with the total of the balances on the individual purchase ledgers.

It can be safely assumed that if the balance on the purchases ledger control account does not agree with the sum of the individual purchase ledger balances, then there are errors that need to be investigated and corrected. Unfortunately, it is also possible that errors have been made that do not cause a discrepancy – for example, a payment might be debited to the wrong supplier's account, which would result in two incorrect balances even if the total payables balance was still correct.

The purchases ledger control account and the purchases ledgers represent liabilities because the balances show how much money is owed by the business. Items that increase what is owed will appear as credit entries and those that reduce the size of the liability are shown as debits.

A list of the most common items that you will encounter are:

Debits		Credits	
Purchases returns	Initially recorded in the purchase returns journal	Balance b/d	The amount owed to suppliers
Payments	Initially recorded in the cash book	Purchases	Initially recorded in the purchase journal
Discounts received	Initially recorded in the cash book	Dishonoured cheques	The money would be owed again
Contras	Usually the subject of a specific journal		

It should be noted that it is possible for a purchases ledger to have a debit balance. The reasons for this include:

- the business has overpaid a purchase invoice
- the business has paid in advance or paid a deposit before the delivery of the goods and the creation of the invoice
- the business has paid the invoice in full but a problem discovered later has resulted in a credit note being received.

Some businesses will offset those debit balances against the credit balances to arrive at one figure while others keep them separate.

KEY TERM

purchases ledger control account: summarises the transactions involving purchases on credit.

WORKED EXAMPLE 3

A business has four credit suppliers whose balances at the start of the month were:

	$
	$
Johnson	980
Lyon	2 345
Siddle	1 680
Warner	525
	5 530

The entries in the journals for that month were:

Purchase journal	$
Johnson	2 010
Lyon	760
Siddle	1 285
	4 055

Purchase returns journal	$
Johnson	430
Lyon	285
Warner	75
	790

Details taken from the cash book were as follows:

	Bank	Discount received
	$	$
Johnson	1 480	20
Lyon	2 315	30
Siddle	1 725	
Warner	525	
	6 045	50

In addition, as Siddle owed the business $400, it was agreed that this would be set off against the amount owed to him (a contra).

Steps to create a purchases ledger control account:

Step 1

Enter the opening balance and the summary of each transaction into the control account – debiting or crediting on the basis of whether the item increases the amount owed (liability) or reduces it.

Step 2

Enter the total debit balance b/d below the sub-total and the credit balance c/d above the sub-total.

CONTINUED

Step 3

Balance off the control account and check that it agrees with the total of the individual purchase ledger balance.

Purchases ledger – Johnson account

Debit		$	Credit		$
Purchases returns		430	Balance b/d		980
Cash book		1 480	Purchases		2 010
Discount received		20			
Balance c/d		1 060			
		2 990			2 990
			Balance b/d		1 060

Purchases ledger – Lyon account

Debit		$	Credit		$
Purchases returns		285	Balance b/d		2 345
Cash book		2 315	Purchases		760
Discount received		30			
Balance c/d		475			
		3 105			3 105
			Balance b/d		475

Purchases ledger – Siddle account

Debit		$	Credit		$
Cash book		1 725	Balance b/d		1 680
Contra (sales ledger control)		400	Purchases		1 285
Balance c/d		840			
		2 965			2 965
			Balance b/d		840

Purchases ledger – Warner account

Debit		$	Credit		$
Purchases returns		75	Balance b/d		525
Cash book		525			
			Balance c/d		75
		600			600
Balance b/d		75			

Note: the total of the balances in the individual purchases ledgers is 1 060 + 475 + 840 = $2 375.

CONTINUED

The purchases ledger control account is produced by posting the total for each transaction into it:

Purchases ledger control account			
Debit		**Credit**	
	$		$
Purchases returns	790	Balance b/d	5 530
Cash book	6 045	Purchases	4 055
Discounts received	50		
Contra (sales ledger control)	400		
Balance c/d	2 375	Balance c/d	75
	9 660		9 660
Balance b/d	75	Balance b/d	2 375

Note: the credit balance in the control account agrees with the total of the credit balances on the individual purchases ledgers.

TIP

The debit balances should be entered into the control account before the control account is balanced off.

ACTIVITY 14.2

A business had the following balances at the start of March 2020:

	$
Customers with credit balances	531
Customers with debit balances	18 270
Suppliers with credit balances	11 263
Suppliers with debit balances	772

The following financial transactions took place during March 2020.

	$
Cash purchases	8 119
Cash sales	14 025
Contra entries	350
Credit purchases	12 568
Credit sales	21 072
Discounts allowed	943
Discounts received	1 071
Dishonoured cheques (from customers)	1 239
Irrecoverable debts	837
Payments to suppliers	11 248
Purchase returns	693
Receipts from customers	23 006
Sales returns	1 485

CONTINUED

Balances at the end of March 2020 were:

	$
Customers with credit balances	195
Customers with debit balances	13 624
Suppliers with credit balances	10 301
Suppliers with debit balances	604

Required

Produce the sales ledger control account and the purchases ledger control account at 31 March 2020.

KEY CONCEPT LINK

Duality: Recognises that every financial transaction has a double (or dual) effect on the position of a business as recorded in the accounts. Do you think that recording the debits and credits in both the trade receivables and payables ledger control accounts and the relevant individual purchase ledgers is a breach of the concept of duality? Why/why not?

14.5 Control accounts and the double-entry model

The individual sales ledgers record individual financial transactions whereas the control accounts show the totals for each type of transaction. What this means is that there is an inequality on the double-entry because the value of the debits does not equal the value of the credits.

This is illustrated with the following sales transactions:

Credit sales	Debit: Sales ledger control account	Debit: individual sales ledgers
	Credit: Sales	
Receipts from credit customers	Debit: Bank	Credit: individual sales ledgers
	Credit: Sales ledger control account	
Discounts allowed	Debit: Discounts allowed	Credit: individual sales ledgers
	Credit: Sales ledger control account	
Irrecoverable debts	Debit: Irrecoverable debts	Credit: individual sales ledgers
	Credit: Sales ledger control account	

The same problem would arise with the purchases ledgers. So given this inequality of debits and credits, the main double-entry system cannot contain both the individual ledgers and the control accounts.

For the purpose of this course, the entries in the individual sales and purchase ledgers should be regarded as part of the double-entry system and the control accounts as memorandum accounts that are there to check the accuracy of the individual trade receivables in the sales ledger and the individual trade payables on the purchases ledger. Of course, should the sales and purchase ledger control accounts balances agree with the total of the individual sales and purchases ledgers, it will be those totals that provide the trade receivables and trade payables balances in the trial balance.

The individual sales and purchases ledgers are also used to provide an accurate and up-to-date record of the transactions involving each customer and supplier as well as the outstanding balances at any point in time so that:

- the right amounts of money can be collected from each customer and late payers can be chased for the correct amounts
- the right amounts of money can be paid to the right supplier at the right time.

14.6 Benefits and limitations of control accounts

Using control accounts provides a number of benefits including:

- indicating that errors have been made if the totals of the balances in the individual ledgers do not agree with the balances on the control accounts
- indicating which part of the accounting system contains errors if there is a difference on a trial balance
- if a business has a large number of credit customers and suppliers, then the trial balance will contain a few large control account balances rather than a huge number of small ones
- improving internal control
- The business accounts may not be maintained using a full double-entry system (see Chapter 16).

However, there are some limitations in using them:

- they may contain errors
- they do not guarantee the accuracy of individual ledger accounts, which may contain compensating errors
- they may add to business costs as someone with specialist accounting knowledge is required to verify their accuracy.

However, the benefits of using them outweigh the limitations, which is why most businesses use them.

14.7 How to reconcile control accounts with sales ledgers

When there is a difference between the balance on a control account and the total of the balances in the ledger it controls, the cause must be found and the necessary corrections made. Only when this has been done can the control accounts and the individual ledgers be said to have been reconciled.

All errors need to be corrected but only some of them may be shown up because the control account balance does not agree with the total of the individual ledger balances.

Errors that do not cause a discrepancy between the control account and the individual ledgers include:

- **Error of omission**: this will not appear in either the individual ledger *or* the control account. Both records will be wrong but our reconciliation will still agree.
- **Error of original entry**: this will be repeated in both the individual ledger *and* the control account. Both records will be wrong but our reconciliation will still agree.

However, other errors will cause a discrepancy between the control account and the individual ledgers and these include:

- If an item is copied incorrectly from a book of prime entry to a individual sales or purchases ledger, the control account will *not* be affected, and an unsuccessful attempt

KEY TERMS

error of omission: an error where the financial transaction has not been recorded at all.

error of original entry: an error where the amount is entered incorrectly in one of the books of prime entry for a transaction.

to reconcile the total of the individual ledger balances with the control account balance will reveal that an error has been made.

- If a total in a book of prime entry is incorrect, the control account will be incorrect *but* the individual sales or purchases ledgers will not be affected. The unsuccessful attempt to reconcile the total of the individual ledger balances with the control account balance will reveal that an error has been made.

In Worked example 4, we are going to investigate how the correction of errors might be needed to reach:

a a correct total balance in the individual ledgers

b a correct balance in the control account that should agree with the results of **a**

c a corrected profit figure

d accurate asset or liability figures in the statement of financial position.

WORKED EXAMPLE 4

A company has a total balance on its sales ledger control account of $33 240 but the total of its individual ledgers adds up to $32 180.

a An investigation revealed the following errors involving the individual ledgers:

1 An irrecoverable debt of $525 had been entered into the control account but not in the relevant individual ledger.

2 A payment of $2 200 from a customer had been entered twice into the relevant individual ledger.

3 A settlement discount of $175 had been entered on the wrong side of the relevant individual ledger.

4 A set-off of $400 had been correctly entered into the control account but put on the wrong side of the relevant individual ledger.

		$
Total of individual sales ledgers:		32 180
Error **1**	Subtract	(525)
Error **2**	Add	2 200
Error **3**	Subtract	(350) [1]
Error **4**	Subtract	(800)
Revised total to agree with control account:		32 705

Note:

[1] When dealing with an error where an item has been put on the wrong side, it is necessary to make a correction for twice the amount – in this case, the first $175 removes the damage caused by the error and the second $175 has the effect that we were originally trying to achieve.

b There were other errors that had affected the sales ledger control account:

5 A credit sale of $260 to Aylott had been entered into the sales journal twice by mistake.

6 A set-off entry for $150 had been omitted from the sales ledger control account.

7 An irrecoverable debt of $125 had been entered into the Clarke individual ledger but had not been recorded in the sales ledger control account.

CONTINUED

Adjustments that need to be made to the sales ledger control account are as follows:

Sales ledger control account			
Debit		Credit	
	$		$
Original balance b/d	33 240	Error 5: Sales	260
		Error 6: Purchases ledger control account	150
		Error 7: Irrecoverable debts	125
		Revised balance c/d	32 705
	33 240		33 240
Revised balance b/d	32 705		

c   The provisional draft profit figure was $25 000 and the business sets its allowance for irrecoverable debts at 4% of trade receivables.

The original allowance for irrecoverable debts was 4% × 33 240 = $1 330

The new allowance for irrecoverable debts is 4% × 32 705 = $1 308

	$
Original profit figure	25 000
Add the reduction in allowance for irrecoverable debts	22
Revised profit figure	25 022

d   The trade receivables figure that would appear in the statement of financial position is:

	$	$
Trade receivables	32 705	25 000
Add: reduction in allowance for irrecoverable debts	(1 308)	31 397

ACTIVITY 14.3

A company has a total balance on its sales ledger control account of $24 350 but the total of its individual ledgers adds up to $25 270. An investigation revealed the following errors:

1   A payment of $3 250 from a credit customer had been entered as $2 350 in the relevant individual ledger.

2   A sales return of $230 had been entered on the wrong side of the relevant individual ledger.

3   A settlement discount of $85 had been entered twice in the relevant individual ledger.

4   A set-off of $620 had been omitted from the relevant individual ledger.

5   A sales return of $120 from C Newbury had been entered in the sales returns journal twice in error.

6   In the cash book, the column for receipts from trade receivables had been undercast by $1 000.

CONTINUED

7   The account of D Doherty totalling $95 had been written off in the individual ledger but not in the control account.

The draft profit figure was $12 600 and the company sets its allowance for irrecoverable debts at 6% of trade receivables.

Required

Show the:

a   Corrected total balance for the individual ledgers.

b   Corrected sales ledger control account balance.

c   Corrected profit figure.

d   Corrected trade receivables figure that would appear in the statement of financial position.

14.8 How to reconcile control accounts with purchases ledgers

When dealing with purchases, the process is very similar to sales except that:

- The purchases ledgers and the purchases ledger control account are recording liabilities. So all balances will be on the credit side.

- There will be no irrecoverable debts or allowance for irrecoverable debts to deal with.

- The trade payables figure in the statement of financial position will be the balance in the purchases ledger control account.

WORKED EXAMPLE 5

A company has a total balance on its purchases ledger control account of $30 300 but the total of its individual ledgers adds up to $29 230.

a   An investigation revealed the following errors:

1   A payment of S240 to Mortimer had been correctly entered into the individual ledger but was recorded as $420 in the cash book.

2   A purchase of $400 from Snape had been entered in the purchase journal twice in error.

3   A set-off of $225 against the sales ledger control account had been entered into the wrong side of the purchases ledger control account.

Purchases ledger control account			
Debit		**Credit**	
	$		$
Error 2: purchases	400	Balance b/d	30 300
Error 3: contra (sales ledger control account)	450	Error 1: cash book	180
Balance c/d	29 630		
	30 480		30 480
		Balance b/d	29 630

b   Further investigation revealed the following errors:

1   A settlement discount of $55 had not been entered into the relevant individual ledger.

2   A purchase invoice totalling $865 had not been entered into the relevant individual ledger.

3   A payment of $760 to a supplier had been entered as $670 in the relevant individual ledger.

4   A purchase return of $160 had been entered onto the wrong side of the relevant individual ledger.

			$
Total of individual purchases ledgers:			29 230
Adjustment for **1**		Subtract	(55)
Adjustment for **2**		Add	865
Adjustment for **3**	760 – 670	Subtract	(90)
Adjustment for **4**	2 × 160	Subtract	(320) [1]
Revised total to agree with control account:			29 630

Note:

[1]   When dealing with an error where an item has been put on the wrong side, it is necessary to make a correction for twice the amount.

14.9 Verification of balances using external information

While it can be very reassuring to know that the total balance on the control account agrees with the sum of the balances on the individual ledgers, there is no guarantee that the system is free from error. If internal checks cannot be relied on, then the business can make use of external documentation including:

- *Reconciliations with statements of account*: it is quite likely that statements of account will be received from most, if not all, suppliers. The business can tick off items in the individual purchases ledgers against the statement of account to see if there are any obvious errors. Note that it is possible there will be some timing differences, for example:
  - the business may have recorded a payment and claimed a settlement discount but this had not been received by the supplier in time to be included in the statement of account
  - the supplier may have included invoices or credit notes on the statement of account that have yet to be recorded by the business.
- *Formal requests from suppliers and customers*: **auditors** send out letters to credit suppliers and customers requesting information about the outstanding balance at a particular date. If there is a difference between that reported by the client and the balance according to the customer/supplier, then a reconciliation can be produced to ensure that the differences are due to timing differences rather than genuine errors.

> **KEY TERM**
>
> **auditor:** a person authorised to examine, review and verify financial records to ensure that they are accurate and that the information provided by a business represents a 'true and fair view' of its performance and financial state.

REFLECTION

How effective do you think that reconciling control accounts with the total of the individual ledgers is in ensuring that no bookkeeping errors have been committed? How often do you think this exercise should be carried out? Why?

THINK LIKE AN ACCOUNTANT

Usefulness of control accounts

Giuseppe's friend had shown him how to produce control accounts and explained how the reconciliation could be used to detect errors. But when he produced the sales ledger and purchases ledger control accounts covering the last six months, he uncovered significant discrepancies between those balances and the total balances on the relevant subsidiary ledgers. Finding the errors was taking a long time. Why has it taken so long for Giuseppe to find the errors that have been made over the last six months? What do you think Giuseppe should do to make his life easier?

Figure 14.2: Control accounts can be produced to help detect errors.

EXAM-STYLE QUESTIONS

1   The following items have appeared in the purchases ledger control account:

i   discounts received

ii   purchases

iii   payments to suppliers.

Which of the following would appear as a debit in the purchases control account?

A	i and ii	C	i and iii
B	ii and iii	D	All of them	[1]

2   The debit balance on the sales ledger control account at 30 June is $81 630. The following errors and adjustments have been discovered:

	$
Discounts allowed omitted from the control account	1 125
Sales returns not recorded in the control account	830
Increase in provision for irrecoverable debts	270

What is the total of the balances in the sales ledger?

A $79 405

B $79 675

C $83 585

D $83 855   [1]

CONTINUED

3   The following statements relate to the sales ledger control account and the individual sales ledgers:

   i   If a credit sale were not recorded in the sales journal at all, then there would be a difference between the control account balance and the total of the individual sales ledgers.

   ii   If money received from Customer A was credited to Customer B's account, then this would be shown up when the business tried to reconcile the control account balance and the total of the individual sales ledgers.

Which of the following is a fair reflection of those statements?

   A   both statements are false

   B   both statements are true

   C   only i is true

   D   only ii is true   [1]

4   On 31 May 2020, Indira had a total balance on her sales control account of $15 375, but the total of the individual ledgers added up to $14 205. An investigation revealed the following errors:

   i   Discounts allowed of $640 had been entered on the wrong side of the sales ledger control account.

   ii   A cheque for $220 from a customer had been entered on the debit side of that customer's sales ledger.

   iii Bank receipts from customers of $17 385 had been entered in the control account as $17 835.

   iv An irrecoverable debt of $425 had not been recorded anywhere at all.

   v   The total in the sales journal had been overcast by $600.

   vi A sales return of $685 had been entered in that customer's sales ledger as $865.

Required

   a   State *two* reasons why a credit customer might have a credit balance on their account.   [2]

   b   Prepare the corrections or adjustments that need to be made in the sales control account to arrive at a corrected trade receivables balance.   [6]

   c   Prepare the adjustments that need to be made to the total subsidiary sales ledger balances when the errors shown above are corrected (a table has been provided).

			$
Original total of individual sales ledgers:			
Error	Workings	Add/subtract	
Revised total to agree with control account:			

                                                                   [5]

   d   Explain why the fact that the balance on a sales ledger control account agrees with the total of the balances on the individual sales ledgers does not guarantee that the system is totally correct.   [7]

SELF-EVALUATION CHECKLIST

After studying this chapter, complete a table like this:

You should be able to:	Needs more work	Almost there	Ready to move on
Identify and explain entries in control accounts, including how the sales ledger control account and the purchases ledger control account can help detect errors.			
Prepare sales ledger control accounts and purchases ledger control accounts by recording the total of each type of financial transaction from relevant journals and the cash book.			
Explain methods using internal procedures and external documentation to identify errors, such as reconciliations with statements of account and formal requests from suppliers and customers.			
Identify the effect on the financial statements of the correction of errors.			
Explain the benefits and limitations of control accounts, including how they simplify the trial balance.			
Reconcile the control account balance with the total of the subsidiary ledgers, remembering it cannot guarantee that no errors have been made.			

〉 Chapter 15

The correction of errors

This chapter covers syllabus part of section AS Level 1.4 and 1.5

LEARNING INTENTIONS

In this chapter you will learn how to:

- identify and explain how some errors can be corrected using journals and other errors result in a trial balance not balancing
- prepare ledger accounts and journal entries to correct errors using a suspense account
- identify the effect on the financial statements of the correction of errors.

ACCOUNTING IN CONTEXT

Errors in the trial balance

Olivia had been working at the firm of accountants for several months and her managers had entrusted her with preparing the trial balance and a first draft of the financial statements for a client. One of the client's office staff had made the bookkeeping entries for the year and had already balanced off the individual ledgers. Olivia had made a number of end-of-year adjustments and then she had produced the trial balance, where she discovered that the debit column and the credit column differed by thousands of dollars.

Discuss in a pair or a group:

* What types of error might have been made by the client's employee (or Olivia herself) that caused a difference between the debit and credit columns of the trial balance?

* Should Olivia go ahead and produce a first draft of the financial statements?

Figure 15.1: Olivia had produced the trial balance and discovered that the debit and credit columns differed by thousands of dollars.

15.1 Using the journal to correct errors

While no two situations are ever quite the same, it is worth asking the following questions:

1 How has the transaction been recorded?

2 How should the transaction have been recorded and what is the difference between what has been done and what should have been done?

3 What adjustments are required to correct the error?

WORKED EXAMPLE 1

A business had a trial balance that balanced, but on closer examination the following errors (see Chapter 6) and omissions were discovered:

1 A cheque received from a credit customer for $4 675 had not been recorded at all.

2 Rent and rates of $1 200 had been recorded in the wages and salaries account by mistake.

3 A sale of a motor vehicle for $6 250 had been recorded in the sales account – the bank entry was correct.

4 Drawings from the bank of $750 had been recorded in both accounts as $570.

5 A payment made to a credit supplier for $845 had been debited to the bank account and credited to the purchases ledger control account.

6 The Rent and rates account had been underadded by $1 000 and the Purchases account had been overadded by $1 000 in the trial balance.

CONTINUED

TIP

If the business does not use control accounts, then journals involving trade receivables and trade payables should probably be referred to by name and description, e.g. Johnson (a trade receivable) or Masood (a trade payable).

1   This is an *error of omission* – nothing has been recorded. The solution is to record the transaction, so the journal would be:

	Dr	Cr
Details	$	$
Bank	4 675	
Sales ledger control account		4 675

Narrative: Correction of an error of omission of a cheque received from a credit customer.

2   This is an *error of commission* – Wages and salaries has been debited when it should have been Rent and rates. The solution is to take the entry out of Wages and salaries and put it into Rent and rates.

	Dr	Cr.
Details	$	$
Rent and rates	1 200	
Wages and salaries		1 200

Narrative: Correction of an error of commission – a Rent and rates expense was posted to the Wages and salaries account.

3   This is an *error of principle* – the wrong type of account has been used. The solution is to take the entry out of Revenue and put it into Motor vehicles at cost.

	Dr	Cr
Details	$	$
Revenue	6 250	
Motor vehicles at cost		6 250

Narrative: Correction of an error of principle – a disposal of a non-current asset was treated as a sale of goods.

TIP

Errors of original entry always yield a difference that is divisible by 9 but can be difficult to see. If you have a difference, divide it by 9 to check.

4   This is an error of *original entry* – the wrong figure has been used. There are two ways to deal with this:

   a   Reverse the entry completely to remove the problem and then record the correct postings – the journal will have four entries.

   b   Calculate the difference in the figures and post the difference (in this case 750 − 570 = $180). You must take care when deciding whether the original entries were excessive or insufficient as this will decide whether the original posting needs to be partially reversed or added to.

	Dr	Cr
Details	$	$
Drawings	180[1]	
Bank		180[1]

Narrative: Correction of an error of original entry – drawings of $750 was recorded as $570.

Note:

[1]   In this case, the original posting was insufficient so the correction involved more debiting of drawings and more crediting of the bank account.

CONTINUED

TIP

Identify the type of error – this will help you to determine the correction that needs to be made.

5 This is an *error of reversal* – the solution is to record the transaction correctly but for double the amount. In this case, the first $845 removes the problem caused by the error and the second $845 ensures that the effect of the transaction is recorded.

Details	Dr $	Cr $
Purchases ledger control account	1 690	
Bank		1 690

Narrative: Correction of an error of reversal – a payment to a supplier was entered on the wrong sides of both the bank and the control account.

6 This is a compensating error – this means that there are two or more unconnected errors that have numerically cancelled each other out, so the debit and credit column totals in the trial balance still agree. To correct these, you need to check whether the account has a debit or credit balance and whether that balance is overadded (too big) or underadded (too small). In this case, Rent and rates is a debit balance that is too small, so we need to debit that account for the difference: $1 000. Purchases is also a debit balance but the figure shown is too big, so we need to credit that account $1 000.

Details	Dr $	Cr $
Rent and rates	1 000	
Purchases		1 000

Narrative: Correction of a compensating error where the Rent and rates account had been underadded and the Purchases account had been overadded.

ACTIVITY 15.1

A business had a trial balance that balanced, but on closer examination the following errors and omissions were discovered:

1 Motor expenses of $425 had been credited to the bank account and debited to the motor vehicles at cost account.

2 A purchase for $2 450 had not been recorded at all – a cheque had been used to pay for these goods.

3 A discount of $280 given to a credit customer had been entered in the relevant accounts as $820.

4 A cheque payment to a credit supplier of $3 290 had been recorded in the books as $2 390.

5 $1 800 had been paid to casual staff as overtime. Although this had been entered into the bank correctly, it had been recorded in the office expenses account.

6 A cheque for $1 145 from a credit customer had been debited to the sales ledger control account and credited to the bank.

Required

Indicate which types of error these are and prepare the journals required to correct them. Narratives are not required.

15.2 What is a suspense account?

Suspense accounts are used by accountants for two main reasons:

1   As somewhere to put items that are unusual enough for it to be initially uncertain what it is or how to treat it. When it has been correctly identified or a decision about its treatment has been made, it can be transferred to the correct place by journal. An example might be an invoice relating to the purchase of a non-current asset where there are several items being charged for and it is not certain which of the items should be regarded as capital expenditure and which as revenue expenditure.

2   As a temporary account to help deal with errors that have caused a difference between the debit and credit columns in the trial balance. Its creation will enable the business to continue operating while an investigation takes place as well as providing an account that can be used to correct these errors. As will be seen, the suspense account should have a zero balance (and disappear) once all corrections have been made.

This chapter is only concerned with the second reason.

> **KEY TERM**
>
> **suspense account:** an account opened to record a difference between the debit and credit totals of the trial balance.

15.3 When a suspense account should be opened

A suspense account should be opened only when attempts to find the cause of a difference on a trial balance have been unsuccessful. The following checks should be carried out before opening a suspense account:

a   Check the additions of the trial balance.

b   If the difference is divisible by 2, look for a balance of half the difference that could be on the wrong side of the trial balance, for example a difference of \$960 may be caused by 'office expenses \$480' being entered on the credit side of the trial balance.

c   If the difference is divisible by 9, look for a balance where digits have been reversed – an error or original entry, for example a difference of \$270 may be caused by \$7 142 entered in the trial balance as \$7 412.

d   Check the totals of sales ledger balances and purchases ledger balances against the control accounts, if these have been prepared.

e   Check the extraction of balances from the ledgers.

If the cause of the difference has still not been found, and a statement of profit or loss and a statement of financial position are required urgently, a suspense account can be opened.

15.4 Opening and using a suspense account

A suspense account is opened in the general ledger with a balance on whichever side of the trial balance has the smaller total. If the trial balance has a debit column adding up to \$1 000 000 and a credit column totalling \$980 000, then a suspense account would be created with a credit balance of \$20 000.

It is vital to learn which types of error should involve the suspense account, including:

• *Single entries*: where only half of the financial transaction has been posted, for example the payment of wages has been entered as a credit in the bank account, but no other entry has been made on the debit side of an account.

• *Same side entries*: when both entries have been made on the same side of two separate accounts, for example the payment of wages has been credited to both the bank account and the wages account.

• *Unequal entries*: the entries have been made on the correct sides of the accounts but the figures differ, for example debit wages \$450, credit bank \$500.

- *Balancing off/arithmetical errors*: resulting in the balance on one or more accounts being over or underadded.

KEY CONCEPT LINK

Duality: How does the suspense account enable the accountant, when correcting errors, to maintain the concept of duality?

WORKED EXAMPLE 2

Poseidon constructed a trial balance and discovered that it did not balance. They created a suspense account that had a credit balance of $3 359. On closer inspection, the following errors and omissions were discovered:

1   Being the recording of a cheque received from a credit customer into the sales ledger control account / relevant customer's ledger.
2   Being the correction of an entry made on the wrong side of the discount received account.
3   Being the correction of an erroneous figure being posted into the electricity account.
4   Being the correction of an entry made to the wrong side of the purchase account.
5   Being the correction of an entry made to the wrong side of the purchase ledger control account.
6   Being the correction of an under-casting / under-stating of the rent and rates account.

The double entry included in the journals needed to correct these errors, plus the narratives, would be:

1

	Dr	Cr
Details	$	$
Suspense	6 800	
Sales ledger control account		6 800

This is a single entry – so the correction requires one entry in a nominal ledger account. The suspense account enables the journal to balance.

2

	Dr	Cr
Details	$	$
Suspense	330	
Discounts received		330

Both entries are on the same side, but only one – the discount – is wrong. As it is a reversal, this will involve doubling the amount to correct it. The suspense account enables the journal to balance.

3

	Dr	Cr
Details	$	$
Suspense	27	
Electricity		27

The expenses account had been debited by $27 too much and as the other entry was correct, only one nominal ledger account could be corrected. The suspense account enables the journal to balance.

CONTINUED

4

Details	Dr $	Cr $
Purchases	4704	
Suspense		4704

Both entries are on the same side – the purchases account is wrong. As it is a reversal, this will involve doubling the amount. The suspense account enables the journal to balance.

5

Details	Dr $	Cr $
Suspense	1316	
Purchases ledger control account	.	1316

Both entries are on the same side – the control account is wrong. As it is a reversal, this will involve doubling the amount. The suspense account enables the journal to balance.

6

Details	Dr $	Cr $
Rent and rates	410	
Suspense		410

The rent and rates account is the only one that is wrong and so only one account can be corrected. The suspense account enables the journal to balance.

The entries in the suspense account will be as follows:

	Suspense account				
	Debit			Credit	
		$			$
1	Sales ledger control account	6800		Balance per trial balance	3359
2	Discounts received	330	4	Purchases	4704
3	Electricity	27	6	Rent and rates	410
5	Purchase ledger control account	1316			
		8473		Balance b/d	8473

TIP

The suspense account may initially get bigger as you start making corrections – this will be caused by the order in which the errors are dealt with. It will only 'disappear' when all of the corrections have been made.

ACTIVITY 15.2

An accountant has constructed a trial balance and discovered that it does not balance. She creates a suspense account that has a credit balance of $4656. On closer inspection, the following errors and omissions were discovered:

1   Bank charges of $38 had been entered in the bank account but nowhere else.

2   The purchases account had been over-cast by $2500.

CONTINUED

3   $1 700 of discounts allowed, although entered correctly in the sales ledger control account, had been credited to the discounts received account.

4   A cash sale of $1 551 had been correctly entered in the revenue account but had been entered as $1 155 in the bank account.

5   A purchase of machinery for $3 140 had been debited in both the machinery at cost and bank accounts.

6   A discount of $145 from a supplier, although posted correctly to the discounts received account, had been entered as a credit in the purchases ledger control account.

Required

a   Show the journals required to correct these errors (narratives are required).

b   Create the suspense account.

15.5 When to use a suspense account

The causes of the difference on the trial balance must be investigated at the earliest opportunity and the errors corrected. However, not all errors will require a suspense account to be used.

In real life, if there is still a small balance on a suspense account after all reasonable attempts have been made to find the difference, a business may decide that the amount involved is not material. It will save further time and expense in searching for errors by writing the balance off to the statement of profit or loss. Of course, if that is done, there is the possibility that a small difference could be two very large errors that are nearly compensating for each other.

It is quite likely that there will be a combination of errors, some of which require the suspense account and some of which do not. You will need to be able to tell the difference. The questions you should ask yourself are:

- Did the debits equal the credits when the original entries were made? If the answer is 'no', then the suspense account is required.

- How may accounts have a problem because of this error? If the answer is '1' then the suspense account is required.

WORKED EXAMPLE 3

Munroe constructed a trial balance and discovered that it did not balance. He was forced to create a suspense account with a debit balance of $620. On closer inspection, the following errors and omissions were discovered:

1   A receipt of $1 355 from a credit customer had been credited to both the Sales ledger control account and the bank.

2   A sale of a motor car for $1 840 had been credited to sales.

3   A cheque payment of $795 relating to Rent and rates had been entered in the books as $759.

4   A cash sale of $1 890 had been recorded in the bank account only.

5   Wages and salaries had been overadded by $200.

6   $605 paid for Insurance had been entered into the Heat and light account.

CONTINUED

The journals needed to correct these errors with supporting explanations are as follows:

1

Details	Dr $	Cr $
Bank	2 710	
Suspense		2 710

This is a partial error of reversal – both entries were made on the credit side and only the bank account is wrong. The reversal means that the amount needs to be doubled and the suspense account enables the journal to balance.

2

Details	Dr $	Cr $
Sales	1 840	
Motor car		1 840

An error of principle where the debit and credit entries were equal so the suspense account is not required. The correction involves adjustment to the two accounts affected by the error.

3

Details	Dr $	Cr $
Rent	36	
Electricity		36

An error of original entry (transposition error) where two accounts have received postings that were too small – so the suspense account is not required.

4

Details	Dr $	Cr $
Suspense	1 890	
Sales		1 890

A single entry, so only one account needs to be corrected – the Suspense account is required to balance the journal.

5

Details	Dr $	Cr $
Suspense	200	
Wages and salaries		200

Only one account is wrong and needs to be corrected – the Suspense account enabled the journal to balance.

CONTINUED

6

Details	Dr $	Cr $
Insurance	605	
Heat and light		605

An error of principle where the debit and credit entries were equal so the Suspense account is not required. The correction involves adjustment to the two accounts affected by the error.

The entries in the Suspense account will be as follows:

Suspense account				
Debit			**Credit**	
	$			$
Balance per trial balance	620	1	Bank	2710
4 Sales	1890			
5 Wages and salaries	200			
	2710		Balance b/d	2710

TIP

Remember that the suspense account will only be required if the original debit and credit entries were not equal or only one account requires correcting.

15.6 Errors and profit

The suspense account can enable the business to continue operating while an investigation into where the errors are takes place. If a set of provisional financial statements has been prepared, then it is possible that the profit figure will need changing, as well as the current asset or current liability sections in the statement of financial position.

WORKED EXAMPLE 4

Suppose that Munroe had a provisional profit figure of $12600 for the year ended 30 June 2020. The journals used in Worked example 3 will mean that this will have changed:

Calculation of corrected profit for the year ended 30 June 2020	Increase	Decrease	
	$	$	$
Profit per draft statement of profit or loss			12600
Error 1 No effect on profit			
Error 2 Decrease in sales		1840	
Error 3 No effect on profit			
Error 4 Increase in sales	1890		
Error 5 Decrease in wages and salaries	200		
Error 6 No effect on profit			
	2090	1840	250
Revised profit for the year			12850

ACTIVITY 15.3

A business had constructed a trial balance and discovered that it did not balance. A suspense account was created with a debit balance of $435. On closer inspection, the following errors and omissions were discovered:

1   A payment of $340 to a credit supplier had been debited to both the bank account and the purchases ledger control account.

2   A discount of $72 had been correctly entered in the sales ledger control account but entered in the correct discount account as $27.

3   A cheque receipt of $485 from a credit customer had been credited to the bank and debited to the sales ledger control account.

4   Purchases returns had been overadded by $1 000.

5   A cheque for $1 730 from a credit customer had been entered in the books as $1 370.

6   A sales return of $315 had been entered in the credit side of both the sales returns account and the sales ledger control account.

7   A purchase of a motor vehicle for $800 had been entered in the motor expenses account.

8   A cheque payment to a credit supplier of $560 had been entered in the purchases ledger control account only.

The business had produced a provisional profit figure of $8 745 for the year ended 31 May 2020.

Required

a   Produce the journals needed to correct these errors (narratives are required).

b   Produce the suspense account.

c   Create a statement that shows the revised profit figure once the corrections have been made.

15.7 Errors, current assets and current liabilities

In addition to having an effect on profit, the correction of these errors will change some of the values shown in the statement of financial position. It would be useful to see what effect correcting any errors will have on the current assets and current liabilities.

WORKED EXAMPLE 5

A business had the following list of balances at 28 February 2020:

	$
Accrued expenses	720
Bank overdraft	1 385
Cash	255
Inventory at 28 February 2020	7 610
Prepaid expenses	340
Trade payables (purchase ledger control account)	4 895
Trade receivables (sales ledger control account)	6 120

CONTINUED

Journals used to correct a number of errors were as follows:

		$	$
Error 1	Bank	520	
	Suspense		520
Error 2	Suspense	1 075	
	Trade receivables (sales ledger control account)		1 075
Error 3	Rent and rates	370	
	Bank		370
Error 4	Motor expenses	180	
	Cash		180
Error 5	Bank	6 000	
	Bank loan		6 000
Error 6	Trade payables (purchase ledger control account)	840	
	Bank		840

If we have not been given the net current assets figure, we will need to find it. In this case, we would need to list the current assets and liabilities and find the difference:

	$	$	$
Current assets:			
Inventory at 28 February 2020	7 610		
Trade receivables (sales ledger control account)	6 120		
Cash	255		
Prepaid expenses	340	14 325	
Current liabilities:			
Trade payables (purchase ledger control account)	4 895		
Bank overdraft	1 385		
Accrued expenses	720	7 000	
Net current assets			7 325

These journals will have an impact on the value of items in the financial statements. In order to minimise the chances of making a mistake, you could lay out your adjustments like this:

Current assets:		
Inventory at 28 February 2020	No change	7 610
Trade receivables (sales ledger control account)	6 120 − 1 075 =	5 045
Cash	255 − 180 =	75
Prepaid expenses	No change	340
Current liabilities:		
Trade payables (purchase ledger control account)	−4 895 + 840 =	−4 055
Bank overdraft	−1 385 + 520 − 370 + 6 000 − 840 =	3 925
Accrued expenses	No change	−720

CONTINUED

So, the revised current assets and current liabilities would look like this:

Current assets:	$	$	$
Inventory at 28 February 2020	7 610		
Trade receivables (sales ledger control account)	5 045		
Bank	3 925		
Cash	75		
Prepaid expenses	340	16 995	
Current liabilities:			
Trade payables (purchase ledger control account)	4 055		
Accrued expenses	720	4 775	
Net current assets			12 220

If we were given the net current assets as one figure ($7 325) then we could insert it into a statement like this:

Calculation of net current assets at 28 February 2020	Decrease Dr	Increase Cr	
	$	$	$
Net current assets per draft statement of financial position			7 325
Error 1 Increase in bank account	520		
Error 2 Decrease in trade receivables (sales ledger control account)		1 075	
Error 3 Decrease in bank		370	
Error 4 Decrease in cash		180	
Error 5 Increase in bank	6 000		
Error 6 Decrease in trade payables (purchase ledger control account)	840		
Error 6 Decrease in bank		840	
	7 360	2 465	4 895
Revised net current assets			12 220

Notes:

1 If only a net current assets figure is provided and details of individual current assets or liabilities are not given, then using a statement like that shown here will be the only way of calculating the revised net current assets.

2 Debits will increase net current assets as they either increase assets or reduce liabilities.

3 Credits will reduce net current assets as they either reduce assets or increase liabilities.

4 Adjustments made to the sales and purchases ledger control accounts would also require the appropriate entries to be made to the relevant subsidiary ledger accounts.

ACTIVITY 15.4

A business had the following list of balances at 30 April 2020 and had prepared a provisional set of financial statements at that date:

	$
Accrued expenses	342
Bank (money in the account)	2 196
Cash	437
Inventory at 30 April 2020	9 210
Prepaid expenses	715
Trade payables (PLCA)	9 163
Trade receivables (SLCA)	11 024

Some errors were then discovered and the journals used to correct them were as follows:

		$	$
Error 1	Bank	961	
	Sales ledger control account		961
Error 2	Suspense	283	
	Accrued expenses		283
Error 3	Suspense	54	
	Cash		54
Error 4	Purchases ledger control account	1 342	
	Suspense		1 342
Error 5	Sales ledger control account	180	
	Discounts allowed		180
Error 6	Rent and rates	425	
	Bank		425

Required

a   Show the provisional net current assets before the correction of the errors.

b   Show the revised net current assets once the errors have been corrected.

c   Create a statement that shows the effect of each correction on the net current assets. Ensure it confirms your answers to **b**.

REFLECTION

'Given that the two columns in the trial balance might agree even though there are several types of error that have been committed, this means that producing a trial balance at the end of each month is a complete waste of time.'

Do you agree with this statement? Discuss your comments with another learner. Do they agree with you?

THINK LIKE AN ACCOUNTANT

Any final errors?

Olivia has examined everything and discovered several errors – most had been committed by the client's employee. The debit column in the trial balance now agrees with the credit column and Olivia feels ready to prepare the first draft of the financial statements. Does the fact that the debit column in the trial balance now agrees with the credit column mean that everything is now correct? Why/why not?

Figure 15.2: Olivia has discovered a number of errors committed by the client's employee.

EXAM-STYLE QUESTIONS

1   The purchase of a van for $4 000 has been debited to the purchases account. Which of the following statements is true?

    A   This is an error of commission and will reduce the profit for the year if not corrected.

    B   This is an error of commission and will increase the profit for the year if not corrected.

    C   This is an error of principle and will reduce the profit for the year if not corrected.

    D   This is an error of principle and will increase the profit for the year if not corrected.   [1]

2   A cheque for $4 370 had been received from a credit customer. It had only been recorded in the bank account. What would be the journal entry needed to make the necessary correction?

		Debit		Credit
A	Purchases ledger control account	$4 370	Suspense	$4 370
B	Suspense	$4 370	Purchases ledger control account	$4 370
C	Sales ledger control account	$4 370	Suspense	$4 370
D	Suspense	$4 370	Sales ledger control account	$4 370

[1]

3   The following errors were identified:

    i   Motor expenses of $525 were correctly entered in the suspense account but entered in the bank account as $552.

    ii   A cheque for $800 received that related to a cash sale had been debited to sales and credited to the bank account.

    iii   A credit note for $420 received from a supplier had been recorded in the purchases returns journal as $240.

    Which errors could be corrected without using a suspense account?

    A   i and ii   **B**   i and iii   **C**   ii and iii   **D**   ii only   [1]

CONTINUED

4   Unai had produced a trial balance and had created a suspense account with a credit balance of $2 540. On inspection, a number of errors had been revealed:

1   A settlement discount of $80, given to a customer, had been credited to both the sales ledger control account and the discount allowed account.

2   The wages and salaries account had been overadded by $3 000.

3   A payment of $300 for wages and salaries had been credited to the bank and debited to office expenses.

4   A purchase of fixtures and fittings for $2 100 by cheque had been recorded as debit purchases and credit bank.

5   An irrecoverable debt of $510 had been recorded debited to both accounts.

6   The owner removing $450 for his own use had been debited to the bank and credited to drawings.

7   A cheque payment of $727 for motor expenses had been recorded in both accounts as $772.

8   A payment of $1 320 to credit suppliers had been recorded in the bank account only.

Unai had produced some draft financial statements that showed a loss for the year of $3 295 and net current assets of $7 160.

Required

Prepare:

a   The journals required to make the necessary corrections (narratives not required).   [8]

b   The suspense account.   [6]

c   A statement showing the revised profit (or loss) for the year.   [7]

d   A statement showing the revised net current assets figure.   [7]

SELF-EVALUATION CHECKLIST

After studying this chapter, complete a table like this:

You should be able to:	Needs more work	Almost there	Ready to move on
Identify and explain that some errors can be corrected using journals and other errors result in a trial balance not balancing and so require the creation of a suspense account.			
Prepare ledger accounts and journal entries to correct errors using a suspense account so that once all corrections are completed, the suspense account has a zero balance and the two columns of the trial balance agree.			
Identify the effect on the financial statements of the correction of errors: all errors have the capacity to distort the profit figure or the valuation of assets and liabilities in the financial statements. Once all errors have been corrected, the financial statements can be produced.			

Chapter 16

Incomplete records

This chapter covers part of syllabus sections AS Level 1.5 and A Level 3.1

LEARNING INTENTIONS

In this chapter you will learn how to:

- apply a range of techniques to find missing figures in order to produce financial statements
- calculate profit or loss from statements of affairs
- prepare control accounts to find missing figures
- account for transactions involving non-current assets
- prepare the statement of profit or loss and statement of financial position from incomplete records.

ACCOUNTING IN CONTEXT

Filling in the gaps

Many firms of accountants prepare accounts for their clients when there is not a full set of records to work from. The accountant will receive a box from their client containing a mixture of invoices and till receipts, a cheque book and paying-in book, bank statements, and a notebook containing the list of customers and the amounts of money received. There may also be a box containing some coins and a small exercise book that has recorded details of petty cash payments.

An experienced accountant will go through the information supplied and be able to work out all of the different figures required to produce the financial statements using a variety of techniques.

Discuss in a pair or a group:

- Why do many self-employed small business owners not maintain full double-entry accounting systems?

- Why is this likely to cost them a lot of money?

- How could small business owners save money when it comes to the preparation of financial statements?

Figure 16.1: Accountants sometimes prepare accounts for their clients when there is not a full set of records to work from.

16.1 What are incomplete records?

Business owners often only record transactions using **single-entry bookkeeping**, so they have **incomplete records**. Other businesses will have kept few records or will just put all paperwork into boxes and deliver them to the accountant.

The accountant will use a variety of techniques in order to be able to piece together the evidence presented by the client. They can then produce a set of accounts that will accurately represent what has happened during the year.

16.2 How to calculate capital and profit or loss

If the business has not kept enough records for a statement of profit or loss to be prepared, then the accounting equation may be used to calculate a profit or loss figure (see Section 8.4).

The effect of profit on a sole trader's capital can be summarised as:

Profit increases capital while losses reduce capital.

If the opening and closing capital can be identified, then a reconstruction of the Capital and liabilities section of the statement of financial position will help to identify the profit, because we know that:

	Opening capital
+	Capital introduced
+	Net profit
−	Drawings
=	Closing capital

However, we shall be rearranging this to make it more user-friendly.

The first stage in the process of calculating the profit is to identify the capital by listing the assets and liabilities in a **statement of affairs**.

KEY TERMS

incomplete records: any method of recording financial transactions that is not based on the double-entry model.

single-entry bookkeeping: a method of bookkeeping where only one aspect of each financial transaction is recorded.

statement of affairs: a list of the business assets and liabilities at a point in time, usually prepared to calculate the capital of the business at that point in time.

WORKED EXAMPLE 1

Jane has been a mobile hairdresser and beauty technician for a few years. She has never kept records of her takings and payments but wishes to know how much profit or loss she has made in the year ended 30 June 2020.

A list of her current assets and current liabilities at the start and end of her financial year was as follows:

	1 July 2019	1 June 2020
	$	$
Equipment (net book value)	1 295	1 180
Inventory of hair and beauty supplies	540	575
Amounts owing from clients	275	310
Prepaid expenses	150	95
Balance at bank/(overdraft)	(490)	360
Trade payables for supplies	330	245
Accrued expenses	85	95

Jane has drawn $200 per week from the business for personal expenses.

Jane also introduced equipment valued at $500 to the business and paid for it out of her own personal bank account.

Step 1

Use a statement of affairs to calculate Jane's opening and closing capital:

Statements of affair [1]				
	1 July 2019		30 June 2020	
	$	$	$	$
Assets:				
Equipment (net book value)		1 295		1 180
Inventory of hair and beauty supplies		540		575
Amounts owing from clients		275		310
Prepaid expenses		150		95
Balance at bank [2]		–		360
		2 260		2 520
Liabilities: [4]				
Creditors for supplies	330		245	
Bank overdraft [2]	490		0	
Accrued expenses	85	(905)	95	(340)
Capital [3]		1 355		2 180

Notes:

[1]   It is not essential to produce the statement of affairs in this style – a list of assets and liabilities will achieve the same result.

[2]   The bank account was a current liability on 1 July 2020 and a current asset at 30 June 2020.

[3]   While the business has grown by $825 during the year, this is not her profit figure because of the drawings that she has taken and the equipment that she introduced.

[4]   With a business like Jane's, it is possible that some clients might have paid in advance and this would have been regarded as prepaid income, which is a current liability.

CONTINUED

Step 2

Calculate Jane's profit (or loss). This can be done either by a reconstructing the Capital and liabilities section from a statement of financial position or preparing Jane's capital account and using the profit or loss figure as a balancing item.

The Capital and liabilities section on the statement of financial position can be rearranged as follows:

	$
Closing capital at 30 June 2020	2180
Add: Drawings in year to 30 June 2020 (52 × $200)	10400
	12580
Deduct opening capital at 1 July 2019	(1355)
Deduct value of equipment introduced	(500)
Profit for the year ended 30 June 2020	10725

We might decide to construct Jane's capital account and use the balancing figure to find the profit or loss:

	Jane capital account					
	Debit			**Credit**		
		$				$
30 Jun 20	Drawings	10400	1 Jul 19	Balance b/d		1355
30 Jun 20	Balance c/d	2180	30 Jun 20	Equipment introduced		500
			30 Jun 20	Profit for the year (balancing figure)		10725
		12580				12580
			1 Jul 20	Balance b/d		2180

Note: the balancing figure in the account is a profit for the year because it is increasing Jane's capital. Had the balancing figure been a debit entry, this would have represented a loss as it would be reducing Jane's capital.

16.3 Using control accounts

Control accounts can be used to identify missing figures, as long as there aren't too many. In this chapter, we will look at three possibilities – sales, purchases and expenses.

WORKED EXAMPLE 2

Sales ledger control accounts

Suppose a client had provided the following information:

	$
Opening trade receivables	32140
Closing trade receivables	28675
Receipts from trade receivables	396050
Credit sales	?
Sales returns	5465
Discounts allowed	4970
Irrecoverable debts (written off)	8760

CONTINUED

It would be possible to prepare a control account and use it to find the missing figure by:

1   Inserting the opening balance and the transactions we do have details of

2   Inserting the closing balance c/d and b/d

3   Inserting the 'larger side' totals on both sides

4   Identifying the missing figure on the 'smaller side' as the balancing figure.

Sales ledger control account

Sales ledger control account			
Debit		**Credit**	
	$		$
Opening balance b/d (1)	32 140	Sales returns (1)	5 465
Credit sales (4)	411 780	Bank (1)	396 050
		Discounts allowed	4 970
		Irrecoverable debts (1)	8 760
		Closing balance c/d (2)	28 675
	(3) 443 920		(3) 443 920
Closing balance c/d (2)	28 675		

Notes:

1   This approach can be used regardless of which figure was missing. If receipts had been the missing figure, then the approach would have been identical except that the debit side would have been the larger side and the receipts figure would have been the final balancing figure.

2   This approach cannot be used if there is more than one missing figure.

Purchases ledger control accounts

Suppose a client had provided the following information:

	$
Opening payables	5 785
Closing payables	10 195
Credit purchases	?
Purchases returns	1 245
Payments to trade payables	89 710
Discounts received	2 495

CONTINUED

The approach is exactly the same as for the trade receivables:

Purchases ledger control account				
Debit		**Credit**		
	$			$
Purchases returns (1)	1 245	Opening balance b/d (1)		5 785
Bank (1)	89 710	Credit purchases (4)		97 860
Discounts received (1)	2 495			
Closing balance c/d (2)	10 195			
(3)	103 645		(3)	103 645
		Closing balance b/d (2)		10 195

Notes:

[1] If payments to trade payables had been the missing figure, then the approach would have been identical except that the debit side would have been the larger side and the receipts figure would have been the final balancing figure.

[2] This approach cannot be used if there is more than one missing figure.

Expenses

Suppose the client has provided the following information relating to rent, rates and insurance:

	$
Opening rent accrued	450
Opening insurance prepaid	725
Bank payments	5 160
Rent, rates and insurance expense for the year	?
Closing rent accrued	510
Closing insurance prepaid	760

The approach is the same as for sales and purchases – the only difference is that there might be far more adjustments at the beginning and end of the period, particularly if the client has grouped several expenses together.

In this case, the expense control account would look like this:

Rent, rates and insurance control account				
Debit		**Credit**		
	$			$
Opening balance b/d (1)	725	Opening balance b/d (1)		450
Bank (1)	5 160	Statement of profit or loss (expense) (4)		5 185
Closing balance c/d (2)	510	Closing balance c/d (2)		760
(3)	6 395		(3)	6 395
Closing balance b/d (2)	760	Closing balance b/d (2)		510

The same issues apply here as for the purchases and sales ledgers.

TIP

If there is more than one figure missing in any control account, then it will be impossible to proceed. Examine another part of the system and, if enough of those missing figures are revealed elsewhere, you can finish off the control account.

ACTIVITY 16.1

Julia, a trader, has provided you with the following information relating to parts of her business:

	$
Opening accrued motor expenses	260
Opening prepaid motor expenses	890
Opening trade payables	24 110
Opening trade receivables	11 905
Bank payments for motor expenses	9 015
Credit purchases	??
Credit sales	200 430
Discounts allowed	2 105
Discounts received	3 015
Irrecoverable debts (written off)	3 280
Motor expenses for the year	??
Payments to trade payables	67 900
Purchases returns	4 985
Receipts from trade receivables	??
Sales returns	7 160
Closing accrued motor expenses	440
Closing prepaid motor expenses	565
Closing trade receivables	12 150
Closing trade payables	17 625

Required

Using control accounts, find the receipts from trade receivables, credit purchases and the motor expenses for the year.

16.4 The summary bank account

Most business owners will understand that it is vital to keep records of monies coming into or going out of their business. They will have kept records like bank statements, cheque books, paying-in books, receipts and may even have recorded details into a cash book.

As many transactions will involve the cash or bank account, using that as a 'centre' from which to operate may be a useful way of finding figures.

The summary bank account is another name for the cash book. It serves a number of purposes including:

- forcing the accountant to collate the items involving money coming into the business and money going out of the business so that the totals for each revenue or expense can be identified
- enabling the accountant to find missing figures (or even final balances) – the cash and bank accounts can be used in the same way as the control accounts.

WORKED EXAMPLE 3

Wasim is a sole trader who runs a small shop. The only financial records that he has are bank paying-in book counterfoils, cheque book counterfoils and records of trade receivables and trade payables. Wasim has made notes summarising his transactions with the bank and cash transactions in the year ended 31 December 2019 as follows:

- Bank receipts: cheques received from customers $11 375, takings paid into the bank $9 740.
- Bank payments: suppliers $8 210, wages $4 910, rent and rates $3 600, electricity $1 530, purchase of shop fittings $840, drawings $???
- Cash receipts: sales to customers $31 390
- Cash payments: takings paid into the bank $9 740, suppliers $6 230, postage and stationery $390, other expenses $1 435, drawings $???
- Wasim's cash balance on 1 January 2019 was $245 and on 31 December 2019 was $110.
- Wasim's bank balance on 1 January 2019 was $2 680 and on 31 December 2020 was $525 (both have money in the account).

Wasim regularly took cash out of the till and withdrew money from the bank for his own purposes, but he has no idea how much.

The summary bank account includes only those amounts actually received and spent and is a cash book summary with columns for cash and bank.

The steps are very similar to those seen with the sales and purchases ledger control accounts:

Step 1

Insert the opening balances and all known transactions. Remember that any cash banked needs to be recorded twice – once as a cash payment and once as a bank receipt.

Step 2

Insert the closing balances (if known).

Step 3

Add up the value of transactions on each side and insert the larger side's total into both sides.

Step 4

Identify the missing figure as the balancing figure on the smaller side – in this case, the drawings.

TIP

The cash and bank accounts are different accounts even though they are so close together. Concentrate on one at a time to avoid placing items in the wrong columns.

Cash book

Debit	Cash	Bank	Credit	Cash	Bank
	$	$		$	$
Opening balance b/d (1)	245	2 680	Paid into bank (1)	9 740	
Sales (1)	31 390	11 375	Suppliers (1)	6 230	8 210
Cash banked (1)		9 740	Wages (1)		4 910
			Rent and rates (1)		3 600
			Electricity (1)		1 530
			Shop fittings (1)		840
			Postage and stationery (1)	390	
			Other expenses (1)	1 435	
			Drawings (4)	13 730	4 180
			Closing balances c/d (2)	110	525
(3)	31 635	23 795	(3)	31 635	23 795
Closing balance b/d (2)	110	525			

ACTIVITY 16.2

Jasmina is a general trader who runs a small shop. Her cash and bank transactions were as follows:

1   Bank receipts: cheques received from customers $33 080, takings paid into the bank $7 650.

2   Bank payments: suppliers $11 475, wages $6 600, rent and rates $2 850, electricity $1 140, drawings $400 per week.

3   Cash receipts: sales to customers $???

4   Cash payments: takings paid into the bank $7 650, suppliers $3 305, administrative expenses $1 265.

5   Jasmina's opening cash balance was $395 and closing cash balance was $240.

6   Jasmina's opening bank balance was $4 210 (overdrawn) and closing bank balance was $???

Required

Prepare Jasmina's cash book showing clearly the:

a   amount of cash received from customers

b   the closing bank balance.

16.5 Dealing with non-current assets

A business may have a number of non-current assets and these will need to be depreciated. There may also have been new assets bought during the year and details of these will be included in the summary bank account. How these are dealt with depends on how much information has been provided.

WORKED EXAMPLE 4

Situation 1: Abbie's business has a car that cost $21 000 and which at the start of the year had a net book value of $13 800. By the end of the year, the net book value was $10 200. She had not bought or sold any non-current assets.

Depreciation for the year = 13 800 − 10 200 = $3 600.

Situation 2: Jim's business had equipment that cost $36 000 and which at the start of the year had a net book value of $24 600. By the end of the year, the cost was $58 000 and the net book value was $39 100. He had not sold any non-current assets.

Cost has increased by 58 000 − 36 000 = $22 000, which may be a figure that you have been searching for elsewhere.

Depreciation for the year is a bit more complicated as the accumulated depreciation needs to be calculated at the start and end of the accounting year:

Opening accumulated depreciation = 36 000 − 24 600 = $11 400

Closing accumulated depreciation = 58 000 − 39 100 = $18 900

Depreciation for the year = 18 900 − 11 400 = $7 500

Of course, it is possible that the depreciation policy might be provided.

> **TIP**
>
> If there have been no acquisitions (or disposals) of non-current assets, then a lot of information can be gathered by calculating differences between opening and closing balances.
>
> Remember: cost − accumulated depreciation = net book value.

CONTINUED

Situation 3: Rudolf's business had a vehicle (A) that he had bought for $32 000 and which had been depreciated by $18 400 at the start of the year. Depreciation was based on a residual value of $6 000 and a useful life of five years.

Halfway through the year, Rudolf bought a second vehicle (B) for $41 000 and expected to get $8 000 for it at the end of its six-year useful life. Depreciation on all vehicles is applied on a monthly basis and uses the straight-line method.

In this case, we just follow the instructions:

$$\text{Depreciation on vehicle A} = \frac{(32\,000 - 6\,000)}{5} = \$5\,200$$

$$\text{Depreciation on vehicle B} = \frac{(41\,000 - 8\,000)}{6} \times \frac{6}{12} = \$2\,750 \text{ total} = \$7\,950$$

$$\text{Cost of motor vehicles} = 32\,000 + 41\,000 = \$73\,000$$

$$\text{Accumulated depreciation} = 18\,400 + 7\,950 = \$26\,350$$

The motor vehicles would appear in the statement of financial position as:

	Cost	Accumulated depreciation	Net book value
	$	$	$
Motor vehicles	73 000	26 350	46 650

ACTIVITY 16.3

Calculate the depreciation expense and prepare the details that would appear in the non-current assets section of the statement of financial position in the following situations:

Situation 1: On 1 July 2019, the business owned vehicles that had cost $18 600 and which had a net book value of $5400. On 2 April 2020, a vehicle was bought at a cost of $23 400. On 30 June 2020, the net book value was $19 700. No vehicles were sold during the year.

Situation 2: A business had a machine (A) that had been bought for $65 000 and which had been depreciated by $47 100 at the start of the year. Depreciation was based on a residual value of $11 000 and a useful life of eight years. Three months into the year, a second machine (B) was bought for $36 000. It was expected to last for five years after which it would have a residual value of $4000. Depreciation on all machines is applied on a monthly basis and uses the straight-line method.

KEY CONCEPT LINK

Duality: Recognises that every financial transaction has a dual effect on the position of a business as recorded in the accounts. How important is having a good knowledge of double-entry when preparing the financial statements of a client who has not kept full accounting records?

16.6 How to prepare a statement of profit or loss and a statement of financial position from incomplete records

No two businesses or the information provided are ever quite the same, so you might have to approach the situation slightly differently each time.

WORKED EXAMPLE 5

Fred Brassic has not kept full accounting records but has provided the following information:

	1 April 19	31 March 20
	$	$
Motor vehicles (cost $12 000)	9 000	?
Equipment (cost $6 000)	5 400	?
Inventory	3 000	4 200
Trade receivables	2 560	1 980
Bank account (with money in it)	1 815	?
Trade payables	3 745	2 105
Rent (accrued)	320	460
Rates (paid in advance)	175	130

Fred puts all of his receipts and payments through the business bank account and during the year, the following transactions occurred:

	$
Receipts from trade receivables	82 380
Cash sales	8 565
Payments to trade payables	49 615
Drawings	12 000
Wages and salaries	7 650
Rent and rates	4 210
Admin expenses	5 625
Heat and light	1 400
Motor expenses	2 035
Equipment	4 000
Cash purchases	13 100

During the year, Fred returned faulty goods worth $885 to his (credit) suppliers and received discounts of $405. Fred gave discounts to his (credit) customers totalling $740 and received faulty goods back amounting to $1 295.

Depreciation is charged on the following basis: 25% reducing balance on vehicles and 10% straight-line on other assets. A full year's depreciation is to be charged on all items owned at the end of the year.

Required

Produce a statement of profit or loss and a statement of financial position for Fred for the year ended 31 March 2020.

CONTINUED

Answer

Step 1

Fred's capital at 1 April can be calculated using a statement of affairs. Unfortunately, as there are too many missing figures at 31 March 2020, it is impossible to find his capital at the end of the year.

Statements of affairs		
	1 April 2019	
	$	$
Assets:		
Motor vehicles (net book value)		9 000
Equipment (net book value)		5 400
Inventory		3 000
Trade receivables		2 560
Bank		1 815
Prepaid expenses		175
		21 950
Liabilities:		
Trade payables	3 745	
Accrued expenses	320	(4 065)
Capital		17 885

Step 2

Produce the payments and receipts account, which in this case seems to just consist of a bank account:

	Debit			Credit	
		$			$
1 Apr 19	Balance b/d	1 815	31 Mar 20	Trade payables	49 615
31 Mar 20	Trade receivables	82 380		Drawings	12 000
	Cash sales	8 565		Wages and salaries	7 650
				Rent and rates	4 210
				Admin expenses	5 625
				Heat and light	1 400
				Motor expenses	2 035
				Equipment	4 000
31 Mar 20	Balance c/d	6 875		Cash purchases	13 100
		99 635			99 635
			1 Apr 20	Balance b/d	6 875

Note: in this case, the only missing figure that could be obtained here was the closing bank balance, but it did enable a lot of useful items to be listed that will be used later.

CONTINUED

Step 3

Control accounts can now be used to find items such as:

- credit sales
- credit purchases
- the rent and rates expense for the year where there are multiple adjustments for accruals and prepayments.

Sales ledger control account					
Debit			**Credit**		
		$			$
1 Apr 19	Balance b/d	2 560	31 Mar 20	Bank	82 380
31 Mar 20	Credit sales	[1] 83 835		Sales returns	1 295
				Discount allowed	740
			31 Mar 20	Balance c/d	1 980
		86 395			86 395
1 Apr 20	Balance b/d	1 980			

Note:

[1]   + cash sales of 8 565 = total sales $92 400

Purchases ledger control account					
Debit			**Credit**		
		$			$
31 Mar 20	Bank	49 615	1 Apr 19	Balance b/d	3 745
	Purchases returns	885	31 Mar 20	Purchases	49 265
	Discounts received	405			
31 Mar 20	Balance c/d	2 015			
		53 010			53 010
			1 Apr 20	Balance b/d	2 105

Note:

[1]   + cash purchases of 13 100 = total purchases 62 365

Rent and rates account					
Debit			**Credit**		
		$			$
1 Apr 19	Balance b/d	175	1 Apr 19	Balance b/d	320
31 Mar 20	Bank	4 210	31 Mar 20	Statement of profit or loss (expense)	4 395
31 Mar 20	Balance c/d	460	31 Mar 20	Balance c/d	130
		4 845			4 845
1 Apr 20	Balance b/d	130	1 Apr 20	Balance b/d	460

CONTINUED

Notes:

1 The sales and purchases ledger control accounts could not have been prepared without details of payments from and receipts into the bank. If we had needed the control accounts to calculate the payments and receipts, we would have needed to have done these as step 2.

2 These control accounts only helped us to calculate credit sales and purchases. Any cash transactions needed to be added.

3 As there was only one figure for rent and rates, these two expenses had to be combined.

Step 4

Non-current assets need to be dealt with. The expense needs to be calculated and the non-current section of the statement of financial position needs to be produced:

Depreciation on motor vehicles (reducing balance) = 25% × 9 000 = $2 250

Depreciation on equipment (straight-line) = 10% × (6 000 + 4 000) = $1 000

Total = $3 250

	Cost	Accumulated depreciation	Net book value
	$	$	$
Non-current assets:			
Motor vehicles	12 000	5 250	6 750
Equipment	10 000	1 600	8 400
	22 000	6 850	15 150

Note: Fred applied a full year's depreciation on all of the equipment owned at the end of the year. The fact that we do not know when the $4 000 was spent makes no difference to our calculations.

Step 5

The statement of profit or loss can now be produced. Collate information from the control accounts, payments and receipts accounts and other information provided by the client.

CONTINUED

Statement of profit or loss for Fred Brassic for the year ended 31 March 2020			
	$	$	$
Revenue			92 400
Less: Sales returns			(1 295)
			91 105
Less: Cost of sales			
Opening inventory		3 000	
Purchases	62 365		
Less: Purchases returns	(885)	61 480	
		64 480	
Less: Closing inventory		(4 200)	(60 280)
Gross profit			30 825
Discount received			405
			31 230
Less: Expenses			
Administrative expenses		5 625	
Depreciation		3 250	
Discounts allowed		740	
Heat and light		1 400	
Motor expenses		2 035	
Rent and rates		4 395	
Wages		7 650	
Total expenses			(25 095)
Profit for the year			6 135

Step 6

The statement of financial position can now be produced:

Statement of financial position for Fred Brassic at 31 March 2020	Cost	Accumulated depreciation	Net book value
	$	$	$
Non-current assets:			
Motor vehicles	12 000	5 250	6 750
Equipment	10 000	1 600	8 400
	22 000	6 850	15 150
Current assets:			
Inventory		4 200	
Trade receivables		1 980	
Other receivables		130	6 310
Total assets			21 460

CONTINUED

Capital and liabilities:		17 885
Opening capital		6 135
Net profit	(12 000)	12 020
Drawings		
Current liabilities:		2 105
Trade payables		6 875
Bank overdraft	460	9 440
Other payables		21 460

REFLECTION

Do you think that applying the techniques that you saw in this chapter would be easier if you were dealing with a real client? What might be some of the problems that you would have to overcome to be able to produce a set of financial statements for the type of clients described in this chapter? Discuss your thoughts with another learner.

THINK LIKE AN ACCOUNTANT

Out of chaos comes order...

Despite accountants trying to help their clients to keep better books and records to record their financial transaction, many small business owners still do not enjoy 'doing the books'. They would rather be out selling their products. How might the difficulties encountered by the accountant in sorting out and collating paperwork provided by a client affect whether the financial statements really do provide a true and fair view of the client's business?

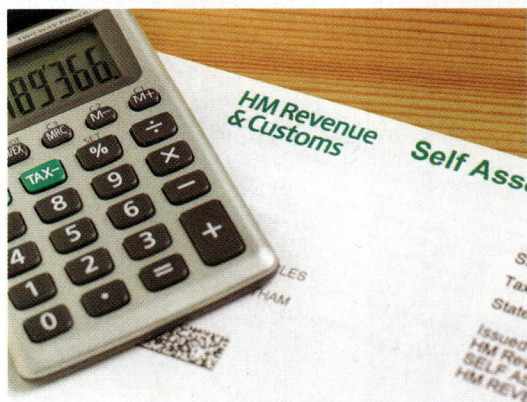

Figure 16.2: Many small business owners do not enjoy 'doing the books' and would rather be selling their products.

EXAM-STYLE QUESTIONS

1 Freda commenced business with $12 000 that she had saved over the years and $5 000 that she had inherited from an uncle. She used some of this money to purchase office equipment for $11 000 and bought a motor vehicle for $24 000 using a bank loan.

How much was Freda's capital?

A $6 000   B $12 000   C $17 000   D $41 000   [1]

2 At 1 January 2019, Hani's business assets were valued at $73 000 and his liabilities amounted to $18 000. At 31 December 2019, Hani's assets amounted to $84 000 and included a new motor vehicle that he had brought into the business on 21 October 2019 when it was valued at $20 000.

His trade payables at 31 December 2019 totalled $23 000 and his drawings during the year were $42 000.

What was Hani's profit for the year ended 31 December 2019?

A $2 000   B $22 000   C $28 000   D $42 000   [1]

3 At 1 May 2019, Ricardo's trade payables amounted to $37 840. In the year to 30 April 2020, he made credit purchases of $246 540. He received discounts of $4 445 and returned goods worth $6 860 to suppliers. His trade payables at 30 April 2020 were $41 430.

How much did Ricardo pay to his credit suppliers during the year ended 30 April 2020?

A $222 755   B $224 785   C $227 200   D $231 645   [1]

Practice question

4 Artur has not kept a full set of accounting records but has provided the following information relating to the year ended 30 June 2020:

	1 July 19	30 June 20
	$	$
Accrued expenses (rent)	700	750
Bank (money in account)	2 465	3 145
Inventory	11 085	13 210
Motor vehicles (cost $17 500)	13 125	?
Office furniture (cost $9 600)	7 440	?
Prepaid expenses (insurance)	1 375	1 540
Trade payables	5 210	4 930
Trade receivables	8 845	9 765

Artur puts all of his receipts and payments through the business bank account and during the year, the following transactions occurred:

	$
Cash purchases	27 145
Cash sales	81 230
Drawings	????
Insurance	2 910
Office furniture	4 800 bought on 30 September 2019
Payments to creditors	49 165
Receipts from trade receivables	50 095
Rent and rates	8 600
Wages and salaries	16 720

CONTINUED

Discounts given to customers for prompt payment were $870 and those received from suppliers were $1 215. There were irrecoverable debts totalling $715.

Artur kept all credit notes received from suppliers – these totalled $2 400, while customers returned goods totalling $1 420.

Depreciation is charged using the straight-line method on the following basis: 20% on vehicles and 15% on office furniture. Depreciation is charged on a monthly basis.

Required

a   Calculate Artur's capital at 1 July 2019.   [3]

b   The summary bank account showing clearly the drawings for the year.   [6]

c   Prepare the sales ledger control account and the purchases ledger control account showing clearly the credit sales and the credit purchases.   [9]

d   The rent and rates and the insurance accounts clearly showing each expense for the year.   [6]

e   The calculation of depreciation for the year.   [4]

f   Prepare a statement of profit or loss for the year ended 30 June 2020.   [10]

g   Prepare a statement of financial position at 30 June 2020.   [12]

SELF-EVALUATION CHECKLIST

After studying this chapter, complete a table like this:

You should be able to:	Needs more work	Almost there	Ready to move on
Know why accountants need to be able to apply a range of techniques to find missing figures to produce final accounts for many small business.			
Calculate profit or loss from statements of affairs: identifying the capital by listing the assets and liabilities.			
Use control accounts to find missing figures such as sales, money received from debtors or even expenses.			
Deal with transactions involving non-current assets, remembering that how you deal with them depends on how much information has been provided.			
Prepare the statement of profit or loss and statement of financial position from incomplete records, remembering that the order in which techniques are applied depends on what information is available.			

> Chapter 17

Incomplete records:
Further considerations

This chapter covers part of syllabus sections AS Level 1.2, 1.5 and A Level 3.1, 3.2

LEARNING INTENTIONS

In this chapter you will learn how to:

- prepare a trading account and use mark-ups or margins to deduce missing figures
- use 'dummy inventory figures' to provide a starting point when you are not given *either* of the opening or closing inventory figures
- calculate the amount of inventory lost, stolen or destroyed after an accident
- value inventory in accordance with recognised accounting concepts
- assess the advantages and disadvantages of keeping a full double-entry accounting system.

ACCOUNTING IN CONTEXT

Finding the missing purchases figure

One of the accountant's tasks when they have not received many records from their clients might be to calculate some of the key figures in the financial statements by working backwards. Using a few simple formulas can help them to calculate the missing figures.

Some business owners use a formula of their own to calculate how much they should charge for their goods. It might not be written down anywhere or even be very scientific, but it is what they use to greater or lesser success. An example might be just doubling the price they pay for the goods when they sell them on. If the customers are happy the business owner is happy too … although their accountant might not be!

Figure 17.1: Accountants sometimes work backwards to calculate some of the key figures in financial statements.

Discuss in a pair or a group:

- Why might the lack of a purchases figure cause the accountant a problem?
- Even if the accountant overcomes this problem, why might there still be a problem?
- Why might the accountant not be happy with the client's formula?

17.1 Using trading account structures

To find sales, purchases and inventory figures the trading part of the statement of profit or loss could be created. Information that is known can be inserted into the structure and then knowledge of how those figures relate to each other can be used to find the other items.

WORKED EXAMPLE 1

Suppose two businesses have provided the following figures:

	Business 1	Business 2
	$	$
Revenue	70 000	120 000
Opening inventory	12 600	17 800
Purchases	47 100	?
Closing inventory	?	19 100
Gross profit	20 800	41 400

Step 1

Sketch out the trading account structure and insert the figures that you know – these have been labelled as (1)

> ## CONTINUED
>
> ### Step 2
>
> Use your knowledge of how the trading account works to find the missing figures. In this illustration, these have been labelled in the order in which they have been found, e.g. (2), (30), etc.
>
> | Business 1: | $ | $ |
> |---|---|---|
> | Revenue | | 70 000 (1) |
> | Less: Cost of sales: | | |
> | Opening inventory | 12 600 (1) | |
> | Purchases | 47 100 (1) | |
> | | 59 700 (3) | |
> | Closing inventory | (10 500) (4) | 49 200 (2) |
> | Gross profit | | 20 800 (1) |
>
> (2)   70 000 − 20 800 = 49 200
>
> (3)   12 600 + 47 100 = 59 700
>
> (4)   59 700 − 49 200 = 10 500
>
> | Business 2: | $ | $ |
> |---|---|---|
> | Revenue | | 120 000 (1) |
> | Less: Cost of sales: | | |
> | Opening inventory | 17 800 (1) | |
> | Purchases | 79 900 (4) | |
> | | 97 700 (3) | |
> | Closing inventory | (19 100) (1) | (78 600) (2) |
> | Gross profit | | 41 400 (1) |
>
> (2)   120 000 − 41 400 = 78 600
>
> (3)   78 600 + 19 100 = 97 700
>
> (4)   97 700 − 17 800 = 79 900
>
> **Note:** when working backwards 'up the back', the opposite in terms of adding and subtracting is done to when working 'down the page'. This approach may provide you with one or more of the missing figures that you needed to be able to construct the control accounts.

ACTIVITY 17.1

The following information is available for Businesses A, B, C and D:

	Business A	Business B	Business C	Business D
	$	$	$	$
Revenue	56 700	73 120	69 135	?
Opening inventory	7 200	8 350	11 490	6 175
Purchases	35 600	?	39 815	?
Closing inventory	?	9 875	?	8 040
Cost of sales	?	?	42 085	37 395
Gross profit	22 200	34 310	?	54 110

Required

Produce the trading account for each of these four businesses and use them to find the missing figures.

17.2 Margins and mark-ups

Sometimes the business has kept so few records that techniques like constructing sales and purchases ledger control accounts cannot be used because too many figures are missing. One approach to this is to use **margins** and **mark-ups**, which are slightly different ways of measuring gross profit.

Margins and mark-ups can be applied to the cost, profit and selling price of individual items – many businesses will use margin or mark-up percentages to determine selling price. However, in this chapter, we will concentrate on how these concepts allow us to find missing items at the end of an accounting year.

17.3 Finding margins and mark-ups

Margin is gross profit expressed as a percentage or fraction of total revenue or selling price. This is shown by:

$$\text{Margin percentage} = \frac{\text{Gross profit}}{\text{Selling price}} \times 100$$

Mark-up is gross profit expressed as a percentage or fraction of cost of sales. This is shown by:

$$\text{Mark-up percentage} = \frac{\text{Gross profit}}{\text{Cost of sales}} \times 100$$

KEY TERMS

margin: the gross profit expressed as a percentage or fraction of selling price.

mark-up: the gross profit expressed as a percentage or fraction of the sales cost.

TIP

Take note of which is being used as there is a difference between say a 25% margin and a 25% mark-up.

> ## WORKED EXAMPLE 2
>
> **Suppose a business provides the following information:**
>
> | | $ |
> |---|---|
> | Revenue | 24 000 |
> | Cost of sales | 18 000 |
> | Gross profit | 6 000 |
>
> The *margin* is: $\dfrac{\text{Gross profit}}{\text{Selling price}} \times 100 = \dfrac{6\,000}{24\,000} \times 100 = 0.25 \times 100 = 25\%$
>
> The *mark-up* is: $\dfrac{\text{Gross profit}}{\text{Cost of sales}} \times 100 = \dfrac{6\,000}{18\,000} \times 100 = 0.3333 \times 100 = 33.33\%$
>
> We may wish to express these items as fractions so we could reduce them down to their lowest form:
>
> $$\text{Margin} = \frac{6\,000}{24\,000} = \frac{1}{4}$$
>
> $$\text{Mark-up} = \frac{6\,000}{24\,000} = \frac{1}{3}$$
>
> It is worth noting that some businesses will sell goods for several times what they paid for them – many mail-order businesses use a 'rule of 3' where they charge three times the cost. In this case, the mark-up percentage would be 200%. However, margins will always be less than 100% – unless the business is getting its products for free.

> ### TIP
>
> You need to know the formula for calculating the margin and the mark-up. Take care to apply the right one as they will give significantly different outcomes.

17.4 Using margins to find missing figures

It may be that the business has provided even less information than in Section 17.3 and there are too many gaps to be able to find the missing figures. In this situation, it may be possible to use your knowledge of margins to deduce some of the missing figures.

The crucial fact is that everything is expressed as a percentage (or fraction of sales) and so the sales figure represents 100% or $\frac{1}{1}$.

The cost of sales is the difference between the revenue and gross profit, so:

- If the margin is 20%, the cost of sales must be 80% (100 − 20)
- If the margin is 35%, the cost of sales must be 65% (100 − 35)
- If the margin is $\frac{1}{3}$, the cost of sales must be $\frac{3}{5}\left(\frac{5}{5} - \frac{2}{5}\right)$
- If the margin is $\frac{1}{4}$, the cost of sales must be $\frac{3}{4}\left(\frac{4}{4} - \frac{1}{4}\right)$ and so on

WORKED EXAMPLE 3

A business has provided information that has been put into a trading account:

	$	$
Revenue		120 000
Less: Cost of sales:		
Opening inventory	15 000	
Purchases	??	
	??	
Closing inventory	(21 000)	
Cost of sales		(??)
Gross profit		??

At this stage, there are too many missing figures – without either the gross profit or the cost of sales, it is impossible to proceed.

However, if we are told that this business uses a profit margin of 40%, we can find some of these missing figures:

	$	$	%	Fraction
Revenue		120 000	100%	$\frac{5}{5}$
Less: Cost of sales:				
Opening inventory	15 000			
Purchases	78 000 [3]			
	93 000 [2]			
Closing inventory	(21 000)			
Cost of sales		(72 000) [1]	60%	$\frac{3}{5}$
Gross profit		48 000 [1]	40%	$\frac{2}{5}$

Notes:

[1] Cost of sales = 100 − 40 = 60% $\left(\text{or } \frac{5}{5} - \frac{2}{5} = \frac{3}{5}\right)$ so both gross profit and cost of sales can be calculated as 40% and 60% of $120 000.

[2] 72 000 + 21 000 = 93 000

[3] 93 000 − 15 000 = 78 000

TIP

Occasionally, you may not have a revenue figure to work from. As long as either the cost of sales or gross profit is known, then this is not a problem.

If you divide the item you know by the percentage it represents, then you will find out what 100% is. In this case:

   $48 000 / 40% or 0.40 = $120 000 or

   $72 000 / 60% or 0.60 = $120 000

ACTIVITY 17.2

The following information was available for three businesses.

Business	A	B	C
	$	$	$
Revenue	300 000	?	500 000
Opening inventory	28 000	11 000	24 000
Purchases	204 000	?	?
Closing inventory	?	9 000	18 000
Gross profit	?	45 000	?
Margin/fraction	30% $\left(\frac{3}{10}\right)$	25% $\left(\frac{1}{4}\right)$	45% $\left(\frac{9}{20}\right)$

Required

Produce the trading account for each of these three businesses and use them and your knowledge of margins to find the missing figures.

17.5 Using mark-ups to find missing figures

If the business is using a mark-up, the approach to finding missing figures is exactly the same as for margins. The only difference is that it is the cost of sales figure that is 100% and the sales figure will be 100 + the mark-up percentage.

WORKED EXAMPLE 4

A business has provided information that has been put into a trading account.

It uses a mark-up of 40% $\left(\text{or } \frac{2}{5}\right)$:

	$	$	%	Fraction
Revenue		560 000	140% [1]	$\frac{7}{5}$
Less: Cost of sales:				
Opening inventory	17 000			
Purchases	406 000 [4]			
	423 000 [3]			
Closing inventory	(23 000)			
Cost of sales		(400 000) [2]	100%	$\frac{5}{5}$
Gross profit		160 000 [2]	40%	$\frac{2}{5}$

Notes:

[1] 100% + 40% = 140%

[2] $560 000/140%$ or $1.40 = $400 000$ and $40\% \times 400 000 = $160 000$

Or inverting the fraction $560 000 \times \frac{5}{7} = $400 000$ and $\frac{2}{5} \times 400 000 = $160 000$

[3] 400 000 + 23 000 = $423 000

[4] 423 000 − 17 000 = $406 00

KEY CONCEPT LINK

True and fair view: Financial statements are designed to give a true and fair view of the financial position to internal and external stakeholders. If you have had to use information about mark-ups or margins to deduce a crucial figure such as purchases or closing inventory, how easy might you find it to convince the tax authorities that the financial statements represent a true and fair view of your business?

17.6 Inventory lost in fire or by theft

The methods used for preparing accounts from incomplete records are also used to calculate the value of inventory lost in a fire or by theft when detailed inventory records have not been kept (or have been destroyed by the fire).

WORKED EXAMPLE 5

A business suffered a major theft and needs to submit an insurance claim. The relevant figures up to the time of the theft were as follows:

	$
Revenue	19 360
Opening inventory	3 000
Purchases	15 000
Closing inventory (before theft)	?

The inventory-take after the theft revealed that the closing inventory was in fact $2 100 and it is known that the firm operates a profit margin of 25%.

What was the value of inventory stolen?

Answer

Step 1

Produce the trading part of the statement of profit or loss using the information given about the mark-up or margin.

Step 2

Subtract the amount of inventory left with the closing inventory figure (that existing before the theft) appearing in the trading account. This will give you the amount of inventory stolen.

	$	$	
Revenue		19 360	100%
Less: Cost of sales:			
Opening inventory	3 000		
Purchases	15 000		
	18 000		
Closing inventory	(3 480) (1)		
Cost of sales		(14 520) (2)	75%
Gross profit		4 840 (1)	25%

CONTINUED

Notes:

[1]   Gross profit = 25% × 19 360 = $4 840

[2]   Cost of sales = (100 − 25) = 75% × 19 360 = $14 520

[3]   Closing inventory = 18 000 − 14 520 = $3 480

Inventory stolen therefore = 3 480 − 2 100 = $1 380

17.7 Inventory – using 'dummy figures'

It is possible you might not be given *either* of the opening or closing inventory figures, only some indication of how inventory levels have increased or decreased during the period. There is a simple, temporary, solution.

WORKED EXAMPLE 6

A business can only provide the following information:

     Revenue $171 300

     Mark-up   50%

During the year, inventory had increased by $5 280.

The key to solving this problem is to insert two inventory figures that agree with the change in the amount of inventory. Any two figures will work as long as the closing inventory figure is $5 280 larger than the opening inventory.

Once the inventory figures are in place, the trading account can be completed in the normal way:

	$	$	
Revenue		171 300	150%
Less: Cost of sales:			
Opening inventory	10 000 [2]		
Purchases	119 480 [4]		
	129 480 [3]		
Closing inventory	(15 280) [2]		
Cost of sales		(114 200) [1]	100%
Gross profit		57 100 [1]	50%

Notes:

[1]   171 300/150% = $114 200, so 171 300 − 114 200 = $57 100 gross profit

[2]   'dummy inventory' figures chosen to show an increase of $5 280

[3]   114 200 + 15 280 = $129 480

[4]   129 480 − 10 000 = $119 480

This approach has allowed purchases to be found.

Should either of the actual inventory figures be found, they can replace the dummy figures that we used.

ACTIVITY 17.3

Calculate the purchases in the following situations:

Situation 1:

Revenue	$75 600
Margin	40%

During the year, inventory had increased by $4 200.

Situation 2:

Revenue	$213 800
Mark-up	60%

During the year, inventory had decreased by $4 190.

17.8 The importance of valuing inventory in accordance with recognised accounting principles

There are three possible ways in which inventory may be valued:

- cost price
- selling price
- what it is considered to be worth.

The third way should be ruled out immediately as it completely contradicts the 'money measurement' concept. 'Worth' is also a matter of opinion. Using selling price also has its problems because using it can contradict several important accounting concepts.

WORKED EXAMPLE 7

Sammy started a new business selling one product. During the year, he sold 2 000 units for $25 each. Sammy bought 2 400 units for $15 each and an inventory-take confirmed that there were 400 units in the warehouse at the end of the year. Sammy's expenses totalled $12 000.

The statements of profit or loss if the closing inventory is valued at cost and selling price will appear as follows:

Inventory valued at cost ($15 per unit)			Inventory valued at selling price ($25 per unit)		
	$	$		$	$
Revenue		50 000	Revenue		50 000
Cost of sales:			Cost of sales:		
Opening inventory	0		Opening inventory	0	
Purchases	36 000		Purchases	36 000	
	36 000			36 000	
Less: Closing inventory	(6 000)	(30 000)	Less: Closing inventory	(10 000)	(26 000)
Gross profit		20 000	Gross profit		24 000

CONTINUED

Valuing the inventory at selling price goes against three important accounting principles:

- *Prudence*: valuing the inventory at selling price has increased its value, which reduces cost of sales and increases profit. There is no guarantee that the 400 units of inventory will be sold for $25. It is possible that the item might go out of fashion or these units might be reaching a 'sell by' date and need to be sold for less.

- *Matching*: valuing the inventory at $25 effectively accounts for the profit on those units this year when they will actually be sold next year, which also contradicts:

- *Realisation*: this concept states that positive events (that make profit) cannot be accounted for until they have actually happened. Those 400 units have not been sold at a profit yet.

Eliminating 'worth' and 'selling price' leaves cost as the only real basis for valuing inventory as, in theory, it is a definite value that does not contradict the main accounting principles.

17.9 Valuation of inventory at the lower of cost and net realisable value

In most situations, inventory is valued at cost. The inventory-take establishes the quantity of each item, the business has paperwork to identify the cost per unit, and the two are multiplied together to find the total value for each product held as inventory.

However, suppose that there are items that are likely to be sold at less than cost price because they are obsolete, near their 'sell by' date or damaged. Can they still be valued at cost when concepts like prudence indicate that negative events must be accounted for as soon as they are recognised?

The principle of inventory valuation is set out in International Accounting Standard 2 (IAS 2). International Accounting Standards are generally accepted standards used when preparing and presenting financial statements. They set out the way in which items should be treated in the financial statements.

IAS 2 (see Chapter 22 for more details) states that 'inventories should be valued at the lower of cost and **net realisable value**'.

Net realisable value varies:

- *Wholesaling or retailing*: where a business buys a product, adds a mark-up or margin and sells at a higher price.

  In this case, the selling price is the net realisable value.

- *Manufacturing*: where the business is making a product involving a combination of material, labour and other costs. As the product goes through the various processes, the costs will grow.

  In this case, net realisable value is the selling price minus all future costs that will be incurred to complete it.

- *Repair or modification*: where the business has a damaged item or one that is going to need to be changed to make it saleable.

  In this case, net realisable value is the selling price minus all future costs that will be incurred in making it saleable.

IAS 2 requires that the business examines all of its inventory and applies the lower of cost and net realisable value to every type of inventory. IAS 32.2 states that if the business is not going to recover the cost of finished products (the net realisable value is lower), it can use **replacement cost** to value the materials used – in this context, the raw materials used in the manufacture of a product.

> **KEY TERM**
>
> **net realisable value:** the selling price of a product minus any costs incurred in bringing it to a saleable condition (e.g. repairs) and/or actually selling it.
>
> **replacement cost:** the amount that a business would have to pay to replace an asset according to its current worth.

WORKED EXAMPLE 8

John runs a shop selling menswear and has just completed an inventory-take. His inventory-take of suits shows:

Style	Number of suits	Cost $	Selling price $	Comments
A	45	160	240	Sells quickly.
B	20	175	280	Sells quickly.
C	15	210	180	End of line – will not be replaced when sold.
D	25	120	200	One-off purchase – will need $30 of work to make them saleable.
E	40	190	300	Five are damaged so only the trousers can be sold for $80 each.

John also had some men's shirts valued at $4 260. However, it was later discovered that this figure included some shirts that had been valued at $1 064, which was the selling price. John applies a mark-up of 40% on shirts.

Suits: The application of IAS 2 will involve considering each style of suit individually.

Style A: Inventory should be valued at the lower of cost and selling price, so we have:

   45 suits × 160 = $7 200

Style B: The same as Style A where this product is being sold for more than cost price – the valuation will be:

   20 suits × 175 = $3 500

Style C: The selling price is lower than cost, so in this case net realisable value is used:

   15 suits × 180 = $2 700

Style D: Work is needed to make the product saleable, so the net realisable value is:

   200 – 30 = $170, which is higher than the cost, so the valuation is:

   25 suits × 120 = $3 000

Style E: 35 of the suits will be valued at cost, which is lower than selling price. However, five of the suits can only be valued at the 'trousers price', which is lower than cost (it is assumed that the jackets are worthless). So the valuation is:

   (35 × 190) + (5 × 80) = 6 650 + 400 = $7 050

Shirts: The selling price is greater than cost, so the inventory value needs to be reduced so that all of the shirts are valued at cost. The cost of those shirts is:

   1 064 / 140% = $760

The total valuation of the shirts is:

   4 260 – (1 064 – 760) = 4 260 – 304 = $3 956

ACTIVITY 17.4

Theo manufactures furniture that he sells to stores. A recent inventory-take showed the following results:

Item	Number	Costs $	Selling price $	Comments
Tables	15	230	450	
Chairs	30	70	140	Incomplete – will cost $20 to finish them.
Cupboards	12	300	250	Original customer went out of business so they are being sold at a lower price to create workshop space.
Wardrobes	18	175	320	Two are not to the required standard (wrong size) and will be sold for $160 each.

Required

Calculate Theo's total inventory figure.

17.10 The advantages and disadvantages of keeping full accounting records

Keeping full accounting records has some advantages and disadvantages.

Advantages

- It allows the financial statements to be prepared quickly and soon after the year end.
- It allows for the financial statements to be prepared more often than once a year, which can help the manager run their business more efficiently.
- It helps to provide some protection against errors and possible fraud by employees. If financial statements are prepared regularly, inventory losses or cash losses can be picked up earlier and corrective action taken.
- The accuracy of the records kept can be improved.
- There may be a legal requirement to keep certain records. For example, payroll records for employees where regular payments of deductions made from their wages and salary have to be paid over to the government.

Disadvantages

- The time it takes to set them up and maintain them.
- Cost – the purchase of a computer package for accounting can be expensive and the business owner may have to go on a training course.
- Often business owners lack the knowledge of how to prepare double-entry accounts, so they employ a specialist. This adds to the business costs.

REFLECTION

How practical do you think it is using mark-ups and margin information to help find items such as purchases and inventory? What are some of the issues that might make using these techniques difficult to apply? Discuss your thoughts with another learner.

THINK LIKE AN ACCOUNTANT

The final outstanding queries

Sometimes, one of the last figures to be calculated in a set of incomplete records is the closing valuation for inventory. If the client hasn't been able to supply accurate records of purchases and sales, the accountant could have difficulty calculating the figure to include in the financial statements. If a client has used selling price to value their inventory, why is this a problem? How could the accountant deal with this issue?

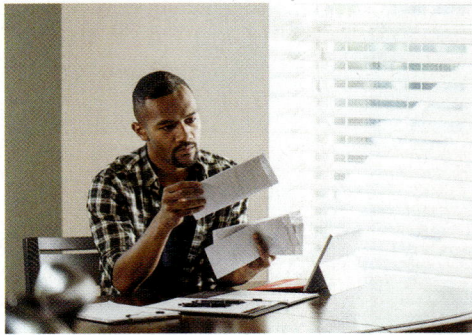

Figure 17.2: If a client has used selling price to value their inventory, why is this a problem?

EXAM-STYLE QUESTIONS

1   A business has an item of inventory that cost $600 to buy. It was damaged and $90 has to be spent on it to bring it to a saleable condition. It will then be sold for $550.

At what cost should it be valued for inventory purposes?

A $460

B $550

C $640

D $690   [1]

2   Included in the inventory of a business are three items. Details of them are:

Item	Cost	Net realisable value	Replacement cost
	$	$	$
1	6 000	4 400	5 200
2	3 100	5 700	4 000
3	4 300	4 900	5 100

What is the total value of the three items for inventory purposes?

A $11 800

B $13 400

C $14 300

D $15 000   [1]

CONTINUED

3 A business had suffered a fire and only managed to recover $4600 of inventory. Information just before the fire was:

	$
Revenue	137 940
Opening inventory	25 870
Purchases	76 900
Mark-up	90%

Required

a Calculate the value of inventory destroyed by the fire.   [5]

b Explain how inventory should be valued according to IAS 2.   [2]

c Explain the main difference between a mark-up and margin.   [3]

[Total: 10]

Practice question

4 On 1 December 2019 and 30 November 2020, Toure's assets and liabilities were as follows:

	1 Dec 19	30 Nov 20
	$	$
Fixtures and fittings (cost $30 000)	24 000	?
Motor vehicle	0	?
Inventory	12 540	10 985
Trade receivables	6 870	8 105
Bank (money in the account)	2 305	?
Trade payables	9 890	11 045
Insurance (prepaid)	655	870
Rent (accrued)	1 050	580

Toure had not kept full accounting records but provided the following information:

1 Revenue for the year was $347 040.

2 The business operates on a mark-up of 60%.

3 Discounts for the year were: allowed $1 725 and received $990.

4 A motor vehicle was bought on 31 May 2020 for $13 000 (paid by cheque).

5 Cheques amounting to $10 260 were paid in respect of rent, rates and insurance.

6 Irrecoverable debts of $2 070 were written off during the year. In addition, on 30 November 2020, Toure wanted to create an allowance for irrecoverable debts of $260.

7 Depreciation is: 20% of cost on fixtures and fittings and 25% of cost on the motor vehicle (both applied on a monthly basis).

8 Wages and salaries of $56 985 and $4 570 for electricity were paid by cheque.

CONTINUED

9   Toure took drawings of $32 600 during the year.

    a   Calculate Toure's capital at 1 December 2019. [4]

    b   Use a trading account to calculate the purchases for the year. [4]

    c   Use a purchases ledger control account to find out the amounts paid to suppliers and a sales ledger control account to find the amounts received from customers during the year. [8]

    d   Use another control account to find out the rent, rates and insurance expense during the year. [4]

    e   Prepare a bank account. [4]

    f   Calculate the depreciation for the year and the resulting accumulated depreciation on the non-current assets. [4]

    g   Produce a statement of profit or loss and a statement of financial position for Toure for the year ended 30 November 2020. [22]

SELF-EVALUATION CHECKLIST

After studying this chapter, complete a table like this:

You should be able to:	Needs more work	Almost there	Ready to move on
Construct a trading account and use mark-ups or margins to deduce missing figures.			
Use 'dummy inventory figures' to provide a starting point when you are not given *either* of the opening and closing inventory figures.			
Find the amount of inventory lost, stolen or destroyed by finding the difference between the closing inventory figure before the incident and the amount that remained.			
Value inventory in accordance with recognised accounting concepts: IAS 2 states that cost should be valued at the lower of cost and net realisable value, which prevents profit being recorded before it is realised.			
Know the advantages and disadvantages of keeping a full double-entry accounting system.			

〉 Chapter 18

Partnership accounts

This chapter covers part of syllabus sections AS Level 1.1 and 1.5

LEARNING INTENTIONS

In this chapter you will learn how to:

- explain why people form partnerships
- calculate the profit shares as set out in a partnership agreement
- apply the Partnership Act 1890
- prepare partnership capital accounts and current accounts
- prepare the partnership appropriation account to distribute profit
- prepare the statement of profit or loss and statement of financial position for a partnership
- evaluate the advantages and disadvantages of partnerships, including the disadvantage of unlimited liability.

ACCOUNTING IN CONTEXT

Mahendra's clothing company

Mahendra has run his own business manufacturing men's clothing for a number of years. He met an old friend Duleep who owns his own business manufacturing and selling men's shoes. The friends agreed that setting up their own businesses had been a good decision although being a sole trader was hard work and stressful.

The two friends discussed the possibility of joining their businesses together and forming a partnership. Both men agreed to think about it some more.

As the weeks passed, Mahendra decided he really liked the idea and wanted to discuss it some more with Duleep.

Figure 18.1: Mahendra and his friend discussed the possibility of joining their businesses together to form a partnership.

Discuss in a pair or a group:

- Why might Mahendra and Duleep find operating as sole traders hard work and stressful?

- What might be the benefits of joining together as a partnership?

- What might be some of the disadvantages of forming a partnership?

18.1 What are partnerships?

In a **partnership** there is a need to ensure that the partners are in agreement about their rights and responsibilities and how the partnership is to operate. The main issues include:

- how much capital each person will bring to the partnership

- the roles that will be carried out by each partner

- how the profits will be be shared

- how new partners will be admitted if the partnership expands

- what happens when a partner leaves, retires or dies – or the whole partnership is dissolved

- how decisions will be made and disputes resolved.

Often, a **partnership agreement** is drawn up to ensure that all partners know their rights and responsibilities and how the business will operate day-to-day. The agreement will be in writing, possibly by deed (a formal legal document), although verbal agreements are not unknown. One advantage of having a partnership agreement is that many disputes can be resolved without the need to involve the courts.

Where there is no partnership agreement, some guidance is provided by the **Partnership Act 1890**. This chapter will largely concentrate on the financial issues surrounding capital and the appropriation (sharing out) of the profit or losses. Unless the partnership agreement states otherwise, the main provisions of the Partnership Act 1890 are as follows:

- All partners are entitled to contribute equally to the capital of the partnership.

- Partners are not entitled to interest on the capital they have contributed.

- Partners are not entitled to salaries.

KEY TERMS

partnership: two or more people carrying on a business together with a view to making a profit.

partnership agreement: an agreement, usually in writing, setting out the terms of the partnership.

Partnership Act 1890: the rules that govern a partnership in the absence of a formal partnership agreement.

- Partners are not to be charged interest on their drawings.
- Partners will share profits and losses equally.
- Partners are entitled to interest at 5% per annum on loans they make to the partnership.

18.2 Advantages and disadvantages of partnerships

There are a number of advantages and disadvantages that can arise from being in a partnership:

Advantages

- The capital invested by the partners is often more than can be raised by a sole trader.
- Partners are likely to have a wider range of knowledge, experience and expertise in running a business than a sole trader.
- A partnership may be able to offer a greater range of services to its customers (or clients).
- The business does not have to close down or be run by inexperienced staff in the absence of one of the partners; the other partner(s) will provide cover.
- Losses are shared by all partners.

Disadvantages

- A partner doesn't have the same freedom to act independently as a sole trader does – decisions may have to be agreed that may be a problem if the partners have different views on how the business should develop and operate.
- Partners generally have 'unlimited liability', which means that they are personally responsible for making good on all losses and debts of the business – this can extend to their losing personal assets.
- A partner may be legally liable for the acts of the other partner(s), even if those acts were committed without all of the partners' knowledge.

18.3 The appropriation account

In partnerships, the division of the profit earned (or loss incurred) between the partners can be shown by preparing an **appropriation account**.

The **appropriation** account is a continuation of the statement of profit or loss. It begins with the profit or loss for the year brought down from the statement of profit or loss. The following methods of dividing profits between partners must be treated as appropriations of profit in the appropriation account.

If there is no partnership agreement then profits and losses are shared equally. There is no other appropriation of profit. However, if the partners draw up a partnership agreement, then the following have to be considered:

- interest on partners' drawings
- partners' salaries
- interest on partners' drawings
- interest on partners' capital
- share of the residual profit.

> **KEY TERMS**
>
> **appropriation account:** an account prepared after the statement of profit or loss that shows how the profit for the year is divided between each partner.
>
> **appropriation:** the sharing out of something – in this case, the profit made by the partnership.

> **KEY CONCEPT LINK**
>
> **Business entity:** A business is a separate legal entity from the owner of a business. The accounting records must relate only to the business and not to the personal assets and spending of the owner. How is the idea of business entity maintained when dealing with practical issues such as the appropriation of profit?

Interest on partners' drawings

Interest on drawings operates as a type of 'fine', which is designed to deter partners from taking excessive amounts of money out of the business.

Partner's salaries

A partner may carry out a large proportion of the day-to-day work and wish to be rewarded for it. One solution is for that partner to have a larger share of the profit. However, the profit share could become the 'loss share'. This would mean that the partner doing all of the work would be paying more if, through no fault of their own, a loss was made.

Choosing to be paid a **salary** means that the partner's work is recognised. It should be noted that this type of salary is an appropriation of profit and should not be confused with wages and salaries paid to employees, which is an expense in the statement of profit or loss. Partners are not employees.

Interest on partners' capital

Interest on capital recognises that if partners do not invest their capital in the partnership, their money could earn interest in some other form of investment. The partnership agreement should state the rate of interest to be paid. Interest on capital is payable even if the firm does not make a profit.

Sharing the residual profit (or loss)

If they are mentioned in a partnership agreement, all of the previous appropriations must be honoured, even if there is no profit to cover them. If there is profit left, then this is shared between the partners in the proportions laid out in the partnership agreement. If there is a deficit after the other appropriations have been made, then the profit shares become 'loss shares'.

Interest on partners' loans to the firm

A partner may have loaned the business money – rather than investing it as capital – and may expect to be repaid at a particular point in time. In this case, the interest agreed should be regarded as an expense in the statement of profit or loss. It is not an appropriation of profit.

18.4 Capital and current accounts

Many partnerships will use two types of account to record the partners' capital balances:

1   The **capital account**, which is used to record long-term capital account balances. It will include the capital introduced by each partner and any long-term capital withdrawn by them (cash or assets such as a car or equipment). As will be seen later in this chapter,

> **KEY TERMS**
>
> **interest on partners' drawings:** a charge or fine imposed on partners, usually as a percentage of drawings, designed to deter partners from removing too much money from the business.
>
> **partner's salary:** a share of the partnership profit for the year paid to one or more of the partners in addition to their normal share of the profit for the year.
>
> **interest on capital:** a share of the profit for the year usually based on a percentage of the amount of fixed capital each partner has contributed to the partnership.
>
> **capital account:** an account that shows a partner's (long-term) investment in the business.

when partnerships change or there is a major revaluation of assets, the capital account will be used to show the adjustments to each partner's investment in the business. A change that results in a partner's capital account balance increasing is recorded as a credit entry and any transactions that reduce the partner's capital account balance are recorded as debits.

2 The **current account**, which records shorter-term changes to the owners' capital including the appropriation of profit and drawings. Interest on a loan from a partner may also be recorded in this account. Any items that result in a partner's current account balance increasing is recorded as a credit entry and any items that reduce the partner's current account balance is recorded as a debit.

While it is always expected that capital accounts and current accounts will have credit balances indicating a positive amount invested in the business, it is possible for a current account to have a debit balance. This would suggest that either the partner's drawings were too large in the previous period, or that their share of the profit was too small to cover any drawings.

> **KEY TERMS**
>
> **current account:** an account that shows a partner's share from profit and loss appropriation account such as interest on capital, salaries and profit etc minus drawings and interest on drawings.

WORKED EXAMPLE 1

Wayne and Michael are in partnership as fitness instructors. The profit for the year ended 31 December 2019 was $57 000. Other information was available:

	Wayne	Michael
	$	$
Capital account balance	60 000 (credit)	80 000 (credit)
Current account balance	15 100 (debit)	7 600 (credit)
Drawings for the year	16 000	24 000

If there was no partnership agreement, then the profits would have been shared equally and the appropriation account would have looked something like this:

Appropriation account for Wayne and Michael year ended 31 December 2019		
Profit for the year		57 000
Less: Profit shares		
Wayne	28 500	
Michael	28 500	(57 000)
		0

Note: the Partnership Act 1890 states that, in the absence of a partnership agreement, profits must be shared equally.

The current accounts would look like this:

	Current accounts					
	Wayne	Michael		Wayne	Michael
	$	$		$	$
Opening balance b/d	15 100		Opening balance b/d		7 600
Drawings	16 000	24 000	Profit share	28 500	28 500
Closing balance c/d		12 100	Closing balance c/d	2 600	
	31 100	36 100		31 100	36 100
Closing balance b/d	2 600		Closing balance b/d		12 100

> **TIP**
>
> The appropriation account is shown immediately after the statement of profit or loss and uses the profit or loss for the year as its starting point.

> **TIP**
>
> Look carefully to see whether the opening balances on the current accounts are debits or credits.

> **TIP**
>
> Appropriations giving the partners profit are credit entries in the current account and those taking it away are debits.

CONTINUED

If there are more than three or four partners, it might be more convenient to show the accounts separately.

The capital accounts, in the absence of any major changes, would look like this:

	Wayne	Michael		Wayne	Michael
	$	$		$	$
Closing balance c/d	60 000	80 000	Opening balance b/d	60 000	80 000
	60 000	80 000		60 000	80 000
		12 100	Closing balance b/d	60 000	80 000

The bottom half of the statement of financial position that shows the capital and liabilities would look like this:

			$
Capital and liabilities:			
	Wayne	Michael	
Capital accounts	60 000	80 000	140 000
Current accounts	(2 600)	12 100	9 500
			149 500
Current liabilities:			
Trade payables			?
Total capital and liabilities			?

Note: Wayne has a debit balance on his current account and this is shown as a negative figure in the statement of financial position.

Suppose there had been a partnership agreement that specified the following:

1 Profits are to be shared 30:70.

2 Interest on drawings is to be charged at 6%.

3 Interest on capital is to be paid at 5%.

4 Wayne is to be paid a salary of $15 000.

> **TIP**
>
> Debit balances on current accounts are shown as negative figures on the statement of financial position.

CONTINUED

The appropriation account would have looked like this:

Appropriation account for Wayne and Michael year ended 31 December 2019		
	$	$
Profit for the year		57 000
Add: Interest on drawings:		
Wayne (6% × 16 000)	960	
Michael (6% × 24 000)	1 440	2 400
		59 400
Less: Appropriation of profit		
Interest on capital:		
Wayne (5% × 60 000)	3 000	
Michael (5% × 80 000)	4 000	(7 000)
		52 400
Salaries: Wayne	15 000	(15 000)
Profit available for distribution		37 400
Profit share (30:70):		
Wayne	11 220	
Michael	26 180	(37 400)
		0

TIP

Look to see if there is a partnership agreement. If there is, all appropriations must be made, even if there is no profit to cover it.

Note: although not a movement of cash, the interest on drawings is effectively a fine where the partners are 'putting money' back into the business and this adds to the amount of profit available for distribution.

The current accounts would look like this:

Current accounts	Wayne	Michael		Wayne	Michael
	$	$		$	$
Opening balance b/d	15 100		Opening balance b/d		7 600
Drawings	16 000	24 000	Interest on capital	3 000	4 000
Interest on drawings	960	1 440	Salaries	15 000	0
			Profit share	11 220	26 180
Closing balance c/d		12 340	Closing balance b/d	2 840	
	32 060	37 780		32 060	37 780
Closing balance b/d	2 840		Closing balance b/d		12 340

Note: the capital account will not have been affected in any way because all appropriations go through the current account.

CONTINUED

The bottom half of the statement of financial position that shows the capital and liabilities would look like this:

Capital and liabilities:			
	Wayne	Michael	
Capital accounts	60 000	80 000	140 000
Current accounts	(2 840)	12 340	9 500
			149 500
Current liabilities:			
Trade payables			?
Total capital and liabilities			?

WORKED EXAMPLE 2

Des, Gallas and Terry are partners whose profit-sharing ratio is 4:3:1. As at 1 August 2019, the balances on their capital and current accounts were as follows:

	Capital	Current
	$	$
Des	80 000	5 250
Gallas	60 000	12 100
Terry	20 000	18 350

The partnership made a profit of $12 000 during the year ended 31 July 2020 and the partners' drawings were Des $18 000, Gallas $14 200 and Terry $15 400.

The partnership agreement had specified the following:

- Interest on drawings was to be charged at 10% per year.
- A salary of $5 000 was to be paid to Des and $14 400 to Terry.
- Interest on capital to be paid at 5% per year.

CONTINUED

The appropriation account would look like this:

Appropriation account for Des, Gallas and Terry year ended 31 July 2020		
	$	$
Profit for the year		12 000
Add: Interest on drawings:		
Des (10% × 18 000)	1 800	
Gallas (10% × 14 200)	1 420	
Terry (10% × 15 400)	1 540	4 760
		16 760
Less: Appropriation of profit		
Interest on capital:		
Des (5% × 80 000)	4 000	
Gallas (5% × 60 000)	3 000	
Terry (5% × 20 000)	1 000	(8 000)
		8 760
Salaries: Des	5 000	
Terry	14 400	(19 400)
'Loss' available for distribution		(10 640)
Loss share (4:3:1):		
Des $\left(\frac{4}{8} \times 10\,640\right)$	5 320	
Gallas $\left(\frac{3}{8} \times 10\,640\right)$	3 990	
Terry $\left(\frac{1}{8} \times 10\,640\right)$	1 330	10 640
		0

Notes:

1   Even though the business has made a profit, the appropriations set out in the partnership agreement must still be honoured even after all of the profit has been distributed. The profit available for distribution has become a deficit – as if there was a loss to be distributed – and so the partners' profit shares have become 'loss shares'.

2   If the partnership had actually made a loss for the year, the appropriations would still have been honoured. The only difference would have been that the loss share figures would have been larger.

CONTINUED

The current accounts would look like this:

Current accounts							
	Des	Gallas	Terry		Wayne	Michael	Terry
	$	$	$		$	$	$
Drawings	18 000	14 200	15 400	Opening balance b/d	5 250	12 100	18 350
Interest on drawings	1 800	1 420	1 540	Interest on capital	4 000	3 000	1 000
Loss share	5 320	3 990	1 330	Salaries	5 000		14 400
Closing balance c/d			15 480	Closing balance c/d	10 870	4 510	
	25 120	19 610	33 750		25 120	19 610	33 750
Closing balance b/d	10 870	4 510		Closing balance b/d			15 480

The bottom half of the statement of financial position that shows the capital and liabilities would look like this:

Capital and liabilities:

	Des	Gallas	Terry	
Capital accounts	80 000	60 000	20 000	160 000
Current accounts	(10 870)	(4 510)	15 480	100
				160 100
Current liabilities:				
Trade payables				?
Total capital and liabilities				?

ACTIVITY 18.1

Sasha, Fatima and Roop are in partnership. The profit for the year was $14 000 and the partnership agreement specified the following.

1   Profits are to be shared 50:30:20.
2   Interest on drawings is to be charged at 8%.
3   Interest on capital is to be paid at 5%.
4   Sasha is to be paid a salary of $9 000 and Fatima is to be paid a salary of $13 000.

Other information was available:

	Sasha	Fatima	Roop
	$	$	$
Capital account balance	100 000	25 000	65 000
Current account balance	12 500 (credit)	1 500 (debit)	4 800 (credit)
Drawings for the year	14 000	10 000	18 000

Required

a   Show the appropriation account, clearly setting out how the profit has been divided up between the partners.

b   Show the current accounts for the partners, clearly setting out the entries needed to record the appropriations of the profit.

c   Show the capital section of the statement of financial position.

18.5 Partnership financial statements

Worked example 3 shows how the appropriation account and the capital/current accounts fit into the overall preparation of the financial statements.

WORKED EXAMPLE 3

Olga and Pavel are in partnership. The trial balance and other information at 31 March 2020 were as follows:

	$	$
Administration expenses	23 190	
Bank		10 555
Capital account – Olga		52 000
Capital account – Pavel		27 000
Current account – Olga		10 125
Current account – Pavel	3 720	
Drawings – Olga	15 300	
Drawings – Pavel	24 900	
Fixtures and fittings at cost	13 250	
Accumulated depreciation on fixtures and fittings		3 975
Inventory at 1 April 2019	12 435	
Loan from Olga		35 000
Office equipment at cost	18 600	
Accumulated depreciation on office equipment		8 370
Premises	90 000	
Purchases	151 670	
Sales		317 120
Selling expenses	13 090	
Trade payables		14 165
Trade receivables	25 630	
Wages and salaries (employees)	86 525	
	478 310	478 310

CONTINUED

TIP

Debit interest on a partner's loan to the firm in the statement of profit or loss and credit it to the partner's current account.

Additional information at 31 March 2020

1   Inventory is valued at $14110.

2   Selling expenses of $885 were prepaid and administrative expenses of $560 were accrued.

3   Depreciation is to be provided using the straight-line method: 10% on fixtures and 15% on office equipment.

4   The loan has a rate of interest of 8% and is not due to be repaid until 2025.

The statement of profit or loss is produced in exactly the same way as for a sole trader:

Statement of profit or loss for Olga and Pavel for the year ended 31 March 2020		
	$	$
Revenue		317120
Less: Cost of sales		
Opening inventory	12435	
Purchases	151670	
	164105	
Less: Closing inventory	(14110)	(149995)
Gross profit		167125
Less: Expenses		
Administrative expenses (23190 + 560)	23750	
Depreciation (1325 on fixtures, 2790 on equipment)	4115	
Interest on loan	2800	
Selling expenses (13090 – 885)	12205	
Wages and salaries	86525	
Total expenses		(129395)
Profit for the year		37730

The partnership agreement made the following arrangements:

1   Interest on drawings is 10%.

2   Interest on capital is 5%.

3   Pavel is to receive a salary of $18000.

4   Profits are to be shared between Olga and Pavel in the ratio of 3:2.

CONTINUED

	$	$
Profit for the year		37 730
Add: Interest on drawings:		
Olga (10% × 15 300)	1 530	
Pavel (10% × 24 900)	2 490	4 020
		41 750
Less: Appropriation of profit		
Interest on capital:		
Olga (5% × 52 000)	2 600	
Pavel (5% × 27 000)	1 350	(3 950)
		37 800
Salaries: Pavel	18 000	(18 000)
Profit available for distribution		19 800
Profit share:		
Olga $\left(\dfrac{3}{5} \times 19\,800\right)$	11 880	
Pavel $\left(\dfrac{2}{5} \times 19\,800\right)$	7 920	(19 800)
		0

The current accounts will look like this:

Current accounts						
	Olga	Pavel			Olga	Pavel
	$	$			$	$
Opening balance b/d		3 720	Opening balance b/d		10 125	
Interest on drawings	1 530	2 490	Interest on capital		2 600	1 350
			Interest on loan		2 800	
Drawings	15 300	24 900	Salaries			18 000
			Profit share		11 880	7 920
Closing balance c/d	10 575		Closing balance c/d			3 840
	27 405	31 110			27 405	31 110
Closing balance b/d		3 840	Closing balance b/d		10 575	

Note: although the interest on Olga's loan is an expense that affects the profit for the year, it has been credited to Olga's current account on the basis that it does not appear to have already been paid and so is owed to her.

TIP

Complete the double entries from the appropriation account to the partners' current accounts and transfer the end-of-year balances on the partners' drawings accounts to their current accounts. If the business does not use current accounts, then these entries will have to be made in the partners' capital accounts instead.

CONTINUED

These new current account balances can be entered into the statement of financial position:

Statement of financial position for Olga and Pavel at 31 March 2020			
Non-current assets:	Cost	Accumulated depreciation	Net book value
	$	$	$
Non-current assets:			
Premises	90 000	0	90 000
Fixtures and fittings	13 250	5 300	7 950
Office equipment	18 600	11 160	7 440
	121 850	16 460	105 390
Current assets:			
Inventory		14 110	
Trade receivables		25 630	
Other receivables		885	40 625
Total assets			146 015

Capital and liabilities:			
	Olga	Pavel	
Capital accounts	52 000	27 000	79 000
Current accounts	10 575	(3 840)	6 753
			85 753
Non-current liabilities:			
Loan – Olga			35 000
Current liabilities:			
Trade payables		14 165	
Bank overdraft		10 555	
Other receivables		560	25 280
Total capital and liabilities			146 015

ACTIVITY 18.2

Saami and Tulu are in partnership. The trial balance and other information at 31 March 2020 was as follows:

	$	$
Bank	40 172	
Capital account – Saami		47 400
Capital account – Tulu		31 800
Current account – Saami		7 175
Current account – Tulu		22 970
Drawings – Saami	19 500	
Drawings – Tulu	23 100	
Inventory at 1 April 2019	24 017	
Loan from Tulu (repayable 2026)		28 000
Motor expenses	12 828	
Motor vehicles at cost	27 400	
Accumulated depreciation on motor vehicles		8 220
Office equipment at cost	13 240	
Accumulated depreciation on office equipment		5 296
Office expenses	19 710	
Premises		
Purchases	127 601	
Sales		226 983
Trade payables		8 209
Trade receivables	36 815	
Wages and salaries (employees)	41 670	
	386 053	386 053

Additional information at 31 March 2020

1   Inventory was valued at $23 592.

2   Motor expenses of $210 were prepaid and office expenses of $545 were accrued.

3   Depreciation is to be provided on the following basis: 20% straight-line on office equipment and 30% reducing balance on motor vehicles.

4   The loan had a rate of interest of 7%.

The partnership agreement made the following arrangements:

5   Interest on drawings was 8%.

6   Interest on capital was 10%.

7   Saami was to receive a salary of $18 000.

8   Profits were to be shared between Saami and Tulu in the ratio of 1:2.

CONTINUED

Required

a   Produce a statement of profit or loss for the year ended 31 March 2020.

b   Produce an appropriation account showing clearly that the profit or loss for the year has been shared between the partners in accordance with the partnership agreement.

c   Produce the current accounts for Saami and Tulu showing clearly the balances at 31 March 2020.

d   Prepare the statement of financial position at 31 March 2020.

REFLECTION

Do you think that the advantages of being involved in a partnership (as opposed to being a sole trader), outweigh the disadvantages? Why/why not? Discuss your views with another learner.

THINK LIKE AN ACCOUNTANT

What's mine is mine

Mahendra and Duleep and their advisers are now discussing what should be included in the partnership agreement. Duleep has recently inherited $100 000 from an uncle and so could introduce far more assets, including the money, to the partnership. However, Duleep does not want to work so hard on a day-to-day basis while Mahendra is willing to take on more of the day-to-day responsibility.

It seems that there are several ways in which the profit could be appropriated – interest on capital, salaries and share of profit – but it doesn't seem likely that there would be an instant agreement. Who would be most likely to want interest on capital included? Why? Who would be most likely to want a salary? Why? Would the partners simply want a larger share of the profit? Why/why not?

Figure 18.2: Mahendra and Duleep are discussing what should be included in the partnership agreement.

EXAM-STYLE QUESTIONS

1 The following ways of appropriating the profit appeared in a partnership agreement:

i   profit share

ii   salaries

iii interest on capital

iv   interest on drawings.

The business made a loss of $21 000.

Which of these would have appeared as debit entries in the partners' current accounts?

A   i and ii

B   i and iv

C   ii and iii

D   iii and iv   [1]

2 Connery and Moore are partners who share profits and losses in the ratio of 3:1. They are allowed interest at 6% per annum on capital account balances. Other information is as follows:

	Connery	Moore
	$	$
Capital account	20 000 credit	80 000 credit
Current account	3 000 credit	5 000 debit

The partnership has made a profit for the year of $36 000. How much is Moore's total share of the profit for the year?

A $9 000

B $12 030

C $12 255

D $12 300   [1]

3 Dalton and Lasenby are in partnership. Dalton is also entitled to a salary of $12 000 per annum. Profits and losses are shared 40:60. The partnership has made a profit for the year of $39 000. How much is Dalton's total share of the profit for the year?

A $10 800

B $15 600

C $22 800

D $27 600   [1]

4 Sven and Steve are in partnership. The profit for the year was $75 000 and the partnership agreement specified the following.

A   Profits are to be shared 25:75.

B   Interest on drawings is to be charged at 10%.

C   Interest on capital is to be paid at 6%.

D   Sven is to be paid a salary of $20 000.

CONTINUED

Other information was available:

	Sven	Steve
	$	$
Capital account balance	60 000 (credit)	40 000 (credit)
Current account balance	11 000 (credit)	16 000 (credit)
Drawings for the year	16 000	23 000

Required

a   Prepare the:

    i   Appropriation account showing clearly how the profit has been divided up between the partners.   [8]

    ii   The current accounts for the partners, showing clearly the entries needed to record the appropriations of the profit.   [6]

    iii The capital section of the statement of financial position.   [4]

b   Explain *one* reason why Sven may have opted for a salary rather than a larger profit share.   [2]

c   Explain *two* benefits that Sven and Steve might gain from being in a partnership.   [4]

SELF-EVALUATION CHECKLIST

After studying this chapter, complete a table like this:

You should be able to:	Needs more work	Almost there	Ready to move on
Know that people form partnerships to combine resources or skills, share the workload and decision making or to raise more finance.			
Know how profits are shared when it is set out in a partnership agreement.			
Know where to apply the Partnership Act 1890.			
Prepare partnership capital accounts (that always has a credit balance) and current accounts (that can have either a debit or credit balance).			
Prepare the partnership appropriation account to distribute profit.			
Prepare the statement of profit or loss and statement of financial position for a partnership.			
Know the advantages and disadvantages of partnerships, including the disadvantage of unlimited liability.			

> Chapter 19

Partnership changes

This chapter covers part of syllabus section A Level 3.1

LEARNING INTENTIONS

In this chapter you will learn how to:

- calculate the revaluation of assets prior to a change in a partnership
- explain the difference between purchased and inherent goodwill
- prepare partnership capital and current accounts as a result of the creation and elimination of goodwill
- calculate changes part way through an accounting year
- prepare the necessary entries to account for the dissolution of a partnership
- evaluate business decisions based on possible changes in the composition of a partnership.

ACCOUNTING IN CONTEXT

Sweets and cakes

Nushi and Rani have been selling home-made sweets and cakes for several years and their business has been steadily expanding. They like making the products and the business is providing them with a good profit. However, they are starting to think that selling their products from a market stall in their local town is limiting their capacity for growth and that the business would never make a fortune.

They decide they need a third person, someone who shares their love of baking and who can help them to expand as well. There would be no point if the business didn't get bigger as they would have to share their profit three ways instead of two.

Discuss in a pair or a group:

What characteristics might a possible new partner have if Nushi and Rani are to consider them suitable to join their partnership?

Figure 19.1: Nushi and Rani are starting to think that selling their cakes from a market stall in their local town is limiting their capacity for growth.

19.1 How to account for the revaluation of assets in a partnership

At certain times throughout the life of the partnership, the partners may realise that some of the assets, probably land, are now well below the market value and that other assets may be overvalued. The partners will probably also do a **revaluation of assets** just before the admission of a new partner or the retirement of an existing partner. This is done either to ensure that the business a new partner is buying into is being valued fairly or that a partner leaving is fairly rewarded for their part in building up the value of the business.

A revaluation is carried out using the following steps:

Step 1 Create a **revaluation account**. This will be a temporary account, like the disposals account that will exist to help the accountant carry out a revaluation – it will disappear when the task is finished.

Step 2 Debit: Revaluation account

Credit: Asset accounts

This will remove the old valuations of the assets.

Step 3 Debit: Asset accounts

Credit: Revaluation accounts

This will insert the new valuations of the assets.

Step 4 Debit: Liability accounts

Credit: Revaluation account

This will remove the old valuations of the liabilities.

Step 5 Debit: Revaluation account

Credit: Liability accounts

This will insert the new valuations of the liabilities.

> **KEY TERMS**
>
> **revaluation of assets:** adjustments made to the value of the partnership assets to reflect their market value.
>
> **revaluation account:** an account used to assist with making the entries required to adjust the value of assets and liabilities.

The remaining balance on the revaluation account will represent a profit or loss on revaluation, which will be shared between the partners in their current profit-sharing ratio and entered into the partners' *capital* accounts. As these revaluations do not involve the movement of cash, it is traditional to regard any profit or loss from the revaluation as an addition or subtraction from long-term capital – so the current account would not be used.

Step 6   Profit on revaluation:

Debit: Revaluation account

Credit: Capital accounts *or*

For a loss on revaluation:

Debit: Capital accounts

Credit: Revaluation accounts

WORKED EXAMPLE 1

George and Shaun are in business, sharing the profits and losses in the ratio 3:2.
Their summarised statement of financial position at 31 March 2020 is as follows:

			$000	$000	
Non-current assets:					
Property				80	Revised valuation $120 000
Plant and machinery				30	Revised valuation $27 000
				110	
Current assets:					
Inventory				9	Revised valuation $8 000
Trade receivables				12	Revised valuation $10 000
Bank account				5	
Total assets				26	
				136	
Capital and liabilities					
	George	Shaun			
Current accounts	60	60		120	
Capital accounts	[4]	13		9	
				129	
Current liabilities:					
Trade payables				7	Revised valuation $6 000
Total capital and liabilities				136	

CONTINUED

In order to do this, they will create a revaluation account and make the necessary entries to remove and insert the new values. The steps are shown in brackets.

Revaluation account (1)			
	$000		$000
Property – old value (2)	80	Property – new value (3)	120
Plant and machinery – old value (2)	30	Plant and machinery – new value (3)	27
Inventory – old value (2)	9	Inventory – new value (3)	8
Trade receivables – old value (2)	12	Trade receivables – new value (3)	10
Trade payables – new value (5)	6	Trade payables – old value (4)	7
Profit on revaluation – George (6)	21		
Profit on revaluation – Shaun (6)	14		
	172		172

Notes:

1   It is possible that there could have been a major devaluation of the assets. This might result from the property losing value because an event has happened that has made the location less attractive. In this case, the balancing items would have been on the credit side of this account – representing losses on revaluation. The partners' capital accounts would have been debited in the profit sharing ratios.

2   It is also possible to cut down on the entries in the revaluation account by just posting the changes in asset and liability values. There is nothing wrong with this but, unless you are very confident, this short-cut could increase the probability of you making an error. The revaluation account would have looked like this:

Revaluation account (1)			
	$000		$000
Plant and machinery – decrease	3	Property – increase in value	40
Inventory – decrease in value	1	Trade payables – decrease	1
Trade receivables – decrease	2		
Profit on revaluation – George (6)	21		
Profit on revaluation – Shaun (6)	14		
	41		41

CONTINUED

The profit on revaluation is now credited to each partner's capital account as follows:

	George	Shaun	Capital accounts	George	Shaun
	$000	$000		$000	$000
Balance c/d	81	74	Balance b/d	60	60
			Profit on revaluation	21	14
	81	74		81	74
			Balance b/d	81	74

The revised statement of financial position looks like this:

	George	Shaun	$000	$000
Non-current assets:				
Property				120
Plant and machinery				27
				147
Current assets:				
Inventory				8
Trade receivables				10
Bank account				5
Total assets				23
				170
Capital and liabilities				
Current accounts	81	74		155
Current accounts	[4]	13		9
Trade payables				6
Total capital and liabilities				170

ACTIVITY 19.1

Ernst and Irma are in business, sharing the profits and losses in the ratio 3:1. Their summarised statement of financial position at 30 April 2020 is as follows:

	$000	$000	
Non-current assets:			
Property		125	Revised valuation $180 000
Plant and machinery		55	Revised valuation $41 000
		180	
Current assets:			
Inventory	21		Revised valuation $17 000
Trade receivables	33		Revised valuation $28 000
		54	
Total assets		234	
Capital and liabilities			

	Ernst	Irma		
Capital accounts	120	75	195	
Current accounts	3	19	22	
			217	
Current liabilities:				
Trade payables			17	Revised valuation $13 000
Total capital and liabilities			234	

Required

a Prepare a revaluation account to show the profit or loss on revaluation.

b Prepare the partners' capital accounts.

c Prepare the revised statement of financial position.

19.2 Goodwill

Using the money measurement principle, businesses are not supposed to include items in their financial statements if there is no definite valuation available. This also complies with the Prudence principle, where a business should not record any event that might yield profit or an increase in the business's value until it is realised.

However, business owners recognise that businesses often have characteristics that can be regarded as assets because they give that business a definite advantage over businesses that don't have those characteristics.

Examples of those characteristics might include:

- a good reputation
- a well-trained work force
- an experienced management team
- an established list of clients
- strong product brands.

As far as many business owners are concerned, their businesses will be worth far more than the cash value of the assets on the statement of financial position. They would certainly not want to sell their business for that amount. The excess value of a business over and above the value of items on the statement of financial position is known as **goodwill** and is regarded as an **intangible asset** because it has no physical form, unlike items such as premises or motor vehicles.

There are two types of goodwill to consider:

- **Purchased goodwill**, which arises when a business is bought. If the purchaser pays more for the business than the net book value of the net assets it buys, then the difference is goodwill. The International Accounting Standards allow this type of goodwill to be shown as an intangible non-current asset in the statement of financial position. If goodwill clearly has a fixed useful life it is depreciated each year until it is written off. If not, the asset is tested for impairment annually. This is dealt with more fully in Chapter 22.

- **Inherent goodwill**, which is goodwill that has not been paid for and so does not have an objective value. It is someone's best estimate or guess of the value of the business's goodwill. Goodwill is always accounted for:

  - when the existing partners agree to change the profit-sharing ratio

  - when an existing partner retires from the partnership

  - when a new partner is admitted into the partnership.

The reason for this is to ensure that the partners responsible for building up the goodwill are rewarded for their efforts and those who are inheriting the benefits of that goodwill pay to do so. It is assumed that the characteristics that form the basis of the goodwill will, all other things being equal, help the business to make more profit. IAS 38 (Intangible assets) was issued to provide guidance about how goodwill should be reported in financial statements (see Chapter 26).

KEY TERMS

goodwill: an intangible non-current asset. It is the difference between the purchase price of a business and a fair value of its assets and liabilities.

intangible assets: assets that do not have a physical form or cannot be 'seen'.

purchased goodwill: goodwill that has a definite valuation because money has changed hands and the excess of the amount paid over the value of the net assets is a matter of fact.

inherent goodwill: this is goodwill that has been recognised as existing, but has not been paid for. It does not appear in the financial statements.

KEY CONCEPT LINK

Money measurement: Financial accounts only include transactions that can be expressed in terms of money. Can it be claimed that the treatment of goodwill complies with the concept of money measurement? Why/why not?

WORKED EXAMPLE 2

Sukhi and Jeevan are partners who share profits and losses 2:3. On 1 July 2020 they agreed that if they were to sell their business, they would want $350 000. The assets and liabilities of the business at that time were:

	$
Premises	175 000
Fixtures and fittings	37 000
Motor vehicles	28 000
Inventory	7 845
Trade receivables	19 100
Cash and bank (debit balances)	6 015
Trade payables	5 830
Accrued expenses	765

What, in the opinion of the partners, is the value of the goodwill?

CONTINUED

The first step is to find the value of the net assets and a statement of affairs could be used to find this:

Statements of affairs – 1 July 2020		
	$	$
Assets:		
Premises		175 000
Fixtures and fittings		37 000
Motor vehicles		28 000
Inventory		7 845
Trade receivables		19 100
Cash and bank		6 015
		272 960
Liabilities:		
Trade payables	5 830	
Accrued expenses	765	(6 595)
Capital		266 365

In the opinion of the partners. Goodwill is valued at 350 000 – 266 365 = $83 635.

Given that goodwill is an asset that belongs to the partners, the entries made to record it – assuming that it is 'purchased' goodwill – would be:

Debit: Goodwill 83 635

Credit: Capital – Sukhi 33 454

Credit: Capital – Jeevan 50 161

ACTIVITY 19.2

Tomas and So-May are partners who share profits and losses equally. On 1 July 2020, they agreed that if they were to sell their business, they would want $250 000. The assets and liabilities of the business at that time were:

	$
Accrued expenses	1 105
Bank overdraft	4 090
Inventory	12 435
Land and buildings	114 000
Office equipment	27 600
Motor vehicles	19 450
Prepaid expenses	730
Trade payables	5 830
Trade receivables	19 100

Required

a   Calculate the net assets of the business.

b   Calculate the value of the goodwill.

19.3 Changes in profit-sharing ratios

Sometimes a partnership change does not involve the admission of a new partner or the retirement of an existing one. It may be that the partners have just decided to change the partnership agreement, in particular the profit shares. Some of the partners will receive a greater benefit as their profit shares increase while others will receive less benefit than before. Accounting for goodwill is a way of ensuring that those gaining from the change compensate those who are losing out. Given that it is likely that all of the partners have helped to make the partnership successful and helped to create the goodwill, this is only fair.

WORKED EXAMPLE 3

Pierce and Tim are partners who share profits and losses equally. However, on 1 January 2020, they agreed to share profits and losses on a 2:1 basis. At that date, the value of the net assets of the business was $260 000, but the partners agreed that the business was actually worth $335 000.

The capital accounts before the change were:

	$
Pierce	72 000
Tim	108 000

There are a number of steps needed to make the change:

Step 1

Calculate the amount of goodwill.

Step 2

Create a goodwill account and:

    Debit: Goodwill

    Credit: Partners' capital accounts (in the old profit-sharing ratios)

Step 3

Eliminate the goodwill by:

    Debit: Partners' capital accounts

    Credit: Goodwill (in the new profit-sharing ratios)

Step 1

In this case, goodwill is $335\,000 - 260\,000 = \$75\,000$.

Goodwill			
	$		$
Capital – Pierce (2)	37 500	Capital – Pierce (3)	50 000
Capital – Tim (2)	37 500	Capital – Tim (3)	25 000
	75 000		75 000

CONTINUED

Capital accounts	Pierce	Tim		Pierce	Tim
	$	$		$	$
Goodwill (3)	50 000	25 000	Balance b/d	72 000	108 000
Balance c/d	59 500	120 500	Goodwill (2)	37 500	37 500
	109 500	145 500		109 500	145 500
			Balance b/d	59 500	120 500

Notes:

1. Pierce has seen his profit share go up from $\frac{1}{2}$ to $\frac{2}{3}$ and in return, he has seen his capital balance fall by $72\,000 - 59\,500 = \$12\,500$.

2. Tim has seen his profit share go down from $\frac{1}{2}$ to $\frac{1}{3}$ and in return, he has seen his capital balance increase by $120\,500 - 108\,000 = \$12\,500$.

19.4 Admission of a new partner

While a new partner might be welcome because of the extra skills or finance that they bring to the business, the existing partners will almost certainly still want them to buy into the goodwill. The use of the goodwill and capital accounts is very similar to that seen with the change in the profit-sharing ratios.

Step 1   Calculate the amount of goodwill.

Step 2   Create a goodwill account and:

Debit: Goodwill

Credit: Partners' capital accounts (in the old profit-sharing ratios)

Step 3   Record the money brought in by the new partner:

Debit: Bank

Credit: New partner's capital

Step 4   Eliminate the goodwill by:

Debit: Partners' capital accounts

Credit: Goodwill (in the new profit-sharing ratios)

WORKED EXAMPLE 4

At the start of the year (1 February 2020), Avram and Roy were partners sharing profits in the ratio 60:40. Their capital and current accounts were all credit balances as follows:

	Capital	Current
	$	$
Avram	63 000	2 140
Roy	39 000	6 730

Sam joined the partnership on 1 February 2020 and it was agreed that the new profit-sharing ratio ought to be 40:30:30 (Avram:Roy:Sam).

CONTINUED

Sam contributed capital of $55 000 in the form of a cheque and it was agreed at the time of his joining the partnership that although the net assets shown on the statement of financial position amounted to $142 000, the business was worth $212 000.

The steps are shown in brackets:

(1)   Goodwill = 212 000 − 142 000 = $70 000

Goodwill				
	$			$
Capital – Avram	42 000	Capital – Avram		28 000
Capital – Roy	28 000	Capital – Roy		21 000
		Capital – Sam		21 000
	70 000			70 000

> **TIP**
>
> The admission of a new partner – just like the change in the profit-sharing ratio – will have no effect on the existing partners' current accounts.

Capital accounts	Avram	Roy	Sam		Avram	Roy	Sam
	$	$	$		$	$	$
				Balance b/d	63 000	39 000	
Goodwill (4)	28 000	21 000	21 000	Goodwill (2)	42 000	28 000	
Balance c/d	77 000	46 000	34 000	Bank (3)			55 000
	105 000	67 000	55 000		105 000	67 000	55 000
				Balance b/d	77 000	46 000	34 000

Notes:

1 Sam has effectively paid 55 000 − 34 000 = $21 000 to join the partnership, which is fair because he now has a 30% share of the profit that theoretically will be larger because of the goodwill created by Avram and Roy.

2 Avram and Roy have seen their capital balances increase – this represents compensation for reducing their share of the profits.

ACTIVITY 19.3

Alana and Harry share profits equally. Their capital account balances are $25 000 and $35 000, respectively.

Roberta joined the partnership and brings with her a cheque for $20 000. The new profit-sharing ratio is to be Alana 40%, Harry 40% and Roberta 20%.

Goodwill has been agreed at $25 000.

Required

Prepare the goodwill account and the partners' capital accounts, showing clearly the entries required as a result of the change in profit shares.

19.5 Retirement of an existing partner

It is possible that a partner may leave, retire or die. Whatever the circumstances, the steps required to record the change are the same:

Step 1 Calculate the amount of goodwill.

Step 2 Create a goodwill account and:

Debit: Goodwill

Credit: Partners' capital accounts (in the old profit-sharing ratios)

Step 3 The current account balance of the partner who is leaving is transferred to the capital account. Depending on whether the current account has a debit or credit balance, the entries will be:

Debit: Current account

Credit: Capital account

or

Debit: Capital account

Credit: Current account

Step 4 Eliminate the goodwill by:

Debit: Partners' capital accounts

Credit: Goodwill (in the new profit-sharing ratios)

Step 5 Record the entries needed to eliminate the departing partner's capital account. Depending on whether the partnership has the money to pay that partner off, there may be several possibilities:

Debit: Partner's capital account

Credit: Bank

However, it may be agreed that the capital account is converted into a loan that will be paid off over time, in which case the entries will be:

Debit: Partner's capital account

Credit: Partner loan

WORKED EXAMPLE 5

Ancelotti, Grant and Hodgson are partners who share profits 40:40:20. Their capital and current accounts on 31 May 2020 were as follows:

	Capital	Current
	$	$
Ancelotti	60 000	2 470
Grant	30 000	7 105
Hodgson	50 000	(3 570)

It came as something of a shock when Grant announced that he wished to retire. Goodwill was agreed at $75 000 and the new profit sharing ratio was to be Ancelotti 55% and Hodgson 45%.

It was decided that Grant's capital would be converted to a loan account.

TIP

Look to see whether the departing partner's current account is a debit or credit balance.

CONTINUED

Goodwill has been given and so does not need to be calculated.

Goodwill			
	$		$
Capital – Ancelotti	30 000	Capital – Ancelotti	41 250
Capital – Grant	30 000		
Capital – Hodgson	15 000	Capital – Hodgson	33 750
	75 000		75 000

> **TIP**
>
> Look to see whether the departing partner's capital will be settled by cheque (credit bank) or by conversion to a loan.

Capital accounts	Ancelotti	Grant	Hodgs		Ancelotti	Grant	Hodgs
	$	$	$		$	$	$
Goodwill (4)	41 250		33 750	Balance b/d	60 000	30 000	50 000
Loan – G (5)		67 105		Goodwill (2)	30 000	30 000	15 000
Balance c/d	48 750		31 250	Current (3)		7 105	
	90 000	67 105	65 000		90 000	67 105	65 000
				Balance b/d	48 750		31 250

Current accounts	Ancelotti	Grant	Hodgs		Ancelotti	Grant	Hodgs
	$	$	$		$	$	$
Balance b/d			3 570	Balance b/d	2 470	7 105	
Capital (3)		7 105					
Balance c/d	2 470						3 570
	2 470	7 105			2 470	7 105	
Balance b/d			3 570	Balance b/d	2 470		

Loan – Grant			
	$		$
		Capital – Grant	67 105

Note: if Grant's current account balance had been a debit balance, then the entries needed to close off his account would have been the opposite and his capital account balance that was converted to a loan would have been 60 000 − 7 105 = $52 895.

ACTIVITY 19.4

Donata, Eugene and Frederica are partners in a landscape gardening business who share profits 5:3:2. Their capital and current accounts on 31 May 2020 were as follows:

	Capital	Current
	$	$
Donata	80 000	(4 120)
Eugene	50 000	3 875
Frederica	70 000	6 090

It came as something of a shock when Donata announced that she wished to retire. Goodwill was agreed at $90 000 and the new profit sharing ratio was to be Eugene 60% and Frederica 40%.

It was decided that Donata would have all the money that she was due converted into a loan.

Required

Show the following accounts to record Donata's retirement:

a   Goodwill

b   Capital accounts

c   Current accounts

d   Donata loan account.

19.6 Appropriation of profit

It is likely that a change in a partnership will take place during the year rather than at the beginning or end. Whether it is simply a case of the same partners changing the terms of a partnership agreement, or the admission or retirement of a partner, this will create a problem concerning how the profits and losses should be appropriated.

Certain principles need to be followed:

- The situation should be treated as two separate partnerships – one before the change and one after.

- It is possible that the business might be highly seasonal in nature and so a large proportion of the profit may be made at certain times of the year and you should look for information that might tell you this. However, this information is rarely available and so the profit or loss for the year is treated as if it was made at a constant rate – in other words, the proportion of profit attributed to before and after the change should reflect the proportion of the year falling before and after the change.

- Some of the arrangements specified in the partnership agreement may refer to annual amounts – these should be fractionalised to reflect the number of months falling before and after the change.

WORKED EXAMPLE 6

Chrissi and Hugh are partners who shared profits on a 50:50 basis. Their trading year runs from 1 January to 31 December and the profit for the year was $52 000. On 1 October, Neil joined the partnership. The old and new partnership agreements made the following arrangements:

1 January – 30 September:

- Interest on drawings was 4%
- Salary: Chrissi $15 000 per year
- Interest on capital was to be 8% per year
- Profit was to be shared 50:50.

1 October – 31 December:

- Interest on drawings was 4%
- Salary: Chrissi $15 000 and Neil $10 000 per year
- Interest on capital was to be 8% per year
- Profit was to be shared Chrissi 30%, Hugh 40% and Neil 30%.

Other information was available:

	1 Jan to 30 Sep	1 Oct to 31 Dec
	$	$
Capital Account – Chrissi	40 000 credit	60 000 credit
Capital Account – Hugh	70 000 credit	80 000 credit
Capital Account – Neil	0	30 000 credit
Current Account – Chrissi	8 800 credit	?
Current Account – Hugh	10 200 credit	?
Current Account – Neil	0	?
Drawings – Chrissi	17 000	8 000
Drawings – Hugh	9 000	3 000
Drawings – Neil	0	7 000

As the partnership change took place nine months into the year and the new partnership has existed for just three months, the profit of $52 000 will be split between the two periods on a 9/12 and 3/12 basis.

TIP

If a partner has joined or left the partnership during the year, it is unlikely that they will receive anything for the period they were not there.

CONTINUED

The appropriation account is best set out in sections so that the arrangements set out by the partnership agreement can be acted on. For Chrissi, Hugh and Neil, the appropriation account would look like this:

	1 Jan to 30 Sep		1 Oct to 31 Dec		1 Jan to 31 Dec	
	$		$		$	
Profit to be appropriated		39 000		13 000		52 000
Interest on drawings [1]:						
Chrissi	(680)		(320)		(1 000)	
Hugh	(360)		(120)		(480)	
Neil	–	1 040	(280)	720	(280)	1 760
Salaries [2]:						
Chrissi	11 250		3 750		15 000	
Neil	–	(11 250)	2 500	(6 250)	2 500	(17 500)
Interest on capital [3]:						
Chrissi	2 400		1 200		3 600	
Hugh	4 200		1 600		5 800	
Neil	–	(6 600)	600	(3 400)	600	(10 000)
Profit available		22 190		4 070		26 260
Share of profit [4]:						
Chrissi	11 095		1 221		(2 084)	
Hugh	11 095		1 628		(2 477)	
Neil	–	(22 190)	1 221	(4 070)	1 221	(26 260)
		0		0		0

TIP

Look to see whether the capital account balance has changed – the effect of creating and eliminating goodwill is likely to have changed the capital account balance.

Notes:

[1] The whole percentage is applied unless the interest rate is expressed per year (in this case 4%).

[2] Fractionalised into $\frac{9}{12}$ and $\frac{3}{12}$ of the yearly amount.

[3] Fractionalised into $\frac{9}{12}$ and $\frac{3}{12}$ of the yearly amount – in this case, 6% and 2%. These are based on the capital account balance for that part of the year.

[4] This is based on the profit available after the appropriations required by the partnership agreement have been carried out. If one period has large salaries (and other appropriations) and the other does not, it is possible for one part of the year to have profit shares and the other half to have 'loss shares'.

The total columns are going to be useful for completing the current accounts, which look like this:

	Chrissi	Hugh	Neil		Chrissi	Hugh	Neil
	$	$	$		$	$	$
Drawings	25 000	12 000	7 000	Balance b/d	8 800	10 200	
Interest on drawings	1 000	480	280	Salaries	15 000		2 500
				Interest on capital	3 600	5 800	600
				Profit share	12 316	12 723	1 221
Balance c/d	13 716	16 243		Balance c/d			2 959
	39 716	28 723	7 280		39 716	28 723	7 820
Balance b/d			2 959	Balance b/d	13 716	16 243	

19.7 The dissolution of a partnership

The partners may come to a point in time when they no longer wish to carry on trading, and in this situation they face two choices:

1 *Realisation*: the partnership is bought out by another business and all assets and liabilities are transferred over to that business. It is possible that the partners will take over some of the assets and might pay off some of the liabilities. This possibility will be dealt with in Chapter 28.

2 *Dissolution*: in this situation, the assets are sold off to a number of different people and the proceeds are used to pay off liabilities such as the trade payables. The balance in the bank account is shared out between the partners who then go their separate ways. This is the situation that we are going to consider and much of what needs to be done involves the creation of a **realisation account**.

There are several steps involved in the dissolution of a partnership:

Step 1 All the assets to be sold are debited to the realisation account at their book values. The entries are:

Debit: Realisation account

Credit: Assets accounts

Step 2 Any money received from the sale of those assets is recorded as:

Debit: Bank

Credit: Realisation account

Step 3 All the liabilities to be paid are credited to the realisation account at their book values. The entries are:

Debit: Liability accounts

Credit: Realisation account

Step 4 Any money paid out to settle liabilities is recorded as:

Debit: Realisation account

Credit: Bank

Step 5 If a partner decides to take an asset (for example, a car) then a valuation for that asset must be agreed by the partners. That valuation will require the following entries:

Debit: Partner's capital account

Credit: Realisation account

Step 6 Any expenses arising from the dissolution – this would include such things as legal or accountancy fees – need to be paid for. The entries for this are:

Debit: Realisation account

Credit: Bank

Step 7 There are two possibilities at this point. Either there will be a profit or a loss on dissolution and entries are needed to close off the realisation account:

1 A profit on dissolution will involve the following entries:

Debit: Realisation account

Credit: Partners' capital accounts

2 A loss on dissolution will involve the following entries:

Debit: Partners' capital accounts

Credit: Realisation account

KEY TERMS

dissolution of a partnership: the process by which all the assets of the partnership are sold and liabilities paid when the partnership ceases trading.

realisation account: an account prepared when a partnership is ceasing to trade, to record the book value of the assets and liabilities and how much is received for them if sold, or paid out in respect of liabilities.

In both cases, the profit or loss will be split in accordance with each partner's profit share.

Step 8 The balances on the partners' current accounts are transferred to their capital accounts. If the current account has a credit balance, the entries are:

Debit: Current accounts

Credit: Capital accounts

Step 9 The balances on their capital accounts are then closed by making the following entries:

Debit: Capital accounts

Credit: Bank

It is possible that a partner may have a debit balance on their capital account. In which case, they would need to pay money into the partnership. The entries in this situation would be:

Debit: Bank

Credit: Partner's capital account

If everything has gone to plan, both accounts should show a zero balance.

The closing or dissolving of a partnership business will now be illustrated in Worked example 7.

TIP

Make sure that the partners' capital accounts are closed by a transfer to or from the bank account as, in reality, this is the most common practice.

WORKED EXAMPLE 7

Dean and Mikali are in business, sharing the profits and losses equally. Their summarised statement of financial position at 31 March 2020 is as follows:

			$000	$000
Non-current assets:				
Property				120
Motor vehicles				35
				155
Current assets:				
Inventory			27	
Trade receivables			19	
Bank			5	51
Total assets				206
Capital and liabilities:				
	Dean	Mikali		
Capital accounts	80	95		175
Current accounts	[2]	11		9
				184
Current liabilities:				
Trade payables				22
Total capital and liabilities				206

CONTINUED

After a series of major disputes, the partners decided to dissolve the business:

1   The property was sold for $152 000.
2   Dean agrees to take one of the vehicles at a value of $7 000. The remaining vehicles are sold for $32 000.
3   The inventory is sold for $25 000 and the partners collected $18 000 from the trade receivables.
4   They pay their trade suppliers $22 000.
5   The expenses of dissolving the partnership amounted to $1 000.

The dissolution of a partnership will be carried out by creating a Realisation account and using journals to transfer or remove balances from the ledgers.

Step 1: Remove the assets of the business. The journals for this will be:

	$000	$000
Realisation account	120	
Property		120
Realisation account	35	
Motor vehicles		35
Realisation account	27	
Inventory		27
Realisation account	19	
Trade receivables		19

Step 2: Record the receipts from the disposal of those assets. The journals for this will be:

	$000	$000
Bank (sale of property)	152	
Realisation account		152
Bank (sale of vehicles)	32	
Realisation account		32
Bank (sale of inventory)	25	
Realisation account		25
Bank (from trade receivables)	18	
Realisation account		18

Step 3: Remove the liabilities of the business. The journals will be:

	$000	$000
Trade payables	22	
Realisation account		22

> **TIP**
>
> When dealing with a dissolution, it is worth producing all of the relevant ledger accounts so that you can follow all of the debits and credits through and reduce the likelihood of errors. It will also make it easier to find the problem if you do end up with a difference.

CONTINUED

Step 4: Record the money paid to settle those liabilities. The journal will be:

	$000	$000
Realisation account	22	
Bank		22

Step 5: Record the removal of any assets by the owners – in this case, Dean is taking a motor vehicle valued at $7 000. The journal will be:

	$000	$000
Capital – Dean	7	
Realisation account		7

Step 6: Record the expenses incurred in dissolving the partnership. The journal will be:

	$000	$000
Realisation account	1	
Bank		1

Step 7: Record the profit or loss made on the dissolution. This is identified by examining the difference between the value of the debit entries in the realisation account and the credit entries. If the debit side is larger, the partners have made a loss on the dissolution, which will reduce their capital account balances. In this case, it is the credit side that is larger which means a profit has been made on the dissolution and as seen in the following journal, the result is an increase in the partners' capital account balances.

	$000	$000
Realisation account	16	
Realisation account	16	
Capital account – Dean		16
Capital account – Mikali		16

The realisation account should now have a zero balance.

Step 8: The partners' capital account balances are transferred to their capital accounts. The journal will be:

	$000	$000
Capital account – Dean	2	
Current account – Dean		2
Capital account – Mikali	11	
Current account – Mikali		11

Step 9: The partners' capital account balances are paid off from the bank account. The journal will be:

	$000	$000
Capital account – Dean	87	
Bank		87
Capital account – Mikali	122	
Bank		122

CONTINUED

The partners' capital accounts and the bank account should now have a zero balance.

Realisation account	$000		$000
Property (1)	120	Bank – sale of property (2)	152
Motor vehicles (1)	35	Bank – vehicles (2)	32
Inventory (1)	27	Bank – sale of inventory (2)	25
Trade receivables (1)	19	Bank – trade receivables (2)	18
Bank – trade payables (4)	22	Trade payables (3)	22
Bank – expenses of sale (6)	1	Capital Dean – vehicle (5)	7
Profit on dissolution:			
Dean (7)	16		
Mikali (7)	16		
	256		256

Capital accounts	Dean	Mikali		Dean	Mikali
	$000	$000		$00	$000
Current accounts (8)	2		Balance b/d	80	95
Vehicle taken (5)	7		Current accounts (8)		11
Bank (9)	87	122	Profit on realisation (7)	16	16
	96	122		96	122

The bank account can now be completed to show the complete closure of the partnership:

Bank account	$000		$000
Opening balance	5	Trade payables (4)	22
Sale of property (2)	152	Expenses of sale (6)	1
Sale of vehicles (2)	32	Capital – Dean (9)	87
Sale of inventory (2)	25	Capital – Mikali (9)	122
Trade receivables (2)	18		
	232		232

REFLECTION

Do you think that the idea of creating and eliminating goodwill when a new partner is admitted or an old one leaves is a good idea? Why/why not?

THINK LIKE AN ACCOUNTANT

A lack of goodwill over goodwill

Gabriel and Raphael have been in partnership selling fishing equipment for a number of years. They are in negotiations with Michael regarding his admission to the partnership. Michael possesses a number of skills that would benefit the partnership as well as $100 000 that he is prepared to invest as capital.

Negotiations had been going well until the subject of goodwill was raised. All three agree that the business is worth more than the value of the net assets stated in the statement of financial position, but the valuations placed on that goodwill by Gabriel, Raphael and Michael are so far apart that it seems reaching an agreement quickly is unlikely. In fact, what had started out as a friendly discussion has definitely started to turn unpleasant. What characteristics might the business possess that has generated goodwill? Are Gabriel and Raphael likely to place a high or low value on that goodwill? Why? Is Michael likely to place a high or low value on that goodwill? Why?

Figure 19.2: Gabriel and Raphael have been in partnership selling fishing equipment for a number of years.

EXAM-STYLE QUESTIONS

1 The summarised statement of financial position for A and B in partnership is given.

	$		$
Non-current assets	72 000	Capital accounts	
Net current assets	28 000	Partner A	64 000
		Partner B	36 000
	100 000		100 000

A and B shared profits and losses in the ratio of 3:2 and have decided to revalue some of the assets. Some non-current assets that were valued at $25 000 are to be valued at $40 000 and some of the current assets that were valued at $17 000 are now to be valued at $14 000.

What is the new balance on A's capital account?

A $56 800

B $58 000

C $70 000

D $71 200

[1]

CONTINUED

2 D and E are partners, sharing profits and losses equally. Their capital balances are: D $30 000 and E $40 000. F joins the partnership, paying in a cheque for $50 000. Goodwill is agreed at $21 000 for her share of the goodwill. Profits and losses are to be shared equally between D, E and F. Which of the following shows the partners' capital accounts on the admission of F as a partner?

	D	E	F
	$	$	$
A	30 000	40 000	50 000
B	33 500	43 500	43 000
C	37 000	47 000	36 000
D	51 000	61 000	28 000

[1]

3 K, L and M were partners, sharing profits and losses equally. K retired and L and M continued in partnership, sharing profits and losses equally. Goodwill was valued at $75 000 but was not shown in the books. Which entries will record the adjustments for K's retirement in the books?

	Capital accounts		
	K	L	M
	$	$	$
A	No adjustment	Credit 37 500	Credit 37 500
B	Credit 25 000	Debit 12 500	Debit 12 500
C	Debit 25 000	Credit 12 500	Credit 12 500
D	No adjustment	Debit 37 500	Credit 37 500

[1]

4 Auric and Gert are in partnership, sharing the profits and losses equally. Their statement of financial position at 31 May 2020 is as follows:

Statement of financial position at 31 May 2020	
	$000
Non-current assets:	
Property	80
Motor vehicles	35
	115
Current assets:	
Inventory	17
Trade receivables	21
	38
Total assets	153
Capital and liabilities:	
Capital accounts:	
Auric	60
Gert	70
	130

CONTINUED

Current liabilities:	
Trade payables	16
Bank overdraft	7
	23
Total capital and liabilities	153

The partners did not operate current accounts.

Additional information

1   On 1 November 2016, they admit Sakata as a partner. The new profit sharing ratio is to be Auric 40%, Gert 40% and Sakata 20%.

2   Sakata will pay $60 000 into the bank as his capital.

3   The goodwill is valued at $50 000. No goodwill account is to appear in the books.

4   Auric and Gert also revalue the assets at the same date. The property is to be revalued at $145 000, the inventory at $14 000 and the trade receivables at $19 000.

Required

a   Explain why it is necessary to revalue the assets of a partnership when a new partner is admitted.   [3]

b   Prepare the following:
   i   revaluation account   [4]
   ii   partners' capital accounts after the revaluation of assets and introduction of Sakata as a partner have taken place.   [6]

c   Explain your treatment of goodwill in the partners' capital accounts on the admission of Sakata as a partner.   [3]

SELF-EVALUATION CHECKLIST

After studying this chapter, complete a table like this:

You should be able to:	Needs more work	Almost there	Ready to move on
Account for the revaluation of assets prior to a change in a partnership – usually the admission or retirement of a partner.			
Explain the difference between purchased (has a definite valuation because money has changed hands) and inherent goodwill (acknowledged by the business owner to exist).			
How to prepare partnership capital and current accounts as a result of the creation and elimination of goodwill arising because of a change in profit-sharing ratios or the admission/retirement of a partner.			
Account for changes part-way through an accounting year – most notably the effect on the appropriation of profit.			
Make the necessary entries to account for the dissolution of a partnership.			
Evaluate business decisions based on possible changes in the composition of a partnership.			

Chapter 20

Manufacturing accounts

This chapter covers part of syllabus section A Level 3.1

LEARNING INTENTIONS

In this chapter you will learn how to:

- prepare a manufacturing account
- identify the three different classes of inventory
- explain that there may be a profit charged when goods are transferred from the factory to finished goods inventory
- calculate the value of finished goods inventory to use in the statement of financial position.

ACCOUNTING IN CONTEXT

Accounting for chocolate

Julia has been working in the accounts department of a limited company that manufactures chocolates for two weeks.

Julia has spent much of her time checking invoices against purchase orders, delivery notes and price lists to make sure that the company has not been overcharged before entering the details into the purchase daybook. She is surprised by how much cocoa, milk, fruit and nuts the company buys.

However, at college she has learned about the statement of profit or loss and the statement where the cost of sales includes 'purchases'. When she looked at the financial statements for the company for the previous year, there didn't seem to be any mention of purchases in these accounts – where did the purchases go that she was recording on a day-to-day basis?

Figure 20.1: Julia is surprised by how much cocoa, milk, fruit and nuts the company buys.

Discuss in a pair or a group:

- How does this company differ from most of the businesses that you have encountered when studying the statement of profit or loss?

- Why does her employer not have a 'purchases' figure in the cost of sales part of the company's statement of profit or loss?

20.1 What is a manufacturing account?

Many businesses manufacture their own products and this involves several different types of cost being brought together to arrive at the total cost of production. Those costs are put into three main categories – materials, labour and overheads.

Manufacturing accounts are prepared before the statement of profit or loss. The cost of goods manufactured is transferred to the trading section of the statement of profit or loss and replaces the figure for purchases that would be found if the business is buying and selling wholly completed goods.

The **manufacturing account** has to deal with the fact that products may take time to produce and it is quite possible that the business may have three types of inventory:

- **raw materials**

- **work-in-progress**

- **finished/completed goods**

The manufacturing account also has to deal with the fact that when a business makes a product, it must ensure that both direct costs and indirect costs are accounted for.

Direct costs are those that can be linked to the making of the product or the provision of a service. In the case of the chocolate manufacturer, these might include:

- materials – the cocoa, milk, fruit, nuts, cardboard and packaging that make up the chocolates

- production-line workers – the people involved in the manufacturing process itself.

Indirect costs are those costs that are incurred by the business but that are not directly involved in the product itself. Examples might include:

KEY TERMS

manufacturing account: an account used to record the various direct and indirect costs associated with making a product.

raw materials: any materials that will form part of the product but have not yet had anything done to them.

work-in-progress: product that has been started but still requires further work to put it into a state of completeness where it is ready to be sent to the customer.

finished/completed goods: product that is ready to be sent to the customer.

- indirect materials – cleaning materials and lubricants used on the machinery

- labour – managers, supervisors, maintenance or administration staff

- overheads – factory rent and rates, heat and light, depreciation of non current assets and insurance.

The manufacturing account is structured to present the direct and indirect costs in a particular way. However, there are many ways in which management accountants record and use cost information to make decisions. Some of these will be examined in detail in Chapters 32–36.

20.2 How to prepare a manufacturing account

If a full trial balance is provided, then it is essential that all of the items relating to production are identified. The manufacturing account is then prepared as shown in Worked example 1.

WORKED EXAMPLE 1

Gayle is a manufacturer. The following had been extracted from her trial balance at 30 April 2020:

		$
Closing inventory:	raw materials	16 000
	work-in-progress	19 400
	finished goods	21 350
Direct labour (manufacturing wages)		458 900
Factory overheads (indirect costs)		137 500
Opening inventory:	raw materials	16 500
	work-in-progress	18 200
	finished goods	20 600
Purchase of raw materials		257 300
Purchase returns of raw materials		2 000
Royalties		7 500
Revenue		1 200 000

Manufacturing account for Gayle for year ended 30 April 2020		
	$	$
Opening inventory of raw material		16 500
Add: Purchases of raw materials	257 300	
Less: Purchase returns of raw materials	(2 000)	255 300
Less: Closing inventory of raw materials		(16 000)
Cost of raw materials consumed [1]		255 800
Direct labour		458 900
Royalties		7 500
Prime cost [2]		722 200
Factory overheads		137 500
Factory manufacturing cost [3]		859 700
Add: Opening work-in-progress	18 200	
Less: Closing work-in-progress	(19 400)	(1 200)
		858 500
Factory cost of completed goods [4]		

> **TIP**
>
> It is important to memorise the structure of the manufacturing account including the main headings.

CONTINUED

Notes:

[1] *Cost of raw materials consumed* is calculated in the same way as the 'cost of sales' figure in the trading account. It is possible that you might see carriage inwards added to purchases. It is vital that only items relating to raw materials are included here.

Note: any indirect materials like grease, lubricants or cleaning supplies would be included in the factory overheads.

[2] **Prime cost** refers to all of the **direct costs** incurred during the period. You will always see materials and direct (or manufacturing) labour. Royalties are regarded as part of prime cost if Gayle has to pay someone on a 'per unit' basis for using their design, but if it were a fixed amount per period it might be regarded as an **indirect cost**.

If there is a reference to direct expenses, they should be included in the prime cost.

[3] **Factory overheads** are added to the prime cost – be careful that you don't subtract them because the manufacturing account looks a bit like a statement of profit or loss!

[4] **Factory cost of completed goods** – we are now converting the costs incurred during the period into all of the costs relating to items finished during the period. The opening work-in-progress was finished this year and so is added while the closing work-in-progress will be completed next year. Remember, this year's closing work-in-progress will be next year's opening work-in-progress.

The factory cost of completed goods is the item that will replace the purchases figure that the wholesaler or retailer would use. In this case, the first part of the statement of profit or loss would look like this:

	$	$
Revenue		1 200 000
Less: Cost of sales		
Opening inventory (finished goods)	20 600	
Factory cost of completed goods	858 500	
	879 100	
Closing inventory (finished goods)	(21 350)	(857 750)
Gross profit		342 250

KEY TERMS

prime cost: the direct costs of making the product.

direct costs: the costs that are involved in the actual manufacture of the product.

indirect costs: costs that relate to the factory but are not directly associated with the product itself.

factory overheads: indirect costs incurred in the factory that are not directly related to the product itself.

factory cost of completed goods: all of the costs associated with the product actually completed during the accounting year.

ACTIVITY 20.1

Romesh is a manufacturer. The following had been extracted from his trial balance at 30 April 2020:

		$
Closing inventory:	raw materials	48 340
	work-in-progress	20 119
	finished goods	38 461
Direct labour (manufacturing wages)		750 199
Factory overheads (indirect costs)		399 245
Opening inventory:	raw materials	49 780
	work-in-progress	23 640
	finished goods	40 210
Purchase of raw materials		849 789
Purchase returns of raw materials		3 500
Royalties		19 000
Revenue		3 241 000

Required

a   Prepare the manufacturing account for Romesh for the year ended 30 April 2020.

b   Prepare the trading account for Romesh for the year ended 30 April 2020, showing clearly the gross profit.

20.3 Costs relating to the whole business

A manufacturing business might have a factory area that concentrates on manufacturing and an office area that deals with the administrative function. This becomes a problem if the business incurs costs that relate to the whole business and there is no detail about how much of those costs relate to which part of the organisation.

There are good reasons why we want to ensure that the factory and offices each get the right amount of cost, including:

- it will give a better idea of how efficiently each part of the business is controlling its costs

- it will give an accurate figure for production costs that may help business owners to set selling prices or decide whether making the products is likely to be profitable.

Where possible, costs should be allocated to the appropriate part of the business. If this is not possible, then accountants will apportion (or share out) those costs between the different areas using techniques that you will encounter in the management accounting section of this book.

Costs that relate to the factory will appear in the manufacturing account and those that relate to the administrative parts of the business will appear in the 'Less: Expenses' section of the statement of profit or loss.

WORKED EXAMPLE 2

Moin is a manufacturer who had the following costs:

- Rent and rates: $34 500 had been paid in total of which $1 800 was a prepayment. The factory occupies 60% of the business premises, the offices 40%.

  Rent and rates expense = 34 500 − 1 800 = $32 700

  Factory overhead = 60% × 32 700 = $19 620 – this will go into the manufacturing account

  Office expense = 40% × 32 700 = $13 080 – this will go into the statement of profit or loss

- Depreciation of office equipment: Office equipment is depreciated at a rate of 20% per year using the straight-line method.

  Office equipment at cost is $54 100 and the accumulated depreciation is $37 800.

  A $\frac{1}{5}$ of the office equipment is at the factory and $\frac{4}{5}$ is in the main offices.

  Depreciation expense = 20% × 54 100 = $10 820

  Factory overhead = $\frac{1}{5}$ × 10 820 = $2 164

  Office expense = $\frac{4}{5}$ × 10 820 = $8 656

Note: if you are producing accounts for a manufacturing business, you should list all of the individual expenses separately rather than trying to combine them into one figure.

20.4 Factory profit (transfer pricing)

Some businesses will treat different parts of their operations as separate entities where each area is expected to operate as if it were a profit-making organisation. The factory may effectively sell the product it makes to a retailing part of the business who sells to the customers. The price charged by the factory (the **transfer price**) will exceed the cost of production. The profit made by the factory is the **factory profit**.

Organisations will use transfer pricing for a number of reasons including:

- Giving recognition to the factory for its contribution towards helping the business to make a profit. There may be bonus schemes attached to the level of factory profit so the workers are rewarded for good performance.
- If the factory is in a different country (where tax levels are lower) from the administration part of the business, transferring the profit will reduce the overall amount of tax payable.

KEY TERMS

transfer price: the price that one part of an organisation sells its product (or service) to another part of that organisation.

factory profit: the amount added to the factory cost of completed goods to arrive at the transfer price.

KEY CONCEPT LINK

Money measurement: Financial accounts only include transactions that can be expressed in terms of money. Do you think that the idea of transfer pricing promotes the concept of true and fair view or distorts it? Why/why not?

There are problems that arise that may actually conflict with some of the basic accounting principles. These problems include:

- The factory profit will, potentially, appear in the manufacturing account but nowhere else. It will increase the cost of sales in the statement of profit or loss, which will drive down the gross profit and profit for the year for the whole business.
- The closing inventory of finished goods that appears in the statement of financial position will contain 'unrealised profit' – it won't be stated at the original cost to the business as a whole – and this will reduce cost of sales and artificially increase the gross profit and profit for the year.

Clearly, adjustments need to be made to deal with both of these issues.

- *Factory profit*: Adding factory profit is effectively increasing costs and so is, in effect, a debit in the manufacturing account. If that amount is added back to the profit in the statement of profit or loss – effectively a credit – then the overall profit figure is restored to what it would have been if there had been no factory profit.

- *Inventory*: To satisfy the realisation concept, the profit element of any closing inventory needs to be removed so that items in stock at the end of the year are valued at the original cost. It is also essential that the inventory figure included in the statement of financial position be adjusted.

WORKED EXAMPLE 3

Gabrielle is a manufacturer who produced a manufacturing account for the year ended 31 March 2020. The business applies a mark-up of 20%.

	$000
Opening inventory of raw material	27
Purchases of raw materials	412
Less: Closing inventory of raw materials	(23)
Cost of raw materials consumed	416
Direct labour	229
Prime cost	645
Factory overheads	371
Factory manufacturing cost	1 016
Add: Opening work-in-progress	134
Less: Closing work-in-progress	(140)
Factory cost of completed goods	1 010
Factory profit (20% mark-up) [1]	202
Transfer price of completed goods	1 212

Note:

[1] If the business had used a **profit margin** of 20%, then the cost of $1 010 000 would represent the remaining 80% of the transfer price. This means that the transfer price would be:

1 010 000 / 80% = $1 262 500

The factory profit is 1 262 500 – 1 010 000 (or 20% of $1 262 500) = $252 500

The transfer price of completed goods is transferred into the statement of profit or loss.

	$000	$000
Revenue		1 568
Less: Cost of sales		
Opening inventory (finished goods)	245	
Factory cost of completed goods	1 212	
	1 457	
Closing inventory (finished goods)	(276)	(1 181)
Gross profit		387
Less: Expenses		(273)
Profit on trading [2]		114
Add: Factory profit [3]	202	
Less: Unrealised profit on closing inventory [4]	(46)	156
Profit for the year		270

CONTINUED

Notes:

[2] Profit on trading is the profit that has been made from the trading activity and does not include factory profit.

[3] Factory profit has already been calculated but it could have been worked out using the transfer price. Care needs to be taken about whether the business has used a mark-up or margin:

Mark-up: the profit is:

$$\frac{20}{120} \times 1\,212 = 202$$

Margin: the adjustment is 20% of $1\,212 = 242.4$

[4] The inventory needs to have the factory profit removed and the approach is exactly the same as in [3]. As this is a 20% mark-up, the calculation is:

$$\frac{20}{120} \times 276 = 46$$

> **TIP**
>
> When dealing with transfer pricing, make sure that you know whether you are dealing with a mark-up or a margin.

20.5 Adjusting for unrealised profit included in the inventories of finished goods

Unrealised holding gain needs to be removed from the value of the inventory and treated as a simple subtraction from profit. There is some bookkeeping required to account for this adjustment in the ledgers, as can be seen in Worked example 4.

WORKED EXAMPLE 4

Hughgine is a manufacturer who started trading on 1 May 2017 and has 30 April as his year end. The transfer pricing mark-up has always been 30%. His inventory figures (including the factory profit) were:

	Opening inventory	Closing inventory
	$000	$000
Year ended:		
30 April 2018	0	156
30 April 2019	156	208
30 April 2020	208	195

The closing inventory at the end of one year is the opening inventory for the next, but we need to calculate the unrealised holding profit relating to the inventory value at the end of each year.

Year ended: **Unrealised holding profit $000**

30 April 2018 $\left(\dfrac{30}{130}\right) \times 156 = 36$

30 April 2019 $\left(\dfrac{30}{130}\right) \times 208 = 48$

30 April 2020 $\left(\dfrac{30}{130}\right) \times 195 = 45$

The first step is to create a provision for unrealised profit account. This records a reduction in an asset – rather like the allowance for irrecoverable debts account. This means that the 'balance b/d' figure will always be a credit.

In 2018 (the first year), the entries made to record the removal of the profit element from the inventory valuation and reduce the value of the asset are:

Debit: Statement of profit or loss	36
Credit: Provision for unrealised profit account	36

The account is then balanced off as for any normal ledger.

In 2019 (the second year) the entries need to record the fact that we already have a provision and just need to adjust it. In this case, the provision is increasing and so the entries are:

Debit: Statement of profit or loss	12
Credit: Provision for unrealised profit account	12

Note: the value reflects the amount of the increase as we are just looking to adjust the amount to the required closing value.

In 2020 (the third year) the entries need to again record the fact that we already have a provision and just need to adjust it. However, in this case, the provision is decreasing and so the entries are:

Debit: Provision for unrealised profit account	3
Credit: Statement of profit or loss	3

Rather like a reduction in the allowance for irrecoverable debts, a reduction in the downgrading of an asset can be regarded as 'good news' and so the entry in the statement of financial position is a credit – we are increasing the profit.

The full provision for unrealised profit account looks like this.

Provision for unrealised profit account					
Debit			**Credit**		
		$			$
30 Apr 18	Balance c/d	36	30 Apr 18	Statement of profit or loss	36
		36			36
			1 May 18	Balance b/d	36
30 Apr 19	Balance c/d	48	30 Apr 18	Statement of profit or loss	12
		48			48
30 Apr 18	Statement of profit or loss	3	1 May 19	Balance b/d	48
30 Apr 20	Balance c/d	45			
		48			48
			1 May 20	Balance b/d	45

ACTIVITY 20.2

Esther is a manufacturer who started trading on 1 May 2017 and has 30 April as her year end. The transfer pricing mark-up has always been 25%. Her inventory figures (including the factory profit) were:

	Opening inventory	Closing inventory
Year ended:	$000	$000
30 April 2018	0	350
30 April 2019	350	325
30 April 2020	325	380

Required

a   Calculate the amount of unrealised profit contained within the inventory values at the end of each year.

b   Prepare the provision for unrealised profit account for Esther for each of the three years ended 30 April 2018, 30 April 2019 and April 2020.

20.6 Manufacturing statement of financial position

For a manufacturing business, the statement of financial position is prepared in the same way as for businesses that buy and sell goods. However, there are two areas that need to be considered:

Non-current assets: this will be presented in the same way as any other business.

Inventories: there are now three categories of inventory:

- raw materials
- work-in-progress
- finished goods at cost.

It is vital that the unrealised profit be removed from the inventory valuation.

The current assets section might look like this:

	$000	$000
Current assets:		
Inventory:		
Materials		37
Work in progress		23
Finished goods	42	
Less: Unrealised profit	(12)	30
		90

ACTIVITY 20.3

Ezekiel is a manufacturer. The following is a list of balances at 30 June 2020 after the end of year adjustments, and the manufacturing account and the statement of profit or loss have been produced:

	$000
Accrued expenses	5
Allowance for irrecoverable debts	3
Bank loan (repayable by 2028)	654
Bank overdraft	19
Capital at 1 July 2019	321
Closing inventory: raw materials	41
work-in-progress	23
finished goods (at transfer price)	56
Drawings	80
Office equipment: at cost	82
Office equipment: accumulated depreciation	54
Plant and equipment: at cost	345
Plant and equipment: accumulated depreciation	216
Premises: at cost	760
Premises: accumulated depreciation	38
Prepaid expenses	8
Profit for the year	95
Provision for unrealised profit	16
Trade payables	36
Trade receivables	62

Required

Produce the statement of financial position for Ezekiel at 30 June 2020.

REFLECTION

What was the part of this topic that you found the most difficult or regularly got wrong?

How are you going to address these difficulties? Discuss your strategies with another learner.

THINK LIKE AN ACCOUNTANT

Transfer pricing and inventory valuation

Julia has just got used to the general idea that manufacturing businesses do not operate like those involved in normal retailing or wholesaling, where they just buy and sell goods. However, Julia can't understand the idea of transfer pricing.

Why would the factory part of an organisation add a mark-up to its cost of production and sell the goods at a profit to another part of the same organisation that then spends time removing that profit element from the value of its inventory? It doesn't seem at all logical! Why do businesses bother with transfer pricing? Do you think they should? Why/why not?

Figure 20.2: Manufacturing businesses do not operate in the same way as most wholesale and retailers.

EXAM-STYLE QUESTIONS

1   A company uses transfer pricing. The cost of completed goods was $1 440 000 and the transfer price was $1 920 000. What approach was being used to find the transfer price?

   A   a mark-up of 30%   C   a margin of 20%

   B   a mark-up of 35%   D   a margin of 25%   [1]

2   The following items can appear in the accounts of a manufacturing company:

   i   carriage inwards

   ii   carriage outwards

   iii   depreciation of warehouse machinery

   iv   provision for unrealised profit

   Which items will be included in the manufacturing account?

   A   i and ii

   B   i and iii

   C   ii and iii

   D   ii and iv   [1]

3   A manufacturing company started trading on 1 June 2019. The transfer price of its completed goods was $736 000 where the company uses a mark-up of 15%. 30% of these completed goods were in stock at the end of the year.

   Which of the following statements is true?

   A   factory profit is $96 000, unrealised profit is $28 800

   B   factory profit is $96 000, unrealised profit is $33 120

   C   factory profit is $110 400, unrealised profit is $28 800

   D   factory profit is $110 400, unrealised profit is $33 120   [1]

CONTINUED

4 The following has been extracted from the trial balance for Yateley Limited at 31 July 2020:

	$000	$000
Administration expenses	270	
Heat, light and power	80	
Machinery: at cost	910	
Machinery: accumulated depreciation		455
Maintenance and repairs	70	
Motor vehicles: at cost	128	
Motor vehicles: accumulated depreciation		56
Office equipment: at cost	95	
Office equipment: accumulated depreciation		67
Rent, rates and insurance	90	
Wages and salaries	560	

Additional information at 31 July 2020:

1 Administration expenses of $14 000 were owing but insurance of $5 000 had been paid in advance.

2 Depreciation is to be applied on the following basis:

    a machinery 15% using the straight-line method

    b motor vehicles 25% using the reducing balance method

    c office equipment 10% using the straight-line method

3 Costs are to be apportioned in the following way:

	Prime cost	Factory overheads	Administration
Depreciation – machinery	–	90%	10%
Depreciation – motor vehicles	–	40%	60%
Depreciation – office equipment	–	20%	80%
Heat, light and power	10%	65%	25%
Maintenance and repairs	–	70%	30%
Rent, rates and insurance	–	$\frac{3}{5}$	$\frac{2}{5}$
Wages and salaries	45%	25%	30%

Required

a Calculate the amount of these costs that would be treated as prime cost, as factory overheads and as expenses that would appear in the statement of profit or loss. [9]

CONTINUED

Further information

Yobled Limited uses transfer pricing where a mark-up of 15% is used. The inventory of finished goods (including factory profit) was:

31 July 2019 $83 490

31 July 2020 $73 255

b Produce the provision for unrealised profit account for the year ended 30 July 2020, showing clearly the adjustment that would need to be made in the statement of profit or loss. **[4]**

c Show how the inventory at 31 July 2020 would be shown in the statement of financial position. **[2]**

d Discuss whether Yobled's decision to use transfer pricing is a good one. **[5]**

SELF-EVALUATION CHECKLIST

After studying this chapter, complete a table like this:

You should be able to:	Needs more work	Almost there	Ready to move on
Prepare a manufacturing account to identify the costs of completed goods and know that this feeds into the statement of profit or loss.			
Know there are three different classes of inventory: raw materials, work-in-progress and finished goods.			
Explain that there may be a profit charged when goods are transferred from the factory to finished goods inventory.			
Include the finished goods inventory in the statement of financial position at cost by deducting any unrealised profit included in it.			

> ## Chapter 21

An introduction to limited company accounts

This chapter covers part of syllabus sections AS Level 1.1; 1.5 and A Level 3.1, 3.2

LEARNING INTENTIONS

In this chapter you will learn how to:

- evaluate the differences between limited companies, partnerships and sole traders
- describe legislation like the UK Companies Act 2006 and regulations like IAS 1
- prepare a statement of profit or loss and statement of financial position in line with IAS 1
- explain and account for the main types of share capital and reserves and their characteristics
- explain what debentures are, when they are issued and how they differ from preference shares.

ACCOUNTING IN CONTEXT

Volkswagen

In 2015 the world was shocked by a news announcement that Volkswagen, a well-known and respected auto manufacturer, had been altering their emissions data by activating software to falsify the results. Many millions of vehicles contained this software and buyers had no idea that the emissions breached their own country's pollution standards.

At first, the company denied there was a problem, saying it was a glitch with the software, but then they had to admit that they had manipulated the data.

Many customers and investors felt very betrayed by what had happened and were angry by how long it had taken Volkswagen to admit the fraud.

The company has been fined many billions of dollars in several countries.

Discuss in a pair or a group:

- Why do people buy shares in companies like Volkswagen?

- Why are news announcements like this not good news for the shareholders?

Figure 21.1: In 2015, it was revealed that Volkswagen had been altering their emissions data to falsify the results.

21.1 What is a limited company? [AS]

A **limited company** is an organisation that is owned by shareholders and which, legally, is regarded as a *separate legal entity*.

In Chapter 9, one of the main accounting concepts that we investigated was *business entity* – the idea that we are concerned with the affairs of the business not its owner. While the application of the business entity concept is still true when dealing with limited companies, separate legal entity does have some very major practical implications for its owners (the shareholders) in two ways:

- *Losses and debts*: The owners of a limited company (shareholders) enjoy the benefit of **limited liability**. If a limited company fails then the debts or losses effectively 'die' with the company. The shareholders will lose their investment because their shares will now be worthless and they will be called upon to pay anything that they owe the company.

If someone supplies a limited company with goods on credit and the company fails, then it is likely that the supplier will not be paid if there are insufficient assets to do so. Separate legal entity means that the shareholders are regarded as separate from the company and cannot be chased for payment.

- *Legal action*: Suppose a sole trader sells a defective product to a customer who becomes ill as a result of using it. If the customer sues the business and the customer wins, then any damages will have to be paid by the business and, ultimately, the sole trader.

If the customer had bought the goods from a limited company, then the legal action would have to be taken against the company, not its owners.

KEY TERMS

limited company: a separate legal entity whose existence is separate from its owners; the liabilities of the members are limited to the amounts paid (or to be paid) on shares issued to them.

limited liability: where the owner of the business has his or her responsibility for paying off debts limited either to a specified amount or to the amount of his or her investment.

Advantages and disadvantages of limited companies

Advantages

- *Separate legal entity and limited liability*: Limited companies are legally regarded as separate from their owners, meaning that any debts incurred by the company are the responsibility of the company not the owners (shareholders) who enjoy 'limited liability'. If the company fails, the shareholders will only be required to pay any unpaid amounts relating to their shares, although those shares will be worthless. Unlike sole traders or partnerships, the shareholders' personal possessions cannot be used to pay the debts of the company.

- *Tax efficiency*: Limited companies have far greater flexibility over the way in which profit or income is taxed and, in some cases, tax rates can be significantly lower. For example, in many countries, dividend income is taxed at a lower rate than income tax.

- *Raising finance*: Limited companies can find it easier to borrow money from some banks and financial institutions as they can often be regarded as a lower risk than, say, partnerships. Public limited companies are able to raise large amounts of money through share issues to fund expansion.

- *Professional status*: Limited companies can often be regarded (by other corporations) as more stable and credible organisations and may therefore find customers that would not be willing to deal with sole traders or partnerships.

Disadvantages

- *Complicated and expensive to set up*: Setting up as a limited company involves preparing various documents that need to be submitted to a Registrar of Companies. This involves time and expense.

- *Complex financial statements*: the legal requirements for a limited company are far greater than for sole traders and partnerships. The company has to provide a statement of profit or loss, a statement of financial position, a statement of cash flows, a directors' report and an audit report. These need to be presented in a particular style with notes explaining the underlying principles, policies and procedures. This can be expensive and time-consuming.

- *Auditors*: Larger limited company accounts have to be examined by auditors who will produce a report that includes their opinion on whether the accounts provide a 'true and fair view' of the company. This involves time and expense.

- *Directors and shareholders*: Most (public) limited companies have too many shareholders for them to be able to manage the company effectively. Getting them all together to make decisions (and ones that they will agree on) is difficult. So the shareholders appoint a board of directors to run the company on their behalf. If the directors are not running the business properly, the shareholders may not be aware of problems until they have become too serious to be easily dealt with.

KEY CONCEPT LINK

True and fair view: Financial statements are designed to give a true and fair view of the financial position of the business to internal and external stakeholders. Why do you think it is particularly important that the financial statements of a limited company do provide a true and fair view?

21.2 Partnerships and limited companies compared [AS]

	Partnerships	Limited companies
Number of owners	2–20 (except in certain professional firms such as accountants, lawyers, etc.).	For a public limited company there is no maximum. For a private limited company there is often a restriction on the number of shareholders and this is set out in the Articles of Association (see Section 21.3).
Capital	Determined by the partnership agreement, or the amount of money a sole trader is able to invest from their own savings.	The potential share capital available to a public limited company is unlimited. The share capital for a private limited company will depend on how much money the shareholders have or choose to invest in the business.
Management and ownership	All partners (except those with limited liability) may manage the firm's affairs on a day-to-day basis, although some partners may choose to limit their involvement to that of being an investor.	Limited companies have directors who are employees of the company, appointed by the shareholders to run the business on their behalf. For private limited companies, there might only be two or three directors who are the shareholders. The company may have been formed to take advantage of 'unlimited liability'. Public limited companies appoint directors. The shareholders 'hire and fire' directors at the annual or extraordinary general meeting (usually by voting). Although they are employees of the company, many directors might possess large numbers of shares in the company. It is possible that part of their financial package involves them being awarded or having the right to buy shares in the company. Although someone can be both a shareholder and director, his or her role is quite different as far as the law is concerned.
Taxation	The owners are subject to income tax because their share of the profits is regarded as income.	Companies are liable to pay tax on their profits (in the UK and many countries, this is called corporation tax). The tax payable is treated as an appropriation of profit.
Distribution of profit	Partners share profits and losses in line with the partnership agreement.	Profits are distributed to shareholders as dividends, which are decided at the discretion of the directors. Undistributed profits are retained within the company.

> **KEY TERMS**
>
> **public limited company (PLC):** a company that is authorised to issue shares to the public.
>
> **private limited company:** a company that is not authorised to issue shares to the public.

Most countries have their own Companies Acts. It might be useful to spend a few minutes looking up the relevant laws that have been passed in your country. Companies Acts are designed to protect the interests of creditors and shareholders, including those who might in future become creditors or shareholders.

21.3 How are limited companies formed? [AS]

In the UK, a company is formed when certain documents are registered by people (known as its 'founders') with the Registrar of Companies, and various fees and duties are paid to the Registrar. It is quite common for partnerships to convert into limited companies in order to take advantage of 'limited liability'.

Memorandum and articles of association

These are two of the documents that must be filed with the Registrar of Companies.

The *Articles of Association* is the main constitutional document of a company that defines the existence of the company and regulates the structure and control of the company and its members. It contains such things as:

- liability of members

- directors' powers and responsibilities

- appointment and removal of directors

- issue and transfer of shares

- dividends and other distributions to members

- members' decision making and attendance at general meetings.

The *Memorandum of Association* forms part of the articles and defines the relationship of the company to the rest of the world. It contains information about:

- the name of the company, which must end with the words *public limited company (plc)* if it is a public company, or *Limited or Ltd* if it is a private company. The difference between the two types of company will be explained more fully in Chapter 25.

- a statement that the liability of the company is limited.

Public and private companies

Companies register as either public companies or private companies:

- *Public companies* may offer their shares to the public and may arrange for the shares to be bought and sold on a stock exchange.

- *Private companies* are not allowed to offer their shares to the public and shares cannot, therefore, be bought and sold on a stock exchange.

It is not unusual for small private limited companies to expand to the point where it is not possible to raise the money needed by issuing shares to a chosen number of investors. The directors will often decide that converting the business to a public limited company is the best option.

In the UK, the Companies Act 2006 and some IASs can require public limited companies and private limited companies to:

- prepare different financial statements (and include different information within them)

- treat various accounting issues differently.

The distinction between public and private companies applies in the UK but may not apply in all countries. Therefore, companies will be described as 'Limited' in this book but will be treated as public limited companies unless expressly stated otherwise.

21.4 Share capital and debentures [AS]

The issuing of **shares** has traditionally been an effective way for limited companies to raise money, but they are not the only method.

Ordinary shares (equity)

Most of the shares issued by a company are ordinary shares and the people who own ordinary shares are the owners of the company. The ordinary **share capital** is known as the *equity* of a company.

There are a number of reasons why people (or organisations) might want to own ordinary shares, including:

- being entitled to attend the **annual general meeting (AGM)** and vote on the proposals made by the directors
- receiving a share of the profits in the form of *dividends* – many shareholders treat dividends as an income and a return on their investment
- the hope that the price of the shares will rise and they can then be sold at a profit
- shareholders may receive discounts on the goods and services that the company provides – this is common with retailers.

Ordinary shareholders are paid after other shareholders/creditors. There is no guarantee that the directors will pay out all of the profits in dividends (they may prefer to retain and reinvest the profit). In years where profits are high, ordinary shareholders may receive large dividends after other people have received their (fixed) return, but in years where profits are low, there may be nothing left to pay them. The other hazard is that, should the company fail, ordinary shareholders will be among the last to be paid out when the assets of the company are sold.

Dividends on ordinary shares are usually paid twice per year. An *interim dividend* may be paid when the results of the first half of the year are known and a *final dividend* may be announced and paid after the year end.

There is often a strong link between dividends and the market price of the share. If it is likely that a company will announce a large profit (and so the directors might pay a large dividend), investors will regard owning shares in that company as attractive because they will get a good return on their investment. Extra demand for those shares will cause the market price to rise.

If profits are low, shareholders may feel that there may be little or no dividend and so are likely to want to sell their shares. The extra supply of shares and the lack of people wanting to buy them will cause the share price to fall.

Sometimes even bad news about the company can be enough to make shareholders want to sell their shares, forcing share prices to fall. When Volkswagen, the world's largest car manufacturer, faced problems over the results of its air pollution tests in the United States, investors feared that the huge cost of putting things right and paying any fines/legal costs would damage profits. Volkswagen also faced major damage to its reputation and the price of the company's shares fell by 23–25% in the days that followed.

Debentures

These are formal certificates issued by companies to raise long-term finance and those issued by large public limited companies are often traded on major stock exchanges. The debenture entitles the lender to a fixed rate of interest that must be paid whether the business makes a profit or not. Unlike a dividend that represents an appropriation of profit, the interest on a debenture is treated as an expense (a 'finance cost').

KEY TERMS

share: the smallest division of the total share capital of the company that can be issued in order to raise funds for the company.

share capital: the capital raised by a business by the issue of shares, usually for cash, but may also be for consideration other than cash, such as non-current or current assets.

annual general meeting (AGM): a meeting held after the end of the financial year where all ordinary shareholders are entitled to attend to vote on proposals made by the directors.

Debentures often have a *redemption date* where the company is committed to buy them back (at face value) on or after a certain date.

The difference between ordinary shares and debentures

There are a number of differences between ordinary shares and debentures, including:

Ordinary shares	Debentures
Shareholders are members of the company.	Debenture holders are not members of the company. They are creditors of the company because, at some point in the future, the company will have to repay the debenture to the person, bank or company who lent it.
Share capital is shown in the statement of financial position under equity.	Debentures are shown in the statement of financial position as non-current liabilities unless they are due for redemption within one year, when they must be shown as current liabilities.
Shareholders are the last people to be repaid when a company is wound up.	Debenture holders are entitled to be repaid before the shareholders when a company is wound up.
Dividends may only be paid if distributable profits are available.	Interest on debentures must be paid even if the company made a loss.
Dividends are an appropriation of profit.	Debenture holders receive interest. This is an expense that is shown under finance costs in the statement of profit or loss.

21.5 Share capital and common terms [AS]

There are some terms that you should be aware of when dealing with shares and these include:

- *Issued capital*: the total of the shares that have been issued to the shareholders.
- *Called-up capital*: money required to be paid by shareholders immediately. A newly formed company may not require all the money due from shareholders immediately. If it needs to build a factory and then equip it with machinery, the money could lie idle in the company's bank account until those items have to be paid for. It may require the shareholders to pay only part of the amount due on their shares until further sums are required, when it will call on the shareholders to make further payments.
- *Uncalled capital*: any amount of the share capital not yet called up by the company.
- *Paid-up capital*: the money received from shareholders on the called-up capital. Some shareholders may be late in paying their calls or may fail to pay them at all.
- *Calls in advance*: money received from shareholders who have paid calls before they are due.
- *Calls in arrears*: money due from shareholders who are late in paying their calls.
- *Forfeited shares*: shares that shareholders have forfeited because they have failed to pay their calls. The shares may be reissued to other shareholders.
- *Debenture*: a loan of a fixed amount given to a company. The loan is repayable at a fixed date in the future and carries interest at a fixed rate.
- *Nominal (or par) value*: the face value of a share.
- *Share premium*: the excess over the nominal or par value of a share when it is issued.
- *Interim dividend*: a dividend paid to existing shareholders during the year provided the directors are satisfied that sufficient profits have been earned and the cash is available to pay the dividend.

- *Final dividend*: the dividend the directors recommend should be paid to shareholders after the end of the year. The directors can only propose the dividend. It must be approved by the shareholders at the annual general meeting.

Many of these elements will be examined in Chapters 22, 25 and 31.

21.6 Statement of profit or loss for a limited company [AS and AL]

The way the financial statements of limited companies are prepared is set out in IAS 1. The statement allows income and expenses of a company to be presented in one of two ways:

a in a single statement of profit or loss and other comprehensive income covering the accounting year

b in two separate statements:

 i a separate statement of profit or loss

 ii a statement of other comprehensive income.

IAS 1 permits alternative titles to be used, but for the remainder of this part of the coursebook a *statement of profit or loss* will be used.

WORKED EXAMPLE 1

The following information was extracted from the records of Smith Limited at 31 August 2020:

	$000	$000
Inventories at 1 September 2019	621	
Sales		4 230
Administrative expenses	984	
Distribution costs	505	
Purchases	2 107	
Loss on disposal of non-current assets	41	
8% Bank loan		600
Rent received		85

Notes:

1 Inventory at 31 August 2020 was valued at $747 000.

2 Corporation tax on the profits for the year is estimated to be $152 000.

CONTINUED

3   Administrative expenses of $23 000 had been paid in advance but distribution costs of $19 000 were owing.

Statement of profit or loss for Smith Ltd for year ended 31 August 2020	
	$000
Revenue[1]	4 230
Cost of sales[2]	(1 981)
Gross profit	2 249
Distribution costs[3]	(524)
Administrative expenses[4]	(961)
Profit/(loss) from operations[5]	764
Other income (rent received)[6]	85
Other expenses[7]	(41)
Finance costs[8]	(48)
Profit/(loss) before tax	760
Tax[9]	(152)
Profit/(loss) for the year[10]	608

Notes:

[1]   Revenue is the income generated by the company from its trading activities, in other words, its sales for the year.

[2]   Cost of sales. The detail does not have to be shown here, but show it as a working:

opening inventory + purchases – closing inventory

621 + 2 107 – 747 = 1 981

[3]   Distribution costs include expenses such as salespeople's salaries or expenses, warehousing costs, carriage outwards, depreciation of warehouses or delivery vans, or any other expenses associated with the transfer of goods from the company to its customers.

[4]   Administrative expenses would include office salaries or costs, selling costs not treated as part of the distribution expenses, general depreciation of cars or office equipment. It may also include discounts allowed, provision for irrecoverable debts and irrecoverable debts.

Note: adjustments need to be made for accruals and prepayments:

Administrative expenses = 984 – 23 = 961

Distribution costs = 505 + 19 = 524

[5]   Profit from operations is the profit earned by the company in its day-to-day trading activities. Other sources of income and expenditure, which are not part of its normal trading activities, are shown below this.

[6]   Other income would include such things as profit on disposal of non-current assets, or rental income, where renting property or equipment is not the main object of the company.

[7]   Other expenses would include items not included under either [3] or [4] .
It may include, say, loss on disposal of non-current assets.

CONTINUED

[8] Finance costs would include interest on bank overdrafts or loans, debenture interest or interest on loans from other companies. It also includes dividends paid on redeemable preference shares as these types of share are regarded as a long-term loan of the business.

In this case, finance costs are $8\% \times 600 = 48$

Finance costs are the amount due not the amount paid. There may be a debit figure in the trial balance that relates to the amount of interest already paid.

There may also be finance income. This could be, say, bank interest received.

[9] The tax is payable on the profits the company earns. It may be given either as a figure, or you will be told the percentage rate so you can work it out. If this is the case, the figure will be calculated on the profit before tax.

[10] Profit/(loss) for the year. The ordinary shareholders are the owners of the company. All the profit earned by the company belongs to them. In some companies, this figure is called 'profit or loss attributable to equity holders'. Either term is acceptable.

Note: the layout provided here is for accounts that will be published by the company and available for the general public to look at. There is nothing to stop a limited company using a format similar to that of the sole trader for internal use where the 'cost of sales' and the 'less expenses' are itemised.

21.7 Classifying the expenses [AS]

The limited company may have a large number expenses that need to be put under the *administrative expense* and *distribution cost* headings. In fact, for companies involved in making a product, some of those costs will need to be charged to *cost of sales* (through a manufacturing account) as well.

Many of these expenses will clearly belong to a particular category, for example costs relating to operating a number of delivery vans will obviously be distribution costs, while the office manager's salary would clearly be an administrative expense.

However, there may be some overhead costs like rent and rates that relate to the company as a whole. In this case, a decision needs to be made about how those items should be treated. It may be that a number of these costs need to be shared ('apportioned') between the two or three areas using an appropriate characteristic ('basis of apportionment'). This will be covered in more detail in Chapter 33.

WORKED EXAMPLE 2

The following costs were incurred by Jones Limited during the year ended 30 September 2020:

	$	Apportionment:
Advertising	36000	
Closing inventory of finished goods	25000	
Depreciation of office equipment	51000	20% factory, 50% office, 30% sales
Depreciation of motor vehicles	47000	10% factory, 30% office, 60% sales
Depreciation of machinery	88000	80% factory, 10% office, 10% sales
Directors' remuneration	342000	one-third each
Heat, light and power	35000	60% factory, 25% office, 15% sales
Insurance	18000	55% factory, 25% office, 20% sales
Office expenses	97000	
Opening inventory of finished goods	31000	
Raw materials consumed	167000	
Rent and rates	63000	40% factory, 35% office, 25% sales
Wages and salaries – factory workers	241000	
Wages and salaries – office staff	176000	
Wages and salaries – salesmen	194000	

TIP

Always make adjustments such as accruals and prepayments before you try to apportion the costs between the different categories.

Note: rent and rates of $9000 was accrued while $4000 of insurance had been paid in advance. The classification of costs for Jones Limited would look like this:

	Total	Cost of sales	Admin	Distribution
	$	$	$	$
Advertising	36000	–	–	36000
Closing inventory of finished goods	(25000)	(25000)	–	–
Depreciation of office equipment	51000	10200	25500	15300
Depreciation of motor vehicles	47000	4700	14100	28200
Depreciation of machinery	88000	70400	8800	8800
Directors' remuneration	342000	114000	114000	114000
Heat, light and power	35000	21000	8750	5250
Insurance (18000 – 4000)	14000	7700	3500	2800
Office expenses	97000	–	97000	–
Opening inventory of finished goods	31000	31000	–	–
Raw materials consumed	167000	167000	–	–
Rent and rates (63000 + 9000)	72000	28800	25200	18000
Wages and salaries – factory workers	241000	241000	–	–
Wages and salaries – office staff	176000	–	176000	–
Wages and salaries – salesmen	194000	–	–	194000
Total	1566000	670800	472850	422350

CONTINUED

Note: there may be many costs that require some thought about their classification. Common examples include discounts received, discounts allowed and irrecoverable debts. These are accepted to be administrative expenses because they relate to the paying and collecting of money, which is separate from the actual buying and selling of goods.

ACTIVITY 21.1

The following information was extracted from the books of Patel Limited as at 31 August 2020:

	$	Apportionment
Closing inventory of finished goods	41 000	
Depreciation of office equipment	36 000	15% factory, 60% office, 25% sales
Depreciation of motor vehicles	57 000	$\frac{1}{5}$ factory, $\frac{3}{5}$ office, $\frac{1}{5}$ sales
Depreciation of machinery	124 000	80% factory, 10% office, 10% sales
Heat, light and power	26 000	70% factory, 15% office, 15% sales
Management/director salaries	414 000	one-third each
Office expenses	98 000	
Opening inventory of finished goods	33 000	
Raw materials consumed	356 000	
Rent, rates and insurance	21 000	$\frac{3}{5}$ factory, $\frac{1}{5}$ office, $\frac{1}{5}$ sales
Wages and salaries – factory workers	207 000	
Wages and salaries – office staff	152 000	
Wages and salaries – sales people	97 000	
Warehouse costs – raw materials	102 000	
Warehouse costs – finished goods	125 000	

Other balances included:

	$	$
Sales		2 142 000
Loss on disposal of non-current assets	26 100	
7% Bank loan		480 000
Rental income		19 700

Notes:

1 Office expenses of $17 000 was accrued while $2 000 of insurance had been paid in advance.

2 Corporation tax for the year was $58 800.

Required

a Calculate the cost of sales, administrative expenses and distribution costs for the year ended 31 August 2020.

b Prepare the statement of profit or loss for Patel Limited for the year ended 31 August 2020.

21.8 Dividing up the profit for the year [AS]

Having calculated the net profit for the year, we need to consider what happens to it. There are several possibilities:

- *Dividends*: A limited company can have a large number of owners in the form of shareholders. They will be rewarded for their investment by the company paying them a dividend. For ordinary shares, this will be a certain amount per share (e.g. $0.05), while the preference shareholders will receive their fixed percentage.

- *Retained earnings*: It would be unwise for a company to always pay out all its profit to the shareholders. The directors may wish to use any spare cash to fund expansion of the company and most shareholders will be happy if, long term, they end up with a share of a larger and far more profitable company.

  Most companies, after paying some of the profit as dividend, keep the rest within the company and this is known as *retained earnings*. This is added to the retained earnings from previous years and shown as a separate figure on the statement of financial position.

- *Reserves*: The directors may transfer some of the profits to reserves. Although this is not an actual movement of cash, it does indicate to the shareholders that this is profit that is not going to be distributed for the foreseeable future.

21.9 Statement of financial position for a limited company [AS and AL]

IAS 1 specifies the minimum information that must be shown in the statement of financial position for a limited company.

WORKED EXAMPLE 3

The following balances were extracted from the books of Smith Limited as at 31 August 2020:

	$000	$000
Property, plant and equipment (net book value)	14 076	
Share capital		8 000
Bank loan		6 000
Trade and other receivables	1 102	
Retained earnings at 1 September 2019		753
Bank and cash	197	
Trade and other payables		1 041
Dividends paid	320	
Profit for the year		608

Notes:

1   Inventory at 31 August 2020 was valued at $911 000.

2   Corporation tax on the profits for the year is estimated to be $208 000.

CONTINUED

3   Administrative expenses of $23 000 had been paid in advance but distribution costs of
    $19 000 were owing.

Statement of financial position for Smith Limited at 31 August 2020	
	$
Non-current assets:	
Property, plant and equipment[1]	14 076
Current assets:	
Inventories[2]	911
Trade and other receivables[3] (1 102 + 23)	1 125
Cash and cash equivalents[4]	197
	2 233
Total assets[5]	16 309
Equity and liabilities:	
Equity:[6]	
Share capital	8 000
Retained earnings (753 + 608 – 320)	1 041
Total equity	9 041
Non-current liabilities:	
Bank loan[7]	6 000
	6 000
Current liabilities:[8]	
Trade and other payables (1 041 + 19)	1 060
Tax payable	208
	1 268
Total liabilities[9]	7 268
Total equity and liabilities	16 309

Notes:

[1]   It is usual to present the non-current assets as one figure (the total net book value)
      in the statement of financial position and present all of the supporting information
      in separate notes.

CONTINUED

As will be seen in Chapter 26, a summary of the non-current assets is presented in a table known as the schedule of non-current assets, which might look like this:

Schedule of non-current assets				
	Premises	Plant and machinery	Motor vehicles	Total
	$	$	$	$
Cost				
Cost at 1 April 2019	400000	135000	42000	577000
Add: Revaluation	250000	–	–	250000
Additions during the year	–	50000	21000	71000
Less: Disposals during the year	–	(43000)	(16000)	(59000)
Cost at 31 March 2020	650000	142000	47000	839000
Depreciation				
Accumulated depreciation at 1 April 2019	–	75000	33000	108000
Add: Charge during year	–	28400	11750	40150
Less: Disposals	–	(36500)	(12400)	(48900)
Accumulated depreciation at 31 March 2019	–	66900	32350	99250
Net book value at 31 March 2020	650000	75100	14650	739750
Net book value at 1 April 2019	400000	60000	9000	469000

This table would be supported by notes that explain how the figures were arrived at, including details of cost, expected useful life, residual values and the method of depreciation being used. In this case, the value appearing in the statement of financial position at 31 March 2020 would have been $739750 and shareholders are able to see how and why the net book value has increased from the $469000 that was shown in the previous statement of financial position.

This section will include both tangible assets, such as plant and machinery, motor vehicles and office equipment, and intangible assets, such as purchased goodwill or the cost of developing the company's products and acquiring patents and trademarks.

[2] Inventories could include raw materials, work-in-progress and finished goods in the case of a manufacturing company.

[3] Trade receivables is the amount receivable from customers while other receivables refers to prepayments.

[4] Cash and cash equivalents include short-term deposits as well as bank current accounts. It should be noted that if the company had a bank overdraft then this item would appear under current liabilities.

[5] Total assets is simply the sum of non-current and current assets.

[6] The capital of the company is analysed, showing the separate classes of paid-up capital, share premium and reserves.

Retained earnings = opening retained earnings + profit for the year – dividends

Any transfer to reserves would be a deduction from the retained earnings figure.

CONTINUED

[7] Non-current liabilities are amounts that fall due for payment more than 12 months after the end of the financial year. This includes items such as long-term loans that the company owes. It also includes debentures and redeemable preference shares.

Note: although not shown here, it is also possible for a company to have non-current receivables. This may be something such as a debt that is due to be received more than 12 months after the date of the statement. Such items are shown as a separate heading in the statement.

[8] Current liabilities include trade payables (amounts due to suppliers) and other payables such as accruals. It would also include other short-term borrowings such as a bank loan and the current portion of long-term borrowings, such as that part of a long-term loan which is repayable within 12 months from the date of the statement of financial position. Note that the tax payable is listed separately from the other current liabilities.

[9] Total liabilities is the sum of the equity, non-current and current liabilities.

The format for the statement of financial position is one that is widely used in practice. IAS 1 allows other layouts. However, the layout here will be used for the rest of the book.

ACTIVITY 21.2

The following balances have been extracted from the books of Patel Limited at 31 August 2020:

	$000	$000
Property, plant and equipment (net book value)	8457.4	
Share capital		7000.0
7% Bank loan		480.0
Trade and other receivables	88.5	
Retained earnings at 1 September 2019		812.4
Bank and cash	112.9	
Trade and other payables		209.3
Dividends paid	97.6	
Profit for the year		221.2

Notes:

1 Inventories at 31 August 2020 were valued at $41 000.

2 Office expenses of $17 000 were accrued while $2 000 of insurance had been paid in advance.

3 Corporation tax for the year was $58 800.

Required

Produce the statement of financial position for Patel Limited at 31 August 2020.

21.10 Share issues [AS]

During the course of an accounting year or even at the end of it, the directors may want to issue shares.

Shares issued at 'face value'

Suppose a company already has 400 000 ordinary shares of $1 and on 1 January, the directors decide to issue another 200 000 ordinary shares. If investors pay the nominal or 'face value' of $1 each by cheque, the entries in the ledgers would look like this:

Bank account (extract)			
Debit		**Credit**	
	$		$
1 Jan 20 Ordinary share capital	200 000		

Ordinary share capital account			
Debit		**Credit**	
	$		$
		1 Jan 20 Balance b/d	400 000
		1 Jan 20 Bank	200 000

Shares issued at 'a premium'

There is no guarantee that the market price of shares will bear any relation to the nominal or face value. If the company is profitable, then demand for the shares is likely to be high and this will be reflected in their price. The directors will know this and, as one of the reasons for issuing shares is to raise money, will consider whether they can sell the new shares for more than their face value. It is a balancing act – sell the shares for too low a price and the opportunity to maximise the money raised will be lost. Charge too high a price and not all of them will be sold.

Suppose the company issued the 200 000 shares of $1 each but managed to sell them for $1.50 each. The extra $0.50 received is known as the *share premium* and is entered into a *share premium account* like so:

Bank account (extract)			
Debit		**Credit**	
	$		$
1 Jan 20 Ordinary share capital	200 000[1]		
1 Jan 20 Share premium	100 000[1]		

Note:

[1] One debit entry of $300 000 would have been acceptable.

Ordinary share capital account			
Debit		**Credit**	
	$		$
		1 Jan 20 Balance b/d	400 000
		1 Jan 20 Bank	200 000

Share premium account			
Debit		**Credit**	
	$		$
		1 Jan 20 Bank	100 000

TIP

It is possible that there will already be a balance on the share premium account arising from previous share issues, so take care to examine trial balances and other information provided.

21.11 Dividends [AS]

It is likely that the directors will pay dividends twice per year – an interim dividend partway through the year and a final dividend after the year end. The final dividend is **proposed** by the directors but has to be approved by the shareholders at the AGM, which may be many months after the year end.

Under IAS 10: Events after the Reporting Period, only dividends paid during the year can be recorded in the financial statements and so, in practice, this will mean that the accounts are effectively showing 'last year's final dividend and this year's interim dividend'. The proposed final dividend for this year is disclosed in the notes supporting the final accounts stating that it is subject to the approval of the shareholders at the AGM.

It is likely that when preparing financial statements for a limited company, you will find an item in the debit column of the trial balance that refers to dividends paid as well as some guidance in the additional information that a further dividend was paid but has not yet been accounted for. You will have to make the necessary adjustments where the results will be deducted from the retained earnings figure.

KEY TERMS

proposed dividend: a dividend that has been recommended by the directors of a company but not paid – usually because it has not yet been approved by the shareholders at the Annual General Meeting.

WORKED EXAMPLE 4

The following balances were available for a limited company at 31 July 2020:

	$000	$000
Share capital (ordinary shares of $0.50 each)		4 000
Bank	541	
Dividends paid	160	
Retained earnings at 1 August 2019		753
Profit for the year		635

Additional information

The directors paid a further dividend of $0.03 per share but nothing has been recorded in the books.

Step 1

Calculate the amount of dividend being paid. You should take care to identify how many shares there are as they are not always $1 each.

$$\text{Number of shares} = \frac{4\,000\,000}{0.50} = 8\,000\,000 \text{ shares} \times 0.03 = \$240\,000$$

Obviously, if the shares had been $1 each, then only $4\,000\,000 \times \$0.03$ would have been paid.

CONTINUED

Step 2

Make the necessary adjustments to record the dividend:

Debit: Dividends paid 240 000 (this will mean that $400 000 has been paid in total)

Credit: Bank 240 000 (this will reduce the bank balance to $301 000)

Step 3

Calculate the retained earnings figure:

Opening balance + profit for the year – dividends paid

753 000 + 635 000 – 400 000 = $988 000

21.12 Revaluations [AS]

If a company has owned non-current assets like premises or land and buildings for a long time, it is possible that the valuation will be very different from current market value. Under these circumstances, it is permissible for an adjustment to be made to ensure that the value of the assets in the statement of financial position is appropriate.

WORKED EXAMPLE 5

An extract from a company's books shows the following:

	$	$
Land and buildings: at cost	80 000	
Land and buildings: accumulated depreciation		12 000

The buildings have been professionally revalued at $300 000 and the directors have decided to revalue the buildings in the books. The entries in the books are shown by the following journal entry:

	Dr	Cr
	$	$
Land and buildings: at cost	220 000	
Land and buildings: accumulated depreciation	12 000	
Revaluation reserve		232 000

Note: the buildings are being increased from a net book value of $68 000 to $300 000, an increase of $232 000. The amount already provided for depreciation must be transferred to the revaluation reserve.

As a result of the journal entry, the land and buildings at cost account will now have a balance of $300 000 while the balance on the land and buildings: accumulated depreciation account will be zero. If it is decided to depreciate the land and buildings in future then the annual charge will be based on the revalued amount of $300 000.

In all probability, you will not need to revalue an item that has been depreciated, so your journal is likely to be:

Debit: Asset at cost

Credit: Revaluation reserve

ACTIVITY 21.3

The following balances were available for a limited company at 31 July 2020:

	$000	$000
Property, plant and equipment (net book value)	2 120	
Share capital (ordinary shares of $0.50 each)		6 000
Bank		449
Dividends paid	360	
Share premium account		610
General reserve		500
Retained earnings at 1 August 2019		1 630
Profit for the year		873

Additional information

1 3 000 000 shares of $0.50 each had been issued and cheques for $1.85 million had been received. Nothing had yet been recorded in the accounts.

2 The directors paid a further dividend of $0.03 per share on all shares. Nothing has been recorded in the accounts.

3 Buildings had been valued at $1.20 million but were still recorded in the accounts as being worth $820 000. No depreciation had ever been charged on these buildings.

4 The directors had decided that $300 000 should be transferred to the general reserve.

Required

a Prepare the journals for the four adjustments (narratives are not required).

b Show the revised values of all of the relevant accounts. You should show the retained earnings as they would appear in the statement of financial position.

21.13 Reserves [AS]

There are two classes of reserves: **capital reserves** and **revenue reserves**. The differences between them are important.

Capital reserves

Capital reserves are part of the capital structure of a company; they should never be credited back to the statement of profit or loss and can *never* be used to pay cash dividends to shareholders.

The most common capital reserves, and ones with which you should become familiar, are given next.

Share premium account

This is created when shares are issued at a price that is greater than their nominal or face value. The balance on the share premium account will be shown in the equity section of the statement of financial position and can be very useful when carrying out some of the

KEY TERMS

capital reserves: gains that arise from non-trading activities, such as the revaluation of a company's non-current assets.

revenue reserves: the profits made by a company that have not been distributed to shareholders.

bookkeeping arising from unusual transactions. The UK Companies Act 2006 permits the share premium account to be used for certain specific purposes only:

- to pay up unissued shares to existing ordinary shareholders as fully paid-up bonus shares
- to write off the expenses arising on a new issue of shares at a premium
- to write off any commission paid on a new issue of shares at a premium.

(Some of these topics are covered in Chapter 22, and you will see that there are certain important restrictions on the use of the share premium account to provide for the premium payable on the redemption of shares.)

Revaluation reserve

A company may revalue its non-current assets and any gain on the revaluation must be credited to a revaluation reserve. The gain is an unrealised profit and must not be credited to the statement of profit or loss.

The revaluation reserve may be used to issue shares to existing shareholders of the company as bonus shares.

Capital redemption reserve

This reserve must be created when a company redeems (buys back) any of its shares from existing shareholders using any other method than issuing new shares. The bookkeeping entries for the redemption of shares are not covered in this book.

Revenue reserves

The most common *revenue reserve* is retained earnings.

Retained earnings

This contains all of the profit that has not been distributed to the shareholders. The balance at the end of the year can be found as follows:

Opening balance + profit for the year – dividends paid – any transfers to other reserves

General and other reserves

General and other reserves contain profit that the directors have taken out of retained earnings – effectively, it tells the shareholders that these amounts are unlikely to be distributed as dividends and are going to be used to fund future growth. If the transfer is made to a **general reserve** it suggests that the directors do not have a specific direction in which that profit is going to be invested. However, the profit will sometimes be transferred to a named reserve, for example 'Reserve for replacing plant and equipment', which indicates where the profit is going to be reinvested. Whichever reserve is used, this transfer of profit does not represent a movement of cash. Any money used to fund future projects will need to be taken from the company's bank account.

The creation of revenue reserves reduces the amount of profit available to pay dividends, If the reserves are later considered by the directors to be excessive (and no longer required); however, they can be credited back to retained earnings and become available for the payment of dividends.

All of these reserves will appear in the 'equity' section of the statement of financial position.

> **KEY TERMS**
>
> **general reserve:** a ledger account created to show the amount of retained earnings kept aside by the company to meet future needs, e.g. fund future expansion; it is a bookkeeping adjustment, not an actual movement of cash.

21.14 Adjustments and the financial statements [AS and AL]

It is now time to examine how these adjustments actually influence the preparation of financial statements.

WORKED EXAMPLE 6

The following trial balance had been extracted for Callis at 30 September 2020:

	$000	$000
Property, plant and equipment (net book value)	9133	
Inventories at 1 October 2019	564	
Share capital (ordinary shares of $1 each)		3000
Bank loan		4000
Trade and other receivables	841	
Sales		10219
Administrative expenses	1473	
Distribution costs	829	
Retained earnings at 1 October 2019		1627
Bank		1261
Trade and other payables		449
Purchases	6711	
Dividends paid	565	
Loan Interest	440	
	20556	20556

Additional information

1 Inventory at 30 September 2020 was valued at $702000.

2 Tax on the profits for the year is estimated to be $177000.

3 Property that had been valued at $600000 was now to be valued at $1500000 – this had not been recorded in the books.

4 During the year, ordinary shares with a nominal value of $2000000 had been issued and cheques for $2600000 had been received. Nothing had yet been recorded in the accounts.

5 On 30 September 2020, there were distribution costs owing of $27000.

6 On 30 September 2020, there were prepaid administrative expenses of $12000.

7 The company had decided to transfer $400000 of its retained earnings to general reserve.

CONTINUED

Statement of profit or loss for Callis for the year ended 30 September 2020	
	$000
Revenue	10219
Cost of sales[1]	(6573)
Gross profit	3646
Administrative expenses[2]	(1461)
Distribution costs[3]	(856)
Profit from operations	1329
Finance costs	(440)
Profit before tax	889
Tax	(177)
Profit for the year	712

Notes:

[1]   Cost of sales = 564 + 6711 − 702 = 6573

[2]   Administrative expenses = 1473 − 12 = 1461

[3]   Distribution costs = 829 + 27 = 856

Statement of financial position for Callis at 30 September 2020	
	$000
Assets	
Property, plant and equipment[1]	10033
Current assets:	
Inventories	702
Trade and other receivables[2]	853
Bank[3]	1339
	2894
Total assets	12927
Equity and liabilities:	
Equity:	
Share capital[4]	5000
Share premium	600
Retained earnings[5]	1374
Revaluation reserve	900
General reserve	400
Total equity	8274
Non-current liabilities	
Bank loan	4000
	4000
Current liabilities	
Trade and other payables[6]	476
Tax payable	177
	653
Total liabilities	4653
Total liabilities and equity	12927

CONTINUED

Notes:

[1] Property, plant and equipment = 9 133 + (1 500 − 600) = 10 033

[2] Trade and other receivables = 841 + 12 = 853

[3] Bank = −1 261 + 2 600 = 1 339

[4] Share capital = 3 000 + 2 000 = 5 000

[5] Retained earnings = 1 627 + 712 − 400 − 565 = 1 374

[6] Trade and other payables = 449 + 27 = 476

21.15 Statement of changes in equity [AS and AL]

Limited companies are required to produce a **statement of changes in equity** that bridges the gap between the statement of financial position for two successive years.

IAS 1 allows more than one presentation to be used, the most detailed being shown in Worked example 7.

KEY TERM

statement of changes in equity: a statement showing the changes in a company's share capital, reserves and retained earnings over a reporting period.

WORKED EXAMPLE 7

The balances for the shareholders equity for Callis on 1 October 2019 were as follows:

	$
Share capital	3 000 000
Retained earnings	1 627 000

The events that took place during the year were as follows:

1 Shares with a face value of $2 000 000 were issued and cheques for $2 600 000 had been received.

2 Profit for the year was $712 000.

3 Property previously worth $600 000 was revalued at $1 500 000.

4 There had been a transfer of $400 000 to general reserve.

5 Dividends of $565 000 had been paid.

The statement of changes in equity will look like this:

	Share capital	Share premium	Revaluation reserve	General reserve	Retained earnings	Total equity
	$000	$000	$000	$000	$000	$000
Balance at 1 Oct 19 [1]	3 000				1 627	4 627
Changes in equity:						
Profit for the year					712	712
Revaluation			900			900
Dividends					(565)	(565)
Transfer to reserves [2]				400	(400)	–
Issues of shares	2 000	600				2 600
Balance at 30 Sep 20	5 000	600	900	400	1 374	8 274 [3]

CONTINUED

Notes:

[1] The opening balances on 1 October 2019 will be the values taken from the statement of financial position at 30 September 2019, while the closing balances will be those found in the statement of financial position at 30 September 2020.

[2] The transfer to reserves row should net to zero as profit is being moved from one reserve to another.

[3] The total of $8 274 000 shown is arrived at by adding together the individual figures in the bottom row and those found in the total equity column.

IAS 1 also requires a statement showing details of dividends paid during the year. Only dividends *paid* during the year are included in the financial statements and so the statement of changes in equity could very well include the payment of the final dividend in respect of the previous year and an interim dividend for the current year. It doesn't actually matter to which year the dividend relates. Provided money has left the business as payment of dividends to the shareholders, it is always recorded in the statement of changes in equity.

Proposed dividends are voted on by the shareholders at the AGM and approved by them at that time. The AGM takes place after the end of the final year and the preparation of the accounts for that year. There is always the possibility that the shareholders may not vote to approve the dividend payment. Thus, they are never recorded in the financial statements for the year recently ended. This results in them being paid some months after the end of the financial year, often well into the next financial year. Thus, proposed dividends are *never* shown in the financial statements although they are referred to in a note to the published accounts, as follows:

Dividends for the year ended .... (Note for the published accounts)	This year	Last year
	$000	$000
Amounts recognised as distributions to equity holders during the year:		
Final dividend for last year of $0.04 per share	2 000	1 200
Interim dividend for this year of $0.02 per share	1 000	900
	3 000	2 100
Proposed final dividend for this year of $0.05 per share	2 500	2 000

Note: these types of statement contain details of the information relating to the previous year so that shareholders can compare the dividends being distributed this year with those of the past.

IAS 1 allows for alternative ways of setting out the statement of changes in equity. One such alternative is to prepare a *statement of recognised income and expenses*. This is much less detailed, as it includes such things as the profit for the year and gains on revaluation of non-current assets. It does not include dividends paid or issues of shares. You should be aware of its existence and what it does and does not include.

ACTIVITY 21.4

The balances for the shareholders equity for Rudolph Limited on 1 October 2019 were as follows:

	$000
Share capital	11 000
Retained earnings	879
Share premium	500
Revaluation reserve	635
General reserve	1 100

The events that took place during the year were as follows:

1 Shares with a face value of $2 000 000 were issued and cheques for $2 200 000 had been received.

2 Profit for the year was $2 258 000.

3 Property previously worth $1 240 000 was revalued at $3 700 000.

4 There had been a transfer of $400 000 to general reserve.

5 Dividends of $1 300 000 had been paid.

Required

Prepare the statement of changes in equity for the year ended 30 September 2020.

REFLECTION

Do you consider that the advantages of forming a private limited company outweigh the disadvantages? Why/why not?

THINK LIKE AN ACCOUNTANT

Share and share alike?

We have seen that there are many different ways that someone can invest in a limited company – ordinary shares, preference shares or debentures as well as just loaning the company the money. Which of the various ways, if any, of investing in a limited company might you choose? What factors might you use to help you make a decision?

Figure 21.2: Shares, preference shares, debentures and loaning the company money are just a few of the ways to invest in a company.

EXAM-STYLE QUESTIONS

1   A company has share capital of $150 000 that consists of ordinary shares of $0.25 each. The directors recommend an interim dividend of $0.03 per share. What will be the amount of the interim dividend?

   A $1 125

   B $4 500

   C $18 000

   D $37 500   **[1]**

2   A company has 300 000 ordinary shares of $1 each. It also has $100 000 9% debentures. The profit for the year before finance costs is $42 000. The directors propose to transfer $24 000 to the general reserve. What is the maximum dividend per share that can be paid on the ordinary shares from the remaining profit so that retained earnings are not reduced?

   A $0.03

   B $0.06

   C $0.11

   D $0.14   **[1]**

3   Which of the following will not be shown as equity in the statement of financial position?

   A debentures

   B retained earnings

   C revaluation reserve

   D share premium   **[1]**

Practice question

4   The following trial balance had been extracted from the books of Doominie Limited at 30 September 2020:

	$000	$000
Non-current assets (net book value)	4 708	
Inventories at 1 October 2019	435	
Share capital		2 400
Bank loan		1 000
Trade and other receivables	621	
Sales		7 143
Admin expenses and distribution costs	3 769	
Retained earnings at 1 October 2019		1 146
Bank		445
Trade and other payables		307
Purchases	2 168	
Dividends paid	690	
Loan interest	50	
	12 441	12 441

CONTINUED

Additional information

1   Inventory at 30 September 2020 was valued at $312 000.

2   Corporation tax on the profits for the year is estimated to be $192 000.

3   During the year, ordinary shares with a nominal value of $3 600 000 had been issued and cheques for $4 710 000 had been received. Nothing had yet been recorded in the accounts.

4   On 30 September 2020, there was $50 000 of the interest on the bank loan owing.

5   On 30 September 2020, there were administrative expenses owing of $24 000.

6   The company had decided to transfer $500 000 of its retained earnings to general reserve.

7   The company had bought property for $4 500 000 during the year and paid through the bank, but this had not been recorded in the books.

Required

a   Prepare a statement of profit or loss for the year ended 30 September 2020.   [9]

b   Prepare a statement of financial position at 30 September 2020.   [15]

c   Prepare the statement of changes in equity for the year ended 30 September 2020.   [6]

d   Explain *three* differences between an ordinary share and a debenture.   [6]

e   Explain why it is important that the concept of 'going concern' is applied to the shareholders.   [4]

SELF-EVALUATION CHECKLIST

After studying this chapter, complete a table like this:

You should be able to:	Needs more work	Almost there	Ready to move on
Explain that limited companies are different from partnerships and sole traders as they have 'limited liability' and are run by directors who may not be involved in the decision making and day-to-day running of the business.			
Outline legislation like the UK Companies Act 2006 and regulations like IAS 1 that mean that limited companies have to satisfy far stricter reporting requirements than sole traders and partnerships.			
Produce a statement of profit or loss and statement of financial position in line with IAS 1, remembering to include the effect of the issue of shares.			
Explain and account for the main types of share capital and reserves and their characteristics.			
Know what debentures are, when they are issued and how they differ from preference shares.			

Chapter 22

Limited companies: Further considerations

This chapter covers part of syllabus sections AS Level 1.5 and A Level 3.1, 3.2

LEARNING INTENTIONS

In this chapter you will learn how to:

- explain the features and accounting treatment of bonus issues and rights issues
- explain the advantages and disadvantages of making a bonus or rights issue
- prepare ledger accounts to record an issue of ordinary shares at a par or a premium
- prepare ledger accounts to record a rights issue at par or at a premium
- prepare ledger accounts to record a bonus issue.

ACCOUNTING IN CONTEXT

Curton Plc

Mia Carr has owned shares in Curton Plc for a number of years and is used to receiving letters from the company, usually inviting her to the AGM or occasionally asking her to vote on a particular issue. This one was slightly different:

'Dear Ms Carr,

I am pleased to announce that Curton Plc is making a 1-for-2 rights issue of ordinary shares. According to our records, you hold 800 ordinary shares. We, the directors, are giving you the option of buying 400 shares at a price of $6.25 per share, which is significantly below the current market price.

This offer is available until ….'

Mia wonders whether she should apply for these shares.

Figure 22.1: Mia Carr owns shares in Curton Plc and often receives letters inviting her to vote on issues.

Discuss in a pair or a group:

What factors might Mia have to consider before deciding whether to take up the offer and buy these shares?

22.1 Calculation of the value of ordinary shares

The market price (value) of shares depends on many factors, most notably the investors' views on how attractive an investment the company is. It is fair to say that there are many factors that might influence the investors' views, and therefore the supply and demand, including:

- Past, present and expected future performance of the company itself.
- Economic, political and sociological factors at home and abroad, and whether investors feel that these will make it easier or more difficult for companies to make a profit and therefore pay dividends. Governments increasing interest rates as a policy to control inflation might cause a significant reduction in demand for goods and services and so make it difficult for companies to make a profit.
- Changes in the structure of the markets in which a particular company operates, for example increased competition might make it more difficult for businesses operating in that market to make a profit.
- Rates of return available on other forms of investment will also influence how attractive shares seem to investors.

Since different investors will have different views on how important these factors are, and have their own views on the return they require (and the risks they are prepared to take), it is difficult to arrive at a formula to determine what the market price should be. Often, changes in share prices are not the result of definite facts but the opinions held by existing shareholders and those thinking of investing about what might happen in terms of future profitability and therefore dividends.

However, it is possible to use a measure called 'net asset value', in order to establish some sort of measure of what a company's shares might really be worth.

Net asset value is based on the fact that all the assets of a company belong to the ordinary shareholders. According to the accounting equation:

Assets – Liabilities = Capital

This means that the net assets of the company can be identified by looking at the shareholders' equity section of the statement of financial position. If this is divided by the number of ordinary shares, then some sort of 'share value' can be determined.

KEY CONCEPT LINK

True and fair view: Why do you think shareholders and potential investors need the financial statements of a public limited company to show a true and fair view of that company?

WORKED EXAMPLE 1

The following is an extract from the statement of financial position of Callis Limited at 30 September 2020:

	$000
Total assets	12 927
Equity and liabilities:	
Equity:	
Share capital (5 000 000 share of $1 each)	5 000
Share premium	600
Retained earnings	1 374
Revaluation reserve	900
General reserve	400
Total equity	8 274
Non-current liabilities	4 000
Current liabilities	653
Total liabilities	4 653
Total liabilities and equity	12 927

The net asset value of *one* ordinary share is calculated as follows:

The total of the ordinary share capital and reserves = $8 274 000

The number of ordinary shares is 5 000 000

The net asset value of one ordinary share is $\dfrac{\$8\,274\,000}{5\,000\,000} = \$1.6548$ or $1.65 per share

Note: under the money measurement concept, only allowed items with a definite monetary value can be included in the financial statements. This means that items like non-purchased goodwill, which might actually be of significant value, should not be included in the figures here. So the $1.65 might be significantly lower than the real value of the shares.

ACTIVITY 22.1

The following was taken from the statement of financial position for Rudolph at 30 September 2020:

	$000
Total assets	27 223
Equity and liabilities:	
Equity:	
Share capital (ordinary shares of $0.50 each)	13 000
Share premium	700
Retained earnings	1 437
General reserve	1 500
Revaluation reserve	3 095
Total equity	19 732
Non-current liabilities	4 770
Current liabilities	2 721
Total liabilities	7 491
Total liabilities and equity	27 223

Required

Calculate the asset value per share at 30 September 2020.

22.2 Bonus shares (issues)

The Companies Act 2006 allows companies to use their reserves to issue shares to the ordinary shareholders as fully paid-up shares – this is known as a **bonus share issue**.

While the shareholders do not have to pay for them, the reserves from which these shares are being issued already belong to the shareholders so they are not being given anything that doesn't already belong to them.

A bonus issue involves shareholders being given a number of shares that represents a proportion of their existing holding. For example, a 1-for-2 bonus issue means that someone will be given one share for every two that they already have. So a shareholder with 1 000 shares will be given another 500 free shares. That shareholder will not really see any practical benefit as the market price of the share will quickly fall in proportion to the bonus issue. If the market price of these shares had been $3.00, then it is likely that within a short space of time it will fall to $2.00 and the shareholder will still have an investment worth $3 000.

Bonus issues are made to acknowledge the fact that the reserves belong to the shareholders. They can also be issued to shareholders in place of cash dividends when the company may need to preserve cash for future expansion. It can also correct an imbalance between a share capital that has stayed the same for years while the reserves have grown significantly. Having reserves that exceed the share capital is not regarded as desirable, because it can be

KEY TERM

bonus share issue: an issue of free shares to existing shareholders from the accumulated reserves of the company in the same proportion as the shares held by them.

a reminder of how much retained earnings are not available for distribution as dividends.

If there is a choice of reserves to use, directors will opt to use the capital reserves like the share premium first. This is because, unlike the revenue reserves that can be used for most things, there are restrictions on what capital reserves can be used for (they cannot be used to fund the payment of dividends, for example).

Specification note: the use of the revaluation reserve is specifically excluded from the syllabus although they are commonly used for this purpose because they cannot be used to pay dividends.

WORKED EXAMPLE 2

Suppose the following information has been extracted from the statement of financial position of a limited company. The statement of financial position would look as follows:

	$000
Non-current assets	2 000
Net current assets	600
Total assets	2 600
Equity:	
Share capital (ordinary shares of $1 each)	900
Share premium (capital reserve)	650
Revaluation reserve (capital reserve)	250
General reserve (revenue reserve)	200
Retained earnings (revenue reserve)	600
	2 600

The directors have decided to make a 2-for-3 bonus issue, which means that 600 000 shares will be issued.

Given that the directors will probably want to make use of the capital reserves, they will prioritise the share premium and the revaluation reserve. The journal if the share premium account is used is:

Details	Dr	Cr
	$000	$000
Share premium	600 000	
Share capital		600 000

Narrative: 2-for-3 bonus issue.

CONTINUED

The equity section under this option would then look like this:

Option 1	
	$000
Equity:	
Share capital (ordinary shares of $1 each)	1 500
Share premium (capital reserve)	50
Revaluation reserve (capital reserve)	250
General reserve (revenue reserve)	200
Retained earnings (revenue reserve)	600
	2 600

Operating this way has also provided a number of benefits (some of them only in terms of appearance), including:

- The non-current assets are closer to being covered by the share capital.

- The creation of these new shares may draw attention away from the fact that the directors may not be paying a dividend, which will protect the company's bank account. The non-payment of a dividend may also reduce resentment from employees if they have faced pay freezes or redundancies and see money being paid to outsiders who have done little to generate a profit for the company.

22.3 Rights issues

When a company needs to raise more capital, it may do so by issuing more shares. An invitation to the general public to subscribe for shares is an expensive process because the company must issue a prospectus. The prospectus gives the past history of the company, its present situation and much other information in great detail. In addition, the company must employ lawyers, accountants and auditors to advise and check on the preparation of the prospectus.

There is then the problem of deciding who receives the new shares. This can be tricky if there are applications for more shares than are available (the issue is said to be **over-subscribed**).

If a company restricts the invitation to subscribe for shares to existing shareholders, the requirements are less stringent and less costly. If the company is a private company, it is not permitted to invite the general public to subscribe for shares anyway, and so is limited to its existing shareholders. This is a **rights issue of shares**.

A rights issue entitles existing shareholders to apply for a specified number of shares, depending on how many they already hold. For example, they may apply for one share (or any other number of shares) for every two shares that they already hold (the same 1-for-2 idea that we saw with the bonus issue).

The offer price will be below the price at which shares are currently changing hands on the stock exchange, or their current valuation in the case of private companies.

Shareholders who do not wish to exercise their 'rights' may sell them to some other person who might be willing to buy them (if the cost of the 'rights' plus the share offer price is less than the price at which the shares are already being traded). For example, a rights issue may be offered at $2.50 per share when the price at which the shares are changing hands is $3.20.

KEY TERMS

over-subscribed: when there have been applications for more shares than the number of shares being issued.

rights issue of shares: an issue of shares made for cash. The shares are offered first to existing shareholders, in proportion to the shares held by them.

If the rights can be bought for less than $0.70, the person buying the rights will be able to acquire the new shares at a price below that at which they are being traded.

The accounting entries for a rights issue are no different from those for an ordinary issue of shares.

WORKED EXAMPLE 3

Suppose a company has the following statement of financial position:

	$000
Non-current assets	3 000
Net current assets	500
Total assets	3 500
Equity:	
Share capital (ordinary shares of $1 each)	1 800
Share premium	600
Revaluation reserve	400
General reserve	200
Retained earnings	500
	3 500

The directors decided to make a 1-for-3 rights issue where the shares would be sold for $1.75 (at the time the market price was $2.40 per share). All of the existing shareholders exercised their rights to the shares.

The journal for the rights issue was:

Details	Dr	Cr
	$000	$000
Bank (net current assets) 600 000 × 1.75 =	1 050 000	
Share capital		600 000
Share premium		450 000
Narrative: 1-for-3 rights issue		

The statement of financial position would look like this:

	$000
Non-current assets	3 000
Net current assets	1 550
Total assets	4 550
Equity:	
Share capital (ordinary shares of $1 each)	2 400
Share premium	1 050
Revaluation reserve	400
General reserve	200
Retained earnings	500
	4 550

ACTIVITY 22.2

The following was taken from the statement of financial position of a company at 30 September 2020:

	$000
Non-current assets	1 600
Net current assets	400
	2 000
Equity:	
Share capital (ordinary shares of $0.50 each)	800
Share premium (capital reserve)	300
Revaluation reserve (capital reserve)	500
General reserve (revenue reserve)	100
Retained earnings (revenue reserve)	300
	2 000

1 The directors have decided to make a 1-for-2 bonus share issue. This will use the capital reserves starting with the share premium account.

2 The director have decided to make a 1-for-2 rights issue instead. The shares will be sold for $0.75 each. The current market price is $0.90.

Required

a Show the journal needed to record the bonus share issue and the statement of financial position after that issue has taken place.

b Show the journal needed to record the rights share issue and the statement of financial position after that issue has taken place.

> **TIP**
>
> It is possible that you may need to explain the main differences between a bonus issue and a rights issue.

The main differences between a bonus issue and a rights issue are:

Bonus issue	Rights issue
Shareholders do not pay for the shares.	Shareholders pay for the shares.
The net assets of the company are unchanged.	The company's net assets are increased by the cash received.
All the ordinary shareholders will receive their bonus shares.	Shareholders do not have to exercise their right to subscribe for the new shares.
Shareholders may sell their bonus shares if they do not wish to keep them.	Shareholders may sell their rights if they do not wish to exercise them.

22.4 Redemption of debentures (and shares)

In Chapter 21 we learned that debentures are a form of loan finance that requires the company to pay interest as well as buying them back at a later date. The company may buy them back for their face value ('at par') or may pay more ('at a premium'). Any costs and losses on settling a liability are passed through the statement of profit or loss (or retained earnings).

WORKED EXAMPLE 4

A company has an 8% debenture of $200 000 that it:

a   redeems at par value

b   redeems at a premium of 25%.

The journals would appear like this:

a

	Dr	Cr
	$000	$000
8% debentures	200	
Bank		200
Narrative: amount paid to debenture holders on redemption		

b

	Dr	Cr
	$000	$000
8% debentures	200	
Finance costs share premium (or retained earnings)	50	
Bank		250
Narrative: amount paid to debenture holders on redemption including a premium of 25%		

22.5 Liabilities, provisions and reserves

There are three terms that you will encounter when dealing with limited company accounts that need to be discussed in their own right, not least because the differences between them can be quite subtle. These are:

Liabilities: These are amounts owing by a company to trade or other creditors when the amounts can be determined with substantial accuracy (e.g. trade payables and accrued expenses). As will be seen in Chapter 25, under IAS 37 there will be other occasions when companies will be required to account for a liability. These include when a company is being sued and there is a high probability of it losing and being forced to pay damages and legal fees.

Provisions: These are created to provide for liabilities that are known to exist but of which the amounts cannot be determined with substantial accuracy (e.g. irrecoverable debt provisions). Provisions are created by debiting the amounts to the statement of profit or loss and crediting them to provision accounts. Unfortunately, accountants also use the word 'provision' when making reductions in the values of assets. This alternative meaning is seen when provisions are made for the depreciation of non-current assets (see Chapter 11) and unrealised profit on inventory of manufactured goods (see Chapter 20).

Reserves: These are created from profit set aside and are and not included in the definition of provisions here. They may be created by debiting the appropriation section of a company's statement of profit or loss and crediting reserve accounts. They may also be created by revaluing non-current assets.

22.6 Dividend policy

Before paying or recommending dividends, directors of a company must consider the following important matters:

- whether the amount of distributable profits justifies paying a dividend

- whether there is enough cash available to pay the dividend

- the mood of the shareholders – are they likely to be sympathetic to the directors' wishes to reinvest the profit into the company to help it grow, or will they be more concerned with a quick return

- the effect on share prices – a generous dividend policy may increase the value of shares on the stock exchange, whereas a 'mean' policy will have the opposite effect.

22.7 Other sources of finance for a limited company

There are a number of other sources of finance available to limited companies (and other businesses) apart from the issue of shares. Some of these will now be discussed in more detail.

Bank overdrafts

Bank overdrafts are temporary facilities that allow companies to become overdrawn on their bank accounts. Overdrafts are supposed to be a short-term solution to help businesses deal with temporary cash flow problems although many businesses do seem to be permanently overdrawn. Given that banks earn much of their income from interest (and the rates charged on overdrafts tend to be far higher than on longer-term finance), most bank managers will be quite happy for that situation to exist as long as they are reasonably certain that the amount being borrowed can be paid back.

While interest is calculated daily on the amount by which the business is overdrawn, it is only applied when the business is actually overdrawn. Some banks may offer overdrafts where a flat fee rather than interest is applied, as long as the overdraft is kept below an agreed limit. If the overdraft exceeds the agreed limit, then interest may be applied at a much higher rate.

Banks may cancel overdraft facilities at any time without notice, particularly if the business is breaching the terms and conditions under which the account operates or there is doubt over whether the amount being borrowed can be paid back.

Bank loans

Bank loans are available to a company provided it can satisfy the bank that:

- the funds are required for a project, such as capital investment or expansion that has a reasonable chance of success

- the company will be able to make the repayments on time, including interest

- the company is being properly run – it is not likely to lend people money when it is their incompetence that has caused the need for finance.

If the loan is being used to acquire assets, then it is likely that the legal ownership of those items will pass to the company straightaway. It will appear on the statement of financial position and will incur depreciation as normal. The loan will appear as a (long-term) liability and as the payments are made, part of these will reduce the liability and the interest will appear in the statement of profit or loss.

Bank loans are offered over a time period ranging from 12 months to 15 years and many large loans will be *secured* against the assets of the company, particularly if the loan is being provided to buy those assets. This means that if the business fails to keep up with the repayments then the bank can seize those assets in order to recover its losses.

Smaller bank loans tend to be unsecured, which means that the amount borrowed is not linked to any assets owned or being bought by the borrower. If the borrower fails to keep up with the repayments, the bank will take action to recover the money not seek to take possession of assets.

The rate of interest charged on a loan may be fixed or variable and is a lower rate than that charged on overdrafts. Larger (and longer-term) loans attract a lower interest rate, although factors such as the bank's opinion about how risky the loan is will also be considered. The interest is charged on the full amount of the loan whether it is used or not.

Hire purchase

A **hire purchase** agreement is a method of buying an asset where legal ownership does not pass to the company until all of the repayments have been made.

The concept of *substance over form* can, in special circumstances, be used by companies to justify their putting the asset into the statement of financial position.

Leasing

Leasing is a form of rental that allows a company leasing an asset (the lessee) to use it while the ownership of the asset remains with the company from which it is leased (the lessor). With a pure **lease**, the asset will never become the property of the lessee and the rental is shown in the lessee's statement of profit or loss as an expense. Some companies will enter into a *lease-to-buy* agreement where they will have the option of paying a final amount in order to acquire ownership. The leasing agreement indicates that the lessor is responsible for the repair and maintenance of the assets and will enable the lessee to upgrade to higher specification assets (for a suitable increase in the monthly payments) if the need arises.

Trade payables

Some of a company's finance is provided by its trade and expense payables. This is a short-term form of finance. However, if a company abuses this source of finance, it risks losing the goodwill of its suppliers and sacrificing advantageous credit terms. The creditors may insist that future dealings are on a cash basis, or they may even withdraw supplies or services altogether.

22.8 Deciding how a company is financed

Limited companies will use a mix of all the forms of financing covered in this chapter. The type of financing required will depend on whether the company is investing for the future and needs long-term capital, or whether it is looking for assistance with its current cash flow needs, known as the company's net current assets.

Long-term capital

Long-term requirements should be financed by long-term sources. Financing the acquisition of non-current assets runs the risk that the loans will have to be repaid before the assets in question have generated sufficient funds for the repayment. The non-current assets of a company should be adequately covered by long-term loans, share capital and reserves or, possibly, by long-dated debentures. This will allow the company to generate the funds for repayment by the time the term has expired.

KEY TERMS

hire purchase: a finance or credit agreement where a person has the use of an asset while paying for it in instalments.

lease: a contract outlining the terms under which one party agrees to rent property owned by another party.

Net current assets

As will be seen in Chapter 30, the company should have more current assets than current liabilities (a current ratio exceeding 1:1) if it is to be confident of meeting its day-to-day liabilities. However, it is possible that some of its current assets might not be instantly convertible into cash. Some of the inventory might be slow-moving and some of the trade receivables might be very slow to pay.

The company might consider taking out a loan to cover this, but the repayments will commit them to further cash flow stresses. Potentially short-term problems require short-term solutions – possibly organising an overdraft facility.

REFLECTION

Do you think that deciding the right dividend policy for a public limited company can be quite difficult for the board of directors? Why/why not?

THINK LIKE AN ACCOUNTANT

Raising investment funding

'Even though the company has made increasingly large profits over the last few years, it needs to raise $10 million', stated the Finance Director.

'There are several options available to us including:

- making a traditional issue of ordinary shares
- making a rights issue of ordinary shares
- issuing preference shares
- issuing debentures
- taking out a loan.'

What are the advantages and disadvantages of each of these methods of finance? Which one should the company choose and why?

Figure 22.2: When a company needs to raise money, there are a number of options available to them.

EXAM-STYLE QUESTIONS

1   Which of the following will not be shown as equity in the statement of financial position?

   A   debentures   **C**   revaluation reserve

   B   retained earnings   **D**   share premium   [1]

2   A company has issued 600 000 ordinary shares of $0.50 each. It makes a bonus issue of one share for every two already held. It follows that with a rights issue of two shares for every three already held at $0.80 per share. The rights issue was fully taken up. What was the increase in the share capital account as a result of the bonus and rights issues?

   A $300 000   **B** $360 000   **C** $450 000   **D** $480 000   [1]

CONTINUED

3 A company, which has 400 000 ordinary shares of $1 each, issues 200 000 bonus shares and follows this with a rights issue of 300 000 ordinary shares at $1.80 per share. What is the increase in the share capital and reserves of the company after these transactions?

   A $300 000

   B $500 000

   C $540 000

   D $900 000   **[1]**

4 The following trial balance was provided for Compton Ltd at 30 November 2020:

	$000	$000
Property, plant and equipment (net book value)	2 239	
Ordinary share capital ($0.50 each)		800
Share premium		400
General reserve		300
Sales		13 915
Administrative expenses	3 345	
Distribution costs	941	
Bank loan		600
Trade payables		659
Trade receivables	1 304	
Purchases	8 233	
Inventory at 1 December 2019	1 074	
Loan interest paid	54	
Retained earnings at 1 December 2019		720
Ordinary share dividends	430	
Cash at bank		226
	17 620	17 620

Further information

- Inventory on 30 November 2020 was valued at $987 000.
- Administrative expenses of $37 000 were prepaid at 30 November 2020 while distribution costs of $16 000 were owing.
- Some of the land and buildings which were shown in the books at $880 000 were to be revalued at $1 200 000.
- There had been a 1-for-4 rights issue which had resulted in receipts to the bank of $275 000. Nothing had yet been recorded in the accounts.
- Tax for the year was $288 000.
- $200 000 needs to be transferred to general reserve.

CONTINUED

Required

a   Show the journal required to record the rights issue (narratives are required).   [3]

b   Prepare the statement of profit or loss for Compton for the year ended 30 November 2020.   [11]

c   Prepare the statement of changes in equity for Compton for the year ended 30 November 2020.   [6]

d   Explain *two* differences between a bonus issue and a rights issue.   [4]

Further information

Compton Limited wants to buy non-current assets costing $400 000 but has not decided on how to finance this. The bank is willing to lend the company the money, with monthly repayments amounting to a total of £504 000 over a four-year period, but there is also the option of the company leasing the assets over a four-year period at a cost of $240 000. The useful life of the assets is ten years.

e   Explain *three* main differences between acquiring a non-current asset using a bank loan and using an ordinary leasing agreement.   [6]

SELF-EVALUATION CHECKLIST

After studying this chapter, complete a table like this:

You should be able to:	Needs more work	Almost there	Ready to move on
Explain the features and accounting treatment of bonus issues and rights issues, remembering that a bonus issue is an issue of free shares to existing shareholders from the accumulated reserves of the company so they are not being given anything that doesn't already belong to them, whereas a rights issues is an issue of shares made for cash. The shares are offered first to existing shareholders, in proportion to the shares held by them.			
Explain the advantages and disadvantages both to the company and to its shareholders of the company making a bonus or rights issue.			
Prepare ledger accounts to record an issue of ordinary shares at par or at a premium, a rights issue at par or at a premium, or a bonus issue.			

Chapter 23

Non-profit making organisations (clubs and societies)

This chapter covers part of syllabus section A Level 3.1

LEARNING INTENTIONS

In this chapter you will learn how to:

- distinguish between and prepare the receipts and payments account and the income and expenditure account
- prepare subscription accounts
- prepare the statement of financial position for non-profit making organisations
- define and calculate the accumulated fund
- produce the financial statements for non-profit making organisations.

ACCOUNTING IN CONTEXT

Oldcastle Cricket Club

Majid has been elected as Oldcastle Cricket Club treasurer. He was nominated only two weeks before the annual general meeting. The previous treasurer was offered a job in another country and so had not offered himself for re-election. Several of the other second team players had convinced Majid that as he was a partly qualified accountant, being treasurer would be fairly easy, but now he is not so sure.

From what he has seen of the club's accounts in previous years, Oldcastle Cricket Club's financial statements are quite different from most of those that he has seen at work.

Discuss in a pair or a group:

- What are the main objectives of Oldcastle Cricket Club and how do they differ from the typical client that Majid deals with at work?

- Why is it important that the financial affairs of organisations like Oldcastle Cricket Club be kept tightly under control?

- Why is it important that an accurate set of financial statements be produced every year for organisations like Oldcastle Cricket Club?

Figure 23.1: Oldcastle Cricket Club's financial statements are different from those that Majid has seen at work.

23.1 What are non-profit making organisations?

There are organisations involved in financial activity where profit is not the main priority. These organisations will include charities, where the main priority is to generate money that can be used to fund 'activities' that society would consider to be worthwhile. Examples might include:

- Oxfam – funding efforts to fight global poverty
- World Wildlife Fund (WWF) – looks to protect animals and protect the environment.

Other non-profit making organisations will include clubs like Oldcastle Cricket Club.

These clubs and societies exist to provide facilities for their members to enable them to pursue their interests, or to help their members to support particular projects that they consider worthwhile. While making a profit is not the main objective, raising funds and being financially sensible are essential if the organisation is to have enough money to be able to afford to carry out its main activities and provide good quality facilities for its members.

Another reason why the financial affairs of non-profit making organisations need to be tightly controlled and reporting accurate is that in some cases, that organisation may be responsible for handling vast amounts of money (Oxfam had income in 2018/19 of about US$190m). Clearly, the scope for mismanagement or even fraud in organisations of this size is enormous and so there will be laws and regulations requiring the reporting of accounting information.

Even at a smaller level, for example the average cricket club, the need for control and accurate reporting is still important.

Some clubs or societies have a treasurer who has some accounting knowledge. However, this cannot be relied on and often the only records that are kept are details of money received and spent. In these situations, preparing a set of accounts can be quite similar to the process of producing financial statements from incomplete records that we encountered in Chapter 16.

23.2 Special features of the accounts of non-profit making organisations

There are a number of terms that you will need to know when preparing financial statements for a non-profit making organisation. These are set out here, together with the corresponding term for a sole trader or partnership.

- An **income and expenditure account** takes the place of the statement of profit or loss.
- The words 'surplus of income over expenditure' are used in place of 'profit for the year'.
- The words 'excess of expenditure over income' are used in place of 'loss for the year'.
- The term **accumulated fund** is used in place of 'capital account'.
- A **receipts and payments account** takes the place of a bank account.
- **Subscriptions** take the place of revenue in the income and expenditure account.

Other types of club income may come from dances or the sale of tickets for a particular activity. Incomes and expenses from particular activities are often grouped together in the income and expenditure account so that it is possible to see whether a particular activity, say a social event, has made a surplus or deficit. This may help the committee who runs the club to decide whether to repeat that activity.

Some clubs may even have a shop, for example a cricket club may have a shop that sells cricket equipment and kit. In this case, it is likely that the profit (or loss) arising from this will be found by preparing a trading account and the result will be transferred to the income and expenditure account. A profit from such activities is regarded as an income while a loss will be regarded as expenditure. It is worth noting that some clubs may subsidise the cost of items by deliberately selling them at below cost price.

23.3 Income

The income of a club or society (we will use 'club' in the rest of this chapter to cover all not-for-profit organisations) should be treated in their accounts as set out here.

Subscriptions

In theory, working out subscription income ought to be easy as this involves multiplying the number of members by their annual subscription. Many clubs may have different categories (e.g. juniors, seniors and family memberships) where different fees are paid. A further complication is that some members may pay their membership in advance while others will pay late.

One way of calculating how much subscription income has been earned is to prepare a subscriptions account and use it in a similar way to income accounts (covered in Chapter 10). *Subscriptions in arrears* and *subscriptions in advance* can then be treated as accruals (current asset) and prepayments (current liability). Subscriptions that are never going to be received can be written off as irrecoverable debts.

KEY TERMS

income and expenditure account: the equivalent of the statement of profit or loss that enables the members to determine whether the organisation has made a surplus or deficit.

accumulated fund: the accumulated surpluses made by a club or society over previous years.

receipts and payments account: records the inflows and outflows of money through the cash and bank accounts during a period. It is also the bank account used by clubs and societies.

subscriptions: the amounts paid by members to be part of the club or society.

TIP

Knowledge of these terms is important and should be used correctly. For example, when preparing an income and expenditure account, label the final figure as 'surplus of income over expenditure', not 'profit for the year'.

Although it is preferable that the matching principle be applied, some clubs apply the *cash basis* where the amount of money actually received is treated as the income, regardless of whether it relates to late payments or those made early.

WORKED EXAMPLE 1

Wormingfield Cricket Club is a non-profit making organisation. Members each pay an annual subscription of $50. The numbers of members who had paid their subscriptions early or who were in arrears were as follows:

	1 January 2019	31 December 2019
In arrears	6	9
In advance	12	10

During the year ended 31 December 2019, $6 150 was received in subscriptions. Two members were written off as irrecoverable debts.

The subscriptions account for the year ended 31 December 2019 is shown below:

Subscriptions account					
Debit			Credit		
		$			$
1 Jan 19	Balance b/d [1]	300	1 Jan 19	Balance b/d [2]	600
31 Dec 19	Income and		31 Dec 19	Receipts and payments [3]	6 150
	expenditure [5]	6 500	31 Dec 19	Irrecoverable debts [4]	100
31 Dec 19	Balance c/d	500	31 Dec 19	Balance c/d	450
		7 300			7 300
1 Jan 20	Balance b/d [1]	450	1 Jan 20	Balance b/d [2]	500

Notes:

[1] Subscriptions in arrears are accrued income and therefore an asset – the balance b/d at both ends of the year are therefore debit balances.

[2] Subscriptions in advance are prepaid income and therefore a liability – the balance b/d at both ends of the year are therefore credit balances.

[3] The entries are debit bank (or receipts and payments account), credit subscriptions account.

[4] This assumes that the subscription owed by these members was $50 each. If these have been outstanding for long periods, it is possible that the cost of membership might have changed. What they owed is what should be written off.

[5] This is entered last and is the missing figure that represents the income for the year. Note that the term 'statement of profit or loss' has not been used.

The treasurer should have a list of the members and so will know who has paid and who hasn't, as well as having an idea of how much money should be coming in. If the financial affairs are in a chaotic state, it may be possible to use the subscriptions account to find other figures including:

a the subscriptions paid in advance

b the subscriptions owing at the end of the year

c the amount of money that was banked.

We will be using this information in Worked example 3 in Section 23.5.

ACTIVITY 23.1

A sailing club has 180 members. The annual subscription is $325. At the start of 2019, seven members had paid in advance and six members owed their subscriptions from last year.

During the year the treasurer banked $56 550 for subscriptions received from members including money from four members who had paid in advance for the next year.

Required

a   Prepare the subscriptions account for the year.

b   Explain how the two balances brought down are treated in the statement of financial position.

Life subscriptions and entry fees

Life subscriptions are received as lump sums but should not be credited in full to the income and expenditure account when received. The club should have a policy of spreading this income over a specified period (e.g. ten years). The amounts received should be credited to a separate **life membership** account and credited to the income and expenditure account in equal annual instalments over a period determined by the club committee. Any balance on the account at the end of the year will be carried forward to the next year.

Entry fees are also lump sum payments to the club, but these are paid by new members when they join the club. Clubs will treat that money as income in the year in which the member joins, but occasionally some clubs may treat these in the same way as life subscriptions. They are entered in an entry fees account and credited to the income and expenditure account in equal instalments over a period of time.

KEY TERM

life membership: the amount paid by a member of a club, which entitles them to be members of the club for their lifetime.

WORKED EXAMPLE 2

A club asks all new members to pay an entry fee of $200, in addition to their subscriptions. It is the club's policy to write down the entry fee over five years.

During 2019, eight new members joined, each paying the entry fee of $200. Five decided to just pay their first year's subscription of $120 while the other three decided to pay the life subscription of $600. The club writes off life subscriptions over five years.

At 1 January 2019, the balance on the entry fees account was $3 120 and on the life subscriptions account was $5 400.

The normal subscriptions account will contain the $600 arising from the five members who chose just to pay the first year's membership. The entry fees and the life subscriptions will appear as follows:

Entry fee account					
Debit			**Credit**		
		$			$
31 Dec 19	Income and expenditure [1]	944	1 Jan 19	Balance b/d	3 120
31 Dec 19	Balance c/d	3 776	31 Dec 19	Receipts and payments	1 600
		4 720			4 720
			1 Jan 20	Balance b/d	3 776

CONTINUED

Life subscriptions account					
Debit			Credit		
		$			$
31 Dec 19 Income and expenditure		1 440	1 Jan 19	Balance b/d	5 400
31 Dec 19 Balance c/d[2]		5 760	31 Dec 19	Receipts and payments	1 800
		7 200			7 200
			1 Jan 20	Balance b/d	5 760

Notes:

[1]   Entry fee income = 4 720 / 5 = $944

[2]   Life subscription income = (7 200 / 5) × 4 years = $5 760

In the event of no-one else joining the club or paying a life subscription, these figure would apply for each year until 2023.

As we shall see in Section 23.6, these closing balances are regarded as part of the accumulated fund (the club's equivalent of capital).

Donations

Donations refers to money given to the club by members in addition to their annual subscription or entry fee, or by non-members such as local businesses. If they are general donations, they are treated as general income.

However, sometimes they are donations where the donor has asked that the money be spent on a particular project, for example new showers in the changing rooms in the clubhouse. This often happens when someone who dies leaves a gift to the club in their will.

Specific donations should be credited to an account opened for the purpose and then expenditure on the project relating to the donation or legacy can be debited to the account.

Money received for special purposes should also be placed in a separate bank account to ensure that it is not spent on other things.

At the end of the year, the balance on the 'specific donations account' is listed under the accumulated fund in the statement of financial position. The balance on the bank account may appear under current assets as a separate item. Some clubs also list it as a non-current asset in the statement of financial position.

Other club activities (events)

The club may organise events that are not part of the club's main activities. A cricket club, for example, may organise dinner-dances or quizzes to help raise money for the club or have an annual presentation night to celebrate the achievements of the club and its members. It is usual for the revenues and costs to be collated so that the profit or loss arising from it can be assessed and this will be recorded in the income and expenditure account.

If an element of trading from an activity has taken place then a trading account might be produced to help to identify the profit or loss. This is important as the club's officers may use this information to help to decide whether an activity is worth doing.

A vital source of information for doing this is the receipts and payments account.

> **KEY TERM**
>
> **donations:** money given freely to an organisation. Sometimes donors may stipulate the use of the money.

23.4 Receipts and payments account

This account records the money coming in and going out of the club. It can be regarded as a representation of the club's bank account (in practice, the club may also keep reserves of cash too).

Preparation of the receipts and payments account is very similar to producing the bank accounts – receipts are debits and payments are credits. The account is balanced off in the normal way too.

23.5 Income and expenditure account

This is the club's equivalent of the statement of profit or loss and, if possible, should follow the main accounting principles like matching (accruals). This does mean that items not involving the movement of cash like depreciation and irrecoverable debts will be included and adjustments will need to be made for accrued and prepaid expenses. Assuming that the treasurer has the required expertise, the treatment of all of the items should be the same as for normal trading organisations.

It is therefore quite possible that the change in the club's bank account may not match the size of the **surplus of income over expenditure** or the **deficit of income over expenditure**.

WORKED EXAMPLE 3

Wormingfield Cricket Club had the following receipts and payments account for 2019:

Receipts and payments account			
Debit		**Credit**	
	$		$
Opening balance b/d	2930	Heat, light and water	1235
Subscriptions (general)	6150	Cricket ground maintenance	8210
Subscriptions (life)	500	Presentation night – catering	2135
Donations – general	985	Presentation night – trophies	330
Donation – new showers	2000	Presentation night v – band	400
Ticket sales – presentation night	1760	Grand prize draw [1] – prizes	1240
Ticket sales – grand prize draw [1]	2080	Bar purchases	5615
Match fees (from players)	3250	Materials for new showers	2095
Bar income	7635	New sightscreens (equipment)	3770
		Closing balance c/d	2260
	27290		27290
Closing balance b/d	2260		

Note:

[1] The Grand Prize Draw is a large-scale raffle where members buy numbered tickets. The prizes are awarded to the members owning the numbers of the tickets drawn (unseen) out of a large container.

Further information

1 General subscription income was $6500 and there had been irrecoverable debts of $100 (see Worked example 1).

2 A life subscription is deemed to last for ten years; the balance at the start of the year was $880.

3 Opening bar inventory was $280 and closing bar inventory was $235.

4 Equipment at 1 January was: cost $9 835 and accumulated depreciation $6 780.

5 Depreciation is applied at a rate of 20% per year using the straight-line method and it is assumed that equipment has no residual value.

6 An electricity bill of $240 was owing at the end of 2019 and there was a prepayment on ground maintenance of $625.

7 The committee has decided that the cost of the showers will be written off as an expense, given the donation.

To prepare the income and expenditure, consider any parts of the club that may involve trading. The bar is the obvious activity here and so a trading account is required:

Bar trading account		
	$	$
Revenue (takings)		7 635
Less: Cost of sales		
Opening inventory	280	
Purchases	5 615	
	5 895	
Closing inventory	(235)	(5 660)
Bar profit (income and expenditure account)		1 975

If the club employed someone to run the bar and paid them to do so, then it is likely that the wages would be deducted from the gross profit.

The life subscriptions account would look like this:

Life subscriptions account					
Debit			Credit		
		$			$
31 Dec 19 Income and expenditure		138	1 Jan 19 Balance b/d		880
31 Dec 19 Balance c/d		1 242	31 Dec 19 Receipts and payments		500
		1 380			1 380
			1 Jan 20 Balance b/d		1 242

The presentation night could be presented like this:

	$	$
Ticket sales		1 760
Less: Costs		
Catering	2 135	
Trophies	330	
Band	400	(2 865)
Loss/net cost of event (income and expenditure account)		(1 105)

CONTINUED

The Grand Prize Draw could be presented like this:

	$
Ticket sales	2 080
Prizes	(1 240)
Profit/income from draw (Income and expenditure account)	840

Some clubs may have put all of these figures into the income and expenditure account. The Grand Prize Draw would appear in the income section and the presentation night in the expenditure section.

If there are several figures involved, the treasurer may have to make a judgement about whether inclusion of all of the information might make the accounts difficult to read.

An alternative might be to show the workings as separate notes that support the main income and expenditure account. The same might apply to the depreciation and the two expenses that were adjusted for the accruals and prepayments.

Income and expenditure account		
	$	$
Income:		
Subscriptions: General	6 500	
Life	138	6 638
Bar profit (Income and expenditure account)		1 975
Donations – general		985
Match fees		3 250
Prize draw		840
		13 688
Expenditure:		
Presentation night	1 105	
Heat, light and water (1 235 + 240)	1 475	
Ground maintenance (8 210 – 625)	7 585	
Depreciation 20% × (9 835 + 3 770)	2 721	
Irrecoverable debts	100	
Showers[1]	95	(13 081)
Surplus of income over expenditure		607

Note:

[1]   Most of the cost of the showers was covered by the donation. Had the spending been less than $2 000, then nothing would be recorded in the income and expenditure account and there would have been a credit balance on a 'Donations: Showers' account. Had the showers cost $3 000, then a decision about capitalising the extra $1 000 (and applying depreciation) would need to be made.

ACTIVITY 23.2

Colneford Sports Club is a non-profit making organisation. Members each pay an annual subscription of $120. The numbers of members who had paid their subscriptions early or who were in arrears were as follows:

	1 April 2019	31 March 2020
In arrears	25	19
In advance	12	17

1. During the year ended 31 March 2020, $37 320 was received in subscriptions.
2. The club offers a life subscription option where members can pay $600. The club has decided that this income should be spread over a five-year period. Fourteen members took advantage of this option during the year. The balance on the life subscription account at the start of the year was $3 870.

Required

a. Prepare the subscriptions account to show the general subscription income earned by Colneford Sports Club during the year ended 31 March 2020.

b. Prepare the life subscription account to show the life subscription income earned by Colneford Sports Club during the year ended 31 March 2020.

Further information

Colneford Sports Club operates a bar that serves cold food and drinks and a shop that sells sports equipment and clothing at a subsidised price to its members. Inventory for both of these activities was:

	1 Apr 19	31 Mar 20
	$	$
Bar inventory	585	710
Shop inventory	3 105	2 875

The receipts and payments account for the year was as follows:

Receipts and payments account

Receipts and payments account				
Debit		**Credit**		
	$		$	
Opening balance b/d	1 830	Bar purchases	15 240	
Subscriptions (general)	37 320	Shop purchases	22 310	
Subscriptions (life)	8 400	Dinner dance – catering costs	1 960	
Bar income	23 195	Dinner dance – band	545	
Shop income	18 045	Quiz – cost of prizes	890	
Dinner dance – ticket sales	5 820	Heat and light	2 065	
Quiz income	3 215	Water rates	1 790	
		Rent, rates and insurance	5 240	
		Motor expenses	6 835	
		Wages and salaries (general)	18 600	
		Closing balance c/d	22 350	
	97 825		97 825	
Closing balance b/d	22 350			

CONTINUED

Notes:

1   The club owned a number of non-current assets:

    •   Equipment and furniture: cost $27 400, accumulated depreciation $18 200 (depreciation is to be applied 10% straight-line).

    •   Motor van: cost $16 100, accumulated depreciation $ 9 600 (depreciation is to be applied 25% reducing balance).

2   Heat and light of $720 was owing at 31 March 2020 but $1 420 of insurance had been prepaid.

Required

c   Prepare the bar trading account and the shop trading account for the year ended 31 March 2020.

d   Prepare the income and expenditure account for Colneford Sports Club for the year ended 31 March 2020.

23.6 The statement of financial position

The statement of financial position for a club has many of the same characteristics as that of a sole trader or partnership. In many ways, preparing one is very similar. However, there are some notable differences.

•   *Non-current assets*: In the statement of financial position, it is expected that each category of asset will be represented by three figures (cost, accumulated depreciation and net book value). While it is not wrong to show this amount of detail in the statement of financial position itself, many clubs will just show the net book value and refer members to a supporting note giving all of the information.

•   *Accumulated fund*: Instead of owner's capital, the club will have an accumulated fund which is considered to belong to the members. A *surplus of income over expenditure* during the year will increase the accumulated fund while a *surplus of expenditure* over income will reduce it. Unlike the capital for a sole trader, it is very unlikely that anyone will legitimately take money from the club and so there is no equivalent of drawings.

•   *Life-subscriptions/entry fees/specific donations*: There are likely to be a number of balances on these accounts that represent liabilities because members have paid money into the club and either the income has not been earned yet or the money donated has not yet been used.

It is quite possible that you will not be given the opening balance on the accumulated fund and so may need to prepare a statement of affairs to find it. The approach is the same as we saw in Chapter 16.

WORKED EXAMPLE 4

If we consider Wormingfield Cricket Club, taking many of the figures from Worked example 3), the statement of affairs might look something like this:

	$	$
Pavilion (new figure introduced here)		30 000
Equipment[1]		3 055
Bank		2 930
Bar inventory		280
Subscription (in arrears)		300
		36 565
Life subscriptions	880	
Subscriptions (in advance)	600	(1 480)
Accumulated fund at 1 January 2019		35 085

Note:

[1] Net book value = cost $9 835 – accumulated depreciation $6 780 = $3 055.

The statement of financial position and the supporting notes might look something like this:

	Cost	Accumulated depreciation		Net book value
	$	$		$
Non-current assets:				
Pavilion	30 000	–		30 000
Equipment	13 605 [2]	9 501	[3]	4 104
	43 605	9 501		34 104
Current assets:				
Bar inventory		235		
Subscriptions owing		450		
Bank		2 260		
Other recievables		625		3 570
Total assets				37 674
Capital and liabilities:				
Accumulated fund at 1 January 2019				35 085
Add: surplus of income over expenditure				607
Accumulated fund at 31 December 2019				35 692
Life subscriptions				1 242
Current liabilities:				
Subscriptions prepaid		500		
Other payables		240		740
Total accumulated fund and liabilities				37 674

Notes:

[2] Cost = opening balance $9 835 + equipment bought $3 770 = $13 605

[3] Accumulated depreciation = opening balance $6 780 + expense $2 721 = $9 501

ACTIVITY 23.3

Colneford Sports Club is a non-profit making organisation. The following balances were available:

	1 Apr 19	31 Mar 20
	$	$
Accrued expenses	–	720
Bank	1 830	22 350
Bar inventory	585	710
Equipment and furniture: at cost	27 400	27 400
Equipment and furniture: accumulated depreciation	18 200	??
Life subscriptions	3 870	9 816
Motor vehicles: at cost	16 100	16 100
Motor vehicles: accumulated depreciation	9 600	??
Prepaid expenses	–	1 420
Shop inventory	3 105	2 875
Subscriptions – in arrears	3 000	2 280
Subscriptions – paid in advance	1 440	2 040

Further information

1   Depreciation for the year was: equipment and furniture $2 740 and motor vehicles $1 625.

2   Surplus of income over expenditure was $9 484.

Required

a   Prepare a statement of affairs in order to find the accumulated fund at 1 April 2019.

b   Prepare a statement of financial position for Colneford Sports Club at 31 March 2020.

23.7 How to prepare club accounts

The process of producing a full set of accounts for a club can involve a number of steps.

As with incomplete records, no two situations are quite the same, but there are certain techniques you should make sure you master.

Step 1   Preparation of a statement of affairs – in order to find the accumulated fund.

Step 2   Preparation of general and life subscription accounts – remember that we are dealing with accrued and prepaid income which will determine whether we are dealing with assets or liabilities.

Step 3   Preparation of the receipts and payments (bank) account – in addition to finding a closing balance or a missing figure, this will enable you to identify important items relating to trading, major club events or the buying and selling of non-current assets.

Step 4   Preparation of trading accounts – in order to find the profit or loss made by the club bar or shop, which must then be inserted in the income and expenditure account.

Step 5   Preparation of income and expenditure account – do not forget to:

- Offset income and expenditure from an event and insert the results into the correct part of the account (profit is an income while a loss is expenditure). If there are several items, you could show your workings separately and just include the final results.

- Adjust for accruals or prepayments of expenses and depreciation.

Step 6   Preparation of the statement of financial position.

Activity 23.4 will take you through the whole process.

KEY CONCEPT LINK

Consistency: What items within a club or society's financial statements might be treated in a number of different ways and therefore a consistent approach (or policy) would need to be adopted?

ACTIVITY 23.4

Cropford Sports Club provides recreational activities, refreshments and social events for its members. It also sells sports equipment to its members at reduced prices.

The following list of balances was available:

	1 Apr 19	30 Mar 20
	$	$
Accrued expenses (heat and light)	325	510
Bank (money in account)	3480	??
Bar inventory	1245	1760
Equipment: at cost	24170	??
Equipment: accumulated depreciation	13255	??
Life subscriptions	5120	??
Motor van: at cost	17600	??
Motor van: accumulated depreciation	12200	??
Premises	130000	130000
Prepaid expenses (insurance)	1125	870
Shop inventory	2065	2290
Subscriptions – in arrears	1050	1640
Subscriptions – paid in advance	760	940

CONTINUED

Required

a   Prepare a statement of affairs showing clearly the accumulated fund at 1 April 2019.

Further information

1   The following payments and receipts had been made during the year:

Administration costs $16 430; Bar purchases $8 735; Bar takings $13 295; Club lottery: income $3 080; Club lottery: prizes $1 415; Events: Ticket sales $7 230; Events: Costs $8 160; General subscriptions received $18 210; Heat, light and insurance $6 595; Life subscriptions received $4 930; Purchase of equipment $4 500; Shop purchases $9 485; Shop takings $11 010.

2   Life memberships are spread across five years.

Required

b   Prepare a receipts and payments account showing clearly the bank balance at 31 March 2020.

c   Prepare the general subscriptions and life subscriptions accounts showing clearly the incomes for the year.

d   Prepare the bar and shop trading accounts for the year ended 31 March 2020.

e   Prepare the heat, light and insurance account showing clearly the expense for the year ended 31 March 2020.

Further information

Depreciation is to be applied on the following basis: equipment: 20% using the straight-line method, motor van: 30% using the reducing balance method.

Required

f   Prepare the income and expenditure account for the year ended 31 March 2020.

g   Prepare the statement of financial position at 31 March 2020.

REFLECTION

Apart from accounting knowledge, what skills would you regard as being essential in order to carry out the role of treasurer of a club or society? Discuss your thoughts with another learner.

THINK LIKE AN ACCOUNTANT

Onwards and upwards

Majid, the treasurer, has just finished preparing the financial statements for the AGM next month. Oldcastle Cricket Club's first team has been promoted to a higher division and the second team has won their division, partly due to the 43 wickets that Majid took. Memberships have increased, as have the bar takings and the surplus of income over expenditure was $4 230. There is also just over $5 000 in the club's bank account.

There have been discussions about certain projects that the club might undertake, including:

1 a complete refurbishment of the showers and changing rooms (a local building firm had quoted $8 000 to do the work) as the current ones are in poor repair

2 the replacement of sightscreens that were damaged in storms suffered several weeks ago (costing $2 000)

3 a refurbishment of the kitchen facilities including new equipment – a health and safety inspector has stated that no food could be served again until this has been done (one of the club's sponsors has offered a favourable quotation of $3 000 to do the work).

Figure 23.2: Oldcastle Cricket Club's first team has been promoted to a higher division.

These issues would be discussed at the AGM and Majid knew that the way he presented the financial statements (and the advice he gave) would influence those discussions. What conclusions and recommendations do you think Majid should make at the AGM regarding the three capital projects? Suggest how Oldcastle Cricket Club might go about obtaining the money to carry out all of these projects.

EXAM-STYLE QUESTIONS

1 Which of the following will *not* be found in the accounts of a club?

A accumulated fund

B drawings account

C receipts and payments account

D statement of financial position [1]

2 The following items have been found in the accounts of a non-profit making organisation:

i accrued expenses

ii prepaid expenses

iii subscriptions in arrears

iv subscriptions in advance

Which of the following are liabilities?

A i and iii

B i and iv

C ii and iii

D ii and iv [1]

CONTINUED

3   The following information for a year is extracted from a sports club's accounts:

	$
Subscriptions received	12 600
Sales of equipment to members	3 650
Opening inventory of equipment	680
Closing inventory of equipment	540
Purchases of equipment	2 430
Other expenses	5 200

What was the club's surplus of income over expenditure for the year?

A $7 400

B $7 940

C $8 480

D $8 760   [1]

4   The Long Spike Athletics Club's receipts and payments account for the year ended 31 May 2020 was as follows:

Receipts and payments account			
Debit		**Credit**	
	$		$
Opening balance b/d	2 104	Administrative expenses	1 842
Presentation night – ticket sales	3 215	New equipment purchases	2 210
Raffles – ticket sales	2 039	Presentation night costs	1 963
Snack bar sales	9 211	Prizes for raffles	1 321
Sales of equipment	150	Snack bar purchases	4 298
Subscriptions	4 360	Travelling expenses	1 329
		Wages	2 250
		Closing balance c/d	5 866
	21 079		21 079
Closing balance b/d	5 866		

Further information

1   Snack bar inventories were valued at $327 at 1 June 2019 and $285 at 31 May 2020.

2   At 1 June 2019, subscriptions paid in advance were $320 and $440 at 31 May 2020.

3   At 1 June 2019, subscriptions owing were $240, of which $200 was paid in the year to 31 May 2020. It is the club's policy to write off subscriptions if they have not been received by the end of the year following their due date. Subscriptions owing at 31 May 2020 were $280.

4   The wages were paid to staff serving refreshments in the snack bar.

5   Equipment was valued at $7 420 at 1 June 2019 and at $8 190 at 31 May 2020. Equipment disposals in the year had a net book value of $370.

6   The managing committee is considering whether to introduce a life membership scheme.

CONTINUED

Required

a   Prepare the club's subscriptions account for the year ended 31 May 2020.   **[4]**

b   Prepare the snack bar trading account for the year ended 31 May 2020.   **[6]**

c   Prepare the income and expenditure account for the year ended 31 May 2020.   **[8]**

d   State *two* differences between the financial statements prepared by a non-profit making organisation and a trading business.   **[2]**

e   Advise the club management whether or not they should introduce such a scheme. Justify your answer.   **[5]**

SELF-EVALUATION CHECKLIST

After studying this chapter, complete a table like this:

You should be able to:	Needs more work	Almost there	Ready to move on
Distinguish between and prepare the receipts and payments account and the income and expenditure account, as many clubs will have an income and expenditure account instead of a statement of profit or loss and a receipts and payments account instead of a bank account.			
Prepare subscription accounts, as clubs and societies will generate income from ordinary subscriptions, life memberships and entry fees.			
Prepare the statement of financial position for non-profit making organisations including adjustments, remembering that instead of capital, the club will have an accumulated fund.			
Define and calculate the accumulated fund, ensuring that the surplus of income is added to the accumulated fund but the surplus of expenditure reduces it.			
Produce the financial statements, where necessary applying incomplete records techniques.			

> Chapter 24

Statements of cash flows

LEARNING INTENTIONS

In this chapter you will learn how to:

- explain what a statement of cash flows is and why it is important
- explain the main provisions of IAS 7
- prepare a statement of cash flows in line with IAS 7 and legal requirements
- prepare a statement of financial position using the statement of cash flow.

ACCOUNTING IN CONTEXT

Roger's engineering company

The financial statements for Roger's engineering company had shown a large profit for the year and yet, the business bank account was heavily overdrawn. Twice in the last year, Roger had received a letter from the bank telling him that there would be large bank charges because the overdraft limit had been exceeded. It seemed that every morning, Roger received more reminders and final demands for payment of various bills and he was starting to dread the phone ringing as this was almost invariably another angry supplier wanting to know when he would get paid.

Roger was puzzled. How could it be that the company could be so profitable and yet his cash flow could be so bad that his business might actual be forced to close down?

Discuss in a pair or a group:

- What is the difference between cash flow and profitability?

- What types of item or transaction differ in terms of their effect on the bank account and how they appear in a business' financial statements?

Figure 24.1: Roger's engineering company had shown a large profit for the year and yet, the business bank account was heavily overdrawn.

24.1 What is a statement of cash flows?

A statement of cash flows is one that lists the inflows and outflows of cash for a business over a period of time – the same period as that covered by the statement of profit or loss.

A cash flow is any increase or decrease in the amount of **cash** held by a business. For the purposes of this chapter, cash refers to more than just 'notes and coins'. It also includes positive balances or overdrafts in bank accounts that are *repayable on demand*. On demand means money that can be reclaimed/repaid either immediately or within 24 hours of notice being given.

> **KEY TERM**
>
> **cash:** includes cash in hand and bank deposits repayable on demand, less any overdrafts repayable on demand.

24.2 Why statements of cash flows are important

As discussed in Chapters 7, 18 and 21, the size of the profit made by a business will be of considerable interest to a wide range of people including:

- *Sole traders and partners*: The profit will represent income and debts will be their personal responsibility.

- *Shareholders*: The profit of a company will determine the size of dividends that can be paid out by the directors.

- *Banks and other lenders*: The company's profits may determine how confident these people will be about getting paid their money back as well as whether they will lend money to the business in the first place.

- *Suppliers*: The profitability of the business will help suppliers decide whether they should offer credit facilities.

- *Employees and the local community*: The business may provide employment to a large number of local people. Jobs are more likely to be secure if the business is making a profit.

- *Tax authorities*: The size of the company's profits will determine how much tax needs to be paid.

While it is important to make a profit, most accountants would agree that it is cash flow that determines whether a business survives or not. Profit does not pay the wages, the day-to-day bills or suppliers – cash does. Businesses can survive long term without ever making an operating profit, but many businesses have been forced to close down in a very short space of time because they did not have enough money in their bank accounts to settle debts when they became due.

One of the problems is that even profitable businesses can suffer from major cash flow difficulties. This is because there will be a large number of items that will have a different impact on the size of the bank account and the business's profit figure, not least because of the use of the accruals concept in the measurement of income and expenses.

The following table shows some of the differences:

	Bank account shows	Profitability shows
Purchases/sales	Money changing hands	Invoices received/issued on credit
Expenses	Money paid out	Expenses relating to the period whether paid in advance or in arrears
Non-current assets	When money is paid out on acquisition	Depreciation is spread out over the life of the asset
Irrecoverable debts	Nothing – not a movement of cash (depreciation is a non-cash item)	Expense
Drawings, tax and dividends	Money paid out	No effect – these are appropriations not expenses
Loans	All repayments or taking out of loans	Interest on repayments only
Share issues and introduction of capital	An inflow of money	Nothing – this is not income

This is not a complete list but it does provide some reasons why a business could make a large profit but still experience difficulties because of a lack of cash (or make a loss but still see an increase in the amount of cash it has). A statement of cash flows helps the business and its owners see why this apparent contradiction has happened.

24.3 Statements of cash flows and limited companies

IAS 7: Statement of Cash Flows covers the structure and layout of the statement of cash flows for a limited company. This requires limited companies to produce a statement of cash flows as part of the annual financial statements. It provides guidelines for the format of statements of cash flows.

The statement is divided into three categories:

1   **Operating activities:** These show the main revenue-generating activities of the business, together with the payment of interest and tax.

2   **Investing activities:** These show the acquisition and disposal of long-term assets together with details of interest and dividends received.

> ### KEY TERM
>
> **operating activities:** the main revenue-generating activities of the company – the trading of goods or provision of services.

3   **Financing activities:** These show receipts from the issue of new shares, payments for the redemption of shares and changes in long-term borrowings (loans).

These three categories will be used to explain the change between the cash and cash equivalents at the start of the period and those at the end of the period. In this book and the syllabus, cash and cash equivalents will be deemed to be cash and bank current accounts.

Let us look at how a basic statement of cash flows is constructed.

KEY TERMS

investing activities: the acquisition and disposal of non-current and other long-term assets.

financing activities: receipts from the issue of new shares or long-term loans, also payments made to redeem shares or to repay long-term loans.

WORKED EXAMPLE 1

The statements of financial position for Wright Limited for 31 December 2019 and 2020 were as follows:

	2019 Cost	2019 Depreciation	2019 Net book value	2020 Cost	2020 Depreciation	2020 Net book value
	$	$	$	$	$	$
Non-current assets:						
Land	75 000	–	75 000	125 000[1]	–	125 000
Motor vehicles	22 200	6 200	16 000	39 000	8 900	30 100
			91 000			155 100
Current assets:						
Inventories	7 000			11 000		
Trade receivables	5 000			3 700		
Bank	1 000	13 000		500	15 200	
Current liabilities:						
Trade payables	5 500			7 300		
Tax	1 000	(6 500)		1 500	(8 800)	
Net current assets			6 500			6 400
			97 500			161 500
Equity and liabilities:						
Ordinary shares		80 000			90 000	
Share premium		1 500			2 500	
Revaluation reserve		–			50 000	
Retained profits		11 000	92 500	[2]	16 000	158 500
Non-current liability:						
Debentures			5 000			3 000
			97 500			161 500

Notes:
[1]   During 2020, the land was revalued at $125 000.
[2]   Dividends paid during the year were $2 500.

CONTINUED

The relevant details from the statement of profit or loss were as follows:

Profit from operations	9 400
Interest payable	(400)
Profit before tax	9 000
Tax	1 500
Profit for the year	7 500

The convention adopted is that inflows of cash are shown as positive figures and outflows of cash or items being subtracted are shown in brackets.

Reconciliation of profit from operations to net cash from operating activities for Wright Ltd for the year ended 31 December 2020	
Net cash inflow from operating activities:	$
Profit from operations[1]	9 400
Depreciation for year[2]	2 700
Increase/decrease in respect of inventories[3]	(4 000)
Increase/decrease in respect of trade receivables[4]	1 300
Increase/decrease in respect of trade payables[5]	1 800
Cash generated by operations	11 200
Interest paid (given)	(400)
Tax paid[6]	(1 000)
Net cash from operating activities[7]	9 800

Notes:

[1] The starting point is an assumption that a profit means that more cash came into the business from revenue than went out in expenses – in this case $9 400. A loss would have indicated a net outflow of cash. The rest of this statement provides reasons why this is not entirely true.

[2] Depreciation is added back because it is not an outflow of cash and so the cash flow is better than the $9 400 previously thought. The figure is simply the difference between the closing and opening accumulated depreciation figure (8 900 – 6 200).

[3] Inventories has increased by $4 000 (11 000 – 7 000) and this is regarded as an outflow of cash because the business has spent more on inventory than it has used and that money is tied up in the warehouse. A reduction in inventory would have been regarded as an inflow.

[4] Trade receivables has reduced by $1 300 (3 700 – 5 000), which is good for cash flow because it means that customers have paid more money than the credit sales made during the year. An increase in trade receivables would mean that people had not been paying, which is bad for cash flow.

[5] Trade payables increasing by $1 800 (7 300 – 5 500) is good for cash flow because it means that the company has paid out less money than the amount of goods purchased on credit. This is good for the bank balance, although it may not be good for the relationship with the supplier who is not happy about being kept waiting for their money. A reduction in payables is shown as an outflow as it would mean that the company had paid out more than the value of the credit purchases.

CONTINUED

[6] Tax paid was in this case deduced using common sense. The opening liability was $1 000 and companies have nine months to pay the tax due, so it seems reasonable to assume that this was the amount paid, particularly as the tax for the year of $1 500 matches the closing liability. In later examples, the situation might not be so simple.

[7] This is our assessment of the real net (inflow) of cash arising from our trading activities and increase/decrease to our net current assets. This figure feeds into the main statement of cash flows.

Statement of cash flows for Wright Ltd for the year ended 31 December 2020		
	$	$
Net cash from operating activities [as calculated previously]		9 800
Investing activities:		
Purchases of property, plant and equipment [8]	(16 800)	
Proceeds on disposal of property, plant and equipment	–	
Net cash used in investing activities [11]		(16 800)
Financing activities:		
Proceeds of share Issue [9]	11 000	
Repayment of debentures [10]	(2 000)	
Dividends paid (given)	(2 500)	
Net cash from financing activities [11]		6 500
Net decrease in cash and cash equivalents [12]		(500)
Cash and cash equivalents at the start of the year [13]		1 000
Cash and cash equivalents at the end of the year [13]		500

Notes:

[8] $16 800 is the difference between the costs at the beginning and end of the year (39 000 − 22 200). The cost of land has changed because of a revaluation and so the increase of $50 000 should be ignored because it is not a movement of cash.

[9] The share capital and premium has increased by $11 000 (from a combined total of $81 500 to $92 500), which tells us how much money was received.

[10] The face value of the debentures has fallen by $2 000 indicating that the company has redeemed them – an outflow. It can always be assumed that this redemption took place at 'par value'. If the value of debentures had increased, we would know that an issue of debentures had taken place – an inflow. The same principle applies to loans – repayment is an outflow of cash and taking out a loan is an inflow.

[11] These sections have two possibilities: a net inflow and a net outflow. You should note the labelling of these headings. 'Used in' indicates a net outflow and 'from' indicates a net inflow.

[12] The combined totals of the operating, investing and financing activities will either result in a net increase or net decrease in cash and cash equivalents. This figure should match the change in the opening and closing cash/bank figure.

[13] These are taken straight from the statements of financial position, but you need to take to ensure that both cash and bank balances are used. Obviously, if both items are current assets, the numbers can be added together, but if the bank balance is an overdraft, then the figures will need to be *netted off* against each other.

ACTIVITY 24.1

The statements of financial position for Starman Limited for 30 June 2019 and 2020 were as follows:

	2019 Cost	2019 Depreciation	2019 Net book value	2020 Cost	2020 Depreciation	2020 Net book value
	$	$	$	$	$	$
Non-current assets:						
Premises	80000	–	80000	80000	–	80000
Motor vehicles	51000	22100	28900	83000	35400	47600
Office equipment	29000	18000	11000	49000	23000	26000
			119900			153600
Current assets:						
Inventories		22500			15300	
Trade receivables		9000			7000	
Bank		–	31500		6100	28400
Total assets			151400			182000
Equity:						
Ordinary shares		50000			60000	
Share premium		25000			30000	
Retained profits		18000	93000		16000	106000
Non-current liabilities:						
Bank loan			40000			55000
Current liabilities:						
Trade payables		9000			15000	
Corporation tax		3200			6000	
Bank overdraft		6200	(18400)		–	21000
Total liabilities			58400			76000
Total equity and liabilities			151400			182000

Dividends paid during the year amounted to $11000.

The relevant details from the statement of profit or loss were as follows:

Profit from operations	19000
Interest payable	(4000)
Profit before tax	15000
Tax	(6000)
Profit for the year	9000

Required

a   Prepare a reconciliation of profit from operations to net cash from operating activities for Starman Ltd for the year ended 30 June 2020.

b   Prepare a statement of cash flows for Starman Ltd for the year ended 30 June 2020.

24.4 Disposals and deducing amounts paid

So far, we have been able to find items (e.g. purchases of non-current assets or depreciation) by working out the size of the changes in the relevant figures between the beginning and end of the year. However, things become more complicated when non-current assets are sold as the costs and accumulated depreciation amounts will have been removed from the accounts. There will also be proceeds and a profit or loss on disposal to be considered.

It is also possible that with items like tax, the company may have made payments based on estimates or been required to make payments in advance. To deal with these, use the same approach when dealing with incomplete records – namely constructing 'outlines' into which the known figures can be placed and using them to deduce the missing figures. Once found, these can be inserted into the main statements.

WORKED EXAMPLE 2

The statements of financial position for Upson Limited for 31 October 2019 and 2020 were as follows:

	2019 Cost	2019 Depreciation	2019 Net book value	2020 Cost	2020 Depreciation	2020 Net book value
	$	$	$	$	$	$
Non-current assets:						
Premises	200 000	–	200 000	350 000	–	350 000
Machinery	110 000	81 000	29 000	132 000	83 000	49 000
Fixtures and fittings	87 000	41 600	45 400	84 000	38 300	45 700
			274 400			444 700
Current assets:						
Inventories	23 600			30 900		
Trade receivables	17 800			34 900		
Bank	11 500	52 900		74 400	140 200	
Current liabilities:						
Trade payables	25 500			37 000		
Tax	1 700	(27 200)		1 400	(38 400)	
Net current assets			25 700			101 800
			300 100			546 500
Equity and liabilities:						
Ordinary shares		250 000			300 000	
Share premium a/c		–			20 000	
Revaluation reserve		–			150 000	
Retained profits		10 100			16 500	
Debentures		40 000			60 000	
			300 100			546 500

CONTINUED

During the year, the premises was revalued at $350 000.

Machinery costing $37 000 that had been depreciated by $31 200 was sold for $6 500 and fixtures and fittings costing $28 000 that had been depreciated by $25 700 were sold for $900.

Dividends paid during the year were $3 600.

The relevant details from the statement of profit or loss were as follows:

	$
Profit from operations	19 200
Interest payable	(5 000)
Profit before tax	14 200
Tax	(4 200)
Profit for the year	10 000

It is probably best to deal with the complications arising from the disposal of the non-current assets first and then look at the tax payment.

There are several ways in which the 'outlines' can be set out, but the following approach could be used:

[1]Disposals	Machinery	Fixtures	[2]Depreciation:	Machinery	Fixtures
	$	$		$	$
Cost	37 000	28 000	Opening balance	81 000	41 600
Accumulated depreciation	(31 200)	(25 700)	Add depreciation	33 200	22 400
Net book value	5 800	2 300		114 200	64 000
Proceeds	6 500	900	Less disposals	(31 200)	(25 700)
Profit/(loss) on disposal	$700	$(1 400)	Closing balance	83 000	38 300

[3]Tax	Tax	[4]Purchases:	Machinery	Fixtures
	$		$	$
Opening liability	1 700	Opening balance	110 000	87 000
Add amount for year	4 200	Plus purchases	59 000	25 000
Less amount paid	(4 500)		169 000	112 000
Closing liability	1 400	Less disposals	(37 000)	(28 000)
		Closing balance	132 000	84 000

We now have the necessary items to put into the main statements:

CONTINUED

Reconciliation of profit from operations to net cash from operating activities for Upson Ltd for the year ended 31 October 2020

Reconciliation of profit from operations to net cash from operating activities for Upson Ltd for the year ended 31 October 2020	
	$
Net cash inflow from operating activities:	
Profit from operations	19 200
Depreciation for year	55 600 [2]
Loss on disposal of property plant and equipment	700 [1]
Increase/decrease in respect of inventories	(7 300)
Increase/decrease in respect of trade receivables	(17 100)
Increase/decrease in respect of trade payables	11 500
Cash generated by operations	62 600
Interest paid	(5 000)
Tax paid	(4 500) [3]
Net cash from operating activities	53 100

Statement of cash flows for Upson Ltd for the year ended 31 October 2020		
Net cash from operating activities		53 100
Investing activities:		
Purchases of property, plant and equipment[4]	(84 000)	
Proceeds on disposal of property, plant and equipment	7 400	
Net cash used in investing activities		(76 600)
Financing activities:		
Proceeds of share issue	70 000	
Issue of debentures	20 000	
Dividends paid	(3 600)	
Net cash from financing activities		86 400
Net increase in cash and cash equivalents		62 900
Cash and cash equivalents at the start of the year		11 500
Cash and cash equivalents at the end of the year		74 400

Notes:

[1] In this case, the two disposals have been combined. A loss on disposal is added back while a profit on disposal is subtracted. There are several reasons for this:
   • The profit or loss on disposal is the result of the large or small size of the proceeds, which will be recorded in the main statement of cash flows. Not removing them here will result in double-counting the gain or loss.
   • Disposals of non-current assets are not a day-to-day trading activity and so it is not suitable to leave them in the 'profit from operations' section.

[2] The depreciation charges on each category of non-current assets have been combined to provide one figure for the main statement.

[3] The tax paid is as calculated in the 'outline'.

[4] The purchases of each category of non-current assets have been combined to provide one figure for the main statement.

> **CONTINUED**
>
> It is worth noting that the information that you have access to may be different or may be presented in a different way. In Worked example 1, you were given the following information:
>
> 'Machinery costing $37 000 which had been depreciated by $31 200 was sold for $6 500.'
>
> The information about the machinery could easily have been presented as follows:
>
> Machinery costing $37 000 that had a net book value of $5 800 was sold and a profit on disposal of $700 was made.
>
> As long as you are aware of the relationship between cost, accumulated depreciation and net book value, and you know what profit or loss on disposal means in terms of the proceeds, there should be no problem:
>
> Cost – accumulated depreciation = net book value
>
> This can be rearranged as:
>
> Cost – net book value = accumulated depreciation
>
> 37 000 – 5 800 = $31 200 (which could then be inserted into the relevant 'outlines')
>
> Proceeds =   net book value + profit on disposal
>
> Or   net book value – loss on disposal
>
> For the machinery, this will be:
>
> Proceeds = 5 800 + 700 = $6 500 (that could then be inserted into the statement of cash flows.
>
> For the fixtures and fittings, the information might have been presented as follows:
>
> Fixtures and fittings costing $28 000 which had a net book value of $2 300 were sold. A loss on disposal of $1 400 was made.
>
> Accumulated depreciation = 28 000 – 2 300 = $25 700
>
> Proceeds = 2 300 – 1 400 = $900

ACTIVITY 24.2

A company made a number of disposals during the year.

Required

Complete the following table, which contains some of the information about the items that were sold.

	Original cost	Accumulated depreciation	Net book value	Profit or loss	Proceeds
	$	$	$	$	$
Equipment		23 490	7 160	Profit 3 500	
Machinery	54 000	41 800			9 750
Motor vehicles	28 100		5 650		6 840
Office furniture	11 200		2 870	Loss 2 120	

24.5 Non-current assets – published accounts

So far, detailed information has been provided about the non-current assets including the cost, accumulated depreciation and net book value, while the various categories of assets have been listed separately. However, it is quite possible that if you only have access to the published final accounts but not the supporting notes, the information provided might not give all of this detail.

WORKED EXAMPLE 3

Suppose the information has been provided in the following style:

	2020	2019
	$	$
Non-current assets (net book value)	820 000	727 900

During the year, non-current assets costing $214 000 that had been depreciated by $146 000 were sold and a profit on disposal of $28 200 was made. Depreciation for the year was $85 000.

The information may be presented with the most recent to the left and the oldest on the right.

To calculate missing items like the purchases of non-current assets, construct an 'outline' that reflects all of the possible changes to the net book value. In this example, it might look something like this:

	$	
Non-current assets:		
Opening balance (net book value)	727 900	
+ Purchases	245 100	
	973 000	= 820 000 + 85 000 + 68 000 (see below)
+ Revaluations	–	
– Disposals (net book value)	(68 000)	= 214 000 – 146 000
– Depreciation expense	(85 000)	
= Closing balance (net book value)	820 000	

> **TIP**
>
> Take care. Getting these figures mixed up will cause problems as you will be mistaking increases for decreases and just about every figure that you put into the main statements will be wrong.

Proceeds: The amount of money received from the disposal of a non-current asset is either:

 net book value at time of disposal + profit on disposal or
 net book value at time of disposal – loss on disposal

Here, it is a profit on disposal, so 68 000 + 28 200 = $96 200.

This figure will be shown as an inflow of cash in the 'investing activities' section of the statement of cashflows.

Once these items have been identified, the preparation of the main statements can be carried out in the usual way.

ACTIVITY 24.3

The following information was available for Kaneria Limited:

	2020	2019
	$000	$000
Non-current assets (net book value)	1701	1323

During the year, non-current assets costing $396 000 that had been depreciated by $269 000 were sold and a loss on disposal of $42 000 was made. The value of the buildings had been increased from $200 000 to $500 000 during 2020.

Depreciation for the year was $314 000.

CONTINUED

Required

a Calculate the purchases of non-current assets for the year.

b Calculate the the proceeds arising from the disposals.

24.6 How to prepare a statement of financial position from a statement of cash flows

It is normal to produce a statement of cash flows from the two statements of financial position (and a few other pieces of information). However, it is also possible to prepare a closing statement of financial position using the opening one, the statement of cash flows and a few other pieces of information, as Worked example 4 demonstrates.

WORKED EXAMPLE 4

The statement of financial position for Vieira Limited at 30 November 2019 was as follows:

	Cost	Depreciation	Net book value
	$	$	$
Non-current assets:			
Motor vehicles	22 000	10 500	11 500
Equipment	36 000	16 000	20 000
			31 500
Current assets:			
Inventories	15 000		
Trade receivables	8 000		
Bank and cash	18 800	41 800	
Current liabilities:			
Trade payables	11 000		
Tax	6 000	(17 000)	24 800
			56 300
Equity and liabilities:			
Ordinary shares		20 000	
Retained earnings		16 300	
Bank loan		20 000	
			56 300

Further information

1 A motor vehicle costing $10 000 that had been depreciated by $7 200 was sold for $4 500.

2 Depreciation on motor vehicles during the year was $3 900.

3 Motor vehicles were purchased for $15 600.

4 Equipment costing $14 000 that had been depreciated by $9 600 was sold for $3 500.

5 Depreciation on equipment during the year was $12 600.

6 Equipment was purchased for $28 000.

CONTINUED

The relevant details from the statement of profit or loss were as follows:

	$
Operating profit	13 700
Interest payable	(1 000)
Profit before tax	12 700
Tax	(7 400)
Profit for the year	5 300

The reconciliation of profit from operations to net cash from operating activities and the statement of cash flows for Vieira Limited for the year ended 30 November 2020 were as follows:

	$
Net cash inflow from operating activities:	
Profit from operations	13 700
Depreciation for year	16 500
Gain on disposal of property plant and equipment	(800)
Increase/decrease in respect of inventories	3 000
Increase/decrease in respect of trade receivables	(6 600)
Increase/decrease in respect of trade payables	(3 000)
Cash generated by operations	22 800
Interest paid	(1 000)
Tax paid	(9 200)
Net cash from operating activities	12 600

		$
Net cash from operating activities		12 600
Investing activities:		
Purchases of property, plant and equipment	(43 600)	
Proceeds on disposal of property, plant and equipment	8 000	
Net cash used in investing activities		(35 600)
Financing activities:		
Proceeds of share issue	10 000	
Repayment of bank loan	(5 000)	
Dividends paid	(4 500)	
Net cash from financing activities		500
Net (decrease) in cash and cash equivalents		(22 500)
Cash and cash equivalents at the start of the year		18 800
Cash and cash equivalents at the end of the year		(3 700)

CONTINUED

Non-current assets: The closing balances can be obtained using the 'outline' approach that we saw earlier:

	Motor vehicles	Equipment	
	$	$	
Assets at cost			
Opening balance	22 000	36 000	
Add purchases	15 600	28 000	Given in the question
	37 600	64 000	
Less disposals	(10 000)	(14 000)	Given in the question
Closing balance	27 600	50 000	

	Motor vehicles	Equipment
	$	$
Accumulated depreciation		
Opening balance	10 500	16 000
Depreciation	3 900	12 600
	14 400	28 600
Disposal	(7 200)	(9 600)
Closing balance	7 200	19 000

The net book value can be found by subtracting the accumulated depreciation from the cost.

Current assets and liabilities: Apart from the tax, these can be found by considering the cash flows from operating activities:

Inventories: 15 000 − 3 000 = $12 000 (a reduction of inventory is an inflow of cash)

Trade receivables: 8 000 + 6 600 = $14 600 (an increase in trade receivables is an outflow of cash)

Trade payables: 11 000 − 3 000 = $8 000 (a reduction in trade payables is an outflow of cash)

Tax	$
Opening liability	6 000
Amount in year	7 400
Amount paid	(9 200)
Closing liability	4 200

Capital and loans: This is again a case of examining the changes that have taken place:

Share capital: 20 000 + 10 000 = $30 000 (there is not enough information to be able to identify how much of this might be share premium).

Retained earnings: 16 300 + 5 300 − 4 500 = $17 100

Loan: 20 000 − 5 000 = $15 000 (repayment has reduced the balance)

CONTINUED

The statement of financial position for Vieira Limited at 30 November 2020 will therefore look like this:

	Cost	Depreciation	Net book value
	$	$	$
Non-current assets:			
Motor vehicles	27 600	7 200	20 400
Equipment	50 000	19 000	31 000
			51 400
Current assets:			
Inventories	12 000		
Trade receivables	14 600	26 600	
Current liabilities:			
Trade payables	8 000		
Bank overdraft	3 700		
Tax	4 200	(15 900)	10 700
			62 100
Equity and liabilities:			
Ordinary shares			30 000
Retained earnings			17 100
Bank loan			15 000
			62 100

KEY CONCEPT LINK

Planning and control: Management accounting provides a framework for a business to plan and control its finances and enables informed decision making. How can the production of the statement of cash flows help the business in its planning and control?

REFLECTION

Which do you think is more important, good cashflow or good profitability? Justify your choice to another learner.

THINK LIKE AN ACCOUNTANT

Sorting out the cash flow

Roger's meeting with the accountant had been quite useful. It seemed that there were a number of practical ways that Roger could improve his company's cash flow, including:

- more effective control of his current assets – particularly trade receivables, trade payables and inventory

- deciding how to finance the acquisition of a new motor van costing $30 000.

This all sounded good in practice, but any measures that Roger took would need to work quickly if his business were to survive. What practical measures might Roger use to manage his current assets better and improve his cash flow? What should Roger do regarding acquiring a new motor van, assuming that it is essential that he gets one?

Figure 24.2: Roger's accountant discussed a number of ways to improve the company's cash flow.

EXAM-STYLE QUESTIONS

1   An examination of a company's accounts at the end of the year revealed the following:

	$
Cash from operations	40 000
Increase in trade payables	7 000
Decrease in trade receivables	2 000
Increase in inventories	6 000
Depreciation charge for the year	18 000

What was the profit from operations before interest and tax for the year?

A $19 000   B $37 000   C $61 000   D $73 000   [1]

2   The following relates to the plant and machinery for a limited company:

	At 31 Dec 2020	At 31 Dec 2019
	$	$
Cost	70 000	45 000
Depreciation	(30 000)	(28 000)

During the year plant costing $14 000 was sold at a loss of $5 000. What figure will appear as purchase of non-current assets in the statement of cash flows for the year?

A $34 000

B $36 000

C $37 000

D $39 000   [1]

CONTINUED

3 The following figures have been extracted from the books of a limited company:

	At 31 Aug 2020	At 31 Aug 2019
	$000	$000
Ordinary share capital	400	300
Share premium	80	50
Debenture 2023/2024	30	50
Dividends paid during the year	15	11

What is the cash from financial activities for the year?

A	$85 000	B	$95 000	C	$135 000	D	$146 000	[1]

4 The statements of financial position for Kanu Limited for 30 April 2019 and 2020 were as follows:

	2019 Cost	2019 Depreciation	2019 Net book value	2020 Cost	2020 Depreciation	2020 Net book value
	$	$	$	$	$	$
Non-current assets:						
Premises	90 000	–	90 000	140 000	–	140 000
Motor vehicles	52 000	27 600	24 400	79 000	33 500	45 500
Office equipment	66 000	17 900	48 100	76 000	21 400	54 600
			162 500			240 100
Current assets:						
Inventory	9 800			16 100		
Trade receivables	22 500			15 200		
Bank	1 500	33 800		10 700	42 000	
Current liabilities:						
Trade payables	23 300			23 400		
Tax	11 000	(34 300)		13 000	(36 400)	
Net current assets			(500)			5 600
			162 000			245 700
Equity and liabilities:						
Ordinary shares		100 000			120 000	
Share premium		20 000			30 000	
Retained profits		22 000			25 700	
Revaluation reserve		–	142 000		50 000	225 700
Bank loan			20 000			20 000
			162 000			245 700

CONTINUED

Further information

1   During the year, the land was revalued at $140 000.

2   Vehicles costing $18 000, that had been depreciated by $13 200 were sold for $6 400 and equipment costing $9 000 that had been depreciated by $6 800 was sold for $1 500.

3   Dividends paid during the year were $8 000.

The relevant details from the statement of profit or loss were as follows:

	$
Profit from operations	26 700
Interest payable	(2 000)
Profit before tax	24 700
Less tax	(13 000)
Profit for the year	11 700

Required

a   Prepare a reconciliation of profit from operations to net cash from operating activities for Kanu Limited for the year ended 30 April 2020.   [6]

b   Prepare a statement of cash flows for Kanu Limited for the year ended 30 April 2020.   [10]

c   Explain why it is important for Kanu Limited to produce a statement of cash flows.   [4]

SELF-EVALUATION CHECKLIST

After studying this chapter, complete a table like this:

You should be able to:	Needs more work	Almost there	Ready to move on
Explain what a statement of cash flows is and why it is important. It is possible to be profitable and have very poor cash flow.			
Know the main provisions of IAS 7: Statement of Cash Flows, as it requires companies to produce a statement of cash flows that shows the inflows and outflows of cash and cash equivalents during the year.			
Prepare a statement of cash flows in line with IAS 7 and legal requirements and also prepare a statement of financial position using the statement of cash flow, remembering that the statement of cash flows is broken into operating activities, investing activities and financing activities.			

> Chapter 25

Auditing and stewardship

This chapter covers part of syllabus section A Level 3.2

LEARNING INTENTIONS

In this chapter you will learn how to:

- explain stewardship and the roles and responsibilities of directors
- describe the role and responsibilities of the auditor
- describe the differences between an external auditor and an internal auditor
- explain the difference between a qualified and unqualified audit report
- explain the importance of a true and fair view in respect of financial statements
- explain the main requirements of IAS 8, IAS 10 and IAS 37.

ACCOUNTING IN CONTEXT

Discom PLC

Although Hansie only owned a few hundred shares in Discom PLC, he did like to go to the AGMs. They were normally quite interesting and he was exercising his rights as a shareholder to be there. However, given some of the rumours that had appeared in the financial press, strange things had been going on within the company. Two of the directors had already resigned and Hansie suspected that the meeting could turn out to be quite unpleasant.

An Extraordinary General Meeting has now been be called where there will be a motion to dismiss the board of directors and a recommendation that a special audit be carried out by the auditors.

Discuss in a pair or a group:

- Why are directors needed in a PLC?
- What are the main responsibilities of the directors?
- Who would have called the Extraordinary General Meeting?
- What may have caused the shareholders to want to dismiss the board of directors?
- Why might the auditors be asked to conduct a special audit?

Note: Do not worry if you are unfamiliar with some of these terms. Try looking them up if you have resources available. If not, you will find out what they mean, and the associated issues, in this chapter.

Figure 25.1: Although Hansie only owned a few hundred shares, he liked to go to the AGMs.

25.1 Introduction to published company accounts

There are many groups of people who will have a legitimate interest in the financial statements of a limited company. Many of them are external stakeholders including banks, payables and the tax office.

However, we will concentrate on three groups of people who play a major role in, hopefully, ensuring that a limited company is operating legally and is providing accurate accounting information. These are:

- shareholders
- directors
- auditors.

The roles of each are discussed in detail in the following sections.

25.2 The role of shareholders

The shareholders do not usually manage the company on a day-to-day basis unless they are also directors. Most public limited companies have many shareholders and it would be impractical to get them together regularly to make speedy and effective decisions, particularly as it is unlikely that they would be in complete agreement. However, shareholders do have *two* important duties to perform:

- They appoint the members of the **board of directors**. Each year the company must hold an annual general meeting (AGM). At this meeting the ordinary shareholders, who are the owners of the company, will vote on a number of items put forward by the directors. One of these will be to elect the members of the board of directors.

KEY TERM

board of directors: a group of people elected by a company's shareholders to represent the shareholders' interests and ensure that the company's management acts on their behalf.

- They vote at the AGM on key issues that ensure the effective governance of the company by the directors. By voting on these issues they are giving clear and detailed instructions to the board of directors as to how the company should be managed and what is expected of them as directors. The directors act as **stewards** of the shareholders' investment in the company and, as such, are in a position of trust. Apart from voting on the appointment of directors at the AGM, the shareholders are also asked to vote on other issues such as:

  - the appointment of the company's auditors

  - to approve the dividends proposed by the directors

  - to approve charitable donations by the company.

KEY TERM

steward: someone who is appointed to look after money or property belonging to another person or organisation.

Under company law, the shareholders can also request the directors to convene a special meeting (an Extraordinary General Meeting or EGM) if something is happening of which they disapprove. For example, if they feel that the directors are acting unethically or if they wish to ask the director who is taking this action to resign.

The directors can also convene a special meeting of the shareholders if they have an important decision to make, such as a potentially major change to the company's activities. At this meeting, the directors will ask the ordinary shareholders to vote on their proposal.

25.3 Stewardship: the role of the directors and their responsibilities to shareholders

The directors act as *stewards* of the shareholders' investments in the company; they are in a position of trust. As there is most likely to be more than one director, they are usually referred to as the *board of directors*. Directors are appointed to manage the company day-to-day on behalf of the owners, its ordinary shareholders, and are directly accountable to those shareholders for their actions.

Each year at the AGM the directors must provide a report to the shareholders on the performance of the company, its future plans and strategies, and recommend any dividends. Directors are usually only appointed for a set period – a certain number of years – as set out in the Articles of Association. Once that period has expired, any directors who wish to continue in the role must seek re-election by the shareholders at the AGM. If the shareholders vote not to re-elect a director then he or she must step down and can no longer take part in managing the company.

Overall, the key role of the board of directors is to ensure the prosperity of the company by directing the company's affairs. They must also meet the interests of the shareholders and other stakeholders by ensuring that they (and the company) always act in a responsible and ethical manner.

The directors are also responsible for ensuring that certain documents are prepared and published annually in accordance with the law and accounting regulations. These documents are:

- statement of profit or loss

- statement of financial position

- statement of cash flows

- directors' report

- audit report.

These documents must be sent to the shareholders in advance of every AGM as well as to debenture-holders and every person who is entitled to receive notice of general meetings. The directors must file an annual return, which includes the annual accounts, with the

Registrar of Companies. These returns may be inspected by any member of the public (on payment of a small fee). Apart from shareholders and debenture-holders, other people who may be interested in a company's accounts are:

- trade and other creditors

- providers of long-term finance, such as banks and finance houses

- trade unions, representing the company's workforce

- financial analysts employed by the financial press

- fund managers managing client investments

- stock exchanges.

Directors' report and strategic report

The directors of the company are required by the Companies Act to prepare a report for each financial year. The purpose of the report is to supplement the information given by the financial statements. The directors of a company qualifying as large or medium-sized must also prepare a strategic report, as well as a directors' report, within their annual report.

The **directors' report** contains the following information:

- The names of the directors, together with their responsibilities, interests and shareholdings in the company. The shareholders are entitled to know who have been stewards of their interests during the year.

- Proposed dividends payable by the company. These will be voted on for recommendation by the shareholders at the company's AGM.

- Political donations made by the company. Shareholders may not want their money to be used for political purposes.

- Company policy on the employment of disabled people. Legislation dictates that companies must not discriminate against employees on the grounds of any disability.

- A report on the annual quantity of greenhouse gas emissions from activities for which the company is responsible.

- A statement confirming that all relevant audit information has been provided to the company's auditor and an auditor's independence statement.

- Details of any post year-end important events affecting the company or group.

- Likely future developments in the business, research and development.

- Information on acquisition of own shares.

- Voting rights along with details of the AGM.

- What action the company has taken on employee involvement in the running of the business, and any consultation that has taken place between management and workers on the management and running of the business.

The strategic report contains the following information:

- a fair review of the company's business

- a description of the principal risks and uncertainties facing the company

- analysis using financial key performance indicators

- additional explanations of amounts included in the company's annual accounts.

In addition, for PLCs:

- the main trends and factors likely to affect future performance

- the company's strategy and business model

> **KEY TERM**
>
> **directors' report:** a report prepared by the directors of a limited company at the end of the financial year.

- information about environmental matters, employees and social, community and human rights issues
- information about gender diversity of the directors, the senior managers and the employees of the company.

Companies that qualify for the small companies' exemptions are not required to prepare a strategic report.

Companies with fewer than 250 staff members are not required to give the employee information set out here.

25.4 Roles and responsibilities of auditors

In connection with a limited company there are two types of auditor:

- *Internal auditors*: These are employees of the company, appointed by the directors. In many organisations, internal auditors will be linked to the security function although their main role is to help 'add value' to the company and help the organisation achieve its strategic objectives. They form part of the day-to-day management team of the business. Their key roles are therefore:

  a   evaluate and assess the control systems in place within the company

  b   evaluate information security and risk within the company

  c   consider and test the anti-fraud measures in place in the company

  d   overall, help to ensure that the company meets its strategic and ethical objectives.

- *External auditors*: These examine the systems and records of the company – usually at the year end. External auditors are not employees of the company; they are independent accountants. They are appointed by the shareholders to ensure that the financial statements prepared by the directors are a *true and fair view* of the state of financial affairs of the company. The auditors examine the financial records and systems and prepare an **audit report**, which is presented to the shareholders at the AGM. The shareholders, along with the debenture-holders, are entitled to receive copies of the annual accounts. It is important that shareholders and debenture-holders are sure that the directors can be trusted to conduct the company's business well and that the financial statements and directors' report are reliable.

The shareholders appoint auditors to report at each AGM whether:

a   proper books of account have been kept

b   the annual financial statements are in agreement with the books of account

c   in the auditor's opinion, the statement of financial position gives a true and fair view of the position of the company at the end of the financial year, and the statement of profit or loss gives a true and fair view of the profit or loss for the period covered by the accounts

d   the accounts have been prepared in accordance with the Companies Act and all current, relevant accounting standards.

If auditors are of the opinion that the continuance of a company is dependent on a bank loan or overdraft, they have a duty to mention that fact in their report, as it is relevant to the *going concern concept*.

The auditor's responsibility extends to reporting on the directors' and any strategic report and stating whether the statements in it are consistent with the financial statements. They must also report whether, in their opinion, the report contains misleading statements or information that is incomplete or is difficult to verify.

> **KEY TERM**
>
> **audit report:** an external report prepared by the auditors of a limited company stating whether or not the annual financial statements provide a true and fair view.

Auditors must be qualified accountants and independent of the company's directors and their associates. They report to the shareholders and not to the directors; as a result, auditors enjoy protection from wrongful dismissal from office by the directors.

The structure of the audit report

There is a set format for the auditor's report. It will usually begin with:

> *We have audited the accompanying financial statements of Miggins Limited for the year ended...*

Here, the financial statements include not only the statement of profit or loss and the statement of financial position but also the statement of cash flow and any schedules, say of non-current assets. The audit will have examined the ledgers and bank reconciliation. They will have looked at vehicle log books and title deeds to property, and physically inspected the assets concerned. All the time the auditor is trying to ensure the accuracy and validity of the figures set out in the financial statements.

The report will then set out management's responsibility for the preparation of accurate financial statements. The principle here is that the financial statements have been, and have to be, prepared by the directors. It is not the auditors who prepare the financial statements.

The report then sets out the responsibilities of the directors and auditors in connection with the financial statements. These include:

- that the audit has been conducted in accordance with the auditing standards issued by their professional body in their country
- that the directors are fully aware of their responsibility to prepare accurate financial statements
- that they, as auditors, have taken all the necessary steps to obtain enough information to express their opinion
- that they have also taken into account the relevant IASs and Companies Act provisions as part of their audit.

Qualified and unqualified audit reports

The final stage is for the report to give an opinion on the financial statements. These may take several forms:

Unqualified reports: The auditors will issue an unqualified audit report if:

- in their opinion, the company's financial statements are fairly and appropriately presented and represent a true and fair view of the state of affairs at the year-end date, without any identifiable exceptions
- the financial statements have been prepared in compliance with generally accepted accounting principles, legislation and the accounting regulations
- the auditor believes that all changes, accounting policies, and their application and effects – they may have requested them – have been accurately made and disclosed.

This audit report will be written as:

> ***In our opinion***, *the financial statements give a **true and fair view** of Miggins Limited's affairs at 30 November 2020 and of the profit and cash flows for the 52 weeks ended on that date...*

> *...that they **have been properly prepared** in accordance with the requirements of the Companies Act 2006 and IAS...*

> *...that the **information given in the directors' report is consistent** with the data contained in the financial statements.*

Qualified reports: If, during the course of their audit the auditors found anything which they feel was in doubt or inaccurate they can issue a *qualified* audit report. In this case, at the end, a statement will be inserted that draws the attention of the shareholders to this fact. For example:

> *During the course of our audit we discovered that the method of valuing inventory changed from last year, but no mention of this has been made in the directors' report. We believe that this has had a material effect on the profit stated.*

The offending issues will have been raised with the directors who will have been given the opportunity to make the necessary changes suggested by the auditors. This type of qualified audit report is unusual and can indicate that either the directors have refused or are unable to make the necessary changes.

In extreme cases, the auditors will put something along the lines of:

> **we are unable** *to express an opinion as to whether these accounts represent a true and fair view* … This means vital information could not be verified due to a lack of evidence.

A qualified auditor's opinion represents very bad news for a limited company, particularly the 'unable to express an opinion', as stakeholders are unable to place much, if any, trust on those reports.

Auditors and fraud: A question often raised is whether auditors are legally responsible for identifying fraud. Would they be guilty of negligence if they provided an unqualified audit report and, later, a major fraud was revealed to have taken place? The accounting authorities hold the view that if the auditors have adopted a thorough approach to examining and testing data that makes it reasonably likely that significant error or fraud would be revealed, then they will not be held responsible for problems that remain undetected.

ACTIVITY 25.1

The auditors of Mugs Limited have identified a number of issues with the financial statements and have recommended a number of changes.

After discussion, the directors have told the auditors that they do not accept their proposal to adjust the accounts. They have stated that the accounts they have prepared will be used to obtain additional funding from the bank for expansion. If the accounts are adjusted, they may fail to obtain this funding.

Required

a   Explain the difference between an internal and external audit and the roles and responsibilities of each.

b   Explain what is meant by a true and fair view of the financial statements of a limited company.

c   Explain whether or not the auditors should present a qualified audit report at the AGM.

25.5 The financial statements

The overall objectives of a set of financial statements is that they provide a true and fair view of the profit or loss of the company for the year, and that the statement of financial position likewise gives a true and fair view of the state of affairs of the company at the end of the financial year.

The accounting principle of *substance over form* (see Chapter 9) is one accounting principle intended to give a true and fair view. The Companies Act sets out rules for the presentation of company accounts. If accounts prepared in accordance with those rules do not provide sufficient information to meet the requirement to present a true and fair view then:

- further information must be provided in the financial statements or in the notes supporting those accounts

- if necessary, because of special circumstances, the directors shall depart from the normal rules in order to present a true and fair view and state why they have departed from the normal rules. An example of this is the capitalisation of certain non-current assets that are being used as part of a leasing agreement (where strictly speaking, the ownership of the assets will never change hands).

25.6   Generally accepted accounting principles (GAAP)

Accounting standards form the basis of the regulatory framework and help to ensure that businesses and their accountants comply with the true and fair view concept. All companies are required to comply with accounting standards, or to publish reasons for departing from them.

Company auditors are required to ensure that company accounts are prepared in accordance with the standards and to report any significant departure from the standards to the shareholders. The standards help to increase uniformity in the presentation of company accounts and to reduce the subjective element in the disclosure of information.

International accounting standards have been developed in the form of **International Accounting Standards (IASs)** and *International Financial Reporting Standards (IFRS® Standards)* since 2005, with the aim of harmonising (standardising) financial reporting.

The following table shows the IASs you should be aware of. Some have already been covered in other chapters. The remaining ones, and some aspects of the others not previously mentioned, will be covered here.

IAS	Topic	Covered in
1	Presentation of financial statements	Chapter 21 and 22
2	Inventories	Chapters 17 and 26
7	Statement of cash flows	Chapter 24
8	Accounting policies	Chapter 25
10	Events after the statement of financial position date	Chapter 25
16	Property, plant and equipment	Chapter 26
36	Impairment of assets	Chapter 26
37	Provisions, contingent liabilities and contingent assets	Chapter 25
38	Intangible assets	Chapter 26

> **KEY TERM**
>
> **International Accounting Standards (IASs):** standards created by the International Accounting Standards Board stating how particular types of transaction or other events should be reflected in the financial statements of a business entity.

As we have already discussed in earlier chapters, company law also plays an important part in the way financial accounts are presented. In particular, it makes it a requirement for companies to state that their accounts have been prepared in accordance with applicable accounting standards. If this has not been the case then details must be given as to why not.

This book will examine the IASs that specifically refer to assets in Chapter 26.

25.7 Accounting concepts

Although not an accounting standard, a **conceptual framework** has been developed by the International Accounting Standards Board (IASB), which sets the IASs underlying the preparation and presentation of financial statements.

The framework identifies the typical user groups of accounting statements. The table identifies these user groups (stakeholders) and gives some reasons why they would be interested in the financial statements.

> **KEY TERM**
>
> **conceptual framework:** a system of objectives and ideas that lead to the accounting authorities creating a consistent set of rules.

Stakeholders	Reasons for use
Investors	To assess past performance and the health of the business to decide whether to invest
Employees	To assess performance for future wage and salary negotiations or to determine likely job security
Lenders	To assess performance and health of the business to determine whether there is a risk of not being repaid
Suppliers	To assess whether it is safe to grant credit to the business – is there a risk that the business will not pay what it owes?
Customers	To assess performance in relation to the likelihood of continuity of trading
Government/ Tax office	To assess whether the company is complying with regulations and assessment of taxation liabilities
Public	To assess performance in relation to ethical trading

When preparing financial statements, we assume that they are prepared on a matching basis and that the business is a going concern.

- *Matching* (see Chapter 9): Companies must compile their financial statements (except statements of cash flows) on a matching (accruals) basis. This means that transactions are recorded in the accounting year in which they occur and to which they relate, not when cash is received or paid. Examples include adjusting expenses to reflect the amount incurred or the charging of depreciation across the useful life of non-current assets.

- *Going concern* (see Chapter 9): Financial statements are prepared on the assumption that the business will continue trading for the foreseeable future – even if there is a very real possibility that it will fail. One reason for this is the valuation of assets, particularly the non-current assets. It is quite possible that the disposal value of a business's assets is significantly lower than the net book value of those items. If the value of those assets were to suddenly be adjusted to that lower level because the business was thought to be in difficulties, it might cause panic among the stakeholders, including trade and other payables who might take action to recover the money that they were owed. This could lead to the business failing when it might otherwise have survived.

There are a number of other accounting concepts that you should also consider when preparing the financial statements:

- business entity
- materiality
- consistency
- prudence
- money measurement.

All of these concepts, which were also examined in detail in Chapter 9, are designed to ensure that the information provided in the financial statements is useful to users with four objectives in mind:

- *Relevance*: Information should have the ability to influence the economic decisions of the users of the statements and be provided in time to influence those decisions.

- *Reliability*: Information is reliable if it faithfully represents the facts and is free from bias and material error. It must be complete 'within the bounds of materiality' and prudently prepared.

- *Comparability*: It should be possible to compare information with similar information about the company in a previous period and with similar information relating to other similar companies.

- *Understandability*: Information should be able to be understood by users who have a reasonable knowledge of business and accounting as long as they are willing to study the information carefully.

25.8 IAS 8 Accounting policies, changes in accounting estimates and errors

IAS 8 deals with the treatment of changes in accounting estimates, changes in accounting policies and errors in the financial statements.

Accounting policies: These policies are selected by the directors when the company is preparing and presenting its financial statements. It is essential that any policy they select complies with the relevant accounting standards. Examples of accounting policies can include the method of valuing inventory (e.g. choosing whether to use the FIFO or AVCO method) or the method(s) used to depreciate non-current assets (e.g. straight-line or reducing balance methods).

Accounting estimates: These are an assessment of the net book value of an asset, liability, or related expense. Accountants will frequently consider the expected future benefits and obligations associated with each asset, liability or related expense to determine whether the valuation of these items in the financial statements is valid. It is possible that an accountant may decide that an assessment of the value of an asset, liability or expense is no longer valid and that a change to some of the accounting estimates is required.

Sometimes, the relevant standards are not specific enough. Many only provide a range of acceptable accounting treatments rather than one particular method. In this situation, the directors must use their judgement to give information that is relevant and reliable. They may refer to practise what is normal for their particular industry or seek guidance from their industry's lead bodies (authorities).

Accounting principles: These are the broad concepts that apply to almost all financial statements and include many of the concepts encountered in Chapter 9, including going concern, materiality, prudence and consistency.

Accounting bases: These are the methods developed for applying the accounting principles to financial statements. They are intended to reduce subjectivity by identifying and applying acceptable methods. The general rule is that once an entity adopts an accounting policy then it must be applied consistently for similar transactions. Changes in accounting policies can only occur if the change is required by a standard or if the change results in the financial statements providing more reliable and relevant information. Once any changes are adopted then they must be applied retrospectively to financial statements. This means that the previous figure for equity and other figures in the statement of profit or loss and the statement of financial position must be altered, subject to the practicalities of calculating the relevant amounts.

Examples here include the method and rate used by a company to depreciate its non-current assets or the way in which it values inventory. Does the value include material and labour costs or a proportion of factory overheads or should FIFO or AVCO be used?

Dealing with errors: If the business discovers a material (significant) error in the financial statements, then they must correct it in the next set of financial statements and restate relevant amounts from previous periods if they can be calculated.

In this instance, errors are omissions from (or misstatements in) the financial statements covering one or more prior periods. They might be something as simple as a mathematical mistake made when preparing the accounts. They may also include the failure by directors to use reliable information that was available when the financial statements were prepared and more accurate information has become available.

There are many examples of where errors can have a very significant effect on the financial statements of a business. Some of these include:

Uber (taxi services in the UK): Between 2015 and 2017, the company had taken its 25% commission from the total income of its drivers rather than after tax and other fees had been deducted. The effect on profit of refunding those drivers reduced the company profit by $45–50 million.

Valeant Pharmceuticals: This multinational company based in Canada overadded is revenue by $58 million in 2015–16, and although this amount was a small proportion to its turnover, it was sufficient to result in an investigation by the accounting authorities who concluded that this had been happening for a number of years. Share prices fell by 86% in 2016 and the company was later taken over by Bausch Health Companies Inc.

Tesco (the largest UK supermarket): In 2017, a series of inaccurate reporting involving inventory valuation, amounts paid to suppliers and turnover resulted in profits being overadded by £250 million. This resulted in three directors standing trial for fraud and a total of over £200 million having to be paid in compensation to investors or fines. On 22 September 2017, when the news of the problem was made public, the fall in share prices exceeded a total value of £2 billion.

Changes should only be made to previous accounts if it means that those accounts are more accurate. It is never permissible to change accounting methods in order to achieve a desired result, e.g. achieving a higher or lower profit figure.

25.9 IAS 10 Events after the statement of financial position date

These are events that occur between the year end and the date on which the financial statements are authorised or approved. Directors often have to decide whether they should be included in the financial statements of the year that has just finished, particularly if they are adjustments to existing figures. IAS 10 provides guidance.

The basic principle is that once the financial statements are authorised or approved they cannot be altered.

IAS 10 distinguishes between two types of event, adjusting events and non-adjusting events.

Adjusting events: These are events or conditions *that existed at the year end* that would *materially* affect the financial statements. Alterations can be made to the financial statements to reflect these conditions.

Examples of adjusting events could include:

- the settlement, after the date of the statement of financial position, of a court case that confirms that an obligation existed at the date of the statement of financial position

> **KEY TERM**
>
> **adjusting events:** events where the financial statements can be adjusted because the underlying conditions leading to those events existed at the year end.

- the purchase price or proceeds from the sale of a non-current asset bought or sold before the year end, but not known about at the date of the statement of financial position

- inventories where the net realisable value falls below the cost price

- assets where a valuation shows that impairment is required (see Chapter 26)

- trade receivables where a customer has become insolvent

- the discovery of fraud or errors that show the financial statements to be incorrect.

Non-adjusting events: No adjustment is made to the financial statements for such events. In other words, the items and values included in the financial statements themselves are produced on the basis that these events had not actually happened. However, if these events are material because they could affect the stakeholders' view of the business, they should be disclosed by way of notes to the financial statements.

Examples of non-adjusting events include:

- major purchases of assets

- losses of production capacity caused by fire, floods or strike action by employees

- announcement or commencement of a major reconstruction of the business

- the company entering into significant commitments or contingent liabilities (a liability that may occur depending on the outcome of an uncertain future event and where the value can be reasonably estimated)

- commencing litigation based on events arising after the date of the statement of financial position

- major share transactions, such as the issue of new shares and debentures or capital reductions or reconstructions.

There are three situations in addition to these that require consideration:

a   Dividends declared or proposed after the date of the statement of financial position are no longer recognised as a current liability in the financial statements. They are non-adjusting events and are now to be shown by way of a note to the accounts.

b   If, after the date of the statement of financial position, the directors determine that the business intends to cease trading and that there is no alternative to this course of action, then the financial statements cannot be prepared on a going concern basis.

c   A business must disclose the date when the financial statements were authorised for issue and who gave that authorisation. If anyone had the power to amend the financial statements after their authorisation, then this fact must also be disclosed.

ACTIVITY 25.2

A limited company has a year end of 31 March 2020 and the financial statements were due to be authorised on 31 August 2020.

Indicate whether each of the following represents an adjusting or a non-adjusting event under IAS 10 or needs to be adjusted under IAS 8. Justify your decisions.

1   On 14 May 2020 it was discovered that inventory had been overadded by $72 000 because of a problem with computer software.

2   On 27 June 2020 the size of the directors' bonuses was established at $210 000. A provisional figure of $180 000 had been put into the original draft statements.

3   A customer – who the company had been worried about on 31 March 2020 – had actually gone out of business on 16 September 2020. There was no prospect of any of the $61 000 owed being recovered.

TIP

You may be asked about events occurring after the date of the statement of financial position and for re-drafted financial statements to take account of any changes required as a result of these. You should familiarise yourself with these items as they represent most of the common examples.

CONTINUED

4   On 13 April 2020, the directors had, in response to an unexpected opportunity, bought a factory in France. The factory produced components that the company previously had to buy in.

5   On 8 April, the company was sold faulty goods by a supplier, some of which had caught fire and caused damage. The directors started legal proceedings against that supplier a week later.

25.10 IAS 37 Provisions, contingent assets and contingent liabilities

These items represent uncertainties at the time the financial statements are prepared. They need to be fully accounted for on a consistent basis so that users of the accounts can understand their effect on the accounts.

Provisions: These are liabilities where there is uncertainty about the amount or timing. Provisions should only be shown in the accounts when there are valid grounds for them. If it is likely that a firm will have to make a payment for something and the amount it will have to pay can be reasonably estimated, then it can reasonably bring a provision into the accounts. An example of a provision might be where the company is being sued by customers and has been advised that it will almost certainly lose any court case and have to pay compensation. The only real doubt is over precisely when this will happen or the amount of compensation that they might have to pay.

Liabilities: These are present obligations a business has as a result of past events where the settlement amount is known and is expected to result in a payment being made. For example, a business has a liability to pay its suppliers for goods and services they have provided.

Contingent liabilities: These are possible liabilities to the business, which arise from some past event that is dependent on a series of events that are beyond the business's control. For example, someone may be suing the company for supplying faulty goods and there is a possibility that the company will lose a court case and have to pay damages. The decision and the amount of the payment is outside the company's control.

Note: there can also be *contingent assets* that arise from past events, which will materialise when something happens that is not entirely within the company's control. An example of a contingent asset would be if a company was involved in a lawsuit and expected to win the case and receive compensation. It is a contingent asset because the outcome of the case is not yet known and the amount of compensation that the company might receive is yet to be determined. A contingent asset should *never be recognised in the accounts*, as to do so may be to bring in revenue that may never be realised. However, when the profit is almost certain to arise it is no longer a contingent asset, and it should then be recognised in the accounts and valued at the amount that will be received.

IAS 37 uses three words when it talks about *provisions* and *contingent liabilities*. They are:

- *Probable* – more than a 50% chance that the event will occur. In this case, the amount should be entered in the financial statements as a *provision*. There must also be a note to the accounts giving details of the relevant figures.

- *Possible* – less than 50% chance that the event will occur. In this case no amount is included in the financial statements but a note to the accounts is given about the *contingent liability*.

> **TIP**
>
> Make sure you remember the 50% rule.

- *Remote* – little or no chance of the event occurring. There is no need to even make a note about this item.

The reporting requirements for contingent assets is more restrictive and reflects the prudence concept:

- *Contingent assets with more than a 50% chance of occurring (probable)*: In this case no amount is included in the accounts. However, a note to the accounts is provided about the contingent asset.

- *Contingent assets with less than a 50% chance of occurring (both possible and remote)*: In both cases no amount is included in the accounts, neither is a note to the accounts included.

Clearly, making adjustments under IAS 8. IAS 10 and IAS 37 may well have an impact on the profit reported by the business.

WORKED EXAMPLE 1

The financial statements for Libra Limited had been produced for the year ended 31 August 2020. They showed a profit for the year of $263 000. The directors met to discuss the financial statements before they were to be presented to the shareholders for approval/authorisation. One of the directors has raised the following issues:

i   I have been informed that our revenue figure has omitted a sale for $81 000 made on 17 July 2020. Shouldn't this be included?

ii   Our financial accountant tells me that that some items included in the closing inventory at $42 000 actually have a total selling price of $33 000 (which on 31 August 2020 had been showing in the company's online price list). Do we need to change the accounts for this?

iii I notice in these accounts (year end 31 August 2020) that administrative expenses does not contain an irrecoverable debt of $22 000 that was highly suspected on 31 August 2020 but which was not confirmed until that customer formally went into liquidation on 28 October 2020. Should this irrecoverable debt be included in the 2020 or 2021 accounts?

iv   I see that directors bonuses have been shown as $65 000 in the original statements but we now know that they are going to be $85 000. Does this need to be corrected?

I see that there are two court cases going on at the moment:

v   one where we are being sued – the legal team seems to think that we have a 75% chance of losing this one (which according to our legal team, could cost anything between $50 000 and $300 000) and:

vi   one where we are suing another company. Our legal team think we have a 90% chance of winning this case and we are likely to be awarded $200 000 in compensation.

Do we need to account for these?

The treatment of these items and the effect on profit is as follows:

i   This is a material error and under IAS 8 should be corrected – this will increase the reported profit by $81 000 dollars.

ii   Assuming that the error is regarded as material, under IAS 8 and IAS 2 (which requires inventory to be valued at the lower of cost and net realisable value), the inventory value should be reduced by $9 000 – which will reduce the reported profit.

iii Under IAS 10, this is an adjusting event because the conditions existed at the year-end – so the administrative expenses for 2020 should include the irrecoverable debt and this will reduce the reported profit.

CONTINUED

iv Under IAS 10, this is an adjusting event because the conditions existed at the year-end (it was known that a bonus would be paid, it was just the amount that had not been determined – so again, the expenses should be increased and this will reduce the reported profit.

v The court case where the company is being sued satisfies the over 50% probability rule but the actual cost is very uncertain. Under IAS 37, we would only make a note about the contingent liability because of the uncertainty over the amount of damages that would need to be paid. This would not affect the reported profit.

vi Although there is a high level of certainty about the probability of winning the case and the amount of compensation, IAS 37 will only allow us to make a *contingent asset* note to the accounts. In any event, the prudence concept will only allow positive events to be recorded when they are realised and although this is likely, it is not certain. There will be no effect on the reported profit.

The reported profit figure would be:

	$
Original profit:	263 000
Increased sales revenue (i)	81 000
Reduced inventory value (ii)	(9 000)
Irrecoverable debt (iii)	(22 000)
Increase in directors bonuses (iv)	(20 000)
Revised profit	293 000

KEY CONCEPT LINK

Money measurement: Financial statements only include transactions that can be expressed in terms of money. Does the way in which IAS 37 (Provisions, contingent liabilities and contingent assets) support or contradict the idea of money measurement?

REFLECTION

IAS 37 makes constant reference to a 50% likelihood when deciding whether to make a provision for an event or deciding whether to report a contingent asset or contingent liability. What might be some of the problems in trying to apply that 50% rule?

THINK LIKE AN ACCOUNTANT

Fraud and the audit report

Judy worked for the firm of accountants who, several months previously, had carried out a special audit at Discom PLC following the dismissal of its board of directors. What a mess that had been! As suspected, there had been evidence of fraud and it was likely that some of those directors would go to prison.

Judy's firm had produced a set of financial statements and a large number of problems had been sorted out. It was quite likely, however, that the auditors would present a 'qualified' auditor's opinion stating that there were several significant items where it was impossible to express an opinion as to whether the information available represented a 'true and fair view'.

'This is going to cause some problems!' thought Judy. Why is it important that a company like Discom PLC gets an unqualified auditor's report? What problems is the company likely to experience if they receive a qualified auditor's report?

Figure 25.2: Judy worked for an accounting firm who carried out a special audit at Discom PLC.

EXAM-STYLE QUESTIONS

1   Which of the following statements is false?

   A   internal auditors are employees of the company and will often be linked to that company's security function

   B   external auditors only ever work at the company at the year end when the financial statements are being prepared

   C   the audit report only expresses the auditor's opinion as to whether the financial statements represent a 'true and fair view'

   D   the directors and shareholders would prefer an 'unqualified audit report' to a qualified one   [1]

2   Which of the following is a non-adjusting event?

   A   a non-current asset which is the subject of an impairment review loss

   B   a major customer becoming insolvent three weeks after the end of the financial year

   C   a discovery that the values of some items of inventory have fallen below their cost

   D   the purchase of a new machine costing $500 000 made one month after the end of the financial year   [1]

3   A company is being sued by a customer for defective goods sold to them. The company's solicitors have advised that there is a 75% chance they will lose the case and have to pay the customer compensation of $50 000. How should this be recorded in the annual accounts?

   A   no reference to it is included

   B   a note only is included

   C   a note and a provision of $37 500 is included

   D   a note and a provision of $50 000 is included   [1]

4   The financial statements for Scorpio Limited had been produced for the year ended 30 June 2020. It showed a profit for the year of $421 000. The directors met to discuss the financial statements before they were to be presented to the shareholders for approval/authorisation. One of the directors has raised the following issues:

CONTINUED

i   I notice in these accounts (year end 30 June 2020) that administrative expenses contain an irrecoverable debt of $18 000 that was highly suspected on 30 June but which was not confirmed until that customer formally went into liquidation on 6 August 2020. Why is this irrecoverable debt not being included in the 2021 accounts?

ii I see that there are two court cases going on at the moment … one where we are being sued and one where we are doing the suing. The legal team seems to think that we have a 90% chance of winning 'big damages' in the second one, while they tell me that there is about a 20% chance of losing the first one (in which case it will cost between $750 000 and $1 million). Do we need to account for these?

iii Our financial accountant tells me that that some items included in the closing inventory at $51 000 actually have a total selling price of $39 000 (which on 30 June 2020 had been showing in the company's online price list). Do we need to change the accounts for this?

iv I have been informed that our revenue figure includes a sale for $27 000 that was recorded twice. Does this need to be corrected?

v   I see that directors bonuses have been shown as $111 000 in the original statements but we now know that they are going to be $100 000. Does this need to be corrected?

Required

a   Explain, with reference to relevant IASs, how **i** to **v** should be accounted for.   [15]

b   Calculate the revised profit figure as a result of your opinions in **a**.   [5]

SELF-EVALUATION CHECKLIST

After studying this chapter, complete a table like this:

You should be able to:	Needs more work	Almost there	Ready to move on
Explain stewardship and the roles and responsibilities of directors, appointed by shareholders, of a limited company, including the day-to-day decisions they make.			
Outline the role and responsibilities of the auditor, most importantly that they examine the financial records of the business to ensure that what is being presented represents a 'true and fair view'.			
Outline the differences between an external auditor (independent of the company) and an internal auditor (employees of the company).			
Explain the difference between a qualified and unqualified audit report, remembering that the external auditors will issue a qualified audit report if, during the course of their audit, they find anything which they feel was in doubt or inaccurate.			
Explain the importance of a true and fair view in respect of financial statements, as the overall objectives of a set of financial statements is that they provide a true and fair view of the profit or loss of the company for the year.			
Apply the main requirements of IAS 8: Accounting policies (notes to the financial statements and correction of errors guidelines), IAS 10: Events after the statement of financial position date (rules as to whether financial statements can be updated to reflect these events) and IAS 37: Provisions, contingent liabilities and contingent assets.			

> **Chapter 26**

International accounting standards

This chapter covers part of syllabus section A Level 3.2

LEARNING INTENTIONS

In this chapter you will learn how to:

- explain and apply the main provisions of IAS 2
- explain and apply the main provisions of IAS 16
- explain and apply the main provisions of IAS 36
- explain and apply the main provisions of IAS 38.

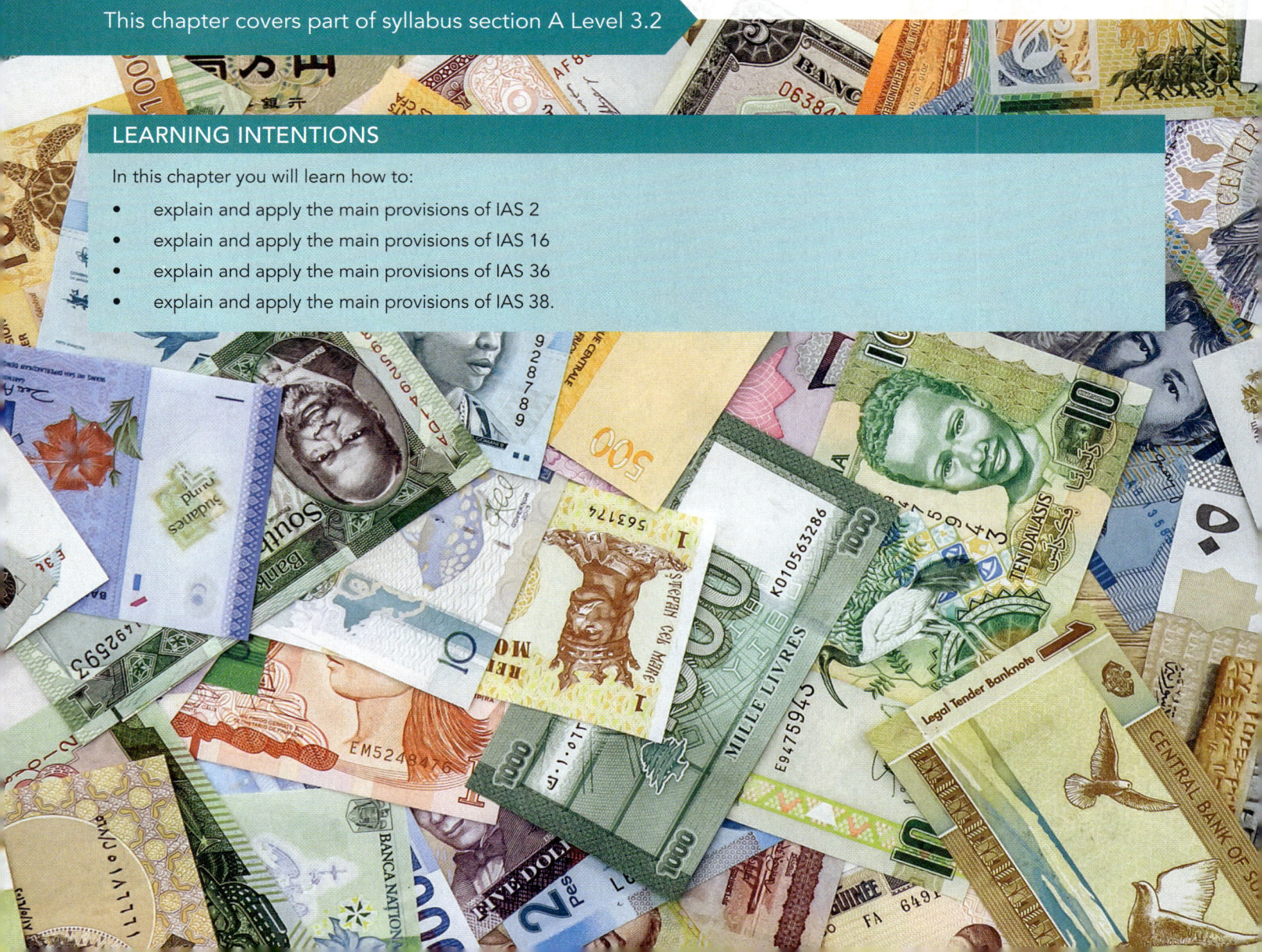

ACCOUNTING IN CONTEXT

Tyrion limited

The directors of Tyrion Limited were unhappy. The first draft of the financial statements showed a profit figure that would not please the shareholders at the Annual General Meeting. One of the directors proposed a number of changes:

- Valuing the closing inventory to selling price would not only reduce cost of sales and improve profit but would also increase the value of the assets in the statement of financial position.

- An increase in the value of the company's properties would also please the shareholders as they would realise that they owned a company worth more than previously thought.

- The company had a good reputation. If that was included as an asset in the statement of financial position, then shareholders would realise that the value of their company was increasing.

Figure 26.1: The directors of Tyrion Limited were unhappy.

Discuss in a pair or a group:

- Should the directors make these changes?

- Which accounting concepts should be considered when deciding whether to make these changes?

26.1 IAS 2 Inventories

Inventory can take a number of different forms. It can be:

- raw materials that will be used in a manufacturing process

- work-in-progress – partly manufactured goods that still require work before they are ready to be sold to the customer

- finished goods – ready to be sold to the customer or that the business has bought for resale to customers.

Inventory valuation

As has been seen in earlier chapters, inventory appears in both of the main financial statements. It appears twice in the trading part of the statement of profit or loss (opening and closing inventory) and as a current asset in the statement of financial position. A correct valuation of inventory is important as it has a major impact on the size of the gross profit as well as the value of the business's assets.

There are two stages to valuing inventory:

- carrying out an inventory count to identify how many of each item the business has

- placing a cash value on those items, which is where IAS 2 provides guidance.

The main principle of IAS 2 is:

Inventories should be valued at the lower of cost and net realisable value.

What is meant by net realisable value depends on the type of business or situation. There are two main variations.

1   *Wholesaling or retailing*: This is where a business buys in a product, adds a mark-up or margin and sells it at a higher price. In this case, the *selling price* is the net realisable value.

2   *Manufacturing*: This is where the business is making a product involving the combination of material, labour and other costs. As the product goes through the various processes, the costs will grow. In this case, net realisable value is the *selling price minus all future costs* that will be incurred in completing it.

IAS 2 requires that the valuation of work-in-progress and finished goods includes not only their raw or direct materials content but also an element for direct labour, direct expenses and production overheads.

The cost of work-in-progress and finished goods therefore consists of:

- direct materials
- direct labour
- direct expenses
- production overheads – these are costs to bring the product to its present location and condition
- other overheads that may be applicable to bring the product to its present location and condition.

The cost of work-in-progress and finished goods excludes:

- abnormal waste in the production process
- storage costs
- selling costs
- administration costs not related to production.
- *Repair or modification*: This is where the business has a damaged item or one that is going to need to be changed to make it saleable. In this case, net realisable value is the selling price minus all future costs that will be incurred in making it saleable. This is virtually identical to the manufacturing situation.

IAS 2 requires that the business examines all of its inventory and applies the lower of cost and net realisable value to every type of inventory.

WORKED EXAMPLE 1

John runs a business that manufactures and sells bats and other cricket equipment. A recent stock-take included the following information:

a   Finished goods

Bats	Number	Cost $	Selling price $	Comments
Standard	45	80	130	
Extra	70	110	180	
Super	20	150	95	End of line – will not be replaced when sold.

In this situation, the Standard and Extra are both being sold for more than they cost to make and so should be valued at cost. However, the Super are being sold for less than cost and so IAS 2 requires them to be valued at the lower selling price.

CONTINUED

The inventory valuation of the bats is:

Bats	Number	Value	Total value	Comments
		$	$	
Standard	45	80	3 600	
Extra	70	110	7 700	
Super	20	95	1 900	

b Work-in-progress: the following items were identified by the inventory count:

Batting gloves	Number	Costs incurred	Further costs	Selling price	Comments
		$	$	$	
Amateur	30	25	15	70	
Pro	15	35	20	50	Discontinued line
Starman	50	40	10	90	

In this case, there are two parts to the process. Firstly, the net realisable value needs to be identified (selling price minus further costs) and, secondly, the lower of cost and net realisable value needs to be identified.

The inventory valuation of the gloves is:

Batting gloves	Number	Costs incurred	Net realisable value	Total value price
		$		$
Amateur	30	25	70 – 15 = 55	750
Pro	15	35	50 – 20 = 30	450
Starman	50	40	90 – 10 = 80	2 000

In this case, one item (the Pro) is going to lose money and a question that is often raised is, 'why finish them off?'

In many cases, the incomplete items might be in the sort of state where they could not be sold at all unless they were finished off. So spending the extra $20 will result in the business receiving $50 of income rather than nothing at all.

If the business bought in finished items and needed to do some work on them prior to selling them (possibly changing the labels or providing different packaging), then the same principle would have applied as to the batting gloves. The net realisable value would still be the selling price minus further costs to be incurred.

c John has a range of items that have been valued at the total selling price rather than original cost price. These items are:

	Current valuation	Profit
	$	
Cricket shirts	1 800	Margin of 30%
Cricket trousers	2 450	Mark-up of 40%

The inventory valuation of these items is:

	Revised valuation	Inventory adjustment
	$	
Cricket shirts	Cost = 70% × 1 800 = 1 260	Reduction 1 800 – 1 260 = 540
Cricket trousers	2 450 / 140% = 1 750	Reduction of 2 450 – 1 750 = 700

> **TIP**
>
> If inventory needs to be adjusted from selling price to cost, read the question carefully as mark-up and margin are not the same and mixing them up will give you very different answers!

ACTIVITY 26.1

Jagvir manufactures and sells camping equipment. A recent inventory-count showed the following results:

Finished items	Number	Cost	Selling price	Comments
		$	$	
Small tents	20	80	135	
Medium tents	12	140	115	Discontinued line – lack of demand
Large tents	24	185	240	

Work-in-progress	Number	Costs incurred	Further costs	Selling price	Comments
		$	$	$	
Single camp beds	50	30	12	75	
Double camp beds	10	40	20	55	Discontinued

Inventory of 'small camping equipment' (accessories) had been valued at $3 800 but this included items shown at their selling price of $900. Jagvir applies a profit margin of 45% on accessories.

Required

a   Calculate the inventory value of the tents.

b   Calculate the inventory value of the camp beds (work-in-progress).

c   Calculate the inventory value of the 'small camping equipment'.

26.2 Inventory valuation methods where items are bought and used on a regular basis

Many businesses buy items on a regular basis. The cost of these items may change as time passes, which can cause problems with the valuation of such inventory.

IAS 2 allows *two* different methods to be used for valuing this type of inventory:

1   *First in, first out (FIFO)*: This method assumes that the first items to be bought (the oldest) will be the first to be used. The value of the remaining inventory will always be the value of the most recently purchased items.

2   *Average cost (AVCO)*: Under this method, a new average value (the weighted average using the number of items bought) is calculated each time a new delivery of inventory is acquired.

Some say that these methods are not supposed to represent the physical movement of inventory but only provide a way of valuing that inventory. However, in reality, many businesses will use methods like batch numbers and 'sell by/use by' dates to ensure that their inventory is used on a FIFO basis in order to minimise the possibility of items deteriorating, going out of date or having to be thrown away. Even in the case of liquid inventory that is stored in large containers, there will be a mixing of old liquid and new liquid, so this represents 'AVCO in practice'. One reason that IAS 2 approves of these methods is that they do represent what happens in practice.

Another possible method of inventory valuation is replacement cost. The replacement cost may be the latest price of the good, or an estimate of what the price will be at some future date. While it is acceptable to use replacement cost to make a decision regarding setting a price or providing a particular customer with a quotation, it is *not acceptable* as a basis for valuing inventory under IAS 2.

IAS 2 also expects inventories that are similar in nature to be valued using the same method. The consistency concept also requires that, once a business has adopted a particular inventory valuation method, it should continue to use that method unless there are good reasons why a change should be made. Under no circumstances can a business change methods just to obtain a desired result like an increase or decrease in a profit figure.

26.3 IAS 16 Property, plant and equipment

This standard deals with the accounting treatment of the non-current assets of property, plant and equipment, and covers:

- the recognition of the assets – when is the item recorded in the accounts and what is its initial valuation

- the calculation of the net book value – what value is placed on these assets in the financial statements

- depreciation charges

- impairment losses – what happens when the value of the asset is below that shown in the accounts.

Property, plant and equipment are tangible assets held for more than one year for use in the production or supply of goods and services, for rental to others or to help the business to carry out its administrative functions.

Although depreciation was discussed in great detail in Chapter 11, it is worth revisiting the topic again so that terms included in IAS 16 can be explained.

WORKED EXAMPLE 2

Suppose a company buys some plant and machinery at a cost of $360 000. It expects the plant to be used for eight years and at the end of that time to be sold for $20 000. The *depreciable amount* will be $340 000. Assuming the company uses the straight-line method of depreciation, then the depreciation recorded in the statement of profit or loss for each year will be:

$$\frac{360\,000 - 20\,000}{8} = \$42\,500$$

- *Depreciation*: This is the allocation of the cost of an asset over its useful life – $42 500 will be written off each year.

- *Depreciable amount*: This is the cost or valuation of the asset, less any residual amount. This will be the figure of $340 000 ($360 000 – $20 000).

- *Useful life*: This is the length of time that the business will use the asset – in this case eight years. Where an asset is depreciated on the basis of the number of units it produces, then the estimated output of the item over its useful life can be used.

- *Residual value*: This is the net amount the business expects to obtain for an asset at the end of its useful life, after deducting the expected costs of disposal – in this case $20 000.

- *Net book value*: This is the amount at which an asset is recognised in the statement of financial position and is often also known as the net book value. In the case of this example, the net book value as the years passed is:

	Cost	Accumulated depreciation	Net book value
	$	$	$
After 1 year	360 000	42 500	317 500
After 2 years	360 000	85 000	275 000
After 3 years	360 000	127 500	232 500

The standard also uses some other terms:

- *Fair value*: This is the amount for which an asset could be exchanged between two knowledgeable and willing parties. If, for example, after five years the company decided to sell the plant, it may offer it to a buyer at $145 000. This might be regarded as a fair value for the item being sold, even if that value bore little or no relation to the net book value.

- *Recognition of assets*: An asset should be recorded in the financial statements when a business is able to use it to generate revenue and can assign a cost to it.

Capital or revenue expenditure?

When dealing with non-current assets, many businesses have to make decisions about whether money spent on them represents capital or revenue expenditure. Capital expenditure refers to the purchasing of an asset that will be included in the statement of financial position and which will almost certainly be depreciated. Revenue expenditure, in this case, refers to money spent on a non-current asset that can be recorded as an expense in the statement of profit or loss.

When the asset is purchased, apart from its original cost, a business may also pay other costs as part of the purchase price. IAS 16 states that the following items should be included as part of the original cost:

- any import duties – taxes directly attributable to bringing the asset to its present location and condition

- the costs of site preparation

- initial delivery and handling costs

- installation and assembly costs

- cost of testing the asset

- professional fees – say architects' or legal fees

- costs incurred in, initially, bringing the asset up to a standard where it can be used – the business may have bought a building in a very poor state of repair and needs to carry out lots of redecoration and repairs to make it usable.

There is also an argument for including training costs if they are incurred at that time and are essential for the asset to be used (it may be significantly different from anything that the employees have used before).

There are also cases where later expenditure may be considered as capital expenditure, including:

- Where parts require replacement at regular intervals, say the seats in an aeroplane, then these costs can be added to the cost of the asset in the statement of financial position and depreciated accordingly.
- Where the asset requires regular inspections in order for the asset to continue operating, then the costs of such inspections can also be added to the cost of the asset in the statement of financial position and depreciated as part of the non-current asset.

Revenue expenditure refers to the day-to-day costs of using the asset and items that are treated in this way include:

- repairs, servicing and redecoration
- warranties that provide (free or low-cost) repairs if the asset breaks down
- insurance
- training costs relating to employees who join the business later.

Some of these will relate to a long period of time, like a three-year warranty, and the accruals concept demands that the cost of this be matched as an expense against each of the three years.

Valuation of the asset

Once the asset has been acquired, the business must adopt one of two models for its valuation:

1 *Cost less accumulated depreciation.*

2 *Revaluation*: The asset is shown at a revalued amount. Revaluations are to be made regularly by suitably qualified people to ensure that the net book value does not differ significantly from the fair value of the asset at the date of the statement of financial position. Unless non-current assets are being bought and sold on a regular basis, revaluations should be undertaken by the business with sufficient regularity (probably every three to five years) to ensure that the net book value is up to date.

If an asset is revalued then every asset in that *class* must be revalued. Thus, if one parcel of land and buildings is revalued then all land and buildings must be revalued. Any surplus on revaluation is reported in the statement of comprehensive income and transferred to the equity section of the statement of financial position as a revaluation reserve; this may not be used to pay dividends to the shareholders.

A reduction in an asset's value will be recorded as:

Debit: Revaluation reserve

Credit: Asset

If there is no revaluation reserve left, then the loss on revaluation will be shown as an expense in the statement of profit or loss.

Depreciation

Under IAS 16, the expected life and residual value of the asset must be reviewed annually. If there is a difference from previous estimates this must be recognised as a change in an estimate under IAS 8 (accounting policies, changes in accounting estimates and errors). Depreciation must also continue to be charged even if the fair value of an asset exceeds its net book value. However, depreciation need not be charged when the residual value is greater than the net book value. Depreciation is included as an expense in the statement of profit or loss.

The business must choose a method of depreciation that reflects the pattern of its usage over its useful economic life. Ideally, once the method has been decided, this should not be changed. It is possible to review the method and if a change in the pattern of usage of the asset has occurred, then the method of depreciation should be changed to reflect this. Such a change would come under IAS 8.

WORKED EXAMPLE 3

Suppose a company buys machinery for $225 000 that is expected to have a useful life of six years, after which it was expected to be sold for $15 000. The company uses the straight-line method of depreciation.

After three years, the machinery was valued at $96 000 and was thought to have a remaining useful life of only two years, after which it would be sold for $10 000.

In this case the annual depreciation expense needs to be calculated:

$$\text{Depreciation per year} = \frac{225\,000 - 15\,000}{6} = \$35\,000$$

After three years, the net book value of the machinery is:

$$225\,000 - (3 \times 35\,000) = \$120\,000$$

If the value of the machinery is only $96 000, then there has been more loss in value than expected, which will be described later in the chapter as 'impairment'. In this case, the impairment is $24 000 and this is treated as an extra amount of expense, bringing the total expense for year 3 to $59 000 and the net book value in the statement of financial position is adjusted to $96 000.

The depreciation for years 4 and 5 is then adjusted to:

$$\frac{96\,000 - 10\,000}{2} = \$43\,000 \text{ per year}$$

If the remaining useful life had been assessed at four years, then the depreciation for years 4 to 7 would be adjusted to:

$$\frac{96\,000 - 10\,000}{4} = \$21\,500 \text{ per year}$$

ACTIVITY 26.2

Vernon bought machinery for $142 000 that is expected to have a useful life of ten years, after which it was expected to be sold for $30 000. The company uses the straight-line method of depreciation.

After four years, the machinery was valued at $88 000 and is thought to have a remaining useful life of five years, after which it would be sold for $20 000.

Required

a   Calculate the initial depreciation expense per year.

b   Calculate the net book value of the machinery at the end of four years after the revaluation review had taken place and the depreciation-related expense for year 4.

c   Calculate the revised depreciation charge per year.

26.4 Disclosure in the financial statements

For each class of property, plant and equipment, the financial statements must show:

- the basis for determining the net book value
- the depreciation method and rate being used
- the useful life of the asset
- the gross net book value at the beginning and end of the accounting year
- the accumulated depreciation and impairment losses at the beginning and end of the accounting year
- additions during the period
- disposals during the period
- depreciation and impairments for the period.

These are likely to be shown by way of a non-current asset schedule and included as a note to the accounts.

WORKED EXAMPLE 4

A company produces its financial statements for the year ended 31 March 2020. The balances on the non-current asset accounts at 1 April 2019 were:

	Cost	Accumulated depreciation	Net book value
	$	$	$
Premises	400000	0	400000
Plant and machinery	135000	75000	60000
Motor vehicles	42000	33000	9000
	577000	108000	469000

The following information was available:

1   During the year, the land and buildings were revalued at $650000. Plant and machinery was bought for $50000 as were new motor vehicles costing $21000.

2   During the year, plant and machinery that had cost $43000 and had a net book value at the time of disposal of $6500 had been part of a trade-in on the new plant and machinery (the effective proceeds on disposal had been $10000). Motor vehicles costing $16000 that had been depreciated by $12400 were sold for $3000.

3   The company policy for depreciation is to charge 20% straight-line on all machines owned at the end of the year and 25% straight-line on all motor vehicles owned at the end of the year. No depreciation is to be charged on items disposed of during the course of the year or on the premises.

CONTINUED

The non-current asset schedule would look like this:

	Premises	Plant and machinery	Motor vehicles	Total
	$	$	$	$
Non-current assets				
Cost:				
Cost at 1 April 2019	400 000	135 000	42 000	577 000
Revaluation	250 000	–	–	250 000
Additions during the year	–	50 000	21 000	71 000
Disposals during the year	–	(43 000)	(16 000)	(59 000)
Cost at 31 March 2020	650 000	142 000	47 000	839 000
Depreciation:				
Accumulated depreciation at 1 April 2019	–	75 000	33 000	108 000
Charge during year[1]	–	28 400	11 750	40 150
Disposals[2]	–	(36 500)	(12 400)	(48 900)
Accumulated depreciation at 31 Mar 2019	–	66 900	32 350	99 250
Net book value at 31 March 2020	650 000	75 100	14 650	739 750
Net book value at 1 April 2019	400 000	60 000	9 000	469 000

Notes:

[1]   Accumulated depreciation on plant and machinery sold = cost – net book value = 43 000 – 6 500 = $36 500

[2]   Depreciation on plant and machinery = 20% × 142 000 = $28 400

Depreciation on motor vehicles = 25% × 47 000 = $11 750

26.5 IAS 36 Impairment of assets

IAS 36 states that non-current assets (including goodwill) should not be recorded in the financial statements at more than their 'recoverable amount'. The recoverable amount is the higher of its fair value (minus selling costs) and the value of the benefits arising from its use (the revenue that it would help to generate).

If the recoverable amount falls below its net book value, then impairment has taken place and companies are required to review their assets particularly if there are indications that a fall in value may have occurred. Examples of indicators might include:

- A fall in the market value of the asset

- damage or obsolescence to the asset

- a major reorganisation casting doubt on the asset's usefulness, for example the business decides not to make a particular product anymore because of a fall in demand for that product.

If impairment is considered to have taken place then the reduction is treated as an *expense in the statement of profit or loss* (unless it is the subject of a previous upwards revaluation, in which case an adjustment to the revaluation reserve should be made. A note should also be made in the bottom section of the statement of profit or loss.

The stages involved in the impairment review are:

1   Calculate the asset's net book value.

2   Compare this with the asset's recoverable amount. The recoverable amount will be the *higher* of:

   •   the asset's fair value less costs to sell

   •   the asset's value in use. This is the present value of future cash flows to the business generated as a result of using the asset.

3   Compare all the values calculated. If *either* measures of the recoverable amount is *higher* than the asset's net book value, then there is no need to reduce the carrying value of the asset. However, if both are lower than the carrying value of the asset, then the carrying value must be reduced but to the higher of the two measures of the recoverable amount.

WORKED EXAMPLE 5

A company examined some of its non-current assets and found the following:

	Net book value	Resale value	Benefits from use
	$	$	$
Asset A	61 600	65 000	83 000
Asset B	47 300	32 000	57 500
Asset C	32 400	19 100	26 500

In the statement of financial position they should be shown at the following values:

Asset	Value in statement of financial position $	Reason
A	61 600	Both measures of recoverable value exceed the net book value so there is no need to show any impairment.
B	47 300	One measure of recoverable amount (benefits from use) exceeds the net book value and so there is no need to show any impairment.
C	26 500	Both measures of recoverable value are below the net book value so the company will need to show impairment of $5 900 as the value of the asset is reduced to the greater of the two ($26 500).

ACTIVITY 26.3

A company examined some of its non-current assets and found the following:

	Net book value	Resale value	Benefits from use
	$	$	$
Asset D	71 400	82 500	61 900
Asset E	102 600	91 700	78 300
Asset F	63 400	70 600	26 500

Required

a   Show the value of each asset that should be shown in the financial statements.

b   Show the amount of impairment that needs to be applied to each asset and in total.

26.6   IAS 38 Intangible assets

An intangible asset is an identifiable non-monetary asset without physical form. An example of this is goodwill and others include patents and trademarks, which have value but cannot be touched (or even seen).

There are three characteristics that must exist for an asset to be identifiable:

1   the business must have control over it

2   it must be able to bring economic benefits to whoever owns it

3   it must be capable of being sold separately from other parts of the business.

An example that would satisfy these requirements is a customer list.

There are three main types of intangible asset that are covered by IAS 38:

1   research and development

2   goodwill

3   patents, copyrights and trademarks.

Research and development

Many businesses will spend money carrying out research and development activities, often in order to create new products that can be sold. This is particularly important in fast-moving industries like mobile phones and computer games consoles where the key to success is to bring out products that have better features than those provided by rival companies. Car manufacturers look to replace a particular model of vehicle every few years.

The main issue covered by IAS 38 is whether research and development expenditure should be written off as an expense in the year in which it is incurred or whether it should be capitalised as an asset. If it is capitalised then the value of this intangible asset must be depreciated. Depreciation of intangible assets is called **amortisation**. Worked example 6 provides a detailed example of the approach used.

There are four ways in which money can be spent on research and development:

Capital expenditure: This may involve the building and equipping of laboratories or testing equipment. This type of expenditure must be treated as a tangible non-current asset.

> **KEY TERM**
>
> **amortisation:** the non-tangible asset equivalent of depreciation where the value of the non-tangible asset is reduced over its life.

Pure research: This is work undertaken to gain new knowledge for its own sake. IAS 38 requires that this expenditure be written off as an expense in the statement of profit or loss in the year in which it is incurred.

Applied research: This is work undertaken to acquire new knowledge directed towards a particular project. Again, IAS 38 requires that this expenditure be written off as an expense in the statement of profit or loss in the year in which it is incurred.

Development: This is work undertaken to produce new or improved products where there is a clearly defined project:

- which is technically possible
- where the benefits will outweigh costs
- which will be completed with the resources available
- which will have a reasonably predictable lifespan where the benefits will be received.

If these conditions are met, then this expenditure can be shown as an intangible asset in the statement of financial position. It will then be offset against the benefits as and when they are received.

WORKED EXAMPLE 6

Suppose a car manufacturer spends $2 million on development of a new model that is expected to generate revenue of $400 million over a four-year period – when the next model will be released. It has been decided that the research and development expenditure should be shown as an asset in the statement of financial position and amortised on a straight-line basis. The manufacturer believes that there will be a residual value at the end of the four years of $200 000.

It is expected that $1.8 million will be amortised over the 4 years and so the annual amortisation will be:

$(2\,000\,000 - 200\,000) / 4 = \$450\,000$ per year, which will be shown as an expense in the Statement of Profit or Loss.

The value of the Research and development asset will be:

Year	Asset value at the start of the year	Amortisation	Asset value at end of year
	($)	($)	($)
1	2 000 000	450 000	1 550 000
2	1 550 000	450 000	1 100 000
3	1 100 000	450 000	650 000
4	650 000	450 000	200 000

If it is believed that the amount of revenue generated by the new model will vary (it might be that sales in Years 2 and 3 will be greater than for Years 1 and 4), it may seem desirable to apply the 'matching concept' in this situation by trying to charge a greater share of the amortisation to the years where the research and development yielded most benefit.

However, there are problems with this approach:

1 The number of cars sold will be difficult to predict and this might lead to distortions in the amount of expense from year to year – Year 4 might show the highest sales but all $1.8 million of amortisation has been applied to Years 1–3.

2 The new model might last longer than four years and so will be generating revenue in Years 5 and 6 when all $1.8 million of amortisation has been applied.

CONTINUED

3   The new model might fail, either in terms of number of cars sold or in terms of number of years. This will mean that the financial statements will be showing an intangible asset as having a large value when in fact, it is worth very little or nothing. This will need to be written off as an expense that will drastically reduce the profit shown in that period.

4   If there is no new model of the vehicle as a result of the expenditure, then the manufacturer will be faced with the problem of writing off $2 million as an expense, which again will distort the profit figure for that year.

As a result of these issues, particularly points 3 and 4, accountants tend to apply the prudence principle and will tend to advise that even development expenditure is written off as an expense in the year in which it is incurred.

Goodwill

IAS 38 only permits 'purchased goodwill' to be recognised in the accounts. This is because of the money measurement concept. Only when something has been bought can its value be established with any certainty. While there is little doubt that goodwill built up by the business is likely to be high, until a new purchaser or partner agrees to its value by paying for it, then that value is just a matter of opinion.

The term used to describe goodwill that has been built up – over a period of time – is 'inherent goodwill'. While there is little doubt that many businesses are actually worth far more than the value of the assets shown in the financial statements, the value of inherent goodwill is a matter of opinion. The owner of the business is likely to value it far more highly than outsiders. IAS 38 follows the money measurement concept and does not allow inherent goodwill to be capitalised.

Once the decision is made that the goodwill is 'purchased goodwill' and can be included in the financial statements as an asset, it is shown at cost less any accumulated amortisation (depreciation) and impairment losses. IAS 38 states that the business must identify the useful life of the goodwill. If it has a limited life, it should be amortised using the straight-line method. In all cases, the residual value should be regarded as zero and the amount of the amortisation should be charged as an expense in the statement of profit or loss. The amortisation period should be reviewed at least annually and any changes to the amounts charged made in line with such a review.

Where goodwill is deemed to have an indefinite life, it will not be amortised but must undergo an annual impairment review that will consider whether or not an indefinite life is still valid in respect of the asset. It is possible that the impairment review might reduce the value of the goodwill significantly or completely and any loss in value arising from such a review is charged as an expense in the statement of profit or loss.

Patents, copyrights and trademarks

These are, effectively, licences that protect a business from having its ideas or designs stolen by a competitor. They do not have a physical form but are legally identifiable. Once registered, they usually cover a specific time period, e.g. 20 years. An industry that use these is pharmaceuticals where companies manufacturing medicines place legal protection on their discoveries.

IAS 38 states that patents, copyrights and trademarks should be *capitalised at cost price* and then amortised over a period not exceeding 20 years.

In every case where amortisation is applied to an intangible asset, details of cost, expected life and amortisation policy should be shown in the notes to the accounts.

The accounting authorities have issued a large number of accounting standards that cover how accounts should present information about assets in the financial statements. These also cover the information that should be provided in the notes to the accounts (this chapter only looks at four of them). As a result, a large amount of time and effort, during auditing and accounts preparation, is spent ensuring that companies comply with these rules.

KEY CONCEPT LINK

True and fair view: Financial statements are designed to give a true and fair view of the financial position, performance and changes in financial position of the business to internal and external stakeholders. How much do you think that the IASs covered in this chapter increase the likelihood of the financial statements showing a true and fair view of the performance and financial position of a company?

REFLECTION

How much do you think that having a regulatory framework, including the presence of a large number of IASs, helps businesses comply with the accounting concept of consistency?

THINK LIKE AN ACCOUNTANT

Company motor vehicles

The Finance Director was appalled. A review of the motor vehicles used by the salespeople had revealed that a vast number of them were in a fairly poor condition given that they were all less than three years old. Even though the company applied depreciation at a rate of 35% per year using the reducing balance method, the net book values were almost certainly far greater than the likely proceeds of any sale.

'I am going to have to have a serious word with the Sales Director – these people are clearly not looking after company property!' he thought.

What should the Finance Director do in terms of accounting for the poor condition of the vehicles?

Figure 26.2: A review of the motor vehicles used by the salespeople had revealed that a vast number of them were in a fairly poor condition.

EXAM-STYLE QUESTIONS

1   How should inventory be valued in a statement of financial position?

A   at the lower of net realisable value and selling price

B   at the lower of replacement cost and net realisable value

C   at lower of cost and replacement cost

D   at lower of cost and net realisable value   [1]

2   A company had the following stock valuations as a result of an inventory count:

	FIFO	LIFO	Selling price
	$	$	$
Product H	2 190	1 980	3 195
Product J	4 325	4 075	4 240
Product K	1 780	1 660	2 680
Total	8 295	7 715	10 115

According to IAS 2, which of the following inventory values should be used by the company?

A $7 715

B $8 210

C $9 295

D $10 115   [1]

3   The company had the following information about its non-current assets to hand:

	Net book value	Resale value	Benefits from use
	$	$	$
Equipment A	53 200	29 200	114 100
Equipment B	31 600	17 200	28 300
Equipment C	32 700	41 300	30 300

The amount of impairment required is:

A $0

B $3 300

C $14 400

D $29 800   [1]

CONTINUED

4 The directors of a company have prepared the following draft statement of financial position at 31 March 2020 and presented it to the company's auditors:

	$000
Non-current assets:	
Tangible[1]	2 300
Intangible – goodwill[2]	270
	2 570
Current assets:	
Inventory[3]	211
Trade receivables[4]	47
Total current assets:	258
Total assets	2 828
Equity and liabilities:	
Share capital and reserves	
Share capital	1 500
Revaluation reserve	650
General reserve	175
Retained earnings	416
Total equity	2 741
Current liabilities:	
Trade payables	50
Bank overdraft	37
Total current liabilities	87
Total equity and liabilities	2 828

During the course of their audit, the auditors discovered the following:

The tangible non-current assets includes land that had a cost of $720 000. This had been revalued by the son of one of the directors who is training to be an architect. He estimated the increase in value to be $180 000. This increase has been included in the revaluation reserve. [1]

The value of goodwill has been estimated at $270 000 by the directors based on their valuation of the excess profits earned because the company has a very good reputation. [2]

Included in inventories are some items that were purchased for $17 000. They can now only be sold for $11 000. [3]

Included in trade receivables is a customer who owes $15 000. The directors know that it is extremely unlikely that this customer will be able to pay anything at all. [4]

Required

a Prepare a revised statement of financial position at 31 March 2020, taking into consideration the information given above and any other relevant matters. [9]

b Explain the adjustments you have made in respect of these items, making reference to any relevant accounting standards. [7]

SELF-EVALUATION CHECKLIST

After studying this chapter, complete a table like this:

You should be able to:	Needs more work	Almost there	Ready to move on
Explain and apply the main provisions of IAS 2: Inventories, where inventory should be valued at 'the lower of cost and net realisable value'. Remember that IAS 2 states that LIFO should not be used in financial accounts.			
Explain and apply the main provisions of IAS 16: Property, plant and equipment, that requires companies to produce a non-current assets schedule that shows the changes of assets at cost, accumulated depreciation and net book value.			
Explain and apply the main provisions of IAS 36: Impairment of assets, that recognises that assets may lose value faster than expected and provides guidance on how impairment ought to be applied.			
Explain and apply the main provisions of IAS 38: Intangible assets, that deals with intangible assets and provides regulations about when research and development expenditure and goodwill should be capitalised and how it should be amortised in the financial statements.			

Chapter 27

Computerised accounting systems

This chapter covers part of syllabus sections AS Level 1.2 and all of A Level 3.4

LEARNING INTENTIONS

In this chapter you will learn how to:

- explain the transfer of accounting data to a computerised system
- explain the safeguards required to ensure that the data is transferred completely and accurately
- explain the use of computerised accounting systems in recording financial transactions and the advantages and disadvantages these systems bring
- explain the measures that can be taken to protect the integrity and security of data within a computerised accounting system.

ACCOUNTING IN CONTEXT

Case study: Ursa Limited

Ursa Limited is a small (private) limited company that sells clothing. Its year end is 31 July. Goods are bought from suppliers and sold to customers on both a cash and credit basis.

The company's accounting system consists of a number of separate systems. Each employee operates her own system on her own computer to which only she has access. At the end of the month, information from those systems is copied onto a special spreadsheet. At the end of the year, when everyone has input their data, the office manager, Mohammed, checks it and then sends the spreadsheet to the company's accountant to prepare the company's statement of profit or loss and statement of financial position. The accountant charges for the services that she provides.

The two directors of Ursa Limited and Mohammed have decided that the current system has a number of problems:

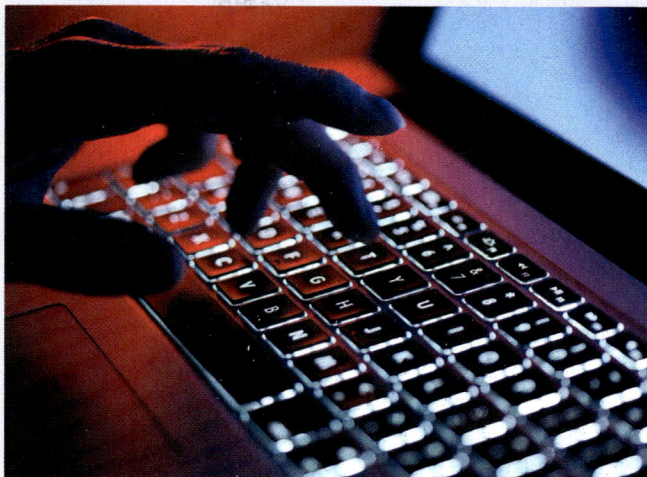

Figure 27.1: Ursa Limited's accounting system consists of a number of separate systems.

- general efficiency – many of the employees are complaining that they are struggling to keep up with their workload

- wasted time – hours have been spent sorting out errors and tidying up the spreadsheet. The accountant also has to spend time sorting out difficulties, which has increased the amount that he charges Ursa Limited.

Mohamed thinks that the company needs a computerised accounting system that links everything together and decides to discuss it further with the two directors.

Discuss in a pair or a group:

What problems might the company be experiencing as a result of the company's use of different systems? You may think of some that have not been mentioned in the case study.

27.1 Introducing a computerised accounting system

There are many computerised accounting packages to choose from depending on the type of business and its requirements. These include:

- Sage Line 50 (suitable for a range of businesses)

- Accounts IQ (particularly suitable for construction, retail and hospitality)

- Xero (particularly suitable for small businesses)

The steps that a business is likely to go through in either case are very similar and this chapter will be using the Ursa Limited situation to examine the possible process.

Step 1 Decide which accounting package (system) to choose.

The directors of Ursa Limited need to decide whether a general accounting package is required or whether a program needs to be designed to meet the company's specific needs. This will depend on factors such as the size and nature of the business. Ursa Limited is a business that sells clothing. There is nothing exceptional about the type of business or its size and so a general accounting package would certainly be able to carry out all of the different parts of the

> **KEY TERM**
>
> **computerised accounting system:** a set of programs that allow the accounts to be prepared using a computer. An alternative to manual bookkeeping.

accounting function. Some industries might be so specialised that specific programs might need to be designed, but this isn't one of them.

Step 2 Decide who to buy the package from.

The directors of Ursa Limited have a choice about where to get the accounting package from, including a local computer shop or from a website on the internet. The decision might depend on a number of factors including choice of packages, price, product knowledge and customer service, repairs/maintenance and availability of upgrades.

ACTIVITY 27.1

The following factors can influence the choice of computer system to be purchased:

- choice of packages that meet the business's needs and their speed of availability
- price
- customer service/product knowledge
- repairs/maintenance
- availability of upgrades.

Required

For each factor, explain the likely advantages and disadvantages of:

a buying an accounts packages from a local computer shop

b buying an accounts package online.

Step 3 Computer network or standalone?

Ursa Limited will need to decide whether the accounting package should be installed on an individual computer or on a number of computers that are linked into a network.

The company needs information to be up-to-date and accurate – there should only be one definitive value for any item or ledger balance. If Ursa Limited has the accounts package installed on all computers, and those computers are organised into a network, then as soon as an employee inputs data all relevant parts of the system are updated. Ursa should have the system networked.

Step 4 Installation.

Should the system be installed by specialists or can it be done by the employees themselves? Installing the package on one machine may just be a case of downloading the program and following the instructions. However, the networking of a computer system will require technical expertise, which will take time and money. When making their decision about which package and which supplier to use, the directors may consider whether installation (and servicing/maintenance) will be included and at what cost.

Step 5 Setting up the accounts.

Most computer packages have a list of default account names that can be adapted and added to – they are set out in sections, e.g. non-current assets followed by current assets, current liabilities, non-current liabilities, capital, income (sales) and expenses. Each account name will have a numerical code assigned to it. An example of this:

1001	Freehold land and buildings at cost
1002	Freehold land and buildings accumulated depreciation
1200	Bank current account
3000	Capital
4000	Sales 1
5000	Purchases 1
7000	Wages

You will notice that in this case:

- The four-digit codes enable a large number of new accounts to be created with names that suit the particular requirements of the business. In this case, Ursa Limited could create account codes for a lot of assets or expenses if required.

- Some of these descriptions given are pretty basic, e.g. sales 1. These can be changed to meet the company's needs, e.g. 4001 sales – menswear, 4002 sales – womenswear, and so on.

It is essential that before any information is loaded onto Ursa Limited's new system, the codes that will be required are established and any changes or additions to the default settings are made.

Step 6   Decide on the date to transfer the balances from the manual system to the computer.

The most sensible time will be at the end of their financial year, mainly because there will be a complete trial balance where every ledger balance will be available. Care will need to be taken to make sure that no last minute adjustments are going to be made, however.

It is likely that a large number of the ledgers that have been used all year will be zero because they are income or expense accounts where the balances have been 'transferred to the statement of profit or loss'. It is the statement of financial position that is going to be important because it will contain the balances of asset, liability and capital items that will represent the opening balances for the new year.

Step 7   Balance reconciliation and data entry.

This is one of the most important parts of the process as it is essential that any data entered onto the new system be as accurate as possible. The balances on the statement of financial position are input into the new accounting system as well as the balances on the individual credit customers' and credit suppliers' accounts.

Trade receivables and payables: Arguably, the most important thing to do is to carry out the following reconciliations:

- the sales ledger control account with the total of the individual balances on the credit customers' accounts

- the purchase ledger control account with the total of the individual credit supplier's accounts.

In addition, because the new system is going to be used to monitor and control the credit customers and manage the payment of credit suppliers, the precise details of every outstanding customer and supplier balance need to be known and entered into the system. This will include dates, documents numbers and amounts outstanding.

The accounts clerks will be able to use these details to monitor which parts of any outstanding balance are within agreed terms and conditions and which are late. In the case of the receivables clerk, this information can be used to determine whether action needs to be taken against late payers, while the payables clerk may be able to decide when suppliers need to be paid in order to avoid problems (or to obtain settlement discounts).

Bank and cash: The following reconciliations need to be carried out:

- Complete a bank reconciliation – any adjustments should be carried out if they haven't already been done.

- Reconcile the cash balance in the ledgers with the amount of physical cash.

Inventory: The business should do a physical count of the inventory at the year end. Details of physical quantities and values of every type of inventory will need to be entered onto the new system.

Non-current liabilities: Any non-current liabilities and other liabilities need to be checked before being entered onto the system.

Step 8 Enter the balances onto the new system.

Once all of these checks and reconciliations have taken place, the data can be entered onto the new system and an initial trial balance produced. This should be compared with the final trial balance from the old system to ensure that no major problems have been introduced. Any differences should be investigated.

Step 9 Training.

It is likely that the new accounting package will be significantly different from anything that the employees at Ursa Limited have seen before. Training will be absolutely vital if the benefits of having the new system are to be maximised and expensive mistakes avoided.

This training can take a number of forms including:

- *External training courses*: Employees might attend a programme outside, possibly at a local college.

- *Visiting trainers*: External trainers might visit Ursa Limited to deliver the training.

- *In-house training*: This might be delivered at Ursa Limited by people employed by the company. Many large businesses have departments responsible for delivering a significant amount of the training taking place within that organisation.

ACTIVITY 27.2

Explain the likely advantages and disadvantages of Ursa Limited using the following methods to deliver training on how to use the new accounting system to the accounts staff:

a External training courses

b Visiting trainers

c In-house training.

Step 10 Parallel running.

Unless the old system is known to be producing inaccurate information, many organisations will run both the old and the new systems at the same time for a specified period (at least a month). This is called 'parallel running'.

While the process of entering data onto the systems and downloading information from it may be different, it should be possible to compare what the two systems are producing. If the two systems are producing the same balances on the ledgers, then there should be some assurance that the new system is functioning properly. Major discrepancies should be investigated as this may be an early indication of problems with the new system.

Many organisations take the view that parallel running should continue until both systems are always in agreement although the cost and the amount of practical inconvenience in running two systems at the same time may force the business to accept 'near agreement'.

Another advantage of running systems in parallel is that if something goes wrong or someone makes a mistake that deletes a vast amount of information, the other system will provide a back-up. With new systems, this is always a real possibility.

27.2 The advantages of computerised accounting

There are a number of advantages that computerising the accounting system can bring to the business, including:

- *Speed of processing data (automatic updating)*: Computerised accounting systems should be able to speed up work because data will only need to be entered into one place and the system will automatically update all of the relevant ledgers. For example, every time an invoice is entered into the sales day book, the relevant subsidiary sales ledger and the sales control account will be adjusted virtually instantly.

  Not only will this save time and wages, it will reduce the possibility of errors as only one transaction will be input rather than three entries.

- *Space can be saved*: There will be no need to keep ledgers and books of prime entry, although it is important that a sensible filing system be set up for the reports taken from the computer.

- *Production of documents*: Most businesses will want to produce business documents such as invoices or credit notes quickly and in large quantities. There will also be a need to send out letters (e.g. requests for payment from customers whose balances are overdue). Many accounting packages provide a wide range of styles that can be selected for business documents (like invoices) and letters. Many packages supply specimen examples although there is always an option to upload a preferred 'gapped layout' where the specific names, details and monetary amounts can be added before a particular letter is sent out.

- *Reports and financial statements*: Most accounting packages enable a very wide range of reports to be produced quickly and in a variety of formats to suit the needs of the business. Apart from the trial balance, statement of profit or loss and statement of financial position, Ursa Limited could produce detailed breakdowns of:
  - trade receivables, including an aged receivables schedule that analyses the amount of each credit customer's balance by how long it has been outstanding
  - trade payables, including an aged payables schedule that analyses the amount of each credit supplier's balance by how long it has been outstanding
  - inventory, by individual product.

- *Improved accuracy*: Most accounting packages have built-in safeguards that make it more difficult to make an error. For example, journals cannot be input onto the system if they don't balance. There may also be several stages of checking where the system will ask the user to respond to questions like, 'Are you sure?' before data is entered or deleted.

- *Auditing and fraud prevention*: Many systems will highlight unusual and potentially fraudulent activity – often without the individual user knowing – so that auditors and managers can investigate potential problems.

27.3 The disadvantages of a computerised accounting system

There are also a number of potential disadvantages:

- *Cost*: These can be significant and may include:
  - Purchase of new computers – there may be technician costs if systems are having to be installed and networked.
  - Accounting software – this may involve a one-off purchase but could involve subscription and licence costs.
  - Maintenance or warranties – computer systems may go wrong and the business will need technical support to sort out the problems; warranties from manufacturers or getting repairs done can be expensive.
  - Staff training – this will consist not only of any fees payable to trainers but also the cost of the person's time while they are being trained.

- *Staff training (inconvenience)*: Apart from the cost, there will be problems in deciding when the training should take place. It may be difficult to get everyone together at the same time and, in any event, the training will mean that there will be a period of time where the employees are unavailable to carry out their work.

- *Systems crashing*: Computers may crash because of power-cuts or program failures and it is possible that work will be lost. Many firms will try to limit the possible damage by insisting that employees save and back up their work regularly.

- *Internal threats and privacy (employees)*: Unhappy employees might either steal information to give to competitors, or delete or change information in order to cause damage or hide fraudulent activity. Preventing this from happening may be difficult. Downloading information from the computer and taking it out of the office may be easy because it can be carried on a USB ('memory stick'). There is also a problem that in a small accounts office where one person is responsible for each part of the accounting function, it may be easy to commit and conceal fraud.

  Managers may also be concerned that if every employee has access to the whole system, they will be able to see and change confidential information that directors would rather they couldn't (e.g. payroll records).

- *External threats to the data*: Cyber-attacks are becoming increasingly common and can be very damaging. It is essential that a good anti-virus system be installed and that procedures are in place to reduce the possibility of staff carelessness allowing outsiders to get access to information or the system.

- *Carelessness*: If employees feel that the computerised system has built-in facilities to prevent errors, there is a likelihood that they may take less care over their work and actually make more mistakes.

- *Employee resistance*: Some employees may not welcome change and in extreme cases, the introduction of a new system can result in valuable staff deciding the time is right to leave.

27.4 Protecting the integrity and security of data

Most, if not all, business owners are concerned about keeping their data safe – both in terms of not being corrupted or lost and not being stolen. They know that corrupted or lost data will result in wasted time and increased costs while the data is replaced or recovered. Stolen data might give competitors an advantage or weaken a bargaining position should there be negotiations regarding say the buying and selling of assets.

There are a number of measures that can be employed to help a business protect the security and integrity of its data, including:

- *Installing up-to-date antivirus packages*: Computer viruses come in many forms and cause different types of problem. Some viruses infiltrate a system and start corrupting or stealing data, while others (ransomware) cause the system to shut down. A ransom demand is often received later offering to unlock the system in return for a large cash payment. Spyware viruses can be used to steal confidential data, while yet more viruses are designed to steal money, often by diverting payments into specified and different accounts from the one that the payer intended to use.

  Hackers also use their expertise to illegally gain access ('hack') into a system, sometimes just for the challenge but often with a view to stealing information.

  Anti-virus packages can be installed that can repel viruses or warn people that there is an attempt being made to access the system through a suspicious looking email or a suspect URL link. However, as new viruses are constantly being developed by cyber-criminals, it is essential that any business continues to use the most up-to-date anti-virus packages.

- *Strong passwords and restricted access*: It is essential that passwords are not obvious ('strong') and are regularly changed to prevent illegal access to systems. Restricting employee access to parts of the system that they need to perform their roles will not only limit the number of people who might have the opportunity to steal data, but can also help to narrow down the number of suspects if there has been a problem.

  When employees leave their jobs, they should have their access rights removed immediately in order to reduce the risk of that member of staff committing some malicious action.

- *Automatic lockdown or logging out*: People should not leave their computers unattended, but they often do and they don't always lock or log out of the system. This could provide an opportunity for someone to access information that they do not have a right to. If settings are adjusted so that a computer automatically locks after only two or three minutes of inactivity, then the risk is reduced.

- *Saving and backing-up of work*: Computers systems can crash – sometimes because of a basic problem like a power failure or because of viruses. Saving work regularly will mean less time is wasted as less work has been lost, while backing up work provides insurance against whole files or systems being corrupted or wiped clean by say a virus.

- *Encrypted or restricted USB drives*: Most people are familiar with USB drives (sometimes called 'thumb-drives' or 'memory sticks') and regard them as a very convenient way of transferring data. Some business will insist on employees only using USBs issued by the company that have an encryption password on them. They may ban staff from bringing USBs into work or taking them out of the office. All of these rules and procedures can reduce the risk of people bringing computer viruses into work – for example, if the USB has been plugged into an infected computer, illegally removing sensitive information or providing public access to the information if the memory is lost by the employee while outside the office.

- *Introduce an acceptable use policy*: Many organisations have an acceptable use policy that sets out what its employees should and shouldn't be doing. If an employee only accesses websites relevant to work, they are far less likely to introduce viruses to the system or allow access to hackers.

- *Staff training*: Many businesses will insist that their employees complete regular courses in cyber awareness, many of which are available online.

  This training will provide useful practical tips on how to spot suspicious-looking emails that might be harmful if opened. Large organisations might have an IT department that circulates details to all staff about latest scams and attempts to hack systems, often citing particular examples of suspicious emails that have been recently identified.

- *Disciplinary process*: The business could ensure that the consequences of not following the rules and procedures set out in a staff handbook or acceptable IT use policy are widely known. This could be reinforced by staff training. It is essential all employees know that failure to comply with the rules will result in firm action if a thorough investigation correctly finds them guilty of having committed an offence.

- *Compliance audits and tracking*: Management may need to carry out unannounced audits to ensure that people are following the rules and many systems enable management to identify what files are being downloaded, who is accessing which websites and how the email system is being used. If employees know that their offences could be discovered, they are less likely to commit them.

ACTIVITY 27.3

The directors of Ursa Limited are concerned that once the new computerised system is installed, there may be problems:

- keeping information confidential from outsiders

- preventing information (work) from being lost or deleted

- preventing employees from committing fraud and/or causing malicious damage to the system

- reducing the risk of external hackers accessing the system (or being infected with viruses).

Required

Explain some procedures (or rules) that could be introduced regarding the use of computers that could reduce the risk of these problems happening.

If you have worked in an office with any computer system, you may want to consider some of the rules or procedures that the business had and why they were introduced.

REFLECTION

'It does not matter how sophisticated the computer system installed by a business, if the employees cannot or will not comply with company policy, the potential benefits are limited and the scope for problems could well be greater than if the business had kept a manual accounting system.'

Do you think that this statement is true? Why/why not?

THINK LIKE AN ACCOUNTANT

More problems than before

It had been a couple of months since Ursa Limited had installed a new computerised accounting system and Geraldo, one of the directors, was feeling quite frustrated. The company had bought the new system as the designers stated that it would enable the accounts staff to work more quickly and would help to cut down the number of errors. However, if anything, the number of errors seemed to have increased and people were spending time sorting them out. Geraldo found himself wondering whether there was anything that could be done to ensure that the benefits of the new computerised system were maximised. Discuss what actions Geraldo could take to ensure that the company and its employees are able to make the most effective use of the new computerised accounting system.

Figure 27.2: The new accounting system was causing more problems than before.

EXAM-STYLE QUESTIONS

1   Which of the following statements is *false*?

   A   Introducing a computerised accounting system can help the business to increase its efficiency and cut day-to-day costs.

   B   A computerised accounting system that has built-in safeguards will ensure that the accounts cannot commit errors.

   C   Introducing a computerised accounting system is likely to involve large initial costs but may lead to long-term cost savings.

   D   When introducing a computerised accounting system, for a while it may be sensible for the business to keep the old system and the new system running at the same time.   [1]

2   State *three* advantages and *three* disadvantages of changing to a computerised accounting system from a manual accounting system.   [6]

3   Discuss ways in which the integrity of the accounting data can be ensured during the transfer to a computerised accounting system.   [8]

4   Explain *three* practical measures that a business with a computerised accounting system could introduce in order to protect the integrity and security of its data and how each of those measures would do so.   [9]

SELF-EVALUATION CHECKLIST

After studying this chapter, complete a table like this:

You should be able to:	Needs more work	Almost there	Ready to move on
Explain the transfer of accounting data to a computerised system and the safeguards required to ensure that the data is transferred completely and accurately.			
Explain the use of computerised accounting systems in recording financial transactions and the advantages and disadvantages these systems bring, including the increased speed and accuracy of work and the ability to extract reports quickly and easily versus the costly installation process and the resistance to change.			
Discuss the measures that can be taken to protect the integrity and security of data within a computerised accounting system.			

> Chapter 28

Business acquisition and merger

This chapter covers syllabus section A Level 3.3

LEARNING INTENTIONS

In this chapter you will learn how to:

- explain why business acquisitions and mergers happen
- prepare the journal entries and make entries in the relevant ledger accounts to reflect the acquisition or merger
- calculate goodwill on the acquisition of a business by another entity
- prepare financial statements for the newly formed business entity after the acquisition or merger
- explain the advantages and disadvantages of the acquisition or merger in each situation.

ACCOUNTING IN CONTEXT

Selling clothes

Benjamin and Florence have been in partnership selling clothing for many years. They are not sure whether there is any room for further expansion and in any case, they are both in their late fifties and wondering how much longer they could keep up with the workload. Benjamin had thought about retiring.

Roundwindow PLC, a company that also operates in the clothing industry, wishes to buy the partnership and has offered some cash and shares. The value of the offer is considerably more than the value of the assets in the partnership's financial statements.

Benjamin and Florence are both quite tempted to accept the offer.

Figure 28.1: Benjamin and Florence are tempted to take an offer for their business.

Discuss in a pair or a group:

- What advantages might Benjamin and Florence get from accepting the offer?

- What potential disadvantages might there be if Benjamin and Florence accept the offer?

28.1 Why do business acquisitions or mergers happen?

It is quite common for businesses to combine – whether it is one business actually taking over another or two businesses joining forces as equals. In both cases, the reasons for the combination are likely to be similar.

Companies merge with or **acquire** other companies for various reasons, including:

- *Efficiency gains*: When two businesses combine, there are cost savings that can be made. There is no longer a need to have two of each department. There may also be cost savings on purchasing because the new entity will be buying in larger quantities.

- *Increased expertise*: It is likely that the skill sets owned by the people involved in both businesses will be different and the two business combining will provide greater coverage. The increased size of the business may also justify the new organisation employing specialists.

- *Growth*: **Mergers** can give the acquiring company an opportunity to grow market share by buying out a competitor's business for a certain price. For example, a beer company may choose to buy out a smaller competing brewery, enabling the smaller outfit to produce more beer and increase its sales to brand-loyal customers.

- *Increase supply-chain pricing power*: A business can eliminate an entire tier of costs and protect its market position by buying out one of its suppliers. Taking over one of its distributors will also enable the business to cut out that business's profit-margin and enable the goods to be sold at a lower price.

- *Eliminate competition*: Many mergers or **takeovers** allow a business to eliminate future competition and gain a larger market share. However, the company may have to pay a high price to convince the target company's shareholders to sell their shares and in many countries, the authorities do not approve of anti-competitive behaviour.

KEY TERMS

acquisition: when one business purchases another – for companies, it is when one company purchases most or all of another company's shares to gain control of that company.

merger: where two or more independent businesses combine their assets and form a completely new business.

takeover: another term for acquisition – it is when one company purchases most or all of another company's shares to gain control of that company.

28.2 Mergers vs takeovers

There is often a lot of confusion about the difference between a merger and a takeover – not least because both involve two business entities combining to become one (larger) organisation.

A merger involves the mutual decision of two companies to combine and become one entity where both parties are seen to be equals in making the decision. If two companies merge, the shareholders are offered shares in the new organisation.

An example of a successful merger was when Walt Disney Company joined forces in 2007 with Pixar Entertainment a deal worth $7.4 billion. Walt Disney had been the biggest name in family entertainment for decades, producing a combination of animated and live action classics like Jungle Book, Mary Poppins and The Lion King.

Pixar was a relatively new arrival on the market but by taking advantage of new 'computer-generated animation' enjoyed huge success with films like Toy Story and Finding Nemo.

The merger allowed Disney to consolidate its brand as the biggest provider of family-friendly films and it allowed Pixar to greatly increase its production process and release two new films per year. Pixar films, including Up and WALL-E, have been hugely successful and both parties have clearly benefited from the combining of the two areas of expertise.

A takeover, or acquisition, on the other hand, often involves the purchase of a smaller company by a larger one and is less likely to be a mutual decision. A larger company can initiate a **hostile takeover** of a smaller firm where it buys the smaller company against the wishes of the smaller company's management and shareholders. In an acquisition, the acquiring firm offers a cash price per share to the target firm's shareholders, although shares in the 'acquiring firm' may be offered at a specified conversion rate, e.g. two shares in the acquiring company may be exchanged for every three shares in the company being taken over. Either way, the acquiring company is buying the target company for its shareholders.

Generally, the company being taken over will be managed by the company buying it and may have to significantly change the way it operates.

Not all acquisitions are unwelcome. An example is when the Walt Disney Corporation bought Pixar Animation Studios in 2006. In this case, the takeover was friendly, as Pixar's shareholders all approved the decision to be acquired. Both companies recognised that there were significant benefits for everyone of combining forces, not least the opportunity to dominate the animated feature films market.

> **KEY TERM**
>
> **hostile takeover:** the acquisition of one company by another, against the wishes of the management of the company being taken over who fear being replaced. It is usually accomplished by going direct to the company's shareholders and offering to buy their shares.

28.3 A merger of two businesses

A **merger** is where two existing businesses combine to form a single, larger business. There are several ways in which this could happen, including the merger of two sole traders to form a partnership, or the combination of a sole trader with a partnership (which is different from an admission of a partner to an existing partnership).

Worked example 1 shows how the combination of two sole traders might be accounted for.

WORKED EXAMPLE 1

Suganiya and Ibrahim each operate their own businesses as sole traders. Their summarised statements of financial position at 31 December 2020 were as follows:

	Suganiya	Ibrahim	Suganiya	Ibrahim
			$	$
Non-current assets			70 000	35 000
Current assets				
Inventory	7 000	6 000	12 000	16 000
Trade receivables	4 000	8 000		
Cash and cash equivalents			8 000	5 000
			20 000	21 000
Total assets			90 000	56 000
Capital and liabilities				
Capital accounts			84 000	47 000
Current liabilities				
Trade payables			6 000	9 000
Total capital and liabilities			90 000	56 000

Suganiya and Ibrahim feel that if they operate as a partnership, they can make more profit and, being friends, they are confident that they would work well together.

On 1 January 2021, they decide to create a partnership. They have agreed that the real value of the assets and liabilities of their businesses are as follows:

	Suganiya	Ibrahim
	$	$
Non-current assets	65 000	35 000
Inventory and trade receivables	11 000	14 000
Cash and cash equivalents	8 000	5 000
Trade payables	(6 000)	(9 000)
Net assets transferred to new partnership at agreed values	78 000	45 000

CONTINUED

The accountant has prepared the following statement of financial position at 1 January 2021 to record the opening balances of the new partnership:

Statement of financial position at 1 January 2021	
	$
Non-current assets: (65 000 + 35 000)	100 000
Current assets:	
Inventory (7 000 + 6 000)	13 000
Trade receivables (4 000 + 8 000)	12 000
Cash and cash equivalents (8 000 + 5 000)	13 000
	38 000
Total assets	138 000

	Suganiya	Ibrahim	
Capital accounts	78 000	45 000	123 000
Current liabilities:			
Trade payables (6 000 + 9 000)			15 000
Total capital and liabilities			138 000

All the accountant has done is to combine the value of the assets and liabilities from both businesses and has done so at the *values agreed by the partners*. It is likely that both partners have taken the opportunity to examine the assets and liabilities and have made some adjustments to ensure that they represented fair valuations. These would have to meet with the approval of the other partner.

It would be advisable for Suganiya and Ibrahim to draw up a partnership agreement to deal with issues such as the appropriation of profit and the rights and responsibilities of each partner.

However, it is likely that both Suganiya and Ibrahim would consider that their businesses were worth far more than the value of the assets in the statements of financial position – goodwill needs to be considered. The way in which we would deal with this is similar to how it was dealt with in the admission or retirement of a partner.

Suppose Suganiya and Ibrahim agree that the goodwill for their individual businesses was $60 000 and $40 000 and the partnership agreement states that partnership profits are to be shared equally:

	Suganiya	Ibrahim
	$	$
Net assets at valuation	78 000	45 000
Goodwill created (agreed by the partners)	60 000	40 000
	138 000	85 000
Goodwill written off (new profit sharing ratio)	(50 000)	(50 000)
Revised capital account balances	88 000	35 000

CONTINUED

The agreement by the partners that the goodwill is $60 000 and $40 000, respectively, which indicates that they believe that the value of assets of their part of the business are worth more than the cash value of the tangible assets ($78 000 and $45 000). This is similar to a revaluation in that this is treated as an addition to their capital account balances. Had we presented this in journal form, the entries would have been:

	$000	$000
Goodwill	100	
Capital – Suganiya		60
Capital – Ibrahim		40

The goodwill is then eliminated and, rather like the elimination of goodwill in Chapter 19, the partners are required to reduce their capital balances in the new profit-sharing ratios. There is no specific mention of 'new profit-sharing ratios' so under the Partnership Act 1890 we will use 50:50, so the journal entries would be:

	$000	$000
Capital – Suganiya	50	
Capital – Ibrahim	50	
Goodwill		100

This means that Suganiya's capital balance has increased by $10 000 and Ibrahim's has reduced by $10 000, and there is an element of fairness to this. Suganiya has made a 60% contribution to factors likely to increase the profitability of the partnership but will only take 50% of the profits – the $10 000 represents a form of compensation for this. Ibrahim will benefit from a 50% profit share that his goodwill has only contributed 40% to – he is paying $10 000 to Suganiya for this.

The statement of financial position for the Suganiya Ibrahim business will look like this:

Statement of financial position at 1 January 2021			
			$
Non-current assets (65 000 + 35 000)			100 000
Current assets:			
Inventory (7 000 + 6 000)			13 000
Trade receivables (4 000 + 8 000)			12 000
Cash and cash equivalents (8 000 + 5 000)			13 000
			38 000
Total assets			138 000
	Suganiya	Ibrahim	
Capital accounts:	88 000	35 000	123 000
Current liabilities:			
Trade payables (6 000 + 9 000)			15 000
Total capital and liabilities			138 000

Note: apart from the slight change in the opening capital balances, this is exactly the same as earlier. The totals will still be $138 000.

ACTIVITY 28.1

Garrett and Zhi each operate their own businesses as sole traders but have decided to form a partnership. Their summarised statements of financial position at 31 December 2020 were as follows:

	Garrett	Zhi
	$	$
Non-current assets:	92 000	61 000
Current assets:		
Inventory	9 000	8 000
Trade receivables	12 000	5 000
Cash and cash equivalents	4 000	9 000
	25 000	22 000
Total assets	117 000	83 000
Capital and liabilities:		
Capital accounts	98 000	72 000
Current liabilities:		
Trade payables	19 000	11 000
Total capital and liabilities	117 000	83 000

The partners have agreed that the following revaluations need to be made:

- Garrett's non-current assets should be valued at $120 000.

- Zhi's inventory is only worth $7 000 and trade receivables are only worth $3 000.

- Garrett's trade payables are, in fact, only worth $18 000.

- Goodwill has been agreed at $30 000 for Garrett and $50 000 for Zhi.

- The partners will share profits equally.

Required

a Show the revised statements of financial position for each sole trader before the merger (excluding the goodwill).

b Calculate the opening capital account balances that will appear in the statement of financial position after accounting for goodwill.

c Prepare the statement of financial position for the Garrett–Zhi partnership.

It is quite possible a merger might take place between a sole trader and an existing partnership. Worked example 2 shows how this might be achieved.

WORKED EXAMPLE 2

Fatima and Raki have been in business for a number of years sharing profits and losses equally. Their summarised statement of financial position at 31 March 2020 is as follows:

	Fatima	Raki	$000
Non-current assets:			130
Current assets			78
Total assets			208
Capital accounts	73	65	138
Current accounts	17	22	39
			177
Current liabilities:			31
Total capital and liabilities			208

On 1 April 2020, they agreed to admit Salif, a sole trader, as a partner. It was agreed that Salif would introduce the following assets into the partnership:

	$000
Motor vehicle	25
Inventory	17
Cash	8

Fatima and Raki revalued their non-current assets upwards to $180 000. They also valued goodwill at $70 000. It was agreed that goodwill would be eliminated immediately after Salif's admission.

A partnership agreement was drawn up which stated that Fatima, Raki and Salif would share the profits on a 5:3:2 basis.

The whole process involves a number of steps:

Step 1

Deal with the revaluation of the assets (and liabilities). The double-entry for this will depend on whether assets are increasing or decreasing:

- For an increase:

  Debit: assets

  Credit: partners' capital accounts (in the original profit sharing ratio).

- For a decrease:

  Debit: partners' capital accounts (in the original profit sharing ratio)

  Credit: assets

Step 2

Award the goodwill to the existing partners according to their profit sharing ratios:

  Debit: goodwill

  Credit: partner's capital accounts

CONTINUED

Step 3

Introduce the new partner's assets and open up a capital account for him/her:

> Debit: assets (and/or cash)
>
> Credit: partner's capital account

Step 4

Eliminate the goodwill using the new profit sharing ratios:

> Debit: partners' capital accounts
>
> Credit: goodwill

Step 5

Balance off the capital accounts.

Step 6

Prepare the new (opening) statement of financial position.

The journals required to carry out these steps would be as follows:

Step 1: Revaluation of non-current assets

	$000	$000
Non-current assets	50	
Capital – Fatima		25
Capital – Raki		25

Step 2: Creation of goodwill

	$000	$000
Goodwill	70	
Capital – Fatima		35
Capital – Raki		35

Step 3: Assets introduced by Salif

	$000	$000
Motor vehicles	25	
Inventory	17	
Cash	8	
Capital – Salif		50

Step 4: Elimination of Goodwill

	$000	$000
Capital – Fatima	35	
Capital – Raki	21	
Capital – Salif	14	
Goodwill		70

CONTINUED

These steps are shown in brackets below:

Partners capital accounts							
	Fatima	Raki	Salif		Fatima	Raki	Salif
	$000	$000	$000		$000	$000	$000
Goodwill (4)	35	21	14	Balance b/d	73	65	
Balance c/d (5)	98	104	36	Non-current assets (1)	25	25	
				Goodwill (2)	35	35	
				Motor vehicles (3)			25
				Inventory (3)			17
				Cash (3)			8
	133	125	50		133	125	50
				Balance b/d	98	104	36

(6)				$000
Non-current assets: (130 + 50 + 25)				205
Current assets: (78 + 17 + 8)				103
Total assets				308
	Fatima	Raki	Salif	
Capital accounts	98	104	36	238
Current accounts	17	22	–	39
				277
Current liabilities:				31
Total capital and liabilities				308

ACTIVITY 28.2

Pavel and Magda are in partnership, sharing profits and losses in the ratio of 2:1, respectively. Their summarised statement of financial position at 31 December 2020 is as follows:

			$000
Non-current assets:			165
Current assets			90
Total assets			255
	Pavel	Magda	
Capital accounts	96	114	210
Current accounts	[3]	20	17
			227
Current liabilities:			28
Total capital and liabilities			255

They agree to admit Li as a partner with effect from 1 January 2021. The new profit-sharing ratios will be 4:4:2.

The following matters should be taken into account:

1 Pavel and Magda will revalue their non-current assets upwards by $45 000.

2 Goodwill is valued at $60 000. No goodwill account is to remain in the books of account.

3 Li will introduce non-current assets valued at $47 000 and inventory valued at $15 000.

Required

a Complete the capital accounts for Pavel, Magda and Li.

b Prepare the statement of financial position at 1 January 2021 (immediately after the admission of Li to the partnership).

There are other situations where two businesses come together:

- the purchase of the business of a sole trader by a limited company
- the purchase of a partnership by a limited company.

28.4 Purchase of a sole trader by a limited company

A sole trader may sell their business to a limited company. Worked example 3 illustrates how this might be achieved.

One thing to pay particular attention to is whether the company is going to take over the sole trader's cash and bank account – usually they don't – as this will make a major difference to the calculation of any goodwill.

Before any entries for the purchase of a business are made in a company's ledger accounts, the transaction must be recorded in the company's journal.

TIP

Only take into account the assets and liabilities being bought by the limited company when calculating the value of purchased goodwill.

WORKED EXAMPLE 3

Larkfield Limited purchased the business of Mohammed, a sole trader, on 1 October 2020. Mohammed's statement of financial position at that date was:

	$000
Non-current assets:	
Land and buildings	230
Plant and machinery	40
Motor vehicles	35
	305
Current assets:	
Inventory	38
Trade receivables	24
Cash and cash equivalents	13
	75
Total assets	380
Capital and liabilities:	
Capital account	347
Current liabilities:	
Trade payables	33
Total capital and liabilities	380

The net assets were taken over at the following values were agreed:

	$000
Land and buildings	275
Plant and machinery	37
Motor vehicles	28
Inventory	37
Trade receivables	22
Trade payables	(33)
	366

The total of the *agreed* value of the assets purchased by Larkfield Limited amounts to $366 000. Larkfield Limited did not take over Mohammed's cash and cash equivalents, so these are *not* entered in the journal.

Larkfield Limited paid Mohammed $500 000, made up as follows: cash $100 000 and 250 000 ordinary shares of $1 each.

CONTINUED

The accountant of Larkfield Limited prepared the following journal entry to record the purchase of Mohammed's business:

	Dr	Cr
	$000	$000
Land and buildings	275	
Plant and machinery	37	
Motor vehicles	28	
Inventory	37	
Trade receivables	22	
Goodwill [1]	134	
Trade payables		33
Cash and cash equivalents		100
Ordinary share capital		250
Share premium account [2]		150
	533	533

Narrative: purchase of Mohammed's business

Notes:

[1] Goodwill = purchase consideration less value of net assets acquired, which in this case is 500 000 − 366 000 = $134 000.

[2] The shares were valued at 500 000 − 100 000 = $400 000 so the share premium = 400 000 − the nominal value of $250 000 = $150 000 (the shares are effectively being valued at $1.60 each).

The purchase of Mohammed's business on 1 October 2020 for the sum of $500 000 is payable as follows: cash $100 000 and by the issue of 250 000 ordinary shares of $1 at $1.60 per share.

CONTINUED

Larkfield Limited's statement of financial position at 1 October 2020 before it acquired Mohammed's business was as follows:

Statement of financial position at 1 October 2020	
	$000
Non-current assets:	
Land and buildings	400
Plant and machinery	125
Motor vehicles	60
	585
Current assets:	
Inventory	47
Trade receivables	54
Cash and cash equivalents	111
	212
Total assets	797
Equity and liabilities	
Equity:	
Ordinary share capital	600
Retained earnings	142
	742
Current liabilities:	
Trade payables	55
Total capital and liabilities	797

> **TIP**
>
> If you are required to prepare journal entries in a company's books to record the purchase of a business, *do not* show the entries in the books of the business being taken over.

Once Mohammed's assets and liabilities were purchased by Larkfield Limited, the accountant could prepare a statement of financial position.

CONTINUED

In order to do this, the accountant added the journal entries to Larkfield Limited's assets, liabilities, share capital and reserves as follows:

	$000
Intangible non-current assets – goodwill	134
Tangible non-current assets:	
Land and buildings (400 + 275)	675
Plant and machinery (125 + 37)	162
Motor vehicles (60 + 28)	88
	1 059
Current assets:	
Inventory (47 + 37)	84
Trade receivables (54 + 22)	76
Cash and cash equivalents (111 – 100)	11
	171
Total assets	1 230
Equity and liabilities	
Ordinary share capital (600 + 250)	850
Share premium	150
Retained earnings	142
	1 142
Current liabilities:	
Trade payables (55 + 33)	88
Total capital and liabilities	1 230

ACTIVITY 28.3

Bridges Limited purchased the business of Monty, a sole trader, on 30 June 2020.
The statements of financial position of both businesses at that date were as follows:

	Monty	Bridges Limited
	$	$
Non-current assets:		
Premises	140	510
Plant and machinery	57	133
Office furniture and equipment	23	58
	220	701
Current assets:		
Inventory	28	67
Trade receivables	14	33
Cash and cash equivalents	7	69
	49	169
Total assets	269	870
Capital and liabilities		
Capital account	251	
Current liabilities:		
Trade payables	18	
Total capital and liabilities	269	
Equity and liabilities		
Ordinary shares of $1		550
Share premium		155
Retained earnings		126
		831
Current liabilities:		
Trade payables		39
Total capital and liabilities		870

It was agreed that Monty's assets should be valued as follows:

	$000
Freehold property	190
Plant and machinery	55
Office furniture	19
Inventory	26
Trade receivables	13

Bridges Limited did not acquire Monty's bank account. The consideration for the sale
was $460 000. This consisted of $40 000 in cash and the 300 000 ordinary shares of $1
each in Bridges Limited.

CONTINUED

Required

a   Prepare the journal entries in Bridges Limited's books to record the purchase of Monty's business.

b   Prepare Bridges Limited's statement of financial position immediately after the acquisition of Monty's business.

28.5 Purchase of a partnership business by a limited company – the company's point of view

The purchase of a partnership business by a company follows a similar procedure to that for the purchase of a sole trader's business. There is one main complication to consider, however, and that is if an individual partner might have made a loan to the partnership.

In this case, it is usual for the company taking over the business to issue debentures to the partner so that they will continue to receive the same amount of interest that they were receiving before the takeover. This can be illustrated as follows:

Situation 1: a partner has loaned the company $50000 and the interest rate is 6%. The company taking over the partnership issues debentures with an interest rate of 10% and wants to ensure that the partner continues to receive the same amount of interest.

The interest currently being paid is $6\% \times \$50\,000 = \$3\,000$

so the value of debentures that need to be issued $= \$3\,000 \,/\, 10\% = \$30\,000$

or

Situation 2: a partner has loaned the company $80000 and the interest rate is 5%. The company taking over the partnership issues debentures with an interest rate of 10% and wants to ensure that the partner continues to receive the same amount of interest.

The interest currently being paid is $5\% \times \$80\,000 = \$4\,000$

so the value of debentures that need to be issued $= \$4\,000 \,/\, 10\% = \$40\,000$

Worked example 4 looks at a complete takeover of a partnership by a limited company.

> **TIP**
>
> When a debenture is issued to a partner, and the partner is to receive the same amount of annual interest as she or he received before the sale of the firm, check that you have calculated the amount of the debenture correctly.

Ed and Mia are partners in a business who share profits equally. They have accepted an offer from Tully Limited to purchase their business. The statements of financial position for both the partnership and the company at 31 December 2020 are as follows:

Ed and Mia				Tully Limited		
			$000			$000
Non-current assets:				Non-current assets:		
Land and buildings			170	Land and buildings		420
Fixtures and fittings			21	Fixtures and fittings		63
Office machinery			35	Office machinery		80
			226			563
Current assets:				Current assets:		
Inventory			18	Inventory		67
Trade receivables			24	Trade receivables		45
Cash and cash equivalents			9	Cash and cash equivalents		39
			51			151
Total assets			277	Total assets		714
Capital and liabilities				Equity and liabilities:		
	Ed	Mia				
Capital accounts	80	118	198			
Non-current liability:						
10% Loan from Ed			60			
Current liabilities:				Current liabilities:		
Trade payables			19	Trade payables		36
Total capital and liabilities			277	Total equity and liabilities		714

It has been agreed that the partnership assets are to be valued as follows:

	$000
Land and buildings	210
Fixtures and fittings	18
Office machinery	30
Inventory	17
Trade receivables	21

CONTINUED

Tully Limited has agreed to take over all of the assets and liabilities of the business, with the exception of the partnership bank account, and will settle the purchase price as follows:

1   A payment of cash, $25 000.

2   8% debentures issued to Ed to ensure that he continues to receive the same amount of interest annually as she has received from the partnership.

3   The balance to be settled by an issue of 200 000 ordinary shares of $1 in Tully Limited, valued at a price of $1.50 per share.

Step 1   Calculate the value of the debentures needed to ensure that Ed receives the same amount of interest as he was getting from his partnership loan.

Interest = $60 000 × 10% = $6 000

Value of debentures = 6 000 / 8% = $75 000

Step 2   Calculate the value of the goodwill. This will be based on the agreed value of the assets and liabilities:

	$000	$000
Land and buildings	210	
Fixtures and fittings	18	
Office machinery	30	
Inventory	17	
Trade receivables	21	
Trade payables		19
Cash and cash equivalents		25
Debenture for Ed		75
Ordinary share capital		200
Share premium account		100
Goodwill[1]	123	
	419	419

Note:

[1]   Purchase price was 25 + 75 + 200 + 100 = 400

Assets acquired were 210 + 18 + 30 + 17 + 21 − 19 = 277

Goodwill = 400 − 277 = $123 000

CONTINUED

Step 3 The statement of financial position for Tully Limited immediately after the purchase of the partnership can now be produced. You will notice that a lot of the work involves combining the assets and liabilities of the partnership and the limited company.

	$000
Intangible non-current assets (goodwill)	123
Tangible non-current assets:	
Land and buildings (420 + 210)	630
Fixtures and fittings (63 + 18)	81
Office machinery (80 + 30)	110
	944
Current assets:	
Inventory (67 + 17)	84
Trade receivables (45 + 21)	66
Cash and cash equivalents (39 − 25)	14
	164
Total assets	1 108
Equity and liabilities:	
Ordinary shares of $1 each (500 + 200)	700
Share premium (200 × 0.50)	100
Retained earnings	178
	978
Non-current liability:	
8% debentures (issued to Ed)	75
Current liabilities:	
Trade payables (36 + 19)	55
Total equity and liabilities	1 108

One practical issue that will need to be resolved is how much cash and how many of the ordinary shares Ed and Mia are going to take.

The goodwill is *purchased goodwill* as the total amount paid by the limited company exceeded the net book value of the assets acquired by them. It doesn't matter whether that payment was for cash, shares or debentures. As we saw in IAS 38, this goodwill can be shown in the company's statement of financial position. It is likely that Tully will look to write off (amortise) that goodwill either during the next period or over a number of years.

Until the purchase takes place, any goodwill (sometimes referred to as inherent goodwill) is only a matter of opinion, and even if everyone agrees that a particular business has certain characteristics that have significant commercial value, IAS 38 does not allow it to be included in the financial statements.

If the amount paid for a business is less than the fair value of its separable net assets, the difference is called *negative goodwill*. This is known as a bargain purchase and the profit is recognised immediately in the statement of profit or loss of the company buying the business.

28.6 Purchase of a partnership business by a limited company – the partnership's point of view

When a limited company takes over a partnership, the partnership is effectively dissolved. The steps are:

Step 1   Remove the current accounts by transferring the balances to the partners' capital accounts.

Step 2   Deal with any loans from partners by calculating the amount of debentures that need to be issued.

Step 3   Open up a realisation account and use it to remove the assets and liabilities of the business. This will enable you to identify the profit or loss on realisation.

Step 4   Prepare the partners' capital accounts and identify how much each partner is entitled to take away from the dissolution of the partnership.

Step 5   Make the necessary entries in the ledger to record the partners receiving their shares and any monies from the bank, if there is any left.

WORKED EXAMPLE 5

Marg and Victor are partners in a business who share profits equally. They have accepted an offer from Wilson Limited to purchase their business. The statement of financial position for the partnership at 31 December 2020 is as follows:

			$000
Non-current assets:			
Land and buildings			180
Motor vehicle			24
Office machinery			45
			249
Current assets:			
Inventory			33
Trade receivables			42
Cash and cash equivalents			11
			86
Total assets			335
Capital and liabilities			
	Marg	Victor	
Capital accounts	89	154	243
Current accounts	12	[8]	4
			247
8% Loan – Marg			50
Current liabilities:			
Trade payables			38
Total capital and liabilities			335

CONTINUED

Wilson Limited has agreed to take over all of the assets and liabilities of the business, with the exception of the partnership bank account and the motor vehicle that Victor is going to take. The company will settle the purchase price as follows:

1   A payment of cash, $50 000.

2   Marg will be issued with 10% debentures that will ensure that she continues to receive the same amount of interest as she did before.

3   The balance will be settled by an issue of 300 000 ordinary shares of $1 in Wilson Limited, valued at a price of $1.20 per share.

Step 1   There current accounts balances need to be transferred to the partner's capital accounts.

Current accounts					
	Marg	Victor		Marg	Victor
	$000	$000		$000	$000
Balance b/d		8	Balance b/d	12	
Capital account	12		Capital account		8
	12	8		12	8

Step 2   Dealing with the Marg loan:

Interest currently received = 8% × 50 000 = $4 000

Value of debentures to be issued = 4 000 / 10% = $40 000

Step 3   Prepare the realisation account in the partnership books:

Realisation account			
	$000		$000
Land and buildings[1]	180	Trade payables[1]	38
Motor vehicle[1]	24	Cash	50
Office machinery[1]	45	Shares (including premium)	360
Inventory[1]	33	Capital – Victor (motor vehicle)	24
Trade receivables[1]	42	Debentures – Marg[3]	40
Profit on realisation – Marg[2]	94		
Profit on realisation – Victor[2]	94		
[4]	512		512

Notes:

[1]   The values of the assets and liabilities are those in the statement of financial position not the agreed values that might have been used to calculate Wilson's goodwill. From the partners' point of view, we are regarding any difference as profit (or loss) on realisation rather than goodwill.

[2]   The profit or loss on realisation is split between the partners in their profit-sharing ratios.

[3]   The debentures given to Marg are regarded as part of the purchase price of the partnership but will actually be debited to her current account. The loan itself will be converted to Marg capital in Step 3.

CONTINUED

[4] If there are expenses to pay in connection with the realisation of the partnership, these should be debited to the realisation account and credited to the partnership bank account. This will reduce both the profit on dissolution and the bank account.

Step 4   It is now possible to prepare the partners' capital accounts and the movements on the bank account as follows:

Capital accounts	Marg	Victor		Marg	Victor
	$000	$000		$000	$000
Realisation – vehicle		24	Balance b/d	89	154
Current account		8	Current account	12	
Debentures	40		Loan – Marg	50	
Balance c/d	205	216	Profit on realisation	94	94
	245	248		245	248
			Balance b/d	205	216

Bank		$000			$000
Balance b/d		11	Balance c/d		61
Realisation account		50			
		61			61
Balance b/d		61			

Step 5   Paying off the partners will involve making entries to reflect that they will be taking away cash and shares in Wilson Limited.

The value of shares being offered is $360 000 (including the premium of $0.20) while the amount of cash available is $61 000. This is a total of $421 000.

Marg is entitled to a total pay-off of $205 000 and Victor is entitled to $216 000 – also a total of $421 000. It is now down to the partners to agree on the form of their pay-off, which might look something like this:

Capital accounts	Marg	Victor		Marg	Victor
	$000	$000		$000	$000
Bank	25	36	Balance b/d	205	216
Shares in Wilson	180	180			
	205	216		205	216

Bank		$000			$000
Balance b/d		61	Capital – Marg		25
			Capital – Victor		36
		61			61

28.7 Conversion of own business

Sometimes a sole trader or a partnership may decide to convert their business into a limited company. This is done by forming a new company that purchases the business.

WORKED EXAMPLE 6

Sanna is as a sole trader. On 1 October 2020 she decided to form a limited company to take over her business. She will hold ordinary shares of $1 in the company as her capital.

Sanna's summarised statement of financial position at 1 October 2020 was as follows:

	$
Non-current assets	40 000
Net current assets	25 000
	65 000
Capital account	65 000

The summarised statement of financial position of the new company is:

Sanna Limited	
	$
Non-current assets	40 000
Net current assets	25 000
	65 000
Share capital	
Ordinary shares of $1	65 000

Sanna has transferred all the assets and liabilities of her 'old' business to a new limited company and, in return, she has replaced her old capital account with shares: ordinary shares of $1 each.

Sanna is the only shareholder. She can run the business herself as the only director. The only practical differences are that she will have to set up the company officially, possibly have her accounts audited and present the financial statements in a more structured format. (Having her accounts audited would depend on the jurisdiction in her country as not all countries require audits for small companies.) The key advantage is limited liability, which she didn't have as a sole trader.

28.8 Purchasing a business or purchasing of the assets of a business

It is also possible that a buyer only wishes to acquire the assets of an organisation, and the organisation being bought out will cease to trade. Alternatively, the buyer may only wish to buy some of the assets, and the seller will still own their business and may have to make a decision as to whether they can continue to trade. In either of these situations, there will be no goodwill paid.

KEY CONCEPT LINK

Business entity: The accounting records must relate only to the business and not to the personal assets and spending of the owner. Why is it so important to maintain this separation of business and the owner(s), particularly when there is a merger or a takeover taking place?

THINK LIKE AN ACCOUNTANT

Business valuation

Benjamin and Florence had started negotiations with Roundwindow Limited regarding the sale of their clothing business. Florence had suggested that $100 000 for goodwill should be added to their statement of financial position in order to ensure that Roundwindow Limited were aware of the true value of the business. Her view was:

'We have a good reputation, a strong customer-base and a very experienced workforce – all these things should be recognised as they have taken us years to build them up!' Should the partners include the $100 000 in their financial statements to cover goodwill?

Why/why not?

Figure 28.2: Negotiations begin about the sale of the clothing business.

REFLECTION

How much of a problem would it be if a company wished to buy a partnership and some of those partners were in favour of being bought out and others were completely against the idea? How might this problem be overcome?

EXAM-STYLE QUESTIONS

1   The following is information about the assets and liabilities of a business:

	Book value	Market value
	$	$
Non-current assets	120 000	145 000
Current assets	53 000	49 000
	173 000	
Current liabilities	(18 000)	18 000
	155 000	

Goodwill is valued at $40 000. What should be paid for the net assets of the business?

A $191 000

B $195 000

C $216 000

D $220 000

[1]

CONTINUED

2 A company paid $960 000 to acquire the business of a sole trader. The sole trader's assets and liabilities were valued as follows:

Non-current assets	800 000
Current assets	120 000
Current liabilities	70 000
Non-current liability	300 000

How much was paid for goodwill?

A $110 000

B $210 000

C $310 000

D $410 000 [1]

3 The statement of financial position of a sole trader is as follows:

	$
Non-current assets	
Goodwill	60 000
Plant and machinery	200 000
Net current assets	100 000

A company purchased the business, paying for the plant and machinery and the net current assets, at the valuations shown here. The company settled the purchase price by issuing 300 000 ordinary shares of $1 at $1.50 per share. How much did the company pay for goodwill?

A $0

B $60 000

C $90 000

D $150 000 [1]

4 Queen Limited purchased the business of Ruy Lopez, a sole trader, on 30 June 2020. The statements of financial position of both businesses at that date were as follows:

	Ruy Lopez	Queen Limited
	$	$
Non-current assets:		
Premises	–	440
Motor vehicles	40	75
Office equipment	32	110
	72	625
Current assets:		
Inventory	57	94
Trade receivables	24	65
Cash and cash equivalents	13	31
	94	190
Total assets	166	815

CONTINUED

	Ruy Lopez	Queen Limited
	$	$
Capital and liabilities		
Capital account:	131	
Current liabilities:		
Trade payables	35	
Total capital and liabilities	166	
Equity and liabilities		
Ordinary shares of $0.50		500
Share premium		55
Retained earnings		189
		744
Current liabilities:		
Trade payables		71
Total capital and liabilities		815

It was agreed that Ruy Lopez's assets should be valued as follows:

	$000
Motor vehicles	36
Office furniture	30
Inventory	54
Trade receivables	22

Queen Limited did not acquire Ruy Lopez's bank account. The consideration for the sale was $190 000. This consisted of $20 000 in cash and the 200 000 ordinary shares of $0.50 each in Queen Limited, valued at $0.85 each.

Required

a Prepare the journal entries in Queen Limited's books to record the purchase of Ruy Lopez's business. [5]

b Prepare Queen Limited's statement of financial position immediately after the acquisition of Ruy Lopez's business. [10]

c Explain:

- the difference between inherent goodwill and purchased goodwill
- how goodwill should be accounted for in the financial statements of a business according to IAS 38. [4]

d Explain *three* reasons why a merger or a takeover might take place. [6]

SELF-EVALUATION CHECKLIST

After studying this chapter, complete a table like this:

You should be able to:	Needs more work	Almost there	Ready to move on
Discuss why business acquisitions and mergers happen (including gaining access to new markets, achieving efficiency gains or to protect the distribution chain) and the difference between the acquisition of a business and a merger of two businesses.			
Prepare the journal entries and make entries in the relevant ledger accounts to enable goodwill to be calculated and to transfer the assets and liabilities to the 'new entity', or the business carrying out the takeover, or to show the sole trader's or partners' departure from the business.			
Account for the value of goodwill on the acquisition of a business by another entity, understanding the difference between purchased and inherent goodwill.			
Prepare financial statements for the newly formed business entity after the acquisition or merger.			
Discuss the advantages and disadvantages of the acquisition or merger in each situation.			

> **Chapter 29**

Ethics and the accountant

This chapter covers part of syllabus section A Level 3.2

LEARNING INTENTIONS

In this chapter you will learn how to:

- explain the need for an ethical framework in accounting
- explain the fundamental principles of integrity, objectivity, professional competence and due care, confidentiality and professional behaviour
- explain how the ethical behaviour of accountants and auditors impacts the business and other stakeholders
- describe approaches that can be used by organisations to promote ethical behaviour
- describe the social implications of decision making, especially 'corporate social responsibility'.

ACCOUNTING IN CONTEXT

The accounts junior

While Jamal was working on producing a provisional set of final accounts, one of the partners asked him to reduce the closing inventory figure by $10 000. When Jamal asked whether there was a reason for the adjustment, the partner got angry and told him to 'just do it!'

Jamal's probationary period would finish the following month, and he wasn't sure what to do. There didn't seem to be a good reason for adjusting the inventory, but he really did want to keep his job.

Discuss in a pair or a group:

- Why might making the inventory adjustment be a problem?
- Should Jamal follow the instructions of the partner?

Figure 29.1: Jamal didn't see a good reason to adjust the inventory figure.

29.1 The need for ethical behaviour and guidelines

The **ethics** of an organisation are 'the moral principles or standards that govern the conduct of the members of that organisation'. While it is expected that an organisation and the people that work for it will obey the law and accounting regulation, there is an expectation that they will exhibit 'good behaviour'.

People place trust in accountants including:

- clients relying on the accountant preparing their financial statements accurately (and in accordance with laws and the accounting framework) and ensuring that they pay the minimum (but legal) amount of tax
- banks and other investors relying on the information contained within those financial statements being accurate so that they can decide whether to lend money to the business
- suppliers needing to decide whether they are going to offer credit facilities.

If the accountant has a reputation for being principled and trustworthy, these stakeholders will feel more able to place their trust in that accountant.

All professional accounting bodies have ethical guidelines for their members and investigate any allegation of behaviour likely to harm their reputations.

It would be unfair to say that all unethical behaviour is committed by immoral or dishonest people. There may be many other reasons why people may not do the right thing including:

- *Being put under personal pressure*: Jamal from the Accounting in Context feature might know what he should do (refuse to adjust the inventory figure) but is being pressured by a partner at his accounting firm. He may have a lot to lose, for example, his job by refusing the request.
- **Conflicts of interest**: someone may face a conflict of interest where they are receiving demands from two or more parties that are incompatible. An example of this might be where an accountant has a number of clients and knows that if he or she provides good professional advice to one of those clients, it will have a negative effect on another of his clients. It will be impossible to please all of those parties. They may (wrongly) meet the demands of the more dominant force or find that they are so confused that their ability to make a rational or right decision is impaired.

KEY TERM

ethics: the moral principles or standards that govern the conduct of a person or organisation that knows the difference between right and wrong behaviour.

conflicts of interest: where a person is faced with demands from two or more people or organisations that are incompatible

A further problem is that what is regarded as morally acceptable and what is not can vary at a number of levels including:

- *National level*: Different attitudes to certain behaviours will exist in different parts of the world. In India, a public servant convicted of bribery can receive a prison sentence of three to seven years plus a fine, while in South Africa, the High Court can impose up to a life sentence. In other regions, offering a bribe in order to be awarded a contract may almost be compulsory.

- *Corporation level*: The directors and owners of different organisations, even in the same industry, may hold different views about what represents ethical behaviour. This may even extend to who they will or won't do business with. Some business are happy to use suppliers even if they know that the working conditions in their factories or the way that they source raw materials is bad for the environment, while others may refuse to trade with those suppliers, even though they may charge lower prices.

- *Department level*: Attitudes to ethical behaviour may vary between departments. This may reflect the personality of the department manager rather than the organisation as a whole. Some sales managers might insist that in order to obtain a sale, it is acceptable to exaggerate or lie to customers or try to sell goods or services that they do not really need, while other managers might insist on a policy of total honesty and may even take disciplinary action against staff who do show dishonest behaviour.

- *Personal level*: Individuals will have very different personal views that may well have been developed as a result of factors including age, gender, race, creed or religious beliefs. Some individuals may have strong views on issues such as veganism, for example, which might make it difficult for them to provide sound impartial advice to clients whose businesses are involved in those types of goods or service.

It is therefore very unlikely that everyone will take exactly the same view when faced with a situation that is not covered by specific rules or laws.

As a result of this, **professional bodies** or **industry lead bodies** issue ethical codes of conduct that they expect their members to follow. Examples from within the UK accounting industry include the Institute of Chartered Accountants of England and Wales (ICAEW) who have issued a 'Code of Ethics', and the Association of Accounting Technicians (AAT) who have issued the Code of Professional Ethics.

Most guidelines or codes issued by professional bodies emphasise the need to go beyond the requirements of laws and regulation. They will mention the need to strive for 'the highest standards' and will actively seek to discipline members who fall short of the required standards or whose behaviour threatens to harm the reputation of that professional body. The reasons for doing this include:

- Protecting the members themselves – someone acting ethically is less likely to get into trouble and is better equipped to defend themselves if there is a problem later.

- Protecting the organisation and its stakeholders – there is less likelihood of legal action or financial problems if the accountant is always striving to protect principles like 'true and fair view' which will help the organisation to maintain good links with its stakeholders.

- Protecting the reputation of the professional body itself.

While no two ethical codes are exactly the same, most of them emphasise the same five fundamental principles: integrity, objectivity, professional competence and due care, confidentiality and professional behaviour. As we will see, there will be a great deal of overlap of the principles because many unethical forms of behaviour will threaten or breach more than one of the fundamental principles.

Anyone working in a business environment could be faced with situations where they are required to make an ethical decision and this may not always be easy. Professional

> **KEY TERMS**
>
> **professional bodies:** organisations that have members operating in a particular industry.
>
> **industry lead bodies:** organisations that control the way in which industries are run and the way in which people working in those industries operate.

bodies recognise this and work on the principle that if their members look to apply ethical principles to the way they work, they are less likely to encounter problems later and will protect their own reputations and that of the profession.

29.2 Integrity

Examples of an accountant displaying **integrity** might include:

- *Communicating all information factually whether good or bad*: Sometimes it may be tempting to leave out the bad news and only tell the client what you think he or she wants to hear. Sometimes leaving out information can have legal implications too. In the UK, the Fraud Act 2006 has three categories of fraud, including false representation (telling lies) and failure to disclose (leaving out facts that might have changed someone's decision). The third type of fraud is 'abuse of position', which is where someone is dishonestly taking advantage of a person who may be old, ill or unable to manage their own affairs, relying on them to take care of their best interests. It is likely that your country will have similar laws. An accounting example of this would be when filling out a bank loan application for a client, leaving out negative information that might result in the bank rejecting that client's application.

- *Avoiding compromising situations*: This means refusing gifts that might be seen by an outsider to be a bribe. An accounting example of this might involve how you deal with a situation where, at the end of a job, a client offers you a season ticket in the executive box of your favourite sports team to thank you for the work that you have done. Declaring that the offer has been made to the management would display integrity.

- *Avoiding conflicts of interest*: This will be discussed more fully in the next section of this chapter but could also include declaring a possible conflict of interest, e.g. stating in a job interview situation that there is a personal connection with one of the candidates and offering to step aside.

- *Recognising and communicating one's personal and professional limitations*: An accounting example of this would be if a manager asks an accounts junior to produce a bank reconciliation because the junior has passed an accounts course where these were on the syllabus. The junior knows that they have never managed to get a bank reconciliation to agree! Showing integrity might involve admitting that they do have the skills and knowledge to perform the task to the required standard.

- *Avoiding certain activities*: These activities could prevent them from performing their duties or could discredit the profession or organisation. They may involve lifestyle choices outside of work. It might not be considered appropriate if an accountant who is responsible for looking after his client's financial affairs was to get involved in practices such as buy to let, for example, where people buy properties just to rent them out, as this might be regarded as exploitative.

As with many of the fundamental principles, it is as important that an accountant is *seen* to be entirely honest as it is knowing in themselves that they are.

One main technique in maintaining integrity, particularly if one is placed in an awkward situation, is to ask one simple question: 'Do I need to tell someone about this?'

In many cases, that someone may be a line manager. From a practical point-of-view, if an awkward situation is declared early, then your position is often far easier to defend if there is a later accusation made.

> **KEY TERM**
>
> **integrity:** being straightforward and honest in all of your dealings.

ACTIVITY 29.1

In each of the following situations, explain:

- why the principle of integrity is being threatened or breached
- what the person should do in order to ensure that any problems are avoided.

Situation 1: At the end of a successful job, the client has brought in a case of expensive wine (or a large bunch of flowers and chocolates) to thank you for your efforts.

Situation 2: Your company has obtained a new client and you are going to be involved in the work. Unfortunately, the job is going to require you to perform tasks that you have absolutely no experience of or training in.

Situation 3: You have been invited to a party weekend in a large city that may well involve vast amounts of drinking and various forms of riotous behaviour. The travel schedule will involve you arriving back home at 6.30 a.m. on Monday morning. Your employer expects you to take part in a very important meeting, involving some important clients, at 9 a.m. on Monday morning.

Situation 4: A friend of yours from a previous employer has telephoned you to offer you some temporary work that you can fit in at the weekend. It appears that your previous employer (who works in the same line of business as your current firm) has a staffing emergency.

29.3 Objectivity

There are a number of reasons why someone's **objectivity** can be threatened, including:

- *Self-interest*: There may be an advantage to be gained in not being objective, e.g. gaining a promotion or keeping a job.

- *Self-review*: Someone is less likely to be objective if they are reviewing their own work. If someone realises that they have committed an error, they might be tempted to conceal the fact rather than bringing it into the open. In any event, a review by someone not involved in the original work often increases the chances of an error being detected, as a fresh pair of eyes might notice something unusual that has been missed by the person doing the original work.

- *Advocacy*: This is where someone's opinions, preferences and beliefs are allowed to affect their judgements, e.g. it may be difficult to do the best possible job if your beliefs mean that there is an in-built disapproval of the client's line of business (say, selling tobacco or alcohol).

- *Familiarity or trust*: This is where someone may be influenced because of a connection with family or friends. This could be because they find themselves dealing with a business that employs a family member or a friend. Sometimes, they might be contacted by someone they know who has approached them specifically in order to ask them to do something or make a decision in their favour.

- *Intimidation*: There may be a temptation to make a decision because there may be an actual or feared threat being made by an employer or client.

In many cases, the difference between self-interest and intimidation can be a fine line. In the Accounting in Context feature, the partner made reference to Jamal coming to the end of his probation period. Was Jamal facing a self-interest risk to his objectivity (a promise that he would be offered permanent employment) or being threatened (refusal would cost him his job)? It is difficult to tell, but the main point is there was pressure being put on Jamal to make the wrong decision.

KEY TERM

objectivity: being impartial and unbiased – making a decision based on the facts or evidence or taking an action because it is the right thing to do.

An accountant should not only avoid those influences but be seen to avoid those influences. It is not enough for that accountant to know that they are being objective – sometimes referred to as 'independence of mind'. People need to see that the accountant is actively avoiding situations that might compromise their objectivity – sometimes referred to as being 'independent by appearance'. If that accountant is an employee in a company, then one practical action that should be taken if there is a possible risk to objectivity, is to declare the possible problem to management. Management will then need to decide whether they find the risk acceptable or not.

It may be that the accountant has to be removed from the situation and given other jobs, but this is far better than keeping quiet and management finding out later.

ACTIVITY 29.2

In each of the following situations, explain:

- which risk to objectivity is being displayed and why
- what the person should do in order to ensure that any future problems are avoided.

1   You work for a firm of accountants and the organisation has recently obtained a new client – a partnership of builders. There is every likelihood that you will be involved in this work. One of the partners happens to be your brother-in-law.

2   One of your clients at your accounts firm has telephoned you regarding the final accounts that you produced for him. It seems that he is applying for a loan and feels that a larger profit figure is required. He has suggested that if you cannot comply with his request, he will take his business to another firm of accountants and tell the partners why.

3   You have recently changed jobs. A client from your previous firm has changed accountants due to a series of problems and disputes, and approached your current employer. The job has been accepted and there is every chance that you are going to be asked to work on this client's books.

29.4 Professional competence and due care

An accountant needs to ensure that she or he has the *professional knowledge and skills* to ensure that the service provided is both *competent* and in accordance with latest *legislation and industrial standards*.

Satisfying the **professional competence** element of this principle will involve:

- *Initially obtaining the skills and knowledge* necessary to be able to work to a professionally competent level. This may involve being a learner attending day-release or evening courses at a college or other training provider.

- Undertaking *Continuing Professional Development (CPD)*, which is training or other activities designed to help someone keep up-to-date with changes in laws, regulations and techniques. Laws and industrial standards change and failure to keep up-to-date may get the accountant into trouble – possibly even leading to legal action or getting sued by an angry client. Most professional bodies require their members to carry out CPD and keep a record of what has been done. Failure to provide evidence of CPD can result in severe disciplinary action (even withdrawal of membership).

Accountants should also avoid undertaking work that they know they are not competent to do. For example, members of the Association of Chartered Certified Accountants (ACCA)

KEY TERM

professional competence: having the skills, knowledge and understanding to be able to perform a task to the appropriate professional standard.

or the Institute of Chartered Accountants of England and Wales (ICAEW) are not, in themselves, allowed to offer legal services to their clients.

Due care simply means that members should act diligently – that is, they should take care to be accurate, thorough and carry out their duties to the highest possible standard. Many professional bodies will make reference to excellence in their guidelines as there is a perception that 'professional standard' is the bare minimum that should be provided.

If an employee is asked to perform work when they do not have the skills and knowledge to do it, then they should disclose the fact to their manager as failure to do so may give the impression that they are qualified. This would be a form of dishonesty (breaching the integrity principle). It is also likely that if the employee does try to do the work without adequate training or support, the work will not be carried out to the required standard. Ultimately, it is the management's responsibility to ensure that they are only using employees who are capable of performing a given task, which may involve organising the relevant training.

29.5 Confidentiality

It is highly likely that in performing her or his duties, the accountant will have access to highly sensitive information about the clients and their businesses. Some of this information will be of a personal nature while some might involve commercially sensitive secrets that would place the business at a serious disadvantage if it fell into the hands of competitors.

Clients have a right to expect that their accountant will keep this information safe and will respect their **confidentiality** and many firms of accountants are more likely to dismiss employees for breaching this principle than for making (serious) errors. While the Ethical Guidelines issued by different professional bodies may vary slightly, there are certain principles common to all:

- Information gained during the course of one's duties should not be disclosed to anyone who does not have a right to it – we will discuss where disclosures can be made a little later in this section.

- Information cannot be used for one's own personal benefit or the benefit of third parties, e.g. buying shares in a company because you have information indicating that the share price will rise in the next few weeks is not allowed. In many countries, this is actually a criminal offence. In Singapore, **insider trading** carries a penalty of up to seven years in prison plus a maximum fine of $250 000.

- Confidentiality applies even after a business relationship has ended. An ex-client has an equal right to expect you to respect their confidentiality as an existing client. This is also true of ex-employees, which means that if someone changes their job, they should not be revealing information acquired at the previous company to their new colleagues (including details of terms and conditions).

- If an accountant is managing staff, it is essential that the importance of confidentiality be impressed on them. New staff need to be made aware of company policy regarding keeping information safe while existing staff should be constantly reminded of their need to maintain confidentiality.

However, there are circumstances under which disclosures can be made. They could be placed in the category of 'can', 'should' and 'must' and include:

- *With the person's permission*: Sometimes an organisation like a bank might make a request for personal information about a client or employee. That person has applied for a loan or mortgage and the bank wishes to confirm the income figure that they put on the application.

KEY TERMS

due care: the care that a competent person (accountant) would reasonably expect to take in order to perform a task to the required professional standard.

confidentiality: not disclosing (keeping secret) sensitive information that would not be available to the public.

insider trading: where someone uses information not available to members of the public for their own benefit or the benefit of third parties.

Assuming that it can be established that it is the bank making the request (and not a scam being committed by fraudsters), a decision has to be made about whether the information is given. The safest approach is to contact the person concerned and ask whether they are happy for you to share that information – preferably in writing. Once permission has been received, the information *can* be shared.

- *Evidence of wrongdoing*: An employee may uncover evidence that their company is committing something wrong, e.g. the illegal pollution of a local river or a breach of health and safety rules. Many countries have laws that protect an employee if they report this wrongdoing to the authorities, but the degree of protection varies. In South Africa, informing the authorities of wrongdoing (**whistleblowing**) is covered by the Protected Disclosures Act 2000 that protects workers from dismissal or any prejudice or detriment if they disclose information to specified persons in good faith. The dismissal of employees for making protected disclosures is rendered automatically unfair. Compensation of up to 12 months' salary may be claimed for detrimental treatment, or up to 24 months' salary for an automatically unfair dismissal.

This type of disclosure might be regarded as a *should disclose* but many employees will recognise that although they cannot officially be victimised because of that disclosure, it is possible that unscrupulous employers might make life uncomfortable in other ways, e.g. the quality of their work and overall competence is suddenly and constantly being called into question or the employer finds an unrelated minor issue that they can use to initiate disciplinary proceedings which may eventually force a resignation.

It is therefore recognised by most professional bodies that an employee needs to think carefully before they take the step of whistleblowing, particularly if they are not 100% sure that there is wrongdoing.

- *Legal requirements*: An employee may have a legal duty to disclose information and this can take a number of forms:

  - Law courts may summon an accountant as a witness – failure to answer questions will be seen as breaking the law ('contempt of court').

  - Police or law enforcement agencies may require information as part of an investigation – this should be given.

  - Tax authorities may require information – this should be given.

  - Specific laws in many countries make certain disclosures mandatory – **money laundering** is a very good example. In the UK, the law requires that anyone even *suspecting* money-laundering must report their suspicions to the National Crime Agency (or get the Money Laundering Reporting Officer if their company has one to do it). Not doing so will be regarded as committing an offence called 'failure to disclose' that, in the UK, carries a maximum sentence of five years in prison.

In popular films, money laundering is portrayed as a criminal committing a robbery and trying to move the money around to make it difficult to trace, but for legal purposes it is defined as 'all forms of handling or possessing criminal property (including the proceeds of one's own crime) and the facilitating of any handling or possession of criminal property'.

In practice, suspicions of money laundering might be raised by any activity that looks as though it might involve a large-scale fraud. This could include unusual movements of money that bear little relation to the normal activities of the business or transactions (sales or expenses) that appear to be fictional.

- *Demands by professional bodies*: An accountant may be asked to attend an investigation or disciplinary hearing organised by his or her professional body. He or she may face questions from a panel or committee that require the disclosure of

KEY TERMS

whistleblowing: in some countries this is referred to as a public disclosure (or similar) where someone, often an employee, reports wrongdoing to the authorities.

money laundering: all forms of handling or possessing criminal property (including the proceeds of one's own crime) and the facilitating of any handling or possession of criminal property.

potentially sensitive information. The ethical guidelines of any profession will say that the accountant must provide that information.

It should be noted that, in the case of these last two circumstances, the wishes of the client or employer are irrelevant. The information must be provided, even if the client or employer tells the accountant not to cooperate.

ACTIVITY 29.3

In each of the following situations, indicate what you should do (or what information should be disclosed, if any). You should justify your opinion.

1   An estate agent has written to request confirmation of one of your client's income who has applied to rent a property. What should you do?

2   You receive a formal demand from the tax authorities for information used in producing the tax return of one of your clients. What should you do?

3   A new receptionist provides her banking details by email. She asks you to pass it on to the payroll department. The email contains details of rates of pay and benefits provided by her previous employer. What should you do?

4   A friend who works for a small business has been offered a large contract to supply goods to a company who happens to be a client of your firm. You know that the company is in financial difficulties and would certainly struggle to pay for those goods. This would cause your friend's small business serious difficulty. What should you do?

5   You have been working on the payroll of a client and you discover that there are people mentioned on the list of employees that do not exist. What do you do?

6   You discover that one of your clients has been receiving money from invoices issued to customers who appear to be fictional. What do you do?

29.6 Professional behaviour

Professional behaviour can take many forms but can be summarised by asking one simple question: 'Is this the sort of behaviour that would be regarded by an outsider as appropriate to a member of the accounting profession?'

Some of the suggestions below could be regarded as fairly vague although they are all important. Clients are people and maintaining their confidence in you is vital. Whether it is fair or not, their initial level of confidence will often be based on early impressions based on your appearance and general attitude.

- *Image and credibility*: Does the member give the impression that they have the suitable skills and do they fulfil the client's expectations? This can involve dressing and talking appropriately, which may seem shallow because the quality or smartness of an accountant's clothing will have absolutely no bearing on their ability. However, clients are people and people often feel that they can place greater faith in someone that looks or sounds the part.

- *Courtesy and communication skills*: Do they apply suitable courtesy, particularly in communicating with clients? Simple things like using someone's title rather than their first name (until invited to use it) can avoid annoying the client while the professional relationship is still being established.

- *Appearing ethical*: Throughout this chapter, we have emphasised that it is as important to be seen to be ethical as it is to actually behave ethically. It is vital that a client feels they trust the accountant to 'do the right thing'.

- *Quality and range of services*: Services need to be offered to the highest possible standard and clients should only be offered the services that they need. It is not ethical to generate fee income by carrying out work that the client does not need.

As we have already suggested, any breach of the previous four principles will almost certainly also represent a lack of professional behaviour.

29.7 Promoting ethical behaviour

Employees are likely to face conflicting pressures or situations where the ethical approach is not obvious, and so it is inevitable that mistakes will be made. It is also possible that, if a situation is not covered by law or specific rules and regulations, some employees may behave in an unethical manner. It is therefore vital that employers use a variety of measures in order to ensure that their staff are aware of what is expected and are looking to apply ethical principles as often as possible. These measures could include:

- *Clear written guidelines*: Many organisations will issue a staff handbook. The handbook will contain a copy of the rules, policies and procedures as well as providing guidance regarding how the company expects its employees to behave. It is likely that staff will be asked to sign a document to confirm that they have read and understood what is expected of them, which prevents people being able to claim ignorance of the offences or the possible consequences if disciplinary proceedings are later called as a result of poor behaviour. It is not uncommon for junior clerks to talk about the work that they have been doing when meeting socially, which can lead to breaches in confidentiality. If there are clear guidelines that this behaviour is not acceptable, it should reduce the possibility of this happening.

- *Regular reviews*: Laws, rules and regulations change as well as what is regarded as sensible or acceptable by the industry or society as a whole. In most organisations, policies and procedures will be regularly reviewed and if necessary updated. An accounting example of this would be the need for UK and EU accountants in practice to review the way they collected, used, stored and disposed of sensitive information when the General Data Protection Regulations were introduced in May 2018. These replaced the Data Protection Act 1998, so if accountants had continued to follow the earlier requirements, they would have risked serious breaches of the new ones.

- *Induction training*: New employees usually have to complete induction training. This training will provide the newcomer with information about the business, systems and policies, their job role and the rules governing conduct at work. Induction can be a good opportunity to ensure that new staff are aware of the fundamental ethical principles and what is or isn't acceptable behaviour.

- *Refresher training*: People can slip into bad habits and so it is good to ensure that they are reminded of what represents ethical behaviour and, at least as importantly, what doesn't.

- *Disciplinary process*: It is important that any rules regarding behaviour are supported by a structured and logical disciplinary process that ensures every possible breach of the rules or ethical principles is investigated in a thorough but fair way. Employees should be aware – possibly from the staff handbook – what the penalties for poor behaviour are and should be entitled to expect that these will be applied fairly regardless of who is involved. This may deter poor behaviour that, in the case of accounting firms, might include breaches of confidentiality and inappropriate use of the firm's or the client's money.

- *Reporting process*: Many organisations have reporting mechanisms that will enable employees to report poor behaviour including bullying. It may involve taking out a grievance through human resources. If people are aware that their behaviour might be reported, they might think twice before behaving unethically. Like any other places of work, in accounting firms, there will be occasions when senior or experienced members of staff treat their junior colleagues unfairly.

- *Setting an example*: Sometimes called 'tone at the top', the theory is that if employees see their managers setting a good example, they are more likely to behave more ethically themselves. An accounting example of this might be where managers and senior staff ensure that they are seen to be completely honest when claiming expenses.

29.8 Social aspects of decision making

In recent years, there has been a greater emphasis on environmental and social (welfare) issues, largely fuelled by reports issued by organisations like the Brundtland Commission.

The aim of the Brundtland Commission was to unite countries to pursue *sustainable development* together and in its report in 1987, it defined *sustainability* as 'meeting the needs of the present without compromising the ability of future generations to meet their own needs'.

The Commission outlined three key components of sustainable development:

- economic growth
- environmental protection
- social equality.

These three factors have often been referred to as the *triple-bottom-line* and are used in ethical guidelines issued by professional accounting bodies. While much of what the Brundtland Commission said really referred to governments and nations, the underlying principles can be applied at the 'individual business level'.

The intention is that when businesses make decisions they shouldn't just focus on the financial implications of those decisions – although making a profit is important – but they should also consider whether that decision will have a positive or negative effect on the environment and the people involved.

In many cases, all three elements of the triple-bottom-line may be involved in a decision and sometimes those elements will be in conflict, e.g. a good environmental decision may increase costs or a sound financial decision may have a negative impact on employees or people living in the local community. Sometimes those elements work together, e.g. a decision that is good for the environment may also benefit the local people.

The International Ethics Standards Board for Accountants (IESBA) states in their ethical guidelines that accountants have a duty to *society as a whole* and in terms of the triple-bottom-line, this means that the client should be advised of the advantages of considering all three elements when making a decision.

Areas that might be considered include:

1 *Financial factors*: Will this decision lead to increased profitability that will increase the wealth of owners, employees and the local economy?

2 *Environmental factors*: Will the decision result in the conservation of energy (resources), the reduction of emissions or other pollution and will it increase the opportunity to reduce waste or increase the amount of recycling of materials?

3 *Social factors*: These can be promoted in many ways including:

- ensuring decent pay and conditions – both within the organisation and trading partners. Not obtaining supplies from businesses whose working conditions are poor is the ethical choice.

- Preserving the local economy through protecting employment and providing job security.
  - giving something back to the community, which could include sponsoring local events or organisations or providing facilities
  - reducing the level of pollution caused by the business's activities
  - donating to local charities.

In recent years, many businesses have recognised that they have a responsibility to demonstrate **corporate social responsibility (CSR)**. Some large companies have actively used their commitment to CSR as part of their promotional activity. In South Korea, Samsung joined with the Korea International Volunteer Organisation to bring solar-powered lanterns to areas where electricity is scarce as part of a 'Bringing light to Ethiopia' project.

Whether this is the result of accountants reminding directors of their responsibilities is highly debateable, but it does not alter the fact that accountants have a moral and ethical duty to make sure that their clients are aware of the ethical choices when making a major decision.

> ### KEY TERM
>
> **corporate social responsibility (CSR):** a philosophy where a business organisation takes the view that they have a moral responsibility to behave ethically by assessing whether the impact they have on people, society and the environment could be more positive, and then taking the appropriate action.

KEY CONCEPT LINK

True and fair view: How important do you think that having managers and employees behaving ethically can have a real impact on how much the financial statements of a business provide a true and fair view of the performance and financial position of that business? Justify you views to another learner.

THINK LIKE AN ACCOUNTANT

Not declaring all the income

Lee was 100% certain that one of his clients had sources of income that had not been declared on their tax return. Unfortunately, when he had reported it to one of the partners at the accounting firm, he had been told to mind his own business. When Lee had stated that knowingly not declaring income amounted to tax evasion, the partner had got quite angry and had said, 'if you don't like the way we operate, you can always find somewhere else to work!'

Lee's parents had brought him up to believe that 'honesty was the best policy!' Right now Lee wasn't quite so sure. What are some of the ethical courses of action that Lee should consider? What should Lee actually do? Why?

Figure 29.2: Lee was certain that his client was not declaring all sources of income on his tax return.

REFLECTION

Do you think it is realistic to expect employees to always behave ethically when faced with a difficult situation, just because they know what the ethical guidelines and fundamental principles are? Why/why not? Discuss your opinions with another learner.

EXAM-STYLE QUESTIONS

1 Which fundamental principle of ethics requires an accountant to undertake training or other activities in order to keep their knowledge and skills up-to-date?

   A   confidentiality

   B   integrity

   C   objectivity

   D   professional competence and due care   [1]

2 Romesh claimed $20 in travelling expenses when he had, in fact, got a lift in a colleague's car. Apart from professional behaviour, which fundamental principle of ethics has Romesh breached?

   A   confidentiality

   B   integrity

   C   objectivity

   D   professional competence and due care   [1]

3 Brigitta is a qualified accountant who buys supplies for Rainham Limited. She is currently negotiating a contract with a potential supplier, Harrow PLC. Brigitta's contact at Harrow PLC has suggested that if she gives Harrow PLC the contract, she and her family will receive a two-week holiday to Disneyland Florida.

   Which type of risk is this to Brigitta's objectivity?

   A   familiarity

   B   intimidation

   C   self-interest

   D   self-review   [1]

4 Ekim & Co is a firm of accountants. The partners of the firm want to ensure that all of their employees behave ethically and apply the highest professional standards. A set of Ethical Guidelines has been issued to every member of staff, who were also given some training to ensure that every employee was familiar with the partners' expectations.

   a   Explain *two* reasons why it is important that the employees at Ekim & Co behave ethically.   [4]

   b   Kane is a junior accounts assistant at Ekim & Co. He has been asked by one of his managers to produce a bank reconciliation statement for one of the clients.

      Kane did study a finance course at college but never really understood bank reconciliation statements. What is worse is that there are 23 pages of cash book and 37 sheets of bank statements.

      Explain how Kane might behave unethically in the situation, referring to *two* fundamental ethical principles that would be breached if he does the wrong thing.   [5]

CONTINUED

c   Explain what Kane should do in this situation.   [2]

d   Explain *one* ethical solution to this problem assuming that Kane has taken the action that you recommended in **c**.   [2]

e   Apart from issuing guidelines and providing training, explain *one* other way that the management at Ekim & Co could try to ensure that their staff behave ethically.   [2]

SELF-EVALUATION CHECKLIST

After studying this chapter, complete a table like this:

You should be able to:	Needs more work	Almost there	Ready to move on
Explain the need for an ethical framework in accounting, explaining how it protects the accountant, her or his organisation and the client, and inspires confidence in the profession.			
Explain the fundamental principles of integrity, objectivity, professional competence and due care, confidentiality and professional behaviour that all accounting bodies use.			
Explain how the ethical behaviour of accountants and auditors impacts the business and other stakeholders, including where there are difficulties in identifying an ethical course of action.			
Outline approaches that can be used by organisations to promote ethical behaviour, including written guidelines, regular reviews, induction training, refresher training, disciplinary processes and reporting processes.			
Know the social implications of decision making, especially corporate social responsibility (CSR).			

> Chapter 30

Accounting information for stakeholders

This chapter covers syllabus section AS Level 1.6

LEARNING INTENTIONS

In this chapter you will learn how to:

* identify and explain the differing requirements for information of interested parties
* discuss and analyse the information required by these different interested parties
* calculate profitability, liquidity and efficiency ratios and interpret them to evaluate and comment on the business.

ACCOUNTING IN CONTEXT

The Shoe Company

Sunita had worked at The Shoe Company (a manufacturer) for ten years and was worried. The financial statements for the year ended 30 June 2020 had just been published and they showed a large loss. Fred, who worked in the accounts office, had told her that the finance director had instructed the staff in trade payables to delay paying suppliers for as long as possible as there were 'cash flow problems'.

During the first three years, the company had given ordinary shares to employees as a bonus. Sunita had nearly 1 000 shares and knew that they had been worth about $5 each when she last received a dividend cheque in 2017. Sunita had no idea what they were worth now. She was more concerned about how the company's results might affect her and the 800 local people employed there.

Discuss in a pair or a group:

How might events at The Shoe Company affect Sunita and other people?

Figure 30.1: The company's financial statements for the year show a large loss.

30.1 Stakeholders

Stakeholders can be categorised in a number of ways. The simplest way is to divide them up by whether they are *internal stakeholders* (people or groups within the business) or *external stakeholders* (people or groups affected by the business).

KEY TERM

stakeholder: a person or organisation that has a legitimate interest in a business or who can be affected by that business.

Internal stakeholders

These and their reasons for being interested in the financial statements might include:

User	Reasons for interest
Owner of the business (sole trader or partners) These are the people directly involved in the day-to-day running and management of the business.	• To assess the overall performance of the business – any profit is their income and any loss is their personal responsibility. • To identify which areas have performed well and which have performed badly and be able to take appropriate action. • To make decisions including whether to expand or discontinue (part of) the business.
Existing shareholders The owners of limited companies will not generally be involved in the day-to-day running of the business.	• To assess the overall performance of the business – the level of profit will have a major impact on the size of any dividends and the share price. • To determine how well the directors have been looking after their company. • To consider the security of their investment and make decisions about whether to continue holding shares in the company or consider alternative investment opportunities.
Managers and directors	• Often the salary or bonus paid to these employees is based on the performance of the business in certain key areas. • Directors may be relying on keeping the shareholders satisfied with their performance – they could be voted out at an AGM or EGM.
Employees	• They will be concerned about whether their jobs are secure or whether there is likely to be an increase in their pay.

External stakeholders

These and their reasons for being interested in the financial information about a company might include:

User	Reasons for interest
Lenders	• The financial statements will be used to help determine whether a loan or overdraft should be granted to the business. • If a bank loan or overdraft has already been granted the bank will want to assess the business's ability to repay what is owed.
Potential shareholders/ investors	• These may wish to assess whether the business is likely to provide a good return on their investment.
Suppliers to the business (trade payables)	• The statements will help to decide whether credit facilities should be granted to the business and, if they already have, will provide an indication as to whether they are likely to be paid.
Customers of the business	• Customers will want to be reassured that the business will be around for the foreseeable future so that they have a dependable supplier.
Government/local authorities *(including public and environmental bodies)*	• The level of taxes will be determined by the profits of the business. • The financial statements will be used to determine whether grants can be given. • Whether the business is doing and spending enough on issues like reducing pollution/ emissions, recycling and protecting the environment.
Local community	• The business may provide major employment in a particular area. • Many (small) businesses might be dependent on trade from employees, e.g. a sandwich shop may provide much of the workforce with their lunch. • They will be interested in whether or not the business is operating ethically towards its workers, customers and the environment.
Trade unions	• Their job is to protect the rights, terms and conditions of their members – the employees. Unions will be interested in the business's profitability as it will affect their ability to negotiate changes to pay and conditions.

KEY CONCEPT LINK

True and fair view: Financial statements are designed to give a true and fair view of the financial position, performance and changes in financial position of the business to internal and external stakeholders.

Identify some of the groups of users of financial statements who rely on those statements giving a true and fair view of the performance and financial position of the business. How and why might they suffer if the financial statements do not reflect the company's true position?

30.2 Limitations of financial statements

As we have already seen, governments have passed laws and the accounting authorities have issued a large range of standards in order to (where possible) ensure that:

• information is presented in a certain way

• items are treated in a standard way.

The Companies Acts and accounting standards require companies to add numerous notes to their financial statements to throw more light on the items in the accounts.

However, despite this, the published accounts of limited companies have a number of limitations when communicating information:

- Users may have an inadequate knowledge of accounting and finance and so do not understand the financial statements. Even qualified accountants may need to interpret the figures before they are able to understand their significance.

- The information they give is not complete – legislation and accounting standards recognise that companies cannot reveal everything because it would give competitors an unfair commercial advantage.

- The comparability of financial statements is only relative because there are a number of acceptable alternative methods when dealing with issues like depreciation, allowances for irrecoverable debts and inventory valuation. In any case, companies are allowed to depart from accounting standards if such departure is justified by the nature of their business and will improve the quality of the information provided by the accounting statements.

- Published accounts may not be published for many months after the end of the financial year they cover and many circumstances may have changed. The state of the economy or government might have changed, the level of competition in the market may have improved or worsened, new technologies may have been developed or customers' tastes may have changed. All of these factors may make it easier or more difficult to make a profit.

- The scale of the numbers when comparing two business may be quite different and this may make it difficult to identify the relative quality of performance.

  The directors' report may help to overcome some of the limitations of the financial statements, but not completely.

  In order to be able to analyse and interpret the financial statements, many users will calculate widely accepted accounting ratios.

  Before we look at particular ratios, there are certain underlying principles that need to be considered:

- *Industrial standards and comparability*: Different industries operate in different ways and so what is regarded as an acceptable figure will vary considerably. It will be meaningless to compare the ratios for a large supermarket with those of high-class department stores like Harrods or Fortnum & Mason in London's West End. Ratios should only be used to examine companies in the same industry or the same company over successive accounting years (comparing 'like with like').

- *Context*: Ratios are only meaningful if they are given some context. A company may see an improvement in its ratios from 2019 to 2020 but could still be performing at a very poor level compared to the rest of the industry! Consideration also needs to be given to the objectives of the company as it is possible that maximising profit is not the only (or even main) objective.

- *Percentages, proportions and raw numbers*: Most ratios express items as percentages or ratios and sometimes, it is tempting to lose sight of the raw numbers involved. As we shall see, sometimes it is better to have a small percentage of a large number than a large percentage of a small one!

We will now look at some of the most common measures under the headings of profitability, liquidity and efficiency. You should note that although most of the following examples involve limited companies, accounting ratios can be used to analyse the financial statements of sole traders and partnerships too.

30.3 Calculation and evaluation of ratios

Profitability ratios

There are a number of ratios that will enable the users of the accounts to determine whether the company has performed well or not.

1 **Gross profit margin (%)** – this ratio measures the amount of profit made on the goods being sold. The formula is:

$$\frac{\text{Gross profit}}{\text{Revenue}} \times 100$$

2 **Mark-up (%)** – this is an alternative approach to the gross profit margin where the profit on the goods is expressed as a percentage of cost of sales. The formula is:

$$\frac{\text{Gross profit}}{\text{Cost of sales}} \times 100$$

In simple terms, the bigger these figures are, the better, although much depends on the reasons for any changes between the figures for say 2019 and 2020. The two elements of these ratios are revenue (selling price) and cost of sales (purchase price) and factors that might increase or decrease these include:

- *Level of competition*: Increased competition will probably force selling prices down while reduced competition may well allow the business to raise its prices.

- *Level of demand for the product*: Increased demand will allow the business to raise its prices while reduced demand will probably force the business to set lower prices.

- *Pricing strategies*: The business may decide to adopt an aggressive pricing strategy to undercut the competition and grab market share. The prices may reflect whether the business wishes to attract customers at the high or low end of the market.

- *Availability of suppliers/goods*: The purchase price of supplies may reflect the availability of goods. If there is a local or world shortage of a product, its price is likely to rise while a plentiful supply is likely to see prices fall. Agricultural products and oil are commodities that reflect this.

- *Scale of activities*: Bulk discounts may be available if the business expands and buys its supplies in greater quantities.

3 **Operating expenses to revenue ratio (%)** – this shows what percentage of revenue is being spent on operating expenses as a whole although this formula can be adapted to identify what percentage of revenue is being spent on a particular expense (e.g. selling and distribution costs). The formula is:

$$\frac{\text{Operating expenses}}{\text{Revenue}} \times 100$$

In general terms, the smaller these figures are, the better. There is a basic implication that a small expense percentage means that either costs are being effectively controlled or money is being spent wisely in particular areas. Many mail order businesses spend quite a lot of money on advertising/promotion (by monitoring the advertising percentage as a whole and examining the figures for each type of advertising activity, it is possible to identify which areas are performing well – the ones with the smallest expense to revenue percentage).

However, one factor does need to be considered. If a cost is fixed in nature, it will not change in size. The expense percentage will be determined entirely by the level of revenue rather than how effectively the money is being spent!

4   **Profit margin (%)** – this tells us how much profit (per \$100 of revenue) has been made after all operating costs and expenses have been deducted. The formula is:

$$\frac{\text{Profit for the year + other income}}{\text{Revenue}} \times 100 \text{ or } \frac{\text{Profit for the year (after interest)}}{\text{Revenue}} \times 100$$

As with many of these profitability ratios, the bigger the figure, the better. The main factors affecting this ratio will be:

- *Gross profit margin (%)*: if this is large, then the profit margin is more likely to be large.

- *Expenses*: smaller expenses contribute to a larger profit figure.

5   **Return on capital employed (ROCE) (%)** – this is one of many ratios that gives some indication of how much of a return investors could receive on the money they have tied up in the company. The formula is:

$$\frac{\text{Profit from operations}}{\text{Capital employed}} \times 100$$

where Capital employed = issued shares + reserves + non-current liabilities

For sole traders or partnerships, the formula would be:

$$\frac{\text{Profit for the year}}{\text{Capital employed}} \times 100$$

As has already been suggested in Chapters 21, 22 and 25, the amount of profit available to be distributed and how much is actually given can be two very different things.

Interpretation and evaluation of ratios

In common with liquidity and efficiency, there are some basic principles you need to master if you are to interpret and evaluate the ratios properly. These include:

- Having a clear understanding of what each ratio shows.

- Identifying the factors that might have caused each ratio to be high or low, compared to either previous values or the industrial average.

- Knowing whether those factors were the result of conscious actions by the business or due to external factors beyond the business's control. There is a difference between deliberately charging lower prices to increase sales and having to charge lower prices because of increased competition.

- Knowing for each ratio what is an acceptable value. Different industries work in different ways – for example, a supermarket is likely to work on far lower gross profit margins than a department store. It is always useful to have industrial averages for comparison as it is possible to have shown improvement between 2019 and 2020 but still be performing poorly or show a deterioration but still be outperforming other businesses operating in that industry.

- Understanding what the implications of the change in the ratio are and being able to determine what effect this is likely to have on a particular group of stakeholders.

Worked example 1 shows how these ratios can be calculated in a particular situation and how they might be interpreted and evaluated.

WORKED EXAMPLE 1

Extracts from the final statements for Junaid Limited for the years ended 30 November 2019 and 2020 were as follows:

	2020	2019
	$000	$000
Revenue	9 600	7 000
Cost of sales	(5 088)	(4 130)
Gross profit	4 512	2 870
Operating expenses	(2 112)	(1 750)
Profit from operations	2 400	1 120
Interest payable	(600)	(675)
Profit before tax	1 800	445
Tax	(450)	(85)
Profit for the year	1 350	360
Shareholders' equity	12 000	12 000
Long-term loans	8 000	9 000

Additional information

1   During the year, one of the company's main competitors went out of business and Junaid Limited was able to grab their market share. The resulting expansion meant that Junaid was able to obtain bulk discounts on many of its supplies.

2   Fuel prices increased by 10% during the course of the year.

3   Administration expenses were largely fixed in nature.

The ratios are as follows:

	2020	2019
Gross profit margin	$\frac{4\,512}{9\,600} \times 100 \quad = 47.00\%$	$\frac{2\,870}{7\,000} \times 100 \quad = 41.00\%$
Mark-up	$\frac{4\,512}{5\,088} \times 100 \quad = 88.68\%$	$\frac{2\,870}{4\,130} \times 100 \quad = 69.49\%$
Operating expenses to revenue %	$\frac{2\,112}{9\,600} \times 100 \quad = 22.00\%$	$\frac{1\,750}{7\,000} \times 100 \quad = 25.00\%$
Operating profit margin %	$\frac{2\,400}{9\,600} \times 100 \quad = 25.00\%$	$\frac{1\,120}{7\,000} \times 100 \quad = 16.00\%$
or		
Profit margin %	$\frac{1\,800}{9\,600} \times 100 \quad = 18.75\%$	$\frac{445}{7\,000} \times 100 \quad = 6.36\%$
ROCE	$\frac{2\,400}{20\,000} \times 100 = 12.00\%$	$\frac{1\,120}{21\,000} \times 100 \ = 5.33\%$

Interpretation and evaluation

- The *gross profit margin* improved considerably from 41% to 47% (and the mark-up percentage did too). This was probably due to two factors. The major competitor going out of business enabled Junaid Limited to increase its market share, and it is likely that the company was able to charge higher prices than in 2019. The extra volume of trade also enabled the company to obtain bulk discounts from its suppliers and this again, increases the gross profit percentage.

> **CONTINUED**
>
> - The *profit margin* percentage also showed great improvement (increasing from 16% to 25%) and again was the result of the higher gross profit percentage and a proportional reduction in the operating expenses (from 25% to 22% of revenue).
>
> - The improvement in the *operating expenses as a percentage of revenue* (from 25% to 22%) was the net result of two factors. Revenue increased significantly between 2019 and 2020 and because the administration expenses were fixed, the percentage of revenue that they represented fell. However, fuel prices increased by 10% during 2020 and although the company cannot be blamed for circumstances beyond its control, this would have increased operating expenses and reduced the profit margin.
>
> - As a result of the increased profitability, the *return on capital employed* improved considerably from 5.33% to 12%. This was the result of the greater profits made by Junaid Limited and implies that the various investors have received a far better return on their investment in 2020 than they did the previous year. Whether this increase represents a better return for shareholders will also depend on what returns are available on alternative investment opportunities. The improvement in this ratio and the greater level of profit indicates that the interest payable on the reduced level of non-current liabilities is (and should to be) less of a burden on the business.

When interpreting and evaluating accounting ratios, it is essential to use the right language. Merely stating that one ratio is bigger or smaller than another (or has increased or decreased) is not regarded as evaluation. This is because not all ratios follow the principle of, 'the bigger is better' – for example, you want your expenses as a percentage of revenue to be as small as possible. Unless you provide an explanation to support bigger or smaller, the person reading your report may have doubts about whether you know how these ratios work. It is better to use terms such as improved/worsened if you are looking at ratios for two years, or better/worse when comparing two businesses. Your evaluation will also be improved if you are able to provide information about the factors that have caused the change in the ratios and the implications for the business of the result.

Interpretation and evaluation (two businesses)

Whether calculating the ratios for one business over two years or two businesses for the same year, the approach is the same. However, the way in which those ratios are evaluated is slightly different.

Suppose we had calculated the ratios for Inzimam and Haq for 2020 and arrived at the following figures:

	Inziman	Haq
Gross profit margin (%)	40	37
Operating expenses (%)	28	24
Operating profit margin (%)	12	13
ROCE (%)	5	8

The main difference in how these ratios are interpreted is that instead of using phrases such as 'improved' or 'worsened', we are going to use words like 'better than' or 'worse than' before going on to explain the factors that may have caused the difference. Avoid words such as 'higher' or 'lower' because with some ratios, a bigger value is better and for others, a smaller value represents a better performance.

In the case of Inzimam and Haq, the interpretation might appear as follows (the reasons have been provided for illustrative purposes and do not relate to any particular question):

- The *gross profit margin* of 40% for Inzimam was better than the 37% achieved by Haq. The main reason for this was that Inzimam buys his goods in larger volumes and achieved bulk discounts that were not available to Haq.

- However, the *operating profit margin percentage* of 12% for Inzimam was not as good as Haq's 13% and the main reason for that was that Haq had maintained tighter control on its operating expenses, which accounted for only 24% of revenue rather than the 28% spent by Inzimam.

- The return on capital employed of 8% for Haq suggests that shareholders will be receiving a better return than those investing in Inzimam where the ROCE was only 5%. The reason that Haq has outperformed its rival is that its profit increased significantly between 2019 and 2020 and its share capital is smaller than Inzimam's.

Note that if industrial averages been available, comparisons could have been made with those too.

ACTIVITY 30.1

Extracts from the final statements for Freddy Limited for the years ended 30 November 2019 and 2020 were as follows:

	2020	2019
	$000	$000
Revenue	1 600	1 200
Cost of sales	(1 008)	(744)
Gross profit	592	456
Operating expenses	(440)	(363)
Operating profit	152	93
Interest payable	(12)	(15)
Profit before tax	140	78
Tax	(45)	(26)
Profit for the year	95	52
Shareholders equity	300	285
Long-term loans	240	300

Required

a Calculate the following ratios for 2019 and 2020. Industry averages for 2020 have been given in brackets:

Gross profit margin (35%)

Mark-up % (54%)

Operating expenses to revenue % (25%)

Profit margin % (10%)

Profit margin % after interest (7%)

Return on capital employed (20%)

b Explain whether the profitability of Freddy Limited has improved between 2019 and 2020 and whether the directors can be satisfied with the company's performance.

Liquidity ratios

Profitability is important to any business, but many accountants will argue that it is the ability to pay debts when they fall due that is more likely to keep a business going than whether it reports a profit or loss for the year.

Liquidity is a measure of how well the company is able to pay short-term debts, particularly trade payables. There are two main ratios that will provide an indication of how well placed a business is to meet its obligations:

1. **Current ratio** – this looks at the relationship between current assets and current liabilities. The formula is:

$$\frac{\text{Current assets}}{\text{Current liabilities}} = \text{xxx:1 (the answer is presented as a ratio, e.g. } 1.50:1)$$

    Note how this ratio is expressed; it is important that you express it in this way. What this ratio tells us is the value of current assets (resources that can quickly be turned into cash) for every $1 of current liability that might need to be paid quickly.

    What represents a secure position will vary from industry to industry, and 1.50–2.00:1 is often regarded as a 'comfort zone' where a business can be regarded as unlikely to suffer cash flow difficulties. Obviously, if the business is known to be quite profitable, it is less likely that its trade payables will be nervous about whether they are going to get paid.

    Businesses in some industries are able to operate with very low current ratios. An example of this is Tesco (the UK's largest supermarket), which had a current ratio of 0.92 at August 2020. There were three reasons why Tesco – and other supermarkets – are able to operate with very low current ratios:

    -   The business is very profitable and so it is unlikely that any lenders or trade payables would become nervous and consider demanding instant repayment of monies owed.

    -   For many of its trade payables, Tesco represents a very large customer who might decide to stop buying their products if that supplier upset it. It is unlikely that most of those payables would risk this, even if Tesco were to start taking too long to pay them.

    -   All of their sales are for cash, not credit, so Tesco does not have to wait to receive the cash.

    Other industries operate with very high current ratios. In the USA, the industrial average for 'death care services' (which provides funeral and related services) was assessed by Forbes (an American business magazine) as being 4.9 – mainly as a result of large trade receivables on the Statement of financial position. Specialist clothing stores averaged 4.5 because of large amounts of inventory.

    Many accountants will suggest that if this ratio is too high (say 5.00 or 6.00:1), then it is likely that the business has too much money tied up in current assets and should be diverting those resources into more productive areas, e.g. cash into bank accounts that yield interest.

    However, there is a second ratio that takes a more cautious view!

2. **Acid test ratio** – sometimes also known as the liquid capital or quick ratio, the acid test ratio makes the assumption that, in an emergency, inventory cannot be relied on to provide cash quickly. This is because a lot of businesses make many of their sales on a credit basis and, if it is taking time to sell the inventory and more time to collect the money from the trade receivables, this could be too late to satisfy the trade and other payables. The formula is:

$$\frac{\text{Current assets} - \text{inventory}}{\text{Curret liabilities}} = \text{xxx}:1 \text{ (the answer is presented as a ratio)}$$

The acid test value is also expressed as a ratio and any figure above 1.00:1 is often regarded as in the 'comfort zone'. Values lower than 1.00:1 might suggest that cash flow problems are more likely, although other factors will come into effect including profitability.

There are some examples of companies operating quite successfully with very low acid test ratios. Tesco plc (holding over 30% of the grocery market) had a ratio of 0.66:1 for the year ended 31 August 2019 and there is no likelihood of liquidity issues because:

- inventory sells very quickly

- most customers pay immediately not on extended periods of credit

- Tesco plc represents a large customer to most of its suppliers and most would not risk being 'de-listed' (dropped) by applying pressure to them

- they are highly profitable.

In any case, many businesses would (if faced with an emergency) be able to raise quick cash by selling inventory, even if it had to give a substantial discount.

It is worth noting that if there is a huge difference between these two ratios, then the business might be carrying too much inventory. Having too much money sitting idle as inventory is never good for cash flow.

WORKED EXAMPLE 2

Extracts from the statements of financial position for Jamshed Limited for 30 November 2019 and 2020 were as follows (all values in $000s):

	2020		2019	
	$000	$000	$000	$000
Current assets:				
Stock	160		175	
Trade receivables	125		120	
Bank	0	285	50	345
Current liabilities:				
Trade payables	115		90	
Bank overdraft	80		0	
Tax	40	235	75	165
Net current assets		50		180

	2020	2019
Current ratio	$\frac{285}{235} = 1.21:1$	$\frac{345}{165} = 2.09:1$
Acid test ratio	$\frac{285 - 160}{235} = 0.53:1$	$\frac{345 - 175}{165} = 1.03:1$

CONTINUED

Interpretation and evaluation

The liquidity of Jamshed Limited has worsened significantly between 2019 and 2020 as both ratios have dropped considerably and are now well below the accepted 'comfort zone benchmarks' of 1.50–2.00:1 for the current ratio and 1.00:1 for the acid test. This, and the fact that the bank account has seen a reduction of $130 000 and is now heavily overdrawn, suggests that the company is more likely to have cash flow problems if the trade payables become nervous and start applying pressure. In any case, this trend cannot be allowed to continue. Further deterioration may even result in the business failing altogether as a result of not being able to pay its suppliers and day-to-day expenses.

Efficiency ratios

These ratios give the user an indication as to how well the resources of the business are being used to generate revenue or how well vital parts of the business are being managed.

1 **Non-current asset turnover (times)** – this ratio shows how fully the non-current assets are being used in generating revenue. The formula is:

$$\frac{\text{Net revenue}}{\text{Total net book amount of non-current assets}} = \text{xxx time}$$

Note that the ratio is expressed in times and the greater the figure, the more fully (and efficiently) the business is considered to be using its resources. You should note that this ratio can be quite misleading if care isn't taken to examine whether the business owns, rents or leases its non-current assets.

Suppose we have two companies who operate in an identical way but one owns land and buildings worth $8 million and the other rents them:

	Company A	Company B
	$000	$000
Revenue	40 000	40 000
Non-current assets	10 000	2 000
Non-current asset turnover	4.00 times	20.00 times

These figures give the impression that Company B is making far better use of the resources at its disposal when, in fact, they are both operating at the same level.

2 **Inventory turnover (days)** – this ratio gives an indication as to how long, on average, the business is taking to sell its inventory. This is important for a number of reasons including:

- Inventory is money tied up in the stockroom – holding too much slow-moving inventory is likely to harm cash flow. The cost of storage may also be high.

- Slow-moving inventory is not earning profit and its presence may be depriving the business of the chance to hold other inventory that would have been faster moving.

- Many types of inventory have a limited life-span – it may become obsolete or may spoil if kept for too long.

The formula for inventory turnover is:

$$\frac{\text{Average inventory}}{\text{Cost of sales}} \times 365 = \text{xxx days}$$

where, dependent on what information has been provided:

$$\text{Average inventory} = \frac{(\text{opening} + \text{closing inventory})}{2}$$

or closing inventory if that is the only figure available

Longer turnover periods imply poor inventory management because:

- If too much stock is being held, the average inventory period will rise and so will the turnover period.
- If the wrong inventory is being held, it won't sell and the low cost of sales figure will cause the turnover period to rise.

We can conclude that a short turnover period implies good inventory management!

As with many accounting ratios, what represents an acceptable level depends on the industry – supermarkets will expect food products to sell within a few hours or days whereas businesses selling larger items like furniture or electrical goods may expect inventory to sell far more slowly.

3 **Rate of inventory turnover (times)** – this ratio gives an indication as to how many times the average item of inventory will sell during the year. Its formula is:

$$\frac{\text{Cost of sales}}{\text{Average inventory}} = \text{xxx times}$$

In this case, the larger the figure, the better the inventory management is considered to be.

Interestingly, if the results of these two inventory ratios are multiplied together, the result should be 365 (a useful check of accuracy).

4 **Trade receivables turnover (days)** – this ratio gives an indication as to how long it is taking, on average, for the credit customers to pay what they owe. The formula is:

$$\frac{\text{Trade receivables}}{\text{Credit sales}} \times 365 = \text{xxx days}$$

Sometimes, only the total revenue figure is provided, with no indication of the breakdown between cash and credit sales. In this case, the total sales can be used. A business would hope that the proportion of sales made on credit has not changed significantly between one year and the next (or between the business and what is typical for the industry) if it is to make meaningful comparisons.

As with the inventory turnover period, shorter is better as it means that the business is waiting less time to receive its money. The period can also be interpreted as an indication of how effective the credit control procedures are, although again different industries may offer different periods of credit.

When you are comparing the figures for two periods or against the industrial average, you should consider whether there has been a conscious change in company policy. One cannot criticise the performance of the credit controller if, say, the company actively offered longer periods of credit in order to attract new customers!

5 **Trade payables turnover (days)** – this ratio gives an indication as to how long it is taking, on average, for the company to pay its suppliers. The formula is:

$$\frac{\text{Trade payables}}{\text{Credit purchases}} \times 365 = \text{xxx days}$$

Sometimes, only the total purchases figure is provided, with no indication of the breakdown between cash and credit sales. Occasionally, only the cost of sales figure is available. In this case, the total purchases or cost of sales must be used, which is not ideal!

Unlike most of the other ratios, it is not always immediately obvious whether a short or long turnover period is desirable. A short turnover period will keep suppliers happy and may earn cash discounts but paying early is not good for cash flow. Taking time to pay may be good for cash flow but may not lead to a good relationship with suppliers.

Most accountants will suggest that the ideal balance is one where the business takes the longest period to pay without upsetting the trade payable, which may now have you casting your mind back to the chapter on ethics!

WORKED EXAMPLE 3

Extracts from the final statements for Irfan Limited for the years ended 30 November 2019 and 2020 were as follows:

	2020		2019	
	$000	$000	$000	$000
Revenue		600		450
Opening inventories	40		30	
Purchases	420		300	
Closing inventories	(50)	(410)	(40)	(290)
Gross profit		190		160
Trade receivables		54		48
Trade payables		42		18
Non-current assets		120		150

Note: we are assuming that all purchases and sales are on credit. There had been no change in company policy regarding inventory, trade receivables or trade payables.

The industrial averages and agreed trading terms were as follows:

Inventory turnover: 36 days or 10.14 times

Trade receivables turnover: 30 days

Trade payables turnover: 30 days

The ratios are as follows:

	2020	2019
Inventory turnover (days)	$\frac{45}{410} \times 365 = 40.06$ days	$\frac{35}{290} \times 365 = 44.05$ days
Rate of inventory turnover (times)	$\frac{410}{45} = 9.11$ times	$\frac{290}{35} = 8.29$ times
Trade receivable turnover (days)	$\frac{54}{600} \times 365 = 32.85$ days	$\frac{48}{450} \times 365 = 38.93$ days
Trade payables turnover (days)	$\frac{42}{420} \times 365 = 36.50$ days	$\frac{18}{300} \times 365 = 21.90$ days

CONTINUED

Interpretation and evaluation

- *Inventory turnover (days)* – the reduction in this ratio from 44 days to 40 days (and increase in the turnover from 8.29 to 9.11 times) suggests a slight improvement in the efficiency with which the inventory is being managed, even though the stock levels have increased. This efficiency might reflect either that a more appropriate amount of stock is being held given the volume of trade, or that 'the right type of items' are being held. However, the company is still taking longer to move its inventory than the industrial average (36 days), which implies that there is still scope for improvement.

  Overall, an improvement in this ratio also implies that in proportion to revenue, less capital is being tied up in inventory in 2020 than it was in 2019. From a cash flow point of view, this should be regarded as positive.

- *Trade receivable turnover (days)* – the reduction in this ratio from 39 days to 33 days suggests an increase in the efficiency of debt collection, particularly as there appears to be no policy changes regarding the granting of credit (e.g. periods and limits). Despite this improvement, it still appears that customers are taking marginally too long to pay.

  Overall, an improvement in this ratio also implies that money is flowing into the business's bank account more quickly, which is good for cash flow.

- *Trade payables turnover (days)* – from a cash flow point of view, long periods are regarded as good news as it means the company is retaining its money for longer, which is good from a cash flow point of view. At first glance, this ratio seems to reflect an improved situation as the company is retaining its money for 36 days rather than 22 days. However, it is highly possible that suppliers might become irritated by what appears to be an increased tendency towards late payment (30 days is the agreed credit period) and so care needs to be taken that the trade payable turnover period is not extended further, as this may result in lost discounts or even a total refusal by suppliers to process further orders.

> **TIP**
>
> Take care to express ratios in their proper forms, e.g. 40%, 2.10:1 or 32.20 times.

ACTIVITY 30.2

Extracts from the financial statements for Anderson Limited and Harmison Limited for 2020 are as follows:

	Anderson		Harmison	
	$000	$000	$000	$000
Revenue		900		700
Opening inventory	52		29	
Purchases	509		345	
Closing inventory	(48)	513	(31)	(343)
Gross profit		387		357

CONTINUED

	Anderson $000	Anderson $000	Harmison $000	Harmison $000
Non-current assets:		870		545
Current assets:				
Inventory	48		31	
Trade receivables	73		45	
Bank	29	150	29	105
		1 020		650
Shareholders equity:				
Share capital	350		300	
Share premium	0		70	
Retained earnings	50	400	130	500
Non-current liabilities:				
Bank loan		500		100
Current liabilities:				
Trade payables	104		20	
Tax	16	120	30	50
		620		150
Total equity and liabilities		1 020		650

Required

a   Calculate the following ratios:
- Current ratio
- Acid test ratio
- Non-current asset turnover (times)
- Inventory turnover (days)
- Rate of inventory turnover (times)
- Trade receivables turnover (days)
- Trade payables turnover (days).

b   Explain which company has the best liquidity ratios.

c   Explain which company has the best efficiency ratios.

d   State which company might be the best investment.

TIP

Never just refer to a ratio as increasing or decreasing as bigger is not always better. Take care to comment on whether it has improved or worsened.

30.4 Trend analysis and inter-firm comparisons

Individual ratios covering one period are of relatively little value. Investors would far rather have access to ratios covering several years so that they can see whether the company is improving or not. Having access to industrial averages and ratio values for other firms in the same industry will also be useful in helping investors decide whether they should continue with their investment or move their money into ventures that might provide a better return (investment ratios will be discussed in Chapter 31).

Trade associations collect information from their members and publish the statistics as averages for the trade or industry.

As we have already suggested, comparisons will only be meaningful if they involve companies who operate in the same industry and, ideally, they should also involve businesses of a similar size – large companies may operate quite differently from small businesses.

30.5 The benefits and limitations of ratios

Using ratios can provide a number of benefits including:

- Enabling managers to build up a trend of performance over a number of years, which can help with making comparisons between different years and between different businesses in the same trading sector.
- It helps identify where improvements need to be made for the future.

However, there are a number of limitations in using accounting ratios, including:

- To be useful and reliable, ratios must be reasonably accurate. They should be based on information in accounts and notes to the accounts. Some useful information may not be disclosed in the accounts in order to protect commercial secrets. Equally, some account headings may not indicate the contents clearly.
- Information must be timely to be of use. It may not be available until many months after the end of a company's financial year and circumstances may have changed significantly.
- Ratios do not explain the cause of the changes in the results but may indicate areas of concern that require further investigation.
- Ratios do not recognise seasonal factors in business – profit margins may change during the year.
- Items like inventory, trade receivables and trade payables are unlikely to remain at constant levels throughout the year. In fact, given that many companies have their year ends during less busy times of the year, it is possible that these items will be at their lowest level and so can distort the ratio values.
- Companies, even in the same trade, will have different policies for such matters as providing for depreciation, irrecoverable debts, profit recognition, transferring profits to reserves and dividend policy.

30.6 Limitations of using financial statements

There is an accounting framework consisting of Companies Acts and a large number of accounting standards that are designed to ensure that the financial statements are produced in, as far as possible, the same way. Theoretically, this will enable the users of the reports to make meaningful comparisons and good decisions.

However, there are a number of factors that might reduce the consistency, completeness and reliability of the financial statements. These include:

- Financial reports may be too old to be useful. There will be a time delay of several months between the end of the financial year and the date on which the accounts are presented to shareholders at the annual general meeting. Circumstances may have changed significantly – both internally and externally (examples might include developments in the industry, general political and economic conditions, changes in fashion, level of competition and market demand).
- Accounting rules do not require confidential information that might provide an unfair advantage to competitors to be disclosed. The undisclosed information might contain important clues to how the company has performed.

- While additional notes explain how items in those financial statements have been arrived at, companies may differ in their classification of many items of income and expenditure and the notes may not be in sufficient detail to identify the differences. This will mean that users are not comparing 'like-with-like'. The size of the business may mean that there are different thresholds for deciding when to treat an item as capital or revenue expenditure. A small business would certainly capitalise an item costing $1 000 while an international company might write it off as an expense.

- Where accounting standards apply to a particular business, the directors may adapt them or even ignore them, provided they have good reason for doing so.

- A company may own its extensive properties or it may operate solely from rented accommodation. One will pay no rent, while the other may be burdened with very high rental payments. One will show the item in the statement of financial position, while the other will show it in their statement of profit or loss. We have already seen how this can affect the non-current asset turnover figures and may render any comparison between two companies meaningless.

- Companies in the same line of business are often not comparable. For example, some may simply retail their goods, while others manufacture and retail them. Some companies may act as manufacturers and wholesalers only.

- The financial accounts and reports of companies in countries where there is high inflation can be seriously misleading if the accounts have been based on historic costs.

- The directors may present the financial statements in a way that gives an overly favourable impression using techniques known as **window dressing** and income smoothing.

30.7 Window dressing and income smoothing

Given that company directors are 'hired and fired' by the shareholders, it is only natural that they should want the financial statements to reflect favourably on them. There may also be bonuses at stake! This may lead to window dressing where (sometimes dubious) tactics are used to make the figures look better than they really are. Examples of 'window-dressing' include:

- reducing trade payables in the statement of financial position by drawing cheques at the end of the financial period to pay the creditors but not posting the cheques until the start of the next financial year.

- reducing the trade receivables in the statement of financial position by pressing them to pay before the end of the financial period.

Other methods of window dressing, such as changing the bases of calculating depreciation of non-current assets and the provision for irrecoverable debts, of inventory valuation, etc., are not permissible and contravene accounting standards. They may even amount to fraud.

Income can be subject to 'window-dressing' techniques, sometimes referred to as *income smoothing*. Income should be recognised as soon as it is realised and not before. Such techniques might include:

- *Invoice timing*: If a business expects that income next year might be poorer than this year, the directors might order the delay of issuing invoices related to goods and services being provided this year until the following year to improve next year's figures. This contravenes the realisation concept and auditors would be very likely to object!

- *Payment by instalments*: Customers may be invoiced in one period where payment is due in the next period. Directors may be tempted to defer the income to when the money is received – a clear breach of the realisation concept.

> **KEY TERM**
>
> **window dressing:** the misleading presentation of financial statements, designed to create a more favourable impression of a situation than is justified.

- *Projects spanning two or more periods*: This is common in building projects. A company carrying out work under a contract which spans two or more financial periods is required to spread the anticipated profit on the contract over the financial periods concerned. The amount of profit to be credited in each year is calculated by a formula which apportions the profit according to the amount deemed to have been earned in each period, less a prudent provision for any future unanticipated losses. However, directors could try to apportion the profits in a way that suits their purposes – clearly not something that can possibly be approved of.

Therefore, while most of these schemes are likely to earn disapproval from any self-respecting auditor, it is worth bearing in mind that any set of financial statements will almost certainly contain a degree of opinion and judgement. This means that any comparison between accounts of two companies needs to be treated with a fair degree of caution.

REFLECTION

How reasonable is it for the users of a company's financial statements to expect that what they are analysing hasn't, to some extent, been presented in a way designed to reflect well on the board of directors?

ACCOUNTING IN CONTEXT

The shoe company's ratios

Analysis of The Shoe Company's financial statements indicated that the inventory turnover period, trade receivables turnover period and trade payables turnover period were all poor as were the current and asset test ratios. The directors had announced that they would welcome any suggestions as to how these could be improved. Suggest measures that could be introduced in order to improve these ratios and ease the company's cash flow problems.

Figure 30.2: The Shoe Company's finances have taken a turn for the worst.

EXAM-STYLE QUESTIONS

1 Extracts from the statement of profit or loss for two years for a manufacturer are given in this table:

	Year 2	Year 1
	$	$
Revenue	600 000	440 000
Gross profit	180 000	143 000

What might explain the change in the gross profit margin in year 2?

A   a market shortage of some raw materials used in manufacture

B   an increase in the sales price

C   an increase in inventory

D   suppliers offering bulk discounts on raw materials   [1]

2 What is the effect on the current ratio and acid test ratio of a business if it uses cash to buy inventory?

	Current ratio	**Acid test ratio**
A	decrease	decrease
B	decrease	increase
C	no change	decrease
D	no change	increase

[1]

3 The opening inventory was $42 000, closing inventory was $48 000, sales were $720 000 and the cost of sales was $438 000.

What was the inventory turnover (in days)?

A   22.81 days   B   37.50 days   C   45.63 days   D   75.00 days   [1]

4 Extracts from the final statements for Hilfenhaus Limited for the years ended 30 November 2019 and 2020 were as follows:

	2020		2019	
	$000	$000	$000	$000
Revenue		1 200		1 050
Opening inventories	41		31	
Purchases	810		710	
Closing inventories	(51)	(800)	(41)	(700)
Gross profit		400		350
Trade receivables		180		90
Trade payables		150		100

Required

a   Calculate the following ratios:

- Inventory turnover (days)
- Trade receivables turnover (days)
- Trade payables turnover (days)   [6]

b   Evaluate whether the efficiency of Hilfenhaus Limited has improved or worsened in 2020.   [6]

c   Explain *two* assumptions that you have had to make about the information provided when calculating your ratios in **a**. You should indicate how those assumptions may affect your evaluation in **b**.   [6]

SELF-EVALUATION CHECKLIST

After studying this chapter, complete a table like this:

You should be able to:	Needs more work	Almost there	Ready to move on
Identify and discuss the differing requirements for information of interested parties, who will use the information for a variety of reasons including judging performance and paying dividends, decision making, assessing return on investment or deciding whether jobs are secure.			
Communicate and analyse the information required by these different interested parties, who may use it to decide whether to lend money or offer credit to the business.			
Calculate profitability, liquidity and efficiency ratios and interpret them to evaluate and comment on the business. Take care to comment on whether a ratio has improved or worsened.			
Suggest possible measures to improve the profitability, liquidity and efficiency of an organisation by analysing the ratios.			

> Chapter 31

Analysis and communication of accounting information

This chapter covers syllabus section A Level 3.5

LEARNING INTENTIONS

In this chapter you will learn how to:

- calculate the following ratios: working capital cycle, net working assets to revenue, interest cover, gearing ratio, earnings per share, price/earnings ratio, dividend yield, dividend cover and dividend per share
- analyse and evaluate the results and draw conclusions
- make appropriate recommendations to interested parties on the basis of the analysis undertaken
- evaluate the interrelationships between ratios.

ACCOUNTING IN CONTEXT

Aravinda's new business

Aravinda had been in business for several months and his sales had been expanding rapidly. Customers seemed to like the products and the fact that Aravinda kept such a wide range of inventory. They were also happy with the fact that they could buy on credit – that is how Aravinda had attracted many of them in the first place!

Being a new business, most of Aravinda's suppliers were insisting on payment before they fulfilled his orders. Aravinda was finding it difficult to pay his day-to-day running costs like wages. Even though a roughly drafted statement of profit or loss suggested that he was making a good level of profit, he was rapidly running out of cash.

What was going wrong?

Discuss in a pair or a group:

* Is Aravinda right to be concerned about his business? Why?

* What are the causes of his problems?

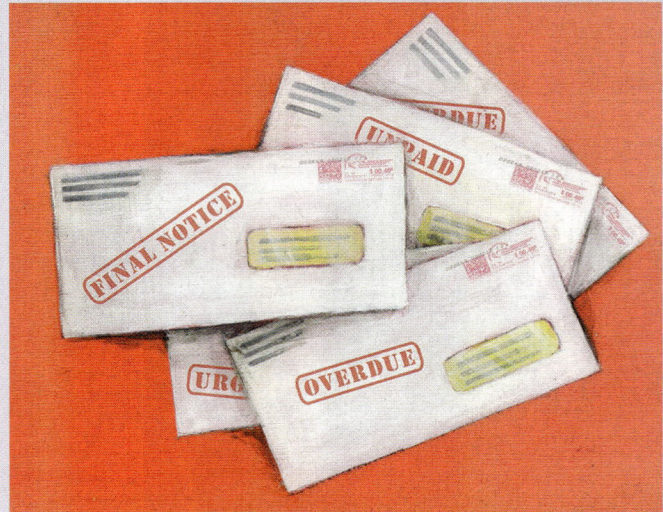

Figure 31.1: Aravinda was finding it difficult to pay his day-to-day running costs.

31.1 Overtrading

If a (new) business fails to attract enough customers, it is going to struggle to survive. However, businesses can also struggle with liquidity problems if they expand too quickly as Worked example 1 demonstrates.

WORKED EXAMPLE 1

Brassic sets up in business and during the first few weeks, his purchases, sales and expenses are:

	Sales	Purchases	Expenses	Profit
	$	$	$	$
Week 1	2 000	1 000	600	400
Week 2	3 000	1 500	600	900
Week 3	4 000	2 000	600	1 400
Week 4	5 000	2 500	600	1 900
Week 5	6 000	3 000	600	2 400

At first glance, Brassic looks to have a very profitable business that is expanding rapidly. However, suppose further investigations reveal that being a new business, Brassic is having to pay for his purchases straightaway, but in order to attract new customers, he has had to offer them four weeks' credit – so cash from week 1's sales will not be received until week 5 and week 2's sales will not be received until week 6. It becomes clear that Brassic's cash flow is not going to be very healthy:

CONTINUED

	Sales inflow	Purchases	Expenses	Net cash flow
	$	$	$	$
Week 1	0	1 000	600	(1 600)
Week 2	0	1 500	600	(2 100)
Week 3	0	2 000	600	(2 600)
Week 4	0	2 500	600	(3 100)
Week 5	2 000	3 000	600	(1 600)

Assuming that sales and purchases continue to rise at the same rate, it will be many weeks before the inflows even match the outflows. Also, we have not even considered how much money Brassic may have tied up in inventory or how long that inventory will take to sell, both of which will further damage his cash flow.

Brassic has seen a net outflow of $11 000 in the first five weeks and unless he had injected large amounts of money into the business, he might be struggling to stay in business while he waits for the inflows to 'catch up' (week 7 was the first week that generated more inflows than outflows). The expansion of his business only served to make things worse and this represents **overtrading**.

> **KEY TERM**
>
> **overtrading:** the (rapid) expansion of a business that does not have the financial resources to support such an expansion.

31.2 The working capital cycle

Accounting ratios can be used to identify whether a business is in danger of overtrading.

In Chapter 30 we encountered four ratios that were presented as a measure of efficiency. Three of them can also be used to assess how long it takes cash to circulate round the business. These are:

Inventory turnover (days) $\dfrac{\text{Average inventory}}{\text{Cost of sales}} \times 365$

Trade receivables turnover (days) $\dfrac{\text{Trade receivables}}{\text{Credit sales}} \times 365$

Trade payables turnover (days) $\dfrac{\text{Trade payables}}{\text{Credit purchases}} \times 365$

These can be combined to represent the working capital cycle.

Working capital cycle (days) =

inventory turnover + trade receivables turnover – trade payables turnover

Suppose the values of these ratios for two business are as follows:

	Inventory turnover (days)	Trade receivables turnover (days)	Trade payables turnover (days)	Working capital cycle (days)
Business A	25	+60	–45	40
Business B	20	+35	–60	–5

The working capital cycle is suggesting that Business A is more likely than Business B to be overtrading or suffering liquidity problems. Business B is probably in quite a good position as far as cash flow is concerned. If we consider a single transaction for each business:

- Business A buys the inventory at the start of day 1. After taking 25 days to sell it and 60 days to collect the debt, the money is received on day 85 while the supplier is being paid on day 45. The business has paid out money 40 days before it gets paid and is therefore in the same position as Brassic was (in danger of overtrading or liquidity problems).

- Business B buys the inventory at the start of day 1. After taking 20 days to sell it and 35 days to collect the debt, the money is received on day 55 while the supplier is not being paid until day 60. The business has received its money five days before the suppliers need to be paid – a far healthier position.

The working capital cycle makes the simplistic assumption that the trade receivables turnover period and the trade payables turnover period can be treated as completely independent items. In reality, this may not be true. If customers are taking a long time to pay then this will harm the business's cashflow, which will result in it not being able to pay its suppliers on time. Of course, if customers are paying quickly then the business has the choice of whether to pay its debts quickly. This might depend on factors including whether there are cash discounts on offer for prompt payment.

Whether it has liquidity problems or not, the owners of any business will want to ensure that the current assets and current liabilities are being managed efficiently and there are a number of actions that can be taken to improve all three elements, including:

Inventory:

- Only place orders for items that are moving quickly.
- Consider order sizes – for example, whether any bulk discount justifies how much money is being tied up in the warehouse.
- Consider discontinuing items that are not selling – do not reorder.
- Sell off discontinued items or those nearing their sell by date – even if selling prices have to be reduced.
- Offer significant discounts for cash buyers.
- Consider a just-in-time (JIT) approach to inventory – whether customers will be prepared to wait for goods that are ordered when required. This approach is common with large items such as motor cars.

Trade receivables:

- Be selective on which customers will get credit.
- Credit limits should be large enough to satisfy requirements but not so large that excessive amounts are owed.
- Do not be too generous with credit periods.
- Consider offering cash discounts to encourage prompt payment.
- Have a logical chase-up procedure where degrees of lateness trigger certain actions – an aged receivables schedule is useful.
- Apply the procedures rigorously – if customers think they can get away with late payment, they will pay late!

Trade payables:

- Do not pay before the deadline – money in our bank account is better than in someone else's.
- Consider the trade-off between obtaining a cash discount and the effect on cash flow.
- Keep communicating with suppliers, particularly if payment is likely to be late. Silence can make payables nervous and it may be possible to come to an agreement that prevents legal action.

ACTIVITY 31.1

Extracts from the financial statements for Virat for the year ended 30 November 2020 was as follows:

	2020	
	$000	$000
Revenue (all on credit)		628
Opening inventories	66	
Purchases (all on credit)	410	
Closing inventories	(70)	(406)
Gross profit		222
Trade receivables		97
Trade payables		33

Required

a   Calculate the inventory turnover, trade receivables turnover and trade payables turnover and use them to calculate the working capital cycle. Round all of your answers to the nearest day.

b   Suppose that Virat introduces a number of measures to improve his management of the current assets and current liabilities, and achieves the following:

- Inventory turnover reduced by 15 days

- Trade receivables turnover reduced by 10 days

- Trade payables turnover increased by 20 days

Comment on how this is likely to affect his cash flow position.

c   Explain two possible problems arising from actions that Virat might have taken to achieve these changes.

31.3 More solvency ratios

In Chapter 30 we encountered two main solvency ratios – the current ratio and the acid test ratio – and although you are going to need to remember them from your AS Level, there are other ratios that can be used to assess whether the business is financially healthy.

1   **Net working assets to revenue (sales)** – this ratio gives an indication as to how efficiently the net working assets are being used to generate sales. The formula is:

$$\frac{\text{Net working assets}}{\text{Revenue (sales)}} \times 100 = xx\%$$

where net working assets = inventories + trade receivables – trade payables

The general view is that the smaller the value of this ratio, the better. This is because a low percentage indicates that these assets are being used efficiently to generate a large amount of revenue and implies that the business does not have too much money tied up in inventory or trade receivables. Of course, if that value has been achieved because the level of working assets is very small, then it is possible that the business may be in danger of suffering cash flow problems – the current and acid test ratios (see Chapter 30) will provide an indication of whether this is the case.

2   **Interest cover** – this ratio is of particular interest to debenture-holders and other lenders and it gives them an idea of how well-equipped the business is to meet its interest payments. The formula is:

$$\frac{\text{Profit from operations}}{\text{Interest payable}} = \text{xxx times}$$

The larger the interest cover, the better as it provides a safety margin against a fall in profits. As well as reassuring lenders, this ratio will also be of concern to the ordinary shareholders who know that dividends are only going to be paid if there is sufficient profit left after all finance costs have been paid.

3   **Gearing ratio** – this ratio gives an indication as to how reliant the business is on external fixed cost capital. The formula is:

$$\frac{\text{Fixed cost capital}}{\text{Total capital}} \text{ which can be written as}$$

$$\frac{\text{Fixed cost capital}}{\text{Issued share capital} + \text{all reserves} + \text{non-current liabilities}} \times 100 = \text{xx\%}$$

It is accepted that the lower the gearing ratio, the better. There are a number of reasons for this, including:

- High gearing is associated with high risk. Fixed cost capital requires the payment of significant amounts of interest, which may account for a large proportion of the profits of the business and lenders may be concerned that a fall in profits may make it difficult for the business to cover the interest payments. This, in turn, may cause those lenders to wonder whether they should continue to lend the business money.

- Fixed cost capital (e.g. loans) will often require the amount borrowed to be paid back over a scheduled period and so there might be significant monthly repayments that have to be met, regardless of how well the business is performing. This could cause cash flow problems. A company that is low geared will have much of its finance in the form of capital and reserves. This means that there is no obligation for the company to repay amounts borrowed and dividends will only be paid when there is profit (and cash) available to do so.

- If a lender did decide to call in a loan, there is a greater likelihood – assuming that the company was not obviously about to fail – that a company with low gearing would be able to raise the necessary finance through a share issue (possibly a rights issue). This is because it would almost certainly be easier asking shareholders to increase their investment by a relatively small proportion than by a large proportion.

A company is often described as highly geared if the gearing is more than 50%. If it is less than 50%, it is low geared while exactly 50% is neutral gearing.

There are actions that a company can take in order to improve its gearing ratio, including:

- issuing more ordinary shares
- repaying a loan
- issuing ordinary shares and using the money to pay off the loan
- retaining profits or transferring them to reserves.

Extracts from the financial statements for two companies, Daffodil Limited and Tulip Limited, for the year ended 31 December 2020, were as follows:

	Daffodil Ltd	Tulip Ltd
	$000	$000
Revenue (sales)	1 200	1 500
Profit from operations	216	279
Finance costs (interest)	60	45
Inventory	45	75
Trade receivables	60	100
Trade payables	30	55
Ordinary share capital	400	600
Share premium	80	150
General reserve	110	200
Retained earnings	130	420
Long-term bank loan	500	200
Debentures	300	300

The solvency ratios are as follows:

Daffodil Limited   **Tulip Limited**

Net working assets to revenue

$$\dfrac{\text{Net working assets}}{\text{Revenue (sales)}} \times 100$$

$$\dfrac{45 + 60 - 30}{1\,200} \times 100 = 6.25\%$$

$$\dfrac{75 + 100 - 55}{1\,500} \times 100 = 8.00\%$$

These figures suggest that Daffodil Limited is making better use of the net working assets at its disposal. However, we do not know what the current or acid test ratios are as we do not have details of cash, bank or accruals and prepayments.

Interest cover

$$\dfrac{\text{Profit from operations}}{\text{Interest payable}}$$

$$\dfrac{216}{60} = 3.60 \text{ times}$$

$$\dfrac{279}{45} = 6.20 \text{ times}$$

These figures indicate that Tulip Limited has a better interest cover and is better equipped to meet its interest payments.

Gearing

$$\dfrac{\text{Fixed cost capital}}{\text{Share capital + all reserves + non-current liabilities}}$$

$$\dfrac{800}{400 + 320 + 800} \times 100 = 52.63\%$$

$$\dfrac{500}{600 + 770 + 500} \times 100 = 26.74\%$$

Tulip Limited is a low geared company and this is preferable to Daffodil's high gearing.

As with any other ratios, these can be used to assess whether the same company has improved or worsened over time.

ACTIVITY 31.2

Extracts from the financial statements for Rose Limited for the years ended 31 December 2019 and 2020 were as follows:

	2020	2019
	$000	$000
Revenue (sales)	2 120	1 600
Profit from operations	444	317
Finance costs (interest)	90	95
Inventory	96	48
Trade receivables	147	102
Trade payables	72	45
Ordinary share capital	1 130	880
Share premium	290	240
General reserve	300	300
Retained earnings	675	490
Long-term loans and debentures	900	1 100

Required

a   Calculate the net working assets to revenue, interest cover and gearing ratios for Rose Limited for 2019 and 2020.

b   Comment on whether each ratio has improved or worsened, in each case giving a reason for the change.

31.4 Investment ratios

Limited companies have shareholders who will be particularly interested in whether they are getting a good return on their investment or whether they should sell their shares. There will also be people who are considering whether to buy shares in a particular company. A number of investment ratios can help these people to make a decision including:

1   **Earnings per share** – earnings are the profit left for the ordinary shareholders after interest, tax and preference dividends have been provided for in the statement of profit or loss. Ordinary dividends are paid out of earnings and any amounts not distributed will increase the retained earnings or may be transferred to the general reserve, which will increase the value of the shares in the statement of financial position. Either way, the greater the earnings per share, the better it is for the shareholders. Earnings per share are expressed in cents (e.g. $0.05 per share) and are calculated using the formula:

$$\frac{\text{Profit for the year}}{\text{Number of issued ordinary shares}} = \$\text{xx per share}$$

2   **Price/earnings ratio** – this is a measure of how confident investors are in the future performance of a company. The higher the price/earnings ratio, the more confidence investors have in the company earning increasing profits in the future, which may well lead to ordinary shareholders receiving a larger dividend. This is because if shares are regarded as desirable, they will be traded at a higher market price than if people

regard them as a poor investment opportunity. The price/earnings ratio calculates what multiple of the price being paid for the shares on the market is of the earnings per share. It is calculated using the formula:

$$\frac{\text{Market price per share}}{\text{Earnings per share}} = \text{xxx times}$$

3   **Dividend per share** – so far, the ratios have calculated the potential return on investment based on the amount of profit that the business has generated. However, shareholders will really only be concerned about the amount that they actually receive. Dividends are expressed as cents per share and this ratio uses the formula:

$$\frac{\text{Annual ordinary dividend}}{\text{Number of issued ordinary shares}} = \$0.\text{xx per share}$$

where the ordinary dividend = interim dividend paid + final dividend proposed

Clearly, the larger the figure, the better. However, when using this ratio, there are several things that need to be considered:

- The annual ordinary dividend represents dividends *relating to the year* and is not the figure that appears in the statement of changes in equity, which shows the *amount paid*.

Shareholders will be interested in the return they are getting on the amount of money they have tied up in the company, which is reflected by the market price. While a dividend per share of $0.10 in Company A may look twice as good as a figure of $0.05 for Company B, A's shareholders may not be so happy if the market price of their shares is $5.00 while those in B are $1.25. This is one of the reasons why the next dividend ratio is used.

4   **Dividend yield ratio** – this ratio to show what return the shareholders are actually getting and is based on the market price at the end of the year, which may or may not reflect the price throughout the year. The formula used is:

$$\frac{\text{Annual ordinary dividend per share}}{\text{Market price per share}} \times 100 = \text{xx\%}$$

where the ordinary dividend = interim dividend paid + final dividend proposed

Again, the larger the figure the better. Investors can then compare the dividend yield with the returns available from other investments, e.g. depositing money into interesting-bearing bank accounts.

5   **Dividend cover** – this ratio shows the number of times the profit, out of which dividends may be paid, covers the dividend actually being paid. The formula used is:

$$\frac{\text{Profit for the year available to pay ordinary dividend}}{\text{Annual ordinary dividend}} = \text{xxx times}$$

where the annual ordinary dividend = interim dividend paid + final dividend proposed

Deciding whether a figure is good or not will depend on the context. A low dividend cover may indicate poor profits. Certainly, a low profit will almost certainly result in little or no dividend being paid. However, it may well be that the directors have decided to pay a generous dividend this year following relatively low ones in previous years. Shareholders will need to examine the previous financial statements to determine whether this is the case. A high dividend cover may reflect a lack of generosity on the part of the directors who are seeking to reinvest the profits, which is likely if the company is expanding or looking to expand. And a high dividend cover is likely to be regarded by some shareholders as demonstrating a mean dividend policy.

TIP

When dealing with ratios that involve numbers of shares, take care to examine the nominal value of the shares. Share capital of $300 000 will represent 300 000 shares only if they are shares of $1.00 each. If they were shares of $0.50 each, then there would be 600 000 shares to consider or at $0.25 each, there would be 1.2 million shares to consider.

WORKED EXAMPLE 3

Extracts from the final statements for Bairstow Limited and Foakes Limited for the year ended 30 November 2020 were as follows:

	Bairstow Limited	Foakes Limited
	$000	$000
Operating profit	680	455
Interest payable	(110)	(80)
Profit before tax	570	375
Tax	(120)	(65)
Profit for the year	450	310
Share capital	600	500

Notes:

1   Bairstow

- The ordinary shares have a nominal value of $0.50 each and at 30 November 2020 had a market value of $4.00 each.
- An interim dividend of $120 000 was paid during the year and a final dividend of $180 000 had been proposed.

2   Foakes

- The ordinary shares have a nominal value of $0.25 each and at 30 November 2020 had a market value of $2.10 each.
- An interim dividend of $70 000 was paid during the year and a final dividend of $130 000 had been proposed.

The investment ratios are as follows:

	Bairstow Limited	**Foakes Limited**
Earnings per share:		
$\dfrac{\text{Profit for the year}}{\text{Number of issued ordinary shares}}$	$\dfrac{450}{1\,200} = \$0.375$ per share	$\dfrac{310}{2\,000} = \$0.155$ per share
Price/earnings ratio:		
$\dfrac{\text{Market price per share}}{\text{Earnings per share}}$	$\dfrac{400}{0.375} = 10.67$ times	$\dfrac{2.10}{0.155} = 13.55$ times
Dividend per share:		
$\dfrac{\text{Annual ordinary dividend}}{\text{Number of issued ordinary shares}}$	$\dfrac{300}{1\,200} = \$0.25$ per share	$\dfrac{200}{2\,000} = \$0.10$ per share
Dividend yield:		
$\dfrac{\text{Annual ordinary dividend per share}}{\text{Market price per share}} \times 100$	$\dfrac{0.25}{4.00} \times 100 = 6.25\%$	$\dfrac{0.10}{2.10} \times 100 = 4.76\%$
Dividend cover:		
$\dfrac{\text{Profit for the year available to pay ordinary dividend}}{\text{Annual ordinary dividend}}$	$\dfrac{450}{300} = 1.50$ times	$\dfrac{310}{200} = 1.55$ times

---

CONTINUED

Comments

Earnings per share and *dividends per share*: at first glance, both of these ratios seem to favour Bairstow Limited, but you should remember that the market price of the shares is very different so the dividends per share is not a fair reflection of the return actually obtained by the shareholders. Also, earnings per share only looks at what the shareholder might get in the unlikely event of the directors distributing all of the available profit in dividends.

Price/earnings ratio: the higher figure for Foakes Limited seems to suggest that 'the market' is more confident in the future prospects of this company despite the dividend yield for 2020 favouring Bairstow Limited.

Dividend yield: the shareholders in Bairstow Limited appear to have enjoyed a better return on their investment, although how this compares with returns available on alternative investment opportunities is not known.

Dividend cover: the companies have very similar figures, which suggests a relatively generous dividend policy by both sets of directors.

Note: it is difficult to come to any definite conclusions because:

- We don't know whether these two businesses are in the same industry and even if they are, we have no industrial averages to work from.

- We only have one set of figures rather than trends to look at.

- We do not have access to the full sets of financial statements, which would include information that might give an indication of what has been happening to each of these companies and what their plans and expectations are.

ACTIVITY 31.3

Extracts from the financial statements for Dhoni Limited and Karthik Limited for the year ended 30 November 2020 were as follows:

	Dhoni Limited	Karthik Limited
	$000	$000
Operating profit	1 598	3 169
Interest payable	(185)	(223)
Profit before tax	1 413	2 946
Tax	(283)	(531)
Profit for the year	1 130	2 415
Share capital	5 000	3 500

Notes:

1 Dhoni:
   - The ordinary shares have a nominal value of $1.00 each and at 30 November 2020 had a market value of $0.90 each.
   - An interim dividend of $120 000 was paid during the year and a final dividend of $150 000 had been proposed.

2 Karthik:
   - The ordinary shares have a nominal value of $0.50 each and at 30 November 2020 had a market value of $1.50 each.
   - An interim dividend of $130 000 was paid during the year and a final dividend of $290 000 had been proposed.

CONTINUED

Required

a   Calculate, for *both* companies, the following ratios:

- earnings per share
- dividend yield
- price/earnings ratio
- dividend cover.
- dividend per share

b   Use the ratios to comment on which company presents the best return for its shareholders.

31.5 Limitations of financial statements and the use of accounting ratios

In Sections 30.5 to 30.7, the benefits and limitations of using financial statements and accounting ratios to analyse them were discussed at some length. We do not propose raising all of those points again, but you may wish to revisit them.

KEY CONCEPT LINK

True and fair view: Even if the financial statements of a profitable company provide the 'most true and fair view possible' and analysts state that a company will provide a good return on investment, can someone thinking of buying shares in that company be guaranteed to make money on those shares? Why/why not?

REFLECTION

What do you consider to be the biggest problem in using accounting ratios to analyse a company?

ACCOUNTING IN CONTEXT

Investing an inheritance

Geoff could not believe his good fortune. His Great Uncle Ernest died and left Geoff $25 000 in his will. What was really surprising was that Geoff had only met Ernest on two occasions.

The question was, what was Geoff going to do with the money? Ernest had made large amounts of money over the years by having a good instinct about buying the right 'stocks and shares', but Geoff had heard tales of other people who had made heavy losses too. His wife wanted him to put the money into a long-term bank account, but Geoff quite fancied the excitement of trading on the stock exchange. How could Geoff make money by buying and selling shares? Is there a relationship between the returns from different investment opportunities (e.g. bank accounts and ordinary share ownership) and the level of risk? How could Geoff maximise his chances of making money by buying and selling shares?

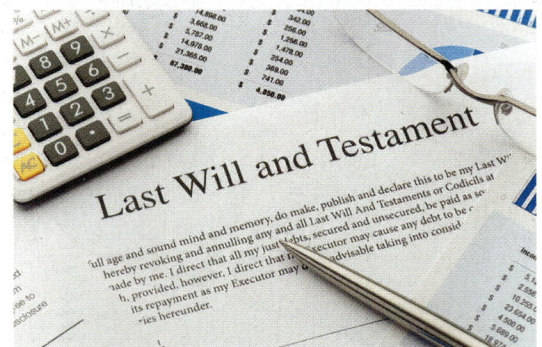

Figure 31.2: Geoff is surprised to learn he has inherited a large sum from his Great Uncle Ernest.

EXAM-STYLE QUESTIONS

1 A business has the following accounting ratios: inventory turnover 32 days, trade receivable turnover 41 days and trade payables turnover 55 days.

What is the working capital cycle period?

A	18 days	**C**	64 days	
B	46 days	**D**	128 days	**[1]**

2 The following are balances taken from the statement of financial position of a company:

	$000
8% debentures	500
General reserve	180
Issued share capital	600
Long-term bank loan	245
Retained earnings	344
Share premium	275

What is the company's gearing ratio?

A	11.42%	**C**	34.75%	
B	23.32%	**D**	43.14%	**[1]**

3 The following information was available for Carnation Limited and Lily Limited at 31 December 2020:

	Carnation Limited	Lily Limited
	$000	$000
Profit for the year	198	120
Ordinary share capital	450[1]	300[2]

Notes:

[1] The share capital of Carnation Limited consisted of ordinary shares of $0.50 each where the market price at 31 December 2020 was $1.25. Paid or proposed dividends relating to 2020 amounted to $72 000.

[2] The share capital of Lily Limited consisted of ordinary shares of $0.25 each where the market price at 31 December 2020 was $0.75. Paid or proposed dividends relating to 2020 amounted to $36 000.

Required

a Calculate, for *both* companies, the following ratios at 31 December 2020:

- earnings per share
- price/earnings ratio
- dividend per share
- dividend yield
- dividend cover. **[10]**

b Evaluate which company represents the best investment opportunity. **[5]**

c Explain *two* reasons why directors may decide to pay a low dividend. **[4]**

d Explain *three* limitations of using accounting ratios to analyse financial statements. **[6]**

SELF-EVALUATION CHECKLIST

After studying this chapter, complete a table like this:

You should be able to:	Needs more work	Almost there	Ready to move on
Calculate the following ratios: working capital cycle, net working assets to revenue, interest cover, gearing ratio, earnings per share, price/earnings ratio, dividend yield, dividend cover and dividend per share, ensuring you can also analyse and evaluate the results, and draw conclusions.			
Make appropriate recommendations to interested parties on the basis of the analysis undertaken, so existing shareholders and potential investors can decide whether ordinary shares in a particular company represent a good investment opportunity.			
Evaluate the interrelationships between ratios, ensuring you understand the importance of examining a variety of financial ratios and not just a single ratio.			

> Part 3

Cost and management accounting

Chapter 32

Costing of materials and labour

This chapter covers syllabus section AS Level 2.1

LEARNING INTENTIONS

In this chapter you will learn how to:

- explain that accounting can be split into financial accounting and management accounting, and that cost accounting is part of management accounting
- describe the management of inventory using just-in-time
- define a cost unit as the unit of output of a business to which costs can be charged, and give suitable examples
- analyse costs into direct and indirect costs
- analyse direct and indirect materials using FIFO and AVCO methods
- analyse direct and indirect labour.

ACCOUNTING IN CONTEXT

Eat it while it's fresh

The food industry uses a huge amount of raw materials. Materials such as salt can last for a long time but others, such as fruit and milk, perish quickly. Businesses that buy perishable goods must use or sell them promptly to minimise wastage.

Nestlé is one of the world's largest manufacturers of food products. It buys sugar, cocoa, dairy products and many other raw materials and then uses them to manufacture a wide range of food and refreshments including cereals, coffee, chocolate and baby food. Nestlé's best-known brands include KitKat, Nescafé and Maggi. Although the company is based in Switzerland, its goods are produced and sold around the world.

Nestlé's inventory was valued at over $9 billion in 2018. It must value its inventory at the lower and cost or net realisable value. In most situations, the lower figure is usually cost. The cost of buying inventory varies over time.

Figure 32.1: Nestlé is one of the world's largest manufacturers of food products.

Nestlé's raw materials are valued using a method called First In, First Out, which assumes that inventory is used in manufacturing in the order in which it is purchased. This is a sensible assumption given the perishable nature of its raw materials.

Discuss in a pair or a group:

- Why is it important to use and sell your oldest inventory first in the food industry?
- Can you think of other products that also need to sell their oldest inventory first?
- What kind of products don't need to sell the earlier inventory first?

32.1 The purpose of cost and management accounting

Accounting can be split into two broad areas: financial accounting and **management accounting**. Part II of this book covers financial accounting; that is the recording and reporting of historical information. Part III focuses on management accounting.

Cost accounting is an important part of management accounting.

The way data is collected and presented in management accounting is different from the way it is collected and presented in financial accounting.

With management accounting, the organisation is gathering and analysing information that will be used as a basis for making decisions affecting the future performance and profitability of the firm.

There is some overlap between management and financial accounting. For example, information collected in relation to the cost of part-completed units of product will allow it to accurately value inventory in the financial statements.

Manufacturing accounts are prepared as part of the company's financial accounting system (see Chapter 20). They provide us with information about prime cost, overheads and the cost of producing goods. This information is also used substantially in cost accounting to establish costs per unit and give information to managers to help them make informed decisions such as deciding selling prices.

KEY TERMS

management accounting: the process of preparing reports and accounts that can be used by managers as a basis for making decisions about the future performance of the business.

cost accounting: a method of accounting where all the costs associated with a particular activity or product are collected together, classified and recorded.

32.2 Direct and indirect costs

In Section 20.2, we saw that a distinction is made in manufacturing accounts between direct costs and indirect costs. Cost accounting makes substantial use of direct and indirect cost information.

Direct costs include:

1   direct materials (those materials from which goods are made, and carriage inwards paid on the materials)

2   direct labour (the wages of workers who actually make goods)

3   direct expenses (will vary with the number of products such as royalties and licence fees).

Indirect costs include:

1   indirect materials purchased for the factory, (e.g. cleaning materials, lubricating oil for any machinery)

2   indirect wages – the wages of all factory workers who do not actually make the finished goods (such as factory managers, supervisors, store staff and cleaners)

3   indirect expenses (will not vary with the number of products such as rent, heating and lighting, depreciation of machinery).

Cost accounting requires both materials purchased and wages paid to be classified as direct or indirect.

If materials are used as part of the finished product, they are direct materials. For example, if a manufacturer produces jeans, then one pair of jeans is the **cost unit**. The cost of the cotton, zip(s) and button(s) that go into producing one finished pair of jeans are the direct materials cost per unit.

If the business issues overalls to its workers to use while making the jeans, the cost of these materials is indirect. The overalls can be used a number of times during the manufacturing process.

32.3 Direct and indirect materials

Manufacturing businesses may purchase a range of items that are used in making a product. The cost of buying these items may vary over time and between suppliers. Changes in cost affect the value that is placed on inventory.

When considering a manufacturing company, IAS 2 (see Chapter 20) allows *two* different methods to be used for valuing direct materials inventory. They are:

•   **first in, first out (FIFO)**

•   **average cost (AVCO)**.

Using FIFO to value inventory

This method assumes goods are used in production or sold in the order in which they are received from the supplier.

A manufacturer will purchase inventory. When the inventory is received by the business it may be kept temporarily in a storeroom before being issued for use in production when required.

TIP

Classifying costs into direct and indirect costs is an important feature of management accounting.

KEY TERMS

cost unit: the unit of output of a business to which costs can be charged, such as a computer for a computer manufacturer or an item of clothing for a dressmaker.

first in, first out (FIFO): a method of inventory valuation that assumes that the first items to be purchased will be the first to be used in production and sold.

average cost (AVCO): a method of inventory valuation that uses a weighted average to calculate the value of inventory each time new inventory is purchased.

WORKED EXAMPLE 1

At 1 June, the inventory of grape juice, which is a material used in production of soft drinks, consisted of 80 litres that cost $0.60 per litre. The receipts of the material from the suppliers and the issues of the material to production in June were:

Date	Receipts from suppliers	Purchase price per litre	Issues to production
	litres	$	litres
2	100	1.00	
6			70
15	200	1.20	
22			200
24	50	1.40	
30			80

Required

Calculate the value of the direct materials issued to production and the remaining inventory throughout June using the FIFO method.

Answer

Table 32.1 shows how issues and inventory are valued using FIFO.

Table 32.1: Valuing issues and inventory using FIFO

Date	Receipts		Issues		Inventory	
	Litres	Price per litre	Litres	Value ($)	Litres	Value ($)
June 1					80	80 × 0.60 = 48
2	100	1.00			80 + 100 = 180	80 × 0.60 = 48 100 × 1.00 = 100 Total 148 [1]
6[2]			70	70 × 0.60 = 42	180 − 70 = 110	10 × 0.60 = 6 100 × 1.00 = 100 Total 106
15	200	1.20			110 + 200 = 310	10 × 0.60 = 6 100 × 1.00 = 100 200 × 1.20 = 240 Total 346
22			200	10 × 0.60 = 6 100 × 1.00 = 100 90 × 1.20 = 108 Total 214	310 − 200 = 110	110 × 1.20 = 132
24	50	1.40			110 + 50 = 160	110 × 1.20 = 132 50 × 1.40 = 70 Total 202
30			80	80 × 1.20 = 96	160 − 80 = 80	30 × 1.20 = 36 50 × 1.40 = 70 Total 106

CONTINUED

Notes:

[1] The receipt on 2 June increased the total inventory to 180 litres. The costs of the two components are added together to arrive at an inventory value of $148.

[2] The issue on 6 June reduced the total inventory to 110 litres. Using FIFO, the 70 litres issued came from the first items in inventory, the 80 litres at 1 June. This left 10 litres of those items and 100 litres of the items received on 2 June. These were valued at their respective purchase price per litres. This process can be followed with each subsequent receipt and issue. In each case, the items issued are taken from the first items delivered that are still left in inventory. Thus, first in, first out (FIFO).

> **TIP**
>
> The layout shown in an inventory valuation table can seem time consuming but is essential to help avoid errors.

Using AVCO to value inventory

Unlike FIFO, the AVCO method does not assume a particular order in which goods are issued from inventory into production. When calculating the value of issues and inventory using AVCO, the weighted average cost of inventory is calculated *every time new goods are received*.

The weighted average cost of inventory formula is:

$$= \frac{\text{Total cost of inventory}}{\text{Number of units of inventory}}$$

WORKED EXAMPLE 2

The process of valuation using AVCO will now be demonstrated using the data from Worked example 1.

Required

Calculate the value of the direct materials issued to production and the remaining inventory throughout June using the AVCO method.

Answer

Table 32.2 shows how issues and inventory are valued using AVCO.

Table 32.2: Valuing issues and inventory using AVCO

Date	Receipts		Issues		Inventory	
	Litres	Price per litre	Litres	Value ($)	Litres	Value ($)
June 1					80	80 × 0.60 = 48
2	100	1.00			80 + 100 = 180	(100 + 48) = 148
6			70	(70 × 0.822) = 58[1]	180 − 70 = 110	(148 − 58) = 90
15	200	1.20			110 + 200 = 310	330[2] (240 + 90) ÷ 310 = 1.065 per kg
22			200	(200 × 1.065) = 213	310 − 200 = 110	110 × 1.065 = 117
24	50	1.40			110 + 50 = 160	187[3] (117 + 70) ÷ 160 = 1.169 per kg
30			80	(80 × 1.169) = 94	160 − 80 = 80	93 (80 × 1.169)

CONTINUED

Notes:

[1] After the receipt of goods on 2 June, a weighted average cost of inventory is calculated. On that date, there was 180 litres in inventory at a total cost of $148. Thus, the weighted average cost per litres was:

$$\frac{\text{Total cost of inventory}}{\text{Number of units of inventory}} = \frac{\$148}{180} = \$0.822 \text{ per litre}$$

This value was then used to calculate the cost of the issue of inventory on June 6:

70 litres × $0.822 = $58 (rounded to the nearest dollar).

[2] A new average cost per litre was calculated after the receipt of goods on June 15. This was applied to the issue on June 22.

[3] Finally, a new weighted average cost was calculated after the receipt on June 24. This was applied to the issue on June 30 and the closing inventory on that date.

TIP

The weighted average cost of inventory needs to be calculated when new goods are received not when goods are issued or sold.

Be aware that figures often need to be rounded when using AVCO, such as to three decimal places.

ACTIVITY 32.1

Jessie's business had no inventory at the start of August. The following purchases and issues to production were made during August.

Date	Quantity received	Price per unit ($)	Quantity issued
August 2	100	10.20	
8			70
10	200	10.40	
18			120
30			50

Required

a   Calculate the quantity and value of the inventory throughout August using each of the following methods:

  i   FIFO

  ii   AVCO.

b   Which method gives the higher inventory valuation at the end of August? Why does this occur?

REFLECTION

When answering Activity 32.1, was the method giving the higher inventory valuation the one you expected? What would you expect to happen if the price per unit stayed constant or decreased over time? Discuss your answers with another learner to see whether you agree.

Perpetual and periodic inventories

Perpetual inventory is a method of inventory valuation, such as FIFO and AVCO, that maintains a continuous balance of inventory available after each transaction.

Periodic inventory is a method of inventory valuation that is often used in small businesses that just need a valuation of their inventory at the end of the financial year.

KEY TERMS

perpetual inventory: a method of inventory valuation that maintains a continuous balance of inventory available after each financial transaction.

periodic inventory: a method of inventory valuation that only shows the balance of inventory at intervals, such as each week or each month.

WORKED EXAMPLE 3

Using the data in Worked example 1, calculate the value of the inventory at 30 June on a periodic basis using:

i   the FIFO method

ii the AVCO method.

Answer

First, calculate the number of units in inventory at 30 June:

Units available (80 + 100 + 200 + 50)	430
Less: units issued (70 + 200 + 80)	(350)
Balance of units	80

Then the valuations can be calculated as follows:

i   Inventory valuation using FIFO:

The 80 units of inventory must be the most recent purchases under the FIFO, so it must be the 50 units bought on 24 June at $1.40 each and the remaining 30 units come from the inventory purchased on 15 June at $1.20 each.

50 at latest price $1.40	$70
+ 30 at previous price of $1.20	$36
Inventory value at 30 June	$106

ii Inventory valuation using AVCO:

The total cost of the opening inventory and purchases must be calculated first:

Valuation	Units	Unit cost ($)	Total ($)
Opening inventory	80	0.60	48
Purchase	100	1.00	100
	200	1.20	240
	50	1.40	70
Total	430		458

Then the weighted average cost per unit can be calculated:

$$\text{Weighted average cost per unit} = \frac{\text{Total cost of inventory}}{\text{Number of units of inventory}} = \frac{\$458}{430} = \$1.065 \text{ per unit}$$

Finally, the inventory can be valued:

Inventory value at 30 June = 80 units × $1.065 = $85.20

Note: the inventory valuation is the same using either the perpetual or periodic approach for FIFO but not for AVCO.

The effect of method of inventory valuation on profits

FIFO and AVCO give different inventory valuation figures, therefore, the method chosen by a business will affect its financial statements.

While the profits reported each period will be affected, the profit made over the whole life of a business is not changed by the choice of method of valuing inventory. This is demonstrated in the following example.

WORKED EXAMPLE 4

Jumps Limited began business in year 1 and stopped trading at the end of year 4. The following information is given for each of the four years.

	Year 1	Year 2	Year 3	Year 4
	$	$	$	$
Sales	1 000	1 400	1 600	800
Purchases	600	800	700	400
Closing inventory:				
Using FIFO	80	100	90	–
Using AVCO	70	90	80	–

Required

a Calculate the gross profit for each of the four years using:

   i FIFO

   ii AVCO.

b Explain which method resulted in the highest gross profit at the end of year 1.

Answer

a **i**

Statement of profit or loss (using FIFO for valuing inventory)								
	Year 1		Year 2		Year 3		Year 4	
	$	$	$	$	$	$	$	$
Revenue		1 000		1 400		1 600		800
Opening inventory	–		80		100		90	
Purchases	600		800		700		400	
Closing inventory (FIFO)	(80)	(520)	(100)	(780)	(90)	(710)	–	(490)
Gross profit		480		620		890		310
Total gross profit								$2 300

ii

Statement of profit or loss (AVCO)								
	Year 1		Year 2		Year 3		Year 4	
	$	$	$	$	$	$	$	$
Revenue		1 000		1 400		1 600		800
Opening inventory	–		70		90		80	
Purchases	600		800		700		400	
Closing inventory (AVCO)	(70)	(530)	(90)	(780)	(80)	(710)	–	(480)
Gross profit		470		620		890		320
Total gross profit								$2 300

b The FIFO method resulted in the higher gross profit at the end of year 1. This was because the value of the closing inventory was higher using FIFO while the value of opening inventory was the same ($0).

FIFO and AVCO compared

Both FIFO and AVCO are acceptable methods of inventory valuation for the purposes of the accounting standards (IAS 2), so a business must choose which method is most suitable for its own use.

The advantages and disadvantages of FIFO and AVCO are now compared.

FIFO	
Advantages	Disadvantages
1 It is realistic. Materials are used in FIFO order and goods will be sold in that order, especially perishable goods. 2 Prices used are those that have actually been paid for goods. 3 Closing inventory is valued on current price levels. 4 It is relatively simple to calculate.	1 When prices are rising, the closing inventory in the financial accounts will be priced at the latest (higher) prices. This results in lowering cost of sales and increasing gross profit. This is not consistent with the concept of prudence, although is acceptable under IAS 2. 2 Identical items of inventory from batches bought at different times may be used for similar jobs, with the result that job A may be charged for the item at a different price from job B. Therefore, quotations for jobs when materials are based on FIFO may be unreliable.

AVCO	
Advantages	Disadvantages
1 The use of average prices avoids the inequality of identical items being charged to different jobs at different prices. 2 AVCO recognises that identical items purchased at different times and prices have identical values. 3 Averaging costs may smooth variations in production costs, and comparisons between the results of different periods may be more meaningful. 4 Averaged prices used to value closing inventory may be fairly close to the latest prices.	1 The average price must be recalculated after every purchase of inventory. 2 The average price does not represent any price actually paid for inventory.

KEY CONCEPT LINK

Consistency: Both FIFO and AVCO are used extensively in industry. Once a method is chosen by a business it should not be changed, unless doing so gives a more realistic value of the business. This is in line with IAS 2 and the concept of consistency because it enables a business's performance to be compared from one year to the next.

It is quite common in manufacturing companies to have inventories of indirect materials, such as drill bits or saw blades. FIFO and AVCO methods of inventory valuation can apply to indirect materials as well as direct materials. A computerised accounting system easily allows inventory records to be maintained using either FIFO or AVCO.

32.4 Just-in-time management of inventory

When inventory is received from a supplier, it is kept temporarily in storage. The inventory will then be issued for use in production as and when it is needed. FIFO and AVCO methods of inventory valuation are typically used by manufacturers to value the raw materials and components that are held before being used in production. If a business does not hold any materials from suppliers in storage, but instead always sends the materials directly to production as soon as they arrive, then the value of inventory of the raw materials or components purchased is zero. As a result, the FIFO and AVCO methods become unnecessary.

As a result of using **just-in-time (JIT)** inventory management, raw materials are not temporarily kept in storage but go straight into the factory and are used immediately.

If this principle is fully met, then the manufacturer holds no inventory of raw materials or components. In practice, businesses that use JIT, such as the car manufacturer Toyota, find it difficult to eliminate inventory altogether; however, using JIT reduces the amount of inventory held.

There are challenges for a business that wants to use JIT to manage its inventory. In particular, the business must be confident that its suppliers are completely reliable and will always deliver good quality raw materials and components on time. If this does not happen it will lead to a shortage of suppliers, which will stop production.

Businesses that do use JIT successfully have lower levels of inventory. These businesses will then benefit from having less cash tied up in inventory and lower storage costs, and the inventory is less likely to be stolen or become damaged.

32.5 Direct and indirect labour

As with materials, labour costs are also classified as direct or indirect. If the wages paid to employees can be linked directly to the cost unit then they are regarded as direct labour.

For example, for a manufacturer that produces jeans, the wages of an employee who is stitching together the components (buttons and zips) of the jeans into the finished product will be treated as direct labour. In order to calculate how much of their hourly rate is charged to each cost unit, the time the worker takes on each product will be calculated.

If a worker is paid $20 per hour and can produce five complete pairs of jeans in an hour, then the direct labour cost per cost unit will be:

$20 ÷ 5 = $4 direct labour per cost unit

Where one pair of jeans is the cost unit.

If there is a supervisor in the factory who is not directly involved in making the finished product, their wages will be treated as an indirect labour cost. As with indirect materials, the total indirect wages is calculated and charged to each cost unit on a predetermined basis. Indirect labour is charged to a cost centre and then included when calculating an overhead absorption rate (see Section 33.3).

There are three ways in which workers can be paid:

a   An hourly rate. This is a common method for paying direct labour.

b   By how much the worker produces (**piece rate**) and is sometimes used for direct labour. It is calculated on the number of units of output (or pieces) the worker makes.

c   A salary. This is a common method for paying indirect labour, such as office staff, factory supervisors or managers.

In addition to these three methods, the employee may receive an additional amount either as an **overtime payment** or a **bonus payment**. An example of an **overtime premium** would be when an employee is paid overtime at a rate of 50% above their normal hourly rate (or time and a half). The extra 50% is the overtime premium. Some businesses treat the overtime premium as indirect labour.

KEY TERMS

just-in-time (JIT): a system of manufacturing that uses the principle that supplies should be received exactly when they are needed in the production process and do not need to be stored by the business beforehand.

piece rate: a wage rate paid to workers based on the number of units of output produced.

overtime payment: an amount paid to an employee for working longer than the time they are contracted to work.

bonus payment: the additional amount paid to an employee for reasons such as producing goods more quickly than the time allowed.

overtime premium: the additional amount given to employees for overtime working. For example, if an employee is paid overtime at a rate of 50% above their normal hourly rate (or time and a half), the extra 50% is the overtime premium.

WORKED EXAMPLE 5

Maria works from home. Her employer sends her 1 000 cards to put into envelopes ready to be posted. Her employer offers Maria two alternative methods of payment:

1 she will be paid $0.50 for each completed envelope and a bonus of $20 if she completes the work within two days

2 she will be paid $0.45 for the first 600 completed and $0.60 for the next 400.

Required

Which payment method should Maria choose? Give reasons for your answer.

Answer

Option 1

Number of units (envelopes)	1 000
× pay per unit	× $0.50
	$500
+ bonus	+ $20
Total pay	$520

Option 2

Pay for first 600 units (600 × $0.45)	$270
Pay for next 400 units (400 × $0.60)	$240
Total pay	$510

Provided she is confident that she can complete the work in two days, she should accept option 1 because her pay will be $10 higher.

A possible problem with piece rate is that work may be rushed, meaning the quality of the finished article may be an issue. Alternatively, workers may take longer than expected to complete the work, which may cause problems with a customer.

Where the piece rate method is used, it is up to management to carefully consider both the time taken and the quality of work produced by the worker.

WORKED EXAMPLE 6

Sam normally works a 37-hour week from Monday to Friday.

For the week ended 30 April, he worked 40 hours from Monday to Friday, and 5 hours on Sunday.

The hourly rate of pay is $12.

Overtime is paid at time and one-third for overtime between Monday and Friday and double time on Sundays.

Required

a Calculate Sam's total pay for the week.

b Calculate Sam's overtime premium.

CONTINUED

Answer

a   Sam's total pay for the week ended 30 April is calculated as follows:

Normal week's pay = 37 hours × $12 = $444

Overtime Monday to Friday

Normal pay per hour	$12
+ one-third of normal rate $\left(\$12 \times \frac{1}{3}\right)$	$4
Overtime rate	$16
Overtime hours (40 actual hours − 37 normal hours)	× 3 hours
Overtime pay for Monday to Friday	$48

Payment for Sunday

Overtime rate for Sunday ($12 × 2)	$24
Sunday hours	× 5 hours
Payment for Sunday	$120

Total pay for the week

Normal week's pay	$444
Overtime pay Monday to Friday	$48
Payment for Sunday	$120
Total pay for the week	$612

ACTIVITY 32.2

Amara usually works a 40-hour week. She is paid $16 per hour. If she works overtime, she is paid time and a half for every extra hour worked.

She is expected to produce an average of 6 completed units per hour. Provided the work is satisfactory, for every unit she produces in excess of 6 per hour she receives a bonus of $3.

For the week ended 7 October, Amara worked 44 hours. In that time, she made 284 acceptable units.

Required

Calculate the following:

a   Amara's basic pay for the week

b   the amount paid in overtime, clearly showing the overtime premium

c   the amount of bonus paid for excess production

d   Amara's total gross pay for the week ended 7 October.

A business may need to decide whether to offer bonuses and/or overtime to staff regularly, occasionally or not at all. To do this, it can be helpful to weigh up the advantages and disadvantages of offering bonuses and overtime payments.

Should a firm offer bonuses and overtime payments? Some of the advantages and disadvantages are now compared.	
Advantages	Disadvantages
1 Bonuses and overtime can increase productivity if the work is of the correct standard.	1 Bonuses may cause workers to rush at the expense of quality. Work should be checked before any payment is approved.
2 Overtime can offer flexibility that allows a business to change production levels and manage busy periods or staff shortages.	2 If the extra production cannot be sold, the firm will incur increased inventory holding costs.
3 Workers can produce a greater number of units to sell and may increase total profit.	3 Extra costs are incurred. It may not be possible to pass these onto the customers.

THINK LIKE AN ACCOUNTANT

Earning a wage

Large businesses will typically use a range of employment types and contracts for different workers in the same organisation. Some staff will have full-time, permanent contracts while others have temporary work; some may have bonuses or overtime payments while others do not.

Within the accounting profession, employment contracts and pay varies widely. Typically, those with a formal accounting qualification earn substantially more than those who are part-qualified or unqualified. Accountants often receive financial benefits as well as their salary. Common examples include pension contributions, performance or profit bonuses and health care.

Carry out some research into careers in accounting. See if you can find out the average pay of new entrants into the profession in your country. What qualifications can be studied and how do employers support staff while they are training?

Figure 32.2: Large businesses will typically use a range of employment types and contracts within an organisation.

EXAM-STYLE QUESTIONS

1   A business use the AVCO method to value its inventory.

	kilos	Cost per kilo ($)
1 May inventory	500	12
Purchases in May	200	14
Sales in May	600	

What is the value of the inventory at the end of May?

A $677

B $1 200

C $1 257

D $1 400   [1]

2   Amir works a basic 35-hour week at $10 per hour plus time and a half for any overtime. He is expected to produce 8 units per hour. He is paid a bonus of $1 for every extra unit produced. Last week Amir worked 40 hours and produced 360 units. What was Amir's gross pay for the week?

A $350

B $390

C $425

D $465   [1]

CONTINUED

3 A business bought and sold goods as follows:

	Bought Units	Unit price ($)	Sold Units
May 1	40	4.00	
3	20	4.80	
6			24
8	40	6.00	
9			32

What is the value of the inventory at 9 May based on FIFO?

A $179.20   B $192.00   C $259.20   D $264.00

4 State two examples of indirect costs.   [2]

5 Lewis's business had an inventory of 160 units at $5 each at 31 July. He sells his product at $12 per unit. The following information is available for August.

Date	Quantity received	Price per unit ($)	Sales quantity
5	100	6	
10			120
15	180	7	
20			100

Required

a   Calculate the value of the inventory at the end of August using the AVCO method on a perpetual basis.   [10]

b   Calculate the gross profit for August.   [6]

SELF-EVALUATION CHECKLIST

After studying this chapter, complete a table like this:

You should be able to:	Needs more work	Almost there	Ready to move on
Explain that accounting can be split into financial accounting and management accounting, and that cost accounting is part of management accounting.			
Describe the management of inventory using just-in-time, which can substantially reduce inventory of raw materials and components.			
Define a cost unit as the unit of output of a business to which costs can be charged, and give suitable examples.			
Analyse costs into direct and indirect costs, as cost accounting requires both materials purchased and wages paid to be classified as direct or indirect.			
Analyse direct and indirect materials using FIFO and AVCO methods, remembering that the method used by a business affects the profits reported each period.			
Analyse direct and indirect labour, ensuring you consider that workers can be paid by the hour, using a piece rate system or through an annual salary, and that they may also receive overtime payments and bonuses.			

> Chapter 33

Absorption costing

This chapter covers part of syllabus section AS Level 2.2

LEARNING INTENTIONS

In this chapter you will learn how to:

- describe the absorption costing method for calculating the cost of making one unit of a product
- allocate and apportion overheads into cost centres to calculate unit cost
- analyse under-absorption and over-absorption of overheads
- use absorption cost data to support selling price decisions
- evaluate the usefulness of using absorption costing.

ACCOUNTING IN CONTEXT

The cost of making steel

Tata Steel is one of the world's largest iron and steel producing companies. It is part of the Tata group and has its headquarters in India. This multinational company has grown rapidly and has large manufacturing plants across Europe, South East Asia and parts of Africa.

All manufacturing businesses have both direct and indirect costs. Tata Steel's direct costs will include raw materials and the wages of the workers who make the pipes. Tata Steel will also have high production overheads as it has large factories and invests heavily in plant and equipment. It will therefore incur indirect costs such as maintenance and depreciation of plant and equipment. There will also be indirect wages for the workers in a factory not directly involved in production including managers, supervisors and warehouse staff.

Tata Steel produces a wide range of products that are used in many manufacturing industries from car-making to construction. Tata Steel sets prices for every one of its products. When deciding prices, managers will want to know the direct costs of manufacturing the product.

Figure 33.1: Tata Steel has large manufacturing plants across Europe, South East Asia and parts of Africa.

Managers also consider the indirect costs when setting prices for each product. This can be complex when a business produces many different products. Ultimately, both the direct and indirect costs must be included in the total cost if a profit is to be made.

Discuss in a pair or a group:

* What other production overheads might Tata Steel have?
* Why is it important that Tata Steel invests heavily in its plant and equipment?
* Why is it easier to set prices for a business with one product than with many different products?

33.1 What is absorption costing?

Manufacturers need to know how much it costs to make all their products and how much it costs to make each individual product. The cost of making one product is called the **unit cost**.

Knowing the unit cost of each product is very useful for a business. It helps management to plan and control its costs and to make good decisions about its operations and products. One very important decision is what selling price it should charge for its products.

If only one type of good has been produced, the unit cost can easily be found simply by dividing the total factory cost by the number of units produced. However, many manufacturing businesses make more than one type of product, so calculating the unit cost needs to be done differently.

Absorption costing is a method for calculating the cost of making one unit of a product by attributing overheads into cost units as well as the direct costs. Profit statements prepared using absorption costing can be found in Section 35.9.

A **cost centre** is usually a department, but may be a process, an item of equipment (a machine) or person (e.g. a marketing manager). Cost centres are a useful aspect of management accounting that help to control expenditure.

KEY TERMS

unit cost: the average cost of producing one unit of a product or service.

absorption costing: a method for calculating the cost of making one unit of a product that involves apportioning overheads into cost units.

cost centre: any part of a business to which costs may be attributed, such as a department.

33.2 How to apportion overheads to cost centres

There are two main types of cost centre:

1 **Production cost centres**: for example, a whole factory or a stage in production, such as assembling components, painting and packaging.

2 **Service cost centres**: for example, stores for inventory, building and plant maintenance or a canteen.

Allocation of overheads to cost centres

Some overheads, such as indirect labour or materials, can be identified with specific cost centres and are allocated to them. This is called **allocation of costs**.

Examples of overheads which may be identified with, and allocated to, specific cost centres include:

- metal, plastic, components and so on – production department

- paint – paints shop

- packing materials – packing department) (take care though as sometimes these may be regarded as direct materials; you will be told whether or not they are direct or indirect items

- maintenance of handling equipment – the stores or warehouse

- food – the canteen.

Apportionment of production overheads to production cost centres

Some overheads can't be identified with specific cost centres and are apportioned to cost centres on suitable bases. This is called **apportionment of costs**.

Examples of suitable bases of apportionment	
Production overhead	Suitable basis of apportionment
Heating and lighting (when not separately metered to the cost centres), rent, insurance of buildings	Floor area
Insurance of plant, machinery and other assets	Cost or replacement values of assets
Depreciation	Cost or net book value of assets

KEY TERMS

production cost centres: cost centres directly involved in producing goods.

service cost centres: cost centres that are not involved in the production of goods but provide services for the production cost centres.

allocation of costs: charging overheads directly to the cost centre(s) that can be clearly identified with them.

apportionment of costs: the process of charging costs that can't be identified with specific cost centres to cost centres using a suitable basis.

TIP

You may be given the basis on which to apportion overheads. Other times you may have to decide a suitable basis of apportionment yourself.

WORKED EXAMPLE 1

Tiddly Toys Ltd makes children's dolls. It has three production cost centres: moulding, painting and packaging.

The following information is available:

	Moulding	Painting	Packaging
Floor area (square metres)	1000	500	500
Plant and machinery at cost ($000)	50	30	20

Forecast expenditure for the year ended 31 December 2021 is as follows:

	Moulding	Painting	Packaging
	$	$	$
Direct materials	50000	10000	6000
Direct labour	80000	40000	20000
Indirect labour	12000	5000	2000

	$
Overheads: Factory rent	40000
Factory maintenance	6000
Heating and lighting	4000
Depreciation of plant and machinery	12000

> **TIP**
>
> Remember that factory overheads are indirect costs.

Required

a   Apportion the indirect costs and overheads to each cost centre.

b   Calculate the total cost of production for each cost centre.

Answer

a   The overhead apportionment will be as follows:

Expense	Basis of apportionment	Total	Moulding	Painting	Packaging
		$	$	$	$
Indirect labour	Allocation	19000	12000	5000	2000
Rent[1]	Floor area	40000	20000	10000	10000
Maintenance	Floor area	6000	3000	1500	1500
Heating and lighting	Floor area	4000	2000	1000	1000
Depreciation[2]	Cost	12000	6000	3600	2400
Apportioned overheads [3]		81000	43000	21100	16900

Step 1: choose suitable basis for appointment e.g. floor area for rent.

Step 2: calculate the emount of each overhead to apportion to each cost centre. See notes 1 and 2.

Step 3: total the overheads apportioned to each cost centre. See note 3.

CONTINUED

Notes:

[1] The overhead rent is split using floor area as the basis of apportionment. The total rent expense was $40 000. The total floor area of the three cost centres is 2 000 (1 000 + 500 + 500) square metres. The cost per square metre for rent is therefore:

$$\frac{\$40\,000}{2\,000} = \$20 \text{ per square metre}$$

Thus, the total cost to apportion to moulding will be the number of square metres it occupies: (1 000) × $20 = $20 000.

[2] Depreciation of plant and machinery is $12 000. The total cost of the plant and machinery is $100 000 (50 000 + 30 000 + 20 000).

The cost of plant and machinery in the moulding department is $50 000, so the calculation for moulding is:

$$\frac{\$12\,000}{\$100\,000} \times \$50\,000 = \$6\,000$$

[3] Check that the totals across the bottom of any table always add up, i.e. $43 000 + $21 100 + $16 900 = $81 000. This is important, as a mistake at this stage will affect the rest of the calculation.

b Using the figures from part **a**, it is now possible to calculate the total cost per cost centre including direct expenditure:

Expense	Total	Moulding	Painting	Packaging
	$	$	$	$
Direct costs:				
Materials	66 000	50 000	10 000	6 000
Labour	140 000	80 000	40 000	20 000
Total direct cost	206 000	130 000	50 000	26 000
Apportionment of overhead	81 000	43 000	21 100	16 900
Total cost per cost centre	287 000	173 000	71 100	42 900

TIP

When calculating the overheads apportioned to each department, the answer is unlikely to come out as a round figure in every case. Round the figures up or down, but always make sure the totals for each department add across to the overall total for the expense.

ACTIVITY 33.1

Lively Limited manufactures a single product which passes through two stages of production: machining and assembly.

Forecast expenditure for the year ended 31 December 2021 is as follows:

	Machining	Assembly
	$000	$000
Direct materials:	80	10
Direct labour	100	40
Indirect labour	12	5

CONTINUED

		$000
Factory expenses:	Heating and lighting	60
	Maintenance	40
	Insurance	20
Plant and machinery:	Depreciation	80
	Repairs	28

Additional information

1   The machining department has a floor area of 400 square metres and the assembly department has a floor area of 200 square metres.

2   Plant and machinery at cost is $60 000 for the machining department and $10 000 for assembly.

Required

a   Calculate the total overhead cost for each department using suitable bases for apportionment.

b   Calculate the total cost of production for each department.

Apportionment of service cost centre overheads to production cost centres

The costs of running service departments that support production, such as canteens or human resources departments, are also overheads that must be included in the total cost of goods produced. These service costs must be apportioned to the production departments on suitable bases.

Examples of suitable bases of apportionment	
Service cost centre	Basis of apportionment
Stores	Number or value of inventory orders
Staff canteen	Number of people
Building maintenance	Area occupied
Plant and machinery maintenance	Number or value of machines

There are a number of ways of apportioning service cost centre overheads to production cost centres. The simplest and quickest way is the elimination method.

When using the elimination method, firstly, the costs from one of the service departments are apportioned to the other cost centres. That service department cost centre is then eliminated from future apportionments.

Secondly, the costs from the next service department must be apportioned to the remaining cost centres. That service department cost centre is then eliminated from future apportionments.

If there are more than two service cost centres, the process is repeated until the last service cost centre is apportioned to the production cost centres.

WORKED EXAMPLE 2

XYZ Limited has two production departments (assembly and finishing) and two service departments (canteen and maintenance) for which the following information is available:

	Assembly	Finishing	Canteen	Maintenance
No. of machines	200	100	50	–
No. of staff	40	20	10	5
Overheads ($000)	100	60	30	30

Required

Apportion the two service departments' overheads to the production departments using appropriate bases.

Answer

This business has two service cost centres. The costs of the two service department cost centres are apportioned to the other cost centres as follows.

	Assembly	Finishing	Canteen	Maintenance
	$	$	$	$
Overheads	100 000	60 000	30 000	30 000
First apportionment*	17 143 [1]	8 571	4 286	(30 000)
Second apportionment**	22 857 [3]	11 429	(34 286) [2]	–
	140 000	80 000	–	–

*Based on 350 machines.

**Based on 60 staff (40 + 20), the number of staff in each *production* cost centre.

Notes:

[1]   The total costs allocated to the maintenance department is $30 000. The total number of machines is 350 (200 + 100 + 50). Thus, the costs to apportion to the assembly department is:

$$\frac{\$30\,000}{350} \times 200 = \$17\,143$$

[2]   As the canteen does some work for the maintenance department (provides food for the workers of that department), some of the overheads of the maintenance department are apportioned to the canteen. As a result, the total costs of the canteen now increase from $30 000 to $34 286. It is important to remember to add this before apportioning the costs of the canteen.

[3]   Similarly, the costs of the canteen can now be apportioned. This is based on the number of staff.

The canteen costs apportioned to the assembly department is:

$$\frac{\$34\,286 \times 40}{60} = \$22\,857$$

ACTIVITY 33.2

Yums Limited has two production departments: bakery and packaging. It also has two service departments: stores and canteen. The following information is provided.

	Bakery	Packaging	Canteen	Stores
Overheads ($000)	120	80	40	10
No. of staff	30	20	10	5
No. of stores requisitions	80	20	40	–

Required

Apportion the service department overheads to the production departments using appropriate bases.

REFLECTION

When answering Activity 33.2, how did you decide the appropriate bases to use? Were they different for each service cost centre? If so, why? If you could have had any further information, were there any other bases that might have been suitable? Why is it necessary to apportion the service department overheads to the production departments? Discuss your answers with another learner to see whether you agree.

33.3 Absorption of overheads into cost units

Once overheads have been apportioned to specific cost centres, the next step is to calculate the **overhead absorption rate (OAR)** for each cost centre that can then be used to calculate the amount of overhead to be absorbed by each cost unit.

OARs are calculated for future periods. They can be used to decide future selling prices for the product(s). Calculations are based on planned volumes of output and budgeted or forecast overhead expenditure.

The amount of overhead absorbed by a cost unit can be calculated in a number of different ways. Methods include the following:

1 Units of output method

2 Direct labour hours method

3 Machine hours method.

Units of output method

This method is most suitable for a business that produces one product only.

The overhead absorption rate formula is:

$$\frac{\text{Budgeted overheads}}{\text{Budgeted number of units}}$$

The result will be an OAR per unit.

KEY TERM

overhead absorption rate (OAR): the rate at which overheads apporticned to a cost centre are charged to the cost unit passing through it.

WORKED EXAMPLE 3

A magazine publisher produces one type of magazine only. The budgeted output for September is 30 000 copies of the magazine. The publisher has the following budgeted costs:

Overheads $36 000 per month

Direct materials $1.10 per magazine

Direct labour $0.80 per magazine

Required

a   Calculate the amount of overhead absorbed by each unit of production.

b   Calculate the budgeted unit cost for one magazine.

Answer

a   The unit overhead absorption rate = $\dfrac{\$36\,000}{30\,000} \times = \$1.20$ per magazine

This is the amount of overhead absorbed by each unit of production.

b   The cost per unit =

Direct materials	$1.10
Direct labour	$0.80
Total direct costs	$1.90
Overhead absorbed	$1.20
Total cost per magazine	$3.10

The budgeted unit cost of each magazine is $3.10.

Direct labour overhead absorption rate method

This method can be used by a business that produces more than one product.

This method should be used where a cost centre is labour intensive. A cost centre is labour intensive when it relies more heavily on labour than machinery and the labour cost is greater than the cost of using machinery.

The direct labour hours overhead absorption rate formula is:

$$\frac{\text{Budgeted overheads}}{\text{Budgeted direct labour hours}}$$

The result will be an OAR per direct labour hour.

WORKED EXAMPLE 4

Softy Ltd makes two products: cushions and pillows. The manufacturing of both products are labour intensive. The budgeted output for September is as follows:

Cushions: 10 000 units

Pillows: 6 000 units

Each cushion requires $1\frac{1}{2}$ direct labour hours to make, and each pillow requires $\frac{3}{4}$ direct labour hours to make.

CONTINUED

The Softy Ltd has budgeted overheads of $58 500 per month and the following budgeted unit costs for September:

	Cushions	Pillows
Direct materials	$1.30	$1.50
Direct labour	$1.60	$1.70

Required

a   Calculate the direct labour hour overhead absorption rate.

b   Calculate the amount of overhead absorbed by *each* cushion and *each* pillow.

c   Calculate the total amount of overhead absorbed by all the cushions and by all the pillows.

d   Calculate the unit cost for each product.

Answer

a   The total number of direct labour hours required to produce 10 000 cushions and 6 000 pillows is:
$$\left(10\,000 \times 1\tfrac{1}{2}\right) + \left(6\,000 \times \tfrac{3}{4}\right) = 19\,500 \text{ hours}$$

If Softy Ltd's budgeted overheads for September are $58 500, the overhead absorption rate is:
$$\frac{\$58\,500}{19\,500} \times \$3 \text{ per direct labour hour}$$

b   The overhead absorbed per unit is:

i   for one cushion: $\$3 \times 1\tfrac{1}{2} = \$4.50$

ii   for one pillow: $\$3 \times \tfrac{3}{4} = \$2.25$

c   The total overhead is fully absorbed as follows:

	$
Cushions: 10 000 × $4.50	45 000
Pillows: 6 000 × $2.25	13 500
Total overhead absorbed	58 500

d

	Cushions	Pillows
Direct materials	$1.30	$1.50
Direct labour	$1.60	$1.70
Total direct costs	$2.90	$3.20
Overhead absorbed	$4.50	$2.25
Unit cost	$7.40	$5.45

ACTIVITY 33.3

A business manufactures two products: A and B. The number of direct labour hours required for each unit is: A 1.5 hours; B 0.6 hours.

In November, the company plans to produce 5 000 of product A and 6 000 of product B. The estimated overhead expenditure for November is $130 000.

Required

a Calculate the direct labour overhead absorption rate per unit of:

   i product A

   ii product B.

b Show how the overhead for November is absorbed by the planned production for the month.

Machine hour overhead absorption rate method

This method can also be used by a business that produces more than one product. This method should be used where a cost centre is capital intensive. A cost centre is capital intensive when it relies more heavily on machinery than labour and the cost of using machinery is greater than the labour cost.

The machine hours overhead absorption rate formula is:

$$\frac{\text{Budgeted overheads}}{\text{Budgeted machine hours}}$$

The result will be an OAR per machine hour.

WORKED EXAMPLE 5

Hussain's business has six machines that are used eight hours each day in a five-day working week.

The budgeted overheads for a 12-week period are $41 760.

Required

Calculate the machine hours OAR.

Answer

The number of machine hours in a 12-week period is 2 880 (6 machines × 8 hours per day × 5 days × 12 weeks) machine hours.

Therefore, the machine hour absorption rate is:

$$\frac{\$41\,760}{2\,880} = \$14.50 \text{ per machine hour}$$

Worked example 6 is a detailed example of the absorption of overheads with OARs for more than one cost centre.

WORKED EXAMPLE 6

Shirtzy Limited manufactures two styles of shirt called Stripy and Spotty. Each requires processing in the company's two production cost centres: colouring and stitching.

The following information is available from the company's budget for the next month:

Production departments	Colouring	Stitching
Budgeted overheads	$32 000	$28 000
Budgeted machine hours	16 000	6 000
Budgeted direct labour hours	4 000	8 000

Budgeted machine and labour hours:

	Product Stripy	Product Spotty
Machine hours per unit for colouring	3	2.5
Direct labour hours per unit for stitching	2	3.6

Budgeted direct costs per unit:

	Stripy ($)	Spotty ($)
Direct materials	3.00	3.20
Direct labour	4.00	4.50

Required

a Choose the most suitable overhead absorption rate base for each cost centre.

b Calculate the overhead absorption rate for each cost centre.

c Calculate the amount of overhead absorbed by each style of shirt.

d Calculate the unit cost for each product.

Answer

a The colouring department (cost centre) is machine intensive because it uses more machine hours than labour hours. The stitching department (cost centre) is labour intensive because it uses more labour hours than machine hours.

b The OARs are:

$$\text{Colouring OAR:} \frac{\$22\,000}{16\,000} = \$2 \text{ per machine hour}$$

$$\text{Stitching OAR:} \frac{\$28\,000}{8\,000} = \$3.50 \text{ per direct labour hour}$$

c Using the appropriate overhead absorption rate for each production department calculated in part b, the overheads absorbed by each product can be calculated as follows.

OAR per unit	Colouring	Stitching	Overhead absorbed per unit
Stripy	($2 × 3) = $6[1]	($3.50 × 2) = $7	$13
Spotty	($2 × 2.5) = $5	($3.50 × 3.6) = $12.60[2]	$17.60[3]

TIP

Often both direct labour and machine hours are given for one cost centre. Always choose the higher figure as your OAR base. For example, if direct labour hours are forecast to be 10 000 and machine hours to be 90 000, choose machine hours OAR.

CONTINUED

[1]   Each stripy shirt requires three machine hours in the colouring department. Thus, the total overheads that will be charged to each stripy shirt as it passes through that department is three machine hours × $2 per machine hour = $6.

[2]   Each spotty shirt requires 3.6 direct labour hours when it is being worked on in the stitching department.

The overhead that will be charged to each spotty shirt as it is worked on in that department is:

3.6 direct labour hours × $3.50 per hour = $12.60

[3]   The total overhead charged or absorbed by each product as it passes through the two departments is:

Stripy shirt $6 + $7 = $13

Spotty shirt $5 + $12.60 = $17.60

d   The unit cost is calculated by adding the overhead cost of each product to its direct materials and direct labour costs.

Total cost per unit	Stripy	Spotty
	$	$
Direct materials	3.00	3.20
Direct labour	4.00	4.50
Overhead	13.00	17.60
Total unit cost	20.00	25.30

Note: the unit cost calculated is a factory cost as nothing has been added to cover other overheads, such as selling and distribution, administrative or finance costs. Some businesses will also add a percentage to the factory cost to contribute towards covering these other overheads.

33.4 Under- and over-absorption of overheads

Overhead absorption rates are calculated on planned levels of production and budgeted overhead expenditure. It is likely that the actual volume of goods produced and the actual overhead expenditure will differ from the forecasts. The result will be that overhead expenditure will be either under-absorbed or over-absorbed.

Under-absorption occurs when:

*   actual expenditure is higher than budgeted expenditure

*   and/or the actual production level is less than the planned level. In this case, not enough overhead has been charged to production.

Over-absorption occurs when:

*   actual expenditure is lower than budgeted expenditure

*   and/or the actual production level is more than the planned level. In this case, too much overhead has been charged to production.

Over- or under-recovery needs to be monitored over time because it impacts on the profit of a business.

KEY TERMS

over-absorption: if production is more than planned or expenditure is less than budgeted, too much overhead will be charged to production, i.e. there is an over-absorption of overheads.

under-absorption: where production is less than planned or expenditure is more than budgeted, not enough overhead will be charged to production, i.e. there is an under-absorption of overheads.

It is now possible to see whether the total budgeted production level will recover the total budgeted overhead.

WORKED EXAMPLE 7

A business uses direct labour hours to calculate its overhead absorption rate. It has the following information for January 2022:

Budgeted labour hours	1 000
Actual labour hours	950
Budgeted overheads	$20 000
Actual overheads	$17 000

Required

Calculate the amount of overhead over- or under-absorbed.

Answer

Step 1: Calculate the OAR (**note:** this is based on the budgeted figures).

$$\frac{\$20\,000}{1\,000} = \$20 \text{ per direct labour hour}$$

Step 2: Calculate the amount of overhead recovered.

Actual labour hours × OAR

950 × $20 = $19 000

Step 3: Calculate the under-/over-absorption.

Overhead recovered – Actual overheads

$19 000 – $17 000 = $2 000 over-recovery of overheads (over-absorption)

If the overheads recovered are less than actual overheads, there is under-absorption.

If overheads recovered are greater than actual overheads, there is over-absorption.

> **TIP**
>
> The calculation of overhead recovered is the actual direct labour hours × OAR, where the OAR is calculated from the *budgeted* figures. A common mistake is to calculate the OAR based on *actual* figures and use that to calculate over- or under-absorption.
>
> It is important to clearly identify over- or under-absorption. If actual overheads are greater than overhead recovered, there is under-absorption and vice versa for over-absorption.

33.5 Using absorption costing to decide selling price

Once the unit cost has been calculated, it is possible to add an element of profit to arrive at a possible selling price for each product. The addition of something for profit is designed to cover all other overheads incurred by the business and leave some profit for the business.

WORKED EXAMPLE 8

Jasper produces a single product. The factory cost of each unit has been calculated as $130. Jasper always marks up the cost of an order by 40% to calculate the selling price.

Required

Calculate the selling price of Jasper's product.

Answer

Cost per unit	$130
Mark-up (40% of $130)	$52
Selling price	$182

> **WORKED EXAMPLE 9**

Jasmine's business makes picture frames. The factory cost of each unit is \$20. Jasmine always aims to earn a gross profit margin of 50% on each unit.

Required

Calculate the selling price of each picture frame.

Answer

$$\text{Gross profit margin} = \frac{\text{Gross profit per unit}}{\text{Selling price}} \times 100$$

Selling price = cost + gross profit per unit

Therefore

$$\text{Selling price} = \$20 + \left(\frac{50}{100} \times \text{selling price} \right)$$

$$\text{Selling price} = \frac{\$20}{0.5}$$

Selling price = \$40

> **TIP**
>
> Take care to note whether any selling price calculation is based on mark-up or profit margin. Mark-up is expressed as a fraction of cost while margin is expressed as a fraction of the selling price or revenue (see Chapter 17).

KEY CONCEPT LINK

Planning and control: Management accounting is used to plan and control the finances of a business. Absorption costing is a management accounting tool that is used to calculate the unit cost. It provides important information that enables management to make more informed decisions about possible selling prices.

33.6 The usefulness of absorption costing

Absorption costing is a useful method of calculating the unit cost. As well as using the unit cost as a basis to set selling prices, the unit cost can also be used by management to inform many decisions about costs such as whether to cut costs or spend money.

However, managers must also consider non-financial factors when making such decisions. Non-financial factors can be many and varied, and will depend on the circumstances in which the business finds itself. A business's relationship with its customers or the actions of competitors may affect the selling price that a business chooses, while the skills and experience of employees may affect decisions to cut staff costs.

In Worked example 9, absorption costing indicated that Jasmine should charge \$40 for each picture frame. However, she may have non-financial reasons for charging different prices to some or all of her customers. She may choose to give a discount to friends and family, or to reduce prices if a new competitor is also selling at a lower price.

The main benefits and limitations of using absorption costing are now shown. Some of these are considered further in later chapters of this book.

Benefits of absorption costing	Limitations of absorption costing
• Absorption costing is useful for long-term decisions such as selling prices because the fixed costs of a business must be covered if it is to be profitable.	• The bases of apportionment are often generalised. Activity-based costing can be a more realistic method (see Chapter 36).
• Inventory can be valued using absorption costing and so can be used when preparing a business's financial statements.	• Under-absorption and over-absorption of overheads can arise. This impacts on the accuracy of the profits reported.
• Absorption costing is straightforward to calculate where there is only one product. It is also more straightforward to calculate than activity-based costing (see Chapter 36).	• Other costing methods are more useful for short-term decision making (see Chapter 35).

Information used in absorption costing is based on planned or budgeted information about the future rather than historic figures. This is necessary so that the business can use the information to make decisions such as what selling prices to charge. However, using budgeted information means that numbers used are not likely to be wholly accurate and are subject to change over time. As a result, costing information needs to be regularly updated.

The next three chapters will consider alternative methods of costing that are more appropriate for some pricing and other business decisions.

THINK LIKE AN ACCOUNTANT

Making informed choices

Management accounting is all about giving managers the financial information they need to be able to make decisions that are good for the business. It's so important that some larger businesses will have specific departments in the organisation dedicated solely to cost and management accounting. Calculating the unit cost can help managers to decide a suitable selling price for a product or even whether to continue to manufacture a product at all.

We all make choices. Some choices may be trivial: what shall we eat for dinner; should I buy chocolate or sweets today? Other choices may be hugely important to us: do I want to have children; should I buy this house? However important the decision, if we have useful information about the options that we have, then we are more likely to make good choices.

Think of a situation in which you have had to carry out some research before you made a decision that has affected your life. How did you find out the information you needed? Were there any drawbacks or difficulties in obtaining the information you needed? Do you think that your research helped you make a better decision?

Figure 33.2: The more information we have, the more likely we are to make better informed choices.

EXAM-STYLE QUESTIONS

1 A business with a single product has the following information available:

	$ per unit
Direct materials	18
Direct labour	20

Two hours of direct labour go into making each unit. Factory overheads are absorbed at $4 per direct labour hour. The company requires a selling price per unit to achieve a 50% mark-up.

What is the selling price per unit?

  A $42   **B** $46   **C** $66   **D** $69   [1]

2 A business provides the following information:

Budgeted machine hours	11 000
Actual machine hours	10 000
Budgeted overhead expenditure	$165 000
Actual overhead expenditure	$159 500

What is the overhead absorption rate based on machine hours?

  A $14.50   **B** $15.00   **C** $15.95   **D** $16.50   [1]

3 A business provides the following information:

Actual machine hours	100
Actual overhead expenditure	$19 000
Budgeted machine hours	110
Budgeted overhead expenditure	$18 500

Which of the following correctly describes the overhead absorbed?

	Under-absorbed	Over-absorbed
A	$1 727	
B		$1 727
C	$2 182	
D		$2 182

  [1]

4 A manufacturer produces a single product. It has two production departments (assembly and finishing) and one service department (canteen) for which the following budgeted information is available:

	Assembly	Finishing	Canteen
No. of staff	40	20	10
Overheads ($000)	120	260	40
Machine hours	6 000	4 000	–
Labour hours	5 000	10 000	–

Budgeted direct costs per unit:

	$
Direct materials	5
Direct labour	7

The canteen overheads are apportioned to the production cost centres on the number of staff per department.

CONTINUED

Required

a   Explain the difference between overhead allocation and overhead apportionment. [4]

b   Apportion the canteen overheads to the production departments. [6]

c   Choose the most suitable overhead absorption rate for each production cost centre. Give reasons for your chosen bases. [4]

d   Calculate the overhead absorption rate for each production cost centre. [4]

e   It takes two hours to assemble a product and one hour to finish a product.
Calculate the total amount of overhead absorbed by each product. [4]

f   Calculate the unit cost. [4]

g   Orders have a mark-up of 40%. Calculate the budgeted selling price of a single unit of product. [4]

SELF-EVALUATION CHECKLIST

After studying this chapter, complete a table like this:

You should be able to:	Needs more work	Almost there	Ready to move on
Describe the absorption costing method for calculating the cost of making one unit of a product, ensuring you can define cost units and cost centres.			
Allocate and apportion overheads into cost centres, then use appropriate overhead absorption rates to calculate the unit cost.			
Analyse under-absorption and over-absorption of overheads, remembering that if actual overheads are greater than overheads recovered then there is under-absorption and vice versa for over-absorption.			
Use absorption cost data to support selling price decisions, as it is possible to add an element of profit to the unit cost to arrive at a selling price for a product.			
Evaluate the usefulness of using absorption costing, taking care to cover both the benefits and the limitations.			

> Chapter 34

Unit, job and batch costing

This chapter covers part of syllabus section AS Level 2.2

LEARNING INTENTIONS

In this chapter you will learn how to:

- assess the difference between continuous and specific order operations
- apply unit costing, job and batch costing methods
- apply unit, job or batch costing principles to manufacturing and service businesses
- prepare costing statements that can be used as a basis for management decisions.

ACCOUNTING IN CONTEXT

Pictures and pricing

Zac runs a profitable photography business, started six years ago. He used his savings and took out a loan that allowed him to buy the specialist camera, lighting and other equipment that he needed to operate. He now regularly travels within a 100-mile radius of his home to take photographs at weddings and other events.

Apart from the cost of albums, prints and USB sticks, Zac has few direct material costs. His biggest cost is direct labour. This includes his own time preparing for events, the event itself and post-production where he edits the photos and produces albums. A six-hour wedding can take Zac about 20 hours of his time.

He runs a website where he promotes his business and gives potential customers information about his services and pricing. When setting prices for each photoshoot, Zac aims to cover his costs including at least $40 per hour for his time. He considers other factors, such as competitor prices, before making a final decision on the price he will quote to a customer.

Figure 34.1: Zac runs a profitable photography business, started six years ago.

Discuss in a pair or a group:

- Why might Zac's business have few direct material costs? Give examples of other businesses that may have few direct material costs.

- What overheads is Zac's business likely to have?

- Do you know what a quote is? If not, research this term. Why is it important to know the cost of a job before providing a quote?

- In addition to cost, why might a business consider other factors before making pricing decisions?

34.1 Continuous and specific order operations

Costing systems can be applied to different types of business including:

- public or privately owned organisations

- manufacturers of goods such as motor cars or breakfast cereals

- providers of services such as hospitals, hotels or accountants.

Each type of business must choose a costing system that suits its particular operation; no one system will serve every type of business.

The operations of a business may be classified as either **continuous** or **specific order**. Continuous (or process) operations are typically those in which a single type of good is produced and the cost units are identical. Production may involve a sequence of continuous or repetitive operations. Examples include oil refining, production of mineral water and the manufacture of goods on an assembly line such as phones, cans of food and plastic toys.

Continuous operations involve a product passing through a number of processes or different operations. For example, when making steel, the raw material will pass through a furnace, then be rolled out into sheets of metal and then cut to size. The final product would probably then be packed before being sent to customers.

Specific order operations are those that are performed in response to special orders received from customers and may be classified according to whether the operations consist of individual jobs, or the production of batches of identical units for a customer.

34.2 Unit costing

Some businesses have continuous operations such as a manufacturer with assembly lines producing the same type of biscuit or a water treatment company that improves water quality until its good enough for us to drink.

For these types of business, **unit costing** can be used. A single unit may be a single item, but a manufacturer of large volumes of a single product may find it more convenient to regard a number of items as a single unit. For example, for a company producing hundreds of thousands of packets of breakfast cereal, the unit may be, say, 1 000 packets. Other examples of cost units are a pallet of bricks in brick making (a pallet is a wooden platform on which a given number of bricks is stacked after manufacture), and barrels for the output of oil wells.

> **KEY TERM**
>
> **unit costing:** the costing method to find the cost of a single cost unit.

WORKED EXAMPLE 1

Froth Limited produces a single type of shampoo. The following information is for the business for one year:

Number of bottles of shampoo produced:	50 000
Direct labour	$20 000
Direct materials	$30 000
Indirect expenses	$75 000

Required

Calculate the unit cost of producing one bottle of shampoo.

Answer

The cost per bottle of shampoo is:

$$\frac{\$20\,000 + 30\,000 + 75\,000}{50\,000} = \$2.50 \text{ per unit}$$

All the costs have been added and divided by the number of units produced to find the cost of a single unit.

ACTIVITY 34.1

Slurp Limited manufactures cans of soup. Its cost unit is 1 000 cans of soup. The following information is given:

Number of cans of soup produced	3 500 000
Direct materials	$350 000
Direct labour	$200 000
Overheads	$1 200 000

Required

Calculate the cost of one cost unit of soup.

34.3 Job costing

For a business that receives specific or special orders from customers, **job costing** can be used. Each order becomes a cost unit and can be costed as a separate job. Examples of jobs include repainting a house, repairing a bicycle or servicing a motor vehicle.

A price for the job can be determined once the cost is known. This price can be given to a customer as a quotation (quote) for the job. The customer then decides whether to place the order.

If the job goes ahead, the costs will be recorded on a job card as they are incurred. There is no set format for a job card that all businesses must follow, but each job card should show the costs of a job broken down into direct materials, direct labour, direct expenses where necessary and indirect costs. Each of these can be divided further into separate cost centres if appropriate.

> ### KEY TERM
>
> **job costing:** a costing method that calculates the cost of meeting a specific customer order or job.

WORKED EXAMPLE 2

Table Tops Limited has been asked to quote a price to install a new kitchen in a house at 7 High Street. The following information is available for the job:

The kitchen units and other materials needed are expected to cost $4 000. Two employees will need to work 40 hours each at $20 per hour to install the kitchen.

Overheads are absorbed at a rate of $30 per direct labour hour.

A mark-up of 30% on cost is required for each order.

Required

a   Calculate the price to be quoted.

Answer

a

	Estimated costs
	$
Direct materials	4 000
Direct labour (2 × 40 hours × $20)	1 600
Overhead ($30 × 80 hours)	2 400
Total cost	8 000
Add: Profit (30% of cost)	2 400
Amount of quotation	10 400

Note: the overheads are an indirect cost that probably relate to the cost of, say, running vans that the kitchen fitters work from. There may also be some loose tools, or perhaps they relate to office costs. These costs will be incurred whether or not Table Tops Limited undertakes this order.

Additional information

The quote has been accepted by the customer and the job goes ahead. It is given the job number 76 so that it can be clearly distinguished from other jobs. The actual direct materials cost was $3 600 and the two employees each took 42 hours to complete the work at $20 per hour.

Required

b   Prepare a job card for the kitchen installation.

c   Identify reasons for the difference between estimated and actual profit.

CONTINUED

Answer

b

Job no. 76 Installation of kitchen at 7 High Street	Estimated	Actual
	$	$
Materials	4 000	3 600
Labour	1 600	1 680 [1]
Overhead	2 400	2 520 [2]
Total cost	8 000	7 800
Add: Profit [3]	2 400	2 600
Amount of quotation	10 400	10 400

Notes:

[1] 42 hours × 2 workers × $20 = $1 680

[2] 42 hours × 2 workers × $30 = $2 520

[3] When the job had been completed, the actual costs entered on the job card show that actual cost was $200 ($8 000 − $7 800) less than the estimated cost. The amount of the quotation is the same in the actual and estimated column, therefore the actual profit made is $2 600 instead of $2 400.

c Actual profit is $200 higher than estimated profit. This is because of an underspend of $400 on materials. However, direct labour hours were higher than expected leading to an overspend of $80 on direct labour and there was an overspend of $120 on actual overheads, which are based on direct hours.

Job cards provide useful information about costs that can be used when quoting for similar jobs in the future. They also give managers information to identify which areas have caused an overspend or underspend on the job. Managers can then investigate the causes of this and take corrective action for future jobs.

Classifying costs for each job is one of the advantages of cost accounting over financial accounting to the decision makers of a business. In the financial accounts, the costs for a particular job will be lost in among all the other labour, materials and overhead costs, giving managers more limited opportunities to analyse the cause of any differences or plan for the future.

KEY CONCEPT LINK

Planning and control: Job cards give managers information to control costs by identifying which costs have caused an overspend or underspend on each job. Managers can then investigate the causes of this and take corrective action for future jobs.

ACTIVITY 34.2

Vinay makes suits and other items of clothing, individually tailored for each customer. He has been asked by a customer, Raj, to make an outfit for a special occasion. Vinay estimates that the project will require four hours of his time, which he charges at $80 per hour plus ten hours of his assistant's time, which he charges at $20 per hour. Overheads are recovered at the rate of $25 per labour hour. Material is expected to cost $130 and Vinay aims to set his prices at 30% above the cost of a job.

Required

a   Prepare a statement to show the amount Vinay will charge for this job.

Additional information

The customer has looked at Vinay's quote. He has offered Vinay a fee of $1 100 for the work instead.

Required

b   Advise Vinay whether he should accept the work. Justify your answer.

34.4 Batch costing

Unlike job costing, **batch costing** is used where production involves a number of identical items rather than just one. All the costs incurred are charged to the batch and the cost per unit is found by dividing the cost of the batch by the number of units in the batch.

KEY TERM

batch costing: a costing method to find the ccst of a batch of items produced.

WORKED EXAMPLE 3

Seats Limited receives an order for 500 office chairs at a negotiated price of $40 000 for the batch of 500.

Seats Limited has three production departments for which the following information is given:

Machining:	OAR $30 per machine hour
Finishing:	OAR $20 per direct labour hour
Assembly:	OAR $15 per direct labour hour

The budgeted costs incurred in the production of 500 office chairs were:

Direct materials	$5 000
Direct labour:	
Machining	130 hours at $10 per hour
Finishing	200 hours at $12 per hour
Assembly	100 hours at $11 per hour

160 machine hours were required in the machining department for the batch of chairs.

Seats Limited charges its administration expenses at 30% on the total cost of production.

CONTINUED

Required

a   Calculate the cost of producing the batch.

b   Calculate the profit from producing the batch.

Answer

The process of calculating the cost of the batch is identical to the approach taken in Section 34.3. The batch cost, cost per chair and profit per chair are calculated as follows:

Costs for batch of 500 chairs		
	$	$
Direct materials		5 000
Direct labour:		
Machining (130 × $10)	1 300	
Finishing (200 × $12)	2 400	
Assembly (100 × $11)	1 100	4 800
Prime cost		9 800
Production overheads:[1]		
Machining (160 × $30)	4 800	
Finishing (200 × $20)	4 000	
Assembly (100 × $15)	1 500	10 300
Cost of production		20 100
Add: Administration costs[2]		6 030
a Total cost of batch of 500 chairs		26 130
b Profit		13 870
Price[3]		40 000

Notes:

[1]   The charge for production overheads is based on the number of hours (direct labour or machine) multiplied by the overhead absorption rate.

[2]   ($20 100 × 30%) = $6 030. This is an illustration of a business adding something to the factory cost of production to cover other overheads incurred.

[3]   In this case, the price has been agreed at the outset as $40 000. Having analysed the job costs, the managers can see that they will expect to make a profit of $13 870 if everything goes to plan.

In Worked example 3, we do not know whether or not $13 870 is a satisfactory level of profit for the business. However, analysing in advance in this way will give them scope to think about asking for an increase in the price they will get, or where they can cut back on costs to increase the profit. Once again, we are seeing that costing allows a business to *plan* its future activities.

TIP

Take care to note whether any selling price calculation is based on mark-up or profit margin. Mark-up is expressed as a fraction of cost while margin is expressed as a fraction of the selling price or revenue (see Chapter 17).

ACTIVITY 34.3

Pink Ink Limited has received a request for a quote for 60 boxes of pens. Each box contains 100 pens.

Pink Ink Limited has two production departments for which the following information is given:

Moulding	OAR $5 per direct labour hour
Finishing	OAR $8 per direct labour hour

The budgeted costs incurred in the production of 60 boxes of pens were:

Direct materials	$700
Direct labour:	
Moulding	10 hours at $14 per hour
Finishing	8 hours at $15 per hour

A mark-up on cost of 40% is required for all sales.

Required

a   Calculate the cost of manufacturing the batch of 60 boxes of pens.

b   Calculate the cost of one pen.

c   What price should be quoted for the batch of 60 boxes of pens?

TIP

Unlike financial accounting, with costing there is no set format that must be used. There are some formats presented which may help. When you set out your work, make sure it is clearly labelled and that all your calculations are shown.

REFLECTION

When answering Activity 34.3, how did you decide how to treat the cost of setting up the machinery for the batch? Discuss with another learner the similarities and differences between job and batch costing.

THINK LIKE AN ACCOUNTANT

To quote or not to quote

Price quotations are used regularly in some industries. A potential customer contacts the supplier giving details of what they require and asking for a price. The supplier then decides what price they want to charge. This price is based on cost and allowing for some profit.

As individuals, we request detailed, written quotes from time to time. We might ask a garage for a quote to repair a car before we agree to go ahead with the work; or we may request several quotes for home insurance before we decide which to buy. We should study the quotes received carefully noting the price and exactly what goods or services we will receive before making a final decision on who to buy from.

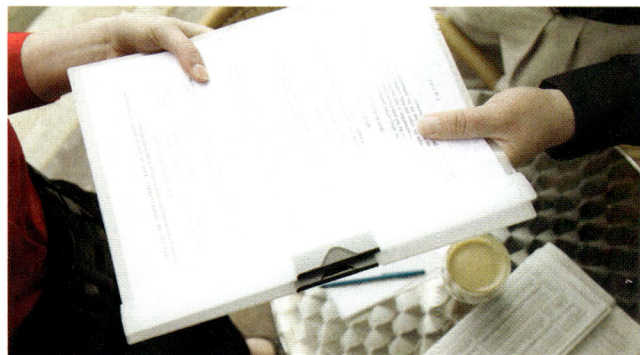

Figure 34.2: Price quotations are used regularly in some industries.

For most day-to-day purchases, individuals do not seek detailed, written quotes. Why don't individuals request quotes for most day-to-day purchases? Why are quotes appropriate for house insurance and car repairs? Can you think of any other examples of when you have requested a quote? Why was it necessary?

EXAM-STYLE QUESTIONS

1 Sam runs a web design business. He thinks it will take 60 hours to complete job 24. Direct labour is $30 per hour for the first 10 hours and $25 per hour for any further hours. Overheads are absorbed at a rate of $10 per direct labour hour. Sam adds 20% to his costs so that his business can earn a profit.

What selling price should be quoted for the job?

A $430

B $2 150

C $2 580

D $2 880 [1]

2 Which of the following should use batch costing?

A   designing a set of ten birthday cards

B   generating electricity

C   oil refining

D   painting the walls of a house [1]

3 Explain the difference between job costing and batch costing. [2]

4 A toy manufacturer has received an order to manufacture 3 000 toy figures. The figures pass through two departments: moulding and finishing. The following budgeted information is given:

	Moulding	Finishing
Direct materials per figure	$2	–
Direct labour rate per hour	$14	$12
Budgeted overhead expenditure	$8 000	$5 000
Budgeted machine hours	130	–
Budgeted direct labour hours for the batch	30	60

A mark-up on cost of 30% is required for all sales.

Required

a   Explain the difference between continuous and specific order operations. [4]

b   Calculate suitable overhead absorption rates for each department. [6]

c   Prepare a costing statement showing the budgeted *total* cost of producing the batch of 3 000 toy figures and the price to be quoted for the batch. [10]

d   Calculate the cost of *one* toy figure. [2]

Additional information

The client is unhappy with the price they have been quoted. They offer to pay $23 000 instead.

Required

e   Advise the toy manufacturer whether or not they should accept a price of $23 000 for the work. Justify your answer by discussing the advantages and disadvantages of accepting or rejecting the order. [8]

SELF-EVALUATION CHECKLIST

After studying this chapter, complete a table like this:

You should be able to:	Needs more work	Almost there	Ready to move on
Assess the difference between continuous and specific order operations, as each type of business must choose a costing system that suits its particular operation; no one system will serve every type of business.			
Apply unit costing (appropriate for businesses that have continuous operations), job and batch costing methods (more appropriate for specific order costing).			
Apply unit, job or batch costing principles to manufacturing and service businesses, building on the work on absorption costing covered in Chapter 33.			
Prepare costing statements that can be used as a basis for management decisions such as how much to quote for a job.			

Chapter 35

Marginal costing

LEARNING INTENTIONS

In this chapter you will learn how to:

- analyse the behaviour of variable, semi-variable, fixed and stepped costs
- calculate contribution, the contribution to sales ratio and marginal costs
- calculate the break-even point
- interpret and analyse break-even information
- evaluate cost-volume-profit data, pricing and other management decisions
- prepare costing and profit statements using marginal costing
- reconcile reported profits using marginal costing and absorption costing
- assess the limitations of cost-volume-profit analysis and marginal costing.

ACCOUNTING IN CONTEXT

Cool hats for hot weather

Leah studied fashion at college and is now planning to start her own business making and selling sunhats that she's designed. Carrying out market research and talking to a small business advisor at her local bank has given her some useful information to support the set-up of the business.

Leah will make the hats herself at home. The main material will be cotton along with accessories such as buttons, bows and badges. She intends to rent a small kiosk in a nearby shopping centre where she can display her hats and will benefit from passing shoppers. She would also like to sell her hats online but is concerned that the delivery costs of posting hats out to her customers might be high and the hats might get damaged in transit.

Figure 35.1: Leah is planning to start her own business making and selling sunhats that she's designed.

Leah is aware that she has limited money available to start the business. Family will support her with most of the initial set-up costs of the business. The bank is then willing to provide a small start-up loan as well. Leah knows that she must make enough in sales revenue to cover the running costs of the business and be able to afford the loan repayments to the bank each month.

The small business advisor has recommended that she uses break-even analysis to help decide selling prices and calculate how many hats she must make and sell to make a profit.

Discuss in a pair or a group:

*   Which costs will increase as Leah makes and sells more hats?

*   Which costs will stay the same even if Leah makes and sells more?

*   The more hats Leah sells, the more profit her business will make. Is this statement always true? Give reasons for your answer.

*   In addition to cost, what other factors might Leah consider before making pricing decisions?

35.1 The behaviour of costs

In management accounting, costs can be classified in different ways depending on how managers want to use the information. In Chapter 33, costs were classified into direct and indirect for use in absorption costing.

This chapter classifies costs into fixed, variable, semi-variable and stepped costs. This classification considers how costs change with different levels of output or sales. This classification is used in marginal costing.

Variable costs

For example, if 1 kg of material is required for one unit of production, 2 kg will be required for two units produced, 10 kg for ten units and so on.

Other direct costs are also deemed to vary in proportion to the number of units produced and may be called **variable costs**. For example, royalties (an amount that has to be paid to the person or company who designed the product) are a direct expense. If a royalty of $0.10

> **KEY TERM**
>
> **variable cost:** a cost which varies in direct proportion to changes in the level of output.

has to be paid for every unit produced, the royalties payable will always be equal to the number of units produced times (×) $0.10.

Direct labour is also considered to be a variable cost. If workers are paid a piece rate according to the amount they produce, then direct wages are proportionate to output and these are variable costs. If direct workers are paid a fixed or basic wage regardless of their output, all wages paid to direct labour will not be in relation to output, but we still treat them as being proportionate to production and thus deem them to be variable costs.

Variable costs can be shown in a graph. For example, if variable costs are $5 per unit then the total variable costs will rise with output as shown in Figure 35.2.

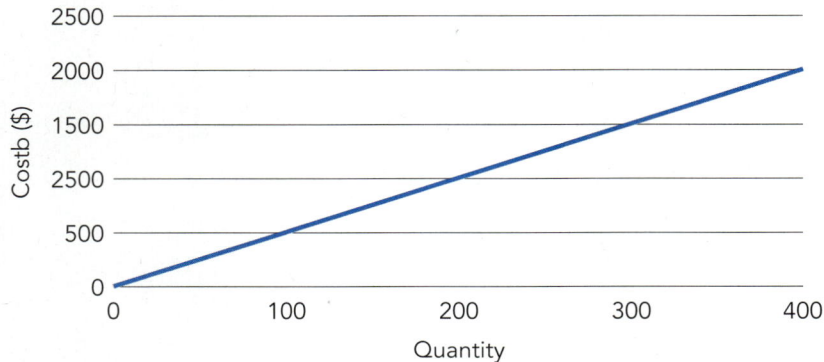

Figure 35.2: Variable costs.

Fixed costs

A **fixed cost** is a cost that remains unchanged within a certain level of activity or output. Rent payable is an example of a fixed cost. It is fixed by a rental agreement and will not change with output. Straight-line depreciation is another fixed expense.

Fixed costs can also be shown in a graph. For example, if fixed costs per month are $500, the graph is shown in Figure 35.3.

KEY TERM

fixed cost: a cost that remains unchanged within a certain level of activity or output.

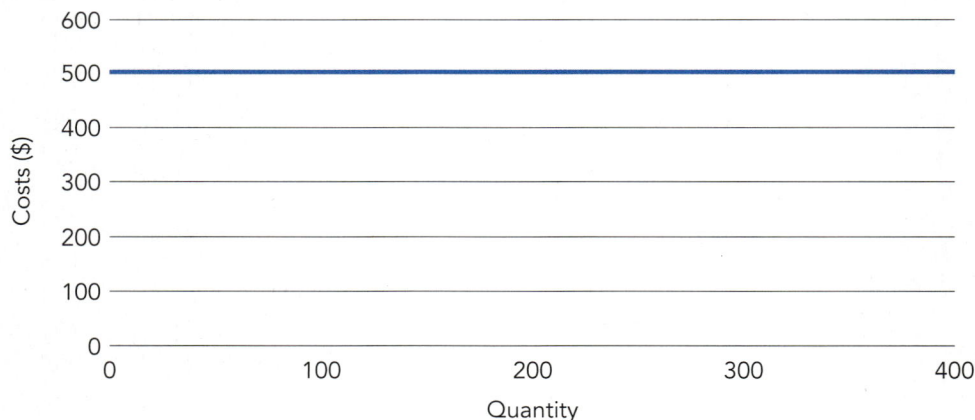

Figure 35.3: Fixed costs.

It is important to remember that even fixed costs are only fixed within certain limits. For example, it may be possible to increase the number of units produced only if additional machines are purchased, and that will increase the total depreciation charge. If production is increased still further and more machines have to be purchased, it may be necessary to lease more factory space and the rent will increase. Fixed costs then become **stepped costs** and may be represented by a chart such as the example in Figure 35.4.

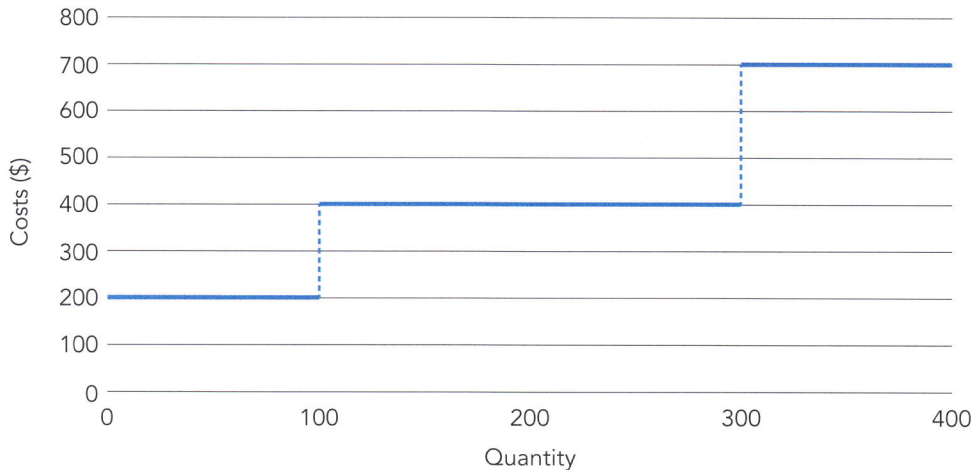

Figure 35.4: Stepped costs.

KEY TERM

stepped costs: fixed costs that are only fixed within certain limits and will increase to a higher level when that limit is reached.

Note: when the output reached 100, it was necessary to buy an additional machine in order to increase production, and the depreciation of machinery charge therefore increased. When output reached 300, a further machine was bought, and it was necessary to rent additional factory space so that both the depreciation charge and the rent increased. Looking at the fixed cost line, it moves upwards at output levels 100 and 300, making the whole line look like steps, hence the term *stepped fixed costs*.

Semi-variable costs

Some costs are classed as **semi-variable costs**. An example of this is a telephone. The fixed element may be the line rental, which must be paid whether any calls are made or not. The variable element would be the call charges, which will increase each time a call is made.

35.2 Marginal cost

For many management decisions it is useful to know the **marginal cost** of a unit of production. Marginal cost is based on the principle that an additional unit of production will result in an increase in the variable costs but not the fixed costs. *Marginal cost of production* is therefore the total of the variable costs of production.

For example, if a business produces 50 units per month and has fixed costs of $1 000 per month and variable costs of $10 per unit then the cost per unit is:

$$\frac{(\$1\,000 + (50 \times \$10)}{50} = \$30 \text{ per unit}$$

However, the marginal cost is only $10 per unit.

Contribution is an important part of marginal costing. It is called contribution because it is the contribution that each unit of production makes towards covering the fixed costs and providing a profit. In total, contribution is the difference between the total revenue and total variable costs.

KEY TERMS

semi-variable cost: a cost that contains an element of both a variable and a fixed cost within it.

marginal cost: the cost of making one extra unit of output.

The **contribution per unit** formula is:

Selling price per unit (SP) – variable costs per unit (VC)

KEY TERM

contribution per unit: the difference between the selling price and variable cost of a unit of output.

WORKED EXAMPLE 1

The business aims to sell its products for $480 each.

Required

Calculate the following:

i   Variable cost per unit

ii Contribution per unit

iii Profit

Answer

	$	$
Selling price		480
Less variable cost per unit:		
Direct labour	20	
Direct materials	100	
Direct expenses	10	
Variable overheads	40	170
Contribution per unit		310
Total contribution (contribution per unit × volume)		31 000
Less fixed overheads		23 000
Profit		8 000

Marginal costing and pricing

The price at which a good may be sold is decided by a number of factors. The need to make a profit is the focus; however, businesses also consider demand from customers and prices that competitors are charging.

Marginal costing can help management to decide on pricing policy. Worked example 1 used the marginal cost of production, but some expenses, such as selling expenses, may also be variable.

An example is salespeople's commission based on the number of units sold. When variable selling expenses are included in marginal cost, the result is the **marginal cost of sales**.

KEY TERM

marginal cost of sales: the variable costs of production and selling of making one extra unit of output.

	$000
Direct materials	100
Direct wages	80
Direct expenses	30
Marginal cost of production	210
Variable selling expenses	15
Marginal cost of sales[1]	225
Other fixed expenses	175
Total cost	400

Note:

[1] Although the selling expenses will only be incurred when the goods are sold, they should be regarded as part of the marginal cost of sales.

Contribution to sales ratio (C/S ratio)

The **contribution to sales ratio (C/S ratio)** is a useful tool for calculating profit at different levels of sales.

For example, using the figures from Worked example 1, the C/S ratio is:

$$\frac{\$310}{\$480} \times 100 = 64.6\%$$

If the sales increase to $60 000, then the total contribution will be $38 760 (60 000 × 64.6%). Assuming fixed costs remain the same at this level of output, the profit will increase to $15 760 ($38 760 − $23 000).

KEY TERM

contribution to sales ratio (C/S ratio): the proportion of sales revenue that contributes towards the fixed costs and profit of a business.

TIP

The contribution to sales (C/S) ratio can be used to calculate the answers to many problems. The use of the C/S ratio avoids the need to spend time calculating marginal cost.

WORKED EXAMPLE 2

A business produces 2 000 units of a product. The following information is available.

	Total ($)
Revenue	140 000
Variable or marginal costs	88 000
Fixed costs	22 000

Required

a Calculate:
   i contribution per unit
   ii profit.
b Calculate the profit or loss at the following levels of output:
   i sales increased to 2 100 units
   ii sales reduced to 1 900 units
   iii sales reduced to 800 units.
c Calculate the contribution to sales ratio.
d Calculate the profit or loss if sales revenue increases to $168 000.

Answer

a

	Total	Per unit
	$	$
Revenue	140 000	70.00
Variable or marginal costs	(88 000)	(44.00)
Contribution (revenue − variable costs)	52 000	26.00
Fixed costs	22 000	(44.00)
Profit (contribution − fixed costs)	30 000	

   i Contribution per unit = $26.
   ii Profit = $30 000.

CONTINUED

b **i** If sales increased to 2 100 units:

The contribution from 2 100 units is $2\,100 \times \$26 = \$54\,600$.

Profit = contribution – fixed costs = $\$(54\,600 - 22\,000) = \$32\,600$.

   ii If sales reduced to 1 900 units:

The contribution from 1 900 units will be $1\,900 \times \$26 = \$49\,400$

Profit = $\$(49\,400 - 22\,000) = \$27\,400$.

   iii If sales reduced to 800 units:

The contribution from 800 units will be $800 \times \$26 = \$20\,800$

Loss = $\$(20\,800 - 22\,000) = \$1\,200$.

c The C/S ratio is:

$$\frac{\$26}{\$70} \times 100 = 37.14\%$$

d In this question we are told the sales revenue instead of the level of output. Therefore, using the C/S ratio:

Total contribution = $\$168\,000 \times 37.14\% = \$62\,400$

Profit = $\$62\,400 - \$22\,000 = \$40\,400$

ACTIVITY 35.1

The marginal cost statement for the production of 4 000 units of a product is as follows.

	$
Selling price	24
Less variable cost per unit	10
Contribution per unit	14
Contribution × volume	56 000
Less fixed costs	30 000
Gross profit	26 000

Required

a Calculate the profit or loss from the sale of:

   i 5 000 units

   ii 2 000 units.

b Calculate the contribution to sales ratio.

c Calculate the profit or loss if sales revenue increases to $132 000.

REFLECTION

When answering Activity 35.1, discuss with another learner what happens to profit as output changes.

35.3 The break-even point

The **break-even point** occurs when total revenue equals total costs. It is particularly useful for managers to know the break-even point of a product when making decisions about pricing and production levels.

The break-even formula is:

$$\frac{\text{Fixed costs}}{\text{Contribution per unit}}$$

This break-even formula calculates the number of units that must be produced and sold before the fixed costs are covered. At the break-even point, total contribution will equal total fixed costs.

If a business produces and sells below its break-even point, then it will make a loss. If a business produces and sells above its break-even point, then it will make a profit and is said to have a **margin of safety**.

The margin of safety formula is:

Sales quantity – break-even quantity

Knowing a business's margin of safety can be useful to managers as it helps them to understand the amount by which output could fall short before the business risks making a loss.

KEY TERMS

break-even point: the point at which a business makes neither profit nor loss. It is the point at which total contribution is equal to total fixed costs.

margin of safety: the difference between budgeted or actual output and the break-even quantity.

TIP

The margin of safety can be calculated using either the actual or budgeted figures depending on what managers are trying to find out.

WORKED EXAMPLE 3

The following information relates to the production of a product:

	$
Selling price per litre	80
Marginal cost per litre	50
Total of fixed costs	87 000

The business currently produces and sells 4 000 litres.

Required

Calculate:

a   the break-even quantity

b   the margin of safety

c   the break-even revenue.

Answer

a   **Step 1**

Calculate the contribution per unit (in this case litres are the units):

The contribution per litre is $(80 − 50) = $30.

Step 2

Divide the fixed costs by the contribution per litre to find the break-even point:

$$\text{Break-even point} = \frac{\$87\,000}{30} = 2\,900 \text{ litres}$$

b   Margin of safety = 4 000 − 2900 = 1 100 litres

CONTINUED

c   The revenue at which the product will break even is 2900 litres × $80 (selling price per unit) = $232 000.

Note: if we had not already calculated the break-even output then the answer to part **c** may also be found by using the contribution to sales ratio.

The contribution to sales ratio is:

Contribution per $ of selling price = $30 ÷ 80 = 37.5%.

This is used to calculate the break-even point in revenue, as follows:

$$\frac{\text{Total fixed costs of } \$87\,000}{\text{Contribution pper } \$ \text{ of selling price } 37.5\% \text{ or } 0.375} = \$232\,000$$

35.4 Break-even charts

A **break-even chart** is prepared by plotting the total budgeted revenue from the sale of various volumes of a product against the total cost of production. The break-even point occurs where the sales line cuts the total cost line and there is neither profit nor loss.

KEY TERM

break-even chart: a diagrammatic representation of the profit or loss to be expected from the sale of a product at various levels of activity.

TIP

It's important that you can interpret a break-even chart, but you are not required to know how to draw a break-even chart.

WORKED EXAMPLE 4

A business manufactures one type of product. A total of 10 000 units are made and sold each month.

The information is shown in the break-even chart in Figure 35.5.

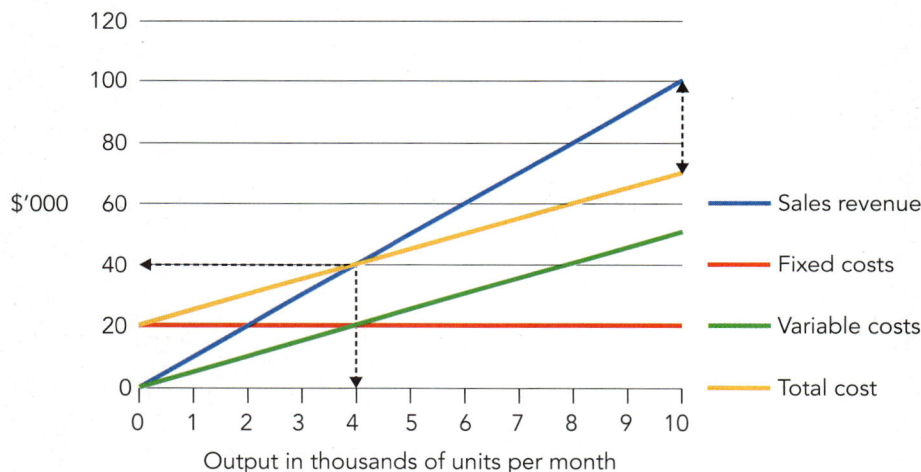

Figure 35.5: Break-even chart.

Required

Use the break-even chart to state the following:

a   break-even quantity

b   break-even revenue

c   profit

d   margin of safety.

> **CONTINUED**

Answer

The break-even point is where the revenue and total costs lines intersect.

a The output at the break-even point is 4000 units.

This can be read from the *x*-axis at the break-even point.

b The revenue at the break-even point is $400000.

This can be read from the *y*-axis at the break-even point.

c At 10000 units, the revenue is $100000 and total cost is $70000. The distance between those two lines shows the profit of $30000 (shown by the purple dotted line on the break-even chart).

d Margin of safety = 10000 − 4000 = 6000 units

This is the difference between the break-even quantity and 10000 units.

The break-even chart can be used to show the effect of a change in any of the variables: fixed costs, variable costs and selling price.

For example, a business has variable costs of $6 per unit and selling price of $8. If fixed costs increase from $500 to $800 the break-even chart will change as shown in Figure 35.6.

The difference between the revenue line and the total cost line *before* the break-even point represents the loss that will be made if the output falls below 400 units. The area *beyond* the break-even point represents profitable levels of sales.

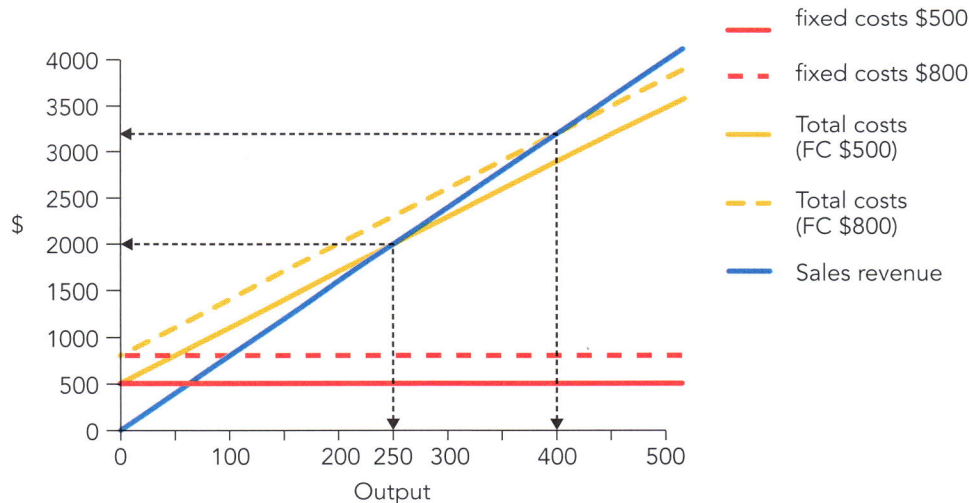

Figure 35.6: Break-even when fixed costs increase.

Total costs will increase by the same amount as the fixed costs. This affects the break-even point, which will occur further to the right of the chart. Therefore, higher fixed costs result in higher break-even points.

CONTINUED

A change in the variable cost per unit will change the angle of the variable cost line. The same is true for a change in selling price.

For example, if the fixed costs remained at $500 but the selling price is increased from $8 to $10 the break-even chart will change as shown in Figure 35.7.

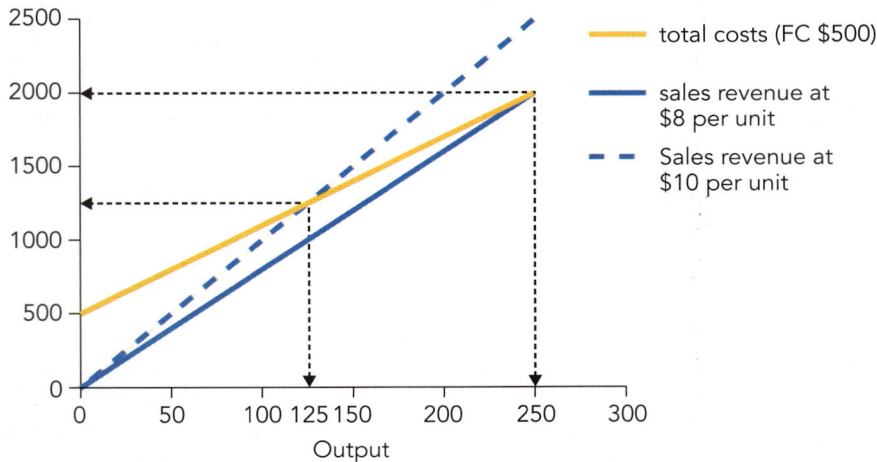

Figure 35.7: Break-even at different selling prices.

An increase in selling price increases the gradient of the revenue line. Cost lines are unaffected but the break-even point moves to the left. This means that less needs to be sold to break even.

Selling price has risen by $2 ($10 – $8) but variable costs have remained the same. Therefore, contribution per unit will also rise by $2.

Profit and break-even points are said to be sensitive to changes in both prices and cost. This aspect will be considered later in Section 35.8.

35.5 Profit/volume charts

Break-even charts may also be drawn to show only the profit or loss at each level of output. The cost and revenue lines are omitted. The break-even chart can be drawn as a **profit/volume chart** instead.

For example, a product with $50000 fixed costs per month, selling price of $400 and variable cost of $100 per unit will have the profit/volume chart as shown in Figure 35.8.

KEY TERM

profit/volume chart: a type of break-even chart that only shows the profit or loss at each level of output.

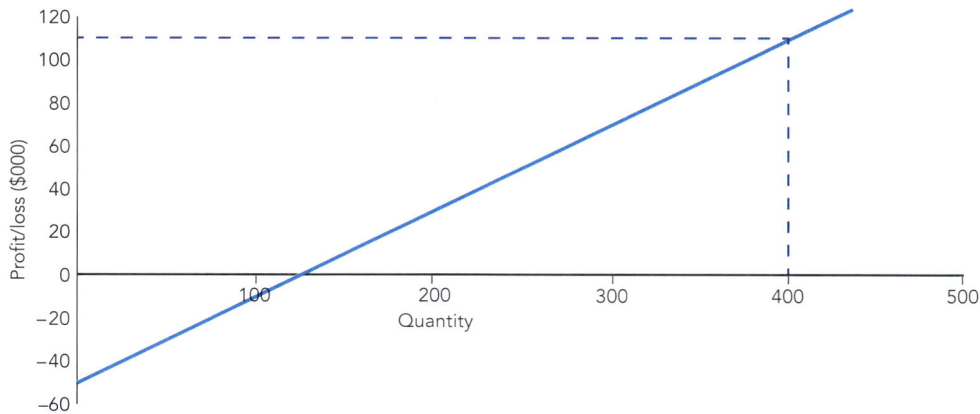

Figure 35.8: Profit/volume chart.

At zero output, the loss equals the total of the fixed costs, $50 000. At 400 units, the profit is equal to $110 000. A straight line joining the two points intersects the output line at the break-even point, which is 125 units.

35.6 The limitations of break-even and profit/volume charts

Break-even charts are useful visual aids for the study of the effect of changes in output, costs and revenues on the break-even point, especially for managers with little accounting knowledge. The charts, however, have their limitations:

- They assume the variable cost per unit is constant at all levels of output. This is not always true in practice. For example, variable costs per unit may fall as output increases if suppliers give bulk discounts.
- Fixed costs do not always stay the same. Some costs may be stepped costs that are only fixed within certain limits.
- Costs may be semi-variable and are not easily classified as fixed or variable. For break-even to work, the fixed and variable elements must be separated and added in with the appropriate fixed or variable figures.
- They assume the selling price is constant at all levels of output. However, for some products more revenue may only be achieved if customers are given discounts from the selling price.
- A break-even or profit/volume chart can only be applied to one product at a time.
- A chart can be time consuming to prepare.
- The charts may mislead people whose accounting knowledge is limited, but trained accountants will know when to make allowances for the charts' limitations.

35.7 Supporting management decision making with marginal costing

Marginal costing focuses on the cost of producing and selling one additional unit. Knowing the marginal cost of a product is useful information for managers that need to make decisions about any of the scenarios shown in Figure 35.9.

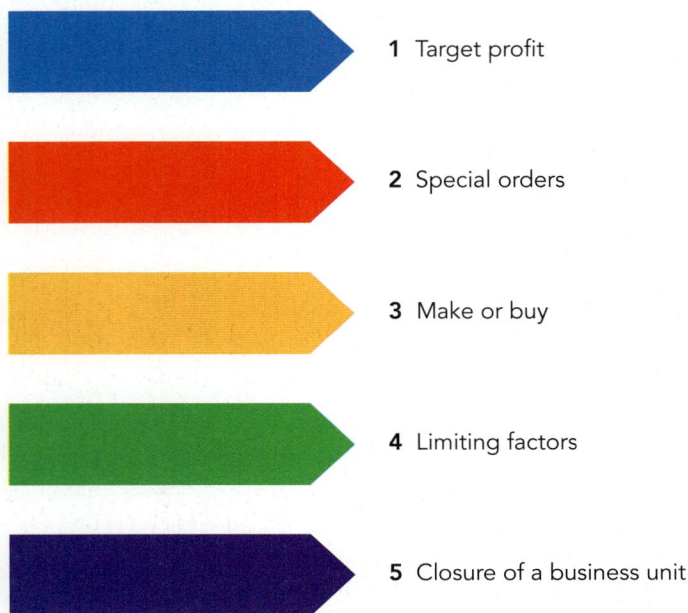

1 Target profit

2 Special orders

3 Make or buy

4 Limiting factors

5 Closure of a business unit

Figure 35.9

KEY CONCEPT LINK

Planning and control: Marginal costing provides managers with financial information to help make decisions and plan for a range of possible scenarios that the business might face. Scenarios can include what to do if a customer offers to pay a low price for goods and what to do if the business has a resource in short supply.

Target profit

1 Target profit

If the managers of a business have an amount of profit that they are aiming to achieve, then marginal costing can be used to calculate the sales quantity needed to achieve this level of profit.

The formula is similar to the break-even formula with the target level of profit added to the fixed costs.

The formula for the target profit output level is:

$$\frac{\text{Fixed costs} + \text{target profit}}{\text{Contribution per unit}}$$

For example, a business has a target profit of $30 000 per year. The selling price of its product is $100, variable costs per unit of $20 and fixed costs of $50 000 per year.

The break-even quantity $= \dfrac{50\,000}{(\$100 - \$20)} = 625$ units per year

Quantity needed to achieve $30 000 profit $= \dfrac{50\,000 + 30\,000}{(\$100 - \$20)} = 1\,000$ units per year

Special orders

2 Special orders

There are occasions when an individual order may be accepted below the normal selling price. This may be considered when there is spare capacity in the factory and other orders are not affected.

Businesses set their selling prices to cover all of their costs including the fixed costs. However, for special orders, the general rule is that the selling price must exceed the marginal cost of production. This will allow the additional order to make a **positive contribution** towards the fixed costs and profit of the business.

Special orders at below the usual selling price can be especially useful in the following circumstances:

- to maintain production and avoid redundancy among a skilled workforce during a period of poor trading
- to promote a new product
- to dispose of inventory that is slow-moving or no longer useful.

KEY TERM

positive contribution: the contribution (selling price – variable costs per unit) is above zero.

WORKED EXAMPLE 5

Light Up Limited makes lamps that it normally sells at $100 each. It currently has spare capacity in the factory.

The following information is available:

	$
Direct material per unit	30
Direct labour per unit	40

CONTINUED

Fixed expenses will not be affected by the additional production.

The following requests have been made by potential customers.

a   500 lamps for which the customer is prepared to pay $90 per lamp

b   2 000 lamps at $60 each.

Required

Should Light Up Limited agree to the special orders?

Answer

Calculate the impact of each option:

a   Order for 500 lamps at $90 each:

- contribution per unit $(90 − 70) = $20
- additional contribution from order: $10 000 (500 units × $20 per unit).

    This order should be accepted as the contribution is positive.

b   Order for 2 000 lamps at $60 each:

- contribution per unit $(60 − 70) = ($10 loss).

The contribution is negative, which would reduce profit, so Light Up Limited should *not* accept the order for 2 000 lamps at $60 each.

The company would make a loss of $20 000 (2 000 units × $10 loss per unit) on the order and so should not accept it. In this case, the marginal cost of sales is greater than the selling price.

> **TIP**
>
> If fixed costs will also change for a special order, remember to take this into account in your calculation.

ACTIVITY 35.2

Sew with Zo Limited normally sells reels of cotton for $1 300 per 1 000 reels of cotton. The following information is given:

	$
Per 1 000 reels of cotton:	
Direct materials	400
Direct labour	600

The company has received orders for:

a   5 000 reels of cotton at $950 per 1 000 reels of cotton

b   3 000 reels of cotton at $1 100 per 1 000 reels of cotton.

The additional production will not require any additional fixed expenses.

Required

Advise which of the two orders, if any, Sew with Zo Limited should accept.

Make or buy decisions

3 Make or buy

A manufacturer may find that it's more profitable to buy goods from another supplier than make the goods itself. This involves a 'make or buy' decision. It may be relevant for goods that are already being produced, or to the introduction of a new product.

The decision will be based mainly on whether the cost of buying the goods from another supplier is more or less than the marginal cost of production.

The principle in this situation is:

- If the marginal cost of production is above the price quoted by the supplier then buy from the supplier.
- If the marginal cost of production is below the price quoted by the supplier then make the good.

Notice that the marginal cost of sales is not relevant to this type of decision, as any variable selling costs will have to be incurred whether the goods are manufactured or purchased.

WORKED EXAMPLE 6

Carvers Limited makes and sells cabinets for which the following information is available:

	$ per cabinet
Selling price	250
Direct materials	100
Direct labour	80
Variable selling expenses	40

Carvers Limited's fixed overheads are $60 000.

Cabinets may be bought from either Company A for $185 per cabinet or Company B for $150 per cabinet.

Required

Should Carvers Limited continue to make the cabinets or buy them from one of the two possible suppliers?

Answer

The fixed overheads and variable selling expenses are ignored as they will have to be incurred anyway and so do not affect the decision.

The marginal cost of production is $(100 + 80) = $180.

Evaluate each option:

- Purchase of the cabinets from Company A: the current marginal cost of production ($180 per unit) is lower than the purchase price ($185 per unit). Accepting this supplier will have the effect of reducing the contribution by $5 per unit.

Therefore, it is better to continue making than buying from Company A.

- Purchase of the cabinets from Company B: the current marginal cost of production ($180 per unit) is higher than the purchase price ($150 per unit). Accepting this supplier will have the effect of increasing the contribution by $30 per unit.

This appears to be the better option because the marginal cost of production is above the price quoted by the supplier. Therefore, Carvers Limited should buy from Company B instead of making it.

Note: information about the fixed costs is not needed to calculate that this option is the better one, assuming that the fixed costs will be incurred regardless of the decision.

Although the calculations should be made to assess whether the business would benefit financially from making or buying the items, managers often need to take non-financial factors into account before deciding which course of action to take.

CONTINUED

Other non-financial factors that a business should consider before finally deciding to stop making and buy from a supplier instead include the following:

- How certain it is that a supplier can be relied on not to increase its prices. Once a business ceases to manufacture a product, it may not be easy to recommence manufacturing if it no longer has its workers and other resources.

- Whether there is a difference in quality between the manufacturer and a possible alternative supplier.

- Whether the supplier is reliable and will deliver the goods promptly.

- Whether the business has an alternative use for the resources that will become free when it ceases to make the goods. Unless it can use the resources profitably to make another product, it will either have to get rid of the resources (labour, machines, etc.) or increase its unproductive costs.

- Whether the manufacturer will lose the services of a skilled and loyal workforce, which may be difficult to replace at a later date when the need arises.

Limiting factors

4 Limiting factors

Limiting factors include:

- a shortage of materials
- a shortage of labour
- a shortage of demand for a product.

When there is a limited resource, a business making several different products should use the limited resources in a way that produces the most profit.

In other decisions, the contribution per unit has been used to make a decision. However, when making the best use of limited resources, the products must be ranked according to the amount of *contribution they make from each unit of the* **scarce resource**. Production will then be planned to ensure that the scarce resource is concentrated on the highest-ranking products.

KEY TERMS

limiting factor: anything that limits the quantity of goods that a business may produce, such as a shortage of labour.

scarce resource: a resource such as labour or materials that has limited availability.

WORKED EXAMPLE 7

Shortage of material

Quip Limited makes three types of specialist equipment: Product A, Product B and Product C. All three products are made from the same raw material. The following information is given for the products and costs:

	Product A	Product B	Product C
Planned production – units	4 000	6 000	8 000
Selling price per unit	$108	$100	$210
Direct materials per unit	4 kg	8 kg	10 kg
Direct labour hours per unit	3	2	6

CONTINUED

Direct materials cost $6 per kg. Direct labour is paid at $20 per hour.

Fixed costs are $200 000.

The material is in short supply and only 120 000 kg can be obtained.

Required

Prepare a production plan, showing how much Quip Limited should produce of each of its products to maximise its profit.

Answer

Step 1

Calculate the marginal cost per unit and the contribution per unit.

	Product A	Product B	Product C
	$	$	$
Selling price per unit	108	100	210
Direct materials per unit	24	48	60
Direct labour per unit	60	40	120
Marginal cost per unit	84	88	180
Contribution per unit	24	12	30
Ranking [1]	2	3	1

Note:

[1] If the products were ranked on the contribution per unit, the order would be 3, 1 and 2. Thus, if there was no restriction on material, the business would make the products in this order.

Step 2

Calculate the contribution per unit of the limited resource. As this business has a shortage of material, we need to calculate contribution per kg of material.

	Product A	Product B	Product C
kg per unit	4	8	10
Contribution per unit	$24	$12	$30
Contribution per kg [1]	$6	$1.50	$3
Ranking [2]	1	3	2

Notes:

[1] The contribution per kg has been calculated by dividing the contribution per unit by the kg per unit. So, for Product A this is $24 ÷ 4 = $6.

[2] The ranking for producing the products is now Product A, Product C and Product B.

Ranking by contribution per kg of the limiting factor (material) rather than contribution per unit leads to a different order of the products.

Step 3

To make the planned production, Quip Limited will require
$(4\,000 \times 4\,\text{kg}) + (6\,000 \times 8\,\text{kg}) + (8\,000 \times 10\,\text{kg}) = 144\,000\,\text{kg}$ of material, if all the planned production was made. However, as only 120 000 kg of material is available, a new production schedule needs to be prepared. The products will now be produced in the order of contribution per kg of raw material.

CONTINUED

The revised plan of production where direct materials is the limiting factor is as follows.

	Units	Direct materials kg	Contribution per unit	Total contribution and profit [3]
			$	$
Product A	4000	16000	24	96000
Product C	8000	80000	30	240000
Product B [1]	3000	24000	12	36000
		120000		372000
Less: fixed costs				(200000)
Profit [2]				172000

Notes:

[1] There will be enough material to produce all the required Product A and Product C. This will use 96000 of the 120000 kg available. This will leave only 24000 kg. Each unit of Product B takes 8 kg. Thus, only 3000 (24000 ÷ 8) of Product B can be made.

[2] The effect of the shortage of materials is to reduce the amount of Product B produced. As Product B has a positive contribution per unit, the expected profit of $172000 is lower than it would be if all of products were produced.

[3] Note the number of units produced is multiplied by the contribution per unit, not the contribution per kg.

Shortage of direct labour hours

The data for the manufacture of Product A, Product B and Product C is as given for the previous worked example, but this time the number of direct labour hours available is limited to 45000. There is no shortage of material.

Required

Prepare a production plan, showing how much Quip Limited should produce of each of its products to maximise its profit.

Answer

The procedure is identical to the shortage of materials, with the exception that this time the contribution per direct labour hour is calculated.

Step 1

Marginal cost per unit and the contribution per unit are the same figures as calculated in Step 1 of Worked example 7 'Shortage of material'.

Step 2

Calculate the contribution per unit of the limited resource. As this business has a shortage of labour, we need to calculate contribution per direct labour hour.

	Product A	Product B	Product C
	$	$	$
Contribution per unit	24	12	30
Direct labour hours per unit	3	2	6
Contribution per direct labour hour	8	6	5
Ranking	1	2	3

CONTINUED

Step 3

To make the planned production, Quip Limited will require (4 000 × 3 hours) + (6 000 × 2 hours) + (8 000 × 6 hours) = 72 000 hours of direct labour, if all the planned production was made.

However, as only 45 000 hours of direct labour is available a new production schedule needs to be prepared. The products will now be produced in the order of contribution per direct labour hour.

A revised plan of production where direct labour hours is the limiting factor is as follows.

	Units	Direct labour hours per unit	Total direct labour hours	Contribution per unit	Contribution
				$	$
Product A	4 000	3	12 000	24	96 000
Product B	6 000	2	12 000	12	72 000
Product C	3 500	6	21 000	30	105 000
			45 000		273 000
Less fixed costs					(200 000)
Profit					73 000

ACTIVITY 35.3

Glimmer and Gleam Limited makes three specialist cleaning products: Burnish, Dazzle and Shine. The maximum production of each product and the budgeted production information for three months is as follows:

	Burnish	Dazzle	Shine
No. of units	2 000	4 000	1 800
Selling price per unit	$4	$7	$6
Direct materials per unit (litres)	2	3	3
Direct labour per unit (hours)	0.1	0.4	0.2

Direct materials cost $0.50 per litre

Direct labour is paid at $10 per hour

Fixed expenses are $10 000.

Glimmer and Gleam Limited has been informed that only 19 400 litres of material is available.

Required

Prepare a revised production budget that will produce the most profit from the available materials.

Closure of a business unit

5 Closure of a business unit

Another topic where marginal costing is important is the decision whether or not to close a business unit. The business unit might be a department, product or other profit centre and its closure is typically being considered because it is not profitable. Managers will need to consider whether the product or department makes a positive contribution towards the fixed costs and profit of the business.

WORKED EXAMPLE 8

Podmore Limited makes three products. The following data is available:

	Product X	Product Y	Product Z
Per unit:	$	$	$
Selling price	30	19	20
Direct materials	12	6	10
Direct labour	12	10	9
Fixed costs	3	2	2
Profit	3	1	(1)

Note: fixed costs are absorbed on the basis of direct labour hours.

For the next year, Podmore Limited is forecasting the following sales volumes:

Product X	10 000 units
Product Y	8 000 units
Product Z	5 000 units

The directors are concerned that product Z is not profitable and are considering whether or not to stop producing it.

Required

a   Prepare a forecast profit statement showing the expected contribution and profit of the business if product Z is continued.

b   Prepare a forecast profit statement showing the expected contribution and profit of the business if product Z is discontinued.

c   Advise the directors on whether the business should continue to produce Product Z.

Answer

First, calculate the contribution per unit:

	Product X	Product Y	Product Z
Per unit:	$	$	$
Selling price	30	19	20
Direct materials	12	6	10
Direct labour	12	10	9
Contribution	6	3	1

Note: product Z is making a unit loss but a positive contribution.

CONTINUED

a

	Units	Contribution per unit	Total contribution and profit
		$	$
Product X	10 000	6	60 000
Product Y	8 000	3	24 000
Product Z	5 000	1	5 000
			89 000
Less: fixed costs [1]			(56 000)
Expected profit			33 000

Note:

[1]	Product X	$3 × 10 000	=	30 000
	Product Y	$2 × 8 000	=	16 000
	Product Z	$2 × 5 000	=	10 000
				$56 000

b

Forecast profit statement if product Z is discontinued			
	Units	Contribution per unit	Total contribution and profit
		$	$
Product X	10 000	6	60 000
Product Y	8 000	3	24 000
			84 000
Less: fixed costs			(56 000)
Expected profit			28 000

c Podmore Limited should continue to produce Product Z.

Despite making a loss per unit, if the company ceased producing product Z they would actually make $5 000 less profit overall. This reduction in profit would be because the business would no longer have the $5 000 positive contribution that product Z creates. Therefore, the two remaining products have to cover all the fixed costs.

It may also be that people who buy product Z also buy other products, and if it was no longer produced, sales of those may suffer as well, reducing the profit even further.

If the directors could save at least $5 000 of fixed costs by ceasing the production of product Z then it will be worth considering.

35.8 Reported profits using marginal costing and absorption costing

Chapter 32 showed that any difference in valuing closing inventory will produce different profit figures. Therefore, the two methods of costing: marginal and absorption, will also produce different profits, as the closing inventory is valued in two different ways.

WORKED EXAMPLE 10

A company produces a single product. The results for the last month are as follows:

Quantity produced	400
Sales quantity	370
Selling price per unit	$100
Variable costs per unit	$60
Fixed overheads for the period	$3 000

Required

a Prepare a costing statement showing the gross profit for last month if the closing inventory is valued using marginal costing.

b Prepare a costing statement showing the gross profit for last month if the closing inventory is valued using absorption costing.

c Prepare a statement reconciling the profit using marginal costing and absorption costing.

Answer

a

Profit using marginal costing		
	$	$
Revenue		37 000
Variable costs	24 000 (400 x 60)	
Less: closing inventory	(1 800) [1]	
		22 200
Total contribution		14 800
Fixed overheads		3 000
Gross profit		11 800

b

Profit using absorption costing		
	$	$
Revenue		37 000
Variable costs	24 000	
Fixed overheads	3 000	
Less: closing inventory	(2 025) [2]	
Cost of sales		(24 975)
Gross profit		12 025

Notes:

[1] Using marginal costing, fixed overheads are not included in the closing inventory figure. Instead they are treated as period costs and written off in full in the month. Therefore, the closing inventory value is: 30 × $60 = $1 800; where 30 units (400 − 370) is the amount of closing inventory and it is valued at the variable cost per unit of $60.

[2] Using absorption costing some of the fixed overheads are included in the closing inventory. Total production cost of $27 000 is divided by the total production of 400 units to arrive at an inventory value per unit of $67.50 per unit. The closing inventory is, therefore, valued at 30 × $67.50 = $2 025.

CONTINUED

c

	$
Gross profit using marginal costing	11 800
Difference between inventory values (2 025 – 1 800)	225
Gross profit using absorption costing	12 025

The difference in gross profit is $225. This is due to the different way that fixed overheads are treated using absorption and marginal costing.

ACTIVITY 35.5

A company produces a single product. The following information is available:

	$
Unit selling price	100
Unit variable costs	40
Fixed costs per month	30 000

Projected sales are 2 000 units for September. The company will produce 2 600 units. There is no inventory at 1 September.

Required

a   Calculate the profit in September if the closing inventory is valued using marginal costing.

b   Calculate the profit in September if the closing inventory is valued using full absorption costing.

35.9 Non-financial factors

Non-financial factors are factors that affect a decision but are difficult to quantify. In this chapter, marginal costing has been used to make a number of decisions. However, it must be recognised that marginal costing only supports the decision making. Managers also need to consider a wider range of non-financial factors before making a final decision.

Possible non-financial factors include the following:

- Customers – a large or important customer might put pressure on a business to provide goods at special (lower) prices. Despite being unprofitable, a business may agree to this in the short-term, in the hope or expectation that the customer will make future purchases at a higher price.

- Human resources – a business may decide to prioritise avoiding staff redundancies. This encourages mangers to accept special orders at low prices or to avoid closing a business unit unless staff can be redeployed to other parts of the business.

- Suppliers – if a business has a strong or long-standing relationship with a supplier then it might prefer not to make a shift from buying to making a product, despite a possible financial gain.

35.10 Benefits and limitations of marginal costing

Using marginal costing rather than absorption costing has both benefits and limitations. These are now discussed.

Benefits of marginal costing	Limitations of marginal costing
• Fixed costs are not included in the cost of production and therefore there is no arbitrary apportionment of fixed costs. • Contribution provides a reliable measure for short-term decision making. • Marginal costing clearly shows the impact on profit of fluctuations in the volume of sales. • Under-absorption and over-absorption of overheads are not a problem as there is no need to calculate an overhead absorption rate. • The marginal costing technique can be used with standard costing (see Chapter 38).	• Marginal costing is only useful for short-term decision making. • Not all costs can easily be split into fixed costs and variable costs. • Under marginal costing, the fixed costs remain constant and variable costs vary according to the level of output. In reality, the fixed costs do not remain constant and the variable costs do not vary according to the level of output. In the long run, all costs are variable. • Inventory should not be valued using marginal costing for a business's financial reporting because fixed manufacturing overheads are required by IAS 2. • Marginal costing may encourage selling prices that are too low because fixed costs are not considered; however, fixed costs must be covered in the long term. • Marginal costing is most useful for a business that makes a single product. A company making several products will have difficulty allocating fixed costs to each product with any degree of accuracy. This will make it difficult to calculate the break-even point for either a single product or the business as a whole.

In general, marginal costing is widely used for short-term decision making. In the long term, it is essential that fixed costs be covered if a business is to make a profit. Therefore, for longer-term decisions absorption costing is more appropriate as it includes consideration of the fixed costs of a business.

THINK LIKE AN ACCOUNTANT

Running out of time

In management accounting, limiting factors can be used to prioritise production of different products. To make the best use of limited resources, the products are ranked according to the amount of contribution they make from each unit of the scarce resource. In practice, the principles underlying limiting factors can be applied to many more situations.

Consider your own time. There is always a finite number of hours available in the day, so this is a limited resource. How many hours do you make available for work? Do you spend some of your hours studying or pursuing hobbies or other social interests instead of being engaged in paid employment? Think about what affects the decisions you make about how to spend your time. Why might your choices be different from others?

Figure 35.10: There is always a finite number of hours in the day, so this is a limited resource.

EXAM-STYLE QUESTIONS

1   A manufacturer makes and sells 20 000 units each month. It has the following information for November.

Sales revenue $1 450 000
Fixed costs $650 000
Variable costs $300 000

What is the break-even point in units?

A   8 696   B   8 966   C   11 304   D   11 305   [1]

2   Figure 35.11 shows the monthly information for a business that makes and sells 1 000 units per month.

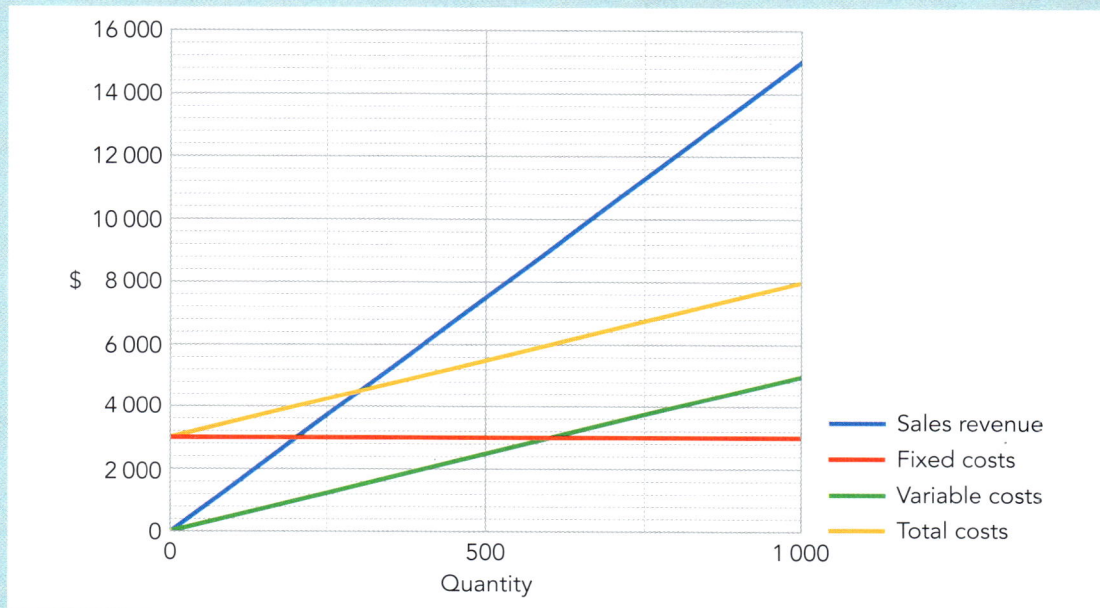

How much profit is made per month?

A $3 000   B $4 500   C $7 000   D $8 000   [1]

3   Information about a product is given:

	Per unit
	$
Selling price	80
Direct materials	30
Direct labour	40

Fixed costs total $40 000 and planned production is 2 000 units. Which action is necessary to break even? Decrease the cost of:

A   direct labour by 15%   C   direct materials by 10%
B   direct labour by 25%   D   direct materials by 20%   [1]

CONTINUED

4   Letters Limited produces three different products. The following budgeted information is available for the next six months:

	Product K	Product L	Product M
Total sales units	8 000	4 000	10 000
Per unit:	$	$	$
Selling price	100	120	80
Direct materials at $6 per kg	(36)	(48)	(24)
Direct labour	(40)	(44)	(30)
Contribution	24	28	26

Total fixed costs are budgeted to be $200 000.

Required

a   Explain what is meant by the term 'limiting factor'.   [3]

b   Calculate the value of the materials required to meet the budgeted sales.   [4]

c   Calculate the total budgeted profit for the next six months.   [6]

Additional information

The directors have been advised that only 48 000 kg of material will be available in the next six months. However, they have existing orders for their products that they feel they should meet. They are considering two options:

1   produce a minimum of 2 000 units of each product in order to meet sales demand

2   not making 2 000 units of each product.

Required

d   Calculate the maximum budgeted profit the company will make:

  i   if a minimum of 2 000 units of each product is made.   [8]

  ii   if no minimum production requirement of any product is put in place.   [4]

e   Advise the directors which course of action they should choose. Justify your answer.   [5]

SELF-EVALUATION CHECKLIST

After studying this chapter, complete a table like this:

You should be able to:	Needs more work	Almost there	Ready to move on
Analyse the behaviour of variable, semi-variable, fixed and stepped costs, particularly when shown on break-even and profit/volume charts.			
Calculate contribution, the contribution to sales ratio (for calculating profit at different levels of sales) and marginal costs.			
Calculate break-even point, where a business's total revenue equals its total costs and it makes neither profit nor loss, and margin of safety (which can be calculated using either the actual or budgeted figures depending on what managers are trying to find out).			
Interpret and analyse break-even information, remembering that a business that produces and sells less than the quantity needed to break even will make a loss and a business that produces and sells above the break-even point will make a profit.			
Evaluate cost-volume-profit data, pricing and other management decisions.			
Prepare costing and profit statements using marginal costing.			
Reconcile reported profits using marginal costing and absorption costing, which produce different inventory valuations and different profit figures.			
Assess the uses and limitations of cost-volume-profit analysis and marginal costing.			

Chapter 36

Activity-based costing (ABC)

This chapter covers syllabus section A Level 4.1

LEARNING INTENTIONS

In this chapter you will learn how to:

- identify what should be in a cost pool and what cost drivers are
- use activity-based costing to allocate overheads to products
- calculate total cost, selling price and profit using activity-based costing
- assess the limitations of activity-based costing
- evaluate management decisions using activity-based costing information.

ACCOUNTING IN CONTEXT

Careful costing

The complexity of manufacturing processes varies greatly between products and between businesses. A small bakery may have straightforward manufacturing processes. The bakery will make and sells loaves of bread each day. It will combine flour, yeast and other raw materials, bake the dough in loaf size portions, then cool and package the bread before selling it. Even if it produces several different products: brown bread, white bread, rolls and so on, the overheads can easily and fairly be split between each product using absorption costing.

Car manufacturers have much more complex manufacturing processes. There are many parts to each vehicle that need to be made and assembled from engines to indicators; wheels to windows. Added to this, many factories make a variety of different models with different features.

Each type of car needs to be carefully costed. The more realistically each type of product is costed, the more useful the information is to the management of the business. The management will use this information to support decisions on selling prices for each model and to calculate profitability of each product. Activity-based costing can be a useful alternative to absorption costing as it is considered a more realistic method.

Figure 36.1: The complexity of manufacturing processes varies greatly between products and between businesses.

Discuss in a pair or a group:

- Think of two other industries with straightforward manufacturing processes such as bread.

- Think of two other industries with complex manufacturing processes such as cars.

- Why is absorption costing not always accurate?

36.1 What is activity-based costing?

Activity-based costing (ABC) can be used as an alternative to absorption costing or marginal costing.

In Chapter 33, we used absorption costing as a method of charging overheads to products. This was done by calculating an overhead absorption rate and then charging that rate to products on the basis of, direct labour hours or machine hours. Absorption costing can lead to inaccurate results, because overheads are not spread fairly among products. Activity-based costing (ABC) aims to give more realistic results than absorption costing because it apportions each overhead in a fairer way by carefully considering how it is used.

Absorption costing uses a single overhead absorption rate for every product. ABC uses a number of different absorption rates for different overheads. ABC tries to identify which specific overheads should be charged to a product, by looking at the activities that are needed to make a product and charging the product with overheads based on how much an activity is used.

ABC carefully considers all the individual overhead costs incurred by each product. These individual costs are grouped together in a **cost pool**.

> ### KEY TERMS
>
> **activity-based costing (ABC):** a method of calculating unit cost that absorbs overhead costs into individual products by focusing on the activities that cause a cost to occur.
>
> **cost pool:** the total of all the costs associated with a particular activity.

For example, if a business uses a forklift truck to unload deliveries from suppliers, then the cost of running the truck is one of the factory overheads. Suppose the individual costs of running the forklift trucks are as follows:

	$
Drivers' wages	60 000
Maintenance costs	20 000
Power and fuel	12 000
Depreciation	8 000
Total forklift truck costs	100 000

The total forklift truck costs of $100 000 represent a cost pool.

A basis for apportioning the cost pool must be identified. This basis should reflect how much of the cost pool a particular product uses. In ABC this is a **cost driver**.

For example, if forklift truck costs are caused or driven by the amount of raw materials received, then an appropriate cost driver would be the volume of raw materials used.

KEY TERM

cost driver: the activity which directly results in a specific cost being incurred.

ACTIVITY 36.1

Identify the most suitable cost driver for each of the following factory overheads:

The first one has been done for you.

Overhead cost		Cost driver	
1	Running a forklift truck	a	Engineering hours
2	Machine set-up	b	Number of inspections
3	Machine maintenance	c	Volume of materials
4	Ordering	d	Number of machine set-ups
5	Quality control	e	Number of orders
6	Engineering	f	Maintenance hours

36.2 How to calculate unit cost using activity-based costing

The steps to calculate the cost per unit using ABC are:

Step 1 Identify the cost pools and associated cost drivers.

Step 2 Calculate the absorption rate for each cost driver, that is the cost driver rates, using the formula:

$$\frac{\text{Cost pool value}}{\text{Number of uses of the cost driver}}$$

Step 3 Use the calculation from Step 2 to apportion the overheads to the products.

Step 4 For each product, add the apportioned overheads to the direct costs to calculate the cost per unit.

TIP

ABC builds on techniques used in absorption costing, so it is useful to review absorption costing before studying ABC.

WORKED EXAMPLE 1

A manufacturer makes two products: Product A and Product B. The budgeted data for one week is as follows.

	Product A	Product B
	$	$
Number of units produced and sold	290	1 440
Number of orders	10	30
Number of production runs	6	24
Direct costs per unit ($)	35	25

Total factory overhead costs:	$
Ordering costs	24 000
Production run costs	13 500

Required

Calculate the total cost per unit for each product using ABC.

Answer

Step 1

Identify the cost pools and the cost drivers for each cost pool.

$24 000 of ordering costs is one cost pool and the number of orders is the cost driver.

$13 500 of production run costs is the second cost pool and the number of production runs is the cost driver.

Step 2

Calculate the cost driver rates.

Ordering costs $\dfrac{\$24\,000}{(10+30)} = \$600$ per order

Production run costs $\dfrac{\$13\,500}{(6+24)} = \$450$ per production run

Step 3

Apportion the overhead to product A and product B.

	Product A		Product B	
		$		$
Ordering	(10 × $600)	6 000	(30 × $600)	18 000
Production runs	(6 × $450)	2 700	(24 × $450)	10 800
Allocated overheads		8 700		28 800

Step 4

Calculate the cost per unit

	Product A		Product B	
		$		$
Overhead cost per unit	($8 700 ÷ 290)	30	($28 800 ÷ 1 440)	20
Add direct cost		35		25
Cost per unit		65		45

ACTIVITY 36.2

Yash manufactures two types of hat, one for winter and one for summer. The budgeted data for three months is as follows.

	Summer hat	Winter hat
Production in units	2 000	500
Direct materials ($)	3 000	1 250
Direct labour ($)	4 000	2 000
Number of quality checks	100	50
Labour hours spent on maintenance	20	20

Total factory overheads:

- $800 for machine maintenance
- $1 500 for quality control

Required

a   Calculate the total cost and the cost per unit for each product using ABC.

b   Calculate the selling price of each type of hat if Yash is aiming for a 60% mark-up on factory cost.

36.3 Making recommendations using activity-based costing

Like absorption costing and marginal costing, ABC is used to allocate overhead costs to each cost unit. Understanding unit costs provides management with important information that supports decision making. Decisions may include setting selling prices, cutting costs and stopping the production of unprofitable products.

ABC is a valuable method of costing for products where reliable information about the cost of each product is important. This might occur where a business has high overheads that make up a large part of the unit cost. Accuracy is also very important for a business that is deciding selling prices with a very small profit margin and needs to have confidence that costs are fully met.

ABC has some particular advantages over other costing methods that mean it can be especially useful for management.

36.4 Advantages and disadvantages of ABC

Advantages of using ABC include:

1   It is a fairer and more realistic allocation of overheads than absorption costing because it focuses on the reason why a product incurs a cost.

2   It gives managers a better understanding of what drives costs; this can lead to more reliable cost information and better control of cost.

3   It allows for the complexity of manufacturing by using more than one cost driver.

4   It is useful for decision making such as setting selling prices. Unlike marginal costing, ABC does consider overheads. ABC is considered more realistic than absorption costing.

The greater accuracy of ABC means that ABC is better at identifying products and areas of high overhead cost. This will direct management to consider the following:

i   reduce overhead costs

ii   stop producing products which do not earn sufficient profit

iii   charge more for more costly products to earn a higher profit.

For a business with a number of different products all sharing common overhead costs, absorption costing sometimes leads to one product subsidising another. In particular, absorption costing will tend to under-price low volume, highly technical products. This is illustrated in Worked example 2.

Although ABC can be useful, there a number of *disadvantages* to using ABC:

1   It is very time consuming to try to work out which specific overhead costs a product incurs and why.

2   It is very difficult to say with certainty which overhead costs are cost drivers for a particular product.

3   It requires a greater degree of analysis of overhead costs than absorption costing. It may not, therefore, be suitable for small businesses where managers often lack the time and expertise to try to establish cost pools and cost drivers.

4   Absorption costing and ABC are both ways of charging overheads incurred to the product produced. If all production made is sold, then whichever method is used, all indirect costs incurred will be charged to each product. The question then becomes, is ABC worth all the effort?

In practice, it is mostly down to management preference, expertise and time available as to which method of absorbing costs a firm uses. Whichever method is chosen, the company should not change it unless there is a valid reason for doing so.

Worked example 2 compares ABC with absorption costing.

WORKED EXAMPLE 2

Letters Limited produces two products A and B. Product A is more expensive to produce and has a higher selling price. Letters Limited is unsure whether to use absorption costing or activity-based costing, and wants to use the more reliable of the two methods. The following budgeted details are available for one month:

	A	B
Units of production and sales	3 000	12 000
Selling price per unit	$200	$100
Direct materials and labour per unit	$100	$50
Direct labour hours per unit	4	3
Number of machine set-ups	80	120
Machine hours	25 000	25 000
Number of orders packed	2 000	3 000

CONTINUED

Budgeted factory overheads:

	$
Machine set-up	84 000
Machine running time	250 000
Packing costs	50 000
Total factory overheads	384 000

Required

a Calculate the following using absorption costing:

  i the budgeted overhead absorption rate using direct labour hours

  ii the budgeted profit per unit.

b Calculate the following using activity-based costing:

  i the absorption rate for each cost driver

  ii the total overhead allocated to product A and product B

  iii the budgeted profit per unit.

c Calculate the difference between the budgeted overhead cost per unit and the budgeted profit per unit using absorption costing and activity-based costing.

d Recommend whether Letters Limited should use absorption costing or activity-based costing.

Answer

a i Traditional absorption costing

The total budgeted direct labour hours are:

Product A   3 000 units × 4   = 12 000 hours

Product B   12 000 units × 3 = 36 000 hours

Total direct labour hours   48 000 hours

Using absorption costing the budgeted overhead absorption rate (OAR) would be:

$$OAR = \frac{\$384\,000}{48\,000} = \$8 \text{ per direct labour hour}$$

ii The budgeted profit per unit would therefore be:

	A	B
	$	$
Selling price	200	100
Direct materials and labour	(100)	(50)
Factory overheads[1]	(32)	(24)
Budgeted profit per unit	68	26

Note:

[1] The factory overhead per unit is calculated by multiplying the hours per unit by the overhead absorption rate. For Product A: $32 (4 hours × $8); for Product B: $24 (3 hours × $8).

CONTINUED

b   i   Step 1   Identify the cost drivers for each activity.

Step 2   Calculate the cost driver rates using the formula:

$$\frac{\text{Cost pool value}}{\text{Number of uses of the cost driver}}$$

Cost driver	Cost	Total number of uses of the cost driver	Cost driver rate
	$		$
Number of machine set-ups	84 000	200 (80 + 120)	420
Machine hours	250 000	50 000 (25 000 + 25 000)	5
Packing costs	50 000	5 000 (2 000 + 3 000)	10

ii   It is now possible to calculate how much of the factory overhead can be charged to each product using ABC.

Product A

Number of units produced: 3 000 units.

Cost driver	Activity overhead absorption rate ($)	Number of activities used	Total factory overheads allocated ($) [1]
Number of machine set-ups	420	80	33 600
Machine hours	5	25 000	125 000
Packing costs	10	2 000	20 000
			178 600

Note:

[1]   The activity rate is multiplied by the number of activities used to arrive at the total factory overhead allocated.

Product B

Number of units produced: 12 000 units.

Cost driver	Activity overhead absorption rate ($)	Number of activities used	Total factory overheads allocated ($)
Number of machine set-ups	420	120	50 400
Machine hours	5	25 000	125 000
Packing costs	10	3 000	30 000
			205 400

TIP

Calculating cost driver rates use in ABC is similar to the way an overhead absorption rate is calculated when using absorption costing in Chapter 33. However, rather than a rate for each department, a rate for each activity has been calculated.

TIP

When tackling a calculation like this, always check that your total overheads allocated to each product adds back to the overall total overheads. In this case, Product A has been allocated with a total of $178 600 of factory costs and Product B $205 400, which together make the total of $384 000.

CONTINUED

iii

	A	B
	$	$
Selling price per unit	200.00	100.00
Direct materials and labour	(100.00)	(50.00)
Factory overheads[1]	(59.53)	(17.12)
Budgeted profit per unit	40.47	32.88

Note:

[1] The factory overhead per unit is the total overhead apportioned divided by the number of units. For Product A: $59.53 ($178 600 ÷ 3 000 units); for Product B $17.12 (205 400 ÷ 12 000 units).

c Comparison of the overhead absorption rates using both methods of overhead absorption:

	A	B
Budgeted unit overhead cost	$	$
Absorption costing	32.00	24.00
ABC	59.53	17.12
Difference	(27.53)	6.88

Comparison of the budgeted unit profit:

	A	B
	$	$
Using absorption costing	68.00	26.00
Using ABC	40.47	32.88
Difference	27.53	(6.88)

d The two methods have resulted in different unit costs and, therefore, unit profits. Using ABC results in:

- higher costs and lower profit for each unit of Product A
- lower costs and higher profit for each unit of Product B.

ABC apportions overheads more realistically. Absorption costing will tend to under-price low volume, highly technical products. In this case, the Product A has low volume and is more expensive to make than Product B.

Using ABC encourages management of the business to reflect on the costs and profits. For example, the higher costs of producing Product A may encourage the managers to consider increasing the selling price of Product A if the market conditions allow. Therefore it is recommended that Letters Limited uses ABC.

Note: This example also highlights some of the disadvantages of ABC. The calculations can be long and complex as can the amount of analysis of the costs and how much each product uses.

KEY CONCEPT LINK

Planning and control: As with the other costing methods, ABC provides managers with financial information to help make decisions and plan for a range of possible scenarios that the business might face. The quality of the information provided means that managers may make more informed decisions on what products to produce and what prices to charge than under absorption costing.

ACTIVITY 36.3

A manufacturer makes two products, X and Y. The following budgeted information is available for each product for one month:

	X	Y
Units of production and sales	3 500	13 000
Selling price per unit	$210	$90
Direct materials and labour per unit	$80	$35
Total budgeted direct labour hours	14 000	26 000
Direct labour hours per unit	4	2

Budgeted factory overheads are $800 000.

Required

a   Calculate the budgeted overhead absorption rate using direct labour hours.

b   Calculate the budgeted profit per unit.

Additional information

The accountant has identified the cost pools and cost drivers for the company. He provides the following analysis:

Activity	Production overhead	X	Y
	$		
Machine maintenance	100 000	3 000 maintenance hours	5 000 maintenance hours
Materials handling	60 000	400 deliveries	600 deliveries
Packing	40 000	600 orders	1 000 orders

Required

c   Calculate the absorption rate for each cost driver.

d   Calculate the *total* cost for product X and product Y using ABC.

e   Calculate the cost per unit for each product using ABC.

f   Calculate using ABC, the profit per unit of each product using ABC.

REFLECTION

When answering Activity 36.3, do you think the cost drivers used in part **c** were the most appropriate ones to use? In practice, could there be any suitable alternatives for production overheads in factories? Discuss your answers with another learner to see whether you agree.

THINK LIKE AN ACCOUNTANT

Choosing the best method

We have looked at three different methods of costing products: absorption costing, activity-based costing and marginal costing. They all provide us with a value for unit cost for a product but each value will be different. None of the answers is wrong. A management accountant will use their judgement to decide which method is best. The answer will depend on the nature of the business and the circumstances that it is in. Can you think of another circumstance where there can be more than one answer? How would you choose the best course of action to take? How would you know if you have chosen the best option?

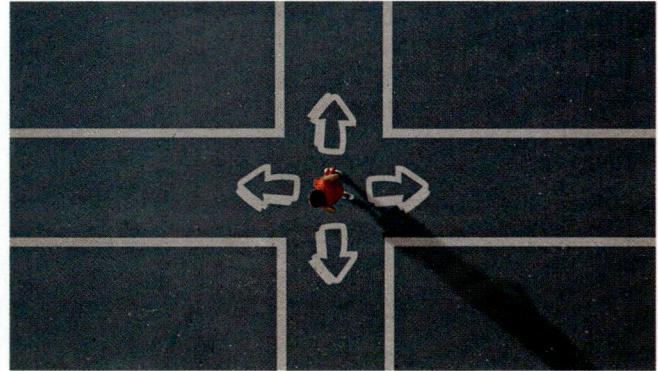

Figure 36.2: A management accountant will use their judgment to decide which method of costing to apply.

EXAM-STYLE QUESTIONS

1   State *two* limitations of using activity-based costing.   [2]

2   Explain the difference between activity-based costing and absorption costing.   [4]

3   Trews Limited produces two types of trousers, Skinny and Baggy. The following budgeted information is available:

	Skinny	Baggy
Production and sales units	16 000	24 000
Machine hours	8 000	16 000
Direct materials per unit	$10	$12
Direct labour per unit	$4	$4

Total production overheads for the next month are budgeted to be $216 000. Trews Ltd uses absorption costing and overheads are absorbed on the basis of machine hours.

The company adds 50% to the unit cost to set the selling price of each product.

Required

a   Calculate the budgeted unit selling price for each product.   [6]

CONTINUED

Additional information

Zara, the managing director of the company, has heard about activity-based costing and has asked the company accountant to investigate whether or not she should use it.

The company accountant has identified that production comprises three activities. She has also calculated the cost of each activity. This information is as follows.

Activity	Production overheads	Skinny	Baggy
	$		
Machine set-up	66 000	50 times	70 times
Machine maintenance	100 000	800 hours	1 200 hours
Quality control checks	50 000	1 000 times	1 500 times

Required

b Calculate the following using activity-based costing:

   i   the budgeted unit cost [4]

   ii   the budged unit selling price. [4]

c Advise Zara whether or not she should change to activity-based costing. Justify your answer by discussing the advantages and disadvantages of changing. [8]

4 Ahmed manufactures two products. He has recently started using activity-based costing (ABC) for allocating the overhead costs to these products. The budgeted data for one month is available as follows:

	Product X	Product Y
Demand (units)	10 000	14 000
Number of orders	20	60
Number of production runs	12	36

	Per unit	Per unit
Direct labour hours	0.75	1.5
Machine hours	2.5	0.5
Direct costs ($)	100	50

Total factory overhead costs	$
Machine maintenance costs	264 000
Ordering costs	54 000
Production run costs	24 000
	342.000

Required

a Calculate the full cost per unit for Product X and Product Y using ABC. [10]

Additional information

Ahmed previously used direct labour hours as a basis to charge overheads to each product.

CONTINUED

Required

b   Calculate the overhead charged to each product using the direct labour hour rate.   [3]

c   Explain the effect that changing the method has had on the overhead cost of each product.   [4]

Additional information

A customer requires 50 units of Product X and has offered to pay Ahmed a total of $8 450 for them. Ahmed uses 40% mark-up on all his products.

Required

d   Advise whether or not Ahmed should accept the offer. Justify your decision using appropriate calculations and considering both financial and non-financial factors.   [6]

e   State two reasons why a business may use ABC for allocating overhead costs.   [2]

SELF-EVALUATION CHECKLIST

After studying this chapter, complete a table like this:

You should be able to:	Needs more work	Almost there	Ready to move on
Identify cost pools (costs that can be grouped together and are influenced by a particular cost driver) and cost drivers (activities that lead to costs).			
Use activity-based costing to allocate overheads to products based on the usage of each overhead.			
Calculate total cost, selling price and profit using activity-based costing.			
Assess the uses and limitations of activity-based costing, highlighting that it can lead to more realistic results than absorption costing because of the way it apportions each overhead but it is more detailed and time consuming to carry out than absorption costing, so for some businesses it is not worthwhile.			
Evaluate management decisions using activity-based costing information, such as setting selling prices.			

Chapter 37

Budgeting and budgetary control

This chapter covers syllabus section A Level 4.3

LEARNING INTENTIONS

In this chapter you will learn how to:

- calculate budgets to plan future activity
- identify and evaluate limiting factors to decide the order in which to prepare budgets
- prepare budgets for sales, production, purchases, labour, trade receivables, trade payables and cash to use to aid the planning and control of a business
- prepare the master budget
- evaluate the advantages and disadvantages of budgetary control and using spreadsheets or specialist accounting software to prepare budgets
- calculate flexible budgets.

ACCOUNTING IN CONTEXT

What does the future hold?

Budgeting is the process of planning future finances. Budgets in various forms have been used for hundreds of years and can be a useful tool for individuals, businesses and governments.

National governments use budgets as part of their planning for the revenue and spending that they control. The budget in the UK is prepared by the Treasury, in India by the Ministry of Finance and in South Africa by the National Treasury. Key information in these national budgets are typically announced to the public each year. Budgets are then used to compare and control actual revenue and spending against expected figures. Governments are held accountable for any differences between figures. So, if a government spends a lot more (or less) on education or health care than expected, it will need to explain why.

It is not a legal requirement for organisations to prepare budgets. However, budgets are widely used in business today. A small new business owner may be encouraged by a bank or other lender to draw up their first cash budget. The bank can then use the information to help decide whether to allow the business to borrow money or open a bank account. A large company may have a whole team of accountants that spend several weeks or months each year preparing budgets on all aspects of the organisation's spending.

Figure 37.1: Budgeting is the process of planning future finances.

Discuss in a pair or a group:

*   Who is responsible for preparing your government's budget?
*   Why is the general public often interested in their country's national budget?
*   Why might large companies choose to spend a lot of money preparing budgets?

37.1 What is budgeting?

A **budget** is a plan of a future activity, expressed in financial terms. A budget should follow from actions taken by management to change the present circumstances and these are expressed in financial terms. For example, if Hussain's sales this year are $100 000 and he aims for sales of his business to grow by 10% each year in future by introducing new products, or by increasing advertising etc., then his budgeted sales for next year will then be $110 000 ($100 000 × 110%) and the following year will be $121 000 ($110 000 × 110%).

A company may use **zero-based budgeting** – setting its budget by analysing existing operations and justifying them on the basis of their use or need to the organisation. In effect, the company starts with a blank piece of paper and builds up every cost from nothing.

An alternative to this is **incremental budgeting**. For example, from its accounts, a company knows that its salaries figure last year was $50 000. It decides it will budget for a 5% increase this year and so sets its salaries budget at $52 500.

There is an argument as to which is the best method. Using incremental budgeting may result in past inefficiencies being built into future plans. Others would argue that using zero-based budgeting is almost impossible without looking back to previous years.

KEY TERMS

budget: a plan of future activity, expressed in financial terms.

zero-based budgeting: using budgeted figures that are justified by analysing existing operations or business needs rather than starting by using figures from previous periods.

incremental budgeting: using last year's budgeted or actual figures as a starting point and adding to it or subtracting from it to reflect changes.

The main budgets used by businesses include the following:

1 Sales
2 Production
3 Purchases
4 Labour
5 Expenditure
6 Trade receivables
7 Trade payables
8 Cash
9 Statement of profit or loss
10 Statement of financial position.

The manager of each department in a business is responsible for the performance of their department. Separate operational or functional budgets must be prepared for each department or activity detailing the department's revenue (if any) and expenses for a given period. Information gained from preparing the functional budgets are then used to prepare a budgeted statement of profit or loss and a budgeted statement of financial position.

37.2 Limiting factors

Limiting factors were discussed in Chapter 35. They are circumstances that restrict the activities of a business. Limiting factors can include:

• limited demand for a product
• shortage of materials, which limits production
• shortage of labour, which also limits production
• shortage of space in which to produce the budgeted amount
• shortage of cash.

Limiting factors *must* be identified before deciding the order in which departmental budgets such as sales and production are prepared.

If the limiting factor is demand for the product, a sales budget will be prepared first. The other budgets will then be prepared to fit in with the sales budget.

If the limiting factor is the availability of materials or labour, the production budget will be prepared first and the sales budget will then be based on the production budget.

If demand for the product is the limiting factor, the order that budgets are prepared is as follows:

	Budget	Information shown in the budget
1	Sales	The budgeted *sales revenue*
2	Production	Manufacturers use production budgets to show the *volume of production* required monthly to meet the demand for sales
3	Purchases	The *volume* and *value of materials purchased*
4	Labour	The *labour hours* and the *labour cost*, i.e. the wages payable to workers involved in the production
5	Expenditure	This budget is optional; it records *payments* that go into the cash budget
6	Trade receivables	*The calculation of trade receivables using information on credit sales, receipts from credit customers and discounts allowed*

	Budget	Information shown in the budget
7	Trade payables	The calculation of trade payables using information on credit purchases, payments to suppliers and discounts received
8	Cash	The calculation of the bank balance using information on receipts and payments
9	Statement of profit or loss	Summarises the *profit or loss*
10	Statement of financial position	Summarises the *financial position*

Budgets **9** and **10** make up the **master budget**. They are the last budgets to be produced as they are prepared using information from other budgets. The master budget is prepared annually.

37.3 How to prepare a sales budget

Demand for a product is often the limiting factor for a business. If this is the case, the first budget to be prepared will be the sales budget.

Sales budgets are based on the budgeted volume of sales *units*. The number of units is then multiplied by the selling price per unit of production to produce the revenue.

Worked example 1 shows the preparation of the various budgets required by the business. It will start with the first stage, the preparation of the sales budget.

> **KEY TERM**
>
> **master budget:** the budgeted statement of profit or loss and the budgeted statement of financial position together.

WORKED EXAMPLE 1

Budge Limited produces and sells one type of product. Sales for the four months from January to April are budgeted in units as follows:

January 1 000; February 800; March 1 100; April 1 300.

The current price per unit is $20. The company plans to increase the price by 5% on 1 April.

Required

Prepare a sales budget for the four months ending 30 April.

Answer

The sales budget is as follows.

	January	February	March	April	Total
Units	1 000	800	1 100	1 300	4 200
Selling price	$20	$20	$20	$21 [1]	
Sales [2]	$20 000	$16 000	$22 000	$27 300	$85 300

Notes:

[1] The price will increase by 5% on 1 April to $21 per unit ($20 × 105%).

[2] The sales value is the units multiplied by the selling price.

37.4 How to prepare a production budget

If demand is the limiting factor, manufacturing companies require production budgets to show the volume of production required monthly to meet the demand for sales.

It is important to check that production is allocated to the correct months. For example, production may be one month before budgeted sales; alternatively, for a perishable product, production may need to be just one day before budgeted sales.

TIP

Remember that production budgets are only needed for manufacturers. The production budget is the second budget to be prepared after sales provided demand is the limiting factor.

WORKED EXAMPLE 2

Continued from Worked example 1

Budge Limited manufactures its goods one month before they are sold. Monthly production is 110% of the following month's sales to provide goods for inventory and to allow for breakages and free samples to promote sales.

Budgeted sales for May are for 1 500 units.

Required

Prepare a production budget for the four months ending 30 April.

Answer

The production budget is as follows.

	December	January	February	March	April
Production for sales (units)[1]	1 000	800	1 100	1 300	1 500
Add: 10% for inventory, breakages and samples	100	80	110	130	150
Monthly production	1 100	880	1 210	1 430	1 650

Note:

[1]   The budgeted sales units have been moved back by one month, as we are told the company will make them one month before they are sold. For example, January's budgeted sales of 1 000 units are moved back to December. As the budgeted sales for May are 1 500 units these will need to be made in April.

ACTIVITY 37.1

Megan and James Limited's sales budget in units for four months ending 31 December is as follows:

September 2400; October 2 500; November 2600; December 2600.

The price per unit will be $10 for the two months to 31 October. The price will be increased to $12 from 1 November.

Required

a   Prepare Megan and James Limited's sales budget for the new product for the six months ending 31 December.

CONTINUED

Additional information

Megan and James Limited manufactures their goods one month before the goods are sold. Monthly production is 110% of the following month's sales. Budgeted sales for January are 2800 units.

Required

b Prepare Megan and James Limited's production budget.

(Keep your answers. They will be needed for Activities 37.3 and 37.4.)

Manufacturers expect to have some loss of materials in the production process. This may be due to breakages or individual items that are below the minimum standard of quality required. It is important that this wastage be built into the production budget, as it will affect how much material needs to be purchased.

WORKED EXAMPLE 3

A business manufactures a product with budgeted sales for next month of 1800 units. There is an opening inventory of 100 units and the company requires a closing inventory of 200 units.

Required

a Prepare a production budget for next month.

Additional information

5% of the production is lost due to damage in the production process.

b Prepare a revised production budget for next month.

Answer

a Without any loss in production the production budget would be:

Budgeted sales units	1800
Opening inventory	(100)
Closing inventory	200
Production required	1900

Notice that the opening inventory of units is deducted from the budgeted sales. There is no need to make them. The closing inventory is added. This is the opposite way around to how opening and closing inventory is shown in the statement of profit or loss.

b The loss due to damage will mean that more units have to be produced to cover the loss.

Production from above	1900
Production to cover loss (1900/95%)	2000

The revised production budget for next month is:

Budgeted sales units	1800
Opening inventory	(100)
Closing inventory	200
Add: Loss in production	100
Production required	2000

TIP

Notice that production is grossed up to achieve the required production. If 5% of 1900 was taken as the amount of extra production, the loss in the production process would not have been covered.

37.5 How to prepare a purchases budget

Having worked out how many units need to be produced to make the goods to be sold, the company now has to buy the raw materials to produce them. This is done using a purchases budget.

A purchases budget may be prepared for either:

- raw materials purchased by a manufacturer
- goods purchased by a trader.

A manufacturing company's purchases budget is prepared from the production budget, while a trader's purchases budget is prepared from the sales budget.

The purchases budget is calculated as follows:

> Units produced per production budget × quantity of material per unit produced × price per unit of material

WORKED EXAMPLE 4

Continued from Worked example 2

Budge Limited purchases its raw materials one month before production. Each unit of production requires 3 kg of material, which costs $2 per kg.

Required

Prepare a purchases budget needed for the production budget in Worked example 2.

Answer

The purchases budget is as follows. Note that the months run from November to March to include the purchases needed for production through to April.

	November	December	January	February	March
No. of units [1]	1 100	880	1 210	1 430	1 650
Material required [2] (kg)	3 300	2 640	3 630	4 290	4 950
Purchases [3]	$6 600	$5 280	$7 260	$8 580	$9 900

Notes:

[1] As the goods are required one month before they are needed in production, the production budget prepared in Worked example 2 has been moved back another month. For example, the 1 100 units to be made in December has been moved backwards by one month to November, the month when the goods are purchased.

[2] Each unit requires 3 kg of material. Therefore, the number of units is multiplied by 3 to give the number of kg purchased.

[3] Each kg costs $2, so the number of kg required is multiplied by $2 to find the total cost of the purchases.

> **TIP**
>
> Take care to ensure that the purchases are made in the correct month. For example, purchases may be one month before production.

37.6 How to prepare a labour budget

After the preparation of the production budget, it may be necessary to prepare a labour budget. The labour budget calculates the wages payable to workers involved in the production.

WORKED EXAMPLE 5

Prem Limited has calculated its budgeted production for the next three weeks. Details are as follows.

Week	Production units
1	1 000
2	1 200
3	1 400

Each unit requires four hours of direct labour. Workers are paid $20 per hour.

Required

Prepare a labour budget for the three weeks.

Answer

The labour budget in hours and value for the three-week period would look like this:

	Week 1	Week 2	Week 3
Production units	1 000	1 200	1 400
Budgeted labour hours required (units × 4)	4 000	4 800	5 600
Budgeted labour cost (budgeted hours × $20)	$80 000	$96 000	$112 000

The budgeted labour cost would then be entered as a payment in the cash budget.

ACTIVITY 37.2

Bajat Limited has the following production budget:

Production budget in units			
September	October	November	December
4 000	4 200	4 400	4 800

- Each unit takes two hours of direct labour.
- Workers are paid $12 per hour.
- 90% of the direct labour is paid in the month, with the remaining 10% paid in the following month.

Required

Prepare the direct labour budget in hours and dollars to show the amount of direct labour each month to be included in the cash budget for October, November and December.

37.7 How to prepare an expenditure budget

An expenditure budget shows the payments for purchased materials (from the purchases budget) plus all other expenditure in the period covered by the budget. An expenditure budget is not essential as the payments can simply be put directly into the cash budget instead. If an expenditure budget is prepared, it makes the cash budget easier to prepare because all of the expenditure payments can be easily transferred straight into the cash budget.

> **TIP**
>
> In an expenditure budget, ensure that you put the payments for the expenditure in the correct month. For example, purchases must be entered in the month they are paid for rather than the month they were bought.

WORKED EXAMPLE 6

Continued from Worked example 4

Budge Limited pays for its raw materials two months after the month of purchase. Its other expenses are as follows:

a Monthly wages of $5 000 are paid in the month in which they are due.

b General expenses are paid in the month in which they are incurred and are to be budgeted as follows: January $6 000; February $7 000; March $6 900; April $7 000.

c Budge Limited pays interest of 8% on a loan of $20 000 in four annual instalments on 31 March, 30 June, 30 September and 31 December.

d A final dividend of $1 000 for the year ended 31 December is payable in March.

Required

Prepare Budge Limited's expenditure budget for January to April.

Answer

The expenditure budget for January to April is as follows:

	January	February	March	April
	$	$	$	$
Purchases [1]	6 600	5 280	7 260	8 580
Wages	5 000	5 000	5 000	5 000
General expenses	6 000	7 000	6 900	7 000
Loan interest	–	–	400	–
Dividend	–	–	1 000	–
Total expenditure	17 600	17 280	20 560	20 580

Note:

[1] Payments for raw materials are made two months *after* the goods are purchased. This means the goods purchased in November will be paid for in January. Those purchased in December will be paid for in February and so on. The figures come from the purchases budget.

TIP

You will not need to produce an expenditure budget itself, but you do need to know the information it contains for the payments section of a cash budget.

ACTIVITY 37.3

Continued from Activity 37.1

Megan and James Limited uses 2 litres of material in each unit of their product. The price of the material is currently $3 per litre, but the company has learnt that the price will be increased to $3.50 in November. The raw materials are purchased one month before production; 3 000 units are budgeted to be produced in January.

Required

a Prepare Megan and James Limited's purchases budget based on its production budget for the five months from August to December.

CONTINUED

Additional information

Megan and James Limited's overheads and other expenses for four months to 31 December are budgeted as follows:

1   Purchases are paid for in the following month.

2   Wages of $3 000 per month are paid in the same month as they are earned.

3   Electricity bills are expected to be received in September for $1 400 and in December for $2 000. The bills will be paid in the month following their receipt.

4   Other expenses are expected to amount to $3 000 per month. They are paid in the month they are incurred.

5   Megan and James Limited has a loan of $10 000 on which interest at 10% per annum is payable in four quarterly instalments on 31 March, 30 June, 30 September and 31 December.

6   The company will purchase equipment in November for $12 000 with immediate payment.

7   A final dividend of $2 000 for the year ended 31 December will be paid in April.

Required

b   Prepare Megan and James Limited's expenditure budget for the four months ending 31 December. (Keep your answer; it will be needed in Activity 37.4.)

37.8 How to prepare a trade receivables budget

The trade receivables budget calculates the amount of cash that will be received from credit customers each month. It has to be prepared after the sales budget but before the cash budget and the master budget. The final balance on the trade receivables budget will appear as the trade receivables figure under current assets in the master budget.

WORKED EXAMPLE 7

Continued from Worked example 6

Budge Limited's sales in November were $18 000 and in December were $19 000.

Of the total sales, 40% are on a cash basis. Of the remainder, 50% are to credit customers who pay within one month and receive a cash discount of 2%. The remaining 10% of credit customers pay within two months.

Required

Prepare Budge Limited's trade receivables budget for January to April.

Answer

The workings required to prepare the trade receivables budget for the period from January to April are as follows. Notice that the workings start at the previous November. This is because, as we have seen, some of the money from November's sales isn't received until January.

CONTINUED

	Working					
	November	December	January	February	March	April
	$	$	$	$	$	$
Sales for the month	18 000	19 000	20 000	16 000	22 000	27 300
Cash sales	7 200	7 600	8 000	6 400	8 800	10 920
Credit sales	10 800	11 400	12 000	9 600	13 200	16 380
Cash received one month after sale [1]		8 820	9 310	9 800	7 840	10 780
Discount [2]		180	190	200	160	220
Cash received two months after sale [3]			1 800	1 900	2 000	1 600

Notes:

[1] The balance of cash received after one month is 50% of the total sales made the previous month less a 2% cash discount. For example, in January, Budge Limited receives cash from 50% of December's sales less 2% cash discounts: $9 310 ($19 000 × 50% × 98%).

[2] The discount figure is 2% of 50% of the sales for the previous month. Thus, in January, the discount is $190 ($19 000 × 50% × 2%).

[3] The balance of cash received after two months is 10% of the total sales made two months before. Thus, in January, Budge Limited will receive $1 800 (10% of November's sales of $18 000).

Trade receivables budget for the period January to April				
	January	February	March	April
	$	$	$	$
Opening trade receivables [1]	13 200	13 820	11 520	14 720
Add: Credit sales for the month	12 000	9 600	13 200	16 380
Less: Cash received [2]	11 190	11 700	9 840	12 380
Less: Discounts allowed	190	200	160	220
Closing trade receivables	13 820	11 520	14 720	18 500

Notes:

[1] Opening balance in January is the total of the credit sales from December ($11 400) plus 10% of sales from November that are still to be paid ($1 800). All other opening balances are the closing balances of the previous month; so, February's opening balance is January's closing balance etc.

[2] Cash received is the total of cash received after one month of sales plus the cash received after two months of sales. For example, for January: $11 190 ($9 390 + $1 800).

The layout of the trade receivables budget starts with the opening balance of trade receivables at the start of the month. The total credit sales for the month are added onto that figure. The cash received in the month and the discount allowed in that month are then deducted. The result is the closing figure for trade receivables. This is carried forward and forms the opening balance at the start of the next month.

37.9 How to prepare a trade payables budget

The preparation of the trade payables budget is similar to that used when preparing the trade receivables budget. The starting point of the calculation is the opening trade payables. Onto this is added the credit purchases for the month. The cash paid and any discount received is deducted to leave the closing trade payables, which is carried forward to the start of the next month.

WORKED EXAMPLE 8

Continued from Worked example 7

Budge Limited pays for its raw materials two months after the month of purchase, as illustrated in the expenditure budget in Worked example 6.

Required

Prepare a trade payables budget for the period January to March.

Answer

The trade payables budget for Budge Limited for the months from January to March is as follows.

	November	December	January	February	March
	$	$	$	$	$
Opening trade payables[1]			11 880	12 540	15 840
Add: Credit purchases for month[2]	6 600	5 280	7 260	8 580	9 900
Less: Cash paid[3]			6 600	5 280	7 260
Closing trade payables			12 540	15 840	18 480

Notes:

[1]   We were told in Worked example 6 that Budge Limited pays for its goods two months after they have been purchased. Therefore, at the beginning of January, Budge Limited will owe its trade payables for goods bought in November ($6 600) and December ($5 280) giving the total of $11 880.

[2]   This information comes from the purchases budget (see Worked example 4).

[3]   January's payment is November's credit purchases; February's payment is December's credit purchases, etc.

37.10 How to prepare a cash budget

Although it is called a cash budget, it really relates to the business bank account. The cash budget includes money received and paid and the months in which the receipts and payments occur. Non-cash items such as depreciation or discounts must never be included.

The information for the cash budget has come from other budgets including the sales, trade receivables and expenditure budgets.

When preparing a cash budget, care must be taken with respect to the following:

- Revenue must be allocated to the months in which the money is received. Receipts from credit customers who are allowed cash discounts must be shown as the amounts after deduction of the discounts. The discounts allowed to customers should not be shown separately as an expense.

- Payments to suppliers (purchases) must be shown in the months in which the payment is made.

- The discounts received from suppliers should *not* be shown separately as income. The reason for this is that no money changes hands in respect of discounts allowed and received. Thus, they must not be entered in the cash budget.

The cash budget is prepared in three stages:

- Total the receipts from all sources, not just revenue. For example include receipts from sale of assets.

- Total the expenditure (payments).

- Calculate the opening and closing cash balances at the end of each month.

WORKED EXAMPLE 9

Continued from Worked example 8

Budge Limited received $5 000 from the sale of a non-current asset in March. The balance at bank on 31 December was $10 000.

Required

Prepare a cash budget for January to April.

Answer

The cash budget prepared for Budge Limited is as follows.

	January	February	March	April
	$	$	$	$
Receipts				
Cash sales[1]	8 000	6 400	8 800	10 920
Credit customers – one month[2]	9 310	9 800	7 840	10 780
Credit customers – two months[3]	1 800	1 900	2 000	1 600
Sale of non-current asset	–	–	5 000	–
Total revenue	19 110	18 100	23 640	23 300
Expenditure[4]				
Purchases	6 600	5 280	7 260	8 580
Wages	5 000	5 000	5 000	5 000
General expenses	6 000	7 000	6 900	7 000
Loan interest	–	–	400	–
Dividend	–	–	1 000	–
Total payments	17 600	17 280	20 560	20 580
Calculation of opening and closing bank balances				
Net receipts (payments) (total receipts minus total payments)	1 510	820	3 080	2 720
Bank balance brought forward	10 000	11 510	12 330	15 410
Bank balance carried forward	11 510	12 330	15 410	18 130

CONTINUED

Notes:

[1] Cash sales are 40% of the total sales for the month. January's sales were budgeted to be $20 000 (see the sales budget in Worked example 1). The cash sales were therefore $20 000 × 40% = $8 000 (this was calculated in the workings for the trade receivables budget in Worked example 7).

[2] In January we receive cash from credit customers of December's sales ($19 000 × 50% × 98%) = $9 310 (this was calculated in the workings for the trade receivables budget in Worked example 7).

[3] The balance of cash received after two months is 10% of the total sales made two months before (this was also calculated in the workings for the trade receivables budget in Worked example 7).

[4] The expenditure was calculated in the expenditure budget (see Worked example 6).

ACTIVITY 37.4

Continued from Activity 37.3

Megan and James Limited's sales in July were $26 000 and in August were $27 000. Of total revenue, 50% is on a cash basis, 40% is received one month after sale and 10% of revenue is received two months after sale.

The bank balance on 31 August was $500 overdrawn.

Required

a Prepare Megan and James Limited's trade receivables budget for the four months ending December.

b Prepare Megan and James Limited's trade payables budget for the four months ending December.

c Prepare Megan and James Limited's cash budget for the four months ending December.

REFLECTION

When answering Activity 37.4, part **c**, how did you calculate the opening and closing balance each month? What do you notice about the balances each month compared to the balances in Worked example 9?

37.11 How to prepare a master budget

A master budget is a budgeted statement of profit or loss and statement of financial position prepared from the information provided by other budgets. The purpose of the master budget is to show management the profit or loss to be expected if their plans for the business are implemented, and the state of the business at the end of the budget period. The master budget is always the last budget produced.

Details of non-current assets that are to be sold or purchased are included in a capital budget, as shown in Worked example 10.

WORKED EXAMPLE 10

Master Limited has the following information available:

Master Limited Statement of financial position at 31 December 2020	Cost	Accumulated depreciation	Net book value
	$	$	$
Non-current assets			
Equipment	10000	6000	4000
Motor vehicles	12000	4800	7200
	22000	10800	11200
Current assets			
Inventory			10800
Trade receivables			33600
Cash and cash equivalents			20600
			65000
Total assets			76200
Equity and liabilities			
Share capital and reserves			
Ordinary shares of $1			50000
Retained earnings			20000
			70000
Current liabilities			
Trade payables			6200
Total equity and liabilities			76200

Additional information

1   Goods are purchased one month before the month of sale.

2   Budgeted purchases and sales for the year ending 31 December 2021 are as follows:

	Purchases	Sales
	$	$
January–March	72000	132000
April–June	96000	156000
July–September	84000	168000
October–December	96000	144000

Sales and purchases accrue evenly over each quarter.

3   Master Limited receives one month's credit on all purchases and allows one month's credit on all sales.

CONTINUED

4 The following expenses will be incurred in the year ending 31 December 2021:

   i rent of $2000 per quarter, paid in advance on 1 January, 1 April, 1 July and 1 October

   ii wages of $8000, payable each month

   iii other expenses of $25000, paid quarterly.

5 A new motor vehicle will be purchased on 1 April 2021 for $10000.

6 A motor vehicle that cost $6000 and has a written down value of $3000 at 31 December 2020, will be sold for $2000 on 1 July 2021.

7 The company depreciates equipment and motor vehicles at 10% per annum on cost at the end of the year.

8 The company's inventory at 31 December 2021 will be valued at $30000.

Required

Prepare the following budgets for the year ending 31 December 2021.

a cash budget

b budgeted statement of profit or loss

c budgeted statement of financial position.

Answer

a

Master Limited Cash budget for the year ended 31 December 2021	Jan/Mar $	Apr/Jun $	Jul/Sep $	Oct/Dec $
Receipts				
Sales	121600[1]	148000[2]	164000	152000
Proceeds from sale of van	–	–	2000	–
	121600	148000	166000	152000
Payments				
Purchases	54200[3]	88000[4]	88000	92000
Rent	2000	2000	2000	2000
Wages	24000	24000	24000	24000
Other expenses	25000	25000	25000	25000
Purchase of motor vehicle	–	10000	–	–
	105200	149000	139000	143000
Net receipts/(payments)	16400	(1000)	27000	9000
Balance brought forward	20600	37000	36000	63000
Balance carried forward	37000	36000	63000	72000

Notes:

[1] Receipts from sales are trade receivables at 31 December 2020: ($33600) $+ \frac{2}{3}$ of sales for January/March = $88000 $\left(\$132000 \times \frac{2}{3}\right)$.

[2] $\frac{1}{3}$ of previous quarter's sales $+ \frac{2}{3}$ of current quarter's sales.

CONTINUED

[3] Trade payables at 31 December 2020: ($6 200) + $\frac{2}{3}$ of purchases for January/March.

[4] $\frac{1}{3}$ of previous quarter's purchases + $\frac{2}{3}$ of current quarter's purchases.

b   As part of the workings, a budgeted statement of non-current assets for the year ended 31 December 2021 is produced as follows:

	Equipment	Motor vehicles	Total
	$	$	$
Cost at 31 December 2020	10 000	12 000	22 000
Additions		10 000	10 000
Disposals		(6 000)	(6 000)
Cost at 31 December 2021	10 000	16 000	26 000
Accumulated depreciation at 31 December 2020	6 000	4 800	10 800
Additions	1 000	1 600	2 600
Disposals	–	(3 000)	(3 000)
Accumulated depreciation at 31 December 2021	7 000	3 400	10 400

This budgeted statement of non-current assets provides the information to include in both the budgeted statement of profit or loss for the depreciation charge for the year, and the budgeted statement of financial position at 31 December 2021.

Master Limited Budgeted statement of profit or loss for the year ending 31 December 2021			
	$	$	$
Revenue [1]			600 000
Less: cost of sales:			
Opening inventory		10 800	
Purchases [2]		348 000	
		358 800	
Closing inventory [3]		(30 000)	(328 800)
Gross profit			271 200
Less: expenditure			
Wages		(96 000)	
Rent		(8 000)	
Other expenses		(100 000)	
Loss on sale of motor vehicle		(1 000)	
Depreciation:			
Equipment	(1 000)		
Motor vehicles	(1 600)	(2 600)	(207 600)
Profit for the year			63 600

CONTINUED

Notes:

[1] The revenue is the total of the sales made in the year
$(132 000 + 156 000 + 168 000 + 144 000).

[2] The purchases figure is the total of the purchases made in the year
$(72 000 + 96 000 + 84 000 + 96 000).

[3] See note 9 in the additional information.

Note that the purchases figure in the budgeted statement of profit or loss reflects when the purchases occur not when payments are made to the suppliers. Similarly the sales figure reflects when the sales occur not when the cash is received.

c

Master Limited Budgeted statement of financial position at 31 December 2021	Cost	Accumulated depreciation	Net book value
	$	$	$
Non-current assets			
Equipment	10 000	(7 000)	3 000
Motor vehicles	16 000	(3 400)	12 600
	26 000	(10 400)	15 600
Current assets			
Inventory			30 000
Trade receivables			48 000 [1]
Cash and cash equivalents			72 000
			150 000
Total assets			165 600
Equity and liabilities			
Share capital and reserves			
Ordinary shares of $1			50 000
Retained earnings			
(20 000 + 63 600)			83 600
			133 600
Current liabilities			
Trade payables			32 000 [2]
Total equity and liabilities			165 600

Notes:

[1] Trade receivables are December sales $48 000 ($144 000 $\times \frac{1}{3}$).

[2] Trade payables are December purchases $32 000 ($96 000 $\times \frac{1}{3}$).

Note: as the master budget is prepared for management, there is no need to present it in line with IAS 1.

37.12 Using spreadsheets for budgeting

Budgets can be produced manually although spreadsheets are now widely used by businesses for preparing budgets.

Using spreadsheets to prepare budgets has a number of advantages and disadvantages, including the following:

Advantages	Disadvantages
Using spreadsheets to produce budgets is quicker than manual budgeting. For example, formulas can be used to calculate discounts or percentages of trade receivables that are expected to be paid each month.	As with any computer-based system, there are potential system failures and potential security breaches.
Coordination between budgets is improved and errors are reduced because worksheets can be linked together. For example, if the production budget is on one worksheet, it can be linked to the purchases budget. Then, if the production budget changes, it automatically changes the purchases budget.	If an error is introduced in one budget it will affect other budgets as worksheets are linked together.
Spreadsheets are versatile and easy to customise to an individual business's needs.	Staff will need training to use spreadsheets. This can be costly to the business.

Specialist accounting software that can be used for preparing budgets is also available for businesses to buy. In practice many businesses, especially smaller ones, still prepare budgets with spreadsheets rather than specialist accounting software. Reasons why many businesses continue to use spreadsheets rather than move to more specialist software include:

- While some staff training is needed to use spreadsheets, this is less than for specialist accounting software.
- Changing systems can be expensive.
- Spreadsheets are more easily available and less expensive to buy than specialist accounting packages.

37.13 Budgetary control

Managers are responsible for planning and controlling a business for the benefit of its owners. Budgets are an important part of the planning and control cycle for a business. The planning and control cycle is sometimes referred to as a planning loop, as shown in Figure 37.2.

Planning

Managers will use the business's aims and information from past performance of the business to plan for the year(s) ahead. Budgets are produced to set out the plans in monetary terms and ensure co-ordination between different parts of the business.

Once the budgets have been prepared the managers are responsible for implementing the plans and meeting the budgets set. For example, the sales manager is responsible for achieving figures in the sales budget etc.

Well-managed businesses have short-term budgets for, say, the year ahead. Small businesses may function well enough with these, but larger businesses need to plan further ahead and may prepare long-term budgets, in addition to the short-term ones, for the next five, ten or even more years ahead. These plans are often known as rolling budgets because, as each year passes, it is deleted from the budget and a budget for another year is added. A budget for one year ahead will be detailed, but budgets for the following years may be less precise because of uncertainty about future trading conditions.

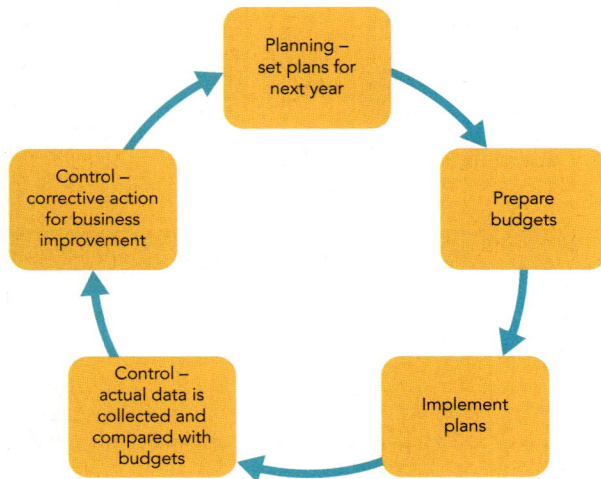

Figure 37.2: The planning and control cycle.

A budget committee, including the accountant, should co-ordinate the departmental budgets to ensure that they achieve top management's plans for the business.

Control

Control involves measuring actual performance, comparing it with the budget and taking corrective action to bring actual performance into line with the budget. It is important that deviations from budget be discovered early before serious situations arise. Annual departmental budgets may be broken down into four-weekly or monthly, or even weekly, periods, and departmental management accounts are prepared for those periods. These management accounts compare actual performance with budget and must be prepared promptly after the end of each period if they are to be useful and feed into future plans.

Comparison between actual and budgeted performance is discussed in Chapter 38.

KEY CONCEPT LINK

Planning and control: Budgets put management plans into financial terms. Actual results are then compared against budgets on an ongoing basis to monitor performance and take corrective action where appropriate.

The behavioural aspects of budgeting

Setting the budget

Budgets are based on the plans for a business. One use of budgets is for setting individual targets for managers and other staff. For example, sales staff may have individual targets for the volume or value of the goods they sell.

Organisations have varied approaches to setting budgets. Some use a top-down approach and others use a bottom-up approach. Managers' commitment and motivation to achieving the budgets can depend on the approach taken.

Top-down budgets are well co-ordinated so that they all fit together as a logical and consistent plan for the whole business. However, departmental managers may not feel committed to keeping to these budgets as they have had little or no say in their preparation and may be of the opinion that the budgets are unrealistic.

KEY TERM

top-down budgets: budgets prepared by top management and handed down to departmental managers, who are responsible for putting them into effect.

Bottom-up budgets can be unsatisfactory because they may not fit together with all the other departmental budgets to make a logical and consistent overall plan for the business. Also, managers tend to base their own budgets on easily achievable targets to avoid being criticised for failing to meet them; this will result in departments performing below their maximum level of efficiency and be bad for the business as a whole.

Ultimately, managers who will be responsible for achieving a budget will be more motivated if they participate in the setting of budgets. This will increase the likelihood that they agree with and accept the figures, and will work hard to achieve them.

> **KEY TERM**
>
> **bottom-up budgets:** budgets prepared by departmental managers.

Working to achieve the budget

It is the responsibility of the managers to ensure that the actual figures are in line with the budgets. Aiming towards a target can be a good way of motivating managers and other employees.

How motivated staff will be can depend on the perceived fairness of the budgeted figures.

If budgets are unrealistic, they can be frustrating and demotivating for staff. If they are too high, staff may think that they are unachievable and stop trying; if they are very low, staff may not think that they need to put in much effort to achieve them.

A motivating budget is often one that is ambitious but seen as achievable and staff may have participated in its planning. This type of budget is most likely to encourage staff to perform at their best.

After actual results are available

Once the actual results become available, budgeted and actual results are compared. This comparison of actual performance against the budget often forms part of the assessment of managers' performance in their jobs. Where actual figures achieve or surpass the budgeted figures, managers may be rewarded. They may receive positive feedback from their line managers and may also receive financial rewards such as bonuses.

There are both advantages and disadvantages that budgeting and budgetary control can bring to a business.

Advantages of budgeting and budgetary control	Disadvantages of budgeting and budgetary control
• It encourages managers to think about the future and the direction in which the business is heading.	• Budgets are time consuming to prepare.
• It encourages managers to be aware of costs and helps identify parts of the business where improvements are required or can be made before the start of a trading period.	• Often the budget process is started some months before the end of the current year. A number of things can happen between that time and the end of the year that will affect the future. Hence, budgets can become out of date very quickly.
• It can motivate managers and other staff. This is especially true if management performance is measured against the budget and if staff are paid a bonus if actual results are better than budgeted.	• Budgets often require specialist knowledge to prepare, especially the cash and master budgets. This can add to the expenses of the business, particularly for small sole traders and partnerships that may not have the necessary expertise.
• Banks and other lenders often require budget information from the business. The cash budget is of particular interest to banks before granting further finance to a business, or to see that their investment is safe. Thus, cash budgets may help in securing finance for the firm.	• If managers are paid on their performance against the budget, they may build in some extra costs or reduce the expected revenue to ensure they always beat it. This is known as 'budgetary slack'.

Advantages of budgeting and budgetary control	Disadvantages of budgeting and budgetary control
• Budget preparation ensures the co-ordination of all the activities of a business.	
• When managers are involved in the preparation of their budgets, they are committed to meeting them. Therefore, they are more likely to be achieved.	
• Budgets avoid 'management by crisis', which describes situations in which managers have not foreseen problems before they arise and prepared for them in advance. These managers spend their time dealing with problems that would never have arisen had they been foreseen.	

Despite the disadvantages of budgeting, budgets are vital to enable managers to do their jobs. All businesses should prepare them, even sole traders.

37.14 Using budgets to support decision making

Regularly setting budgets encourages management to think carefully about their business plans for the future. Those plans are quantified in the budgets. The budgets can then be used throughout the period of the budget to support managers in their decision making so that the business's plans are put into action.

Once all the budgets are set, it becomes easier for decision making to be delegated to individual departmental managers to make day-to-day decisions. These decisions will be more informed. For example, if the human resources manager knows the volume of labour needed and the amount that is budgeted for labour costs, then decisions can be made about the number of staff that need to be recruited (or made redundant), what skills are needed and what the business can afford to pay in wages.

While departmental managers use budgets to support their decision making, they should also take other factors into consideration. Non-financial factors such as changes in competitor behaviour, staff motivation and customer preferences can all influence the decisions that managers need to make.

For example, the purchases budget will clarify the plan for the volume and price of materials. The purchases manager will use this information to support decisions on each purchase. However, they may deviate from the budgeted figures for good reasons, such as a supplier offering much better quality materials for a slightly higher price. It may be a better decision for the business to buy the higher quality products. Using the better quality material might make it easier to work with in the production process, or customers may be happier with the final products. This may improve the reputation of the business.

37.15 Flexible budgets

The budgets produced in this chapter are **fixed budgets**, that is, they are based on a specified amount being produced and sold. The actual number of units produced and sold is likely to be more or less than the number in a fixed budget. As a result, fixed budgets may lose their usefulness as a method of budgetary control.

If budgeted output is different from actual output, we are not comparing like with like. When activity levels change, variable and semi-variable costs also change. If output increases dramatically, fixed costs may also change. Thus, to compare actual results with a fixed budget in these circumstances is useless.

> **KEY TERM**
>
> **fixed budget:** a budget which is not changed when sales, or some other activity, increases or decreases.

To overcome the problems of fixed budgets with a fixed level of production, we can 'flex' budgets to reflect various levels of activity and costs. Flexible budgets are more useful for control purposes as they provide management with information to make more meaningful comparisons between budgeted and actual figures.

Flexible budgets are prepared and used in Chapter 38.

THINK LIKE AN ACCOUNTANT

Planning ahead

Budgets are useful tools for planning. Businesses produce a number of different budgets to help with planning for the months and years ahead. By obtaining information about possible outcomes, calculating possible costs and revenues, and analysing the results, more informed decisions can be made and better outcomes can be achieved.

Budgeting can be useful to individuals as well as businesses. Budgeting for general monthly expenditure can make individuals more aware of their spending and consumption of day-to-day items. Budgets can motivate people to save up for major purchases such as a holiday or new car. Can you think of any occasions when you have budgeted? If so, did you find it useful? Why is budgeting useful for individuals? What might discourage people from budgeting in practice?

Figure 37.3: Businesses produce a number of different budgets to help with planing for the months and years ahead.

EXAM-STYLE QUESTIONS

1   Explain what a fixed budget is.   [2]
2   State three advantages of a budgetary control system.   [3]
3   The sales budget for Raj Limited for the five months to 31 October 2021 is as follows:

	Units
June	400
July	600
August	1 000
September	900
October	800

CONTINUED

Additional information

1 All units are sold for $50. Customers are allowed one month's credit.

2 Monthly production of the units is equal to the following month's sales plus 10% for inventory.

3 Costs per unit are as follows:

Material	2 kg
Cost of material	$5.00 per kg
Labour	2 hours
Labour rate	$14.00 per hour
Absorption rates per unit:	
Variable overhead	$15.00
Fixed overhead	$4.00

4 Materials are purchased one month before they are needed for production and are paid for two months after purchase.

5 Wages and variable overheads are paid in the month they are incurred.

6 Fixed overheads are paid in the following month.

7 The cash book balance at 31 July 2020 is $20 000.

Required

a Prepare the following budgets for the month of August 2020 *only*:

   i   production budget (in units only) [5]

   ii   purchases budget in dollars [5]

   iii a cash budget. [10]

Additional information

The directors of Raj Limited are unsure of the benefits of preparing budgets. They argue that the accountant seems to spend a lot of time working on them and that he should no longer prepare them.

Required

b Advise the directors whether or not the company accountant should continue to prepare budgets for the business. Justify your answer. [5]

CONTINUED

4   The accountant of EJs Limited has provided the following data:

EJs Limited Statement of financial position at 31 December 2020			
	Cost	Accumulated depreciation	Net book value
	$	$	$
Non-current assets			
Plant and machinery	50 000	(10 000)	40 000
Current assets			
Inventory			30 000
Trade receivables			20 000
Cash and cash equivalents			16 000
			66 000
Total assets			106 000
Equity and liabilities			
Equity			
Ordinary shares of $1			80 000
Retained earnings			11 000
			91 000
Current liabilities			
Trade payables			15 000
Total equity and liabilities			106 000

Additional information

1   Sales and purchases for the four months from January to April 2021 are budgeted to be:

	Sales	Purchases
	$	$
January	45 000	20 000
February	60 000	20 000
March	60 000	30 000
April	90 000	30 000

1   50% of sales are to cash customers; one month's credit is allowed to credit customers.
2   The company pays for its purchases in the month following purchase.
3   Selling and distribution expenses amount to 10% of sales and are paid in the month in which they are incurred.
4   Administration expenses are $10 000 per month and are paid in the month in which they are incurred.
5   Inventory at 30 April 2021 is estimated to be valued at $30 000.
6   Additional plant and machinery costing $20 000 will be purchased on 1 February 2021.
7   A dividend of $0.10 per share will be paid on the ordinary shares on 30 April 2021.

Required

a   Prepare a cash budget for each of the four months from January 2021 to 30 April 2021.   [8]
b   Prepare a budgeted statement of profit or loss for the four months ending 30 April 2021.   [8]
c   Prepare a budgeted statement of financial position at 30 April 2021.   [9]

SELF-EVALUATION CHECKLIST

After studying this chapter, complete a table like this:

You should be able to:	Needs more work	Almost there	Ready to move on
Calculate budgets to plan future activity.			
Identify and evaluate limiting factors to decide the order in which to prepare budgets, remembering that if customer demand for a product limits the amount that a business can produce and sell, then the sales budget is the first to be produced.			
Prepare budgets for sales, production, purchases, labour, trade receivables, trade payables and cash to aid the planning and control of a business.			
Prepare the master budget (the budgeted statement of profit or loss and the budgeted statement of financial position together).			
Evaluate the advantages and disadvantages of budgetary control and use spreadsheets or specialist accounting software to prepare budgets.			
Calculate flexible budgets instead of fixed budgets because flexible budgets reflect changes in activity levels.			

> Chapter 38

Standard costing

This chapter covers syllabus section A Level 4.2

LEARNING INTENTIONS

In this chapter you will learn how to:

- calculate standards as the starting point for budgeting and budgetary control
- evaluate the advantages and disadvantages of standard costing
- prepare a flexible budget
- calculate variances for sales, materials, labour and fixed overheads
- prepare statements reconciling standard cost and profits of actual units produced
- analyse actual costs and revenue against standards using variances
- assess the use of standard costing to improve business performance.

ACCOUNTING IN CONTEXT

A clean performance

Faiza owns and runs a small business manufacturing and selling soap. She set up three years ago working from home with some equipment and supplies of raw materials. She sells the soaps at local market stalls, events and online.

When planning the business, she approached her local bank for a business bank account and small loan. The bank's business advisor recommended that she set budgets for the business costs and revenues. Faiza found that comparing her actual and expected performance was very useful.

Initially, Faiza relied heavily on market research and guesswork to estimate the cost of making each bar of soap, the selling price and the amount she could make and sell in her first year. When she compared her actual performance against the budgeted figures, she found there were big differences between the two sets of results.

Faiza used the information to help her to focus on what changes she needed to make to improve the business. At the end of the first year, she changed supplier and negotiated a trade discount. Faiza also updated her budgeted figures so that her budgets for the second year were more realistic and achievable.

At the end of her second year of trading Faiza found that her actual results were closer to her budgets than in the first year. Faiza still found the comparison helpful and resolved to continue to compare actual and budgeted figures.

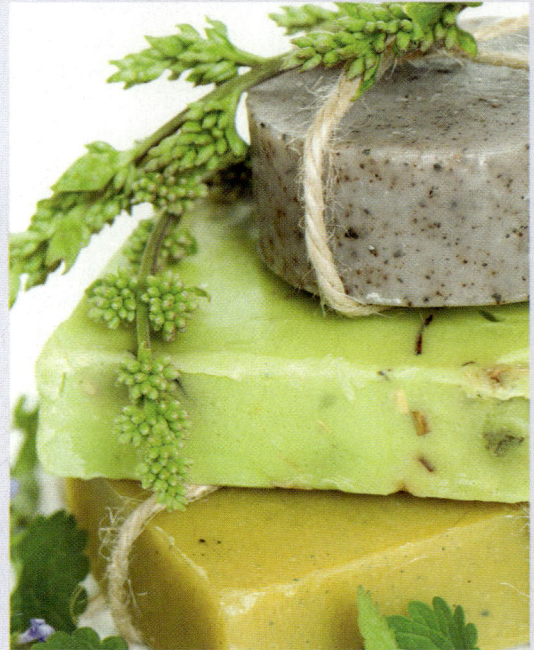

Figure 38.1: Faiza owns and runs a small business manufacturing and selling soap.

Discuss in a pair or a group:

* Why is it useful to compare actual results against budgeted figures?
* Why are Faiza's budgeted figures for the second year likely to be more realistic than for the first year?
* Faiza is keen to continue comparing actual and budgeted figures. Are there any disadvantages of making the comparisons?

38.1 What is standard costing?

A **standard cost** is used by manufacturers when preparing realistic budgets. Standards can also be set for revenue.

Standard costing compares actual costs against standard costs. The differences between actual and standard costs and revenue are known as **variances**.

This comparison will help managers to assess and control costs and take action where needed. For example, a difference between the actual and budgeted cost of materials might show that the purchase price of the materials has increased since the budget was prepared. Possible causes of a significant variance would be investigated. Corrective action might be that the purchasing manager reviews current suppliers or actively seeks additional discounts.

38.2 Setting standards

Standards must be realistic if they are to be useful. Standards will need to be regularly reviewed and kept up to date if they are to be realistic. For example, if new machinery is purchased, direct labour time for production will need to be updated.

KEY TERMS

standard cost: the estimated or budgeted cost of a unit of output or activity.

standard costing: an accounting system that compares actual costs against standard costs, which helps managers to assess and control costs and take action where needed.

variance: the difference between the standard cost and actual cost.

There are various types of standard that businesses might use. The main types of standard and their practical uses are:

- *Ideal standards* are standards that can only be met under ideal conditions. In practice, conditions under which businesses work are rarely ideal, therefore these standards are unrealistic and are unlikely to be attained. As a result, they can demotivate managers and cause them to perform less efficiently. Ideal standards should not be used.

- *Current standards* are based on present levels of performance. This may be inappropriate for the future. They do not offer management or workers any incentive to perform more efficiently. Current standards should only be used when present conditions are too uncertain to enable more appropriate standards to be set.

- *Attainable standards* recognise that there is some wastage of materials and not all the hours worked are productive. Time spent unproductively by workers is called idle time and may occur when machinery breaks down or the machinery has to be 'set up' for a production run. The standards should take account of these factors and give the workers an incentive to use their time and materials efficiently. The standards set should be attainable ones.

Worked example 1 shows how standards are used to prepare budgets.

WORKED EXAMPLE 1

Study Limited makes desks in three sizes: small, medium and large. In April, output is expected to be as follows:

- 200 small desks, which take 30 minutes each to make

- 300 medium desks, which take 1 hour each to make

- 400 large desks, which take $1\frac{1}{2}$ hours each to make.

A standard wage rate paid to direct workers is set at \$15 per hour.

The desks are made from wood. The standard price of the wood is \$20 per metre.

Study Limited has set its budgeted fixed overheads at \$50 000 per month, which are absorbed on the basis of direct labour hours.

The standard selling prices per unit for each product are:

Small desks	\$100
Medium desks	\$150
Large desks	\$200

Required

a   Calculate the standard costs to be charged to production for:

    i   labour

    ii   materials.

b   Calculate the fixed overheads absorption rate.

c   Prepare Study Limited's budgeted profit statement for April.

CONTINUED

Answer

a **i** The standard direct labour cost to make the products in April will be:

	Total standard hours	Total standard wage cost [1]
		$
200 small desks, which take 30 minutes each to make	100	1 500
300 medium desks, which take 1 hour each to make	300	4 500
400 large desks, which take $1\frac{1}{2}$ hours each to make	600	9 000
Total standard hours and wages cost of production	1 000	15 000

Note:

[1] The total standard wage cost for each type of desk is the total standard hours × $15.

ii The standard material cost of production are as follows:

	Total standard material	Total standard material cost [1]
	Metres	$
200 small desks, which each take 2 metres of wood to make	400	8 000
300 medium desks, which each take 3 metres of wood to make	900	18 000
400 large desks, which each take 4 metres of wood to make	1 600	32 000
Total standard quantity and cost of material for production	2 900	58 000

Note:

[1] The total standard material cost for each type of desk is the total standard metres of material × $20.

b Study Limited has set its budgeted fixed overheads at $50 000. It is absorbed on the basis of direct labour hours; therefore, the standard overhead absorption rate is $50 ($50 000 ÷ 1 000 hours).

CONTINUED

c   Study Limited's budgeted profit statement is as follows:

Study Limited Budgeted profit statement for April [1]	Small	Medium	Large	Total
	$	$	$	$
Revenue	20 000	45 000	80 000	145 000
Direct materials	(8 000)	(18 000)	(32 000)	(58 000)
Direct labour	(1 500)	(4 500)	(9 000)	(15 000)
Fixed overhead at $50 per direct labour hour	(5 000)	(15 000)	(30 000)	(50 000)
Budgeted profit	5 500	7 500	9 000	22 000

Note:

[1]   It is not a budgeted statement of profit or loss as not all expenses have been included. This is acceptable as it is for management use and not for publication.

The information to prepare the budgeted profit statement has been built up from the standard data prepared; hence standard costing is the foundation for budgeting and budgetary control.

ACTIVITY 38.1

A manufacturing company uses standard costing for its products: curtains and sheets. Both use the same materials and are made in the same factory.

Estimated production and sales volumes for the next three months are 10 000 sets of curtains and 8 000 packs of sheets.

Standard costing information for the products is as follows:

Details per unit:	Curtains	Sheets
Selling price	$90	$40
Direct materials	5 metres of cotton at $4 per metre	2 metres of cotton at $4 per metre
Direct labour	2 hours at $12 per hour	1 hour at $12 per hour

Total budgeted fixed overheads for the three-month period is $266 000. Fixed overheads are absorbed on the basis of direct labour hours.

Required

Prepare the budgeted profit statement for the next three-month period.

38.3 The advantages and disadvantages of standard costing

Standard costing is an important management tool. It provides a benchmark against which actual performance can be measured.

There are both advantages and disadvantages to using a standard costing system. When used properly, the advantages of standard costing will outweigh the disadvantages and improve the future performance of the business.

Advantages of standard costing	Disadvantages of standard costing
The preparation of budgets is made easier if they are based on standard costs, and the budgets are likely to be more realistic.	It takes time to collect the data needed to prepare the standard cost of a product.
Differences between actual and budgeted results (variances) are easier to identify if standard costs are used.	The standards need to be continually monitored and updated if they are to be useful.
The activities that cause variances are highlighted.	It does not explain the cause of the variances. Further investigation is needed if improvements are to be made.
Calculated standards help the preparation of estimates for the costs of new products and quotations for orders.	There may be factors outside the control of the business which cause the variance. For example, the business may expect material prices to increase by 2%, but inflation may lead to a 4% price increase.
Although standard costing is associated with manufacturing, it can be used in other businesses, including services.	

38.4 The flexible budget

The actual volume of goods produced and sold is not the same as the expected volume on which a budget has been based. Once accurate figures are known, sensible comparisons can be made if 'like is compared with like', and the budget is based on the actual volume of output. This is done by *flexing* the budget after the actual production level is known.

When flexing the budget, the budgeted sales volume is adjusted to the actual sales volume and the variable expenses in the budget is adjusted to take account of the actual volume of goods produced.

It is important to flex the budget for the following reasons:

- It allows comparison of like with like. Comparing actual costs and revenue against figures in a **flexible budget** means that we are comparing figures based on the same level of output. Fixed costs do not vary with output but revenue and variable costs do. Therefore, any variances calculated using figures from a flexible budget will be more meaningful.

- Flexing the budget helps management to take better corrective action and control the business.

> **KEY TERM**
>
> **flexible budget:** a budget that changes to match the actual volume of goods produced and sold.

> **TIP**
>
> Fixed budgets are prepared before production and flexible budgets are prepared after actual production is known.

WORKED EXAMPLE 2

In May, Liu Limited produced the following budget for the production and sale of 20 000 units for the six months ending 31 December.

Budget for 20 000 units, six months ending 31 December	$	$
Revenue		500 000
Variable expenses:		
Direct materials	(50 000)	
Direct labour	(100 000)	
Variable production overheads	(40 000)	
Variable selling and distribution	(10 000)	
	(200 000)	
Fixed expenses	(230 000)	
Total cost		(430 000)
Budgeted profit		70 000

After December, it was found that the actual output and sales for the six months ended 31 December was 28 000 units.

Required

Prepare Liu Limited's flexible budgeted profit statement for the next six-month period.

Answer

The flexible budget for the period is as follows. The budget is flexible by multiplying the revenue

and variable expenses by $\frac{28\,000}{20\,000}$, that is by 1.4.

Flexible budget for 20 000 units, for the six months ending 31 December	$	$
Revenue		700 000
Variable expenses:		
Direct materials	(70 000)	
Direct labour	(140 000)	
Production overheads	(56 000)	
Selling and distribution	(14 000)	
	(280 000)	
Fixed expenses	(230 000)	
Total cost		(510 000)
Budgeted profit		190 000

Note: the revenue and variable costs have all changed as a result of flexing the budget. The fixed expenses have not changed.

TIP

When calculating variances, the first thing you must do is flex the budgeted (or standard) information provided.

Worked example 2 applied flexible budgeting to variable and fixed costs. The variable costs were adjusted but the fixed costs remained the same.

In Section 35.1 we looked at semi-variable costs and stepped costs. A semi-variable cost contains an element of both a variable and fixed cost. Therefore, to flex a semi-variable cost, separate its fixed element from its variable element. The fixed element stays the same while the variable cost is flexed – for example, if Liu Limited has a budgeted telephone expense of $500 that consists of $100 fixed rental and $400 of calls that vary with the level of activity of the business.

The flexed budget telephone expense will be:

$$\$100 + \frac{(28\,000)}{(20\,000)} \times \$400 = \$660$$

A stepped cost is fixed only within a certain limit and will increase to a higher level when that limit is reached.

For example, if Liu Limited had a budgeted labour cost for staff supervision of $300 for the first 9 000 units then another $300 for every 9 000 units of production.

The cost of 0 to 9 000 units = $300; the cost of 9 001 to 18 000 units = $600 ($300 × 2) etc.

Therefore, the original budget for 20 000 units would have a budgeted staff supervision of $900 ($300 × 3) because it falls between 18 001 and 27 000 units.

The flexed budget staff supervision cost is then $1 200 ($300 × 4) because it falls between 27 001 and 36 000 units.

38.5 Variances

A variance is the difference between a standard cost and an actual cost or between budgeted revenue and actual revenue.

Variances are useful for helping management to spot activities that may need intervention if the budgeted profit is to be achieved or to limit any adverse effect on profit.

Variances can be calculated for:

- sales
- direct materials
- direct labour
- variable and fixed overheads.

These variances can be further analysed into sub-variances.

Every variance must be described as either a **favourable variance** (F) or an **adverse variance** (A). A sales variance will be favourable if actual figures are higher than budgeted. A cost variance will be favourable if actual figures are lower than budgeted.

Once the variances have been calculated a flexible budget statement can be prepared. This shows the budgeted and actual results along with the variances. A flexible budget statement is a useful report for management who can use it to help them decide which variances need investigation.

TIP

With all of the variance calculations, a positive number indicates a favourable variance and a negative answer indicates an adverse variance.

KEY TERMS

favourable variance: a variance where the actual cost is less than the standard cost, or where the actual revenue is more than the standard revenue.

adverse variance: a variance where the actual expense is more than the standard cost, or where the actual revenue is less than the standard reve

WORKED EXAMPLE 3

Anya Limited makes one type of product. The budget for September is based on the following standard costs:

Number of units produced and sold:	18 000
Per unit:	
Selling price per unit	$32
Direct materials (kg)	1.25
Cost of material per kg	$4
Direct labour (minutes)	30
Labour rate per hour	$12
Budgeted fixed overheads for the month	$360 000

Required

a   Prepare the budgeted statement of profit or loss for Anya Limited.

Additional information

The actual data for September was as follows:

Number of units produced and sold	20 000
Selling price per unit	$30.60
Direct materials (kg) per unit	1.10
Cost of direct materials per kg	$4.15
Direct labour (minutes)	36
Direct labour rate per hour	$11
Fixed overheads	$370 000

Required

b   Prepare the following statements:

   i   flexible budget September

   ii   actual profit statement for September.

c   Prepare the flexible budget statement for September showing the budgeted and actual data and showing the difference (variance) between the two.

TIP

Remember to flex the budget before calculating the variances. The most common mistake is to calculate the variance by comparing the actual data with the fixed budget.

Answer

a   The budgeted statement of profit or loss:

Budgeted statement of profit or loss 18 000 units in September		
	$	$
Revenue (18 000 × $32)		576 000
Direct materials (18 000 × 1.25 kg × $4)	(90 000)	
Direct labour (18 000 × [30 minutes ÷ 60] × $12)	(108 000)	(198 000)
Contribution		378 000
Fixed overheads		(360 000)
Budgeted profit		18 000

CONTINUED

b **i** It is necessary to flex the budget to reflect the actual level of output and sales. This is, in effect, the new budgeted profit statement for the month.

The flexible budget for the 20 000 units produced and sold:

	Flexible budget 20 000 units	
	$	$
Revenue (20 000 × $32)		640 000
Direct materials (20 000 × 1.25 kg × $4)	(100 000)	
Direct labour (20 000 × [30 minutes ÷ 60] × $12)	(120 000)	(220 000)
Contribution		420 000
Fixed overheads		(360 000)
Flexible budgeted profit		60 000

Note that only the variable costs are flexible to the actual level of output and sales.

ii The actual results:

	Actual results 20 000 units	
	$	$
Revenue (20 000 × $30.60)		612 000
Direct materials (20 000 × 1.10 kg × $4.15)	(91 300)	
Direct labour (20 000 × [36 minutes ÷ 60] × $11)	(132 000)	(223 300)
Contribution		388 700
Fixed overheads [1]		(370 000)
Actual profit		18 700

Note:

[1] The fixed costs are higher than the budget. However, these are the actual results and so the fixed costs for the budget may have been set at a different overhead absorption rate or an unexpected invoice was received.

c From the two sets of data in **b** a flexible budget report for senior management can be prepared.

Flexible budget statement for September:				
	Actual	Budget	Variance	
Units	20 000	20 000		
Revenue ($)	612 000	640 000	(28 000)	Adverse
Direct materials ($)	(91 300)	(100 000)	8 700	Favourable
Direct labour ($)	(132 000)	(120 000)	(12 000)	Adverse
Contribution ($)	388 700	420 000	(31 300)	Adverse
Fixed overheads ($)	(370 000)	(360 000)	(10 000)	Adverse
Profit ($)	18 700	60 000	(41 300)	Adverse

> **TIP**
>
> Variances are shown either without brackets if they are favourable, or in brackets if they are adverse. It is also important to clearly label them as favourable or adverse.

> Variances are shown either without brackets if they are favourable or in brackets if they are adverse.

Understanding the data

The flexible budget report is an important part of management control for a business. It uses flexible figures rather than the master budget data. Some companies may also show the fixed budget data as part of their report, but the comparison between the actual results and the flexible budget is the most important thing.

Variances give management an indication of where to look for the problems. Variances do not tell managers what has caused the variances; this requires further investigation.

ACTIVITY 38.2

Baqri Limited makes one type of product. The following information is available about the standard and actual results for six months to 30 June:

	Standard	Actual
Number of units produced and sold:	12 000	15 600
Per unit:		
Selling price per unit	$22	$20
Direct materials (kg)	1.2	1.0
Cost of material per kg	$4	$3
Direct labour (minutes)	40	30
Labour rate per hour	$12	$14
Budgeted fixed overheads for six months	$110 000	$115 000

Required

Prepare the flexible budgeted profit statement for the six months to 30 June. Show the budgeted and actual data and variances.

38.6 How to calculate sales variances

Actual sales revenue differs from budgeted sales revenue because the actual selling price is different from the standard selling price and/or because the actual volume sold is different. Sales variances highlight the extent of any volume or price differences.

The total sales variance is the difference between actual and budgeted sales revenue. This is caused by the *sales volume variance* (selling more or less than the budget), or the *sales price variance* (selling the goods at a different price than was budgeted). This can be shown diagrammatically as in Figure 38.2.

The variances are calculated as follows:

a *Total sales variance* is the difference between the budgeted sales revenue and the actual sales revenue.

Formula for total sales price variance:

actual sales – (fixed) budgeted sales

b *Sales volume variance* is the difference between the total sales in the original budget and the total sales in the flexible budget.

Formula for sales volume variance:

(actual units sold – fixed budgeted units sold) × standard price

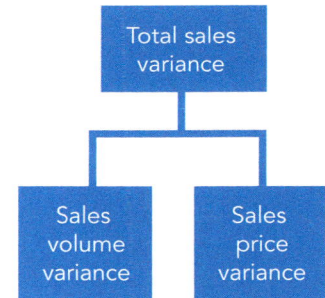

Figure 38.2: Sales variance.

TIP

The total sales variance is equal to the sales volume variance *plus* sales price variance. Knowing this allows you to check whether the sales price and sales volume variances have been calculated correctly.

c   *Sales price variance* compares the actual selling price per unit of the units sold with the standard selling price per unit. It is the difference between the flexible budgeted sales and the actual sales.

Formula for sales price variance:

(actual price − standard price) × actual units sold

WORKED EXAMPLE 4

Continued from Worked example 3

Required

Calculate for Anya Limited for September:

a   the sales volume variance

b   the sales price variance

c   the total sales variance.

Answer

a   Anya Limited's sales volume variance is

$640 000 − $576 000 = $64 000 favourable.

This could also have been calculated using the formula:

(actual sales volume − original budgeted sales volume) × standard price

(20 000 units − 18 000 units) × $32 = $64 000 favourable.

The variance is favourable because actual sales were more than the original amount budgeted.

b   Anya Limited's sales price variance is:

Actual sales − flexible budgeted sales

$612 000 − $640 000 = $28 000 adverse

This could also have been calculated using the formula:

(actual price − standard price) × actual units

($32 − $30.60) × 20 000 units = $28 000 adverse

c   Anya Limited's total sales variance is

actual sales − budgeted sales = $(612 000 − 576 000) = $36 000 favourable.

Alternatively, it can be shown as:

sales volume variance + sales price variance = $64 000 + ($28 000) = $36 000 favourable

Notice here that we are using the sales figures from the original (fixed) budget.

Calculating the variances has identified that having a lower actual selling price has increased the volume Anya Limited sold. The overall effect is higher than expected sales revenue.

38.7 How to calculate direct materials cost variances

As with sales, the variance on the direct materials cost can be due to two things: using more or less material than was budgeted and/or purchasing materials at a higher or lower price than was set in the budget.

This can be shown diagrammatically as in Figure 38.3.

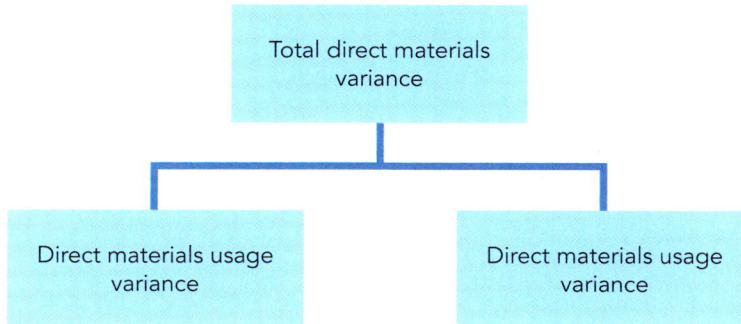

Figure 38.3: Direct materials cost variance.

The total direct materials variance is the difference between actual and budgeted materials. This is caused by the *direct materials usage (volume) variance* (using more or less material than budgeted), or the *direct materials price variance* (purchasing the materials at a different price than was budgeted).

The variances are calculated as follows:

a   *Total direct materials variance* is the difference between the *flexible* budgeted direct materials cost and the actual direct materials cost.

b   *Direct materials usage variance* is the difference between the actual quantity of direct materials used and the quantity of direct materials that should have been used to produce the actual output. The difference between the two figures is multiplied by the standard cost per kg (or other measure of the quantity), that is:

(flexible budget quantity of material – actual quantity of material) × standard cost per unit of material

c   *Direct materials price variance* is the difference between the actual price paid and the budgeted price for the actual quantity used.

If the materials are in kg then the formula is:

(standard price per kg – actual price per kg) × actual quantity in kg

> **TIP**
>
> When calculating material and labour variances, always start with the standard and deduct the 'actual'. This is opposite to the sales variance.

WORKED EXAMPLE 5

Continued from Worked example 4

Required

Calculate for Anya Limited for September:

a   the direct materials usage variance

b   the direct materials price variance

c   the total direct materials variance.

CONTINUED

Answer

a   Anya Limited's total direct materials usage variance is:

(flexible budget quantity of material – actual quantity of material) × standard cost per unit of material

The actual quantity produced and sold was 20 000 units.

The flexible budget quantity of materials is 20 000 × 1.25 kg = 25 000 kg.

The actual usage was 20 000 × 1.10 = 22 000 kg.

The standard cost per kg was $4.

The calculation is, therefore:

(25 000 kg – 22 000 kg) × $4 = $12 000 favourable

b   Anya Limited's total direct materials price variance is:

(standard price per kg – actual price per kg) × actual quantity in kg

The actual price per kg was $4.15.

The budgeted, or standard, price per kg was $4.

The calculation is therefore:

($4.00 – $4.15) × 22 000 kg = $3 300 adverse

c   Anya Limited's total direct materials variance is

flexible budget direct materials – actual direct materials

= $(91 300 – 100 000) = $8 700 favourable

Alternatively, it can be shown as:

$12 000 + ($3 300) = $8 700 favourable

Anya Limited has been more efficient in using the material, or perhaps it was of better quality, as the business has had to pay more for it.

38.8 How to calculate direct labour variances

The calculations of the direct labour variances are similar to those required to calculate the direct materials variances. The only difference is in their names. For direct labour, a *direct labour efficiency variance* is the same thing as a direct materials usage variance. Both measure the efficiency with which the company used the resources.

Similarly, a *direct labour rate variance* measures the price the company paid for labour – the wage rate. This is the same as the direct materials price variance.

This can be shown diagrammatically as in Figure 38.4.

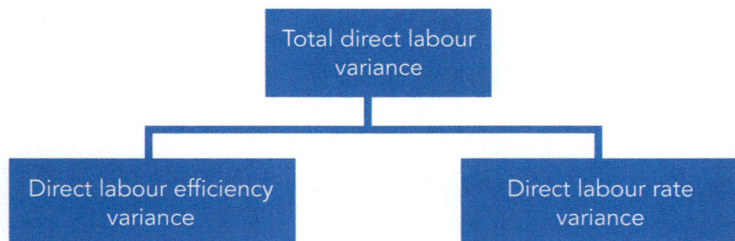

Figure 38.4: Direct labour variance.

The variances are calculated as follows:

a   *Total direct labour variance* is the difference between the flexible budget direct labour cost and the actual direct labour cost.

Formula for total direct labour variance:

(flexible budget labour hours – actual labour hours) × standard wage rate

b   *Direct labour efficiency variance* is the difference between the actual direct labour hours worked and the direct labour hours that *should* have been worked to produce the *actual* output. The difference between the two figures is multiplied by the standard wage rate.

Formula for direct labour efficiency variance:

(flexible budget labour hours – actual labour hours) × standard wage rate

c   *Direct labour rate variance* is the difference between the actual direct labour wage rate and the budgeted direct labour wage rate for the actual hours worked.

Formula for direct labour rate variance:

(standard wage rate – actual wage rate) × actual hours worked

WORKED EXAMPLE 6

Continued from Worked example 5

Required

Calculate for Anya Limited for September:

a   the direct labour efficiency variance

b   the direct labour rate variance

c   the total direct labour variance.

Answer

a   Anya Limited's direct labour efficiency variance is

(flexible budget labour hours – actual labour hours) × standard wage rate

The actual quantity produced and sold was 20 000 units.

The flexible budgeted labour hours is $20\,000 \times (30 \div 60) = 10\,000$ direct labour hours.

The actual usage was $20\,000 \times (36 \div 60) = 12\,000$ direct labour hours.

The standard wage rate is $12.

The calculation is therefore:

(10 000 hours – 12 000 hours) × $12 = $24 000 adverse

b   Anya Limited's direct labour rate variance is:

(standard wage rate – actual wage rate) × actual hours worked

The actual direct labour hour rate was $11 per hour.

The budgeted, or standard, direct labour hour rate was $12 per hour.

The calculation is therefore:

($12 – 11) × 12 000 = $12 000 favourable

CONTINUED

c   Anya Limited's total direct labour variance is

flexible budget direct labour cost – actual direct labour cost

= ($120 000 – $132 000) = $12 000 adverse

Alternatively, it can be shown as:

($24 000) + $12 000 = $12 000 adverse, as identified in the flexible budget

Anya Limited may have used cheaper labour but workers have not been as efficient as predicted.

ACTIVITY 38.3

Action Limited makes one type of product. The following budgeted information is available for January:

	Standard
Number of units produced and sold:	10 000
Per unit:	
Selling price per unit	$8
Direct materials (litres)	1
Cost of material per litre	$5
Direct labour (minutes)	10
Labour rate per hour	$10

The following actual information is available for September:

- sales were 9 000 units at $10 each.
- 9 900 litres of materials were used at a total cost of $44 550.
- 2 250 direct labour hours were used at $11 per hour.

Required

For Action Limited for January:

a   calculate the sales volume variance

b   calculate the sales price variance

c   calculate the direct materials usage variance

d   calculate the direct materials price variance

e   calculate the direct labour efficiency variance

f   calculate the direct labour rate variance

REFLECTION

When answering Activity 38.3, how did you know how to calculate each variance? Did you learn a formula for each or are there other ways to remember how to calculate each variance? Discuss with another learner how you can best learn how to calculate each variance and recognise it as favourable or adverse.

38.9 Calculation of fixed overhead variances

The aim of setting standard costs for fixed overheads is to absorb the amount of fixed overheads into the overall cost of output. Actual costs and levels of production will vary from the standards or budgets set. Thus, there will be an under-(shortfall) or over-(surplus) absorption of overheads. This will be calculated by means of the variances shown diagrammatically in Figure 38.5.

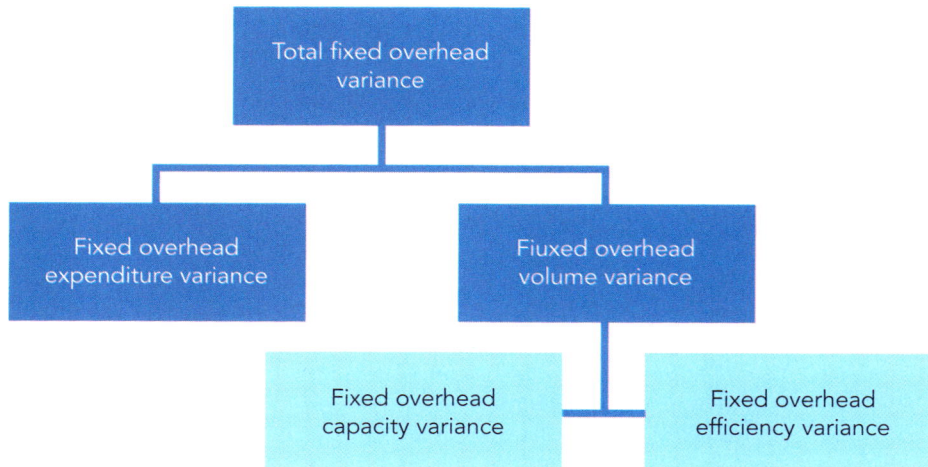

TIP

Only the budgeted fixed overhead absorption rate is used in variance calculations. Never calculate an actual overhead absorption rate.

Figure 38.5: Fixed overhead variance.

Notice from Figure 38.5 that the fixed overhead volume variance is made up of two other variances:

- the fixed overhead capacity variance
- the fixed overhead efficiency variance.

The fixed overhead variances are calculated as follows:

TIP

Note that the budgeted fixed overhead absorption rate will need to be calculated for the fixed overhead volume. capacity and efficiency variances.

a *Fixed overhead expenditure variance*, which is the difference between the actual fixed overheads incurred and the budgeted fixed overheads.

b *Fixed overhead volume variance* is the difference between the standard hours for actual output and the budgeted hours. This difference in hours is then multiplied by the *budgeted* fixed overhead absorption rate (OAR).

Assuming the fixed overheads are absorbed based on direct labour hours, the formula is:

(standard hours for the actual output – budgeted hours) × budgeted OAR

If the fixed overheads are absorbed based on direct materials then the formula will need to be adapted.

Note: the budgeted fixed OAR will be needed to calculate this variance. The OAR will also be needed for the fixed overhead capacity variance and the fixed overhead efficiency variance.

c *Fixed overhead capacity variance* is a sub-division of the volume variance, where actual direct labour hours for actual output differ from the budgeted direct labour hours. Again, this difference in hours is multiplied by the budgeted fixed OAR.

Assuming the fixed overheads are absorbed based on direct labour hours, then the formula is:

(actual direct labour hours – budgeted direct labour hours) × OAR

d *Fixed overhead efficiency variance*, again, is a sub-division of the volume variance, where the actual direct labour hours for the actual output differ from the standard direct labour hours for the actual output. This difference is multiplied by the budgeted fixed OAR.

Assuming the fixed overheads are absorbed based on direct labour hours, then the formula is:

(standard hours for the actual output – actual direct labour hours) × OAR

WORKED EXAMPLE 7

Continued from Worked example 6

Anya Limited uses budgeted direct labour hours to absorb fixed overheads.

Required

Calculate for Anya Limited for September:

a the fixed overhead expenditure variance

b the fixed overhead volume variance

c the fixed overhead capacity variance

d the fixed overhead efficiency variance.

Answer

a Anya Limited's fixed overhead expenditure variance is:

budgeted fixed overheads – actual fixed overheads

= ($360 000 – $370 000) = $10 000 adverse

b The fixed overhead volume variance is:

As the OAR is based on direct labour hours, the formula is:

(standard hours for the actual output – budgeted hours) × budgeted OAR

The budgeted fixed overhead absorption rate per labour hour =

$$\frac{\text{budgeted overheads}}{\text{budgeted direct labour hours}} = \frac{\$360\,000}{9\,000 \text{ hours}} = \$40 \text{ per direct labour hour}$$

Actual output 20 000 units should have taken (20 000 × [30 ÷ 60]) = 10 000 direct labour hours.

Budgeted output 18 000 units should have taken (18 000 × [30 ÷ 60]) = 9 000 direct labour hours.

The calculation is, therefore:

(10 000 hours – 9 000 hours) × $40 = $40 000 favourable

c The fixed overhead capacity variance is:

(actual direct labour hours – budgeted direct labour hours) × OAR

Where:

actual direct labour hours worked = 20 000 units × (36 ÷ 60) = 12 000 direct labour hours.

budgeted direct labour hours = 9 000 direct labour hours.

The calculation is, therefore:

(12 000 hours – 9 000 hours) × $40 = $120 000 favourable

CONTINUED

d The fixed overhead efficiency variance is:

(standard hours for the actual output – actual direct labour hours) × OAR

Where:

actual direct labour hours worked = 12 000.

standard direct labour hours for actual production = 10 000.

The calculation is, therefore:

(10 000 hours – 12 000 direct labour hours) × \$40 = \$80 000 adverse

It is now possible to prepare a summary of the fixed overhead expenditure variances from the calculations made:

	\$
Expenditure variance	(10 000) A
Volume variance*	40 000 F
Total fixed overhead expenditure variance	30 000 F

*The volume variance is sub-divided into:

	\$
Capacity variance	120 000 F
Efficiency variance	(80 000) A
Volume variance	40 000 F

The total fixed overhead variance is positive for Anya Limited. Favourable here means that fixed overheads have been over-absorbed into production as a result of more units being produced and sold than was budgeted for.

The *total fixed overhead variance* is the difference between the fixed overheads absorbed into production (10 000 direct labour hours × \$40 per hour) minus the fixed overheads actually paid. However, the situation is not altogether satisfactory as, despite higher production, the time it took to make the product was in excess of the budgeted time allowed. This has resulted in an adverse fixed overhead efficiency variance.

38.10 Reconciling standard cost and actual cost

After the variances have been calculated, a statement can be prepared reconciling the standard cost of the actual units produced with the actual cost of the units produced. To do this, first it is necessary to calculate the standard cost of production and sales.

WORKED EXAMPLE 8

Continued from Worked example 7

Required

Prepare a statement reconciling the flexible budgeted cost of production with the actual cost of production for Anya Limited.

CONTINUED

Answer

Step 1

Calculate the standard (or budgeted) cost per unit of the product:

	$
Direct materials (1.25 kg per unit × $4)	5
Direct labour (30 min × $12 per hour)	6
Fixed overheads (30 min × $40 per hour)	20
Standard cost per unit	31

Step 2

Calculate the *total* standard cost of actual production and sales:

20 000 units × $31 per unit = $620 000.

Step 3

Prepare the statement reconciling the standard cost of actual production with the actual cost:

Anya Limited Statement reconciling the standard cost of actual production with the actual cost			
	Favourable variances	Adverse variances	Total
	$	$	$
Standard cost of actual production			620 000 [1]
Direct materials usage variance	12 000		
Direct materials price variance		(3 300)	
Direct labour efficiency variance		(24 000)	
Direct labour rate variance	12 000		
Fixed overhead expenditure variance		(10 000)	
Fixed overhead volume variance	40 000 [3]		
	64 000	(37 300)	(26 700)
Actual cost of production [2]			593 300

Notes:

[1] The standard cost of actual production is greater than the figure in the flexible budget by $40 000 ($620 000 − $580 000 [direct materials $100 000 + direct labour $120 000 + fixed overheads $360 000]). This is due to the over-absorption of fixed overheads by the extra production and sales of 2 000 units × $20 per unit = $40 000.

[2] Actual cost of production is the direct materials cost ($91 300) + direct labour cost ($132 000) + actual fixed overheads ($370 000) = $593 300.

[3] The statement could have shown the fixed overhead capacity variance of $120 000 favourable and the fixed overhead efficiency variance of $80 000 adverse, rather than the total volume variance of $40 000 favourable, but not all three variances. If the capacity variance is shown this is a true measure of fixed overheads over-absorbed.

38.11 Reconciling the actual profit with the flexible budget profit

It is now possible to prepare a statement reconciling the flexible budgeted profit for the year with the actual profit for the year. This shows the link between the profit calculated based on standard cost and the actual profit achieved.

WORKED EXAMPLE 9

Continued from Worked example 8

Required

Prepare a statement reconciling the flexible budgeted profit for the year with the actual profit for the year for Anya Limited.

Answer

Anya Limited Statement reconciling the flexible budgeted profit for the year with the actual profit for the year			
	Favourable variances	Adverse variances	Total
	$	$	$
Flexible budget profit for the year			60 000
Sales price variance		(28 000)	
Direct materials usage variance	12 000		
Direct materials price variance		(3 300)	
Direct labour efficiency variance		(24 000)	
Direct labour rate variance	12 000		
Fixed overhead expenditure variance		(10 000)	
	24 000	(65 300)	(41 300)
Actual profit for the year			18 700

Note: only the variances that are reflected in the comparison between the flexible budget and the actual results are included in this statement.

38.12 Causes of variances and their interrelationships

Variances highlight where actual figures differ from standards. Variances do not explain the causes of the differences but do show management where further investigation is required. Once management understands the cause(s) of a variance, they can consider whether there is corrective action that can be taken.

It is important management understands that each variance does not operate in isolation. If action is taken to correct one variance, there can be an effect on another variance. For example, if a business buys cheaper direct materials than the standard, this will result in a favourable direct materials variance. However, if these cheaper materials are of a poorer quality, this might lead to materials being wasted or employees having more work to produce the good to be sold. As a result, the favourable direct materials variance may lead to adverse materials usage and adverse labour efficiency variances.

We now consider what causes variances to be favourable or adverse and their relationships with other variances.

Sales variances

Sales volume variance

A *sales volume* variance means that the actual amount sold was more or less than budgeted.

A *favourable sales volume* variance means that the actual amount sold was more than expected.

Causes of favourable variances

- *increase* in customer demand, for example through improved promotion of the product creating popularity
- selling price has been *reduced* to increase volume
- seasonal sales have *increased* volume
- competition from other businesses has *reduced* or disappeared
- *more* special discounts have been given to selected customers to increase orders.

An *adverse sales volume* variance means that the actual amount sold was less than expected.

Causes of adverse variances

- *decrease* in customer demand, for example due to the goods becoming unfashionable or obsolete
- selling price has been *increased* to pass increased costs onto customers
- seasonal sales have de*creased* volume
- competition from other businesses has *increased*
- *fewer* special discounts have been given to selected customers
- customers have heard that new, improved products will be available soon and are waiting for those.

Other variances that affect sales volume

There is a close relationship between *selling price* and sales volume. Management decides the selling price and knows that this will affect the volume sold. An increase in selling price leads to lower sales volume. Therefore, a favourable sales price variance can lead to an adverse sales volume variance and vice versa.

Sales price variance

A *sales price* variance means that the actual selling price was more or less than budgeted.

A *favourable sales price* variance means that the actual selling price was *higher* than the standard.

Causes of favourable variances

- prices have been increased, for example due to increased costs or inflation
- fewer discounts have been allowed to customers
- improved products have allowed prices to be increased.

An *adverse sales price* variance means that the actual selling price was *lower* than the standard.

Causes of adverse variances

- prices have been reduced, for example to increase sales volume
- some customers have been given price concessions to increase the volume of orders
- competition has necessitated a price reduction
- selling prices have been reduced in seasonal sales.

Other variances that affect sales price

An increase in either *direct materials price* or *direct labour rate* may lead to a management decision to increase the selling price. Therefore, an adverse direct material price variance or an adverse direct labour rate variance can lead to a favourable sales price variance.

Direct materials variances

Materials usage variance

A *materials usage* variance means that the actual amount of material used in production was more or less than expected.

A *favourable material usage* variance means that the actual amount of material used in production was *less* than in the flexible budget.

Causes of favourable variances

- actual materials used were *higher* quality than the standard, resulting in materials that are easier to work with
- actual labour was more *highly* skilled than the standard skill; which may lead to less wastage of the materials.

An *adverse material usage* variance means that the amount of material used in production was more than in the flexible budget.

Causes of adverse variances

- actual materials used were *lower* quality than the standard resulting in materials that are harder to work with
- actual labour was *lower* skilled than the standard skill, which may lead to more wastage of the materials.

Other variances that affect materials usage

Purchasing higher quality materials can lead to an adverse *direct materials price* variance but a favourable direct materials usage variance and vice versa.

Using more highly skilled labour than the standard can lead to an adverse *direct labour rate* variance but a favourable direct materials usage variance and vice versa.

Materials price variance

A *materials price* variance means that the actual price of the material bought was more or less than expected.

A *favourable material price* variance means that the actual purchase price of material was *less* than in the flexible budget.

Causes of favourable variances

- actual materials price falls because the supplier(s) offers new trade or bulk *discounts*
- actual materials price falls because materials bought are of a *lower* quality.

An *adverse material price* variance means that the actual price of materials purchased was *more* than in the flexible budget.

Causes of adverse variances

- actual materials price rises because the supplier(s) passes on their own *increase in costs* sometimes due to inflation
- actual materials price rises because materials bought are of a *higher* quality.

Direct labour variances

Labour efficiency variance

A *labour efficiency* variance means that the actual labour hours were more or less than expected.

A *favourable labour efficiency* variance means that the actual labour time used was less than the standard time allowed.

Causes of favourable variances

- *better* skilled workers were employed who work *more* efficiently than the standard
- *highly* motivated staff
- *good* quality materials and/or machinery for staff to work with.

An *adverse labour efficiency* variance means that the actual labour time used was more than the standard time allowed.

Causes of adverse variances

- *less* skilled workers were employed who work *less* efficiently than the standard
- *low* motivation of staff
- *poor* quality materials and/or machinery breakdowns.

Labour rate variance

A *labour rate* variance means that the actual wage rate was more or less than the standard wage rate.

A *favourable labour rate* variance means that the actual wage rate was *less* than the standard wage rate.

Causes of favourable variances

- actual labour employed was of a *lower* grade than standard.

An *adverse labour rate* variance means that the actual wage rate was *more* than the standard wage rate.

Causes of adverse variances

- actual labour employed was of a *higher* grade than standard
- a wage increase has been given to staff (the standard should be revised).

Fixed overhead variances

- A *favourable fixed overhead expenditure* variance will arise from the actual fixed overhead spend being lower than the budgeted overhead spend, for example because of cost savings made after the budget was set.
- An *adverse fixed overhead expenditure* variance will arise when more has been paid for fixed overheads than was budgeted, for example because of an unexpected cost or a supplier increasing costs more than budgeted. As an example, rent may be increased by a higher figure than was expected when the budget was set.
- A *favourable fixed overhead volume* variance will arise if hours actually worked by direct labour are greater than the direct labour hours budgeted in the master budget.

A new order could have been received that requires extra labour to be employed and therefore extra hours are worked.

- An *adverse fixed overhead volume* variance will arise when the opposite occurs. Fewer direct labour hours were worked than were budgeted for in the master budget.

- A *favourable fixed overhead efficiency* variance arises when the output produced by the direct workers took less time in actual hours than the standard hours set. This may be because higher skilled labour was used. The use of less skilled labour will lead to the opposite.

- An *adverse fixed overhead efficiency* variance arises when the output produced by the direct workers took more time in actual hours than the standard hours set. This may be because lower skilled labour was used.

Note: if fixed overheads are absorbed using machine hours instead of direct labour hours, the comments regarding the fixed overhead volume and efficiency variances will apply to machine hours worked, rather than direct labour hours.

38.13 Using standard costing to support decision making

Managers often have targets for the performance of their area of responsibility. These targets may use budgeted figures. For example, a sales manager will be responsible for the amount sold and may receive a bonus if the budgeted volume is met or exceeded. Managers are therefore responsible for variances that occur in their department. They will be expected to use the information provided by budgets and variances to support decision making to improve the performance of the department and the business.

Standard costing and variance information can be used to support many of the decisions that businesses make. Some examples of these decisions, along with examples of non-financial information that managers may also consider when making decisions, are as follows.

Areas of the organisation	Decisions that can be supported by standard costing information	Non-financial factors that can affect decisions
Sales	<ul><li>Whether the standard selling price needs to be changed.</li><li>Whether sales staff need further training.</li><li>Whether changes are needed to the customer service provided etc.</li><li>How sales staff can be better motivated.</li></ul>	<ul><li>Changes in customer preferences.</li><li>Changes in the competition such as new businesses or improvements in competitors' products and services, and marketing.</li><li>Technological improvements may affect what people buy or how they make purchases such as increases in online sales.</li><li>Changes in the economy, e.g. inflation will affect sales prices; unemployment will affect customer demand for products.</li></ul>
Materials	<ul><li>Whether the standard materials price needs to be changed.</li><li>Whether a change of supplier(s) is appropriate.</li><li>Whether materials are being wasted, and if so, how that wastage can be reduced.</li></ul>	<ul><li>Changes at a supplier will affect the materials purchased. For example, a supplier may become unreliable, provide poor quality materials or no longer offer the materials for sale.</li><li>There may be ethical reasons for changes to materials. For example, some materials may be more environmentally friendly than others.</li></ul>

Areas of the organisation	Decisions that can be supported by standard costing information	Non-financial factors that can affect decisions
Labour	• Whether the standard wage rate needs to be changed. • Whether the business needs to increase or decrease the amount of staff it employs. • Whether the right balance of skills is available and whether further staff training is needed. • Whether there should be a change in the use of overtime hours and/or rates.	• Unexpected events may affect production, for example machine break-down, or adverse weather may affect outside activities. • The availability of appropriate skills in the economy.

Where one variance has an impact on another variance, it is important that department managers do not make decisions in isolation but discuss them across departments to agree the best decision for the business as a whole.

Not all variances need corrective action. Managers focus their attention on the most significant variances. Significant variances are the largest variances, particularly where they are adverse. This is because large variances have the biggest impact on business performance and adverse variances lead to lower than expected profit.

The investigation of all variances in a business can be very time consuming, therefore managers should prioritise variances by taking the following steps:

Step 1 Decide which variances are significant

Step 2 Determine the causes of each significant variance

Step 3 If the cause of the variance can be controlled, then take corrective action

Note: not all variances can be controlled by a business manager. For example, a supplier may increase the price of materials because of inflation. This may make it difficult to find an alternative, cheaper supplier. In this case, it is the standard that will need to be updated for future budgets and variance analysis.

KEY CONCEPT LINK

Planning and control: Variance analysis is an important accounting tool for the control of costs. Managers should carefully consider variances that arise and the causes underlying them. Managers can then make supported decisions to improve business performance and improve the accuracy of future standards and budgets.

THINK LIKE AN ACCOUNTANT

Did you get what you expected?

Plans are useful to steer a way forward but reality rarely matches these plans perfectly.

Variance analysis involves comparing actual against expected results and asking questions about why the two are different. Variance analysis encourages managers to take the opportunity to pause and reflect on what has happened, learn about why reality did not meet expectations and use this reflection to improve plans for the future.

Are the principles of comparing actual against expected results useful to individuals as well as businesses? Can you think of any circumstances where it would be useful to compare expectations against actual outcomes? What might discourage people from making these comparisons?

Figure 38.6: Plans are useful to steer a way forward but reality rarely matches these plans perfectly.

EXAM-STYLE QUESTIONS

1   State two advantages of a standard costing system.   **[2]**

2   Explain two possible causes of an adverse sales volume variance.   **[4]**

3   Tareq makes a single product and uses a standard costing system.
    The budget for the month of July is based on the following standard information.

		Per unit
		$
Direct materials	2.75 kilos at $3 per kilo	8.25
Direct labour	1.5 hours at $5 per hour	7.50
Fixed production overhead		3.75
Standard cost		19.50

Budgeted selling price is $27 per unit.
Budgeted production and sales for July were 10 000 units.
All units produced are sold.
The actual data for the month of July was:

Direct material	26 190 kg which cost $75 951
Direct labour	12 610 hours which cost $65 572
Fixed production overhead	$39 750
Sales revenue	$258 375

Actual production and sales for July were 9700 units.

CONTINUED

Required

a Calculate the following variances for the month of July:

i	Material price	**[2]**
ii	Material usage	**[2]**
iii	Labour rate	**[2]**
iv	Labour efficiency	**[2]**
v	Fixed production overhead expenditure	**[2]**
vi	Sales price	**[2]**
vii	Sales volume	**[2]**

b Prepare a statement reconciling the budgeted profit for 10 000 units with the actual profit for the month of July. **[5]**

Additional information

The supplier of direct materials has announced that he will change his price to $3.10 per kg with immediate effect.

c Assess the implications of this change in material cost based on the actual material used for the month of July. Support your answer with relevant calculations. **[6]**

4 A manufacturer produces one type of product. The budgeted information for October is as follows:

Number of units produced and sold:	10 000
Per unit:	
Selling price per unit	$60
Direct materials (kg)	3
Cost of material per kg	$4
Direct labour (hours)	2
Labour rate per hour	$10
Fixed overheads per unit	$8

Required

a Prepare the statement of budgeted profit statement for October. **[6]**

Additional information

The actual data for October was as follows:

11 000 units were produced and sold at a selling price of $58
The total cost of direct materials was $133 980 at a rate of $4.20 per kg
The direct labour cost was $181 500 at a rate of $11 per hour
Fixed overheads were $100 000

Required

b Prepare the flexible budget statement for the month showing the budgeted and actual data and the difference (variance) between the two. **[9]**

c Calculate the following variances for October:

i	Labour rate	**[2]**
ii	Labour efficiency	**[2]**
iii	Sales price	**[2]**
iv	Sales volume.	**[2]**

d State two possible causes of a favourable labour efficiency variance in October. **[2]**

[Total: 25]

SELF-EVALUATION CHECKLIST

After studying this chapter, complete a table like this:

You should be able to:	Needs more work	Almost there	Ready to move on
Calculate standards as the starting point for budgeting and budgetary control.			
Evaluate the advantages and disadvantages of standard costing, noting that the advantages of standard costing will outweigh the disadvantages and improve the future performance of the business.			
Prepare a flexible budget so that sensible comparisons between budgeted and actual results can be made.			
Calculate variances for sales, materials, labour and fixed overheads.			
Prepare statements reconciling the standard cost and profits of the actual units produced with the actual cost and profits of the units produced.			
Analyse actual costs and revenue against standards using variances; these do not explain the causes of the differences but do show management where further investigation is required.			
Assess the use of standard costing to improve business performance.			

› **Chapter 39**

Investment appraisal

LEARNING INTENTIONS

In this chapter you will learn how to:

- assess whether it is worthwhile to invest funds in a project
- calculate and use accounting rate of return
- calculate and use payback, net present value and internal rate of return
- evaluate the advantages and disadvantages of investment appraisal techniques
- assess investment decisions using investment appraisal techniques
- identify non-financial factors in investment decision making.

ACCOUNTING IN CONTEXT

Investing for a global future

Samsung was established in the 1930s in South Korea producing and selling groceries. It expanded rapidly and is now a huge organisation operating and selling in many countries.

Samsung has diversified into a wide range of different products and services from insurance to electronics to buildings. Its construction work has included high profile projects such as Malaysia's Petronas Towers and Dubai's Burj Khalifa. Its best-known products are its electronic goods including smartphones and tablets.

Much of Samsung's success and growth has come from its willingness to invest time and money in new products and new plant in locations such as India and South Africa. Samsung has also invested through purchasing other existing companies and benefitted from their products and skills.

Figure 39.1: Samsung is now a huge organisation operating and selling in many countries.

Major investments can be risky; large sums of money may be involved and the future is uncertain. Businesses such as Samsung will consider the merits of each potential investment before deciding to go ahead. If a business has many potential projects to consider, it will need to decide which ones to pursue.

Discuss in a pair or a group:

- In addition to these examples, what other products does Samsung make?
- Why might technology products such as smartphones be risky investments?
- What factors do you think Samsung should consider before investing in a new product?
- Do you think the factors will be different when considering other types of investment such as relocating a factory?

39.1 What is investment appraisal?

Businesses invest money in the future of an organisation with the aim of generating success. This success may be greater sales or higher profit through higher revenue or lower costs. Money invested can be for a wide range of varied projects such as introducing new products, a promotional campaign, relocation of a factory, acquiring or replacing an asset, etc.

These projects involve making choices, including whether or not to proceed with the project, which assets to buy, which new products to introduce and so on.

39.2 Investment appraisal techniques

Accounting techniques are essential when investment decisions have to be made, especially if large sums of money are involved and at risk. Investment appraisal techniques assess the financial costs and benefits arising from a project. Techniques available to support investment appraisal decisions are shown in Figure 39.2.

> **KEY TERM**
>
> **investment appraisal:** the process of assessing whether it is worthwhile to invest funds into a particular project.

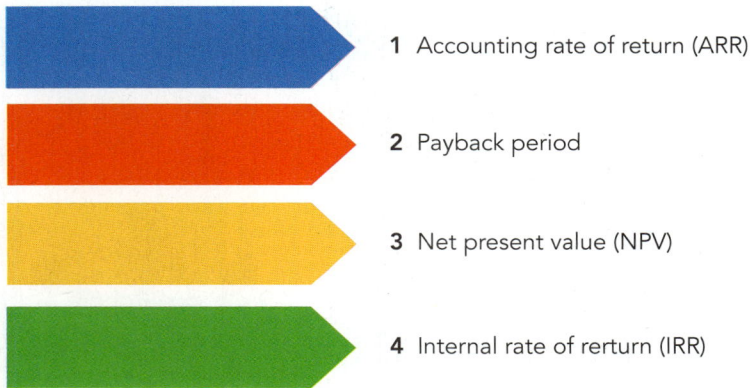

1 Accounting rate of return (ARR)

2 Payback period

3 Net present value (NPV)

4 Internal rate of rerturn (IRR)

Figure 39.2

Accounting rate of return (ARR)

1 Accounting rate of return (ARR)

The **accounting rate of return** is concerned with profitability rather than the cash flow of a project. Average profit is the average of the profit arising directly from the investment expected to be earned over the life of the project.

The steps to calculate the ARR are:

Step 1 Calculate the expected profit over the life of the investment.

Step 2 Calculate the expected average annual profit from the life of the investment using the formula:

$$\frac{\text{total profit over the life of the investment}}{\text{life of the investment}}$$

Step 3 Calculate the average investment using the formula:

$$\frac{\text{the cost of the initial investment} - \text{residual value of the investment}}{2}$$

Step 4 Calculate the ARR using the formula:

$$\frac{\text{average profit}}{\text{average investment}} \times 100$$

A business can compare the ARR of a potential investment with the rate of return that it expects to earn on capital to decide whether the investment will be worthwhile. For example, if a project has an ARR of 20% and the business is currently earning a return on capital employed (ROCE) of less than 20%, the project should improve its overall profitability; if the present ROCE is more than 20%, the project will probably reduce its overall profitability.

> **KEY TERM**
>
> **accounting rate of return:** the average profit from an investment expressed as a percentage of the average capital of the investment.

WORKED EXAMPLE 1

Planners Limited is considering investing in a new machine that will increase the profit of the business. The machine will cost $150 000 and have a life of five years. After that time, it will be scrapped at no value.

The company policy is to depreciate the non-current assets by 20% using the straight-line method.

Expected cash flows from the new machine are:

Year	Cash inflow	Cash outflow
	$	$
1	70 000	30 000
2	75 000	29 000
3	78 000	30 000
4	80 000	31 000
5	84 000	34 000

Required

a   Calculate the ARR for the new machine.

Additional information

Planners Limited currently earns a ROCE of 20% and requires any new investments to earn at least the same percentage.

b   State, with reasons, whether the business should buy the new machine.

Answer

a   **Step 1**

The cash flows and expected profit as a direct result of buying the machine are as follows:

Year	Cash inflow	Cash outflow	Net cash flow [1]	Annual depreciation [2]	Expected annual profit [3]
	$	$			
1	70 000	30 000	40 000	30 000	10 000
2	75 000	29 000	46 000	30 000	16 000
3	78 000	30 000	48 000	30 000	18 000
4	80 000	31 000	49 000	30 000	19 000
5	84 000	34 000	50 000	30 000	20 000
Expected total profit over the life of investment					83 000

> **TIP**
>
> ARR is the only technique in this chapter that takes depreciation of the investment into account. This is because ARR is concerned with profitability; the other techniques are based on cash flows.
>
> If you do not know the rate of depreciation, it would be reasonable to write off the total cost of the non-current asset over the life of the project.

Answer

Notes:

[1]   Net cash flow = cash in – cash out

[2]   Annual depreciation is $30 000 $\left(\dfrac{\$15 000}{5}\right)$

[3]   Annual profit = net cash flow – depreciation

CONTINUED

Step 2

The average profit of the investment of calculating ARR is:

$83 000 ÷ 5 (life of the project) = $16 600

Step 3

The average investment is:

$$\frac{\$150\,000}{2} = \$75\,000$$

Step 4

$$\text{The ARR} = \frac{\$16\,600}{\$75\,000} \times 100 = 22\%$$

b Planners Limited should buy the new machine because the ARR of the new machine is above the company's minimum requirement of 20%. As the ARR is above the current ROCE, the machine should improve the company's overall profitability.

> **TIP**
>
> The average profit figure used in the ARR calculation is the profit for the investment only, not for the business as a whole.

A project may require an increase in net current assets because this may result in increased inventory and trade receivables. Any increase in net current assets will increase the average investment. For example, if a project involves the purchase of a machine at a cost of $60 000, and an increase in net current assets of $40 000, the average investment is:

$$\frac{\$60\,000 + \$40\,000}{2} = \$50\,000$$

The advantages and disadvantages of ARR

Advantages of ARR	Disadvantages of ARR
• The expected profitability of a project can be compared with the present profitability (ROCE) of the business.	• The average annual profit used to calculate ARR is unlikely to be the profit earned in any year of the life of the project.
• ARR is straightforward to calculate.	• The method does not take into account the timing of cash flows. The initial outlay on the project is at risk until the flow of cash into the business has covered the initial cost.
	• ARR ignores the time value of money. Every dollar received now is more useful to a business than a dollar received at a later date.
	• No consideration is taken of the actual life expectancy of a project.
	• Profit is subjective and depends on variable policies such as provisions for depreciation, valuation of inventory, etc.

ACTIVITY 39.1

A manufacturer is proposing to introduce a new product that is expected to produce the following incremental profits over a period of four years:

	$
Year 1	30 000
Year 2	36 000
Year 3	38 000
Year 4	40 000

The project will require the use of a machine that was purchased some years ago at a cost of $25 000, and the use of a second machine that will have to be bought for $150 000. It is estimated that inventory held will increase by $20 000, trade receivables will increase by $15 000 and trade payables will increase by $5 000.

Required

Calculate the accounting rate of return that will be earned from the new product.

Payback period

2 Payback period

When investing in a new project, a business is at risk of being worse off until the initial expenditure on a project has been covered by net cash receipts (cash inflow − cash outflow) from the venture.

Calculation of the **payback period** indicates the time over which the business is at risk. Therefore, payback is concerned with cash flows, not with profitability. Short payback periods are preferred, especially in times of high inflation.

When using the payback method, the net cash flows arising from the project must be calculated. This is the difference between the cash coming in from the project (this could be the revenue or savings) less the cash payments arising from the project. Profitability and depreciation (a non-cash expense) do not enter into the calculations. It is important to consider when the cash comes in and goes out, not when sales or purchases are made.

Future cash flows are the estimated cash receipts less the estimated cash payments attributable to an investment and will be known as net receipts or net payments. If assets purchased for the project are sold at the end of the venture, the proceeds of sale should be included in the net receipts in the last year.

It may also be necessary to consider a build-up of net current assets. This needs to be shown at the start of the project as a cash outflow. At the end of the project, it is brought back into the business as a cash inflow.

The steps to calculate payback are:

Step 1 Calculate the net cash flows for the project.

Step 2 Calculate the cumulative net cash flows from the investment to find out the year that payback occurs.

Step 3 Calculate the portion of the year that will be needed to achieve payback.

KEY TERM

payback period: the period of time it takes for the net cash receipts from a project to pay back, or equal, the total of the funds invested in the project.

TIP

Remember that ARR assesses the profitability of a project while payback focuses on the timing of cash flows.

WORKED EXAMPLE 2

ABC Limited is proposing the manufacture of a new product that will involve the purchase of new plant costing $100 000.

The expected cash flows from the project are as follows:

Required

Calculate the payback period for the new plant.

Answer

The payback period is calculated as follows:

Year	Cash receipts	Cash payments
	$	$
1	78 000	48 000
2	82 000	42 000
3	94 000	44 000
4	100 000	54 000

Steps 1 and 2

Calculate the net cash flow and cumulative net cash flows (at least until they become positive).

> Year 0 is used to indicate that the initial payment of $100 000 occurs at the start of the project.

Year	Cash receipts	Cash payments	Net cash receipts	Cumulative net cash receipts
	$	$	$	$
0		(100 000)	(100 000)	(100 000)
1	78 000	48 000	30 000	(70 000)
2	82 000	42 000	40 000	(30 000)
3	94 000	44 000	50 000	20 000
4	100 000	54 000	46 000	66 000

> The investment will be paid back part way between years 2 and year 3, when the cumulative net cash flow turns from negative to positive.

Step 3

Calculate the portion of the third year that will be needed to achieve payback.

At the end of year 2 $30 000 is still required to pay back the investment. This balance of $30 000 will be received during the third year:

$$\frac{\$30\,000*}{\$50\,000**} = 0.6 \times 12 \text{ months} = 7.2 \text{ months}$$

The payback period is therefore 2 years 8 months. (It is unnecessary to be more precise than this given the figures are estimates of future cash flows.)

* $30 000 is the amount required in year 3 so that the total cash inflows equal the total cost of the asset bought.

** $50 000 is the total of the net cash flows in year 3. It is assumed that the cash flows accrue evenly over the year.

Projects with the same payback period may have different cash flows. For example:

	Project 1	Project 2
	$	$
Year 0 Initial cost[1]	(80 000)	(80 000)
Year 1 Net cash inflow	15 000	30 000
Year 2	25 000	40 000
Year 3	40 000	10 000

Note:

[1] The initial outlay is shown as made in year 0 because it is assumed that cash flows occur on the last day of the year. The initial outlay should be shown as occurring on the first day of year 1, and the last day of year 0 is the nearest we can get to the first day of year 1.

Both projects have a payback period of three years and similar amounts of cash inflows, but project 2 is more attractive as the cash flow is better in the early years.

The use of the term 'year' should not be confused with the accounting year start or end. It relates solely to the start of the project (year 0), the year at which the project starts. This will be at any point during the accounting year.

The simple payback method ignores the time value of money.

The advantages and disadvantages of payback

Advantages of payback	Disadvantages of payback
• Payback is straightforward to calculate.	• The life expectancy of the project is ignored. Once the payback period has been evaluated, the net cash inflows after this time are ignored.
• Payback can compare the relative risks of different projects.	• Projects with the same payback period may have different cash flows.
• Cash flow is less subjective than profitability.	
• Payback highlights the timing and size of cash flows.	
• Short payback periods result in increased liquidity and enable businesses to grow more quickly.	

ACTIVITY 39.2

Jeneric Limited is planning to install a new specialist computer system into the business. It has two choices of replacements: system A or system B, each costing $50000 and both expected to have a useful life of three years. Jeneric Limited is concerned about the risk of the investment and is aiming for a quick recovery of the cost of the original investment.

The following information is available for the systems:

	System A		System B	
	Cash inflow	Cash outflow	Cash inflow	Cash outflow
	$	$	$	$
Year 1	80000	60000	60000	30000
Year 2	90000	70000	80000	60000
Year 3	100000	60000	70000	45000

Required

a   Calculate the payback periods for each of the computer systems.

b   State, with reasons, which computer system Jeneric Limited should purchase.

Net present value (NPV)

> **3** Net present value (NPV)

Net present value is a discounted cash flow method that considers the **time value of money**. This is because, given a choice, a person prefers to have an amount of money now that they can spend or invest, rather than the same amount in the future.

For example, $1 received now is more useful than $1 received some time in the future.

If $100 is invested now at 10% compound interest it will be worth $100 + \left(\dfrac{\$100 \times 10}{100}\right) = \$110$

in one year's time, and in two years' time it will be worth $\$110 + \left(\dfrac{\$110 \times 10}{100}\right) = \$121$.

To put it another way, $110 receivable in one year's time has a **present value** of $100 when discounted at 10%.

The time value of money is important when future cash flows are compared with present cash flows because 'like should be compared with like'. Future cash flows are discounted to present day values so that they can be compared with the initial outlay on a realistic basis.

Cash flows from the full life of a project are considered. This is a positive advantage of using net present value over payback.

The discounting rate taken for net present values is the cost of capital. For example, if money has to be borrowed at 8% interest per annum to finance the investment in a project, the cost of capital is 8% and the future cash flows will be discounted using the factors for that rate. A table of discounting factors can be found in Appendix 1.

KEY TERMS

net present value: the present value of future receipts from a project, less the present value of future payments in respect of the same project.

time value of money: the principle that the same sum of money is worth more now than at some time in the future.

present value: the present or current value of an expected future sum of money.

The steps to calculate NPV are:

Step 1   Calculate the net cash flows for the project for each year.

Step 2   Calculate the discounted cash flows by multiplying the net cash inflow for the year by the discount factor for the year.

Step 3   Calculate the net present value by adding up all the discounted cash flows.

WORKED EXAMPLE 3

Lees Limited is considering a project with an initial cost of $100 000. The company accountant has estimated its net cash receipts from the project for the next five years to be as follows:

Year 1	$30 000
Year 2	$40 000
Year 3	$40 000
Year 4	$46 000
Year 5	$42 000

Lees Limited's cost of capital is 10%. The discount factors for the present value of 10% are:

Year	Discount factor at 10%
0	1.000
1	0.909
2	0.826
3	0.751
4	0.683
5	0.621

TIP

It is a good idea to set out the NPV calculation in a table such as the one in Worked example 3. Always label the columns, especially the net present value.

Required

Calculate the net present value of the project.

Answer

The calculation of the net present value of the project is:

Year	Net cash inflow/(outflow)	Discount factor	Discounted cash flow [1]
	$		$
0	(100 000)	1.000 [2]	(100 000)
1	30 000	0.909	27 270
2	40 000	0.826	33 040
3	40 000	0.751	30 040
4	46 000	0.683	31 418
5	42 000	0.621	26 082
		Net present value [3]	47 850

CONTINUED

Notes:

[1] The discounted cash flow is calculated by multiplying the net cash inflow for the year by the discount factor for the year. For year 1 the discounted cash flow is $30 000 × 0.909 = $27 270.

[2] The discount factor in year 0 is always 1.

[3] The net present value is the total of all the discounted cash flows for years 0 to 5.

The net present value is positive, showing that the project may be undertaken. A negative NPV would mean that the net receipts in present day terms would not cover the initial outlay and the project should not be undertaken. The higher the net present value, the better the project. If two or more projects are being considered, the one with the highest NPV would be preferred to the other(s).

> **TIP**
>
> The discount factor in year 0 is always 1 as the initial cost of the project is already in the present day.

The advantages and disadvantages of NPV

Advantages of NPV	Disadvantages of NPV
• Takes into consideration the time value of money.	• Estimating the most appropriate discount factor can be difficult.
• Uses cash flows that are less subjective than profitability.	• Managers may not fully understand the concept of present value.
• All the cash flows of the project are considered, unlike payback.	

ACTIVITY 39.3

Maya Limited is considering investing in one of two possible projects; project X or project Y. Each project costs $130 000 and will have a five-year life with no residual value at the end of that time.

The net receipts for each project over the five-year period are as follows:

	Project X	Project Y
	$	$
Year 1	50 000	35 000
Year 2	50 000	35 000
Year 3	30 000	35 000
Year 4	25 000	35 000
Year 5	20 000	35 000

CONTINUED

Maya Limited's cost of capital is 12%.

The discount factors at 12% are:

Year	Discount factor at 12%
0	1.000
1	0.893
2	0.797
3	0.712
4	0.636
5	0.567

Required

a   Calculate the net present value of each option.

b   State which project Maya Limited should choose and why.

REFLECTION

When answering Activity 39.3, what is the total net cash flow for each project if discounting isn't used? Why do the projects have different net present values? Discuss with another learner what this activity indicates about the time value of money.

Internal rate of return (IRR)

4 Internal rate of rerturn (IRR)

Net present value does not give the *rate of return* on investment based on discounted values. Therefore, the **internal rate of return** can be more useful to managers making investment decisions, because the IRR does give a rate of return that can be compared with the company's present return on capital.

For example, if NPV at 10% is $14 000 and at 18% is $(6 000), then:

$$\text{IRR} = 10\% + \left(8\% \times \frac{14\,000}{14\,000 + 6\,000}\right) = 10\% + 5.6\% = 15.6\%$$

Therefore, discounted at 15.6%, the investment would have a nil net present value.

The steps to calculate IRR are:

Step 1   Select two discounting rates sufficiently wide apart to give positive and negative net present values.

Step 2   Calculate the net present value for each of the two discount rates chosen in Step 1.

Step 3   Interpolate to find the percentage that will give a nil net present value. (Interpolation means finding an intermediate value between the two discounting rates.)

KEY TERM

internal rate of return: the interest or discount rate at which the net present value of all the cash flows from the project (both positive and negative) equal zero.

Interpolation involves using the formula:

$$P + \left[(N - P) \times \frac{p}{p + n}\right] = \text{IRR}$$

where P is the rate giving a positive net present value

N is the rate giving a negative net present value

p is the positive net present value

n is the negative net present value

WORKED EXAMPLE 4

Continued from Worked example 3

Lees Limited has a net present value of $47 850 when discounted at 10%.

Required

Calculate the internal rate of return for the project.

Answer

Step 1

Lees Limited's project has an NPV of $47 850. This is a positive value. To obtain a negative net present value it needs to be discounted at a higher rate, for example 40%.

Step 2

The calculation of NPV at a discount rate of 40% is as follows:

Year	Net cash inflow (outflow)	Discount factor	Discounted cash flow
	$	40%	$
0	(100 000)	1.000	(100 000)
1	30 000	0.714	21 420
2	40 000	0.510	20 400
3	40 000	0.364	14 560
4	46 000	0.260	11 960
5	42 000	0.186	7 812
	Net present value		(23 848)

Step 3

$$\text{IRR} = 10\% + \left(30\% \times \frac{47 850}{47 850 + 23 848}\right) = 30\%$$

ACTIVITY 39.4

Continued from Activity 39.3

The information is given for Maya Limited in Activity 39.3. Discount factors for 20% are:

Year	Discount factor at 20%
0	1.000
1	0.833
2	0.694
3	0.579
4	0.482
5	0.402

Required

Calculate the internal rate of return for project X.

TIP

When the receipts are constant for a number of consecutive years, the net present value of those receipts may be calculated quickly if the annual amount is multiplied by the sum of the factors for the years concerned.

The advantages and disadvantages of internal rate of return

Advantages of IRR	Disadvantages of IRR
• It takes into consideration the time value of money.	• It needs to consider different discount rates and involves multiple calculations.
• It uses cash flows which are less subjective than profitability.	• Calculating IRR as a percentage means that projects of differing sizes cannot be compared using IRR alone.
• All the cash flows of the project are considered, unlike payback.	
• It gives a rate of return that can be used to make comparisons.	

TIP

When assessing the merits of different techniques, remember that the net present value and internal rate of return have the advantage of taking the time value of money into consideration.

39.3 Capital rationing

In some cases, a company may evaluate a number of projects. However, because of the limited amount of capital it has, the company cannot invest in all the projects at the same time. It must ration its capital in such a way that the projects it invests in maximise the net present value of the company over a period of time.

WORKED EXAMPLE 5

Aarav has evaluated five projects with the following results.

Project	Capital cost	Net present value
	$	$
A	200 000	100 000
B	300 000	80 000
C	500 000	270 000
D	200 000	180 000
E	300 000	100 000

However, he only has a maximum of $500 000 to spend. Aarav needs to decide which projects he should invest in to maximise the net present value.

Required

Which projects should be chosen to maximise the overall net present value?

Answer

Calculate the profitability ratio for each project. This is done by dividing the net present value by the capital cost:

Project	Capital cost	Net present value	Profitability index
	$	$	
A	200 000	100 000	0.50
B	300 000	80 000	0.27
C	500 000	270 000	0.54
D	200 000	180 000	0.90
E	300 000	100 000	0.33

Project D has the greatest profitability index. This would use up $200 000 of the $500 000 available. The remaining $300 000 should be invested in project E. Aarav doesn't have sufficient funds to invest in the next best project, C. Simply investing in C alone will only generate a net present value of $270 000, less than buying D and E.

Therefore, he should invest in projects D and E, as these will yield a total net present value of $280 000. Any other combination will not achieve this amount.

KEY CONCEPT LINK

Planning and control: Investment appraisal techniques give managers financial information about possible future investments. This helps them to plan future investment by making supported decisions based on expected cash flows and/or accounting profits.

39.4 Non-financial factors

Non-financial factors are those factors that affect the decision to undertake a project but are difficult to quantify and are not considered in investment appraisal techniques.

The capital investment appraisal techniques used in this chapter all assess projects on a financial basis either by focusing on cash flow or profitability. Managers should consider the recommendation from investment appraisal methods when making investment decisions. Managers should also consider other relevant factors that can be important to the business and its stakeholders but are more difficult to quantify. Managers will then need to weigh up both the financial and non-financial factors before coming to a final decision.

The specific non-financial factors that may impact on an individual project will vary depending on the nature of the project. Possible non-financial factors include the following:

- Human resources: jobs, motivation, culture and the working environment can all be impacted by new projects. For example, new machinery may result in redundancies and different skills requirements; relocation may suit some staff and not others.

- Environment: projects typically will have some impact on the environment, e.g. on pollution through noise or waste. For example, a change in packaging can have an impact the amount of waste, e.g. manufacturing drinks in glass or plastic bottles.

- Social: projects may affect staff, customers or the general public. For example, a new location for a factory can affect local residents through more traffic, noisy machinery or better job prospects. Residents might protest if unhappy or be supportive if satisfied.

The validity of the data used in an investment appraisal is also an important factor for managers to consider. Future cash flows or profits are estimates and, as such, there is a risk that the numbers used may be inaccurate. The source of the data, length of the project, unexpected actions by competitors or changes in the economy can all affect the accuracy of the numbers used.

Ultimately, managers should be clear on the business's objectives and how the project will fit in with these objectives before arriving at a final decision about any major new project. They can then weigh up the results of investment appraisal calculations, plus any further considerations before coming to a final decision on whether or not to invest.

ACCOUNTING IN CONTEXT

Appraising personal projects

Investment appraisal is all about using estimated financial information to support decision making which involves large sums of money that could affect the success of a business for many years. The better the estimated figures, the more reliable the information management has and so the better the decision is likely to be.

Investment appraisal can be used in personal situations as well as business situations. Consider big choices that people make that have financial implications such as, should I take job X or work for myself? Should I go to university? Should I buy a house?

Financial data can be gathered and used to help make a better decision. Non-financial factors can take on great importance to personal investment decisions and may greatly impact the final decisions made.

Figure 39.3: Investment appraisal can be used in personal situations as well as business situations.

Think of a decision that you might need to make which has large personal financial implications. How could you collect financial data about potential cash flows or profits for the project? How confident can you be about the accuracy of the data? What non-financial factors might be important to consider before making a decision?

EXAM-STYLE QUESTIONS

1 State two advantages the payback method of investment appraisal has over the net present value method of investment appraisal. **[2]**

2 Darsha's business can only invest in any one of the following three projects at one time. Details of the projects are as follows.

Project	Capital cost	Net present value
	$	$
X	200 000	50 000
Y	300 000	60 000
Z	400 000	120 000

Which order should Darsha invest in the projects to maximise the overall net present value? **[4]**

3 A business is proposing to purchase new equipment costing $130 000. The business depreciates equipment at 25% per annum using the straight-line method.

The equipment will earn revenue of $100 000 per annum and involve additional expenditure of $55 000 each year for four years. The company's cost of capital is 10%.

The present value of $1 is as follows:

Year	10%	15%
1	0.909	0.870
2	0.826	0.756
3	0.751	0.658
4	0.683	0.572

Required

Calculate:

a the accounting rate of return **[5]**

b the net present value **[5]**

c the internal rate of return. **[5]**

[Total: 15]

4 A company is planning to produce a new product. In order to make it, the company will have to purchase machine A costing $100 000. This will last for four years, after which it will be scrapped.

The following information is available:

1 Expected sales units will be 12 000 units for each of the four years.

2 The selling price, unit costs and other costs are:

	$	
Selling price per unit	20	This will increase by $1 per annum over the life of the project
Direct costs per unit	16	These will stay the same over the life of the project
Annual fixed overheads (excluding depreciation)	10 000	These will increase by $1 000 per annum over the life of the project

CONTINUED

Required

a   Prepare a table to show the expected annual net cash flows and profits arising from the project.   **[10]**

b   Calculate the following for the project:

   i   payback   **[5]**

   ii   accounting rate of return.   **[5]**

Additional information

The company accountant has also produced the following data for an alternative machine B that could be used for the project. This is as follows:

Capital cost	$140 000
Payback	3 years
Accounting rate of return	30%

The directors can only invest in one project.

Required

c   Advise the directors on which machine they should buy. Justify your answer by using both financial and non-financial factors.   **[5]**

SELF-EVALUATION CHECKLIST

After studying this chapter, complete a table like this:

You should be able to:	Needs more work	Almost there	Ready to move on
Assess whether it is worthwhile to invest funds in a project.			
Calculate and use accounting rate of return to assess the expected profitability of a project.			
Calculate and use payback, net present value and internal rate of return to assess the expected cash flows from a project.			
Explain the advantages and disadvantages of investment appraisal techniques.			
Assess investment appraisal techniques to make supported investment decisions, especially important if large sums of money are involved and at risk.			
Identify non-financial factors in investment decision making, remembering that non-financial factors are not included in investment appraisal calculations but may impact on the final decision that managers make about a potential investment.			

> Chapter 40

Preparing for assessment

LEARNING INTENTIONS

In this chapter you will learn how to:

- understand the structure of the Cambridge International AS & A Level qualifications and how they are assessed
- appreciate what is needed to revise effectively and prepare for assessment
- understand what the assessment objectives are and how learners can demonstrate these clearly in their answers
- know how mark schemes can be used to help prepare effective answers.

Introduction

Understanding Accounting is essential to success at AS and A Level. Preparing for assessments and understanding how you will be assessed will help you to demonstrate your accounting knowledge and skills. This chapter aims to help you with this preparation and understanding.

The information on this page is taken from the Cambridge International syllabus/is based on the 9706 syllabus for examination from 2023. You should always refer to the appropriate syllabus document for the year of your examination to confirm the details and for more information. The syllabus document is available on the Cambridge International website at www.cambridgeinternational.org

The Cambridge International AS & A Level Accounting examination papers
Advanced Subsidiary (AS) Level

- There are two AS Level papers.
- Paper 1 is worth 28% of the AS qualification (14% of the full A Level).
- Paper 2 is worth 72% of the AS qualification (36% of the full A Level).
- The two papers contain different types of question.
    - Paper 1 is 1 hour and consists of 30 multiple choice questions
    - Paper 2 is 1 hour and 45 minutes and consists of 4 structured questions.
- All questions are based on sections 1 and 2 of the syllabus content.
- AS Level papers form part of the full A Level examination.

Advanced (A) Level

- Learners will take 2 hours and 30 minutes of A Level assessment.
- This assessment will be:
    - two papers, one of which is 1 hour and 30 minutes long that assesses financial accounting and a further paper that is 1 hour and assesses cost and management accounting. They are both taken at the end of your A Level course.
- Financial accounting is worth 30% of the A level qualification and assessed through 3 structured questions.
- Cost and management accounting is worth 20% of the A level qualification and assessed through 2 structured questions.

Details of the papers are summarised here.

Paper	Type questions	Duration	Number of questions	Section of syllabus examined
1	Multiple choice	1h	30	1 and 2
2	Structured	1h 45 mins	4	1 and 2
3	Structured	1h 30 mins	3	3
4	Structured	1h	2	4

Help to prepare for examination

There are many useful approaches to help you to prepare for an examination; however, the following points can be followed as a general guide to help you revise and apply the knowledge and skills you have learned in your studies.

- Use the syllabus. It can be useful to tick off each topic as you revise, understand and practise it. The syllabus also explains the structure of the examinations.

- Learn the key concepts and apply them to each part of the content. Key concepts, such as duality and consistency, are stated in the syllabus and are included throughout the coursebook. The concepts will help you understand connections between different parts of the subject content.

- Ensure that your accounting notes are organised. Make sure they give a complete coverage of the syllabus. Use your coursebook or ask your teacher if you find any gaps.

- Plan your revision time. Drawing up a revision timetable can be very useful. It will allow you to allocate time to each topic area and help to avoid running out of time for some topics. Balance your time across all parts of the course and give yourself enough time to study areas that you find particularly difficult.

- Practice the exam-style questions at the end of chapters and in our Cambridge International AS & A Level Accounting workbook. These will help you to apply your skills to more structured, formal questions.

- Make sure that you learn all formulas, such as those for ratios.

- When revising for calculations and account preparation, practise, practise, practise. Remember to check your answers carefully.

- Prepare to make decisions and draw conclusions in written responses, e.g. a discussion. You might feel confident studying, revising, making calculations and preparing accounts, but written questions that require careful analysis and evaluation are just as important. Remember to practice answering lots of these questions to showcase your skills in this area too.

- Practice reading exam-style questions very carefully including any information provided at the start of each question about the business being considered. Underline or highlight the information that you consider to be particularly important.

- Timing is important. It may be helpful to plan how long you intend to spend on each part of any given question so that you don't run out of time. Remember to factor in time to read the question carefully.

- Practice clear presentation in your work – particularly for accounting statements such as the statement of financial position including correct titles and dates. Spacing out each stage of a calculation and showing your workings help to show your understanding.

- Practice checking your work – this is a skill that is often overlooked. Allowing time to check your work gives you an opportunity to spot any mistakes and correct them.

Revision techniques

There are lots of useful approaches and activities you can do to help you revise. You may like to consider trying some of the suggestions that follow:

1 Revise in short sessions, but lots of them. This may help you to concentrate. For example, 4 sessions of 30 minutes each can be more effective than 1 session of 2 hours without a break.

2   Try using lots of different active revision techniques. Ideas include:

- reading and rewriting notes
- producing topic summaries or making mind maps with key words and terms
- testing yourself with simple quizzes that you create and mark yourself, for example lists of definitions, formulas
- make revision cards containing a few key facts, figures or accounts
- practise calculations and the preparation of financial statements and accounts.

Understanding assessment objectives

AS and A Level Accounting are not simply about subject knowledge. You are expected to *analyse and evaluate* this knowledge, especially in relation to business situations.

The key skills in the Cambridge International AS & A Level Accounting syllabus are:

1   **Knowledge and understanding** of the content of the syllabus.

2   **Analysis** of this knowledge in problems and issues. Analysis will include selecting, calculating, interpreting and communicating information and outcomes.

3   **Evaluation** of information. This will involve making business decisions and drawing conclusions. Any recommendations should be based on relevant information.

Full details of the Cambridge International AS & A Level Accounting Assessment Objectives can be found in the syllabus on the Cambridge International website at www.cambridgeinternational.org.

Applying your knowledge and understanding

A good starting point for applying your skills correctly is to read the question carefully so you are clear what is being asked. Use the *command words* and *number of marks* available for a question to help you understand what is needed and how much time you can allow to answer.

a   **Knowledge questions**

These types of question often incorporate command words such as state and identify.

For example, **Chapter 38 Exam-style question 1:**

State two advantages of a standard costing system.   **[2]**

Mark scheme:

Any two advantages. One mark for each advantage. Maximum of two marks.

Make sure that you list the correct number of points, in this case *two* advantages.

b   **Calculations**

Questions requiring calculations typically use command words such as *calculate* and *allocate*. Always clearly show your workings – this means that even if you get your final answer wrong, your understanding can be measured from your workings.

For example, Chapter 39 Practice question 3a

Calculate the accounting rate of return   **[5]**

Mark scheme:

*Average profit per year = $100 000 − $55 000 **(1)** − $32 500 (depreciation)**(1)** = $12 500 **(1OF)***

Average investment = $65 000

*ARR = $12 500/$65 000 **(1)** × 100 = 19.23% **(1OF)***

Even if you are confident that you know how to calculate the ARR, it is easy to make an error as there are multiple calculations needed to arrive at the final answer. Therefore, it is important to always clearly show your workings.

c   Preparation of accounts and statements

Layout and labelling are very important for financial statements. Care must be taken to include the correct descriptors as well as the accurate figures. Use the styles that you have been shown in the coursebook where appropriate. For clarity any calculations needed can be shown separately (e.g. above or below the statement itself) with clear referencing in the document.

For example, Chapter 7 Exam-style question 4

Prepare Umi's statement of profit or loss for the year ended 31 March 2020.   **[15]**

The 15 marks will be given for accurate figures and labelling throughout the statement.

Each mark is for an amount that is clearly identified with a correctly worded label. For example, Gross profit of $133 605 will be given a mark provided both the number and descriptor are correct; the same is true for Loss for the year of $8 543.

Remember that if the profit for the year figure is incorrect because the gross profit was incorrect, it is important to show your working, as parts of the working may be correct even if the answer is wrong.

d   Evaluation, judgement and advice

Questions of this nature require information to be evaluated, conclusions to be drawn and a decision or judgement made. Any decision should be made explicitly with clear justification. Justification may be based on financial and non-financial information.

For example, Chapter 39 Practice question Q4c

Advise the directors on which machine they should buy. Justify your answer by using both financial and non-financial factors.   **[5]**

Mark scheme:

Maximum of 2 marks for reasons for choosing one machine; maximum of 2 marks for reasons for choosing the other machine; 1 mark for decision of either option supported by arguments.

It is important to explain the points you make rather than listing lots of different points. Do not make more points than you need to. Use the stated marks available as a guideline to how many points you need to make. 2 marks available for reasons either way. A supported decision must be given.

Common errors in answering questions

a   Common errors in answering multiple choice questions

- Not answering a question. Answer all questions even if you are not certain of the correct option. It is always worthwhile attempting each question. If you are not sure of the correct answer, start by eliminating any options that you are certain are incorrect then make an educated guess on the remaining options.

- Marking more than one option as correct. If you do this your answer will be wrong as you will have selected at least one wrong answer.

- Spending too long on one question. If you are not sure of the answer, leave it and go back to the question at the end. Check that you have provided a response to all questions.

b   Common errors in answering structured questions

- Not recognising that command words such as *recommend* and *evaluate* require judgement to be shown. You should aim to consider at least two viewpoints or two approaches and then show judgement in discussing them. Usually, a clear decision is asked for.

- Not allocating time effectively – if there are two questions of equal lengths you should allow equal time for each. Allocate time for each question carefully using the number of marks available as a guide. Do not be tempted to focus on calculations instead of questions requiring a written response.

- Failing to apply the calculation findings in one part of a question to the assess answer in the next sub-part.

- Not showing the workings for any calculations. Always show a methodical approach and layout as it will reduce the possibility of errors and allow you to check your answers and spot any mistakes.

- Answering questions that need a fuller evaluative response with short bullet points. Bullet points can be useful for questions that just require short answers; however, for evaluative questions, write answers in prose and in sufficient detail to explain your view and give a supported decision.

- Not fully answering the question set. In particular, if you are asked to discuss both financial and non-financial issues, make sure that you cover both.

>Appendix 1: Table showing net present value of $1

Present value of $1												
Years	5%	6%	7%	8%	9%	10%	11%	12%	13%	14%	15%	16%	17%
1	0.952	0.943	0.935	0.926	0.917	0.909	0.901	0.893	0.885	0.877	0.870	0.862	0.855
2	0.907	0.890	0.873	0.857	0.842	0.826	0.812	0.797	0.783	0.769	0.756	0.743	0.731
3	0.864	0.840	0.816	0.794	0.772	0.751	0.731	0.712	0.693	0.675	0.658	0.641	0.624
4	0.823	0.792	0.763	0.735	0.708	0.683	0.659	0.636	0.613	0.592	0.572	0.552	0.534
5	0.784	0.747	0.713	0.681	0.650	0.621	0.593	0.567	0.543	0.519	0.497	0.476	0.456
6	0.746	0.705	0.666	0.630	0.596	0.564	0.535	0.507	0.480	0.456	0.432	0.410	0.390
7	0.711	0.665	0.623	0.583	0.547	0.513	0.482	0.452	0.425	0.400	0.376	0.354	0.333
8	0.677	0.627	0.582	0.540	0.502	0.467	0.434	0.404	0.376	0.351	0.327	0.305	0.285
9	0.645	0.592	0.544	0.500	0.460	0.424	0.391	0.361	0.333	0.308	0.284	0.263	0.243
10	0.614	0.558	0.508	0.463	0.422	0.386	0.352	0.322	0.295	0.270	0.247	0.227	0.208

	18%	19%	20%	21%	22%	23%	24%	25%				
1	0.847	0.840	0.833	0.826	0.820	0.813	0.806	0.800				
2	0.718	0.706	0.694	0.683	0.672	0.661	0.650	0.640				
3	0.609	0.593	0.579	0.564	0.551	0.537	0.524	0.512				
4	0.516	0.499	0.482	0.467	0.451	0.437	0.423	0.410				
5	0.437	0.419	0.402	0.386	0.370	0.355	0.341	0.328				
6	0.370	0.352	0.335	0.319	0.303	0.289	0.275	0.262				
7	0.314	0.296	0.279	0.263	0.249	0.235	0.222	0.210				
8	0.266	0.249	0.233	0.218	0.204	0.191	0.179	0.168				
9	0.225	0.209	0.194	0.180	0.167	0.155	0.144	0.134				
10	0.191	0.176	0.162	0.149	0.137	0.126	0.116	0.107				

› Ratios

Profitability ratios

Gross profit margin (%) $\dfrac{\text{Gross profit}}{\text{Revenue}} \times 100$

Mark-up (%) $\dfrac{\text{Gross profit}}{\text{Cost of sales}} \times 100$

Profit margin (%) $\dfrac{\text{Profit for the year}}{\text{Revenue}} \times 100$

Can also be expressed as:

$\dfrac{\text{Profit for the year (after interest)}}{\text{Revenue}} \times 100$

Return on capital employed (%) $\dfrac{\text{Profit from operations}}{\text{Capital employed}} \times 100$

Capital employed = issued shares + reserves + non-current liabilities

Expenses to revenue ratio (%) $\dfrac{\text{Expenses}}{\text{Revenue}} \times 100$

Operating expenses to revenue ratio (%) $\dfrac{\text{Operating expenses}}{\text{Revenue}} \times 100$

Liquidity ratios

Current ratio $\dfrac{\text{Current assets}}{\text{Current liabilities}}$

Answer presented as a ratio

Acid test ratio $\dfrac{\text{Current assets – inventory}}{\text{Current liabilities}}$

Answer presented as a ratio

Efficiency ratios

Non-current asset turnover (times) $\dfrac{\text{Net revenue}}{\text{Total net book value of non-current assets}}$

Trade receivables turnover (days) $\dfrac{\text{Trade receivables}}{\text{Credit sales}} \times 365 \text{ days}$

Trade payables turnover (days) $\dfrac{\text{Trade payables}}{\text{Credit purchases}} \times 365 \text{ days}$

Inventory turnover (days)	$\dfrac{\text{Average inventory}}{\text{Cost of sales}} \times 365 \text{ days}$
Rate of inventory turnover (times)	$\dfrac{\text{Cost of sales}}{\text{Average inventory}}$

Solvency and other ratios (A Level only)

Working capital cycle (days)	Trade receivables turnover (days) + inventory turnover (days) − trade payables turnover (days)
Net working assets to revenue (sales) (%)	$\dfrac{\text{Net working assets}}{\text{Revenue (sales)}} \times 100$ Net working assets = inventories + trade receivables − trade payables
Interest cover (times)	$\dfrac{\text{Profit from operations}}{\text{Interest payable}}$
Gearing ratio	$\dfrac{\text{Fixed cost capital}}{\text{Total capital}}$ which is: $\dfrac{\text{Non-current liabilities}}{\text{Issued ordinary share capital + all reserves + non-current liabilities}}$

Investment ratios (A Level only)

Earnings per share	$\dfrac{\text{Profit for the year}}{\text{Number of issued ordinary shares}}$
Price/earnings ratio	$\dfrac{\text{Market price per share}}{\text{Earnings per share}}$
Annual ordinary dividend	Interim dividend paid + final dividend proposed
Dividend yield ratio	$\dfrac{\text{Annual ordinary dividend per share}}{\text{Market price per share}}$
Dividend cover	$\dfrac{\text{Profit for the year available to pay ordinary dividend}}{\text{Annual ordinary dividend}}$
Dividend per share	$\dfrac{\text{Annual ordinary dividend}}{\text{Number of issued ordinary shares}}$

> Glossary

Absorption: where all the allocated and apportioned overheads are charged to units of production.

Absorption costing: a method for calculating the cost of making one unit of a product that involves apportioning overheads into cost units.

Accounting concepts: basic rules for recording financial transactions and preparing final accounts. They are sometimes known as principles.

Accounting equation: an equation that represents the relationship between assets, liabilities and capital.

Accounting rate of return: the average profit from an investment expressed as a percentage of the average capital of the investment.

Accounting system: a system of collecting, storing and processing financial information and accounting data used by managers.

Accrual: an expense that is due within the accounting year but has not yet been paid.

Accumulated depreciation: the cumulative total of all the depreciation that has been charged on the non-current assets.

Accumulated fund: the accumulated surpluses made by a club or society over previous years.

Acquisition: when one business purchases another – for companies, it is when one company purchases most or all of another company's shares to gain control of that company.

Activity-based costing (ABC): a method of calculating unit cost that absorbs overhead costs into individual products by focusing on the activities that cause a cost to occur.

Adjusting events: events where the financial statements can be adjusted because the underlying conditions leading to those events existed at the year end.

Adverse variance: a variance where the actual expense is more than the standard cost, or where the actual revenue is less than the standard revenue.

Allocation of costs: charging overheads directly to the cost centre(s) that can be clearly identified with them.

Allowance for irrecoverable debts: the amount of irrecoverable debts relating to this period's sales and trade receivables figure that a business has estimated it will suffer during the next accounting year.

Allowance for irrecoverable debts account: the account used to account for possible irrecoverable debts that may not be seen until the next accounting year.

Amortisation: the non-tangible asset equivalent of depreciation where the value of the non-tangible asset is reduced over its life.

Annual general meeting (AGM): a meeting held after the end of the financial year where all ordinary shareholders are entitled to attend to vote on proposals made by the directors.

Apportionment of costs: the process of charging costs that can't be identified with specific cost centres to cost centres using a suitable basis.

Appropriation: the sharing out of something – in this case, the profit made by the partnership.

Appropriation account: an account prepared after the statement of profit or loss that shows how the profit for the year is divided between each partner.

Assets: items that are owned by or owed to a business.

Auditor: a person authorised to examine, review and verify financial records to ensure that they are accurate and that the information provided by a business represents a 'true and fair view' of its performance and financial state.

Audit report: a report prepared by the auditors of a limited company stating whether or not the annual financial statements provide a true and fair view.

Average cost (AVCO): a method of inventory valuation that uses a weighted average to calculate the value of inventory each time new inventory is purchased.

Balancing an account: the process of finding which side of a ledger account is the greater and by how much.

Bank reconciliation statement: a statement prepared periodically to ensure that the bank account in the business cash book matches the business bank account shown on the bank statement.

Batch costing: a costing method to find the cost of a batch of items produced.

Board of directors: a group of people elected by a company's shareholders to represent the shareholders' interests and ensure that the company's management acts on their behalf.

Bonus payment: the additional amount paid to an employee for reasons such as producing goods more quickly than the time allowed.

Bonus share issue: an issue of free shares to existing shareholders from the accumulated reserves of the company in the same proportion as the shares held by them.

Book of prime entry: a book used to list all transactions of a similar nature before they are posted to the ledger.

Bottom-up budgets: budgets prepared by departmental managers.

Break-even chart: a diagrammatic representation of the profit or loss to be expected from the sale of a product at various levels of activity.

Break-even point: the point at which a business makes neither profit nor loss. It is the point at which total contribution is equal to total fixed costs.

Budget: a plan of future activity expressed in financial terms.

Capital: the money invested in a business by its owner(s).

Capital account: the account that records the money invested in a business by its owner(s).

Capital expenditure: expenditure incurred in the purchase or improvement of a non-current asset.

Capital reserves: gains that arise from non-trading activities, such as the revaluation of a company's non-current assets.

Capitalised: recording an item as a non-current asset and showing it in the statement of financial position.

Carriage inwards: the additional delivery cost paid by a business in excess of the purchase price of the goods purchased for resale. It is added to the cost of goods by the supplier.

Carriage outwards: the additional cost charged by the seller to deliver goods sold.

Cash: includes cash in hand and bank deposits repayable on demand, less any overdrafts repayable on demand.

Cash book: the book of prime entry used to record all bank, cash and cash discounts. It is also part of the ledger system replacing separate cash and bank ledger accounts.

Cash discount: an allowance given by a seller to a customer to encourage the customer to pay an invoice before its due date for payment.

Commission received: a form of income that is often earned as a result of selling goods on behalf of somebody else.

Computerised accounting system: a set of programs that allow the accounts to be prepared using a computer. An alternative to manual bookkeeping.

Conceptual framework: a system of objectives and ideas that lead to the accounting authorities creating a consistent set of rules.

Confidentiality: not disclosing (keeping secret) sensitive information that would not be available to the public

Conflicts of interest: where a person is faced with demands from two or more people or organisations that are incompatible.

Consistency: financial transactions of a similar nature should be recorded in the same way (that is, consistently) in the same accounting year and in all future accounting years.

Contra (set-off): these arise when two people or businesses owe each other money because they have bought goods or services from each other and they agree to reduce both balances by the lower amount outstanding. Contra entries involve making a debit entry in the relevant purchase ledger and a credit entry in the relevant sales ledger as well as adjusting the purchase ledger and sales ledger control accounts.

Contra entry: the completing of both sides of the double entry within one account or cash book.

Contribution per unit: the difference between the selling price and variable cost of a unit of output.

Contribution to sales ratio (C/S ratio): the proportion of sales revenue that contributes towards the fixed costs and profit of a business.

Control account: a ledger account containing only total amounts – one entry for each type of transaction rather than the details of each individual financial transaction. The two most commonly used are the purchase ledger control account and the sales ledger control account.

Corporate social responsibility (CSR): a philosophy where a business organisation takes the view that they have a moral responsibility to behave ethically by assessing whether the impact they have on people, society and the environment could be more positive, and then taking the appropriate action.

Cost accounting: a method of accounting where all the costs associated with a particular activity or product are collected together, classified and recorded.

Cost centre: any part of a business to which costs may be attributed, such as a department.

Cost driver: the activity that directly results in a specific cost being incurred.

Cost of production: all of the costs associated with the product actually completed during the accounting year.

Cost of sales: the net cost of the goods sold to customers.

Cost pool: the total of all the costs associated with a particular activity.

Cost unit: the unit of output of a business to which costs can be charged, such as a computer for a computer manufacturer or an item of clothing for a dressmaker.

Credit balance: the amount by which the credit side of an account is greater than the debit side.

Credit note: a receipt given to a customer who has returned goods, which can be offset against future purchases.

Credit side: right-hand side of an account where what is given is recorded.

Credit transaction: a financial transaction where no money changes hands at the time of the transaction.

Current account: an account that shows a partner's share from profit and loss appropriation account such as interest on capital, salaries and profit etc minus drawings and interest on drawings.

Current assets: cash and other assets, typically inventory and trade receivables, which are expected to be give rise to cash within 12 months.

Current liabilities: items that the business is due to pay within 12 months.

Debit balance: the amount by which the debit side of an account is greater than the credit side.

Debit side: left-hand side of an account where what is received is recorded.

Deficit of income over expenditure: the equivalent of a loss for the year.

Deposit: money being paid into the bank account.

Depreciate: measuring the loss in value of a non-current asset as a result of factors including age, and wear and tear.

Depreciation: the loss in value of a non-current asset as a result of usage, wear and tear, obsolescence or the passing of time.

Direct costs: the costs that are involved in the actual manufacture of the product.

Direct debit: a regular electronic payment where the payer gives written permission (a direct debit mandate) for the person receiving the money to claim the money by presenting the 'bill'. Usually used when the timing of the payment or the amount is likely to vary.

Directors' report: a report prepared by the directors of a public limited company at the end of the financial year.

Discounts allowed: cash discounts allowed to the customer of goods for prompt payment.

Discounts received: cash discounts received from the supplier of goods for prompt payment.

Dishonoured cheque: a cheque that is not paid, usually because there is not enough money in the payer's account to cover it.

Dissolution of a partnership: the process by which all the assets of the partnership are sold and liabilities paid when the partnership ceases trading.

Donations: money given freely to an organisation. Sometimes donors may stipulate the use of the money.

Double-entry bookkeeping: a system of recording financial transactions that recognises there are two sides (or aspects) to every transaction.

Doubtful debt: a debt due from a customer where it is uncertain whether or not it will be repaid by them.

Drawings: money the business goods or services owner takes out of the business for personal use.

Duality: this recognises that there are two aspects to each financial transaction, represented by debit and credit entries in accounts.

Due care: the care that a competent person (accountant) would reasonably expect to take in order to perform a task to the required professional standard.

Error of omission: an error where the financial transaction has not been recorded at all.

Error of original entry: an error where the transaction is entered incorrectly in one of the books.

Ethics: the moral principles or standards that govern the conduct of a person or organisation that knows the difference between right and wrong.

Expenses: expenditure incurred in running a business on a day-to-day basis.

Factory cost of completed goods: all of the costs associated with the product actually completed during the accounting year.

Factory manufacturing cost: all costs incurred in the factory during the period both direct and indirect.

Factory overheads: indirect costs incurred in the factory that are not directly related to the product itself.

Factory profit: the amount added to the factory cost of completed goods to arrive at the transfer price.

Favourable variance: a variance where the actual cost is less than the standard cost, or where the actual revenue is more than the standard revenue.

Financial statements: the statements that a business is required to produce, normally at the end of an accounting year.

Financing activities: receipts from the issue of new shares or long-term loans, also payments made to redeem shares or to repay long-term loans.

Finished goods/completed goods: product that is ready to be sent to the customer.

First in, first out (FIFO): a method of inventory valuation that assumes that the first items to be purchased will be the first to be used in production and sold.

Fixed budget: a budget that is not changed when sales, or some other activity, increases or decreases.

Fixed cost: a cost that remains unchanged within a certain level of activity or output.

Flexible budget: a budget that changes to match the actual volume of goods produced and sold.

General reserve: a ledger account created to show the amount of retained earnings kept aside by the company to meet future needs e.g. fund future expansion; it is a bookkeeping adjustment, not an actual movement of cash.

Going concern: when there is no intention to discontinue a business in the foreseeable future.

Goods on sale or return: this is not a principle but a very important point in relation to ownership of goods relating to a transaction. When a trader sends goods on sale or return to a customer, no sale takes place until the customer informs the seller that she or he has decided to buy them.

Goodwill: an intangible non-current asset. It is the difference between the purchase price of a business and a fair value of its assets and liabilities.

Gross profit: the profit calculated by deducting the cost of sales from the net sales in the statement of profit or loss.

Hire purchase: a finance or credit agreement where a person has the use of an asset while paying for it in instalments.

Historic cost: financial transactions are recorded at their original cost to the business.

Hostile takeover: the acquisition of one company by another against the wishes of the management of the company being taken over who fear being replaced. It is accomplished by going direct to the company's shareholders and offering to buy their shares.

Impersonal account: any account other than a personal account.

Income and expenditure account: the equivalent of the statement of profit or loss that enables the members to determine whether the organisation has made a surplus or deficit.

Incomplete records: any method of recording financial transactions that is not based on the double-entry model.

Incremental budgeting: using last year's budgeted or actual figures as a starting point and adding to it or subtracting from it to reflect changes.

Indirect costs: costs that relate to the factory but are not directly associated with the product itself.

Industry lead bodies: organisations that control the way in which industries are run and the way in which people working in those industries operate.

Inflation: this is a general rise in the level of prices.

Inherent goodwill: this is goodwill that has been recognised as existing, but has not been paid for. It does not appear in the financial statements.

Insider trading: where someone uses information not available to members of the public for their own benefit or the benefit of third parties.

Intangible assets: assets that do not have a physical form or cannot be 'seen'.

Integrity: being straightforward and honest in all of your dealings.

Interest earned: the income earned from monies that have been invested or lent.

Interest on capital: a share of the profit for the year based on a percentage of the amount of fixed capital each partner has contributed to the partnership.

Interest on partners' drawings: a charge or fine imposed on partners, usually as a percentage of drawings, designed to deter partners from removing too much money from the business.

Internal controls: the presence of systems or procedures that make it more difficult for people to make serious errors or commit fraud without it being detected.

Internal rate of return: the interest or discount rate at which the net present value of all the cash flows from the project (both positive and negative) equal zero.

International Accounting Standards (IASs): standards created by the International Accounting Standards Board stating how particular types of transaction or other events should be reflected in the financial statements of a business entity.

Inventory: the unsold goods of a business involved in buying and selling at a particular point in time.

Investing activities: the acquisition and disposal of non-current and other long-term assets.

Investment appraisal: the process of assessing whether it is worthwhile to invest funds into a particular project.

Invoice: a document that a business issues to its customer asking the customer to pay for the goods or services supplied to them on credit.

Irrecoverable debt: a debt due from a customer that it is expected will never be paid by them.

Job costing: a costing method that calculates the cost of meeting a specific customer order or job.

Journal (or general journal): a book of prime entry for recording financial transactions and events for which there is no other book of prime entry.

Just-in-time (JIT): a system of manufacturing that uses the principle that supplies should be received exactly when they are needed in the production process and do not need to be stored by the business beforehand.

Lease: a contract outlining the terms under which one party agrees to rent property owned by another party.

Ledger: a book or computer file containing accounts.

Ledger account: a history of all financial transactions of a similar nature.

Liabilities: amounts owed by a business.

Life membership: the amount paid by a member of a club, which entitles them to be members of the club for their lifetime.

Limited company: a separate legal entity whose existence is separate from its owners; the debt of the members are limited to the amounts paid (or to be paid) on shares issued to them.

Limited liability: where the owner of the business has his or her responsibility for paying off debts limited either to a specified amount or to the amount of his or her investment.

Limiting factor: anything that limits the quantity of goods that a business may produce, such as a shortage of labour.

Loss: the amount by which expenses exceed the income (or revenue) of the business.

Management accounting: the process of preparing reports and accounts that can be used by managers as a basis for making decisions about the future performance of the business.

Manufacturing account: an account used to record the various direct and indirect costs associated with making a product.

Margin: the gross profit expressed as a percentage or fraction of selling price.

Margin of safety: the difference between budgeted or actual output and the break-even quantity.

Marginal cost: the cost of making one extra unit of output.

Marginal cost of production: the variable costs of production of making one extra unit of output.

Marginal cost of sales: the variable costs of production and selling of making one extra unit of output.

Mark-up: the gross profit expressed as a percentage or fraction of the sales cost.

Master budget: the budgeted statement of profit or loss and the budgeted statement of financial position together.

Memorandum accounts: ledger accounts that are not regarded as part of the main double-entry system even though they are produced using double-entry principles. They are produced to check the accuracy of parts of the accounting system.

Merger: where two or more independent businesses combine their assets and form a completely new business.

Money laundering: all forms of handling or possessing criminal property (including the proceeds of one's own crime) and the facilitating of any handling or possession of criminal property'.

Narrative: something recorded under a journal entry to explain why the journal entry is being made.

Net book value (NBV): the remaining value of the asset (cost – accumulated depreciation).

Net current assets: the amount by which current assets exceed current liabilities.

Net present value: the present value of future receipts from a project, less the present value of future payments in respect of the same project.

Net realisable value: the selling price of a product minus any costs incurred in bringing it to a saleable condition (e.g. repairs) and/or actually selling it.

Net sales: the difference between the original sales made and the amount of refunds that were given.

Nominal account: an account used to record the revenue and expenses of a business. It also relates to an account or accounts that record the revenue of the business from sales.

Non-adjusting events: events where the financial statements cannot be adjusted because the underlying conditions did not exist at the year end.

Non-current assets: items bought by a business that are intended to be used in the business for more than one year.

Non-current liabilities: amounts owed by a business that are repayable in more than one year.

Objectivity: being impartial and unbiased – making a decision based on the facts or evidence or taking an action because it is the right thing to do.

Omitted items: payments and receipts made by the bank that have not been recorded in the cash book.

Operating activities: the main revenue-generating activities of the company – the trading of goods or provision of services.

Other income: income earned by the business from sources other than its main activities.

Other payables: the current liability (money owed by the business) arising from late payment of expenses or early receipt of an income.

Other receivables: the current asset (money owed to the business) arising from early payment of expenses or late receipt of an income.

Over-absorption: if production is more than planned or expenditure is less than budgeted, too much overhead will be charged to production, i.e. there is over-absorption of overheads.

Overdraft: a bank account that has a negative balance. Payments out of the account are greater than receipts into the account.

Overhead absorption rate (OAR): the rate at which overheads apportioned to a cost centre are charged to the cost unit passing through it.

Overadded: a figure that is found by adding up two or more figures but which is higher than the correct figure.

Over-subscribed: when there have been applications for more shares than the number of shares being issued.

Overtime payment: an amount paid to an employee for working longer than the time they are contracted to work.

Overtime premium: the additional amount given to employees for overtime working. For example, if an employee is paid overtime at a rate of 50% above their normal hourly rate (or time and a half) the extra 50% is the overtime premium.

Overtrading: the (rapid) expansion of a business that does not have the financial resources to support such an expansion.

Partnership: two or more people carrying on a business together with a view to making a profit.

Partnership Act 1890: the rules that govern a partnership in the absence of a formal partnership agreement.

Partnership agreement: an agreement, usually in writing, setting out the terms of the partnership.

Partner's salary: a share of the partnership profit for the year paid to one or more of the partners in addition to their normal share of the profit for the year.

Payback period: the period of time it takes for the net cash receipts from a project to pay back, or equal, the total of the funds invested in the project.

Payments unpresented: payments of money from the bank account that have been recorded in the cash book but have not yet appeared on the bank statement.

Periodic inventory: a method of inventory valuation that only shows the balance of inventory at intervals, such as each week or each month.

Perpetual inventory: a method of inventory valuation that maintains a continuous balance of inventory available after each financial transaction.

Personal account: an account relating to a person.

Piece rate: a wage rate paid to workers based on the number of units of output produced.

Positive contribution: the contribution (selling price − variable costs per unit) is above zero.

Posting: the process of recording financial transactions in ledger accounts.

Prepayment: a payment made by a business in advance of the benefits to be derived from it.

Present value: the present or current value of an expected future sum of money.

Prime cost: the direct costs of making the product.

Private limited company: a company that is not authorised to issue shares to the public.

Production cost centres: cost centres directly involved in producing goods.

Professional bodies: organisations that have members operating in a particular industry

Professional competence: having the skills, knowledge and understanding to be able to perform a task to the appropriate professional standard.

Profit: the amount by which the income (or revenue) exceeds the expenses of the business.

Profit (or loss) for the year: the profit (or loss) calculated by adding other income to the gross profit and deducting the business expenses.

Profit/volume chart: a type of break-even chart that only shows the profit or loss at each level of output.

Proposed dividend: a dividend that has been recommended by the directors of a company but not paid – usually because it has not yet been approved by the shareholders at the Annual General Meeting.

Prudence: profits should not be overadded and losses should be provided for as soon as they are recognised.

Public limited company (PLC): a company that is authorised to issue shares to the public.

Purchase returns (returns outwards): purchased goods that are sent back to the supplier who agrees to accept them back and return any money paid.

Purchased goodwill: goodwill that has a definite valuation because money has changed hands and the excess of the amount paid over the value of the net assets is a matter of fact.

Purchases: goods bought from suppliers that will be resold to customers.

Purchases journal: the book of prime entry used to record all purchases bought on credit.

Purchases ledger: the book that contains the individual accounts of all the business's credit suppliers.

Purchases ledger control account: summarises the transactions involving purchases on credit.

Purchases returns: purchased goods that are sent back to the supplier who agrees to accept them back and return any money paid.

Purchases returns journal: the book of prime entry used to record all goods returned to suppliers that have been bought from on credit.

Raw materials: any materials that will form part of the product but have not yet had anything done to them.

Realisation: revenue is recognised or accounted for by the seller when it is earned whether cash has been received from the transaction or not.

Realisation account: an account prepared when a partnership is ceasing to trade, to record the book value of the assets and liabilities and how much is received for them if sold, or paid out in respect of liabilities.

Receipts and payments account: an account that records the inflows and outflows of money through the cash and bank accounts during a period. It is often presented in the style of a (two-column) cash book. Also, it can be the bank account used by clubs and societies.

Receipts unpresented: deposits of money paid into the bank account that have been recorded in the cash book but have not yet appeared on the bank statement.

Reducing balance method: depreciation is calculated as a fixed percentage of the written-down (net book) value of the asset each year.

Rental income: the income earned from allowing someone to use your premises.

Replacement cost: the amount that a business would have to pay to *replace* an asset according to its current worth.

Residual value: the amount that a business will receive for the asset at the end of its useful life – used to be known as scrap value.

Revaluation account: an account used to assist with making the entries required to adjust the value of assets and liabilities.

Revaluation method of depreciation: used to calculate the cost of consumption in the accounting year of small non-current assets such as power tools.

Revaluation of assets: adjustments made to the value of the partnership assets to reflect their market value.

Revenue: the sales of goods or services made by a business.

Revenue expenditure: expenditure on the day-to-day running costs of the business.

Revenue reserves: the profits made by a company that have not been distributed to shareholders.

Rights issue of shares: an issue of shares made for cash. The shares are offered first to existing shareholders, usually in proportion to the shares held by them.

Sales journal: the book of prime entry used to record all sales made on credit.

Sales ledger: the book that contains the individual accounts of all the business's credit customers.

Sales ledger control account: summarises the transactions involving sales on credit.

Sales returns: a customer who has already bought goods sends them back to the seller. A refund is given of any money already paid because goods are faulty or incorrect goods were delivered.

Sales returns journal: the book of prime entry used to record all goods returned from credit customers.

Scarce resource: a resource such as labour or materials that has limited availability.

Segregation of duties: the dividing up of tasks or an accounting function between two or more people in order to strengthen internal controls and reduce the risk of fraud or error.

Semi-variable cost: a cost that contains an element of both a variable and a fixed cost within it.

Service cost centres: cost centres that are not involved in the production of goods but provide services for the production cost centres.

Share: the smallest division of the total share capital of the company that can be issued in order to raise funds for the company.

Share capital: the capital raised by a business by the issue of shares, usually for cash, but may also be for consideration for other than cash, such as non-current or current assets.

Single-entry bookkeeping: a method of bookkeeping where only one aspect of each financial transaction is recorded.

Sole trader: a business that is owned by one person.

Stakeholder: a person or organisation that has a legitimate interest in a business or who can be affected by that business.

Standard cost: the estimated or budgeted cost of a unit of output or activity.

Standard costing: an accounting system that compares actual costs against standard costs, which helps managers to assess and control costs and take action where needed.

Standing order: an electronic payment where the payer gives instruction for his or her bank to pay a regular amount. The amount paid is always the same and takes place on a specific date.

Statement of affairs: a list of the business assets and liabilities at a point in time, usually prepared to calculate the capital of the business at that point in time.

Statement of changes in equity: a statement showing the changes in a company's share capital, reserves and retained earnings over a reporting period.

Statement of financial position: a list of the assets, liabilities, capital and reserves of a business at a particular point in time.

Statement of profit or loss: an account prepared periodically to find the profit or loss made by a business.

Stepped costs: fixed costs that are only fixed within certain limits and will increase to a higher level when that limit is reached.

Steward: someone who is appointed to look after money or property belonging to another person or organisation.

Straight-line depreciation: a method of applying depreciation that assumes that the loss in value will occur at a constant rate.

Subscriptions: the amount paid by members to be part of the club or society.

Subsidiary sales ledger: the book that contains the individual accounts of all the business's credit customers.

Substance over form: the economic substance of the transaction must be recorded in the financial statements rather than its legal form.

Surplus of income over expenditure: the equivalent of the profit for the year and arises where income exceeds expenditure.

Suspense account: an account opened to record a difference between the debit and credit totals of the trial balance.

Takeover: another term for acquisition – it is when one company purchases most or all of another company's shares to gain control of that company.

Time value of money: the principle that the same sum of money is worth more now than at some time in the future.

Timing differences: the delay between items recorded in the cash book and their appearance on the bank statement.

Top-down budgets: budgets prepared by top management and handed down to departmental managers, who are responsible for putting them into effect.

Trade discount: a reduction in the selling price of goods made by one trader to another.

Trade payable: a supplier to whom the business owes money.

Trade receivable: a customer that owes the business money.

Transfer price: the price that one part of an organisation sells its product (or service) to another part of that organisation.

Trial balance: a list of the balances on each account extracted from the ledgers at a particular date. Its purpose is to check arithmetical accuracy of the double entry in the ledger.

True and fair view: the financial statements are accurate and faithfully represent the financial performance and position of the business.

Under-absorption: where production is less than planned or expenditure is more than budgeted, not enough overhead will be charged to production, i.e. there is under-absorption of overheads.

Underadded: a figure that is found by adding up two or more figures but which is lower than the correct figure.

Unit cost: the average cost of producing one unit of a product or service

Unit costing: the costing method to find the cost of a single cost unit.

Unlimited liability: the owner of the business is personally responsible for all of the debts and losses of that business.

Useful life: the amount of time that the business expects to keep the asset – this may be significantly less than its physical life.

Variable cost: a cost that varies in direct proportion to changes in the level of output.

Variance: the difference between the standard cost and actual cost.

Verification: the process of establishing the truth, accuracy, or validity of something.

Warranty: a type of arrangement where the owner of a non-current asset obtain a form of insurance that will pay out for the cost of parts or repairs if there is a problem with the asset.

Whistleblowing: in some countries this is referred to as a public disclosure (or similar) where someone, often an employee, reports wrongdoing to the authorities.

Window dressing: the misleading presentation of financial statements, designed to create a more favourable impression of a situation than is justified.

Withdrawal: money being taken out of the bank account.

Work-in-progress: product that has been started but still requires further work to put it into a state of completeness where it is ready to be sent to the customer.

Zero-based budgeting: using budgeted figures that are justified by analysing existing operations or business needs rather than starting by using figures from previous periods.

> Index

> Acknowledgements

The authors and publishers acknowledge the following sources of copyright material and are grateful for the permissions granted. While every effort has been made, it has not always been possible to identify the sources of all the material used, or to trace all copyright holders. If any omissions are brought to our notice, we will be happy to include the appropriate acknowledgements on reprinting.

Thanks to the following for permission to reproduce images:

Cover MirageC/GI; *Inside* Unit 1 Peter Dazeley/GI; Zoranm/GI; Digital Vision/GI; Unit 2 Chris Griffiths/GI; Budrul Chukrut/SOPA Images/LightRocket/GI; Alex Halada/GI; Unit 3 AndresGarciaM/GI; Martin-dm/GI; Prapass Pulsub/GI; Unit 4 Twomeows/GI; Geber86/GI; Nick White/GI; Unit 5 Eskay Lim/GI; Morsa Images/GI; Vgajic/GI; Unit 6 Reza Estakhrian/GI; Brian Dowling/Contributor/GI; Daniel Sambraus/GI; Unit 7 Marekuliasz/GI; Digital Vision/GI; Triloks/GI; Unit 8 Tetra Images/GI; Tinpixels/GI; RapidEye/GI; Unit 9 Studio Omg/GI; Simon Carter Peter Crowther/GI; Kasayizgi/GI; Unit 10 Digital Art/GI; Wragg/GI; Yongyuan/GI; Unit 11 Jorg Greuel/GI; Alistair Berg/GI; Andipantz/GI; Unit 12 Don Farrall/GI; Westend61/GI; FG Trade/GI; Unit 13 Creativ Studio Heinemann/GI; Sorapong Chaipanya/GI; Image Source/GI; Unit 14 Abstract Aerial Art/GI; Image Source/GI; Kupicoo/GI; Unit 15 Sergii Iaremenko/Science Photo Library/GI; Jose Luis Pelaez Inc/GI; Johannes Mann/GI; Unit 16 Kehan Chen/GI; StanRohrer/GI; Peter Dazeley/GI; Unit 17 MirageC/GI; TravelCouples/GI; Kali9/GI; Unit 18 Lerexis/GI; Westend61/GI; Urbancow/GI; Unit 19 Abstract Aerial Art/GI; Betsie Van der Meer/GI; Yellow Dog Productions/GI; Unit 20 Atlantide Phototravel/GI; Oliver Rossi/GI; Monty Rakusen/GI; Unit 21 D3sign/GI; SusanWoodImages/GI; Moodboard/GI; Unit 22 Carlos Calaff/GI; Traffic_Analyzer/GI; Jose Luis Pelaez Inc/GI; Unit 23 Grant Faint/GI; Loop Images/Universal Images Group/GI; Richard Newstead/GI; Unit 24 Dziggyfoto/GI; Peter Dazeley/GI; GeorgePeters/GI; Unit 25 Thomas Ligart/GI; Thomas Lai Yin Tang/GI; Andersen Ross/GI; Unit 26 Alfexe/GI; Andrew Brookes/GI; Suriyo Hmun Kaew/GI; Unit 27 Henglein and Steets/GI; Andrew Brookes/GI; EmirMemedovski/GI; Unit 28 Jessekarjalainen/GI; Martin Barraud/GI; Helen King/GI; Unit 29 Lawrence Manning/GI; Peter Dazeley/GI; Runstudio/GI; Unit 30 Peter Cade/GI; Epoxydude/GI; Rahul Acharya/GI; Unit 31 Jonathan Kitchen/GI; Fanatic Studio/GI; Courtneyk/GI; Unit 32 Shaunl/GI; D3sign/GI; Bloom Productions/GI; Unit 33 Felix Cesare/GI; STRDEL/GI; Peter Dazeley/GI; Unit 34 Abstract Aerial Art/GI; Kevin Walker/GI; Patrick Lane/GI; Unit 35 DSGpro/GI; Japatino/GI; Peter Dazeley/GI; Unit 36 Fotocelia/GI; Yegor Aleyev\TASS/GI; Klaus Vedfelt/GI; Unit 37 Tuk69tuk/GI; Natdanai Pankong/GI; Martin-dm/GI; Unit 36 Grant Faint/GI; Nadzeya_Kizilava/GI; Compassionate Eye Foundation/John Wildgoose/GI; Unit 37 Andy Roberts/GI; Alex Tai/SOPA Images/LightRocket/GI; Pakin Songmor/GI; Unit 40 Jeffrey Coolidge/GI.

GI = Getty Images.